1993

Children's Writer's & Illustrator's Market

Edited by
Lisa Carpenter

Writer's
Digest
Books

Cincinnati, Ohio

Distributed in Canada by McGraw-Hill Ryerson, 300 Water St., Whitby, Ontario L1N 9B6. Also distributed in Australia by Kirby Books, Private Bag No. 19, P.O. Alexandria NSW/2015 and in New Zealand by David Bateman, P.O. Box 100-242, N. Shore Mail Centre, Auckland 10.

Managing Editor, Market Books Department: Constance J. Achabal; Supervising Editor: Michael Willins.

Children's Writer's & Illustrator's Market.

International Standard Serial Number 0897-9790
International Standard Book Number 0-89879-577-X

Portrait Artist: Leslie Sowers Slaughter
Cover Artist: Thomas Mack

Contents

The Markets

From the Editor

Welcome to the fifth edition of *Children's Writer's & Illustrator's Market* (*CWIM*)! Writer's Digest Books has been publishing this book since 1989 so that you, a writer or artist for children, can have a comprehensive source for marketing your writing and/or artwork for children. Not only does this book supply you with names and addresses of potential publishers of your work, it also provides vital information pertaining to these markets, such as contact names, subject needs and submission guidelines. Using this information may not get you published instantly, but it certainly will give you the edge over other submitters who haven't studied their markets.

Once again, as has been the case since *CWIM*'s debut, the book increased in size for 1993. It contains more than 200 new listings of book publishers, magazines, audiovisual and audiotape markets, special markets, scriptwriter's markets, young writer's/illustrator's markets, contests and resources such as organizations, conferences and workshops.

Wait! There's more!

I don't consider *CWIM* merely a directory. Feedback from readers over the years indicates it's also a major source of practical, how-to marketing information.

Children's writers and illustrators will appreciate the 15-page business section beginning on page 19. Here you will find detailed information on submission formats, agents, contracts and royalties, copyrights and taxes.

Beginning on page 5, editor/author Jean Karl explains the relationship between writer, editor and illustrator when it comes to producing a picture book. Understanding the picture book troika can help you progress in your freelancing career.

Pat Matson Knapp's article beginning on page 15 is a roundup of editors' comments concerning the biggest mistakes writers and illustrators make when submitting their work. In the article, Knapp illustrates how inappropriate submissions not only hurt the chances of the people who send them, but every unpublished author trying to break out beyond the slush pile. If inappropriate submissions continue to congest the offices of publishers, some day the slush pile may be gone too.

Realizing how hard it is to get that first break into publishing, I feel a responsibility for encouraging you to maintain your persistence. New authors and illustrators *are* published, as you will see with three cases in the First Books feature beginning on page 10.

The close-up profiles remain staples of the book. This year we're proud to bring you eight people who have made the business of children their business. Seymour Simon shares with you how writing nonfiction books is just as exciting as fiction; Linda Gondosch allows you to peek into her life as a children's novelist; Peter Catalanotto describes his life as an illustrator and how it led him to become a writer too; Janice Boland, editor at Richard C. Owen Publishers, describes the children's business from a small-press perspective; Ronnie Ann

Herman, art director at Grosset & Dunlap, offers pointers for children's illustrators; Carolyn Yoder advises the best way to approach the editors of the four magazines her company, Cobblestone, publishes; Ron McCutchan, art director of *Cricket* and *Ladybug* magazines, talks about how artists can grab an art director's attention; finally, Jeff Brown points out opportunities for freelance writers with the nationally-syndicated children's radio show he produces.

If anything, this fifth edition proves opportunities for writers and illustrators do exist, even in these tough economic times. Keep in mind, though, that buyers and publishers are getting more and more particular about quality—they won't settle for less than the best from anyone. Nevertheless, considering the fact book sales remained strong even during the Depression, it's clear the thirst for reading is in us all. As writers and illustrators, you know all too well the thirst for creating can be just as strong.

We want you to keep trying to quench that thirst and keep to a minimum the bad taste of rejection you might experience from time to time. The staff at *CWIM* supports you, and understands how hard, and downright frustrating, rejection is.

This book is here to help you, and so are we. Questions or comments about the book, the field, the markets or anything else are welcomed, so feel free to drop us a letter.

Now that you've read pages one and two, it's time to venture on to page three. Here's hoping your journey through *CWIM* will lead you to greater paths into publishing, thus enabling you to someday share your creations with children everywhere!

How to Use Children's Writer's & Illustrator's Market

As a children's writer, illustrator or photographer you may be asking yourself various questions about the 1993 *Children's Writer's & Illustrator's Market*. "How do I use this book to find editors who will buy my work?" "Do I actually need to read every listing in this directory to sell my work?"

It's easy for anyone to open the pages of this book, quickly find the names of numerous contacts who purchase freelance material, and then mail submissions with the hope that an editor will like your work and want to use it. More than likely, if this is your modus operandi, you will end up angering most of the editors you contact. (Pat Matson Knapp's article, Inappropriate Submissions: What Bothers Editors?, beginning on page 15, tells you how to submit your material without aggravating editors.)

The information in this book can help you succeed as a freelancer by providing tips and markets for your work. This book, however, cannot make you a success. Only you can do that. As you turn the pages remember that you are *researching* to find buyers for your work.

In many listings you will find four categories of children's writing/illustrating; they are defined as: "picture books," written/illustrated for preschool-8-year-olds; "young readers" for 5-8-year-olds; "middle readers" for 9-11-year-olds; "young adults" for those 12 years old and older. These age breakdowns may vary slightly from publisher to publisher and they can help you identify buyers who may be interested in your work.

If you have a manuscript about teenage drug users, make sure you identify and contact those book publishers who publish books for young adults. If you have an exciting tale about dragons, princes and princesses that would interest 6-year-olds, search for picture-book or young-reader markets. The Age-level Index in the back of this book can help you quickly accomplish this task.

This directory has over 600 potential buyers for your work and over 200 listings are new this year. All of the new listings are marked with an asterisk [*]. The ability to make the right contacts is essential in getting your work published. The easiest way to do that is narrow down the listings, dissect them until you know which ones publish the type of material you are interested in submitting.

Finding the markets

Many listings use the "Tips" section to describe the freelancing credentials that an editor wants to see. Some editors in this directory are interested in the work of newer, lesser-known writers and illustrators. Others may only be interested in established writers or artists with plenty of credits.

The majority of listings also provide information about the subjects in which they are interested. For example, some editors want manuscripts dealing with multicultural, adventure or contemporary themes. Others want romance, history or religion. Markets also state whether they are seeking fiction and/or nonfiction works. In order to guarantee that you are sending an editor exactly what he wants check to see if submission guidelines are available. This usually is stated, "Ms guidelines available for SASE."

Throughout this book the abbreviations "ms" or "mss" are used to refer to "manuscript" or "manuscripts," respectively. The letters "SASE" stand for self-addressed, stamped envelope, while SAE (self-addressed envelope) is often used in conjunction with IRC (International Reply Coupon). IRCs are required when sending mail to countries other than your own. Many markets require SASEs and it is important to include one if you want your work returned

In the Book Publishers section a solid block [■] may appear before certain listings. This symbol indicates that a market subsidy publishes manuscripts. A double dagger [‡] in the Contests and Awards section indicates that the contest is for students.

If you are a parent or a teacher you may be interested in our Young Writer's/ Illustrator's Markets beginning on page 260. These markets encourage submissions from children and maybe your students or kids have material that could get published in a magazine or book. Some markets, however, require a written statement by a teacher or parent that the work is original. The market also may require an age limit.

Along with information for writers, markets provide plenty of information for photographers and illustrators, usually under the "Photography," "Artwork" or "Illustration" subheads. If you are a photographer, check to see what kind of format a buyer wants to receive. For example, some want 35mm color transparencies, others want b&w prints. Most importantly, note the type of photos a buyer wants to purchase and the procedures for submitting work. It is not uncommon for a market to want a résumé and promotional literature from you, as well as tearsheets from previous work you shot. Listings also note whether model releases and/or captions are required.

Illustrators will find numerous markets in which samples are kept on file for possible future assignments. As with photographers, markets include information regarding subject matter they seek. If you are a writer and an illustrator look for those markets that accept manuscript/illustration packages.

In researching listings you also will find that most supply payment information. Some markets like to pay on acceptance, others prefer to pay on publication. Some pay a flat rate for manuscripts and artwork, others pay advances and royalties. Whatever the case, know how a market operates. This will keep you from being completely shocked when you find out your paycheck won't arrive until your manuscript is published 18 months from the time it was accepted. For more details about contracts and other business tips, see The Business of Children's Writing & Illustrating beginning on page 19.

The popularity of children's writing and illustrating has been growing and growing over the past several years. Every aspect of this book is designed with you in mind and we know you can use this directory to find markets for your work. Thoroughness on our part in putting this edition together, and persistence on your part in finding the right markets for your work, can help you rise above the crowd.

The Picture Book Troika: Writer, Illustrator and Editor

by Jean E. Karl

A *troika*, the dictionary says, is a vehicle drawn by a team of three horses. Troika can describe a picture book, too. It is a vehicle for story and/or information—with pictures as a strong component part—that is moved into being, generally, by three people: writer, illustrator and editor. Often an art director is added to the basic three; production experts are essential for the book to be printed and bound; and for the book to reach its intended audience publicity, promotion and sales people are needed. But the vehicle is started on its way by the basic three. It is these three who must interact well, trust each other, and contribute to the vision of what the completed book ought to be. But though the horses of a real troika may be hitched up at the same time, the people involved in the picture book troika come together one at a time, and in different ways.

The author's task

"I have a really marvelous picture book story to read to you today," Janet says to her writing group. She reads, and the others agree it is a story that ought to be published.

"But I don't know any illustrators," Janet says. "What am I going to do?"

Janet is the first part of the picture book troika—the originator of the book idea, the writer who creates the material. Without her, the book that is to come would never exist. But she does not have to know an illustrator in order for the picture book to happen. What she has to know or find is an editor who likes her story and who wants to make a picture book of it. Janet needs to send her story to publishers, without pictures or even picture suggestions (unless there are elements in the book that are to be carried only in the pictures—in which case, of course, there must be notes as to what will be in those pictures), until she finds an editor who likes it and may want to publish it.

"I know I have to find an editor," Janet says, "but how can I be sure any editor will see my story as I see it and how can I know that the editor will see the pictures as I see them?"

The answer is that maybe no one will ever see Janet's story in quite the same way as Janet sees it. No two people are alike. But if Janet's story has the universality and depth that a good picture book story should have, then the editor in reading that story will see both text and pictures as a book that might come to be, though that book may not be quite the same book as the one Janet sees. Editors are used to reading picture book manuscripts and visualizing them

Jean E. Karl, *founding editor of Atheneum Children's Books, has been an editor for 43 years. She is author of* From Childhood to Childhood, *about the field of children's literature, and she is working on another book,* How to Write & Sell a Children's Picture Book, *due out in the fall of 1994 by Writer's Digest Books.*

as finished books. Janet sees her book in her own terms, but the editor sees the book in publishing terms—in terms of what can be done both in producing the book and in suiting it to the market for picture books. As author and editor work together, in the best possible situations, the two visions of the book become one.

Adding pictures to the package

"Well," says Janet, "I'm not sure I want someone else deciding how my book ought to look. And what about Betty? She's an artist. She wants to do her own pictures. Can't she do them if she wants to? And wouldn't it be a good idea for her to do the pictures for my book, too?"

When it comes to pictures, editors get three kinds of manuscripts: those without pictures (though some will contain suggestions for pictures), those with pictures done by someone other than the author, and those written and illustrated by the same person. A manuscript without pictures is considered for itself: for the originality and aptness of the text, for the author's writing ability, and for the picture possibilities the text presents. Manuscripts that come with pictures are judged by both text and pictures, whether the illustrations are done by the author or by someone else. If the pictures are found wanting, the text may not be taken, even if the editor likes it. The editor will assume that the whole is a package and must be accepted or rejected as such. Furthermore, even if both text and pictures are good, but the illustrator (whether the author or someone else) has finished pictures for the entire book and has done them in a size or technique that does not fit the production needs of that publisher, the book may be rejected. Specifications for finished art are determined by many kinds of production costs the publisher must pay, and book projects are rejected when they, for any reason, will result in a book that must carry a higher price than buyers may be willing to accept.

An interesting problem arises for the editor when a manuscript arrives with poor text by the author but good illustrations by someone else. The editor may contact the illustrator in the hope that he or she might work on another book, but it is often hard to tell an author that a manuscript is not as good as the illustrations. So sometimes the whole matter is just forgotten.

The situation is easier, of course, when the writer and illustrator are one. Writing a story or retelling a folk tale and doing a rough dummy and several sample illustrations is one of the best ways a new illustrator can demonstrate the skills needed to do picture book illustration. Betty might do this—and if she does, she will type the manuscript and maybe make a small dummy showing how the pages fall. Also, she may do two or three sample drawings in several styles to show that she is adaptable. When she is finished, she can simply submit the results to an editor in the same way any other manuscript might be submitted, with a cover letter and a self-addressed stamped envelope for return. Or, if she should decide to make the rounds of art directors and editors with sample illustrations, the dummy and its samples could be shown at the same time. (Though she shouldn't expect anyone to accept the material on the spot—at best, someone might ask to keep it and consider it.) The end of this exercise could be an assignment to illustrate someone else's work, not the book submitted. But that should not matter—not if securing illustration work of some kind has been her objective from the start.

So Betty and those like her may find illustration work by submitting a story with some sample art. But they are better off not illustrating something by a friend, unless that manuscript has already been accepted by a publisher. Janet and writers like her who are not artists themselves are really better off leaving the choice of illustrator to the editor.

"But how do I know that I will like the illustrator the editor chooses? Suppose I hate the pictures? It would be awful if I sold my manuscript and then didn't like the book when it was finished."

That's a chance that all picture book authors take. An author who has never sold a manuscript before may have little input into the finished book. On the other hand, an established writer may have a good deal to say about what goes into a finished book. And if, by some chance, an author is known to understand illustration and illustrators, that person may be given the chance to work with the illustrator on the book.

"But isn't there anything I can do to make sure the pictures are right?" Janet asks frantically.

The editor's insight

Remember, a picture book is the product of a troika. Everyone has a chance for input. The final book is a result of the work of three people. Very few manuscripts arrive at a publisher in perfect shape, no matter how good they may have sounded to their authors when they were sent out. It is an editor's job to help authors perfect their material, to catch a vision of what an author is trying to do and bring the manuscript as close to that vision as possible. Probably even before the manuscript is accepted, Janet will find herself revising certain aspects of her material for the editor. And if the two get on well, when the revision process is ended, Janet may like her text even better than she did when she first sent it in. During revision, she may not have agreed with all of the changes the editor wanted and may have told the editor why. If Janet's explanations were sensible, the editor probably agreed with her. They have established a working relationship — a give and take as both struggle to make the story (or nonfiction text, or whatever) as good as it possibly can be. By the time such an exchange is over, the editor has a good idea of who Janet is, how she feels about her story and about the pictures that ought to illustrate it, and what kind of pictures will best complement the final text.

All along, knowing her own thoughts about the book, and gradually understanding how Janet sees the book, the editor will think about an illustrator. Editors know illustrators, and they work with art directors who know even more illustrators. Together they will search for the appropriate artist. Sometimes editors are looking for a manuscript that will fit the style and interests of a given illustrator, and a manuscript is accepted to be illustrated by that specific person. Other times, the editor simply likes a manuscript and looks for the right person to create the pictures; the person whose style and approach to illustration seems to match the content and atmosphere of the manuscript. When the editor finds an illustrator who seems right for a book — and right for what the editor knows of the author's general feeling about the book — the chosen illustrator is sent a copy of the manuscript, and he or she can decide if the project is of interest and if there is time to manufacture the necessary artwork. If the answer to each of these questions is yes, sometimes the editor will ask for samples of what the illustrator will do, to make sure the choice is right. If the illustrator does not like the manuscript or does not have time to create the pictures, or if the editor does not like the samples, then the editor continues the search for the right artist.

Ideally the editor, in offering the manuscript to the illustrator, spells out the sort of book more or less agreed upon with the author. (However, if they do not see the book in the same way, and the author has signed a contract with the publisher, the editor will have the final say. The editor is responsible to the publishing house and to the author for creating a salable book.) The editor will discuss specific details pertaining to the manuscript, such as whether there is a special background that the illustrator needs to understand or a special place or time that must be pictured (for which the author may have furnished photographs or other source materials). However, the editor will not dictate to the illustrator. Janet may wish that she could sit down with the illustrator and explain what she would like to see in each picture. The editor might like to do that, too. But the editor will not allow herself, the author or even the art director, to do this.

The illustrator's vision

Illustrators are the third part of the troika, and they too have rights in the creation of a picture book. Authors have the ability to create stories or nonfiction texts and to write in a way that makes that material come alive in the mind of a reader. Editors have the ability to read a text, to see its potential, to help the author realize his or her vision of what the text ought to be, and to take the text to an illustrator and see both text and pictures through to a finished book that is more than the sum of the parts. Illustrators have the ability to take a text and, using the visions of authors and editors, add their own sense of life and the world by creating a visual complement to the text. They not only illustrate what is there, but extend it in ways that authors and editors may never have considered.

The illustrator generally creates a dummy first, breaking the text in ways that make possible the illustrations that seem to fit best the vision he or she has of the book. The trim size of the book, the number of pages it will contain, and the amount of color it will have are all determined by the editor, the art director and the production department of the publisher. These all have to do with the price the finished book will have to carry. However, there is some flexibility here, and the illustrator's ideas of size and shape are certainly taken into account. It may not be possible to do exactly what the illustrator wants, but the publisher will try to come as close as possible.

After the illustrator completes a rough dummy, with perhaps one finished piece of art, the editor can see where the illustrator is going and decide if these pictures will create a book that seems to have emerged from one mind and not as the product of a troika. The editor may send the author copies of what the illustrator has done, or have the author view the work in person if he lives close by. But the editor probably will not bring the author and illustrator together. The reason for this is simply that each must be free to create on their own. An author who is too dominant will, even at this stage, inhibit the work of the illustrator, who may as a result not try to realize an extended vision of the work, but only the author's. And the final pictures may be stiff and unnatural. On the other hand, a dominant illustrator can try to influence the author to change the text, to give more picture space or to introduce elements that the illustrator would like to include, and the result may be a story that does not work as well as the initial story and pictures that so dominate the book that the author's work is lost. However, when an editor believes that an author and an illustrator will work well together, the two are sometimes brought together to work out problems between text and illustration—and the result can be very good.

The final product

Eventually the artwork is finished. The editor and the art director may ask for a few corrections and may see things in the pictures that do not agree with the text. But most major changes are made at the dummy stage. Again, the author may be asked to come in to look at the art, or color copies (with colors that may not be true and may lack much of the finished beauty of the art itself) may be sent. At this stage, however, unless the author finds some terrible error, not much change can or will be made. The picture book is all but finished.

Finally the book is printed, bound, and ready to be sold. Whose book is it? It is the author's book because it started with the author's words and the author's view of the world. It is the editor's book because he or she helped the author get the words right by realizing the vision of the perfect text, finding the right illustrator and working with art director and the production department to produce the finished book. It is the illustrator's book because he or she contributed a separate vision to the text and blended that vision with the original to create something that is fuller, richer and more creative than author and editor might have conceived. The finished book could not exist without any one of these contributors, and each needs to realize the right and responsibility of the others to do the very best job possible.

"I guess I never thought about it in quite that way," says Janet. "A troika. And there's no way around it."

None. Unless, instead of getting an advance and a royalty you want to find and pay your own illustrator, find your own printer and pay to have the book printed, and then find a way to sell the books you have published. In the end, three heads may be better than one.

First Books

Success for most writers and illustrators does not come easily. Freelancers are eager to find markets for their work and they know their paths to success will come if they can just get those first bylines. Patience, dedication and hard work eventually will pay off for a talented artist or writer, but the time before that first sale is filled with uncertainty and frustration.

The three people featured in this section have learned much through their beginning experiences. Their publishing exploits are described in the following stories, in which they provide advice for writers and illustrators still trying to get started. After reading about these artists you will know that selling your first book or illustrations requires tenacity and drive. And you will understand the motivation behind those first big sales.

Elizabeth Morgan
Jane Long: A Child's Pictorial History (Eakin Press)

In a letter to *Children's Writer's & Illustrator's Market*, Elizabeth Morgan wrote, "I decided to become a children's book writer in 1989, the same year that the inaugural issue of the *Children's Writer's & Illustrator's Market* came out. For this reason, I feel that we've 'grown up' together, and wanted to let you all know how much your guidance has helped me."

While this book has been a valuable resource to her, the credit really belongs to Morgan. After all, all the resource guides in the world won't get a writer anywhere if the writer isn't motivated. Fortunately, Morgan's persistence is relentless.

As a New Year's resolution in 1989, she decided to become a writer. "At the time my son was three and I decided I could write things that were as good as what I was reading to him." She attempted to write a picture book and found out, though, that it wasn't quite that easy. After receiving 10 rejections, she decided fiction wasn't her thing. Instead, she discovered a knack for nonfiction.

Having found Eakin Press, a publisher that specializes in books about Texas, and being an eighth-generation Texan herself, she decided to compile a photo biography on her favorite Texas heroine, Jane Long. Morgan knew the publisher already had a book on Jane Long, but she believed she could sway the editor by presenting a book which was more factually oriented and illustrated with a lot more photographs than the previous one. She was wrong.

"A wiser writer would have cut her losses and chosen another of the hundreds of fascinating Texas subjects to write about and tried again with this publisher. But nooo! By then I was so wrapped up in the project that I had to find it a home." Morgan tried different publishers, but the manuscript was rejected 23 times. Some of those rejections, however, contained favorable comments and recommendations to contact Eakin Press a second time.

It was at an Austin Writers' League workshop that she learned the key might be in the query. She was advised by David Morgan, an agent leading a class at the workshop, to improve certain areas of her query letter. So she rewrote the query and tried Eakin Press again. This time it worked (a copy of Morgan's revised query letter can be found in the Business of Children's Writing & Illustrating on page 21). "This one was more specific instead of vague," she says of the second query. "It was less self-indulgent in that it was less descriptive of how much I like Jane Long and more forceful and persuasive about why the editor should like her." Her book, *Jane Long: A Child's Pictorial History* (featuring photographs by her sister and writing partner, Nancy Dearing Johnson), was published in fall 1992 and includes a foreward by Texas Governor Ann Richards.

Morgan, a teacher by trade, did loads of reading and research to prepare herself. She read as many books on writing that she could, including *How You Can Make $25,000 a Year Writing No Matter Where You Live* (by Nancy Edmonds Hanson), *How to Write a Book Proposal* (by Michael Larsen) and *Nonfiction for Children: How to Write It, How to Sell It* (by Ellen Roberts). To write the Jane Long photo biography, she read all the books there were on Jane Long. "There aren't very many," she says. She also visited museums, scoured for archival pictures and traveled to various places where her heroine spent her life. In fact, she discovered errors in recorded facts about Long that had been passed down. "Once something is recorded in a book, even though the information may be wrong, it becomes fact," she says.

Having her first experience getting a book published behind her, Morgan says from now on she'll take a different approach to writing her nonfiction books. "Next time I'll send the proposal first before I write the book. However, for my first book, it was necessary for me to write the book first because I wasn't sure if I could."

Now she's doing all she can to promote her first book. Eakin Press markets heavily in Texas schools. Morgan's plans for the near future include a Jane Long tour, or, visiting all the schools in Texas that were named after Jane Long. "Once you sell your first book," she says, "you're the only one who knows how to sell it right. It's important to plan your own marketing strategy."

Morgan doesn't plan to stop at just one book, though. She says she's full of ideas for books with Texas themes. In addition, she's currently marketing a children's book on roller skating and an adult book entitled *Mississippi Mansions*. She got the idea for the latter book while doing research on Jane Long in Mississippi.

Morgan thinks there will be more books down the line for her. "One word to describe me is relentless. I have a lot of motivation and I want to expand my career as a writer. I'm either going to make it or die trying."

—Lisa Carpenter

Cathy Sturm
Whose Toes Are Those (Barrons Educational Series)

As an illustrator, Cathy Sturm is living proof that publishers do take unsolicited art samples seriously, even if it takes a while for a response.

It was a year before Sturm, a graduate of the Art Academy of Cincinnati, heard from Barrons Educational Series about the promotional flier she sent them. It just happened that her style was exactly what they were looking for. Her first picture book, a peek-a-boo novelty book entitled *Whose Toes Are Those* (written by Joyce Elias), was published in November 1992.

Her artistic background includes working as a production artist for a T-shirt company and working in the lettering department of a greeting card publisher. In 1988, when she became a fulltime mother, she decided to make a go of it as a freelancer. "I had been told my style was humorous but cute," she says. "So I got a copy of *Artist's Market* (the 1988 edition—one year before the first edition of *Children's Writer's & Illustrator's Market*) and contacted all the kids' magazines."

Her first illustration job came that year when she did some work for *Humpty Dumpty*. Since then, she's also sold greeting card illustrations, landed some work with *Spark!* and done school posters for Modern Curriculum.

Still, she was interested in landing assignments in book publishing. "I sent out gobs and gobs of letters with my flier. It was so depressing to never hear anything." She even called publishers to make sure they had received her material. "They would all say it was on file," she says, indicating she was not sure whether to believe that response or not. But one day, somebody called her.

Grace Freedson at Barrons Educational Series contacted Sturm to offer her the opportunity to submit an illustration on speculation for a picture book they had just purchased. "She sent me the text of the book and wanted me to illustrate a frog. So I did a full page in pencil with a section of it being in color in order to show my color scheme. When they received it, they absolutely loved it," says Sturm.

Sturm was offered a contract and given the option of being paid by a flat fee or royalties. She opted for royalites, noting that she was told publishers prefer to pay royalties because it provides more of an incentive for illustrators to do their best work (since what they make depends on how many of the books sell). "I received one-third of my advance when I signed the contract, one-third upon delivering sketches and the final one-third upon providing final artwork."

Sturm says that while illustrating the book she learned just how picky picture book publishers were about details, especially educational publishers such as Barrons. She recalls when it came time to discuss her work over the phone with her editor. "I thought she wanted to talk about moving things around in the pictures. I was surprised when she asked me if the monkey I had drawn was a Chinese monkey or an African monkey."

It never occurred to Sturm her animals had to be ethnically correct and consistent in her pictures. For example, when she turned in her illustration of a panda, the picture included a drawing of a green snake. "I was told I couldn't use a green snake. The snake had to be native to China." The same inconsistency showed up when she drew penguins and polar bears in the same picture. "I couldn't do that because penguins live in the South Pole while polar bears are in the North Pole. They never meet," she says.

Looking back, Sturm assures that publishers do look at the art samples they receive and keep on file. She advises illustrators to keep good records of which publishers they have submitted material to. After all, she says, it may take a while. When someone does call, you'll want to remember who they are.

—Lisa Carpenter

Laura Krauss Melmed
The Rainbabies (Lothrop, Lee & Shepard Books)

Laura Krauss Melmed's first published book, *The Rainbabies*, illustrated by Jim LaMarche and published by Lothrup, Lee & Shepard Books, is an original fairy tale. It is a story book/picture book about a childless couple that wishes for a child one rainy night in the light of a full moon. A "moonshower" touches them and they find 12 tiny babies, no bigger than your big toe, in the sparkling light. The couple cares lovingly for them and one day Mother Moonshower takes the babies back. Because the couple cared so well for the tiny babies, they are rewarded with a child of their own.

"As a child I was always fascinated by fairy tales," says Melmed, who read all of Hans Christian Andersen's stories. She says she doesn't write specifically for her children, but always has them in mind. She read a great deal to her three children and believes children's literature is very important. Melmed has a master's degree in early childhood education and taught in the early 1970s in New Orleans.

The First Song Ever Sung, which was actually the first book she wrote, is slated to be published by Lothrup in the fall of 1993. It will be illustrated by a very busy Ed Young, who was awarded the Caldecott Medal in 1990. Having Young associated with the book will add prestige to Melmed's work. Melmed says the inspiration for this book came from her son who asked her the question, "What was the first song ever sung?" The book is her answer to that question. Her husband and friends were impressed with the story and encouraged her to submit it for publication. She did and it was accepted. She also is also under contract with Lothrup to complete two picture books.

Her publishing experiences have been very good, "a combination of lucky circumstances and hard work," she says. Along with her book success she has had poetry published in *Cricket Magazine*, a literary magazine for children. "I would like to write a novel some day, but I don't have a particular idea for one yet," says Melmed, who "sometimes gets lost in the art of writing."

Melmed belongs to the Society of Children's Book Writers & Illustrators and attends workshops at the Writer's Center in Washington DC. Surprisingly, she took her first children's book writing class after her first book was published. She says she is looking for a critique group to get feedback on her writing. "I think it is important to belong to a writing group. Writing can be quite isolating and it's nice to talk with others and share experiences."

She advises writers "to stay in touch with the child dwelling within them, to find ways to reach outward and inward to renew their own sense of wonder about the world and to try to present those feelings and perceptions as a gift to the children for whom they are writing."

Melmed adds, "Don't get discouraged about rejections and don't take it personally. Know your market and what different publishers are publishing before sending your manuscript. It takes lots of perseverance and discipline. Make your writing a priority in your daily routine. Become an informed participant in the publishing of your book."

—Deborah Cinnamon

THE RAINBABIES

BY LAURA KRAUSS MELMED ——— ILLUSTRATED BY JIM LaMARCHE

LOTHROP, LEE & SHEPARD BOOKS 1350 AVENUE OF THE AMERICAS, NEW YORK, N.Y. 10019

Inappropriate Submissions: What Bothers Editors?

by Pat Matson Knapp

The desks of most children's book and magazine editors are piled high with submissions from aspiring writers and artists, but the lion's share of the manuscripts and artwork won't make it past the first read. Why? It's very simple, say editors: Writers and artists often send their work to the wrong publishers. Editors are inundated with inappropriate submissions because many writers and artists submit their work without researching the publishers' needs. Even the most well-crafted young adult mystery won't interest the editor of a publishing company that specializes in young reader picture books. And a science fiction-type illustration is probably not appropriate for a Christian children's magazine.

To identify some of the most common mistakes made by writers and artists when submitting their work, *Children's Writer's & Illustrator's Market* conducted a survey of children's book and magazine editors, asking them to "sound off" about inappropriate unsolicited manuscripts. The survey asked for examples of inappropriate submissions, ways that magazine and book editors deal with them, and suggestions for writers and artists submitting unsolicited work.

Do your homework

By far the most common complaint of editors was that many writers and illustrators just don't do their homework before submitting manuscripts to book publishers or magazines. While many writers and illustrators apparently hope that random submissions will somehow result in that lucky break, they often do little more than irritate the editors who receive them.

"Writers and artists would do themselves, and us, a big favor if they would research the houses to which they'd like to send material," says Kristen Breck, editorial assistant for Chronicle Books. "We often receive chapter books for middle grade/young adult fiction, which we don't publish at all. We receive fantasy and self-help for older readers, too, which we also don't publish."

Janice Boland, editor at Richard C. Owen Publishers, Inc., says her company rejects 98 percent of the manuscripts it receives after reading them only once. "Why? Two main reasons: People don't get our guidelines before they send us their submissions, and people don't read the guidelines once they get them." Boland says her company's guidelines state manuscript criteria quite clearly, but writers still send inappropriate material. "We don't consider holiday themes, but still we receive dozens of Halloween and Christmas tales. We tell authors we do not want cutesy, talking animals. Guess what we get? —Sally Beaver, who wears little pink overalls when she builds dams."

Bradley L. Winch, president of Jalmar Press, strongly encourages writers to

Pat Matson Knapp is a Cincinnati-based journalist and writer who has contributed to HOW magazine and The Artist's Magazine.

know their market before submitting manuscripts. "When you submit a manuscript to me, I need to know that you know what you are talking about," says Winch. "Show me that you know the market—what's available, what sells, why your manuscript deserves to be read by me (and others if eventually published), how you can help promote the title, and your market research on the title. Be thorough. Be professional."

Robert Bittner, assistant editor for Lion Publishing, says, "I'm amazed at how many writers ask us to describe our books to them. Writers need to know what we publish, and they can find out easily through our catalog or a store visit." Robert W. Gordon, vice president of editorial for Players Press, Inc., says some illustrators are also guilty of not doing their research. "Illustrators send what they want but never seem to look at what the publisher uses," he says. "If their style is wrong they send samples anyway."

Editors say writers and illustrators should begin their research by familiarizing themselves with the listings in books such as this one, then matching their manuscript or illustrations with the styles and editorial content of publishers or magazines. Libraries and bookstores are an obvious place to expand your research. Read as many books or magazines in your genre as possible to develop a feel for the market. Once you identify a "target list" of publishers and magazines likely to be interested in your work, gather more information about them by requesting book catalogs and/or submission guidelines—and then read them carefully.

Most book publishers and magazines provide submission guidelines free with a SASE, and most are very explicit about the type of work they consider. In addition to their detailed listings in market directories, some publish author's newsletters to provide more helpful information, and others provide contact information for professional organizations, such as the Children's Book Council and the Society of Children's Book Writers & Illustrators. "We also try to alert first-time authors and artists to common submission mistakes whenever we speak at writer's conferences," notes Stephanie Owens Lurie, senior editor at Little, Brown and Company.

Packaging your submissions

Another pet peeve echoed often by editors was improper packaging of submissions: no SASE or SASE too small to return work in, lack of a cover letter or even a contact name and phone number, original artwork instead of photocopies, and sloppily typed manuscripts.

Laura Walsh, editorial assistant for Philomel Books, says she often receives original artwork or dummies with no postage or insufficient packaging to return them. Wendy S. Larson, assistant to the editor-in-chief for Grosset & Dunlap, also says many writers and artists fail to enclose a SASE or often enclose a letter-size SASE when requesting an 8 × 10-inch catalog. Many publishers quickly file away or discard queries or manuscripts that don't come with a SASE.

"My biggest peeve is with authors who submit manuscripts in care of the editor who worked here five years ago," says Susan Stokes, editor for Woodbine House. "They're obviously using outdated references. Also, people who don't send envelopes large enough to accommodate returning the manuscript."

Sinda S. Zinn, editor of *Junior Trails* magazine, says manuscripts that are typed sloppily and contain numerous spelling errors make a bad first impression with editors. "Writers should give attention to the appearance of their manuscript," she says. "A manuscript neatly typed with few errors gives a more favorable impression than a manuscript with numerous misspellings and typed on paper with several markings."

Many submissions arrive without even the most basic information, such as return addresses, say editors. "Some artists simply send samples, with no cover letter, so I don't know anything about them, or sometimes even how to contact them should I have an assignment," says Susannah C. West, editor of *Hobson's Choice* magazine.

Kristina Russelo, editor of Black Moss Press, says she received a 750-page manuscript, obviously a typed original rather than a photocopy, with two different return addresses, one on the envelope and another on the title page. "How can you respond patiently to such blatant idiocy?"

Again, editors urge you to read their submission guidelines carefully to determine how manuscripts or artwork should be formatted and packaged. The guidelines will tell you if the editor prefers a query letter, cover letter, book proposal, complete manuscript or resume as part of the submission, and in the case of illustrators, how the artwork should be packaged and if they prefer slides or photocopies. (The Business of Children's Writing & Illustrating, on page 19, offers some helpful tips on formatting and packaging your submissions.)

"Talking down" and other pitfalls

A common pitfall for beginning children's writers is the temptation to "talk down" to their readers. "The biggest problem we have with manuscript submissions is authors writing down to teenagers," notes M. Lesa Salyer, editor of *Young Salvationist* magazine. "Very often, they place high school characters in junior high situations and use childhood dialogue! I always remind writers that teens will read 'up' (about characters/situations 'older' than themselves), but they will not read 'down.' "

Christine Clark, editor of *Humpty Dumpty's Magazine*, believes writers talk down to readers when they are trying to communicate a difficult concept. She relates a favorite example: "Our supply of health-related stories and articles is never adequate, so many writers see health-related material as a good way to break in (which it is). But writing about health isn't easy, and a common pitfall is the tendency to talk down to readers. Our favorite bad example of this: a fiction story with anthropomorphized head lice named Hedda and Lyle!"

Clark says writers struggling with a difficult concept, such as health, often take the easy way out by trying to incorporate factual information into a fictional story. "The result is usually a slight, plotless story that doesn't lend itself to illustration," she says. "The better way is often a nonfiction piece with a creative presentation, but many children's writers seem reluctant to try nonfiction."

Other common writing mistakes cited by the editors are loose, rambling prose; manuscripts in verse; "cute" stories about bunnies, puppies or kittens; stories that lack a clear beginning, middle and end; unbelievable characters;

overwriting; stories that depend on coincidence for resolution of the plot; and stories that seem "old-fashioned" and irrelevant to today's world.

"People who want to write children's books should read children's books," advises Janice Boland. "Yes, actually go to the library, sit at one of those little tables, and read, read, read. This isn't the fifties. No more Dick and Jane. Mother is divorced. Father works nights. Tamika has replaced Sally. We don't want grim reality, just reality. Try it! And before you send it out, read it out loud."

The Business of Children's Writing & Illustrating

by Lisa Carpenter

When a writer or illustrator decides to market their freelancing talents they will encounter many unexpected problems, and develop numerous questions about the field of children's writing and illustrating. "What is the proper way to submit my work?" "Do I need an agent?" "How much should I ask for my work?" This section is designed to expose you to the business techniques needed to successfully market your work. It will answer many of your questions and put you on the road to success in the field.

Researching markets

There are two basic elements to submitting your work successfully: good research and persistence. Read through the listings in this book and familiarize yourself with the publications that interest you. Then study the specific needs and the required submission procedures of each publisher or publication. Editors hate to receive inappropriate submissions because handling them wastes precious time. (See article on Inappropriate Submissions beginning on page 15). By randomly sending out manuscripts without knowledge of the markets' needs, you risk irritating the editors. Because editors may remember your name and associate it with inappropriate submissions, this practice actually hurts you more than it helps you.

If you're interested in submitting to a particular magazine, write to request a sample copy. For a book publisher, obtain a book catalog or a couple of books produced by that publisher. By doing this, you can better acquaint yourself with that market's writing and illustration styles and formats.

Most of the book publishers and magazines listed offer some sort of writer's/artist's guidelines. Read these guidelines before submitting work.

Formats for submission

Throughout these listings you will read editors' requests for a query letter, cover letter, book proposal, complete manuscript or résumé as all or part of the initial contact procedure. Any correspondence or submissions should be directed to a specific person. Turnover at publishing companies and magazines is rampant. Therefore, it is a good idea to call the publisher to confirm a contact name before sending anything. There is no need to disturb the contact person by asking to speak with her; merely ask the receptionist or secretary if the person still works there and if she still handles the same manuscripts/artwork.

Query letters. A query letter should be no more than a one-page, well written piece to arouse an editor's interest in your manuscript. Queries are usually required from writers submitting nonfiction material to a publisher. In the query letter you want to convince the editor that your idea is perfect for his readership and that you're the writer qualified to do the job. Include any previous writing experience in your letter plus published samples to prove your credentials, especially any samples that relate to the subject matter about which you're querying.

Many query letters start with a lead similar to the lead that would be used in the actual manuscript. Next, you want to briefly outline the work and include facts, anecdotes, interviews or any other pertinent information that give the editor a feel for the manuscript's premise. Your goal is to entice him to want to know more. End your letter with a straight-forward request to write (or submit) the work, and include information on its approximate length, date it could be completed and the availability of accompanying photos or artwork.

More and more, queries are being used for fiction manuscripts because slush piles at some publishing houses have become virtually uncontrollable. Most initial slush pile reading is performed by editorial assistants and junior editors. However, as the number of submissions continues to skyrocket, several publishers have stopped accepting slush. Though these publishers no longer accept unsolicited submissions, they are still open to queries. For a fiction query you want to explain the story's plot, main characters, conflict and resolution. Just as in nonfiction queries, you want to make the editor eager to see more. (See Elizabeth Morgan's sample query letter on page 21.) Or, for more information on writing good queries, consult *How to Write Irresistible Query Letters*, by Lisa Collier Cool (Writer's Digest Books).

Cover letters. Many editors prefer to review a complete manuscript, especially for fiction. In such a case, the cover letter will serve to introduce you and establish your credentials as a writer plus give the editor an overview of the manuscript.

If an editor asked you for a manuscript because of a previous query make sure you note this fact in your cover letter. Also, if a rejection letter includes an invitation for you to submit other work, mention that fact as well. Editors should understand that the work was solicited.

For an illustrator, the cover letter will also serve as your introduction to the art director and establish your credentials as a professional artist. Be sure to explain what services you can provide as well as what type of follow-up contact you plan to make, if any. If you are sending samples of your work, indicate whether they should be returned or filed. Never send original artwork! If you wish to have the samples returned, include a self-addressed, stamped envelope (SASE) with your submission packet. Cover letters, like the query, should be no longer than one page.

Résumés. Often writers and illustrators are asked to submit a résumé with their cover letter and writing/art samples. Résumés can be created in a variety of formats ranging from a single page listing information to color brochures featuring your art. Keep the résumé brief, and focus on your artistic achievements, not your whole life. On your résumé you want to include your clients and the work you did for them. Also include your educational background and any awards you've won. Do not use the same résumé that you use for a typical job application.

Book proposals. Throughout the listings in the Book Publishers section you will find references to submission of a synopsis, outline and sample chapters.

7803 Kincheon Court
Austin, TX 78749-2880
January 12, 1991

Eakin Press
Attn: Edwin Eakin
P.O. Box 90159
Austin, TX 78709-0159

Dear Mr. Eakin:

As a public school teacher, I know how difficult it can be to capture students' interest in the important events that shaped our state. The television generation is fond of slick formats with succinct wording and vivid illustrations.

My biography of Jane Long brings the Mother of Texas to life with a 5,000 word nonfiction account of her days in Texas under five of its six flags, and how she helped shape the state's destiny.

Thirty photographs and portraits bring the dry, dusty pages of Texas history to the video age. The students are able to see photographs of Jane Long and her famous friends, such as Texas heroes Ben Milam, Sam Houston, Stephen F. Austin, William Barrett Travis, and Mirabeau B. Lamar.

Also photographed are places students can go see today, such as the mansion where she lived in Mississippi, sites of important events of her life in Texas, and modern schools that are her namesakes.

In my research I have come across a number of errors that have been passed down through the years by earlier biographers. My book explains how these errors were discovered and corrected.

Jane Long, the Mother of Texas, has been called the most courageous pioneer of Anglo women in this state. I hope you will want to see my *Jane Long* manuscript and photo collection to find out why. This query was submitted simultaneously to another publisher.

Sincerely

Elizabeth Morgan

This is a sample query letter written by Texas author Elizabeth Morgan. In our First Books feature beginning on page 10 Morgan explains how this letter helped her sell her first book.

Depending on an editor's preference, some or all of these components, as well as inclusion of a cover letter, comprise a book proposal.

A synopsis summarizes the book. Such a summary includes the basic plot of the book (including the ending), is easy to read and flows well.

An outline can also be used to set up fiction, but is more effective as a tool for nonfiction. The outline covers your book chapter by chapter and provides highlights of each. If you are developing an outline for fiction you will want to include major characters, plots and subplots, and length of the book. An outline can run to 30 pages depending on the complexity of your manuscript.

Sample chapters give a more comprehensive idea of your writing skill. Some editors may request the first two or three chapters to see how your material is set up; others may request a beginning, middle and ending chapter to get a better feel for the entire plot. Be sure to determine what the editor needs to see before investing time in writing sample chapters.

Many picture book editors require an outline or synopsis, sample chapters and a variation of roughs or finished illustrations from the author/illustrator. Listings specifying an interest in picture books will detail what type of artwork should accompany manuscripts. If you want to know more about putting together a book proposal, read *How to Write a Book Proposal*, by Michael Larsen (Writer's Digest Books).

Manuscript formats. If an editor specifies that you should submit a complete manuscript for review, here is some format information to guide you. In the upper left corner of your title page, type your legal name (not pseudonym), address, phone number and Social Security number (publishers must have this to file payment records with the government). In the upper right corner you should type the approximate word length. All material in the upper corners should be typed single-spaced, not double. Then type the title (centered) almost halfway down the page with the word "by" two spaces under that and your name or pseudonym two spaces under "by."

The first page should include the title (centered) one-third of the way down. Two spaces under that type "by" and your name or pseudonym. To begin the body of your manuscript, drop down two double spaces and indent five spaces for each new paragraph. There should be 1¼ inch margins around all sides of a full typewritten page. (Manuscripts with wider margins are easier to edit. Also, a page that isn't cramped with a lot of words is more readable and appealing to an editor.) Be sure to set your typewriter on double-space for the manuscript body. From page 2 to the end of your manuscript just include your last name followed by a comma and the title (or key words of the title) in the upper left corner. The page number should go in the top right corner. Drop down two double spaces to begin the body of the page and follow this format throughout the manuscript. If you're submitting a novel, type each chapter title one-third of the way down the page.

When typing text of a picture book, it is not necessary to include page breaks or worry about supplying art. Editors prefer to find the illustrators for picture books. Most of the time, a writer and an illustrator who work on the same book don't know and never meet each other. In this kind of an arrangement, the editor acts as a go-between in case either the writer or illustrator has any problems with text or artwork.

If you are an illustrator who has written your own book, create a dummy or storyboard containing both art and text. Then submit it along with sample pieces of final art (color photocopies — no originals). For a step-by-step guide on creating a good dummy, refer to Frieda Gates' book, *How to Write, Illustrate, and Design Children's Books* (Lloyd-Simone Publishing Company).

For more information on manuscript formats read *Manuscript Submission*, by Scott Edelstein (Writer's Digest Books).

To get an approximate word count for your manuscript, first count the number of characters and spaces in an average line, next count the number of lines on a representative page and multiply these two factors to get your average number of characters per page. Finally, count the number of pages in your manuscript, multiply by the characters per page, then divide by 6 (the average number of characters in a word). You will have your approximate word count.

Mailing and recording submissions

Your primary concern in packaging material is to ensure that it arrives undamaged.

If your manuscript is fewer than six pages it is safe to simply fold it in thirds and send it out in a #10 (business-size) envelope. For a self-addressed, stamped envelope (SASE) you can then fold another #10 envelope in thirds or insert a #9 (reply) envelope which fits in a #10 neatly without any folding at all. Some editors appreciate receiving a manuscript folded in half into a 6x9 envelope. For larger manuscripts you will want to use a 9x12 envelope both for mailing the submission out and as a SASE for its return. The SASE envelope can be folded in half. Book manuscripts will require a sturdy box such as a typing paper or envelope box for mailing. Include a self-addressed mailing label and return postage so it can also double as your SASE.

Artwork requires a bit more packaging care to guarantee that it arrives in presentable form. Sandwich illustrations between heavy cardboard that is slightly larger than the work and tape it closed. You will want to write your name and address on each piece in case the inside material becomes separated from the outer envelope upon receipt. For the outer wrapping you can use either a manila envelope, foam-padded envelope, a mailer with plastic air bubbles as a liner or brown wrapping paper. Bind non-joined edges with reinforced mailing tape and clearly write your address.

You will want to mail material first-class to ensure quick delivery. Also, first-class mail is forwarded for one year if the addressee has moved (which does happen with some magazine and book publishers), and can be returned if undeliverable.

If you are concerned about your material safely reaching its destination, consider other mailing options, such as UPS. If material needs to reach your editor or art director quickly, you can elect to use overnight delivery services.

Occasionally throughout this book you will see the term International Reply Coupon (IRC). Keep in mind foreign markets cannot use U.S. postage when returning a manuscript to you, which therefore renders moot any SASE you may have sent. When mailing a submission to another country (Canada too), include IRC in lieu of U.S. postage. The U.S. post office can help you determine, based on your package's weight, the correct number of IRC to include to ensure its return.

If it is not necessary for an editor to return your work, such as with photocopies of manuscripts or art, don't include return postage. This saves you the cost of extra postage. Instead, track the status of your submissions by enclosing a postage-paid reply postcard (which requires less postage) with options for the editor to check, such as "yes, I am interested" or "no, the material is not appropriate for my needs at this time."

Some writers or illustrators simply set a deadline date. If nothing is heard from the editor or art director by this date, the manuscript or artwork is automatically withdrawn from consideration. Because many publishing houses are overstocked with manuscripts, a minimum deadline should be no less than 3 months.

If you opt for simultaneous submissions, be sure to inform the editor your work is being considered elsewhere. Though it's not set in stone, it is a professional courtesy that is encouraged throughout the field. Most editors are reluctant to receive simultaneous submissions, but understand the frustration experienced by hopeful authors who have to wait many months for a response. In some cases, an editor may actually be more inclined to read your manuscript sooner because he knows it's being considered elsewhere. The Society of Children's Book Writers & Illustrators warns against simultaneous submissions, the feeling being eventually they will cause publishers to quit accepting unsolicited material altogether. Also, since manuscripts that are simultaneously submitted are not specifically tailored to any one publisher, SCBWI feels the act will result in less than serious consideration of work received. The official recommendation of the SCBWI is to submit to one publisher at a time, but wait only three months (note you will do so in your cover letter). If no response is received, then send a note withdrawing your manuscript from consideration. SCBWI considers multiple submissions acceptable if you have a manuscript dealing with a timely issue.

One thing you should never do is use a publisher's fax number to send queries, manuscripts or illustration samples. Only use a fax number after acquiring proper authorization. Don't disrupt the publisher's pace of doing internal business by sending a long manuscript via fax.

Many times writers and illustrators devote their attention to submitting material to editors or art directors, then fail to follow up on overdue responses because they feel the situation is out of their hands. By tracking those submissions still under consideration and then following up, you may be able to refresh a buyer's memory who temporarily forgot about your submission, or revise a troublesome point to make your work more enticing to him. At the very least you will receive a definite "no," thereby freeing you to send your material to another market.

It is especially important to keep track of submissions when you are submitting simultaneously. This way if you get an offer on that manuscript, you will be able to notify the other publishers to withdraw your work from consideration.

When recording your submissions be sure to include the date they were sent, the business and contact name, and any enclosures that were inserted such as samples of writing, artwork or photography. Keep copies of the article or manuscript as well as related correspondence for easier follow up. When you sell rights to a manuscript or artwork you can "close" your file by noting the date the material was accepted, what rights were purchased, the publication date and payment.

Agents

Many children's writers and illustrators, especially those who are just beginning, are confused about whether to utilize the services of an agent. The decision about obtaining an agent's services is strictly one that each writer or illustrator must decide for himself. There are some who are confident enough with their own negotiation skills and feel acquiring an agent is not in their best interest. Still, others scare easily at the slightest mention of business and are not willing to sacrifice valuable writing or illustrating time for the time it takes to market their work. Before you put any thought into whether to contact an agent, read on to become familiar with what an agent can—and cannot—do.

There is enough demand for children's material that breaking into children's publishing without an agent is easier than breaking in with adult titles. In fact, many agents avoid working with children's books because traditionally low advances and trickling royalty payments over long periods of time make children's books less lucrative. Acquiring an agent to market short stories is next to impossible—there just isn't enough of a financial incentive for an agent to be interested.

One benefit of having an agent, though, is it may expedite the process of getting your work looked at, especially with publishers who don't accept unagented submissions. If an agent has a good reputation and submits your manuscript to an editor, that manuscript may actually bypass the first-read stage (which is done by editorial assistants and junior editors) and end up on that editor's desk sooner.

Illustrators who live elsewhere often seek representatives based in New York City when they want their work shown to New York City publishers.

When agreeing to have a reputable agent represent you, keep in mind he should be familiar with the needs of the current market and evaluate your manuscript/artwork accordingly. He should also be able to determine the quality of your piece and whether it is salable. Upon selling your manuscript, your agent should be able to negotiate a favorable contract. Also, sometimes royalty statements can be confusing; your agent should be able to clear up any questions you have about monetary payments. One advantage to having an agent be the "go-between" is his acting as the bad guy during the negotiations. This allows you, as an individual, to preserve your good faith with the publisher.

Keep in mind, though, however reputable the agent is, he has limitations. An agent's representation does not guarantee sale of your work. It just means he sees potential in your writing or art. Though an agent may offer criticism or advice on how to improve your book, he cannot make you a better writer or give you fame.

Agents typically charge a 15 percent commission from the sale of your writing or art material. Such fees will be taken from your advance and royalty earnings. If your agent sells foreign rights to your work, he will deduct 20 percent because he will most likely be dealing with an overseas agent with whom he must split the fee.

Some agents offer reading services. If you are a new writer, you will probably be charged a fee of less than $75. Many times, if an agent agrees to represent you, the fee will be reimbursed (though not always). If you take advantage of an agency's critique service, you will probably pay a range of $25-200 depending on the length of the manuscript. The purpose of a critique service is not to polish the manuscript, but to offer advice based on the agent's knowledge of what sells in juvenile publishing. Prior to engaging in a reading or critique service, you should find out up front what results to expect. Watch out for agencies that derive most of their income from reading and critique services. Unfortunately, there are "quacks" in this business who are more interested in earning their money from services than from selling books. Other standard fees incurred from an agent include miscellaneous expenses such as photocopying, phone bills, postage or messenger services. Before signing a contract with an agent, be sure you know exactly what the terms are, such as what rate of commission is charged and what expenses you will be expected to pay.

Be advised that not every agent is open to representing a writer or artist who doesn't have some sort of track record. Your manuscript or artwork, and query or cover letters, must be attractive and professional looking. Your first impression must be that of an organized, articulate person.

Feel free to investigate an agent before contacting him. Determine how familiar and successful he is with selling to children's publishers. For a detailed directory of literary agents and art/photo reps refer to *Guide to Literary Agents and Art/Photo Reps* (Writer's Digest Books).

Negotiating contracts and royalties

Negotiation is a two-way street on which, hopefully, both the author/artist and editor/art director will feel mutual satisfaction prior to signing a contract.

Book publishers pay authors and artists in royalties, or rather, a percentage of either the wholesale or retail price of each book sold. Usually with large publishing houses, before the book is published, the author or artist receives an advance issued against future royalties. Half of the advance amount is issued upon signing the book contract. The other half is issued when the book is finished. For illustrations, one-third of the advance should be collected upon signing the contract; one-third upon delivery of sketches; and one-third upon delivery of finished art. After your book has sold enough copies to earn back your advance, you will start to get royalty checks. Some publishers hold a reserve against returns. In other words, a percentage of royalties is held back in case books are returned. If you have such a reserve clause in your contract, make sure to be informed of the exact percentage of total sales that will be withheld and the time period the publisher will hold this money. You should be reimbursed this amount after a reasonable time period, such as a year. Royalty percentages vary with each publisher, but there are standard ranges.

For picture books, the writer and illustrator (if two people) should each be able to get $2,000-5,000 advances. Royalties range from 6-10% and are usually split equally between the writer and illustrator. A writer who also does the illustrations usually gets a higher advance ($4,000-7,000) and the full royalty.

Writers of chapter books or middle grade novels should expect royalties of 5-10% and an advance of $3,000-6,000. Illustrators who do 10-15 black and white illustrations and a color cover for these books should get a $3,000-5,000 advance and 2-5% royalties.

Authors of young adult novels can expect a $3,500-6,000 advance with royalty rates of 2-5%. Usually, an artist is paid one flat fee to do one color illustration for the cover.

For all types of books, royalty rates for hardcover books should be higher than percentage rates for paperbacks.

One way to determine a fair advance is to multiply the print run by the cover price and then multiply that figure with the royalty percentage. If you feel the advance is too low, ask for higher royalties.

Price structures for magazines are based on a per-word rate or range for a specific length of article.

Artists have a few more variables to contend with prior to contracting their services. Payment for illustrations can be set by such factors as whether the piece will be rendered in black and white or four-color, how many illustrations are to be purchased and the artist's prior experience. Determine an hourly rate by using the annual salary of a staff artist doing similar work in an economically similar geographic area (try to find an artist willing to share this information), then dividing that salary by 52 (the number of weeks in a year) and again by 40 (the number of hours in a work week). You will want to add your overhead expenses such as rent, utilities, art supplies, etc. to this answer by multiplying your hourly rate by 2.5. Research, again, may come into play to be sure your rate is competitive within the marketplace.

Once you make a sale you will probably sign a contract. A contract is an agreement between two or more parties that specifies the fee to be paid, services to be rendered, deadlines, rights purchased and, for artists, return (or not) of original artwork. Most publishers have a standard contract they offer to writers and illustrators. The specifics (such as royalty rates, advances, delivery dates, etc.) are typed in after negotiations. Though it is okay to conduct negotiations over the telephone, be sure to secure a tangible written contract once both parties have agreed on terms. Do not depend on oral stipulations; written contracts protect both parties from misunderstandings and faulty memories. Look out for clauses that may not be in your best interest, such as "work-for-hire." When you do work for hire, you give up all rights to your creations. There are several reputable children's magazines that buy all rights only, and many writers and illustrators believe it is worth the concession in order to break into the field. However, once you've entered the field of book publishing, it's in your best interest to keep the rights to your work.

Be sure you know whether your contract contains an option clause. This clause requires the author to give the publisher a first look at his next work before marketing it to other publishers. Though it is editorial etiquette to give the publisher the first chance at publishing your next work, be wary of statements in the contract which could trap you. Don't allow the publisher to consider the next project for more than 30 days and be specific about what type of work should actually be considered "next work" (i.e., if the book under contract is a young adult novel, specify that the publisher will only receive an exclusive look at the next young adult novel).

If there are clauses that appear vague or confusing, get some legal advice. The time and money invested in counseling up front could protect you from more serious problems down the road. If you have an agent, he will review any contract.

One final note. When a book goes out of print a publisher will sell any existing copies to a wholesaler who, in turn, sells the copies to stores at a discount. When the books are "remaindered" to a wholesaler the books are usually sold at a price just above the cost of printing the book. When negotiating a contract with a publisher you may want to discuss the possibility of purchasing the remaindered copies before they are sold to a wholesaler. Then you can market the copies you purchased and still make a healthy profit.

Rights for the writer and illustrator

A copyright is a form of protection provided to creators of original works, published or unpublished. The Copyright Act of 1976 (which went into effect January 1, 1978) states that work is protected as soon as it's created.

So the United States may have copyright relations with 80 other countries, in March 1989 Congress amended our copyright law and ratified the Berne Convention, the major international copyright convention. Because of this, most works created after March 1989 that are protected by United States copyright are also protected under the laws of most other countries.

The international recognition of copyright protection provided in the Berne Convention prevents foreign piracy of works copyrighted in the U.S. and allows prosecution of foreign copyright infringers in foreign courts. (Principal countries that haven't yet adopted the convention are China and the former Soviet Union.)

Once works are created, they are protected by the copyright law. However, in order to proceed with an infringement lawsuit, the work must be registered. A person who infringes upon a registered copyright is subject to greater liabilities, even when no damages or profits are made as a result of the infringement. Some feel a copyright notice should be included on all work, registered or not. Others feel it is not necessary and a copyright notice will only confuse publishers about whether the material is registered (acquiring rights to previously registered material is a more complicated process). Most publishers are reputable and will not steal your work; therefore, including a copyright notice on unregistered work is not necessary. However, if you don't feel your work is safe without a copyright notice, it is your right to include one. Including a copyright notice – © (year of work, your name) – should ensure your work against plagiarism.

Registration is a legal formality intended to make your copyright public record. As stated above, registration of work is necessary to file any infringement suits. Also, registration can help you win more money in a court case. By registering work within three months of publication or before an infringement occurs, you are eligible to collect statutory damages and attorney's fees. If you register later than three months after publication, you will qualify only for actual damages and profits.

Keep in mind that ideas and concepts are not copyrightable, but expression of those ideas and concepts are copyrightable. A character type or basic plot outline is not subject to a copyright infringement lawsuit. Also, titles, names, short phrases or slogans, and lists of contents are not subject to copyright protection, though titles and names may be protected through the Trademark Office.

In general, copyright protection ensures you, the writer or illustrator, the power to decide how the work is used and allows you to receive payment for each use. Not only does a copyright protect you, it essentially encourages you to create new works by guaranteeing you the power to sell rights to their use in the marketplace. As the copyright holder you can print, reprint or copy your work; sell or distribute copies of your work; or prepare derivative works such as plays, collages or recordings. The Copyright Law is designed to protect a writer's or illustrator's work (copyrighted on or after January 1, 1978) for his lifetime plus 50 years. If you collaborate with someone else on a written or artistic project, the copyright will last for the lifetime of the last survivor plus 50 years. A writer's heirs may hold a copyright for an additional 50 years. After that, the work becomes public domain. In addition, works created anonymously or under a pseudonym are protected for 100 years, or 75 years after publication, whichever is shorter. Incidentally, this latter rule is also true of work-for-hire agreements. Under work-for-hire you relinquish your copyright to your "employer." Try to avoid agreeing to such terms.

For work published before January 1, 1978, the copyright protection is valid for 28 years with an option to renew the last year of the first term. For most copyrights, the law has extended renewal terms from 28 to 47 years, so these works can now be protected for up to 75 years.

For members of the Society of Children's Book Writers & Illustrators, in-depth information about copyrights and the law is available. Send a self-addressed, stamped envelope to the Society of Children's Book Writers & Illustrators, P.O. Box 66296, Mar Vista Station, Los Angeles CA 90066 and request their brochure, "Copyright Facts for Writers."

For more information about the proper procedure to register works, contact the Register of Copyrights, Copyright Office, Library of Congress, Washington D.C. 20559. The forms available are **TX** for writing (books, articles, etc.); **VA** for pictures (photographs, illustrations); and **PA** for plays and music. To learn more about how to go about using the copyright forms, request a copy of Circular I on Copyright Basics. All of these forms are free. Send the completed registration form along with the stated fee and a copy of the work to the Copyright Office. You can register a group of articles or illustrations if:

- the group is assembled in order, such as in a notebook;
- the works bear a single title, such as "Works by (your name)";
- they are the work of one writer or artist;
- the material is the subject of a single claim to copyright.

It is the publisher's responsibility to register your book for copyright. If you have previously registered the same material, you must inform your editor and supply the previous copyright information. Otherwise, the publisher cannot register the book in its published form.

The copyright law specifies that writers generally sell one-time rights to their work unless they and the buyer agree otherwise in writing. Be forewarned that many editors aren't aware of this. Many publications will want more exclusive rights from you than just one-time usage of your work; some will even require you to sell all rights to your work. Be sure that you are monetarily compensated for the additional rights you give up to your material. It is always to your benefit to retain as much control as possible over your work. Writers who only give up limited rights to their work can then sell reprint rights to other publications, foreign rights to international publications, or even movie rights, should the opportunity arise. Likewise, artists can sell their illustrations to other book and magazine markets as well as to paper-product companies who may use an image on a calendar or greeting card. In some cases, illustrators are now selling original artwork after it has been published. There are now galleries throughout the United States that display the works of children's illustrators.

You can see that exercising more control over ownership of your work gives you a greater marketing edge for resale. If you do have to give up all rights to a work, think about the price you are being offered to determine whether it will compensate you for the loss of other sales.

Rights acquired through sale of a book manuscript are explained in each publisher's contract. Take the time to read through relevant clauses to be sure you understand what each contract is specifying prior to signing. Make sure your contract contains a clause allowing all rights to revert back to you in the event the publisher goes out of business. The rights you will most often be selling to publishers and periodicals in the marketplace are:

● One-time rights — The buyer has no guarantee that he is the first to use a piece. One-time permission to run a written or illustrated work is acquired, then the rights revert back to the creator.

● First rights — The creator offers rights to use the work for the first time in any medium. All other rights remain with the creator. When material is excerpted from a soon-to-be-published book for use in a newspaper or periodical, first serial rights are also purchased.

● First North American serial rights — This is similar to first rights, except that publishers who distribute both in the U.S. and Canada will stipulate these rights to ensure that a publication in the other country won't come out with simultaneous usage of the same work.

● Second serial (reprint) rights — In this case newspapers and magazines are granted the right to reproduce a work that already has appeared in another publication. These rights also are purchased by a newspaper or magazine editor who wants to publish part of a book after the book has been published (such as an excerpt from a just-published biography). The proceeds from reprint rights are often split 50/50 between the author and his publishing company.

● Simultaneous rights — Use of such rights occurs among magazines with circulations that don't overlap, such as many religious publications. Many spiritual stories or illustrations are appropriate for a variety of denominational publications. Be sure you submit to a publication that allows simultaneous submissions, and be sure to state in your cover letter to the editor that the submission is being considered elsewhere (to a non-competing market).

● All rights — Rights such as these are purchased by publishers who pay premium usage fees, have an exclusive format, or have other book or magazine interests from which the purchased work can generate more "mileage" for their interests. (Some magazines that purchase all rights to artwork use the same work again several years later.) When the writer or illustrator sells all rights to a market he no longer has any say in who acquires rights to use his piece. Synonymous with purchase of all rights is the term "work-for-hire." Under such an agreement the creator of a work gives away all rights — and his copyright — to the company buying his work. Try to avoid such agreements; they're not in your best interest. If a market is insistent upon acquiring all rights to your work, see if you can negotiate for the rights to revert back to you after a reasonable period of time. It can't hurt to ask. If they're agreeable to such a proposal, be sure you get it in writing.

● Foreign serial rights—Be sure before you market to foreign publications that you have only sold North American—not worldwide—serial rights to previous markets. If not, you are free to market to publications you think may be interested in using material that has appeared in a U.S. or North American-based periodical.

● Syndication rights—This is a division of serial rights. For example, if a syndicate prints portions of a book in installments in its newspapers, it would be syndicating second serial rights. The syndicate would receive a commission and leave the remainder to be split between the author and publisher.

● Subsidiary rights—These are rights, other than book rights, and should be specified in a book contract. Subsidiary rights include serial rights, dramatic rights, book club rights or translation rights. The contract should specify what percentage of profits from sales of these rights go to the author and publisher.

● Dramatic, television and motion picture rights—During the specified time the interested party tries to sell the story to a producer or director. Many times options are renewed because the selling process can be lengthy.

● Display rights—Watch out for these. They're also known as "Electronic Publishing Rights" or "Data, Storage and Retrieval." Usually listed under subsidiary rights, they're not clear. They refer to many means of publication not yet invented. If a display rights clause is listed in your contract, try to negotiate its elimination. Otherwise, demand the clause be restricted to things designed to be read only. By doing this, you maintain your rights to use your work for things such as games and interactive software.

Business records

It is imperative to keep accurate business records to determine if you are making a profit as a writer or illustrator. You will definitely want to keep a bank account and ledger apart from your personal finances. Also, if writing or illustrating is secondary to another freelance career, maintain separate business records from that career.

If you're just starting your career, you will likely accumulate some business expenses prior to showing any profit. To substantiate your income and expenses to the IRS be sure to keep all invoices, cash receipts, sales slips, bank statements, cancelled checks plus receipts related to travel expenses and entertaining clients. For entertainment expenditures you also will want to record the date, place and purpose of the business meeting as well as gas mileage. Be sure to file all receipts in chronological order; if you maintain a separate file for each month of the year it will provide for easier retrieval of records at year's end. Keeping receipts is important for all purchases, big and small. Don't take the small purchases for granted. Enough of them can result in a rather substantial monetary figure.

When setting up a single-entry bookkeeping system record income and expenses separately. It may prove easier to use some of the subheads that appear on Schedule C (the form used for recording income from a business) of the 1040 tax form. This way you can transfer information more easily onto the tax form when filing your return. In your ledger include a description of each transaction—date, source of income (or debts from business purchases), description of what was purchased or sold; whether payment was by cash, check or credit card, and the amount of the transaction.

You don't have to wait until January 1 to start keeping records, either. The moment you first make a business-related purchase or sell an article, book manuscript or illustrations begin tracking your profits and losses. If you keep records from January 1 to December 31 you are using a calendar-year accounting method. Any other accounting period is known as a fiscal year. You also can choose between two types of accounting methods—the cash method and the accrual method. The cash method is used more often: You record income when it is received and expenses when they are disbursed. Under the accrual method you report income at the time you earn it rather than when it is actually received. Similarly, expenses are recorded at the time they are incurred rather than when you actually pay them. If you choose this method keep separate records for "accounts receivable" and "accounts payable."

Taxes

To successfully (and legally) compete in the business of writing or illustrating you must know what income you should report and deductions you can claim. Before you can do this however, you must prove to the IRS that you are in business to make a profit, that your writing or illustrations are not merely a hobby. Under the Tax Reform Act of 1986 it was determined that you should show a profit for three years out of a five-year period to attain professional status. What does the IRS look for as proof of your professionalism? Keeping accurate financial records (see previous section on business records), maintaining a business bank account separate from your personal account, the time you devote to your profession and whether it is your main or secondary source of income, and your history of profits and losses. The amount of training you have invested in your field is also a contributing factor to your professional status, as well as your expertise in the field.

If your business is unincorporated, you will fill out tax information on Schedule C of Form 1040. If you're unsure of what deductions you can take, request the appropriate IRS publication containing this information. Under the Tax Reform Act, only 80 percent (formerly it was 100 percent) of business meals, entertainment and related tips and parking charges are deductible. Other deductibles allowed on Schedule C include: capital expenditures (such as a computer), car expenses for business-related trips, professional courses and seminars, depreciation of office equipment, dues and publications and miscellaneous expenses, such as postage used for business needs, etc.

If you're working out of a home office, a portion of your mortgage (or rent), related utilities, property taxes, repair costs and depreciation can be deducted as business expenses. To qualify though, your office must be used only for business activities. It can't double as a family room during nonbusiness hours. To determine what portion of business deductions can be taken, simply divide the square footage of your business area into the total square footage of your house. You will want to keep a log of what business activities, and sales and business transactions occur each day; the IRS may want to see records to substantiate your home office deductions. For more information on home office deductions, consult Publication 587 (Business Use of Your Home) from the IRS.

The method of paying taxes on income not subject to withholding is your "estimated tax." If you expect to owe more than $500 at year's end and if the total amount of income tax that will be withheld during the year will be less than 90% of the tax shown on the previous year's return, you will generally make estimated tax payments. Estimated tax payments are made in four equal installments due on April 15, June 15, September 15 and January 15. For more information, request Publication 505, Self-Employment Tax.

Depending on your net income you may be liable for a Social Security tax. This is a tax designed for those who don't have Social Security withheld from their paychecks. You're liable if your net income is $400 or more per year. Net income is the difference between your income and allowable business deductions. Request Schedule SE, Computation of Social Security Self-Employment Tax, if you qualify.

If completing your income tax return proves to be a complex affair, call the IRS for assistance. In addition to walk-in centers, the IRS has various publications to instruct you in various facets of preparing a tax return.

Insurance

As a self-employed professional be aware of what health and business insurance coverage is available to you. Unless you're a Canadian who is covered by national health insurance or a fulltime freelancer covered by your spouse's policy, health insurance will no doubt be one of your biggest expenses. Under the terms of the Consolidated Omnibus Budget Reconciliation Act (COBRA) of 1985, if you leave a job with health benefits, you are entitled to continue that coverage for at least 18 months at the insurer's cost plus a small administration charge. Eventually, though, you will have to search for your own health plan. Also be mindful of the fact you may also need disability and life insurance.

Disability insurance is offered through many private insurance companies and state governments, and pays a monthly fee that covers living and business expenses during periods of long-term recuperation from a health problem. The amount of money paid monthly is based on the writer's or artist's annual earnings.

Before contacting any insurance representative, talk to other writers or illustrators to find out about insurance companies they could recommend. If you belong to a writer's or artist's organization, be sure to contact them to determine if any insurance coverage for professionals is offered to members. Such group coverage may prove less expensive and yield more comprehensive coverage than an individual policy.

Key to Symbols

* *Symbol indicating listing is new in this edition*
■ *Symbol indicating a market subsidy publishes manuscripts*
‡ *Symbol indicating a contest is for students*

Important Market Listing Information

● *Listings are based on questionnaires, phone calls and updated copy. They are not advertisements nor are markets reported here necessarily endorsed by the editor of this book.*
● *Information in the listings comes directly from the company and is as accurate as possible, but situations change and needs fluctuate between the publication of this directory and the time you use it.*
● Children's Writer's & Illustrator's Market *reserves the right to exclude any listing that does not meet its requirements.*
● *This book is edited (except for quoted material) in the masculine gender because we think "he/she," "she/he," "he or she," "him or her" in copy is distracting.*

The Markets

Book Publishers

During a time when businesses of all types are feeling economic pressures, it is surprising that the children's book publishing industry has continued to grow. But the reason for such growth becomes apparent when you consider that parents around the world are concerned with literacy and better education for their children. Adults are willing to cut back on their own material needs to insure that their children receive a good education.

The May 1992 issue of the *Children's Book Insider* reports that married couples with children under 6 years old spent an average of $65.71 in 1990 on books, an increse of 15 percent per year since 1986. "More parents are placing a higher value on education, and choosing to spend their disposable income on books instead of other products for their children," the newsletter reported.

Since the early 1980s the children's book publishing industry has seen steady growth. Children's-only bookstores are popping up all over the United States, over 450 at last count, and retail stores are increasing their stock of children's titles. A survey conducted by Cahners Publishing's research department showed that the amount of retail space devoted to children's books in children's-only stores continues to rise. The results, published in the January 13, 1992 issue of *Publishers Weekly*, show that children's-only bookstores averaged 1,304 square feet of space in 1991 for children's titles. This figure is up from 1,181 square feet in 1990 and 1,099 square feet in 1989. On average, children's-only stores carried 7,901 individual titles in 1991, while general bookstores average 2,739 children's titles.

However, if there is one problem for writers it is that many customers cling to the classics. They search for those stories they remember from childhood and they want to pass those tales on to their children. This causes bookstore operators to be cautious when buying new titles to stock on their shelves.

Multiculturalism

Many new titles that have done particularly well in recent years have been developed around multicultural themes. There's a need to create awareness of other cultures among children. Like everybody else, minority children like to see themselves in books, and they might not view themselves as important if they don't. In the last few years, there has been a great demand for books with ethnic themes. Minority groups want to be represented, while non-minorities seek books to teach their kids about other races and religions.

Some experts predict that by the year 2056 there will be more children of color in the United States than white children. This projection and the changing attitudes in publishing houses have created a viable market for those writers and illustrators who can write interesting, authentic stories using multicultural characters. Publishers are searching for stories that will improve the self-esteem of children and can help children understand different lifestyles.

The push toward a better understanding of different cultures has even resulted in the production of an eight-crayon package containing multicultural colors. Binney & Smith, an Easton, Pennsylvania company that produces Crayola crayons, began producing the eight-pack after teachers and children in Maryland became annoyed that the colors could only be found in the company's 64-pack of crayons.

The August 1992 issue of the newsletter *Children's Writer* reports that publishers are split on the issue of whether a writer must be a member of the ethnic group about which they are writing. Although it certainly helps to be part of a specific ethnic group when writing about the specific culture, some publishers believe that a good writer can transcend any ethnic differences. Others believe writers must be members of the ethnic groups about which they are writing. Otherwise they will risk perpetuating stereotypes through factual errors.

Illustrators able to draw and paint ethnic children are especially in demand, and are practically guaranteed a spot in the field. Multicultural characters should be the main protagonists for entire books and tokenism should be avoided.

The need for writers and illustrators of color prompted HarperCollins Children's Books and Scott Foresman to create the Center for Multicultural Children's Literature. Formed last summer, "the Center will provide a mentoring service for writers and illustrators of color who wish to have their work published in the children's book field," according to an article in the July 27, 1992 issue of *Publishers Weekly*. The Center maintains a list of talented writers and illustrators. Editors seeking new talent can contact the Center and obtain names, phone numbers and tearsheets from a databank. "Manuscripts and illustrations will be matched with mentors based on compatability of style, genre, age level and cultural identity, whenever possible," the article states.

Teaching the trade

One of the keys to writing, whether you are writing multicultural books or nonfiction, is to understand the topic on which you are writing and the audience you are trying to reach.

Remember Dick, Jane and Spot? To the delight of people in the educational field, these superficial characters, long used to teach young children to read, are in grave danger of becoming extinct. Actually, it was the late Theodor Geisel (better known as Dr. Seuss) who originally waged war against Dick and Jane decades ago. His 1957 book, *The Cat in the Hat* is credited with revolutionizing children's reading habits. "That is what I am proudest of, that I had something to do with getting rid of Dick and Jane," he said in 1982. Now Whole Language curriculums, where trade books are used instead of textbooks to teach in the classroom, are currently being implemented nationwide. Teachers are opting to buy trade books from booksellers rather than textbooks. In fact, 30% of all children's-only bookstore sales are to teachers. And it is teachers who can be credited with popularizing titles such as *The True Story of the Three Little Pigs* and *Chicka Chicka Boom Boom*.

Nonfiction books have greatly benefited from the Whole Language movement. Unlike in the past, historical nonfiction no longer contains invented dialogue or fictionalized accounts of events. They have proven to be valuable tools for the classroom. But history and literature are not the only subjects being taught with trade books. Science can also be taught.

In light of the current literature-based curriculums, writers need to become familiar with how to go about composing a book appropriate for the classroom. Children are not patient with boring text (that's why trade books are supposed to be more effective than textbooks), so make sure to write with an upbeat and interesting tone. Humor is a nice touch, as are little-known anecdotes and pieces of trivia.

Who's reading?

The birth rate still remains high and picture books are continuing to sell well. Offspring of the current baby boom are starting to grow up, and early chapter books are coming into prominence because these children are starting to read. Middle readers will be next in line. Some experts predict that as the children of the baby boom reach pre-teen age, young adult titles, now suffering, will once again be in demand. However, others are not so sure. There are questions about what a young adult book is and what a young adult section should consist of. Pre-teens and teenagers are thought to be more sophisticated today than in the past; they don't want books that look childish. Many bypass YA titles altogether and turn to adult titles for recreational reading. To combat this, suggestions have been made to publish YA books with "adult" covers and market them near the adult sections. Time will tell on the YA issue.

Subsidy publishing

Some writers who are really determined to get their work into print, but who receive rejections from all the royalty publishers, look to subsidy publishers as an option. Subsidy publishers ask writers to pay all or part of the costs of producing a book. You will notice some of the listings in this section give percentages of subsidy-published material. Such listings are marked with a solid block (■).

Aspiring writers should strongly consider working only with publishers who pay. They will be active in marketing your work because they profit only through these efforts. Subsidy publishers make their money from writers who pay to have their books published, so be prepared to do your own marketing and promotion. In fact, some operations are more interested in the contents of your wallet than the contents of your book. Though there are reputable subsidy publishers, those considering such services should take a "buyer beware" attitude. Any contracts offered by these houses should be carefully inspected by a lawyer or someone qualified to analyze these types of documents.

If you're interested in publishing your book just to share it with friends and relatives, self publishing is a viable option. In self publishing, an author oversees all of the details of book production. A local printer may be able to help you, or you may want to arrange some type of desk-top computer publishing.

Don't write to order

"Write what you know," or "Write about something that interests you," is the most common advice offered by established authors. Writing about a subject just because there's a demand for it doesn't warrant all the time spent putting it together unless you are truly and sincerely excited about the topic. Otherwise, don't expect your readers to get excited about (or for that matter, finish reading) the material. The same thing goes for illustrators. Creating artwork for children is more challenging than one might think. It's important to draw and paint with the children in mind—not adults. Be sure you are able to show children interacting with each other. Don't underestimate the intelligence of children—they're quick to pick up on substandard material.

And finally, don't treat writing for children as a starter course into the world of "real writing." Creating a children's book is *not* a quick and easy project. Actually, aspects of the craft make writing for this audience more difficult. Writing for children *is* real writing, and what follows in this section are listings of *real* markets—one of which might someday make your dreams of being published a reality.

ADDISON-WESLEY PUBLISHING CO., Trade Dept., One Jacob Way, Reading MA 01867-3999. (617)944-3700. Book publisher. Estab. 1942. Associate Editor: John Bell. Publishes 10 middle reader titles/year. 33% of books by first-time authors.
Nonfiction: Middle readers: science, hobbies, nature/environment. Young readers, young adults: science. "All of our children's books are science activity books." No fiction or picture books. "We don't publish them."
How to Contact/Writers: Nonfiction: Query. Reports on queries in 6 weeks; on mss in 2 months. Publishes a book 2 years after acceptance. Will consider simultaneous submissions.
Illustration: Works with 15 illustrators/year. Will review ms/illustration packages. Will review artwork for future assignments. Prefers "4-color representational art for covers and b&w for interior."
How to Contact/Illustrators: Ms/illustration packages: "Query first." Illustrations only: Send promo sheet." Original artwork returned at job's completion.
Terms: Pays authors in royalties based on retail price. Pays illustrators: by the project. Sends galleys to authors; dummies to illustrators. Book catalog for 7×10 SASE.
Tips: The writer and/or illustrator have the best chance of selling "science activity books *only*. Increasing competition in our field (science projects) means finding more focused and more imaginative books." Also, "Many more book-toy packages have appeared lately. Adults buy them (they're too expensive for most kids that age), so they're being shaped by what adults think kids should like."

ADVOCACY PRESS, P.O. Box 236, Santa Barbara CA 93102. (805)962-2728. Fax: (805)963-3580. Div. of The Girls Incorporated of Greater Santa Barbara. Book publisher. Editorial Contact: Bill Sheehan. Publishes 2-4 children's books/year.
Fiction: Picture books, young readers, middle readers: gender equity, concepts in self-esteem, animal, fantasy, nature/environment. "Illustrated children's stories incorporate self-esteem, gender equity, self-awareness concepts." Recently published *Mother Nature Nursery Rhymes* (32-pages, birth to 6-years), *Mimi Takes Charge, Mimi Makes A Splash* (48-pages, graphic picture books ages 3-8 years). "Most publications are 32-48 page picture stories for readers 4-11 years. Most feature adventures of animals in interesting/educational locales."
How to Contact/Writers: "Because of the required focus of our publications, most have been written in-house." Will review manuscripts in 1-2 months. Include SASE.

Illustration: "Require intimate integration of art with story. Therefore, almost always use local illustrators." Average about thirty illustrations per story. Will review ms/illustration packages.
How to Contact/Illustrators: Ms/illustration packages: Query first.
Terms: Authors and illustrators paid by royalty.

■**AEGINA PRESS/UNIVERSITY EDITIONS, INC.**, 59 Oak Lane, Spring Valley, Huntington WV 25704. (304)429-7204. Book publisher. Estab. 1983. Managing Editor: Ira Herman. Art Coordinator: Claire Nudd. Publishes 3 picture books/year; 4 young reader titles/year; 4 middle reader titles/year; 6 young adult titles/year. 40% of books by first-time authors; 5% of books from agented writers; "over 50% of books are subsidy published."
Fiction: All ages: adventure, animal, fantasy, humor, poetry, religion, romance, science fiction, sports, suspense/mystery. "Will consider most categories." Average word length: picture books—1,000; young readers—2,000; middle readers—10,000; young adults—20,000. Recently published *Tennis Teens*, by Mary Silsby with illustrations by Amy Harold (ages 12+, sports novel); *My Favorite Bedtime Stories*, by Helen Bramos with illustrations by Ann Bramos (ages 4-8, short stories); *A Story from Widg*, by Maddie St. John (ages 5-8, fantasy).
Nonfiction: All ages: animal, history, nature/environment, sports, textbooks. "Will consider all types of manuscripts, especially those usable in classrooms." Recently published *Art, Japanese Style*, by Charlene McCree with illustrations by Jane Thoms (ages 9-11, art and haiku); *Chester's Coloring Book*, by Andrea Ross (ages 4-8, coloring book).
How to Contact/Writers: Fiction/nonfiction: Submit complete ms. Reports on queries in 1 week; on mss in 1 month. Publishes a book 5-6 months after acceptance. Will consider simultaneous submissions.
Illustration: Works with 20 illustrators/year. Will review ms/illustration packages. Will review artwork for future assignments. Primarily uses b&w artwork only.
How to Contact/Illustrators: Ms/illustration packages: query first. Illustrations only: query with nonreturnable samples. "We generally use our own artists. We will consider outside art. Artists should send photocopies or non-returnable samples." Reports on art samples in 1 month. Original artwork returned at job's completion.
Terms: Pays authors in royalties of 10-15% based on retail price. Pays freelance artists per project ($60 minimum). Payment "negotiated individually for each book." Sends galleys to authors. Book catalog available for $2 and SAE and 4 first-class stamps; manuscript guidelines for #10 envelope and 1 first-class stamp.
Tips: "Focus your subject and plotline. For younger readers, stress visual imagery and fantasy characterizations. A cover letter should accompany the manuscript, which states the approximate length (not necessary for poetry). A brief synopsis of the manuscript and a listing of the author's publishing credits (if any) should also be included. Queries, sample chapters, synopses and completed manuscripts are welcome." For the future, "we plan to stress stories for middle readers and older children. Will consider all types, however."

*****AFRICA WORLD PRESS**, P.O. Box 1892, Trenton NJ 08607. (609)771-1666. Book publisher. Editor: Kassahun Checole. Publishes 20-30 picture books/year; 10 young reader and young adult titles/year; 15 middle readers/year. Books concentrate on African-American life.
Fiction: Picture books, young readers: adventure, concept, contemporary, folktales, history, multicultural. Middle readers, young adults: adventure, contemporary, folktales, history, multicultural. Publishes very little fiction.
Nonfiction: Picture books, young readers, middle readers, young adults: concept, history, multicultural. Does not want to see self-help, gender or health books.

How to Contact/Writers: Submit outline/synopsis and 2 sample chapters. Reports in 30-45 days on queries; reports on mss in 3 months. Will consider previously published work.
Illustration: Works with 10-20 illustrators/year. Will review ms/illustration packages. Contact: Kassahun Checole, editor. Will review artwork for future assignments.
How to Contact/Illustrators: Ms/illustration packages: Query. Illustrations only: Query with samples. Reports in 3 months.
Terms: Pays authors royalty based on retail price. Pays illustrators by the project or royalty based on retail price. Book catalog available for SAE; ms and art guidelines available for SASE.

AFRICAN AMERICAN IMAGES, 9204 Commercial, Chicago IL 60617. (312)375-9682. Fax: (312)375-9349. Book publisher. Editor: Jawanza Kunjufu. Publishes 2 picture books/year; 1 young reader title/year; 1 middle reader title/year; 1 young adult title/year. 90% of books by first-time authors.
Fiction/Nonfiction: All levels: black culture.
How to Contact/Writers: Fiction/nonfiction: Submit complete ms. Reports on queries in 1 week; on mss in 3 weeks. Publishes a book 9 months after acceptance. Will consider simultaneous submissions.
Illustration: Editorial will review ms/illustration packages.
How to Contact/Illustrators: Ms/illustration packages: Send 3 chapters of ms with 1 piece of final art. Illustrations only: Send tearsheets. Reports on art samples in 2 weeks. Original artwork returned at job's completion.
Terms: Buys ms outright. Illustrator paid by the project. Book catalog, manuscript/artist's guidelines free on request.

ALADDIN BOOKS/COLLIER BOOKS FOR YOUNG READERS, 24th Floor, 866 Third Avenue, New York NY 10022. (212)702-9043. Paperback imprints of Macmillan Children's Book Group. Book publisher. Estab. 1986. Editor-in-Chief: Whitney Malone. Associate Editors: Julia Sibert, Leslie Ward. Publishes 40 picture books/year; 5 young reader titles/year; 20 middle reader titles/year; 4 young adult titles/year; 25 novelty titles/year. 12% of books by first-time authors; 40% of books from agented writers.
Fiction: "The only *new* original material we publish is novelty material. All other is import or reprint."
How to Contact/Writers: Fiction/nonfiction: Query; submit outline/synopsis and sample chapters. Reports on queries in 4 weeks; on mss in 2 months. Publishes a book 1-2 years after acceptance. Book catalog and ms guidelines available for SASE.
Illustration: Editorial will review artwork for future assignments. Seeks cover artists for paperback fiction for middle grades and young adults. Contact Julia Sibert or Leslie Ward. Uses primarily color artwork. No original picture books.
How to Contact/Illustrators: Ms/illustration packages: query. Illustrations only: query with samples. Reports only if interested. Original artwork returned at job's completion.
Terms: Pays authors royalty of 3-6% based on retail price or flat fee. Offers advances of half of royalty per print run. Pays illustrators royalty of 3-6% based on retail price or flat fee. Ms guidelines available.
Tips: "We are currently concentrating on reprinting successful titles originally published by the hardcover imprints of the Macmillan Children's Book Group. We *rarely* publish original material. We will be publishing fewer young adult titles (Collier imprint) and will be concentrating on several genres for this age group: science fiction, fantasy and

 The solid block before a listing indicates the market subsidy publishes manuscripts.

mysteries. The bulk of our purchases will be novelty projects: lift-the-flaps, musical books, books with an interactive component etc. Other purchases of original material are very rare. We prefer that longer manuscripts be preceded by a query letter and two or three sample chapters. We do not consider picture book manuscripts. Please do not submit more than two short (under 15 typed pages) or one longer manuscript at one time. If you wish to confirm that your manuscript has arrived safely, please include a self-addressed stamped postcard, or send the manuscript via registered mail." Regarding illustrations: "Remember that what appeals to adults may not necessarily appeal to children." (See also Atheneum Publishers, Bradbury Press, Four Winds Press, Margaret K. McElderry Books.)

ALYSON PUBLICATIONS, INC., 40 Plympton St., Boston MA 02118. (617)542-5679. Book publisher. Editorial Contact: Sasha Alyson. Publishes 5 (projected) picture books/year; 1 (projected) young adult title/year. "Alyson Wonderland is the line of children's books. We are looking for diverse depictions of family life for children of gay and lesbian parents."
Fiction: All levels: Books aimed at the children of lesbian and gay parents. "Our YA books should deal with issues faced by kids growing up gay or lesbian." Recently published *A Boy's Best Friend*, by John Alden; *The Day They Put a Tax on Rainbows*, by Johnny Valentine.
How to Contact/Writers: Submit outline/synopsis and sample chapters (young adults); submit complete manuscript (picture books/young readers). Reports on queries in 3 weeks; reports on mss in 3-4 weeks. Include SASE.
Illustration: Send "representative art that can be *kept on file*. Good quality photocopies are OK."
Terms: Prefer to discuss terms with the authors and artists. "We *do* offer advances." Book catalog and/or manuscript guidelines free on request.
Tips: "We only publish kids' books aimed at the children of gay or lesbian parents."

AMERICAN BIBLE SOCIETY, 1865 Broadway, New York NY 10023. (212)408-1235. Fax: (212)408-1512. Book publisher. Estab. 1816. Product Development Manager: Charles Houser. Publishes 2 picture books/year; 4 young reader titles/year; 4 young adult titles/year. Publishes books with spiritual/religious themes based on the Bible.
Nonfiction: Picture books, young readers, middle readers, young adults: religion. Published *Be the Best You Can Be: Achieving Your Potential Through God's Word*, (young adult, Bible passages used to address youth issues).
How to Contact/Writers: "All manuscripts developed in-house; unsolicited mss rejected."
Illustration: Editorial will review artwork for possible future assignments. "Would be more interested in artwork for teens which is influenced by the visual 'vocabulary' of videos."
How to Contact/Illustrators: Ms/illustration packages: "Query first." Illustrations only: Query with samples; arrange a personal interview to show portfolio; send "résumés, tearsheets and promotional literature to keep; slides will be returned promptly." Reports back in 6 weeks. Factors used to determine payment ms/illustration package include "Nature and scope of project; complexity of illustration and continuity of work; number of illustrations." Pays illustrators: $200-30,000; based on fair market value. Sends two complimentary copies of published work to illustrators. Book catalog free on request.
Photography: Photographers should contact Charles Houser. Looking for "Nature, scenic, interracial, intergenerational people shots." Model/property releases required. Uses any size b&w prints; 35mm, 2¼ × 2¼ and 4 × 5 transparencies. To contact, photographers should query with samples; arrange a personal interview to show portfolio; provide résumé, promotional literature or tearsheets.

Terms: Photographers paid by the project (range: $800-5,000); per photo (range $150-1,500).

*APPALACHIAN MOUNTAIN CLUB BOOKS, 5 Joy St., Boston MA 02108. (617)523-0636. Fax: (617)523-0722. Book publisher. Editor: Gordon Hardy. 50% of books by first-time authors; 5% of books from agented authors. Publishes environmental, conservation and oudoor recreation books.
Nonfiction: Young readers: activity books, history, how-to, nature/environment, travel, outdoor recreation. Middle readers, young adults: activity books, history, nature/environment, travel, outdoor recreation. Recently published *Seashells in My Pocket*, by Judith Hansen, illustrations by Donna Sabaka (ages 6 and up, child's nature guide to exploring); *The Conservation Works Book* by Lisa Capone, illustrated by Cady Goldfield (ecology book with humorous sketches for the entire family).
How to Contact/Writers: Fiction: Query; submit outline/synopsis. Nonfiction: Query; submit outline/synopsis. Reports on queries in 1 month; reports on mss in 4 months. Publishes book an average of 6 months after receipt of acceptable ms. Will consider simultaneous submissions and electronic submissions.
Illustration: Works with 2 illustrators/year. Will review ms/illustration packages. Contact: Gordon Hardy, editor. Will review artwork for future assignments. Uses primarily b&w artwork only.
How to Contact/Illustrators: Ms/illustration packages: Query; submit ms with dummy. Illustrations only: Query with samples. Reports in 1 month. Samples returned with SASE.
Photography: Purchases photos from freelancers. Uses cover photos. Model/property releases and captions required. Uses 5 × 8 glossy b&w prints and 35 mm transparencies. To contact, photographers should submit cover letter, stock photo list and color promo piece.
Terms: Pays authors royalty of 6% based on retail price or outright purchase. Offers advances (amount varies with assignment). Pays illustrators by the project (range: $25-50). Photographers paid $25/photo. Sends galleys to authors. Book catalog available for 8½ × 11 SAE and 4 first class stamps; ms guidelines for SASE, art guidelines not available.
Tips: "Make sure writer has an illustrator to propose!" Publishes books that are "outdoor/conservation oriented (New England focus is best)."

*AQUILA COMMUNICATIONS LTD., 8354 Labarre St., Montreal, Quebec H4P 2E7 Canada. (514)738-7071. Book publisher. Manager: Mike Kelada. 100% of books by first-time authors. "We specialize in teaching French as a second language."
How to Contact/Writers: Fiction: Submit outline/synopsis and 5 sample chapters. Nonfiction: Submit outline/synopsis and 10 sample chapters. Reports on queries and mss in 1 week to 2 months. Will consider previously published work.
Illustration: Will review ms/illustration packages. Will review artwork for future assignments. Uses b&w and color artwork.
How to Contact/Illustrators: Ms/illustration packages: Submit ms with copies of artwork. Illustrations only: photocopies of sample artwork. Reports in 3 weeks. Cannot return samples; samples filed.
Photography: Purchases photos from freelancers. Buys stock and assigns work.

■ARCADE PUBLISHING, 141 Fifth Ave., New York NY 10010. (212)475-2633. Subsidiary of Little Brown & Co. Book publisher. President and Publisher: Richard Seaver. Publishes 8-12 picture books/year; 3-5 young reader titles/year; 5-8 middle reader titles/year. 50% of books from agented writers. 25% of books by first-time authors.
Fiction: Young readers, middle readers. Recently published *I Am the Ocean*, by Suzanna Marshak (ages 4-8, picture book).

Nonfiction: Will consider general nonfiction—"all ages." Published *Water's Way*, by Lisa Westberg Peters, illustrated by Ted Rand (ages 4-7, picture book).
How to Contact/Writers: Fiction: Submit complete ms. Nonfiction: Query. Reports on queries in 2 months. Publishes ms 18 months after acceptance. Will consider simultaneous submissions.
Illustration: Will review ms/illustration packages.
How to Contact/Illustrators: "*No* original art—send slides or color photocopies." Illustrations only: Send tearsheets and slides. Reports on ms/art samples in 3 weeks. Original artwork returned at job's completion.
Terms: Pays authors in variable royalties; or buys ms outright for $400-$3,000; "also flat fees per b&w books and jackets." Offers average advance of $2,500. Sends galleys to authors; book catalog for 8 × 10 SASE; manuscript guidelines for SASE.

ARCHWAY PAPERBACKS/MINSTREL BOOKS, 1230 Avenue of the Americas, New York NY 10020. (212)698-7000. Imprint of Pocket Books. Book publisher. Executive Editor: Patricia MacDonald. Publishes originals and reprints. Minstrel Books (ages 7-11) and Archway Paperbacks (ages 12-16).
Fiction: Middle readers: animal, funny school stories. Young adults: contemporary, fantasy, romance, sports, suspense/mystery/adventure, humor, funny school stories.
Nonfiction: Middle readers: animal, sports. Young adults: sports.
How to Contact/Writers: Fiction/nonfiction: Query, submit outline/synopsis and sample chapters. SASE mandatory.
Terms: Pays authors in royalties.

ATHENEUM PUBLISHERS, 866 Third Ave., New York NY 10022. (212)702-2000. Macmillan Children's Book Group. Book publisher. Vice President/Editorial Director: Jonathan Lanman. Editorial Contacts: Gail Paris, Marcia Marshall. Publishes 15-20 picture books/year; 4-5 young reader titles/year; 20-25 middle reader titles/year; 10-15 young adult titles/year. 20% of books by first-time authors; 50% of books from agented writers.
Fiction: Picture books and middle readers: animal, contemporary, fantasy. Young readers and young adults: contemporary, fantasy.
Nonfiction: All levels: animal, biography, education, history.
How to Contact/Writers: Fiction/nonfiction: Query; will consider complete picture book manuscript; submit outline/synopsis and sample chapters for longer works. Reports on queries 6-8 weeks; on mss 3 months. Publishes a book 18-24 months after acceptance. Will consider simultaneous submissions from previously unpublished authors; "we request that the author let us know it is a simultaneous submission."
Illustration: Editorial will review ms/illustration packages.
How to Contact/Illustrators: Ms/illustration packages: query first, 3 chapters of ms with 1 piece of final art. Illustrations only: résumé, tear sheets. Reports on art samples only if interested. Original artwork returned at job's completion.
Terms: Pays authors in royalties of 8-12½% based on retail price. Illustrators paid royalty or flat fee depending on the project. Sends galleys to authors; proofs to illustrators. Book catalog available for 9 × 12 SAE and 5 first-class stamps; manuscript guidelines for #10 SAE and 1 first-class stamp. (See also Aladdin Books/Collier Books for Young Adults, Bradbury Press, Four Winds Press, Margaret K. McElderry Books).

AVON BOOKS/BOOKS FOR YOUNG READERS (AVON FLARE AND AVON CAMELOT), 1350 Ave. of the Americas, New York NY 10019. (212)261-6817. Div. of The Hearst Corporation. Book publisher. Editorial Director: Ellen Krieger. Editorial Contact: Gwen Montgomery. Editorial Assistant: Margaret Draesel. Publishes 25-30 middle reader titles/year; 20-25 young adult titles/year. 10% of books by first-time authors; 20% of books from agented writers.

Fiction: Middle readers: contemporary, problem novels, sports, spy/mystery/adventure, comedy. Young adults: contemporary, problem novels, romance. Average length: middle readers—100-150 pages; young adults—150-250 pages. Avon does not publish preschool picture books.

Nonfiction: Middle readers: hobbies, music/dance, sports. Young adults: music/dance, "growing up." Average length: middle readers—100-150 pages; young adults—150-250 pages.

How to Contact/Writers: Fiction: Submit complete ms. Nonfiction: Submit outline/synopsis and sample chapters. Reports on queries in 2 weeks; on mss in 1-2 months. Publishes book 18-24 months after acceptance. Will consider simultaneous submissions.

Illustration: Very rarely will review ms/illustration packages.

How to Contact/Illustrators: "Send samples we can keep. Need line art and cover art."

Terms: Pays authors in royalties of 6% based on retail price. Average advance payment is "very open." Sends galleys to authors; sometimes sends dummies to illustrators. Book catalog available for 9×12 SAE and 4 first-class stamps; manuscript guidelines for #10 SASE.

Tips: "We have two Young Readers imprints, Avon Camelot books for the middle grades, and Avon Flare for young adults. Our list is weighted more to individual titles than to series, with the emphasis in our paperback originals on high quality recreational reading—a fresh and original writing style; identifiable, three dimensional characters; a strong, well-paced story that pulls readers in and keeps them interested." Writers: "Make sure that you really know what a company's list looks like before you submit work. Is your work in line with what they usually do? Is your work appropriate for the age group that this company publishes for? Keep aware of what's in your bookstore (but not what's in there for too long!)" Illustrators: "Submit work to art directors and people who are in charge of illustration at publishers. This is usually not handled entirely by the editorial department."

BACK TO THE BIBLE, P.O. Box 82808, Lincoln NE 68501. (402)474-4567. Book publisher. Editor: Marcia Claesson.

Fiction: Young Adults/Teens: "Must show how a relationship with Christ can make a difference in the lives of present-day teens." Average word length: 20,000-40,000.

Nonfiction: Young Adults/Teens: Must have biblical emphasis and deal with practical issues for Christian teens. Does not want to see biographies. Average word length: 20,000-40,000.

How to Contact/Writers: Query by mail. Reports on queries in 2 weeks; mss 6-8 weeks. Publishes ms 6-12 months after acceptance.

Illustration: Buys 3 illustrations/year. Preferred theme or style: realistic and/or mood-capturing illustrations; size—no smaller than 8×10. Will review illustration packages. Works on assignment only.

How to Contact/Illustrators: Send résumé and samples. Reports in 2 weeks.

Terms: Buys all rights. Pays 10% royalty on total sales. No upfront fee.

Tips: "At present all book publishing has been temporarily suspended. Contact us in July of 1993 to see what decisions have been made."

*BANCROFT-SAGE PUBLISHING, INC., P.O. Box 355, Marco FL 33969. Contact: Karyne Jacobsen. Book publisher. Publishes 6 middle readers/year; 6 young readers/year. Publishes "strictly nonfiction and illustrated with photography."

Nonfiction: Middle readers: biography, hi-lo, how-to, multicultural, nature/environment, science, sports. Multicultural "titles on family lifestyles in other countries, foods they eat, customs, etc." Average word length: middle readers—5,000. Recently published *Environmental Awareness: Solid Waste*, by M.E. Snodgrass (grades 4-6); *Dinosaur*

Discovery Era, by Elizabeth Sandell (grade 3); *Learning How Gymnastics*, by Jane M. Leder (grades 3-4).

How to Contact/Writers: Nonfiction: Query. Submit outline/synopsis. Reports on queries in 3 months; on mss in 6 months. Publishes book 1 year after acceptance. Will consider simultaneous submissions.

Photography: Purchases photos from freelancers. Contact Karyne Jacobsen. Buys stock. Model/property releases required. Uses 35mm and 2¼ × 2¼ transparencies. To contact, photographers should submit cover letter and stock photo list.

Terms: Pays outright purchase. Photographers paid by the project (range $50-125). Sends galleys to authors. Book catalog not available; ms guidelines not available.

Tips: Looking for "nonfiction — subject matter that can be expanded into a series of 6-10 titles."

*BANDANNA BOOKS, 319-B Anacapa St., Santa Barbara CA 93101. (805)962-9915. Imprint: Little Humanist Classics. Book Publisher. Editor: Sasha Newborn. Publishes 2 young adult titles/year. "Most books have been translations in the humanist tradition. Looking for themes of intellectual awakening."

Fiction: Young adults: history, multicultural, problem novels. Multicultural needs include "cultural encounters." No religious, fantasy. Average word length: young adult — 60,000. Recently published *A Cretan Cycle*, by Marilyn Coffey, illustrated by Kostas Lekakis (ages 14-25, feminist retelling of Greek legends).

Nonfiction: Young adults: biography, history, multicultural. No religious, fantasy. Average word length: young adult — 50,000. Recently published *Sappho*, by N. Browne and illustrated by Jeanne Morgan (ages 14-24, translation of Sappho's poems).

How to Contact/Writers: Nonfiction: Submit outline/synopsis and 1 sample chapter. Reports on queries in 2 weeks; on mss in 2 months. Publishes a book up to a year after acceptance. Will consider simultaneous submissions.

Illustration: Works with 2 illustrators/year. Will review ms/illustration packages. Will review artwork for future assignments. Uses primarily b&w artwork only. Prefers woodblock, scratchboard artwork.

How to Contact/Illustrators: Ms/illustration packages: Submit ms with dummy. Illustrations only: Query with samples, portfolio and tearsheets. Reports back only if interested. Cannot return samples; samples filed. Originals not returned.

Terms: Authors paid "some cash, some books." Offers advances (average amount: $200). Pays illustrators by the project (range: $50-200). Sends galleys to authors. Book catalog not available; ms and art guidelines not available.

BANTAM DOUBLEDAY DELL, 666 Fifth Ave., New York NY 10103. (212)765-6500. Book publisher. "We are accepting only unsolicited manuscripts for picture books. Submit to Picture Book Manuscripts, Doubleday Books for Young Readers, 666 Fifth Avenue, New York, NY, 10103. *All other unsolicited manuscripts are returned to the sender.*"

Illustration: Will review artwork for future assignments (Bantam books only; Dell not reviewing material at this time). Uses artwork for full color books, jacket illustration and paperback book cover illustration. Current projects include a series of young adult hardcover books. Publishes 12-15 books/month. Looking for artists whose work displays ethnic and cultural diversity.

How to Contact/Illustrators: Ms/illustration packages: Submit through agent only. Illustrations only: write or telephone to arrange drop-off of portfolio (appointments not possible). Portfolio drop-off is usually the third week of every month — illustrators

The asterisk before a listing indicates the listing is new in this edition.

should call just to confirm. Samples can be sent to Marva Martin, art director."

BARRONS EDUCATIONAL SERIES, 250 Wireless Blvd., Hauppauge NY 11788. (516)434-3311. Fax: (516)434-3723. Book publisher. Estab. 1945. Acquisitions Editor (picture books): Grace Freedson. Editorial contact (young/middle readers, young adult titles): Grace Freedson. Publishes 20 picture books/year; 20 young reader titles/year; 20 middle reader titles/year; 10 young adult titles/year. 25% of books by first-time authors; 25% of books from agented writers.
Fiction: Picture books/young readers: adventure, animal, contemporary, easy-to-read, health-related, nature/environment, sports, suspense/mystery. Published *Get Ready, Get Set, Read* (beginning reader series).
Nonfiction: Picture books/young readers: activity book, animal, careers, health, history, nature/environment. Middle readers: nature/environment.
How to Contact/Writers: Fiction: Query. Nonfiction: Submit outline/synopsis and sample chapters. Reports on queries in 3-8 weeks; on mss in 6-8 months. Publishes a book 1 year after acceptance. Will consider simultaneous submissions.
Illustration: Editorial will review ms/illustration packages.
How to Contact/Illustrators: Ms/illustration packages: Query first; 3 chapters of ms with 1 piece of final art, remainder roughs. Illustrations only: Tearsheets or slides plus résumé. Reports in 3-8 weeks.
Terms: Pays authors in royalties based on retail price. Illustrators paid by the project based on retail price. Sends galleys to authors; dummies to illustrators. Book catalog, manuscript/artist's guidelines free on request.
Tips: Writers: "We are predominately on the lookout for preschool storybooks and concept books. No YA fiction/romance." Illustrators: "We are happy to receive a sample illustration to keep on file for future consideration. Periodic notes reminding us of your work is acceptable." Children's book themes "are becoming much more contemporary and relevant to a child's day-to-day activities."

BEHRMAN HOUSE INC., 235 Watchung Ave., West Orange NJ 07052. (201)669-0447. Fax: (201)669-9769. Book publisher. Project Editor: Adam Siegel. Publishes 3 young reader titles/year; 3 middle reader titles/year; 3 young adult titles/year. 12% of books by first-time authors; 2% of books from agented writers. Publishes books on all aspects of Judaism: history, cultural, textbooks, holidays.
Fiction: Picture books, young readers, middle readers, young adults: history and religion.
Nonfiction: All levels: history, religion, Jewish educational textbooks. Average word length: young reader—1,200; middle reader—2,000; young adult—4,000.
How to Contact/Writers: Fiction/nonfiction: Submit outline/synopsis and sample chapters. . Reports on mss/queries in 2 months. Publishes a book 2½ years after acceptance. Will consider simultaneous submissions.
Illustration: Will review ms/illustration packages. Will review artwork for future assignments.
How to Contact/Illustrators: Ms/illustration packages: "Query first." Illustrations only: Query with samples; send unsolicited art samples by mail. Reports in 2 months.
Photography: Purchases photos from freelancers. Contact Adam Siegel. Uses photos of families involved in Jewish activities. Uses color and b&w prints. To contact, photographers should query with samples. Send unsolicited photos by mail. Submit portfolio for review.
Terms: Pays authors in royalties of 3-8% based on retail price or buys ms outright for $1,000-5,000. Offers average advance payment of $500. Pays illustrators by the project (range: $500-5,000). Sends galleys to authors; dummies to illustrators. Book catalog free on request.
Tips: Looking for "religious school texts" with Judaic themes.

*BETHEL PUBLISHING, 1819 S. Main, Elkhart IN 46516. (219)293-8585. Book publisher. Contact: Senior Editor. Publishes 1-2 young readers/year; 1-2 middle readers/year.
Fiction: Young readers: animal, religion. Middle readers and young adults: adventure, religion. Does not want to see "New-Age—Dungeon & Dragons type." Recently published *The Great Forest*, by Jean Springer (ages 9-14, religion); *Aaron's Dark Secret*, by Ann Bixby Herold (ages 7-12, religion); *Peace Porridge*, by Marjie Douglas (ages 8-13, religion).
Nonfiction: Young readers, middle readers and young adults: religion.
How to Contact/Writers: Fiction/nonfiction: Query. Submit complete ms. Reports on queries in 3 weeks; on mss in 3 months. Publishes a book 1 year after acceptance. Will consider simultaneous submissions and previously published work.
Illustration: Works with 2 illustrators/year. Will review ms/illustration packages. Will review artwork for future assignments.
How to Contact/Illustrators: Ms/illustration packages: Query. Reports in 1 month. Samples returned with SASE. Originals not returned.
Photography: Purchases photos from freelancers. Contact Senior Editor. Buys stock. Model/property releases required. Uses color and b&w glossy prints; 35mm and 2¼×2¼ transparencies. To contact, photographers should send cover letter.
Terms: Pays authors royalty of 10-18% on wholesale price. Offers advances (average amount: $250). Pays illustrators by the project. Photographers paid by the project. Sends galleys to authors. Book catalog available for 9×12 SAE and 3 first class stamps. Ms guidelines available for SASE. Artist's guidelines not available.

*BLACK MOSS PRESS, 2450 Byng Rd., Windsor, Ontario N8W 3E8 Canada. (519)252-2551. Editor: Kristina Russelo. Publishes 2-4 picture books/year. 75% of books by first-time authors.
Fiction: Picture books: adventure, contemporary, humor. Does not want to see fantasy or food material. Average word length: Picture books—1,000. Recently published *Moving Gives Me A Stomach Ache*, by Heather McKend, illustrated by Heather Collins (ages 3-8, picture book).
How to Contact/Writers: Fiction: Submit complete ms. Reports on queries in 4-6 weeks; reports on mss in 2 months. Publishes book 2 years after acceptance.
Illustration: Works with 3-4 illustrators/year, however, "we aren't really looking for illustrators right now."
Terms: Pays authors royalty of 4-5% based on retail price. Pays illustrators by the project (range: $1,000-1,500). Sends galleys to authors; dummies to illustrators. Book catalog available for 6×8 SAE and 84¢ Canadian first class stamps. Ms guidelines available for SASE; art guidelines not available.
Tips: "Read the books out loud. So many books sound stiff and unnatural. Wants books with a realistic story with an interesting set of characters and strong setting. We will only publish Canadian citizens or landed immigrants."

BLUE HERON PUBLISHING, INC., 24450 NW Hansen Rd., Hillsboro OR 97124. (503)621-3911. Book publisher. Publisher: Dennis Stovall. Publishes 1-2 young adult titles/year. Wants "reprints of YA classics and/or well published authors. Only interested in the previously described from Northwest authors."
Fiction: Middle readers: adventure, animal, contemporary, history, nature/environment. Young Adults: adventure, anthology, animal, contemporary, history, nature/environment. Average word length: young adult—60,000. Published *Death Walk*, by Walt Money (YA, adventure novel); *Morning Glory Afternoon*, by Irene Bennett Brown (YA, historical adventure/romance); and *Angry Waters*, by Walt Morey (YA, adventure).
Nonfiction: Middle readers and young adults: history, nature/environment, writing/publishing.

How to Contact/Writers: Nonfiction: Query. Reports on queries in 4-6 weeks; on mss in 6 weeks. Publishes a book 18 months after acceptance. Will consider simultaneous submissions, electronic submissions via disk or modem and previously published work. **Illustration:** Will review artwork for future assignments (only Northwest artists). Contact Linny Stovall, publisher.
How to Contact/Illustrators: Illustrations only: Query with samples.
Terms: Pays author royalty of 5-8% on retail price. Pays illustrators by the project (range: $100-600). Sends galleys to authors; dummies to illustrators. Book catalog available for 6×9 SAE and 52¢ postage. Ms guidelines available.

BOYDS MILLS PRESS, 910 Church St., Honesdale PA 18431. (717)253-1080. Book publisher. Manuscript Coordinator: Beth Troop. Art Director: Tim Gillner. 5% of books from agented writers. Boyds Mills Press is made up of three imprints: Wordsong publishes poetry books; Caroline House publishes artful picture books; Bell Books publishes educational board books for schools and libraries. In nonfiction, science and environmental issues are covered. "We are just now coming out with a series on rivers."
Fiction: All levels: adventure, animal, contemporary, history, humor, multicultural, poetry, sports. Picture books, young readers, middle readers: folktales. Middle readers, young adults: anthology, suspense/mystery. Multicultural themes vary. "Please query us on appropriateness of suggested topic." Does not want to see fantasy, romance or coming-of-age. Recently published *Six Creepy Sheep*, by Judith Enderle and Stephanie Tessler (ages 2-6, animal); *Grandfather's Day*, by Ingrid Tomey (ages 8-12, contemporary); *Whistling the Morning In*, by Lillian Morrison (all ages, poetry).
Nonfiction: All levels: animal, biography, history, how-to, multicultural, nature/environment, science, sports. Picture books: activity books, arts/crafts, concept. Young readers: activity books, arts/crafts, concept, geography. Middle readers: activity books, arts/crafts, geography. Young adults: geography. Recently published *Yukon River*, by Peter Lourie (ages 8-12, geography).
How to Contact/Writers: Fiction/nonfiction: Submit complete manuscript or submit through agent. Reports on queries/mss in 1 month. Ms publishes 1-2 years after acceptance.
Illustration: Works with 70-100 illustrators/year. Will review ms/illustration packages. Will review artwork for future assignments. Contact Beth Troop, Manuscript Coordinator.
How to Contact/Illustrators: Ms/illustration packages: submit complete ms. Illustrations only: query with samples; send résumé and slides. Originals returned at job's completion.
Terms: Authors paid by royalty or outright purchase. Offers advances. Illustrators paid by the project, royalty. Catalog available for 9×12 SASE. Ms and art guidelines available for free.
Tips: "Picture books are our strongest need at this time."

BRADBURY PRESS, 866 Third Ave., New York NY 10022. (212)702-9809. Imprint of Macmillan Publishing Company. Book publisher. Vice President and Editorial Director: Barbara Lalicki. Art Director: Julie Quan. Publishes 20-25 picture books/year; 5 young reader titles/year; 5 middle reader titles/year. 25% of books by first-time authors; 75% of books from previously published or agented writers.
Fiction: Picture books: animal, contemporary, history. Young readers: animal, contemporary, easy-to-read, history. Middle readers: contemporary, fantasy, history, science fiction, spy/mystery/adventure. Average length: picture books—32 pages; young readers—48 pages; middle readers—112 pages.
Nonfiction: Picture books: animal, history, music/dance, nature/environment. Young readers: animal, biography, education, history, hobbies, music/dance, nature/environment, sports. Middle readers: animal, biography, education, history, hobbies, music/

dance, nature/environment, sports. Average length: picture books—32-48 pages; young and middle readers—48-64 pages.

How to Contact/Writers: Fiction: Query. Nonfiction: Submit outline/synopsis and sample chapters. Reports on queries in 2-3 weeks; on mss in 6-8 weeks. Publishes a book 18 months after acceptance.

Illustration: Will review illustrator's work for future assignments.

How to Contact/Illustrators: Submit ms with color photocopies of art. Illustrations only: Portfolio drop off last Thursday of every month. Reports on art samples only if interested. Original artwork returned at job's completion.

Terms: Pays author in royalties based on retail price. Average advance: varies. Book catalog available for 8×10 SAE and 4 first-class stamps; manuscript and/or artist's guidelines for business-size SAE and 1 first-class stamp.

Tips: Looks for "a strong story, nothing gimmicky, no pop-ups." Trends include "nonfiction for pre-schoolers."

*BREAKWATER BOOKS, Box 2188, St. John's Newfoundland, A1C 6E6 Canada. (709)722-6680. Book publisher. Marketing Coordinator: Loyal Squires. Publishes 3 middle reader titles/year; 2 young adult titles/year.

Fiction: Published *Smoke Over Grand Pré*, by Davison/Marsh (young adults, historical); *Fanny for Change*, by Jean Feather (middle reader); *Borrowed Black*, by Ellen B. Obed (young reader, fantasy).

Nonfiction: Published *A Viking Ship*, by Niels Neerso (young adults).

How to Contact/Writers: Fiction/nonfiction: Submit outline/synopsis and sample chapters; submit complete ms. Publishes a book 2 years after acceptance. Will consider simultaneous and photocopied submissions.

Illustration: Editorial will review ms/illustration packages submitted by authors/artists, ms/illustration packages submitted by authors with illustrations done by separate artists, and illustrator's work for possible use in author's text.

How to Contact/Illustrators: Submit 3 chapters of ms with 1 piece of final art, remainder roughs. Reports on art samples within weeks. Original artwork returned at job's completion.

Terms: Royalties are 10% based on retail price. "Amount varies" for mss purchased outright. Sends galleys to authors; dummies to illustrators. Book catalog free on request.

BRIGHT RING PUBLISHING, 1900 N. Shore Dr., Box 5768, Bellingham WA 98227-5768. (206)734-1601. Estab. 1985. Editor: MaryAnn Kohl. Publishes 1 young reader title/year. 50% of books by first-time authors. Uses only recipe format—"but no cookbooks unless woven into another subject like art, music, science."

Nonfiction: Picture books, young readers and middle readers: activity books involving art ideas, hobbies, music/dance and nature/environment. Average word length: "about 125 ideas/book." Published *Good Earth Art* by Kohl, illustrated by Cindy Gaines (picture book, young reader, middle reader—art ideas). "We are moving into only recipe-style resource books in any variety of subject areas—useful with children 2-12. 'Whole language' is the buzz word in early education—so books to meet the new demands of that subject will be needed."

How to Contact/Writers: Nonfiction: submit complete ms. Reports in 1-6 weeks. Publishes a book 1 year after acceptance. Will consider simultaneous submissions.

"Picture books" are geared toward the preschool—8 year old group; *"Young readers"* to 5-8 year olds; *"Middle readers"* to 9-11 year olds; and *"Young adults"* to those 12 and up.

Close-up

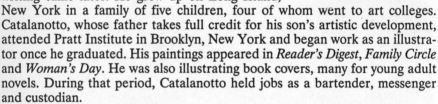

Peter Catalanotto
Writer/Illustrator
Doylestown, Pennsylvania

"My kindergarten teacher asked if I wanted to be
an artist when I grew up. I looked at her slightly
confused and answered, 'I'm an artist now,' " says
Peter Catalanotto, a writer and illustrator of children's books.

Although art was always part of his life's plan,
writing came later. He grew up on Long Island,
New York in a family of five children, four of whom went to art colleges.
Catalanotto, whose father takes full credit for his son's artistic development,
attended Pratt Institute in Brooklyn, New York and began work as an illustrator once he graduated. His paintings appeared in *Reader's Digest*, *Family Circle*
and *Woman's Day*. He was also illustrating book covers, many for young adult
novels. During that period, Catalanotto held jobs as a bartender, messenger
and custodian.

"I was working as an illustrator for six years when an editor suggested I try
picture books. He's been my editor ever since," says Catalanotto. In 1987, he
drew the cover for Judy Blume's *Just as Long as We're Together*, after which the
editor offered him a picture book manuscript, *All I See*. Illustrating *All I See*
prompted Catalanotto to try a story of his own, and in 1988 he wrote and
illustrated *Dylan's Day Out*. He also has written and illustrated *Mr. Mumble*
and *Christmas Always*.

Catalanotto develops his ideas for books by exploring "what ifs?" and attempting to see the world through the eyes of a child. "My editor knows that
the stories I write start with the art," he says. He sees images and writes the
words around them, being careful not to say in words what he's already con-
veyed in his illustrations.

Catalanotto never thought he'd be a writer and was more surprised than
anyone with the advent of his writing career. Writing does not come naturally,
although he enjoys it immensely. "I'm extremely happy doing what I'm doing,"
he says.

It wasn't always easy, though. The first three to five years after Catalanotto
graduated from art school were extremely hard. "I wouldn't wish them on a
dog," he says. He always knew he was entering a competitive field, but didn't
know just how difficult it would be. "I graduated from art school in 1982 but it
wasn't until 1989 that the doubts went away. I finally knew I could make it as
an illustrator," he says.

To aspiring illustrators, Catalanotto says, "Get a thick skin. Chances are the
rejections are going to come." He says that getting published might end one

long road, but it starts another. "When editors and art directors make suggestions on what you've painted, you have to figure out how to be flexible and still stay true to what you do. It's a fine line."

He also advises beginners to develop one style when trying to enter the field. "Most art directors want to know what they're going to get when they hire you. Once you build up a trust through consistency, most art directors will want to see what else you can do," says Catalanotto, who is still developing his own style. He'll make variations in order to accommodate different books. For example, some books will need more tightly rendered images than others; some may use one or two washes of paint; others may require more vivid images and thus several watercolor washes. (Catalanotto always works in watercolor; it's his favorite medium, because of the flexibility.) He also notes that you must appeal to adults as well as children, since children don't buy or review most books.

One thing he misses is time spent painting just for fun. "My schedule really doesn't allow for it," he says. He creates over a dozen book jackets a year and also does illustrations for magazines. The time spent working on a picture book is the closest thing to "just for fun." The work is rewarding and Catalanotto plans to continue working on children's books for a very long time.

"The unique thing about writing and illustrating for children is capturing a child's perspective through your own experiences. To be child-like and not child-ish," he says.

—Donna Collingwood

After Peter Catalanotto worked for six years as an illustrator an editor encouraged him to begin writing children's books. In 1988 he wrote and illustrated his first book, Dylan's Day Out, and since then he has finished two other children's titles, Mr. Mumble, from which comes the above illustration, and Christmas Always.

Illustration: Will review ms/illustration packages. Prefers to review "black line (drawings) for text."
How to Contact/Illustrators: Ms/illustration packages: "Query first." Illustrations only: query with samples; send tearsheets and "sample of ideas I request after query." Reports in 6-8 weeks. Original artwork returned at job's completion.
Terms: Pays authors in royalties of 5-10% based on wholesale or retail price. Pays illustrators $500-1,000. Also offers "free books and discounts for future books." Book catalog, ms/artist's guidelines for business-size SAE and 25¢ postage.
Tips: Illustrators: "Build your portfolio by taking a few jobs at lower pay—then grow. Bright Ring Publishing is not looking for picture books, juvenile fiction, or poetry at this time. We are, however, highly interested in creative activity and resource books for children to use independently or for teachers and parents to use with children. Must work for pre-school through age twelve."

CANDLEWICK PRESS, 2067 Massachusetts Ave., Cambridge MA 02140. (617)661-3330. Book publisher. Editorial Assistant: Susan Halperin. Publishes 80 picture books, 4 young readers, 6 middle readers, and 2 young adult titles/year. 5-50% of books by first-time authors.
Fiction: Picture books: animal, contemporary, fantasy, folktales, history. Young readers, middle readers and young adults: adventure, anthology, animal, contemporary, fantasy, folktales, history, poetry.
Nonfiction: Picture books, young readers and middle readers: animal, biography, history, music/dance, nature/environment. Young adults: animal, biography, history, music/dance.
How to Contact/Writers: Fiction: Query or submit complete ms. Nonfiction: Query or submit outline/synopsis and sample chapters. Reports in 3 weeks on queries; reports in 3 months on mss. Publishes a book 12-18 months after acceptance. Will consider simultaneous submissions.
Illustration: Will review ms/illustration packages. Will review artwork for future assignments. Uses color artwork only.
How to Contact/Illustrators: Ms/illustration packages: submit text with photocopies of artwork. Illustrations only: Send unsolicited art samples by mail; provide tearsheets to be kept on file. Reports only if interested. Include SASE for return.
Terms: Pays authors royalty of 5-10% based on retail price. Offers advances. Pays illustrators royalty of 5-10% based on retail price. Sends galleys to author. Book catalog available for 9×12 SAE and $1.67 postage; ms guidelines available for SASE.

CAPSTONE PRESS INC., P.O. Box 669, N. Mankato MN 56001. (507)387-7978. Book publisher. Publisher: Jean Eick. Publishes 25-30 picture books/year; 25-30 young reader titles/year; 10 middle reader titles/year. 15% of books by first-time authors; 1% from agented authors.
Fiction: Picture books, young readers and middle readers: animal, contemporary easy-to-read, fantasy, history, science fiction, sports, spy/mystery/adventure. Middle readers: problem novels, romance. Published *A Kid's Guide to Living on the Moon*, by Taylor (grade 5, middle reader); *Revolutionary War Soldier*, by Sanford & Green (grade 5, historical fiction); *Definitely from Out of Town*, by Seth Jarvis (grade 5, middle reader).
Nonfiction: Picture books, young readers and middle readers: animal, biography, education, history, hobbies, music/dance, nature/environment, sports. Published *Hot Air Ballooning*, by Costanzo (grade 5, sports); *BMX Bikes*, by Cavstensen (grade 5, sports); *18 Wheelers*, by Maifair (grade 5, sports).
How to Contact/Writers: Fiction/nonfiction: Query. Reports in 2 weeks. Publishes book in "6 months to 1 year depending upon publishing program."
How to Contact/Illustrators: Query first. Submit résumé and photocopies of work. Reports in 2 weeks. Does not return original artwork.

Terms: Outright purchase. Offers advance of one third of purchase price. Illustrators are paid by the project. Does not send galleys to authors; dummies to illustrators.

CAROLINA WREN PRESS/LOLLIPOP POWER BOOKS, 120 Morris Ave., Durham NC 27701. (919)560-2738. Book publisher. Carolina Wren estab. 1976; Lollipop Power Estab. 1971. Both are nonprofit, small presses. Children's Editor: Ruth A. Smullin. Designer: Martha Scotford. Publishes 1 picture book/year. 100% of books by first-time authors.

Fiction: Picture books: multicultural, nonsexist, multiracial, bilingual (English/Spanish). Average length: 30 pages. Recently published *The Boy Toy*, by Phyllis Johnson, illustrated by Lena Schiffman; *Maria Teresa*, by Mary Atkinson, illustrated by Christine Engla Eber; *In Christina's Toolbox*, by Dianne Homan, illustrated by Mary Heine.

How to Contact/Writers: "Query and request guidelines; enclose SASE with request. All manuscripts must be typed, double-spaced, and accompanied by an SASE of appropriate size with sufficient postage. If you do not wish your manuscript returned, you may simply enclose an SASE for our response. Do not send illustrations." Reports on queries/ms in 3 months. Publishes a book 2-3 years after acceptance.

Illustration: Editorial will review ms/illustration packages. Martha Scotford, designer, will review artwork for future assignments.

How to Contact/Illustrators: Query with tearsheets. Reports on art samples only if SASE enclosed. Original artwork returned at job's completion.

Terms: Pays authors in royalties of 5% of print-run based on retail price, or cash, if available. Pays illustrators in royalties of 5% "of print-run based on retail price, or cash, if available." Sends galleys to authors; dummies to illustrators.

Tips: "Lollipop Power Books offer alternative points of view to prevailing stereotypes. Our books show children: girls and women who are self-sufficient, with responsibilities beyond those of home and family; boys and men who are emotional and nurturing and involved in domestic responsibilities; families that use day care or alternative child care; families that consist of one parent only, working parents, or extended families; realistic portrayals of children of all races and ethnic groups, who have in common certain universal feelings and experiences. We believe that children must be taken seriously. Our books present their problems honestly and without condescension. Lollipop Power Books must be well-written stories that will appeal to children. We are not interested in preachy tales where message overpowers plot and character. We are looking for good stories told from a child's point of view. Our current publishing priorities are: a) African-American, Hispanic or Native American characters; b) bilingual books (English/Spanish); c) books that show gay men or lesbian women as ordinary people who can raise children. To request a catalog, send a 9×12 envelope with postage sufficient for 2 ounces."

CAROLRHODA BOOKS, INC., Lerner Publications, 241 First Ave. N., Minneapolis MN 55401. (612)332-3344. Book publisher. Estab. 1969. Submissions Editor: Rebecca Poole. Publishes 5 picture books/year; 25 young reader titles/year; 30 middle reader titles/year. 20% of books by first-time authors; 10% of books from agented writers.

Fiction: Picture books: animal, folktales, multicultural, nature/environment, special needs. Young readers, middle readers: historical, multicultural needs include picture books. Average word length: picture books—1,000-1,500; young readers—2,000. Recently published *Green Beans*, by Elizabeth Thomas with illustrations by Vicki Jo Redensbaugh.

Nonfiction: Picture books: animal, hobbies, nature/environment. Young readers, middle readers: animal, biography, history, hobbies, multicultural, nature/environment, science, social issues, special needs. Multicultural needs include biographies. Average word length: young readers— 2,000; middle readers—6,000. Recently published *American Bison*, by Ruth Berman with photographs by Cheryl Walsh Bellville (ages 7-10, animal photo essay); *Jump at de Sun: the Story of Zora Neale Hurston*, by A.P. Porter, forward by Lucy Ann Hurston (biography, ages 8-11); *The Workers' Detective: A Story about Dr. Alice Hamilton*, by Stephanie Sammartino McPherson with illustrations by Janet Schulz (ages 8-11, biography).

How to Contact/Writers: Fiction/nonfiction: Submit complete ms. Reports on queries in 3-4 weeks; on mss in 3 months. Publishes a book 18 months after acceptance. Will consider simultaneous submissions.

Illustration: Will review ms/illustration packages; will review artwork for future assignments.

How to Contact/Illustrators: Ms/illustration packages: At least one sample illustration (in form of photocopy, slide, duplicate photo) with full ms. Illustrations only: query with samples; send résumé/slides. "We like illustrators to send samples we can keep on file." Reports on art samples only if interested.

Photography: Purchases photos from freelancers. Buys stock and assigns work.

Terms: Buys ms outright for variable amount. Factors used to determine final payment: color vs. black-and-white, number of illustrations, quality of work. Sends galleys to authors; dummies to illustrators. Book catalog available for 9 × 12 SAE and 3 first-class stamps; manuscript guidelines for letter-size SAE and 1 first-class stamp.

Tips: Writers: "Research the publishing company to be sure it is in the market for the type of book you're interested in writing. Familiarize yourself with the company's list. We specialize in beginning readers, photo essays, and books published in series. We do very few single-title picture books and even fewer novels. For more detailed information about our publishing program, consult our catalog. We do not publish any of the following: textbooks, workbooks, songbooks, puzzles, plays and religious material. In general, we suggest that you steer clear of alphabet books; preachy stories with a moral to convey; stories featuring anthropomorphic protagonists ('Amanda the Amoeba,' 'Frankie the Fire Engine,' 'Tonie the Tornado'); and stories that revolve around trite, unoriginal plots. Be sure to avoid racial and sexual stereotypes in your writing, as well as sexist language." (See also Lerner Publications.)

CHARIOT BOOKS, 20 Lincoln Ave., Elgin IL 60120. (708)741-2400. An imprint of Chariot Family Publishing and a division of David C. Cook Publishing Co. Book publisher. Managing Editor: Julie Smith. Book Designer: Dawn Lauck. Publishes 20-30 picture books/year; 6-8 young readers/year; 10-15 middle readers/year; 4-6 young adult titles/year. 5% of books by first-time authors; 5% of books from agented authors. "All books have overt Christian values, but there is no primary theme."

Fiction: Picture books: animal, contemporary, nature/environment, religion. Young readers: adventure, animal, contemporary, history, nature/environment, religion, sports, suspense/mystery. Middle readers: adventure, contemporary, history, religion, sports, suspense/mystery. Young adults: adventure, contemporary, history, problem novels, religion, romance, sports, suspense/mystery. Does not want to see poetry, fantasy or science fiction. Average word length: picture books—1,000; young readers—1,200-1,500; middle readers—6,000-20,000; young adult—25,000. Recently published *The Pet That Never Was*, by Nancy Levene (contemporary, middle reader); *The True Princess*, by Angela Hunt (religion, picture book); *Uncle Alphonso and the Greedy Green Dinosaurs*, by Jack Pearson (animal, young reader).

Nonfiction: Picture books: activity books, animal, biography, nature/environment, religion (Bible stories), devotional. Young readers: activity books, biography, nature/envi-

---

Always include a self-addressed stamped envelope (SASE) or International Reply Coupon (IRC) with submissions.

ronment, religion, devotional. Middle readers: activity books, biography, religion, devotional. Young adults: religion, devotional. Does not want to see textbook, children's sermons. Average word length: picture books—1,000; young readers—1,500-2,000; middle readers—10,000. Recently published *The World's Biggest Chicken*, by Marian Bray (religion-devotional, teen); *When I Grow Up*, by Terry Whalin (religion, picture book). **How to Contact/Writers:** Fiction/nonfiction: Query. Submit outline/synopsis and 2 sample chapters. "For picture books, submit complete manuscript." Reports on queries in 2 months; reports on mss in 3 months. Publishes a book 12-18 months after acceptance. Will consider simultaneous submissions.
Illustration: Will review artwork for future assignments. Contact Dawn Lauck, book designer.
How to Contact/Illustrators: Illustrations only: Query with samples. Reports only if interested. Original artwork returned at job's completion.
Terms: Pays authors royalty, outright purchase. Offers advances on some books. Pays illustrators by the project, royalty. Sends galleys to authors; dummies to illustrators. Ms guidelines available for SASE.

CHARLESBRIDGE, 85 Main St., Watertown MA 02172. (617)926-0329. Subsidiary of Mastery Education. Book publisher. Publishes 4 nonfiction picture books/year. Managing Editor: Elena Dworkin Wright. Publishes nature or science early childhood picture books.
Nonfiction: Picture books: geography, nature/environment, science. No "talking animals, plants, clouds and rainbows. We publish only nonfiction, yet receive many fiction/fantasy manuscripts." Average word length: picture books—1,500. Published: *Will We Miss Them? Endangered Species*, by Alexandra Wright (picture book); *Icky Bug Counting Book*, by Jerry Pallotta (picture book); *At Home in the Rainforest*, by Diane Willow (picture book).
How to Contact/Writers: Nonfiction: Submit complete ms. Reports on mss in 1 month. Publishes a book 1-2 years after acceptance.
Illustration: Works with 5 illustrators/year. Will review ms/illustration packages. Will review artwork for future assignments. Uses color artwork only.
How to Contact/Illustrators: Illustrations only: Query with samples; provide résumé, tearsheets to be kept on file. Reports back only if interested. Does not return original artwork at job's completion.
Terms: Pays authors in royalties or outright purchase. Pays illustrators by the project. Sends galleys to authors.
Tips: Wants "picture books for little kids that have humor and are factually correct."

CHICAGO REVIEW PRESS, 814 N. Franklin St., Chicago IL 60610. (312)337-0747. Book publisher. Editorial Director: Amy Teschner. Art Director: Fran Lee. Publishes 1 middle reader/year; "about 4" young adult titles/year. 50% of books by first-time authors; 10% of books from agented authors. "We publish art activity books for young children and project books in the arts and sciences for ages 10 and up (our Ziggurat Series). We do not publish fiction."
Nonfiction: Young readers, middle readers and young adults: activity books on arts/crafts, geography, nature/environment, science. "We're interested in hands-on, educational books; anything else probably will be rejected." Average word length: young readers and young adult—175 pages. Recently published *The Art of the Handmade Book: Designing, Decorating, and Binding One-of-a-Kind Books*, by Flora Fennimore (ages 10 and up); *Seeing for Yourself: Techniques and Projects for Beginning Photographers*, by Roger Gleason (ages 11 and up); *Exploring The Sky: Projects for Beginning Astronomers, Revised Edition*, by Richard Moeschl (ages 11 and up); *Real Toads in Imaginary Gardens: Suggestions and Starting Points for Young Creative Writers*, by Stephen Phillip Policoff and Jeffrey Skinner (ages 12 and up). Reports on queries/mss in 6-10 weeks. Publishes a

book 1 year after acceptance. Will consider simultaneous submissions and previously published work.

Illustration: Works with 2 illustrators/year. Will review ms/illustration packages. Will review artwork for future assignments.

How to Contact/Illustrators: Ms/illustration packages: Submit 1-2 chapters of ms with corresponding pieces of final art. Illustrations only: Send samples. Reports back only if interested. Original artwork "usually" returned at job's completion.

Photography: Purchases photos from freelancers ("but not often"). Contact Fran Lee, art director. Buys stock and assigns work. Wants "instructive photos. We consult our files when we know what we're looking for on a book-by-book basis." Uses b&w prints.

Terms: Pays authors royalty of 7½-12½% based on retail price. Offers advances ("but not always") of $500-1,500. Pays illustrators by the project (range varies considerably). Photographers paid by the project (range varies considerably). Sends galleys to authors. Book catalog available for SASE; ms guidelines available for SASE.

Tips: "We're looking for original activity books for small children and the adults caring for them—new themes and enticing projects to occupy kids' imaginations and promote their sense of personal creativity. We like activity books that are as much fun as they are constructive. For older kids, age 10 and up, we publish Ziggurat Books—activity books geared to teach a discipline in the arts or sciences. As for the future, we expect parents to become increasingly engaged in their children's educations. Our Ziggurat books are intended to encourage children to pursue interests and talents inspired but not thoroughly covered by their schoolwork or other influences. We think parents are buying our books so their kids can pick up where a particularly exciting lesson or museum visit left off. When a kid becomes curious about say, photography or astronomy, we want to provide the challenging hands-on book that will cultivate enthusiasm while teaching him or her all about that intriguing subject."

*CHILDRENS PRESS, 5440 N. Cumberland, Chicago IL 60613. (312)693-0800. Book publisher. Vice President of Editorial: M.F. Dyra. Creative Director: M. Fiddle. Publishes over 20 picture books and 30 middle readers/year. 5% of books by first-time authors. Publishes informational (nonfiction) for K-6; picture books for young readers K-3.

Fiction: Picture books, young readers: adventure, animal, concept, contemporary, folktales, multicultural. Middle readers: contemporary, hi-lo, humor, multicultural. Young adults: hi-lo. Does not want to see young adult fiction, romance or science fiction. Average word length: picture book—300; middle readers—4,000.

Nonfiction: Picture books: arts/crafts, biography, concept, geography, hi-lo, history, hobbies, how-to, multicultural, nature/environment, science, special needs. Young readers: animal, arts/crafts, biography, careers, concept, geography, health, hi-lo, history, hobbies, multicultural, nature/environment, science, social issues, sports. Middle readers: hi-lo, history, multicultural, reference, science. Average word length: picture books—400; young readers—2,000; middle readers—8,000; young adult—12,000.

How to Contact/Writers: Fiction: Query; submit outline/synopsis or submit outline/synopsis and 1 sample chapter. Nonfiction: Query; submit outline/synopsis. Reports in 2-3 months. Publishes book 18 months after acceptance. Will consider simultaneous submissions.

Market conditions are constantly changing! If you're still using this book and it is 1994 or later, buy the newest edition of Children's Writer's & Illustrator's Market *at your favorite bookstore or order directly from Writer's Digest Books.*

Illustration: Works with 14 illustrators/year. Will review ms/illustration packages. Contact: M. Fiddle, creative director. Will review artwork for future assignments. Uses color artwork only.

How to Contact/Illustrators: Illustrations only: Query with samples or arrange personal portfolio review. Reports back only if interested. Samples returned with SASE. Samples filed. Originals not returned.

Photography: Purchases photos from freelancers. Contact: Jan Izzo, photo editor. Buys stock and assigns work. Model/property releases and captions required. Uses color and b&w prints; 2¼×2¼, 35 mm transparencies. To contact, photographers should send cover letter and stock photo list.

Terms: Pays authors royalty of 5% based on net or outright purchase of $500-1,000. Offers average advances of $1,000. Pays illustrators by the project (range: $1,800-3,500). Photographers paid per photo (range: $50-100). Sends galleys to authors; dummies to illustrators. Book catalog available for SAE; ms guidelines for SASE.

Tips: "Never write down to reader; keep language lively."

CHILDREN'S WRITER'S & ILLUSTRATOR'S MARKET, 1507 Dana Ave., Cincinnati OH 45207. Publication of Writer's Digest Books. Contact: Editor. Publishes annual directory of freelance markets for children's writers and illustrators. Send b&w samples—photographs, photostats or good quality photocopies of artwork. "Since *Children's Writer's & Illustrator's Market* is published only once a year, submissions are kept on file for the next upcoming edition until selections are made. Material is then returned by SASE." Buys one-time rights. Buys 10-20 illustrations/year. "I need examples of art that have been sold to one of the listings in *CWIM*. Thumb through the book to see the type of art I'm seeking. The art must have been freelanced; it cannot have been done as staff work. Include the name of the listing that purchased the work, what the art was used for and the payment you received." Pays $50 to holder of reproduction rights and free copy of *CWIM* when published.

■**CHINA BOOKS,** 2929 24th St., San Francisco CA 94110. (415)282-2994. Fax: (415)282-0994. Book publisher. Independent book producer/packager. Estab. 1960. Senior Editor: Bob Schildgen. 10% of books by first-time authors; 10% of books from agented writers. Subsidy publishes 10%.

Fiction: Picture books: animal, folktales, history, nature/environment, poetry. Young readers: animal, contemporary, folktales, history, nature/environment, religion. Middle readers: animal, contemporary, fantasy, folktales, nature/environment, poetry. Does not want to see subjects "not about China or Chinese Americans."

Nonfiction: Picture books, young readers, middle readers: activity books, biography, hobbies, nature/environment, religion, sports. Average word length: young readers—2,000; middle readers—4,000. Subjects must relate to China or Chinese Americans.

How to Contact/Writers: Fiction/nonfiction: Query; submit outline/synopsis and sample chapters. Publishes a book 9 months after acceptance. Will consider simultaneous and electronic submissions via disk or modem.

Illustration: Editorial will review ms/illustration packages.

How to Contact/Illustrators: Illustrations only: Query with samples.

Photography: Looking for Chinese or Chinese American subjects. Uses color and b&w prints; 35mm and 2¼×2¼ transparencies. To contact, photographers should query with samples.

Terms: Pays authors in royalties of 8-10% based on retail price; buys ms outright for $100-500. Offers average advance payment of "1/3 of total royalty." Pay for illustrators: by the project $100-500; royalties of 8% based on retail price. Pays photographers by the project (range: $50-500); per photo (range: $25-100); royalty of 4-8% based on retail price. Sends galleys to authors; dummies to illustrators. Book catalog free on request; manuscript/artist's guidelines for SASE.

Tips: Looks for "something related to China or to Chinese-Americans."

CHRONICLE BOOKS, 275 Fifth St., San Francisco CA 94103. (415)777-7240. Book publisher. Director: Victoria Rock. Editorial Assistant: Kristen Breck. Publishes 18-20 (both fiction and nonfiction) picture books/year; 2-4 middlegrade nonfiction titles/year. 10-50% of books by first-time authors; 10-50% of books from agented writers.
Fiction: Picture books: animal, anthology, contemporary, easy-to-read, folktales, history, multicultural, nature/environment, poetry, board books and fairytales. Published *Ten Little Rabbits*, by Virginia Crossman and Sylvia Long (picture book); *Mama, Do You Love Me?*, by Barbara Joosse and Barbara Lavallee (picture book).
Nonfiction: Ages 6-12: various categories (primarily natural history, biography and contemporary issues). Recently published *Cities in the Sand: The Ancient Civilizations of the Southwest* (ages 8-12); *Beneath the Waves: Exploring the Hidden World of the Kelp Forest* (ages 8-12); *N.C. Wyeth's Pilgrims* (ages 6-12).
How to Contact/Writers: Fiction and nonfiction: Submit complete manuscript (picture books); submit outline/synopsis and sample chapters (for older readers). Reports on queries in 1-2 months; 2-3 months on mss. Publishes a book 1-3 years after acceptance. Will consider simultaneous submissions, as long as they are marked "multiple submission."
Illustration: Editorial will review ms/illustration packages. "Indicate if project *must* be considered jointly, or if editor may consider text and art separately." Will review artwork for future assignments. Wants "unusual art. Something that will stand out on the shelves. Either bright and modern or very traditional. Fine art, not mass market."
How to Contact/Illustrators: Send samples of artist's work (not necessarily from book, but in the envisioned style). Slides, tearsheets and color photocopies OK. (No original art.) Dummies helpful. Résumé helpful. "If samples sent for files, generally no response—unless samples are not suited to list, in which case samples are returned. Queries and project proposals responded to in same time frame as author query/proposals."
Photography: Purchases photos from freelancers. Works on assignment only. Wants nature/natural history photos.
Terms: Generally pays authors in royalties based on retail price "though we do occasionally work on a flat fee basis." Advance varies. Illustrators paid royalty based on retail price or flat fee. Sends galleys to authors; proofs to illustrators. Book catalog for 9 × 12 SAE and 8 first class stamps; manuscript guidelines for #10 SASE.
Tips: "Chronicle Books publishes an eclectic mixture of traditional and innovative children's books. We are interested in taking on projects that have a unique bent to them—be it in subject matter, writing style, or illustrative technique. As a small list, we are looking for books that will lend our list a distinctive flavor. Primarily we are interested in fiction and nonfiction picturebooks for children ages infant to 8 years, and nonfiction books for children ages 8 to 12 years. At this time we are not publishing any fiction for middlegrade or young adult readers, but we will occasionally look at projects for this age group that are particularly relevant to our publishing program."

CLARION BOOKS, 215 Park Ave. South, New York NY 10003. (212)420-5800. Houghton Mifflin Company. Book publisher. Editor and Publisher: Dorothy Briley. Art Director: Helene Berinsky. Publishes 20 picture books/year; 7 young reader titles/year; 14 middle reader titles/year; 4 young adult titles/year. 10% of books by first-time authors; 15% of books from agented writers.
Fiction: All levels: adventure, animal, contemporary, fantasy, folktales, history, humor, multicultural, nature/environment, science fiction, sports, family stories. Average word length: picture books—50-1,000; young readers—1,000-2,500; middle readers—10,000-30,000; young adults—20,000—30,000.
Nonfiction: All levels: animal, biography, concept, geography, history, multicultural, nature/environment, science, social issues. Average word length: picture books—750-

1,000; young readers—1,000-2,500; middle readers—10,000-30,000.

How to Contact/Writers: Fiction: Send complete ms. Nonfiction: Query. Reports on queries in 1 month; mss in 2-3 months. Publishes a book 18 months after acceptance. Will consider simultaneous submissions.

Illustration: Works with 30 illustrators/year. Will review ms/illustration packages. Will review artwork for future assignments.

How to Contact/Illustrators: Ms/illustration packages: "Query first." Illustrations only: query with samples. Reports on art samples only if interested. Original artwork returned at job's completion.

Terms: Pays in royalties of 10-12½% based on retail price. Offers average advance payment of $2,500-5,000. Pays illustrator royalty of 10-12½% of retail price. Sends galleys to authors; dummies to illustrators. Book catalog, manuscript/artist's guidelines free on request with 8×10 SASE.

*CLOVERDALE PRESS, 96 Morton St., New York NY 10014. (212)727-3370. Independent book producer/packager. Editorial Contact: Jane Thorton. 25% of books by first-time authors; 50% of books from agented writers.

Fiction: Categories for consideration open on all levels. Average word length: picture books—500-1,000; young readers—10,000-15,000; middle readers—20,000-30,000; young adult/teens—30,000-40,000. Published *On The Edge*, by Jesse Maguire (young adult, problem novel); *Caroline Zucker* series, by Jan Bradford (young readers, contemporary); *Animal Inn* series, by Virginia Vail (middle readers, animal/contemporary).

Nonfiction: Picture books, young readers, middle readers and young adults/teens: animal, biography, education, history, hobbies, music/dance, nature/environment, religion, sports and science. Average word length: picture books—500-1,000; young readers—10,000-15,000; middle readers—20,000-30,000; young adult/teens—30,000-40,000. Published *Make the Team: Basketball* (middle readers, sports); *Smart Talk* series (young adult, grooming/manners).

How to Contact/Writers: Fiction/nonfiction: Query or submit outline/synopsis and sample chapters. Reports on queries in 4-6 weeks; mss in 2-3 months. Publishing time for a book "Varies according to publisher—usually about 1 year."

Terms: Pays authors in royalties or purchases outright. Advance varies. Additional payment for ms/illustration package varies. Pays authors and illustrators individually. Illustrators are paid by the project. Sometimes sends galleys to authors and dummies to illustrators. Manuscript guidelines for #10 SAE and 1 first class stamp.

COBBLEHILL BOOKS, 375 Hudson St., New York NY 10014. (212)366-2000. Affiliate of Dutton Children's Books, a division of Penguin Books USA Inc. Book publisher. Editorial Director: Joe Ann Daly. Sr. Editor: Rosanne Lauer. Publishes 6 picture books/year; 14 young reader titles/year; 9 middle reader titles/year; 5 young adult titles/year.

Fiction: Picture books: adventure, animal, contemporary, easy-to-read, sports, suspense/mystery. Young readers: adventure, animal, contemporary, easy-to-read, sports, suspense/mystery. Middle readers: adventure, contemporary, problem novels, sports, suspense/mystery. Young adults: adventure, suspense/mystery.

Nonfiction: Picture books: animal, nature/environment, sports. Young readers: animal, nature/environment, sports. Middle readers: nature/environment.

How to Contact/Writers: Fiction/nonfiction: query. Will consider simultaneous submissions "if we are informed about them."

How to Contact/Illustrators: Illustrations only: Send samples to keep on file, no original art work. Original art work returned at job's completion.

Terms: Pays authors in royalties. Illustrators paid in a flat fee or by royalty. Book catalog for 8½×11 SAE and 2 first class stamps; manuscript guidelines for #10 SASE.

COLORMORE, INC., Box 111249, Carrollton TX 75011-1249. (214)636-9326. Book publisher. Estab. 1987. President: Susan Koch. Publishes 4-6 young reader titles/year. 25% of books by first-time authors.
Nonfiction: Picture books, young readers: history, nature/environment, travel, world cultures and geography. Average word length: 3,000. Published *Colormore Travels – Dallas, Texas – The Travel Guide for Kids*; and *Colormore Travels – San Diego, California – The Travel Guide for Kids*, by Mary Stack (young reader, travel guide/activity book).
How to Contact/Writers: Nonfiction: Submit outline/synopsis and sample chapters; submit complete ms. Reports on queries/mss in 2-4 weeks. Publishes a book 9 months after acceptance.
Illustration: Editorial will review ms/illustration packages. Preference for "8½ × 11 format books, mainly black and white, coloring-type pictures and activities."
How to Contact/Illustrators: Ms/illustration packages: Send "complete ms with 1 piece of final art." Illustrations only: Send "example(s) of black line drawing suitable for coloring." Reports in 2-4 weeks. Original art work returned at job's completion.
Terms: Authors paid a 5% royalty based on invoice price. Ms/illustration packages: 5% royalty. Pays illustrators: 5% royalty based on invoice price. Sends galleys to authors; dummies to illustrators. Ms/artist's guidelines for legal SASE.
Tips: Looking for "a regional/local travel guide with lively, interesting illustrations and activities specifically for kids."

CONCORDIA PUBLISHING HOUSE, 3558 S. Jefferson Ave., St. Louis MO 63118. (314)268-1000. Book publisher. Contact: Ruth Geisler, Family and Children's Resources Editor. Art Director: Ed Luhmann. "Concordia Publishing House publishes a number of quality children's books each year. Most are fiction, with some nonfiction, based on a religious subject."
Fiction/Nonfiction: "Reader interest ranges from picture books to young adults. All books must contain explicit Christian content." Recently published *Little Visits on the Go*, by Mary Manz Simon (family devotional book and audio tape); *The Biggest Bully in Brookdale*, by Carol Gormon (first title in The Tree House Kids series, grades 2-3, first chapter books); *God Loves Me – So What*, by Guy Doud (preteen and teen, Christian living).
How to Contact/Writers: Fiction: Query. Submit complete manuscript (picture books); submit outline/synopsis and sample chapters (novel-length). Reports on queries in 1 month; 2 months on mss. Publishes a book one year after acceptance. Will consider simultaneous submissions.
Illustration: Art director, Ed Luhmann, will review artwork for future assignments.
How to Contact/Illustrators: Illustrations only: Query with samples.
Terms: Pays authors in royalties based on retail price or outright purchase (minimum $500). Sends galleys to author. Manuscript guidelines for 1 first class stamp and a #10 envelope.
Tips: "Do not send finished artwork with the manuscript. If sketches will help in the presentation of the manuscript, they may be sent. If stories are taken from the Bible, they should follow the Biblical account closely. Liberties should not be taken in fantasizing Biblical stories."

COTEAU BOOKS LTD., 401-2206 Dewdney Ave., Regina SK, S4R 1H3 Canada. (306)777-0170. Thunder Creek Publishing Co-op Ltd. Book publisher. Managing Editor: Shelley Sopher. Publishes 1 picture book/year, 9-11 books/year. 50% of books by first-time authors.
Fiction: Picture books, young readers: contemporary, folktales, multicultural. "No didactic, message pieces, nothing religious, no fantasy (especially historical fantasy)." Average word length: picture books – 500. Recently published *The Potter*, by Jacolyn Caton/Stephen McCallum (ages 3-8, picture book).

How to Contact/Writers: Fiction: Submit complete ms. Reports on queries in 1 month; on mss in 4 months. Publishes a book 1-2 years after acceptance. Coteau Books publishes Canadian writers only; manuscripts from the US are returned unopened. In 1992-93 only children's writers from the Canadian Prairies will be considered.
Illustration: Works with 1 illustrator/year. Will review ms/illustration packages. Will review artwork for possible future assignments.
How to Contact/Illustrators: Ms/illustration packages: send "roughs." Illustrations only: send nonreturnable samples. Reports only if interested. Original artwork returned at job's completion. Only Canadian illustrators are used.
Terms: Pays authors in royalties of 5-12% based on retail price. Other method of payment: "signing bonus." Pay for illustrators: by the project (range: $500-2,000) or royalty of 5% maximum based on retail price. Sends galleys to authors; dummies to illustrators. Book catalog free on request with 9 × 12 SASE (IRC).

COUNCIL FOR INDIAN EDUCATION, 517 Rimrock Rd., Billings MT 59102. (406)252-7451. Book publisher. Estab. 1968. Editor: Hap Gilliland. Publishes 1 picture book/year; 1 young reader title/year; 3 middle reader titles/year; 1 young adult title/year. 75% of books by first-time authors.
Fiction: Picture books, young readers, middle readers: adventure, anthology, animal, contemporary, folktales, history, nature/environment, poetry, sports, suspense/mystery. Young adults: adventure, anthology, animal, contemporary, folktales, health-related, nature/environment, poetry, romance, sports. All must relate to Native American life and culture, past and present. Does not want to see "sex, vulgarity or anything not related to American Indian life and culture."
Nonfiction: Picture books, young readers: animal, biography, history, hobbies, nature/environment, sports. Middle readers, young adults: animal, biography, careers, health, history, hobbies, music/dance, nature/environment, sports. All of above must be related to American Indian life and culture, past and present.
How to Contact/Writers: Fiction: Submit complete ms. Nonfiction: Submit outline/synopsis and sample chapters, or submit complete ms. Reports on queries in 2 months; mss in 6 months. "We accept 5% of the manuscripts received. Those with potential must be evaluated by all the members of our Indian Editorial Board, who make the final selection. This board makes sure the material is true to the Indian way of life and is the kind of material they want their children to read." Publishes a book 1 year after acceptance. Will consider simultaneous submissions.
Illustration: "It is doubtful if we will need new artists in the next year." Editor will review ms/illustration packages. "Black-and-white artwork only."
How to Contact/Illustrators: Ms/illustration packages: "Samples sent with manuscript." Illustrations only: Query with samples. Reports on art samples in 3 months "when we report back to author on ms." Original artwork returned at job's completion "if requested."
Terms: Pays authors in royalties of 10% based on wholesale price or buys ms outright for "1½¢ per word." Additional payment for ms/illustration packages "sometimes." Factors used to determine payment for ms/illustration package include "number of illustrations used." Sends galleys to authors. Book catalog/manuscript guidelines available for SASE.
Tips: "For our publications, write about one specific tribe or group and be sure actions portrayed are culturally correct for the group and time period portrayed. What kind of material can we use? These are our preferences, in the order listed: Contemporary Indian Life—exciting stories that could happen to Indian children now. (Be sure the children act like present-day Indians, not like some other culture.) Indians of the old days—authentically portrayed. Be specific about who, where and when. How-to—Indian arts, crafts, and activities. Biography—Indians past and present. History and culture—factual material of high interest only. If you are Indian, express your ideas and

ideals. Folk stories and legends—high interest expressing Indian ideas. Name the specific tribe. Poetry—possibly—if it expresses real Indian ideals. Instructional material and information for teachers of Indian children."

*CRESTWOOD HOUSE, 866 Third Ave,. New York NY 10022. (212)702-9631. Macmillan Children's Book Group. Book publisher. Associate Editor: Barbie Heit. Publishes 70 middle readers/year. 10% of books by first-time authors; 2% of books from agented authors. Publishes "hi-lo nonfiction for reluctant readers."
Nonfiction: Middle readers: biography, careers, hi-lo, history, multicultural, nature/environment, sports. "We publish only in series. Not interested in single titles." Average word length: middle readers—5,000. Recently published *First Families: The Kennedys*; *Cool Classics: Porsche*; *Africa Today: Africa's Struggle to Survive*.
How to Contact/Writers: Nonfiction: Query. Submit outline/synopsis. Reports on queries in 1 month. Publishes a book 1-1½ years after acceptance. Will consider simultaneous submissions.
Illustration: Works with 2 illustrators/year.
Terms: Pays authors outright purchase of $1,000-1,500. Sends galleys to authors. Book catalog available for 9×12 SASE. Ms guidelines not available.

CROSSWAY BOOKS, Good News Publishers, 1300 Crescent, Wheaton IL 60187. Book publisher. Acquisitions Editor: Jennifer Nahrstadt. Production Assistant: Jenny Kok. Publishes 4 middle readers/year; 1-2 young adult titles/year. 10% of books by first-time authors. 3% of books by agented authors.
Fiction: Middle readers: adventure, contemporary, fantasy, multicultural, suspense/mystery. Multicultural needs include positive, contemporary portrayals of ethnic groups. Does not want to see historical fiction. Published *Home By Another Way*, by Nancy N. Rue; *Sadie Rose and the Champion Sharpshooter*, by Hilda Stahl; *Daisy Punkin*, by Hilda Stahl. All books must have spiritual/religious themes.
Nonfiction: Religion, social issues.
How to Contact/Writers: Fiction/nonfiction: Query. Reports on queries in 1 week; on mss in 9 months. Publishes a book up to 1 year after acceptance. Accepts simultaneous submissions.
Illustration: Works with 2-3 illustrators/year. Will review artwork for future assignments.
How to Contact/Illustrators: Query with samples. Submit resume, portfolio or slides. Reports back only if interested. Originals returned to artist at job's completion.
Photography: Purchases photos from freelancers. Contact Jenny Kok. Buys stock. Query with samples.
Terms: Pays by royalty based on wholesale price. Illustrators paid by the project (negotiable). Authors see galleys for review; illustrators see dummies for review. Book catalog for $1.50 and 9×12 SASE. Manuscript guidelines for #10 SASE.

CROWN PUBLISHERS (CROWN BOOKS FOR CHILDREN), 225 Park Ave. S., New York NY 10003. (212)254-1600. Imprint of Random House, Inc. Book publisher. Editor-in-Chief: Simon Boughton. Publishes 20 picture books/year; 10 nonfiction titles/year. 2% of books by first-time authors; 70% of books from agented writers.
Fiction: Picture books: adventure, animal, contemporary, fantasy, folktales, health-related, history, nature/environment, sports. Average word length: picture books—750.

Refer to the Business of Children's Writing & Illustrating for up-to-date marketing, tax and legal information.

Recently published: *The Giraffe That Walked to Paris*, by Nancy Milton; *Ruby Mae Has Something to Say*, by David Small (4-8 years, picture books).

Nonfiction: Picture books, young readers and middle readers: activity books, animal, biography, careers, health, history, hobbies, music/dance, nature/environment, religion, sports. Average word length: picture books—750-1,000; young readers—20,000; middle readers—50,000; Recently published: *Chameleons*, by James Martin and Art Wolfe (4-8 years, picture book); *Children of the Dust Bowl*, by Jerry Stanley (9-14 years, middle reader).

How to Contact/Writers: Fiction/nonfiction: Submit complete manuscript. Reports on queries in 1 month; 2-4 months on mss. Publishes book 2 years after acceptance. Will consider simultaneous submissions.

Illustration: Reviews ms/illustration packages. "Double-spaced, continuous manuscripts; do not supply page-by-page breaks. One or two photocopies of art are fine. *Do not send original art*. Dummies are acceptable.

How to Contact/Illustrators: Photocopies or slides with SASE; provide business card and tearsheets. Reports on ms/art samples in 2 months. Original artwork returned at job's completion. Pays author royalty. Advance "varies greatly." Illustrators paid royalty. Sends galleys to authors; proofs to illustrators. Book catalog for 9 × 12 SAE and 4 first class stamps. Manuscript guidelines for 4¼ × 9½ SASE. Artists' guidelines not available.

*CRYSTAL RIVER PRESS, P.O. Box 1382, Healdsburg CA 95448. Book publisher. Editor-in-Chief: Thomas Watson. Publishes 6-8 picture books/year; approx. 8 young readers/year; 10 middle readers/year; 6-8 young adult titles/year. 70% of books by first-time authors; 30% of books from agented authors.

Fiction: Picture books: adventure, animal, folktales, health, humor, multicultural, nature/environment. Young readers: adventure, animal, anthology, contemporary, fantasy, folktales, health, hi-lo, history, humor, multicultural, nature/environment, poetry, special needs, sports, environmental activity. Middle readers: adventure, animal, anthology, contemporary, fantasy, folktales, health, hi-lo, history, humor, multicultural, nature/environment, poetry, problem novels, religion, romance, science fiction, special needs, sports, suspense/mystery, activity. Young adults: adventure, animal, anthology, contemporary, fantasy, folktales, health, history, humor, multicultural, nature/environment, poetry, problem novels, religion, romance, science fiction, special needs, sports, suspense/mystery. Does not want adult material; no avante-garde or conceptual material. Average word length: picture books—500; young readers—1,500; middle readers—3,000. Soon to be published: *Henry, The Little Kite*; *The Monster in the Mailbox*; *The Place*, all by T.E. Watson.

Nonfiction: Picture books: activity books, animal, arts/crafts, cooking, geography, health, history, hobbies, how-to, multicultural, music/dance, nature/environment, reference, science, self help. Young readers: activity books, animal, arts/crafts, biography, careers, concept, cooking, geography, health, history, hobbies, how-to, multicultural, music/dance, nature/environment, reference, science, self help, social issues, special needs, sports. Middle readers: activity books, animal, arts/crafts, biography, careers, concept, cooking, geography, health, history, hobbies, how-to, multicultural, music/ dance, nature/environment, reference, religion, science, self help, social issues, special needs, sports. Young adults: animal, arts/crafts, biography, careers, geography, health, history, hobbies, how-to, multicultural, music/dance, nature/environment, reference, science, self help, social issues, special needs, sports. Wants themes to be well researched. "Try to remember, we are dealing with young minds." Average word length: picture books: 300-500; young readers: 700-2,000; middle readers: 2,000-5,000. Recently published *Wild Whales*, by T.E. Watson (ages 8-12, environmental nonfiction).

How to Contact/Writers: Fiction: Query; submit complete ms if short; submit outline/ synopsis and 3 sample chapters. Nonfiction: Query; submit complete ms; submit outline/ synopsis. Reports on queries in 3 weeks; reports on mss in 4-8 weeks. Will consider simultaneous submissions, electronic submissions via disk and previously published work.

Illustration: Works with 6-20 illustrators/year. Will review ms/illustration package. Uses both b&w and color artwork.

How to Contact/Illustrators: Ms/illustration packages: Query; submit ms with dummy. Illustrations only: Query with samples; provide resume. Samples returned with SASE; samples filed. Original artwork returned at job's completion.

Photography: Purchases photos from freelancers. Buys stock and assigns work. Uses photos dealing with children, animals, environmental, natural history. Model/property releases and captions required. Uses matte/glossy color and b&w prints, 2¼ × 2¼ and 8 × 10 transparencies. To contact, photographers should submit cover letter, resume, color/b&w promo piece.

Terms: Pays authors royalty of 5-15% based on retail price or makes outright purchase $1,000-5,000. Pays illustrators royalty of 3-15% based on retail price. Photographers paid royalty of 5-15% based on retail price. Sends galleys to authors; dummies to illustrators. Book catalog not available; ms and art guidelines for SASE.

Tips: Sees popularity of audio books growing.

*CSS PUBLISHING, 628 S. Main St., Lima OH 45804. (419)227-1818. Book publisher. Editor: Fred Steiner.

Fiction: Picture books, young readers, middle readers, young adults: religion.

Nonfiction: Picture books, young readers, middle readers, young adults: religion.

How to Contact/Writers: Reports on queries in 1 week; reports on mss in 3 months. Publishes a book 9 months after acceptance. Will consider simultaneous submissions.

MAY DAVENPORT, PUBLISHERS, 26313 Purissima Rd., Los Altos Hills CA 94022. (415)948-6499. Book publisher. Estab. 1976. Independent book producer/packager. Editor: May Davenport. Publishes 1-2 picture books/year; 2-3 young adult titles/year. 99% of books by first-time authors. Seeks books with literary merit. "We are overstocked with picture book/elementary reading material."

Fiction: Middle readers: animal. Young adults: adventure, fantasy, humor, suspense/mystery. Does not want to see "computer tales—children going into the computer world, a pseudo Alice in Wonderland adventure, or a Wizard of Oz fantasy after vaporizing in the computer." Average word length: 20,000-30,000 words. Recently published *Leroy, The Lizzard*, by Claudia Cherness (grades 2-4, paper); *Seymour, The Turtle*, by Andrea Ross, (gr. 2-4, hardcover).

Nonfiction: Activity books to read alone or aloud plus to color. Does not want to see "senior citizens, adventures when they were 4-5 years old and not worth publishing."

How to Contact/Writers: Fiction: Query. Reports on queries in 1-2 weeks; on mss in 2-4 weeks. "We do not answer queries or manuscripts which do not have SASE attached." Publishes a book 6-12 months after acceptance.

Illustration: Works with 1-2 illustrators/year. Will review ms/illustration packages. Will review artwork for future assignments.

How to Contact/Illustrators: Illustrations only: "Send samples for our files for future reference."

Terms: Pays authors in royalties of 15% based on retail price. Pays "by mutual agreement, no advances." Pays illustrators by the project. Book listing, manuscript guidelines free on request with SASE.

Tips: Writers: "Make readers laugh with your imaginative words. However, if you do not have a humorous literary talent, forget it. Try being a stand-up comedian/enne elsewhere." Illustrators: "If your styles of drawing and painting are on file and we have a story which needs your talent, we'll get in touch with you." The trend is "what big publishers want to sell for a profit. If it's folktales from far-away lands, then they publicize it as the thing to read, the trend to buy, and publicity works. Money talks. Children getting their information passively, quickly by print or TV advertisement of trends will not be interested in reading in depth and in writing literature. Such a pity. Perhaps the future will have more computer writers who will depend on the programs to correct their spellings, to put in appropriate punctuation marks, and to select outlines of plots for romance, mystery, etc."

DAVIS PUBLICATIONS, INC., 50 Portland St., Worcester MA 01608. (508)754-7201. Fax: (508)753-3834. Book publisher. Acquisitions Editor: Martha Siegel. Publishes 10 titles total/year. 30% of books by first-time authors. "We publish books for the art education market (elementary through high school), both technique-oriented and art appreciation resource books and textbooks."
Nonfiction: Middle readers, young adults: Activity books about art and art-related textbooks. Multicultural books detailing the arts of other cultures. Recently published *Children and Painting*, by Cathy Weisman Topal; *Basic Printmaking Techniques*, by Bernard Toale; *Exceptional Children, Exceptional Art*, by David Henley; *Design and Drawing*, by Richard L. Shadrin; and *See and Draw*, by Karl V. Larsen.
How to Contact/Writers: Submit outline/synopsis and 1 sample chapter. Reports on queries in 1 month; on mss in 2 months. Publishes a book 1 year after acceptance. Will consider simultaneous submissions and electronic submissions via disk.
Illustration: Works with 1 illustrator/year. "We use a combination of photos and line drawings" (200-300 per nonfiction title). Will review ms/illustration packages. Will review artwork for future assignments.
How to Contact/Illustrators: Query with samples. Reports in 1 month.
Photography: "Rarely" purchases photos from freelancers. "Usually need photos of particular artists, artworks or art forms." Model/property releases and photo captions required. Publishes photo concept books. Uses 5×7 and 8×10 glossy, b&w prints and 4×5 and 8×10 transparencies.
Terms: Pays authors royalties. Pays illustrators by the project. Sends galleys to authors. Book catalog available for SASE; ms guidelines available for SASE.
Tips: Seeking "nonfiction titles on art techniques, media and history/appreciation. We do not publish children's story/picture books; rather, we publish educational books for use by art teachers, art students and amateur artists."

DAWN PUBLICATIONS, 14618 Tyler Foote, Nevada City CA 95959. (916)292-3482. Fax: (916)292-4258. Book publisher. Publisher: Bob Rinzler. Nature and holistic issues.
Nonfiction: All levels: animal, health, nature/environment, health related.
How to Contact/Writers: Nonfiction: Query; submit complete ms; submit outline/synopsis and sample chapters. Reports in 2 months on queries/mss. Publishes a book 1 year after acceptance. Will consider simultaneous submissions and previously published work.
Illustration: Will review ms/illustration packages. Will review artwork for future assignments.
How to Contact/Illustrators: Ms/illustration packages: Query; submit complete package; submit chapters of manuscript. Illustrations only: Query with samples.
Terms: Pays authors royalty. Offers advance. Sends galleys to authors; dummies to illustrators. Book catalog available for 6×9 SASE.

T.S. DENISON CO. INC., 9601 Newton Ave. S., Minneapolis MN 55431. Editor: Baxter Brings. 25% of books by first-time authors. Publishes teacher resource/activity books. "We mostly publish nonfiction."
Fiction: Picture books, young readers, middle readers: history, multicultural, nature/environment, poetry. "Anything that accompanies student activities." Doesn't want "fiction stories without activities for the classroom."

Nonfiction: Picture books, young readers and middle readers: activity books, animal, arts/crafts, careers, history, multicultural, music/dance, nature/environment, reference, science, social issues, textbooks. Average word length: picture books—96 pages; middle readers—150 pages. Recently published *Let's Meet Famous Composers*, by Harriet Kinghorn with illustrations by Margo De Paulis (grades 3-6, teacher resource); *Toddler Calendar*, by Elaine Commius with art by Anita Nelson (Pre-K, teacher resource); *Fairy-Tale Mask*, by Gwen Rives Jones with art by Darcy Myers (grades 1-3, teacher resource).

How to Contact/Writers: Fiction/nonfiction: Query; submit complete manuscript; submit outline/synopsis and 2 sample chapters. Reports on queries/mss in 2 months. Publishes a book 9 months after acceptance. Will consider simultaneous submissions and electronic submissions via disk or modem.

Illustration: Works with 15 illustrators/year. Will review ms/illustration packages. Will review artwork for future assignments.

How to Contact/Illustrators: Illustrations only: Query with samples; arrange a personal interview to show portfolio. Reports in 1 month. Original artwork not returned at job's completion.

Terms: Pays authors royalty of 4-8% based on wholesale price (through stores) or retail price (direct mail). Outright purchase $300-1,000. Pays illustrators by the project (range: $300-400 for covers; $25 for b&w). Book catalog available for 9×12 SAE and 3 first class stamps; ms guidelines available for SASE.

Tips: Wants teacher resource materials.

*DILLON PRESS, INC., 866 Third Ave., New York NY 10022. (212)702-9631. Imprint of Macmillan Children's Book Group. Book publisher. Editor: Joyce Stanton. Publishes 40 middle readers/year. 10% of books by first-time authors; 2% of books from agented authors.

Nonfiction: Middle readers: animal, biography, geography, history, multicultural, nature/environment, science, social issues. Average word length: middle readers—5,000 words. Recently published *Places in American History: The Alamo*; *People in Focus: Malcolm X*; *Ecology Watch: Polar Lands*.

How to Contact/Writers: Nonfiction: Query. Submit outline/synopsis and 2 sample chapters. Reports on queries in 2 months. Publishes a book 1 year after acceptance.

Terms: Pays authors royalty of up to 5% based on retail price; outright purchase $1,000-1,500. Offers advances (average amount: $1,000). Sends galleys to authors. Book catalog available for 9×12 SASE; ms guidelines not available.

■DISCOVERY ENTERPRISES, LTD., 134 Middle St., Lowell MA 01852. (508)459-1720. Fax: (508)937-5779. Book publisher and independent book producer/packager. Executive Director: JoAnne Weisman. Publishes 6 middle readers books/year. 40% of books by first-time authors; subsidy publishes 10%. Publishes all nonfiction picture book biographies in 9×12 full color format—serious histories, but original. "Illustrations are key to the works. Also pen & ink drawings for history series."

Fiction: Picture books, young readers and middle readers: history, nature/environment. Young adults: history.

Nonfiction: Picture books, young readers and middle readers: biography, history, nature/environment, Third World countries. Young adults: biography, history, nature/environment. "No sports, religious leaders or current entertainers for biographies." Average word length: picture books 3,000; young and middle readers 3,000-4,000; young adults 4,000-5,000. Published *Leonard Bernstein: America's Maestro*, by Kenneth M. Deitch (10 and up, picture book biography); *Lucretia Mott: Friend of Justice*, by Kem Knapp Sawyer (8 and up, picture book biography); *W.E.B. DuBois: Crusader for Peace*, by Kathryn Cryan-Hicks (10 and up, picture book biography).

How to Contact/Writers: Fiction: Query. Nonfiction: Query. Submit outline/synopsis and 3 sample chapters. Reports on queries in 4-6 weeks; reports on mss in 6-8 weeks.

Publishes a book 6 months after acceptance. Will consider simultaneous submissions and previously published work.

Illustration: Will review ms/illustration packages. Will review artwork for future assignments. Contact: JoAnne Weisman, executive director. "No preference in medium or style, but artist must be able to do portraits, as these are biographies."

How to Contact/Illustrators: Ms/illustration packages: Submit 2-3 chapters of ms with 4-6 pieces of final art. Send samples of artwork—color copies OK with text. Illustrations only: Query with samples; provide resume, promotional literature and tearsheets to be kept on file. Reports in 4-6 weeks. Original artwork returned at job's completion "but not for 2 years."

Photography: Photographers should contact JoAnne Weisman, executive director. Uses all types of photos. Model/property releases and captions required. Interested in stock photos. Uses 35mm, 2¼ × 2¼ and 4 × 5 transparencies. To contact, photographers should query with samples; provide resume, business card, promotional literature and tearsheets to be kept on file.

Terms: Pays authors royalty of 5-10% based on wholesale price. Offers $1,000 advance. Pays illustrators by the project (range: $600-1,500) or royalty of 5-10% based on wholesale price. Photographers paid per photo (range: $25-400). Sends galleys to authors; dummies to illustrators. Book catalog available for #10 SASE.

Tips: Wants "Neat, clean artwork, presented professionally." For writers, good cover letter, outline and sample chapters necessary. "Watch for grammatical errors. I prefer separate submissions from artists and authors. Carefully research and accurately illustrate art for histories and biographies in any medium." Sees trend toward more nonfiction for use in classrooms to supplement or replace textbooks, as well as more emphasis on multi-racial books, women's history, peace, etc.

DISTINCTIVE PUBLISHING CORP., P.O. Box 17868, Plantation FL 33318-7868. (305)975-2413. Book publisher. Independent book producer/packager. Editor: F. Knauf. Publishes 1-2 books/year. 95% of books by first-time authors.

Fiction: Picture books; adventure, animal, history, nature/environment. Young readers: adventure, animal, history, humor, nature/environment, suspense/mystery, multicultural. "We will consider all submissions." Published *Ships of Children*, by Richard Taylor (middle-young adult, adventure).

Nonfiction: Picture book and young readers: animal geography, biography, careers, history, social issues. "As with fiction we will consider all submissions."

How to Contact/Writers: Nonfiction: Submit complete ms. Reports on queries in 2-4 weeks; reports on mss in 1-3 months. Publishes book 6-12 months after acceptance. Will consider simultaneous submissions and previously published work.

Illustration: Will review ms/illustration packages.

How to Contact/Illustrators: Ms/illustration packages: Submit complete package. Reports in 1 month. Original artwork is returned at job's completion.

Photography: Photographers should contact Alan Erdlee, publisher. Type of photos used depends on project. Model/property release and photo captions required. Interested in stock photos. Publishes photo concept books. Uses 4 × 6 glossy color prints, 2¼ × 2¼ transparencies. To contact, photographer should query with samples; query with resume of credits; provide resume, business card, tearsheets to be kept on file.

Terms: Pays authors royalty based on wholesale and retail price; outright purchase; "each project is different." Offers advances. Pays illustrators by the project or royalty.

 The solid block before a listing indicates the market subsidy publishes manuscripts.

Photographers are paid by the project or per photo. Sends galleys to author; dummies to illustrators. Book catalog available for 9 × 12 SASE.

Tips: Best chance of selling to this market is with adventure and educational mss.

*DORLING KINDERSLEY, INC., 232 Madison Ave., New York NY 10016. (212)684-0404. Book pubilsher. Senior Editor, Children's Books: B. Alison Weir. Publishes 8 picture books/year; 4 young readers/year. 50% of books by first-time authors; 50% of books from agented authors (fiction list only).

Fiction: Picture books: contemporary, folktales, multicultural, nature/environment. Multicultural needs include relationship stories/family stories. Does not want to see fiction with licensed characters. Average word length: picture books—48 pages. "First fiction coming in Spring 1993."

Nonfiction: Young readers: animal, biography (international only), hobbies, how-to, multicultural, music/dance, nature/environment, science. "We produce almost all nonfiction in-house." Does not want to see "manuscripts imitating books we've already published!" Average word length: young readers—32 pages. Recently published Look Closer series, Eyewitness Books and Eyewitness Explorers Guides.

How to Contact/Writers: Fiction/nonfiction: Submit complete ms. Reports on queries/mss in 2 months. Publishes a book 1½ years after acceptance. Will consider simultaneous submissions.

Illustration: Works with 12 illustrators/year. Will review ms/illustration packages. Will review artwork for future assignments.

How to Contact/Illustrators: Submit ms with dummy. Illustrations only: Query with samples; provide promo sheet and tearsheets. Reports only if immediately interested. Otherwise samples go in file. Samples returned with SASE (if requested); samples filed.

Photography: Purchases photos from freelancers. Contact: Dirk Kaufman, designer. Works on assignment only. To contact, photographers should submit cover letter and résumé.

Terms: Pays author royalty based on retail price. Pays illustrators by the project or royalty. Pays photographers by the project. Sends galleys to authors; dummies to illustrators. Book catalog available for 9 × 12 SAE and 3 first class stamps; ms guidelines available for SASE; artist's guidelines not available.

Tips: A writer has the best chance of selling beginning reader nonfiction or creative fiction to this publisher.

DUTTON CHILDREN'S BOOKS, 375 Hudson St., New York NY 10014. (212)366-2600. Penguin USA. Book publisher. Editor-in-Chief: Lucia Monfried. Art Associate: Carolyn Boschi. Publishes approximately 60 picture books/year; 4 young reader titles/year; 10 middle reader titles/year; 8 young adult titles/year. 10% of books by first-time authors.

Fiction: Picture books: adventure, animal, folktales, history, multicultural, nature/environment, poetry. Young readers: adventure, animal, contemporary, easy-to-read, fantasy, suspense/mystery. Middle readers: adventure, animal, contemporary, fantasy, history, multicultural, nature/environment, suspense/mystery. Young adults: adventure, animal, anthology, contemporary, fantasy, history, multicultural, nature/environment, poetry, science fiction, suspense/mystery. Recently published *The Lion and the Little Red Bird*, by Elisa Kleven (ages 3-7, picture book); *Dark Heart*, by Betsy James (ages 10 and up, novel); and *Tyrone Goes to School*, by Susan Saunders and Steve Björkman (ages 7-10, Speedster series for reluctant readers).

Nonfiction: Picture books: animal, history, multicultural, nature/environment. Young readers: animal, history, multicultural, nature/environment. Middle readers: animal, biography, history, multicultural, nature/environment. Young adults: animal, biography, history, multicultural, nature/environment, social issues. Recently published *Wonderful Pussy Willows*, by Jerome Wexler (ages 8 and up, photo essay); *The Story of Christmas*,

Close-up

Linda Gondosch
Writer
Lawrenceburg, Indiana

Like many parents, Linda Gondosch read to her children when they were very little. After the story was over and the children were in bed, however, Gondosch says she just couldn't put the book back on the shelf. "I found myself sitting and looking at it again, rereading it, going back and looking at who wrote it, who illustrated it. And I began to think, 'maybe I could do this.' "

It was not long before she was doing just that, fitting in her writing whenever she could, even though her two preschoolers kept her busy. "I'd write when they were playing, taking naps, watching *Sesame Street*. I even bought them a toy typewriter and they'd sit with me pounding away, writing their own stories."

Now Gondosch's children are in high school and college and her seventh book, *Camp Kickapoo* is due out this spring. Her first book was published in 1984, but by then she'd had about 10 stories published. "I sort of followed the traditional path a lot of writers take by starting with magazines. Although I write fiction, my very first sale was a personal experience story to a small magazine called *Baby Care*. After that I was hooked."

Gondosch writes for 8- to 12-year-olds and 7- to 9-year-olds. Her kids and the neighborhood children have been a constant source of inspiration. When she decided to write her first book Gondosch enrolled in a novel-writing course at Writer's Digest School. "My homework for the class became the book *Who Needs a Bratty Brother*. I was trying to think of something to write and I could hear my children in the next room arguing over who would get the prize in a cereal box. It gave me an idea that became the opening for the book."

By all means, she says, avoid writing down to children. "Don't try to teach a lesson or present a moral . . . . You must see the world through the eyes of a child. When I write I try completely to become the child. Most of my stories are about children in the world today, but a lot also comes from my own childhood. You must be able to remember what it was like to argue with your brother, lose a favorite toy or want your own dog."

The most important advice she would give those interested in writing for children is to study children's books as well as read them. "After you read a book, go back and try to find out what made the story so good. Study how the author grabs the reader's attention, how the plot is developed, how the chapters are broken down, how the characters come alive, at what point in the story the author sets up the conflict and how it is resolved."

—Robin Gee

words from the Gospels of Matthew and Luke, illustrated by Jane Ray (all ages, picture book published in both English and Spanish).

How to Contact/Writers: Fiction/nonfiction: query. Reports on queries in 1 month; on mss in 3 months. Publishes a book 12-18 months after acceptance. Will consider simultaneous submissions.

Illustration: Works with 40-60 illustrators/year. Will review ms/illustration packages. Will review artwork for future assignments.

How to Contact/Illustrators: Ms/illustration packages: Query first. Illustrations only: Query with samples; send resume, portfolio, slides—no original art please. Reports on art samples in 2 months. Original artwork returned at job's completion.

Photography: Purchases photos from freelancers. Assigns work. Wants "nature photography."

Terms: Pays authors royalties of 4-10% based on retail price. Book catalog, manuscript guidelines for SAE. Pays illustrators royalties of 2-10% based on retail price unless jacket illustration—then pays by flat fee. Photographers paid royalty per photo.

Tips: Writers: "We publish high-quality trade books and are interested in well-written manuscripts with fresh ideas and child appeal. Avoid topics that appear frequently. We have a complete publishing program. Though we publish mostly picture books, we are very interested in acquiring more novels for young, middle, and young adult readers. In nonfiction, we are looking for history, general biography, science, and photo essays for all age groups." Illustrators: "We would like to see samples and portfolios from potential illustrators of picture books (full color), young novels (black and white), and jacket artists (full color)." Foresee "even more multicultural publishing, plus more books published in both Spanish and English."

WM. B. EERDMANS PUBLISHING COMPANY, 255 Jefferson Avenue SE, Grand Rapids MI 49503. (616)459-4591. Book publisher. Children's Book Editor: Amy Eerdmans. Publishes 6 picture books/year; 4 young reader titles/year; 4 middle reader titles/year.

Fiction: All levels: religion, fantasy, problem novels, parables, retold Bible stories from a Christian perspective.

Nonfiction: All levels: biography, history, nature/environment, religion.

How to Contact/Writers: Fiction/nonfiction: Query; submit complete manuscript. Reports on queries in 1-2 weeks; mss in 4 weeks.

Illustration: Reviews manuscript packages. Willem Mineur, art director, will review illustrator's work for possible future assignments.

How to Contact/Illustrators: Illustrations only: Submit résumé, slides or color photocopy. Reports on ms/art samples in 1 month. Original artwork returned at job's completion.

Terms: Pays authors in royalties of 5-10%. Pays in royalty for the author. The illustrator receives royalty or permission fee. Sends galleys for review; dummies to illustrators. Book catalog free on request; manuscript and/or artist's guidelines free on request.

FARRAR, STRAUS & GIROUX, 19 Union Square West, New York NY 10003. (212)741-6934. Book publisher. Children's books Editor-in-Chief: Margaret Ferguson. Estab. 1946. Publishes 21 picture books/year; 6 middle reader titles/year; 5 young adult titles/year. 5% of books by first-time authors; 5% of books from agented writers.

Fiction: "Original and well-written material for all ages." Recently published *Weeping Willow*, by Ron White (young adult).

How to Contact/Writers: Fiction/nonfiction: Query; submit outline/synopsis and sample chapters. Reports on queries in 6 weeks; on mss in 12 weeks. Publishes a book 18 months after acceptance. Will consider simultaneous submissions.

Illustration: Will review ms/illustration packages.
How to Contact/Illustrators: Ms/illustration packages: Ms with 1 example of final art, remainder roughs. Illustrations only: Tearsheets. Reports on art samples only if interested. Original artwork returned at job's completion.
Terms: "We offer an advance against royalties for both authors and illustrators." Sends galleys to authors; dummies to illustrators. Book catalog available for 6½ × 9½ SAE and 56¢ postage; manuscript guidelines for 1 first-class stamp.
Tips: "Study our catalog before submitting. We will see illustrator's portfolios by appointment."

*FAWCETT JUNIPER, 201 E. 50 St., New York NY 10022. (212)751-2600. Imprint of Ballantine/DelRey/Fawcett Books. Book publisher. Editor-in-Chief/Vice President: Leona Nevler. Publishes 36 young adult titles/year.
Fiction: Middle readers: contemporary, romance, science fiction. Young adults: contemporary, romance, fantasy.
How to Contact/Writers: Fiction: Query.
Terms: Pays authors in royalties.

*FERON/JANUS/QUERCUS, 500 Harbor Blvd., Belmont CA 94002. Imprint of Simon & Schuster Education Group. Book publisher. Production Director: Karen Gulliver. Publishes 50 special ed., young adult titles/year.
Fiction: Young adults: hi-lo, multicultural, special needs. Average word length: 10,000-15,000.
Nonfiction: Young adults: biography, careers, health, hi-lo, history, multicultural, nature/environment, science, special needs, textbooks.
How to Contact/Writers: Fiction or nonfiction: Query "but, we don't respond to all queries." Reports on queries in 6 months. Reports on mss in 12-18 months.
Illustration: Works with 20 illustrators/year. Will review samples/portfolio. Contact: Karen Gulliver, production director. Will review artwork for future assignments. Uses b&w and color artwork.
How to Contact/Illustrators: Illustrations only: Query with samples, resume, promo sheet, portfolio, slides, client list, tearsheets, arrange personal portfolio review. Reports in 2 months. Samples returned with SASE. "We prefer to keep on file."
Photography: Purchases photos from freelancers. Buys stock images and assigns work. "We don't accept general submissions. We commission as needed." Model/property releases required. Uses wide range of color and b&w prints. To contact, photographers should submit cover letter, résumé, published samples, slides, client list, stock photo list, portfolio, promo piece.
Terms: Pays authors outright purchase, $2,500 minimum. Pays illustrators by the project. Photographers paid by the project. Sometimes sends galleys to authors.
Tips: "Be very sure the house you approach publishes the type of work you do. Make sure your work has solid, carefully crafted development with no dangling details."

*FIFTH HOUSE PUBLISHERS, 620 Duchess St., Saskatoon, Sasketchewan S7K 0R1 Canada. (306)242-4936. Book publisher. Managing Editor: Charlene Dobmeier. Publishes 1 picture book/year; 1 middle reader/year; 1 young adult title/year.
Fiction: "We publish few young adult books but have published in the area of native themes/authors." Recently published *Silent Words*, by Ruby Slipperjack (adult/young adult fiction); *Two Little Girls Lost in the Bush*.

 The asterisk before a listing indicates the listing is new in this edition.

How to Contact/Writers: Fiction: Query; submit outline/synopsis. Reports on queries in 6-8 weeks. Publishes book 1 year after acceptance.
Illustration: Works with 1 illustrator/year. Will review artwork for future assignments. Uses both b&w and color artwork.
How to Contact/Illustrators: Ms/illustration packages: Query. Illustrators only: Query with samples. Reports in 6-8 weeks. Cannot return samples. Original artwork returned at job's completion.
Photography: Purchases photos from freelancers. Works on assignment only. Captions required. To contact, photographers should submit cover letter, published samples for review.
Terms: Sends galleys to authors. Book catalog available for 8 × 10 SAE and 65¢ Canadian first class stamps. Ms guidelines available for SASE. Art guidelines not available.

FOUR WINDS PRESS, 866 Third Ave., New York NY 10022. (212)702-2000. Imprint of Macmillan Publishing Co. Book publisher. Editor-in-Chief: Virginia Duncan. 15-20% of books by first-time authors; 80% of books from agented writers.
Fiction: Picture books: animal, contemporary, humor, fantasy. Middle readers: history, family, contemporary. Average word length: picture books—750-1,500; middle readers—10,000-30,000. "YA books are no longer being considered."
Nonfiction: Picture books: animal, nature/environment, biography, history, concepts. Middle readers: animal, biography, history, hobbies, music/dance, nature/environment, sports. Average word length: picture books—750-1,500; middle readers—10,000-30,000.
How to Contact/Writers: Fiction: Submit outline/synopsis and complete ms. Nonfiction: Query. Reports on queries/mss in 3 months. "Due to volume of submissions received, we cannot guarantee a quick response time or answer queries about manuscript status." Publishes a book 18-24 months after acceptance. "We are *not* reviewing simultaneous submissions."
Illustration: Editorial will review ms/illustration packages.
How to Contact/Illustrators: Picture books: Submit full ms or dummy with art samples (not originals!). Illustrations only: "Illustration portfolios are reviewed every Thursday on a drop-off basis. If you cannot drop off your portfolio, you should mail tearsheets. Your portfolio should contain samples of work that best reflect your technical and creative ability to illustrate a text for children. These samples should include two or three different scenes of animals and/or children rendered in a setting. These should show your ability to handle composition, create interesting characters, and maintain consistency between scenes. Use whatever medium is best suited to your technique. Generally, still life, three dimensional artwork and abstract compositions do not translate well to children's book illustrations." Reports on ms/art samples in 6-8 weeks; art samples only if interested. Original artwork returned at job's completion.
Terms: Pays authors in royalties of 5-10% based on retail price (depends on whether artist is sharing royalties). Pays illustrators by the project; royalties range from 2-5%; "fees and royalties vary widely according to budget for book." Sends galleys to authors; dummies to illustrators. Manuscript and/or artist's guidelines for 1 first-class stamp and a business-size envelope. "No calls, please."
Tips: "The length of your story depends on the age of the child for whom it is intended. There are no fixed lengths. A good story is almost always the right length or can easily be made so." (See also Aladdin Books/Collier Books for Young Adults, Atheneum Publishers, Bradbury Press, Margaret K. McElderry Books.)

FREE SPIRIT PUBLISHING, Ste. 616, 400 First Ave. N., Minneapolis MN 55401. (612)338-2068. Book publisher. Publisher/President: Judy Galbraith. Publishes 3-4 middle reader titles/year; 3-4 young adult titles/year. 80% of books by first-time authors. "Our books pertain to the education and psychological well being of young people."

Nonfiction: Picture books, young readers, middle readers and young adults: health, hobbies, nature/environment, self-esteem, psychology, education. Recently published *If I Ran the Family*, by Lee and Sue Kaiser Johnson (ages 4-9, healthy family issues); *School Power: Strategies for Succeeding in School*, by Jeanne Shay Schumm and Marguerite Radencish (ages 11 and up, education); *The First Honest Book About Lies*, by Jonni Kincher (ages 13 and up, self-help/psychology).

How to Contact/Writers: Nonfiction: Submit résumé, outline/synopsis and sample chapters. Reports on queries in 3 months. Publishes a book 12-18 months after acceptance.

Terms: Pays authors in royalties of 8-12% based on wholesale price. Offers advance payment of $500-$1,000. Sends galleys to authors. Book catalog free on request.

Tips: Does not accept unsolicited artists' or photographers' samples. Wants to see "A book that helps kids help themselves, or that helps adults help kids help themselves."

FRIENDSHIP PRESS, Rm. 860, 475 Riverside Dr., New York NY 10115. (212)870-2497. National Council of Churches of Christ in the USA. Book publisher. Editorial Contact: Margaret Larom. Art Director: Paul Lansdale. Publishes 1-2 picture books/year; 1 young reader title/year; 1 middle reader title/year; 1 young adult title/year. 75% of books commissioned for set themes.

Fiction: Picture books, young readers, middle readers, young adults: multicultural, mission and religion. Average word length: young adults – 20,000-40,000. Book catalog free on request. Published *Pearlmakers*, by Vilma May Fuentes (grades 1-6, stories about the Philippines); *Aki and the Banner of Names*, by Atsuko Gōda Lolling (grades 1-6, stories about Japan).

Nonfiction: Picture books, young readers, middle readers, young adults: activity books geography, multicultural, social issues, mission and religion. Average word length: middle readers – 10,000; young adults – 10,000.

How to Contact/Writers: Fiction and nonfiction: Query. Reports on queries/mss in 3-6 weeks. Publishes a book 18 months after acceptance. Will consider simultaneous submissions. Ms guidelines free on request.

Illustration: Works with 1 illustrator/year. Editorial will review ms/illustration packages. Art Director, Paul Lansdale, will review artwork for future assignments.

How to Contact/Illustrators: Ms/illustration packages: send 3 chapters of ms with 1 piece of final art. Illustrations only: send résumé and tearsheets. Reports only if interested. Original artwork returned at job's completion.

Terms: Buys ms outright for $25-1200. Pays illustrators by the project (range: $25-1,200). Sends galleys to authors; dummies to illustrators. Book catalog and ms guidelines free on request.

Tips: Seeking "a book that illustrates what life is like for children in other countries, especially Christian children, though not exclusively."

*GAGE EDUCATIONAL PUBLISHING COMPANY, 164 Commander Blvd., Agincourt, Ontario M1S 3C7 Canada. (416)293-8141. Imprint: Dancing Sun Books. Book publisher. Publishing Director, Elementary: H. Richardson. Production Manager: A. Kress. Publishes 5 picture books/year. 95% of books by first-time authors. "All books must be applicable to education curricula."

Fiction: Picture books: concept, history (Canadian), multicultural, nature/environment, poetry, special needs. Young readers: concept, history (Canadian), multicultural, nature/environment, poetry. Multicultural themes: "Canadian First nations, Canadian cultural roots and immigrant experiences." Doesn't want "anything not directly linked to curricula." Average word length: picture books – 0-1,200; young readers – 2,500-3,500. Recently published *Jessica and the Lost Stories*, by Jenny Nelson with illustrations by Alice Priestly (picture book, ages 5-8); *The Gift*, by Michael Barnes with illustrations by

Herb Larsen (young readers, ages 8-10); *Island Rhymes*, by Jenny Nelson with illustrations by Herb Larsen (poetry, ages 8-10).

Nonfiction: Picture books: concept, history (Canadian), nature/environment. Young readers: biography (Canadians), concept, history (Canadian), nature/environment. Sees too much "straight factual presentation where there's no stimulation for critical thinking or reader reflection of issues." Average word length: picture books—0-1,000; young readers—2,500-3,500. No nonfiction titles to date—new area for us."

How to Contact/Writers: Fiction/nonfiction: Submit complete ms. Reports on queries in 1-2 months; on mss in 1-3 months. Publishes a book 2 years after acceptance. Will consider simultaneous submissions (if stated).

Illustration: Works with 5-10 illustrators/year. Will review ms/illustration packages. Will review artwork for future assignments. "We have a preference for Canadian illustrators."

How to Contact/Illustrators: Ms/illustration packages: Query. Illustrations only: Query with samples; provide résumé, promo sheet, client list, tearsheets. Reports back only if interested. Samples returned with SASE; samples filed. Return of originals "depends on agreement arranged."

Terms: Pays authors royalty of 5-10% based on net proceeds. Pay for artwork negotiated with book designer and illustrator. Sends galleys to authors. Book catalog not available ("Our catalogs reserved for school systems in Canada); ms guidelines available for SAE with IRCs.

Tips: "Read *Writing Picture Books*, by Kathy Stinson. Attend workshops. Take criticism as offered—a stimulus to improve. Our market is the school market rather than trade. Future is *non-textbook!*"

*LAURA GERINGER BOOKS, 10 E. 53rd St., New York NY 10022. (212)207-7554. HarperCollins Publishers. Editorial Director: Laura Geringer. Publishes 10-12 picture books/year; 2 middle readers/year; 2-4 young adult titles/year. 20% of books by first-time authors; 50% of books from agented authors.

Fiction: Picture books: adventure, animal, contemporary, fantasy, folktales, history, nature/environment, poetry. Young readers: adventure, anthology, animal, contemporary, fantasy, folktales, health-related, history, nature/environment, poetry, sports, suspense/mystery. Middle readers and young adults: adventure, anthology, animal, contemporary, fantasy, folktales, health-related, history, nature/environment, poetry, problem novels, sports, suspense/mystery. Average word length: picture books—250-1,200. Recently published *Bently & Egg*, by William Joyce (ages preschool-3 years, picture book); *The Borning Room*, by Paul Fleischman (ages 10 +, middle grade); *The Tub People*, by Pam Conrad (preschool-3 years, picture book).

How to Contact/Writers: Fiction: Submit complete ms. Reports on queries in 2-4 weeks; reports on mss in 2-4 months. Publishes a book 1½-3 years. Will consider simultaneous submissions.

Illustration: Average number of illustrations used for fiction: picture books—12-18; middle readers—10-15. Will review ms/illustration packages. Will review artwork for future assignments. Contact Laura Geringer or Harriett Barton (art director).

How to Contact/Illustrators: Submit complete package. Illustrations only: Query with samples; submit portfolio for review; provide résumé, business card, promotional literature or tearsheets to be kept on file. Reports in 2-4 weeks. Original artwork returned at job's completion.

Terms: Pays authors royalties of 5-6% (picture book) or 10-12% (novel). Offers advances. Pays illustrators royalties of 5-6%. Sends galleys to authors; dummies to illustrators. Book catalog available for 9×11 SASE; ms guidelines available for SASE.

Tips: "Write about what you *know*. Don't try to guess our needs. And don't forget that children are more clever that what we give them credit for!" Wants "artwork that isn't overly 'cutesy' with a strong sense of style and expression."

*GIBBS SMITH, PUBLISHER, P.O. Box 667, Layton UT 84041. (801)544-9800. Imprint: Peregrine Smith Books. Book publisher. Editorial Director: Madge Baird. Publishes 2 picture books/year. 10% of books by first-time authors. 90% of books from agented authors.

Fiction: Picture books: Christmas. Average word length: picture books—2,000-4,000.

Nonfiction: Picture books: Christmas. Average word length: picture books—2,000-4,000.

How to Contact/Writers: Fiction/nonfiction: Query. Submit complete ms. Reports on queries in 3 weeks; reports on mss in 6-8 weeks. Publishes a book 1-2 years after acceptance. Will consider simultaneous submissions.

Illustration: Works with 2 illustrators/year. Will review ms/illustration packages. Will review artwork for future assignments.

How to Contact/Illustrators: Ms/illustration packages: Query. Submit ms with 3-5 pieces of final art. Illustrations only: Query with samples; provide résumé, promo sheet, slides (duplicate slides, not originals). Reports back only if interested. Samples returned with SASE; samples kept on file. Original artwork returned at job's completion.

Terms: Pays authors royalty of 4-7½% based on wholesale price. Offers advances (average amount: $1,000.) Pays illustrators royalty of 4-7½% based on wholesale price. Sends galleys to authors; dummies to illustrators. Book catalog available for 6×9 SAE and 52¢ postage. Ms/artist's guidelines not available.

Tips: Wants Christmas subjects, either fiction of nonfiction.

*DAVID R. GODINE, PUBLISHER, 300 Massachusetts, Boston MA 02115. (617)536-0761. Book publisher. Estab. 1970. Contact: Editorial Department. Publishes 3-4 picture books/year; 2 young reader titles/year; 3-4 middle reader titles/year. 10% of books by first-time authors; 20% of books from agented writers.

Fiction: Picture books: animal. Young readers: animal, easy-to-read, fantasy, mystery/adventure, folk or fairy tales. Middle readers: animal, fantasy, folk or fairy tales. Published *Cuckoo Clock*, by Mary Stolz (ages 9-11, middle readers); *Sea Gifts*, by George Shannon (ages 8-10, early readers); *A Natural Man*, by Steve Sanfield (ages 8-10, early readers).

How to Contact/Writers: "No unsolicited material being accepted at this time." Reports on queries in 2 weeks; on mss in 3 weeks. Publishes a book 18 months after acceptance.

Illustration: Editorial will review all varieties of ms/illustration packages.

How to Contact/Illustrators: Ms/illustration packages: "Roughs and 1 finished art plus either sample chapters for very long works or whole ms for short works." Illustrations only: "Slides, with one full-size blow-up of art." Reports on art samples in 3 weeks. Original artwork returned at job's completion.

Terms: Pays authors in royalties based on retail price. Number of illustrations used to determine final payment. Pay for separate authors and illustrators: "differs with each collaboration." Illustrators paid by the project. Sends galleys to authors; dummies to illustrators. Book catalog/manuscript guidelines free on request.

GOLDEN BOOKS, 850 Third Ave., New York NY 10022. (212)753-8500. Western Publishing Co. Book Publisher. Editorial Directors: Margo Lundell, Marilyn Saloman.

Fiction: Picture books: animal, easy-to-read. Young readers: easy-to-read. Middle readers: history, sports. Young adult titles: contemporary, sports and series lines.

Nonfiction: Picture books: education, history, nature/environment, sports. Young and middle readers: animal, education, history, nature/environment, sports.

How to Contact/Writers: "Material accepted only through agent."

Illustration: Art directors David Werner and Linda Neilson will sometimes review ms/illustration packages. Will review an illustrator's work for possible future assignments.

How to Contact/Illustrators: Ms/illustration packages: query first.
Terms: Pays authors in royalties based on retail price.

GOSPEL LIGHT PUBLICATIONS, 2300 Knoll Dr., Ventura CA 93003. (805)644-9721. Imprint of Regal Books. Book publisher. Contact: Acquisitions Editor. Publishes 1 picture book/year; 2-3 young reader titles/year; 1 young adult title/year.
Fiction: Picture books and young readers: value-oriented. Published *Smarty the Adventurous Fly*, by Ethel Barrett (ages 3-8, picture book); *Jasper*, by Ethel Barrett (ages 3-8, picture book).
Nonfiction: Picture books, young and middle readers and young adults/teens: religion.
How to Contact/Writers: Fiction/nonfiction: Submit outline/synopsis and sample chapters. Reports on queries in 4-6 weeks; reports on mss in 6-8 weeks. Publishes book 7-12 months after acceptance. Will consider simultaneous submissions.
Illustration: Will review manuscript/illustration packages. Acquisitions editor will review an illustrator's work for possible future assignments.
How to Contact/Illustrators: Submit 3 chapters/1 piece final art. Provide resume and photocopies of work. Reports in 6 weeks. Original artwork returned at job's completion.
Terms: Pays authors royalty based on wholesale price or outright purchase. Sends galleys to authors; dummies to illustrators. Book catalog available for 9 × 12 and 2 first class stamps; ms guidelines available for SASE.

*GREEN TIGER PRESS, INC., 15 Columbus Circle, New York NY 10023. (212)373-8639. Book, calendar and card publisher. Estab. 1970. Publishes 10-15 picture books/year. Also publishes 2-4 calendars and assorted notecards annually.
Fiction: Juvenile and adult picture books. Word length: 250-2,000. Published *Shell of Wonder*, by Harwich and Hay; *Sugar Ships*, by Parsley; *A Visit to the Art Galaxy*, by Reiner.
How to Contact/Writers: Fiction: Submit complete ms to Editorial Committee. Reports on queries/mss in 6 months. Publishes a book 12 months after acceptance. Will consider simultaneous submissions.
Illustration: Editorial will review all varieties of ms/illustration packages.
How to Contact/Illustrators: Ms/illustration packages: Send entire ms, prints, slides or color photocopies of illustrations and dummy. Illustrations only: Send prints, slides or color photocopies. Do not send originals of art work. Reports only if interested. Original art work returned at job's completion.
Terms: Usually pays authors and illustrators a royalty based on retail price. Royalty percentages vary. Book catalog, ms/artist's guidelines free on request.
Tips: "Study the publisher's catalog before submitting." Looking for "32-60 page books—one illustration and one concise paragraph per spread. 'Dreams, visions and fantasies'—not religious or necessarily educational material."

GREENHAVEN PRESS, 10907 Technology Place, San Diego CA 92127. (619)485-7424. Book publisher. Estab. 1970. Senior Editors: Terry O'Neill and Bonnie Szumski. Publishes 40-50 young adult titles/year. 35% of books by first-time authors.
Nonfiction: Middle readers: biography, history, controversial topics, issues. Young adults: biography, history, nature/environment. Other titles "to fit our specific series." Average word length: young adults—15,000-18,000.
How to Contact/Writers: Query only. "We accept no unsolicited manuscripts. All writing is work-for-hire."
Terms/Writers: Buys ms outright for $1,500-2,500. Offers advances. Sends galleys to authors. Book catalog available for 9 × 12 SAE and 65¢ postage.
Tips: "Get our guidelines first before submitting anything."

GREENWILLOW BOOKS, 1350 Ave. of the Americas, New York NY 10019. (212)261-6500. Imprint of William Morrow & Co. Book publisher. Associate Editor: Robin Roy. Art Director: Ava Weiss. Publishes 50 picture books/year; 10 middle readers books/year; 10 young adult books/year.
Fiction: Will consider all levels of fiction; various categories.
How to Contact/Writers: Fiction: Submit complete ms to editorial department. Reports on mss in 2 months. Publishes a book 18-24 months after acceptance. Will consider simultaneous submissions.
Illustration: Will review ms/illustration packages. Will review artwork for future assignments.
How to Contact/Illustrators: Illustrations only: Query with samples, résumé.
Terms: Pays authors royalty. Offers advances. Pays illustrators royalty or by the project. Sends galleys to authors. Book catalog available for 9 × 12 SASE; ms guidelines available for SASE.

GROSSET & DUNLAP, INC., 200 Madison Ave., New York NY 10016. (212)951-8700. Imprint of The Putnam & Grosset Group. Book publisher. Editor-in-chief: Craig Walker. Art Director: Ronnie Ann Herman. Publishes 13 picture books/year; 7 young readers/year; 12 middle readers/year; 5 young adult titles/year; 25 board books/year; 25 novelty books/year. 5% of books by first-time authors; 50% of books from agented authors. Publishes fiction and nonfiction for mass market; novelty and board books.
Fiction: Picture books: animal, concept. Young readers: adventure, animal, nature/environment. Most categories will be considered. "We publish series fiction, but not original novels in the young adult category." Sees too many trade picture books. Recently published *Mike and the Magic Cookies*, by Jon Buller and Susan Schade (grades 2-3, all aboard reading); *The Puppy Who Went to School*, by Gail Herman with illustrations by Betina Ogden (ages 4-8, all aboard book); *Eek! Stories to Make You Shriek*, by Jane O'Connor with illustrations by Brian Karas (grades 1-3, all aboard reading).
Nonfiction: Picture books: animal, concept, nature/environment. Young readers: animal. Recently published *Your Insides*, by Joanna Cole (ages 4-6, human body); *Dinosaur Bones!*, by C.E. Thompson with illustrations by Paige Billin-Frye (ages 4-8, book & mobile); *Zoom!*, written and illustrated by Margaret A Hartelius (ages 4-8, paper airplaine kit).
How to Contact/Writers: Fiction/nonfiction: Query. Reports in 2 weeks on queries; 1-2 months on mss. Publishes book 1-2 years after acceptance. Will consider simultaneous submissions.
Illustrations: Will review ms/illustration packages. Will review artwork for future assignments.
How to Contact/Illustrators: Ms/illustration packages: Query. Illustrations only: Query with samples; send unsolicited art samples by mail; submit portfolio for review; provide promotional literature or tearsheets to be kept on file. Reports only if interested. Original artwork returned at job's completion.
Photography: Photographers should contact Ronnie Ann Herman, art director. Uses photos of babies and toddlers—full color. Interested in stock photos. Publishes photo concept books. Uses color prints; 35mm, 2¼ × 2¼, 4 × 5, and 8 × 10 transparencies. To contact, photographers should query with samples, send unsolicited photos by mail, submit portfolio, provide promotional literature or tearsheets to be kept on file.
Terms: Pays authors royalty or by outright purchase. Offers advances. Pays illustrators by the project or by royalty. Photographers paid by the project or per photo. Book catalog available for 9 × 12 SASE. Ms guidelines available for SASE.

HARBINGER HOUSE, INC., 2802 North Alvernon Way, Tucson AZ 85712. (602)326-9595. Editor: Harrison Shaffer. Publishes 2 picture books/year; 2 young reader titles/year. 25% of books from agented writers.

Close-up

Ronnie Ann Herman
Art Director
Grosset & Dunlap
New York, New York

"I can review a portfolio in about two and a half minutes and tell whether or not I want to see more," says Ronnie Ann Herman, art director of children's books at Grosset & Dunlap. "I'm always looking for artists with an interesting approach. But because I do mass market books, I can't use anything too way out or quirky. My books have to be accessible to a large population."

Herman knows her audience well and she knows what appeals to kids. After nine years in the juvenile art department at Random House, first as senior designer and then as art director, she followed a colleague to Grosset & Dunlap in 1991. Her arrival meant many changes for Grosset, including a new line of easy-to-read books, plus some new books incorporating special projects and unique paper engineering. "For example, one book on dinosaurs contains a perforated, glow-in-the-dark mobile," she muses. "I'm always looking for more clever ideas and new talent."

A freelancer with a clever idea may certainly get a foot in the door, says Herman, but one idea is not enough to secure an assignment. "When I receive a sample I like, I'll often contact the artist and ask to see more." But the artist must be able to show a body of work that reflects a continuity of purpose. "I don't care if illustrators are versatile. I'd rather see someone who has a consistent style that has been developed over time. The artist has to prove that he hasn't just done one great piece—that he is capable of doing it again and repeating the style."

Because many of Grosset's books contain as many as 32 illustrations, Herman looks for illustrators who can carry a narrative through a progression of images. "A book has to have some continuity," she explains. "Each spread isn't just a statement. It has to relate to the spread before it. It's a development. If the story is about one little girl, the illustrator must be able to make each image look like the same little girl. There must be some continuity of character."

Furthermore, it takes a different mind-set to illustrate children's books, she argues, and the artists who do so should be able to draw without photographic references. "I expect my illustrators to know anatomy and to draw well, but I don't just want to see a picture of a child's head drawn from a photograph," she says. "It's great if you can draw this little girl sitting there. But can you make her lying down in bed? Can you draw her swinging? If you're drawing a cat, can you give it character? Can you show it in action?"

Illustrations are not accompaniments, contends Herman. Rather, they are an integral part of each story. In fact, illustrations are so important that they often precede the written word. "I would say that probably as much as 70 percent of the time, we find an artist whose work we like first," she notes, "and then we write a story to go with the illustrations. I visit bookstores often and see portfolios all the time. Sometimes I fall in love with an illustrator when I see a book or samples that he or she has done. Then I come back and have our inhouse staff write a story to go with that artist's work.

"I always visualize exactly how I want a project to look," she says. "Then I hone in on who I think will do the best job." But even after an illustrator has been chosen, it sometimes takes quite a lot of collaboration to get a finished piece. Illustrating for kids' books is not a solitary process for the artist, she warns. "There are times when I'll go through eight to ten sketches for a cover. I have to keep sending them back to the illustrator for changes. And then once I'm satisfied, I have to make sure everyone else likes it: the publisher, the sales force, the marketing team."

Artists should know the market they are approaching, says Herman. "Half the time I get stuff from people who just have no idea what I do," she says with frustration, "and it's not that difficult to find out. Just visit a good children's bookstore. With a little groundwork, you can find out what kinds of books we publish."

And know the audience, she urges. "I always tell my staff, 'Look at books.' You can learn almost everything by what's been done. There's a reason, for example, why certain typefaces are never used. So don't try to create the wheel every time you're making a book."

—*Jenny Pfalzgraf*

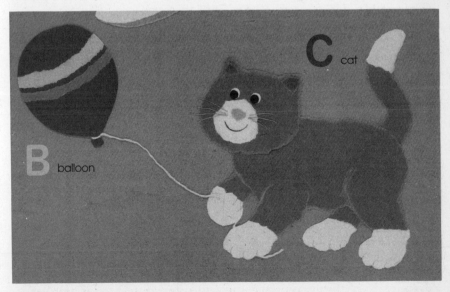

Freelance illustrators who show that they can come up with clever ideas often are the ones hired by Ronnie Ann Herman. The torn paper pictures created by illustrator Bettina Paterson were ideal for the book Baby's ABC.

Fiction: Picture books: Unusual, with a message. Young readers: adventure, regional, ethnic, history, nature/environment. Recently published *Lizards on the Wall*, by Buchanan (ages 4-8).

Nonfiction: Picture books: nature, regional. Young readers: animal, history, nature/environment, geography.

How to Contact/Writers: Fiction/nonfiction: Submit outline/synopsis and sample chapters. Reports on queries in 4-5 weeks; on mss in 7-9 weeks. Publishes a book 18-24 months after acceptance. Will consider simultaneous submissions. Send postage for return of materials.

Illustration: Will review ms/illustration packages.

How to Contact/Illustrators: "For picture books and young readers only: Color copies of minimum of 3 pieces of art." Illustrations only: Color copies. Reports on art samples in 6 weeks. Send SASE or postage for return of materials.

Terms: Pays authors in royalties based on net receipts. Advance payment is negotiable. Pay for illustrators: "royalties based on net receipts or flat fee." Sends galleys to authors; sometimes sends dummies to illustrators. Guidelines for SASE. Book catalog $1 on request.

Tips: Looks for "manuscripts with a particular, well-articulated message or purpose." Illustrators: Looks for "art of imagination and skill that has something special."

HARCOURT BRACE JOVANOVICH, 1250 Sixth Ave., San Diego CA 92101. (619)699-6810. Children's Books Division which includes: HBJ Children's Books, Gulliver Books, Voyager Paperbacks, Odyssey Paperbacks, Jane Yolen Books. Book publisher. Attention: Manuscript Submissions, Children's Books Division. Publishes 40-45 picture books/year; 15-20 middle reader titles/year; 8-12 young adult titles/year. 20% of books by first-time authors; 50% of books from agented writers.

Fiction: Picture books, young readers: animal, contemporary, fantasy, history. Middle readers, young adults: animal, contemporary, fantasy, history, problem novels, romance, science fiction, sports, spy/mystery/adventure. Average word length: picture books—"varies greatly"; middle readers—20,000-50,000; young adults—35,000-65,000.

Nonfiction: Picture books, young readers: animal, biography, history, hobbies, music/dance, nature/environment, religion, sports. Middle readers, young adults: animal, biography, education, history, hobbies, music/dance, nature/environment, religion, sports. Average word length: picture books—"varies greatly"; middle readers—20,000-50,000; young adults—35,000-65,000.

How to Contact/Writers: Fiction/nonfiction: Query; submit outline/synopsis and sample chapters; submit complete ms for picture books only. "Only HBJ Children's Books accepts unsolicited manuscripts." Reports on queries/mss in 6-8 weeks.

Illustration: Editorial will review ms/illustration packages. Art Director of Children's Books, Michael Farmer, will review an illustrator's work for possible future assignments.

How to Contact/Illustrators: Ms/illustration packages: picture books ms—complete ms acceptable. Longer books—outline and 2-4 sample chapters. Send several samples of art; no original art. Illustrations only: Résumé, tearsheets, color photocopies, color stats all accepted. "Please DO NOT send original artwork or transparencies. Include

---

Market conditions are constantly changing! If you're still using this book and it is 1994 or later, buy the newest edition of Children's Writer's & Illustrator's Market *at your favorite bookstore or order directly from Writer's Digest Books.*

SASE for return, please." Reports on art samples in 6-10 weeks. Original artwork returned at job's completion.
Terms: Pays authors in royalties based on retail price. Pays illustrators by the project. Sends galleys to authors; dummies to illustrators. Book catalog available for 9×12 SASE; manuscript/artist's guidelines for business-size SASE.
Tips: "Become acquainted with HBJ's books in particular if you are interested in submitting proposals to us."

HARPERCOLLINS CHILDREN'S BOOKS, 10 E. 53rd St., New York NY 10022. (212)207-7044. Contact: Submissions Editor. Creative Director: Harriet Burton. Book publisher.
Fiction: Picture books, young readers, middle readers, young adult: adventure, animal, anthology, concept, contemporary, fantasy, folktales, hi-lo, history, humor, multicultural, nature/environment, poetry, problem novels, romance, science fiction, special needs, sports, suspense/mystery. Recently published *The Magic Wood*, by Henry Treece (ages 6 and up, picture book); *The Noisy Giants' Tea Party*, by Kate and Jim McMullan (ages 3-8, picture book).
Nonfiction: Picture books, young readers, middle readers, young adults: activity books, animal, arts/crafts, biography, concept, geography, hi-lo, history, hobbies, multicultural, music/dance, nature/environment, reference, science, social issues, sports. Recently published *Marie Curie & Radium*, by Steve Parker (ages 8-12); *The Pigman & Me*, by Paul Zindel (ages 12 up, young adult); *The Moon of the Deer*, by Jean Craighead George (ages 8-12, middle reader).
How to Contact/Writers: Fiction/nonfiction: query, submit outline/synopsis and sample chapters. Reports on mss in 2-3 months.
Illustration: Works with 50 illustrators/year. Will review ms/illustration packages (preferable to see picture books without art); illustrator's work for possible future assignments. (No original art, please).
How to Contact/Illustrators: Ms/illustrations packages: query first. Query with samples, portfolio, slides, arrange personal portfolio review.
Terms: Pays authors in royalties based on retail price. Illustrators paid by the project, royalty based on retail price.

HARVEST HOUSE PUBLISHERS, 1075 Arrowsmith, Eugene OR 97402. (503)343-0123. Book publisher. Manuscript Coordinator: Mary Connor. Publishes 5-6 picture books/year; 3 young reader titles/year; 3 young adult titles/year. 25% of books by first-time authors.
Fiction: Christian theme. Picture books: easy-to-read. Young readers: contemporary, easy-to-read. Middle readers: contemporary, fantasy. Young adults: fantasy, problem novels, romance. Recently published *My Very First Bible*, illustrated with text; *Search of Righteous Radicals*, by Sandy Silverthorne (ages 4-12).
Nonfiction: Religion: picture books, young readers, middle readers, young adults.
How to Contact/Writers: Fiction/nonfiction: Query; submit outline/synopsis and sample chapters; submit complete ms. Reports on queries in 2-4 weeks; on mss in 6-8 weeks. Publishes a book 1 year after acceptance. Will consider simultaneous submissions.
Illustration: Editorial will review ms/illustration package and artwork for future assignments.
How to Contact/Illustrators: Ms/illustration packages: "3 chapters of ms with 1 piece of final art and any approximate rough sketches." Illustrations only: "résumé, tearsheets." Submit to Fred Renich, production manager. Reports on art samples in 2 months. Original artwork returned at job's completion.
Terms: Pays authors in royalties of 10-15%. Average advance payment: "negotiable." Pays illustrator: "Sometimes by project." Sends galleys to authors; sometimes sends dummies to illustrators. Book catalog, manuscript/artist's guidelines free on request.

HENDRICK-LONG PUBLISHING COMPANY, P.O. Box 25123, Dallas TX 75225. Book publisher. Contact: Joann Long, Vice President. Publishes 1 picture book/year; 4 young reader titles/year; 4 middle reader titles/year. 20% of books by first-time authors.
Fiction: All levels: history books on Texas and the Southwest. No fantasy or poetry. Recently published *Boomer's Kids*, by Ruby Tolliver with illustrations by Lyle Miller (ages 12 and above); *The Adventures of Jason Jackrabbit*, by M.M. Dee with illustrations by Donna Newsom (ages 6-9); *Swept Back to a Texas Future: An Original Historical Musical*, by Peggy Purser Freeman with illustrations by Holly Haas (grades 4 and 7).
Nonfiction: All levels: history books on Texas and the Southwest. Recently published *Trails of Tears: American Indians Driven from Lands*, by Jeanne Williams with illustrations and map by Michael Taylor (ages 12 and above); *Miss Ima and the Hogg Family*, by Gwen Cone Neeley, photographs from archives and museums (ages 12 and above).
How to Contact/Writers: Fiction and nonfiction: Query with outline/synopsis and sample chapter. Reports on queries in 1 month; mss in 2 months. Publishes a book 18 months after acceptance. No simultaneous submissions. Include SASE.
Illustration: Number of illustrations used for fiction and nonfiction: picture books-22; middle readers-11; young readers-11. Uses primarily black & white artwork only. Editorial will review ms/illustration packages. Will review artwork for future assignments.
How to Contact/Illustrators: Query first. Submit résumé, promotional literature, photocopies or tearsheets—no original work sent unsolicited. Material kept on file. No reply sent.
Terms: Pays authors in royalty based on selling price. Advances vary. Sends galleys to authors; dummies to illustrators. Book catalog for $1, 52¢ postage and large SAE; manuscript and artist's guidelines for 1 first class stamp and #10 SAE.

HERALD PRESS, 616 Walnut Ave., Scottdale PA 15683. (412)887-8500. Mennonite Publishing House. Estab. 1908. Publishes 1 young reader title/year; 2-3 middle reader titles/ year; 1-2 young adult titles/year; 1 picture storybook. Editorial Contact: S. David Garber. Art Director: Jim Butti. 20% of books by first-time authors; 3% of books from agented writers.
Fiction: Young readers: religious, social problems. Middle readers: religious, social problems. Young adults: religious, social problems.
Nonfiction: Young readers: religious, social concerns. Middle readers: religious, social concerns. Young adults: religious, social concerns.
How to Contact/Writers: Fiction/nonfiction: "Send to Book Editor, the following: (1) a one-page summary of your book, (2) a one- or two-sentence summary of each chapter, (3) the first chapter and one other, (4) your statement of the significance of the book, (5) a description of your target audience, (6) your vita, and (7) a self-addressed stamped envelope for return of the material. You may expect a reply in about a month. If your proposal appears to have potential for Herald Press, a finished manuscript will be requested. Herald Press depends on capable and dedicated authors to continue publishing high-quality Christian literature." Publishes a book in 12 months. Will consider simultaneous submissions but prefer not to.
Illustration: Will review ms/illustration packages. Will review artwork for future assignments.
How to Contact/Illustrators: Illustrations only: Query with samples. Send résumé, tearsheets and slides.
Photography: Purchases photos from freelancers. Contact Jim Butti. Buys stock and assigns work.
Terms: Pays authors in royalties of 10-12% based on retail price. Pay for illustrators: by the project; $220-600. Sends galleys to authors. Book catalog for 3 first class stamps; manuscript guidelines free on request.
Tips: "We invite book proposals from Christian authors in the area of juvenile fiction. Our purpose is to publish books which are consistent with Scripture as interpreted in

the Anabaptist/Mennonite tradition. Books that are honest in presentation, clear in thought, stimulating in content, appropriate in appearance, superior in printing and binding, and conducive to the spiritual growth and welfare of the reader."

HOLIDAY HOUSE INC., 425 Madison Ave., New York NY 10017. (212)688-0085. Book publisher. Vice President/Editor-in-Chief: Margery Cuyler. Assistant Editor: Ashley Johnson. Publishes 30 picture books/year; 7 young reader titles/year; 7 middle reader titles/year; 3 young adult titles/year. 20% of books by first-time authors; 10% from agented writers.
Fiction: Picture book: animal, sports, folk tales. Young reader: contemporary, easy-to-read, history, sports, spy/mystery/adventure. Middle reader: contemporary, fantasy, history, sports, spy/mystery/adventure. Published *Red Sky at Morning*, by Andrea Wyman (middle reader, novel); *Critter Sitters*, by Connie Hiser (young reader, chapter book); and *The Disappearing Bike Shop*, by Elvira Woodruff (young reader/middle reader, short novel).
Nonfiction: Picture books: biography, history, nature. Young reader: biography, history, nature/environment, sports. Middle reader: biography, history, nature/environment, sports. Published *African Elephants*, by Dorothy Hinshaw Patent (young reader, nature/environment); *The Wright Brothers*, by Russell Freedman (middle reader, historical).
How to Contact/Writers: Fiction/nonfiction: Submit complete ms. Reports on queries in 4-6 weeks; on mss in 8-10 weeks. Publishes a book 10 months after acceptance. Will consider simultaneous submissions.
Illustration: Editorial will review ms/illustration packages. Tere Lo Prete, art director, will review an illustrator's work for possible future assignments.
How to Contact/Illustrators: Ms/illustration packages: Query first. Illustrations only: send résumé, and tearsheets. Reports within 6 weeks with SASE or only if interested (if no SASE). Original art work returned at job's completion.
Terms: Manuscript/artist's guidelines for #10 SASE.

HENRY HOLT & CO., INC., 115 W. 18th St., New York NY 10011. (212)886-9200. Book publisher. Editor-in-Chief/Assistant Publisher: Brenda Bowen. Publishes 15-20 picture books/year; 40-60 young reader titles/year; 6 middle reader titles/year; 6 young adult titles/year. 5% of books by first-time authors; 40% of books from agented writers.
How to Contact/Writers: Fiction/nonfiction: Submit complete ms. Reports on queries/mss in 2 months. Publishes a book 12-18 months after acceptance. Will consider simultaneous submissions.
Illustration: Editorial will review ms/illustration packages.
How to Contact/Illustrators: Ms/illustration packages: Random samples OK. Illustrations only: Tearsheets, slides. Do *not* send originals. Reports on art samples only if interested. If accepted, original artwork returned at job's completion.
Terms: Pays authors in royalties based on retail price. Pays illustrators royalties based on retail price. Sends galleys to authors; dummies to illustrators.

HOMESTEAD PUBLISHING, Box 193, Moose WY 83012. Book publisher. Editor: Carl Schreier. Publishes 8 picture books/year; 2 young reader titles/year; 2 middle reader titles/year; 2 young adult titles/year. 30% of books by first-time authors; 1% of books from agented writers.
Fiction: Average word length: young readers—1,000; middle readers—5,000; young adults—5,000-150,000.
Nonfiction: Picture books: animal (wildlife), biography, history, nature/environment. Young readers: animal (wildlife), nature/environment. Middle readers: animal (wildlife), biography, history, nature/environment. Young adults: animal (wildlife), history,

nature/environment. Average word length: young readers—1,000; middle readers—5,000; young adults—5,000-100,000.
How to Contact/Writers: Fiction/nonfiction: Query; submit outline/synopsis and sample chapters. Reports on queries/mss in 4 weeks. Publishes a book 1 year after acceptance. Will consider simultaneous submissions.
Illustration: Will review ms/illustration packages. Prefers to see "watercolor, opaque, oil" illustrations.
How to Contact/Illustrators: Ms/illustration packages: "Query first with sample writing and art style." Illustrations only: "Resumes, style samples." Reports on art samples in 1 month. Original artwork returned at job's completion with SASE.
Terms: Pays authors in royalties of 5-10% based on wholesale price. Outright purchase: "depends on project." Offers advances. Pay for illustrators: $50-10,000/project; 3-10% royalty based on wholesale price. Sends galleys to authors; dummies to illustrators.

HOUGHTON MIFFLIN CO., Children's Trade Books, 2 Park St., Boston MA 02108. (617)725-5000. Book publisher. VP/Director: Walter Lorraine. Senior Editor: Matilda Welter; Editor: Audrey Bryant. Coordinating Editor: Laura Hornick. Art Director: Amy Bernstein. Averages 50-55 titles/year. Publishes hardcover originals and trade paperback reprints (some simultaneous hard/soft).
Fiction: All levels: all categories except religion. "We do not rule out any theme. Though we do not publish specifically religious material." Recently published *The Widow's Broom*, by Chris Van Allsburg (picture book).
How to Contact/Writers: Fiction: Submit complete ms. Nonfiction: Submit outline/synopsis and sample chapters. Reports on queries in 2 weeks; on mss in 1-8 weeks.
Illustration: Works with 60 illustrators/year. Will review ms/illustration packages. Will review artwork for future assignments.
How to Contact/Illustrators: Query with samples (colored photocopies, fine), résumé; provide slides and tearsheets.
Terms: Pays standard royalty; offers advance. Book catalog free on request.
Tips: "The growing independent-retail book market will no doubt affect the number and kinds of books we publish in the near future. Booksellers are more informed about children's books today than ever before."

HUMANICS PUBLISHING GROUP, (formerly Humanics Limited), 1482 Mecaslin St. N.W., Atlanta GA 30309. (404)874-2176. Book publisher. Acquisitions Editor: W. Arthur Bligh. Publishes 4 picture books/year. 50% of books by first-time authors.
Fiction: Picture books: contemporary, easy-to-read, adventure, self-image, self-esteem, multicultural. Average word length: picture books—250-350. Recently published *The Planet of The Dinosaurs*, by Barbara Carr, Ph.D.; *The Adventure Of Paz In The Land Of Numbers*, by Miriam Bowden.
Nonfiction: "Educational materials, teacher supplementary texts, activities, project books." Author degree should equal M.A., M.Ed. or Ph.D. Average word length: 1,000-5,000. Recently published *Earthquakes*, by Maria Valeri-Gold, Ph.D. and Steven Gold.
How to Contact/Writers: Fiction/Nonfiction: Submit outline/synopsis and sample chapters or submit complete ms. No response for queries without SASE. Expect response 3 months after submission has been sent; 6 months for queries. Simultaneous submissions OK.

"Picture books" are geared toward the preschool—8 year old group; "Young readers" to 5-8 year olds; "Middle readers" to 9-11 year olds; and "Young adults" to those 12 and up.

Illustrator Elivia Savadier, of Chestnut Hill, Massachusetts, wanted to portray peace, protection and love between a mother and her child when she created this illustration for Treasure Nap, *by Juanita Havill. Published in 1992 by Houghton Mifflin Company, the book has helped Savadier garner more work in trade.*

Illustration: Illustrations are the author's responsibility. They are not entirely necessary prior to the acceptance stage, but they do not hurt.

How to Contact/Illustrators: Illustrations only: Send résumé, tearsheets, slides, photographs, color photocopies. "Do not send original artwork for preliminary contact. When an illustrator has been hired, he/she will receive artwork back once the project has been completed."

Terms: Pays authors in royalties of 3-10% based on wholesale price. Outright purchase is a possibility. "Book catalog free upon request, but a 9 × 12 SASE envelope is required with 98¢ postage; manuscript/artist's guidelines will fit in #10 SASE with 29¢ postage."

Tips: "Send a cover letter and synopsis, along with résumé and/or vitae. Writers should have some academic/educational background. Manuscripts should be creative, innovative and well written. Too many great ideas come by way of poorly written or conceived means. Stories that are geared toward intellectual and social development, or self esteem are what we are seeking. Illustrators should take chances; the more abstract, the more fantastic, the better. If you want your manuscript back, enclose proper postage and 9 × 12 SAE."

■**HUNTER HOUSE PUBLISHERS,** P.O.Box 2914, Alameda CA 94501. Book publisher. Independent book producer/packager. Editorial Manager: Jennifer D. Trzyna. Assistant Editor: Lisa Lee. Publishes 1 young adult title/year. 80% of books by first-time authors; 5% of books from agented writers; 50% subsidy published.

© Humanics Children's House.

Playful dinosaurs and vivid colors of the rainbow bring to life an imaginary world of giant creatures drawn by Alice Bear, of Lake Park, Florida. Bear received $100 for her artwork, which appears in Barbara Carr's The Planet of the Dinosaurs, *published by Humanics Children's House.*

Nonfiction: Young adults: self-help, social issues. Books are therapy/personal growth-oriented. Does not want to see "fiction; illustrated, picture books." Published *Feeling Great* (rev. ed.), by Rocklin/Levinson (young adults, alternatives to drug use); *Turning Yourself Around: Self-Help Strategies for Troubled Teens*, by Kendall Johnson, Ph.D.

How to Contact/Writers: Nonfiction: Query; submit outline/synopsis and sample chapters. Reports on queries in 1-2 weeks; on mss in 1-2 months. Publishes a book 18 months after acceptance. Will consider simultaneous submissions.

Illustration: Works with 1 illustrator/year. Will review ms/illustration packages. Will review artwork for future assignments. Uses primarily b&w artwork only.

How to Contact/Illustrators: Illustrators only: Query with samples. Provide résumé and client list. Contact Lisa Lee.

Terms: Pays authors in royalties based on wholesale price or outright purchase. Pays illustrators by the project. Sends galleys to authors. Book catalog available for 9 × 12 SAE and 65¢ postage; manuscript guidelines for standard SAE and 1 first-class stamp.

Tips: Wants therapy/personal growth workbooks.

*HUNTINGTON HOUSE PUBLISHERS, P.O. Box 53788, Lafayette LA 70505. (318)237-7049. Book publisher. Editor-in-Chief: Mark Anthony. Publishes 2 young readers/year. 100% of books by first-time authors. "All books have spiritual/religious themes."

Fiction: Picture books: folktales, religion. Young readers: folktales, history, religion. Middle readers and young adults: contemporary, folktales, history, religion. Does not want to see romance, nature/environment, multicultural. Average word length: picture books—12-50; young readers—100-300; middle readers—4,000-15,000; young adults/teens—10,000-40,000. Recently published *Greatest Star of All*, by Greg Gulley and David Watts (9-11 years, adventure/religion).

Nonfiction: Picture books: animal and religion. Young readers, middle readers and young adults/teens: biography, history and religion. No nature/environment, multicultural. Average word length: picture books—12-50 ; young readers—100-300; middle readers—4,000-15,000; young adult/teens—10,000-40,000. Recently published *To Grow By Storybook Readers*, by Marie Le Doux and Janet Friend (preschool—8 years, textbook).

How to Contact/Writers: Fiction/nonfiction: Query. Submit outline/synopsis and 2 sample chapters. Reports on queries in 1 month; on mss in 2 months. Publishes a book 8 months after acceptance. Will consider simultaneous submissions.

Illustration: Works with 2 illustrators/year. Will review ms/illustration packages. Will review artwork for future assignments.

How to Contact/Illustrators: Ms/illustration packages: Query; submit ms with dummy. Illustrations only: Query with samples; send resume and client list. Ms/illustration packages: reports in 1 month. Illustrations only: reports only if interested. Samples are returned with SASE; samples filed. Original artwork returned at job's completion.

Photography: Purchases photos from freelancers. Contact: Managing Editor. Buys stock images. Model/property releases required. To contact, photographers should submit cover letter and resume to be kept on file.

Terms: Pays authors royalty of 10% based on wholesale price. Pays illustrators by the project (range: $50-250) or royalty of 10% based on wholesale price. Sends galleys to authors; dummies to illustrators. Book catalog available for #10 SAE and 2 first class stamps; ms guidelines for SASE; artist's guidelines not available.

HYPERION BOOKS FOR CHILDREN, 114 Fifth Avenue, New York NY 10011. (212)633-4400. An operating unit of Walt Disney Publishing Group, Inc. Book publisher. Editorial Director: Andrea Cascardi. 30% of books by first-time authors; 40% of books from agented authors. Publishes various categories.

Fiction: Picture books, young readers, middle readers and young adults: adventure, anthology (short stories), animal, contemporary, fantasy, folktales, history, poetry, science fiction, sports, suspense/mystery. Middle readers and young adults: problem novels, romance. Published *Rescue Josh McGuire*, by Ben Mikaelsen (ages 10-14, adventure).

Nonfiction: All trade subjects for all levels.

How to Contact/Writers: Fiction: Submit complete ms. Nonfiction: Query. Submit outline/synopsis and 2 sample chapters. Reports on queries in 1 month; reports on mss in 3 months.

Illustration: Average number of illustrations used for fiction and nonfiction: "Picture books are fully illustrated throughout. All others depend on individual project." Will review ms/illustration packages. Will review artwork for future assignments. Contact Ellen Friedman, art director.

How to Contact/Illustrators: Ms/illustration packages: Submit complete package. Illustrations only: provide résumé, business card, promotional literature or tearsheets to be kept on file. Reports back only if interested. Original artwork returned at job's completion.

Photography: Photographers should contact Ellen Friedman, art director. Publishes photo essays and photo concept books. To contact, photographers should provide résumé, business card, promotional literature or tearsheets to be kept on file.

Terms: Pays authors royalty based on retail price. Offers advances. Pays illustrators and photographers royalty based on retail price or a flat fee. Sends galleys to authors; dummies to illustrators. Book catalog available for 9 × 12 SAE and 3 first class stamps; ms guidelines available for SASE.

INCENTIVE PUBLICATIONS, INC., 3835 Cleghorn Ave., Nashville TN 37215. (615)385-2934. Editor: Jan H. Keeling. Approximately 20% of books by first-time authors.
Nonfiction: Young reader/middle reader/young adult: education. Recently published *Cooperative Learning Teacher Timesavers*, by Imogene Forte (grades 1-6, plans, aids and ideas); *Teacher's Gold Mine II*, by Michener and Muschlitz (grades 1-6, ideas and activities).
How to Contact/Writers: Nonfiction: Submit outline/synopsis and sample chapters. Usually reports on queries/mss in approximately 1 month. Publishes a book 18 months after acceptance. Will consider simultaneous submissions.
Terms: Pays in royalties or outright purchase. Book catalog for SAE and 90¢ postage.
Tips: "We buy only teacher resource material. Please do not submit fiction!"

JALMAR PRESS, 45 Hitching Post Dr., Bldg. 2, Rolling Hills Estates CA 90274. (310)547-1240. Fax: (310)547-1644. Subsidiary of B.L. Winch and Associates. Book publisher. Estab. 1971. President: B.L. Winch. Publishing Assistant: Jeanne Iler. Publishes 3 picture books and young reader titles/year. 10% of books by first-time authors. Publishes self-esteem (curriculum content related), drug and alcohol abuse prevention, peaceful conflict resolution, stress management and whole brain learning materials.
Fiction: All levels: concept, self-esteem. Does not want to see "fiction children's books that have to do with cognitive learning (as opposed to affective learning)." Recently published *Scooter's Tail of Terror: A Fable of Addiction and Hope*, by Larry Shles (ages 5-105). "All submissions must teach (by metaphor) in the areas listed above."
Nonfiction: All levels: activity books, concept, how-to, textbooks within areas specified above.
How to Contact/Writers: Fiction/nonfiction: Submit complete ms. Reports on queries in 1 month; on mss in 1-6 months. Publishes a book 6-12 months after acceptance. Will consider simultaneous submissions.
Illustration: Works with 1-4 illustrators/year. Editorial will review ms/illustration packages.
How to Contact/Illustrators: Ms/illustration packages: Submit complete package. Illustrations only: Send unsolicited art samples by mail. Reports in 2 weeks. Originals returned upon job's completion.
Terms: Pays authors 7-12% royalty based on net receipts. Average advance "varies." Pay for illustrators: buyout or share in royalties with author. Book catalog free on request.
Tips: Wants "thoroughly researched, tested, practical, activity-oriented, curriculum content and grade/level correlated books on self-esteem, peaceful conflict resolution, stress management, drug and alcohol abuse prevention and whole brain learning. Books bridging self-esteem to various 'trouble' areas, such as 'at risk,' 'dropout prevention,' etc."

*JEWISH LIGHTS PUBLISHING, P.O. Box 237, Woodstock VT 05091. (802)457-4000. A division of LongHill Partners, Inc. Book publisher. President: Stuart M. Matlins. Publishes 1 picture book/year; 1 young readers/year; 1 middle readers/year; 1 young adult title/year. 50% of books by first-time authors; 50% of books from agented authors. All books have spiritual/religious themes.
Fiction: Picture books: multicultural, religion. Young readers, middle readers and young adults: religion. "We are not interested in anything other than religion/spiritual."
Nonfiction: All levels: religion. Recently published *God's Paintbrush*, by Rabbi Sandy Eisenberg Sasso and Annette Carroll Compton (K-4, spiritual).
How to Contact Writers: Fiction/nonfiction: Query. Submit outline/synopsis. Reports on queries in 1 month; on mss in 3 months. Publishes a book 6 months after acceptance. Will consider simultaneous submissions and previously published work.
Illustration: Works with 3 illustrators/year. Will review ms/illustration packages. Will review artwork for future assignments.

How to Contact/Illustrators: Query. Illustrations only: Query with samples; provide résumé. Reports in 1 month. Samples returned with SASE; samples filed. Original artwork not returned at job's completion.

Terms: Pays authors royalty of 10% of revenue received. Offers advances. Pays illustrators by the project or royalty. Pays photographers by the project, per photo or royalty. Sends galleys to authors; dummies to illustrators. Book catalog available for 9 × 12 SAE and 59¢ postage; ms and artist's guidelines not available.

JEWISH PUBLICATION SOCIETY, 1930 Chestnut St., Philadelphia PA 19103. (215)564-5925. Editor-in-Chief: Dr. Ellen Frankel. Editor: Bruce Black. Book publisher.

Fiction: "All must have Jewish content." Picture books, young readers, middle readers and young adults: contemporary, folktales, history, poetry, problem novels, religion, romance, sports.

Nonfiction: "All must have Jewish theme." Picture books: biography, history, religion. Young readers, middle readers, young adults: biography, history, religion, sports.

How to Contact/Writers: Fiction/nonfiction: query, submit outline/synopsis and sample chapters. Will consider simultaneous submissions (please advise).

Illustration: Will review ms/illustration packages.

How to Contact/Illustrators: Ms/illustration packages: query first or send three chapters of ms with one piece of final art, remainder roughs. Illustrations only: query with photocopies; arrange a personal interview to show portfolio.

Terms: Pays authors in royalties based on retail price.

Tips: Writer/illustrator currently has best chance of selling picture books to this market.

BOB JONES UNIVERSITY PRESS/LIGHT LINE BOOKS, 1500 Wade Hampton Blvd. Greenville SC 29614. (803)242-5100 ext. 4315. Book publisher. Contact: Mrs. Gloria Repp, Editor. Publishes 4 young reader titles/year; 4 middle reader titles/year; 4 young adult titles/year. 50% of books by first-time authors.

Fiction: Young readers: animal, contemporary, easy-to-read, history, sports, spy/mystery/adventure. Middle readers: animal, contemporary, history, problem novels, sports, spy/mystery/adventure. Young adults/teens: contemporary, history, problem novels, sports, spy/mystery/adventure. Average word length: young readers—20,000; middle readers—30,000; young adult/teens—50,000. Recently published *The Treasure of Pelican Cove*, by Milly Howard (grades 2-4, adventure story); *Right Hand Man*, by Connie Williams (grades 5-8, contemporary)

Nonfiction: Young readers: animal, biography, nature/environment. Middle readers: animal, biography, history, nature/environment. Young adults/teens: biography, history, nature/environment. Average word length: young readers—20,000; middle readers—30,000; young adult/teens—50,000. Published *With Daring Faith*, by Becky Davis (grades 5-8, biography); *Morning Star of the Reformation*, by Andy Thomson (grades 9-12, biography).

How to Contact/Writers: Fiction: "Send the complete manuscript for these genres: Christian biography, modern realism, historical realism, regional realism and mystery/adventure. Query with a synopsis and five sample chapters for these genres: Fantasy and science fiction (no extra-terrestrials). We do not publish these genres: Romance, poetry and drama." Nonfiction: Query, submit complete manuscript or submit outline/synopsis and sample chapters. Reports on queries in 3 weeks; mss in 2 months. Publishes book "approximately one year" after acceptance. Will consider simultaneous and electronic submissions via disk or modem.

Terms: Buys ms outright for $1,000-1,500. Book catalog and ms guidelines free on request.

Tips: "Write something fresh and unique to carry a theme of lasting value. We publish only books with high moral tone, preferably with evangelical Christian content. Stories should reflect the highest Christian standards of thought, feeling and action. The text should make no reference to drinking, smoking, profanity or minced oaths. Other unacceptable story elements include unrelieved suspense, sensationalism and themes advocating secular attitudes of cynicism, rebellion or materialism."

■**JORDAN ENTERPRISES PUBLISHING CO.**, 6457 Wilcox Station, Box 38002, Los Angeles CA 90038. Midwest address: P.O. Box 15111, St. Louis MO 63105. Book publisher. Estab. 1989. Managing Editor: Patrique Quintahlen. Publishes 2 picture books/year; 1 young reader title/year; 1 middle reader title/year; 1 young adult title/year. 90% of books by first-time authors; 95% of books from agented writers; 1% subsidy published.

Fiction: All levels: adventure, concept, contemporary, fantasy, folktales, health, hi-lo, history, multicultural, nature/environment, poetry, problem novels, romance, science fiction, special needs, sports, suspense/mystery. "No mystery, horror, feminist or sexist." Average word length: picture books—2,000; young readers—3,000; middle readers—2,500; young adults—20,000. Recently published *The Strawberry Fox* and *The Christmas Toy Welcome*.

Nonfiction: All levels: activity books, animal, arts/crafts, biography, careers, concept, cooking, geography, health, hi-lo, history, hobbies, how-to, multicultural, music/dance, nature/environment, reference, religion, science, self-help, social issues, special needs, sports, textbooks.

How to Contact/Writers: Fiction/nonfiction: Query; submit outline/synopsis and sample chapters. Reports on queries in 4 months; on mss in 9-12 months. Publishes a book 1 year after acceptance. Will consider simultaneous and electronic submissions via disk or modem.

Illustration: Works with 3-5 illustrators/year. Editorial will review ms/illustration packages. Will review artwork for future assignments.

How to Contact/Illustrators: Ms/illustration packages: Query first. Illustrations only: Query with samples. Reports on art samples in 4 months. Original artwork returned at job's completion.

Photography: Photographers should contact Patrique Quintahlen. Needs photos showing nature, art, school, dances, Christmas settings; "various culturally diverse photos with complimentary scenery." Model/property releases and photo captions required. Publishes photo essays and photo concept books. Uses 8×11 color, b&w prints; 35mm, 2¼×2¼, 4×5 transparencies. To contact, photographers should query with samples; provide résumé, promo sheet or tearsheets to be kept on file.

Terms: Pays authors in royalties of 4-8% based on retail price. Buys ms outright for $200-2,000. Offers average advance payment of $500. Pay for illustrators: By the project, $60-$600 or 2 to 3% royalties based on retail price for juvenile novels. Photographers paid by the project (range: $60-600); per photo (range: $10-200); by royalty of 1-2% based on retail price. Sends galleys to authors; dummies to illustrators.

Tips: Wants "Inspiring fantasy picture books and fantasy juvenile novels. Devote 95% of your time to finding an agent once you've completed a manuscript. We are searching for writers who are experienced in using the four stages of writing, and who have written inspiring fantasy stories for children. The gift of imagination combined with professional skills and techniques are a splendid mind set for creating modern classics."

JOY STREET BOOKS, 34 Beacon St., Boston MA 02108. (617)227-0730. Imprint of Little, Brown and Company. Editor-in-Chief: Melanie Kroupa. Publishes 20-25 picture books/year; 5-10 young reader/middle reader/young adult titles/year.

Fiction/Nonfiction: All levels: various categories.

How to Contact/Writers: Fiction/nonfiction: Submit outline/synopsis and sample chapters or submit complete ms. Reports on queries in 2-4 weeks; on mss in 4-8 weeks.

Publishes a book 18 months after acceptance. Will consider simultaneous submissions if informed, but prefers single submissions.

Illustration: Will review artwork for future assignments.

How to Contact/Illustrators: Illustrations only: Query with samples.

Terms: Pays authors in royalties or outright purchase. Book catalog for 8 × 10 SASE; ms guidelines for legal-size SASE.

Tips: Looking for "good middle-grade fiction and strong nonfiction."

JUST US BOOKS, INC., Suite 22-24, 301 Main St., Orange NJ 07050. (201)672-7701. Fax: (201)677-7570. Imprint of Afro-Bets Series. Book publisher; "for selected titles" book packager. Estab. 1987. Vice President/Publisher: Cheryl Willis Hudson. Publishes 4-6 picture books/year; "projected 6" young reader/middle reader titles/year. 33% books by first-time authors. Looking for "books that reflect a genuinely authentic African or African-American experience. We try to work with authors and illustrators who are from the culture itself." Also publishes *Harambee*, a newspaper for young readers 6 times during the school year. (Target age for *Harambee* is 10-13.)

Fiction: Picture books, young readers, middle readers: adventure, contemporary, easy-to-read, history, multicultural (African-American themes), sports. Average word length: "varies" per picture book; young reader — 500-2,000; middle reader — 5,000. Wants African American themes. Gets too many traditional African folktales. Recently published *Jamal's Busy Day*, by Wade Hudson, illus. by George Ford (ages 6-9, picture book).

Nonfiction: Picture books, young readers, middle readers: activity books, biography, concept, history, multicultural (African-American themes). Recently published *Book of Black Heroes Vol. 2: Great Women in the Struggle*, by Toyomi Igus; *Afro-Bets First Book About Africa*, by Veronica F. Ellis.

How to Contact/Writers: Fiction/nonfiction: Query or submit outline/synopsis for proposed title. Reports on queries in 6-8 weeks; on ms in 8 weeks "or as soon as possible." Publishes a book 12-18 months after acceptance. Will consider simultaneous submissions (with prior notice).

Illustration: Works with 4-6 illustrators/year. Editorial department will review ms/illustration packages ("but prefer to review them separately"). Will review artwork for future assignments.

How to Contact/Illustrators: Ms/illustration packages: "Query first." Illustrations only: Query with samples; send résumé, promo sheet, slides, client list, tearsheets; arrange personal portfolio review. Reports in 2-3 weeks. Original artwork returned at job's completion "depending on project."

Photography: Purchases photos from freelancers. Buys stock and assigns work. Wants "African American themes — kids age 10-13 in school, home and social situations for *Harambee* (newspaper)."

Terms: Pays authors royalty or outright purchase. Royalties based on retail price. Pays illustrators by the project or royalty based on retail price. Sends galleys to author; dummies to illustrator. Book catalog for business-size SAE and 65¢ postage; ms/artist's guidelines for business-size SAE and 65¢ postage.

Tips: "Multicultural books are tops as far as trends go. There is a great need for diversity and authenticity here. They will continue to be in the forefront of children's book publishing until there is more balanced treatment on these themes industry wide." Writers: "Keep the subject matter fresh and lively. Avoid "preachy" stories with stereotyped characters. Rely more on authentic stories with sensitive three-dimensional characters." Illustrators: "Submit 5-10 good, neat samples. Be willing to work with an art director for the type of illustration desired by a specific house and grow into larger projects."

KAR-BEN COPIES, INC., 6800 Tildenwood Lane, Rockville MD 20852. (301)984-8733. Fax: (301)881-9195. Book publisher. Estab. 1975. Editor: Madeline Wikler. Publishes 10 picture books/year; 10 young reader titles/year. 20% of books by first-time authors. **Fiction:** Picture books, young readers, middle readers: Jewish Holiday, Jewish storybook. Average word length: picture books—2,000. Recently published *Jeremy's Dreidel*, by Ellie Gellman with illustrations by Judith Friedman (ages 6-8); *A Turn for Noah*, by Sue Remeck Topek with illustrations by Sally Springer (ages 3-5); *Fins & Scales-A Kosher Tale*, by Debby Miller, with illustrations by Karen Ostrove (ages 4-8) **Nonfiction:** Picture books, young readers, middle readers: religion-Jewish interest. Average word length: picture books—2,000. Published *Two by Two: Favorite Bible Stories*, by Harry Araten (ages 5-8); *Kids Love Israel*, by Barbara Sofer (adult, family travel guide); *Alef Is One*, by Katherine Kahn (grades K-3, a Hebrew counting book). **How to Contact/Writers:** Fiction/nonfiction: Submit complete ms. Reports on queries in 2 weeks; ms in 6 weeks. Publishes a book 1 year after acceptance. Will consider simultaneous submissions. "We don't like them, but we'll look at them—as long as we *know* it's a simultaneous submission." **Illustration:** Works with 6-8 illustrators/year. Will review ms/illustration packages. Will review artwork for future assignments. Prefers "4-color art to any medium that is scannable." **How to Contact/Illustrators:** Ms illustration packages: Send whole ms and sample of art (no originals). Illustrations only: Tearsheets, photocopies, promo sheet or anything representative that does *not* need to be returned. Enclose SASE for response. Reports on art samples in 4 weeks. **Terms:** Pays authors in royalties of 5-10% based on net sales. Offers average advance payment of $1,000. Pays illustrators royalty of 5-10% based on net sales. Sends galleys to authors. Book catalog free on request. Ms guidelines for #10 SAE and 1 first class stamp. **Tips:** Looks for "books for young children with Jewish interest and content, modern, non-sexist, not didactic. Fiction or nonfiction with a *Jewish* theme—can be serious or humorous, life cycle, Bible story, or holiday-related."

KNOPF BOOKS FOR YOUNG READERS, 8th Floor, 225 Park Ave., South, New York NY 10003. (212)254-1600. Random House, Inc. Book publisher. Estab. 1915. Publisher: J. Schulman; Associate Publisher: S. Spinner. 90% of books published through agents. **Fiction:** Upmarket picture books: adventure, animal, contemporary, fantasy, retellings of folktales, original stories. Young readers: adventure, animal, contemporary, nature/environment, science fiction, sports, suspense/mystery. Middle readers: adventure, animal, fantasy, nature/environment, science fiction, sports, suspense/mystery. Young adult: adventure, contemporary, fantasy, science fiction—very selective; few being published currently. **Nonfiction:** Picture books, young readers and middle readers: animal, biography, nature/environment, sports. **How to Contact/Writers:** Fiction/nonfiction: submit through agent only. Publishes a book in 12-18 months. Will consider simultaneous submissions. **Illustration:** Will review ms/illustration packages (through agent only). Art Director will review an illustrator's work for possible future assignments. **Terms:** Pays authors in royalties. Book catalog free on request.

KRUZA KALEIDOSCOPIX, INC., Box 389, Franklin MA 02038. (508)528-6211. Book publisher. Picture Books Editor: Jay Kruza. Young/middle readers editorial contact: Russ Burbank. Art Director: Brian Sawyer. Publishes 4 picture books/year; 2 young reader titles/year; 1 middle reader title/year. 50% of books by first-time authors.

Fiction: Picture books: animal, fantasy, history. Young readers: animal, fantasy, history. Average word length: picture books—200-500; young readers—500-2,000; middle readers—1,000-10,000.
Nonfiction: Picture books: animal, history, nature/environment. Young readers: animal, history, nature/environment, religion. Middle readers: biography, sports.
How to Contact/Writers: Fiction/nonfiction: Query; submit outline/synopsis and sample chapters; submit complete ms. Reports on queries/mss in 2-8 weeks.
Illustration: Will review artwork for future assignments. Prefers to see "realistic" illustrations.
How to Contact/Illustrators: Illustrations only: "Submit actual work sample photocopies in color, and photos." Reports on art samples only if interested.
Terms: Buys ms outright for $250-500. Pay for illustrators: $25-100/illustration. Ms/artist's guidelines available for #10 SASE.
Tips: Writers: "Rework your story several times before submitting it without grammatical or spelling mistakes. *Our company charges a $3 reading fee per manuscript* to reduce unprepared manuscripts." Illustrators: "Submit professional looking samples for file. The correct manuscript may come along." Wants ms/illustrations "that teach a moral. Smooth prose that flows like poetry is preferred. The story will be read aloud. Vocabulary and language should fit actions. Short staccato words connote fast action; avoid stories that solve problems by the 'wave of a wand' or that condone improper behavior. Jack of Beanstalk fame was a dullard, a thief and even a murderer. We seek to purchase all rights to the story and artwork. Payment may be a lump sum in cash."

LEE & LOW BOOKS, INC., 14th Floor, 228 East 45th Street, New York NY 10017. (212)867-6155. Fax: (212)490-1846. Book publisher. Publisher: Philip Lee. Publishes 6-8 picture books/year. "The company only publishes books on multicultural subjects."
Fiction: Picture books: adventure, contemporary, history, multicultural, nature/environment, sports, suspense/mystery. Young readers: adventure, anthology, contemporary, folktales, history, multicultural, nature/environment, sports, suspense/mystery. Middle readers: adventure, anthology, contemporary, history, multicultural, nature/environment, problem novels, sports, suspense/mystery. Does not want to see stories using animals as main characters. Average word length: picture books—1,000.
Nonfiction: Picture books, young readers, middle readers: biography, history, multicultural. Average word length: picture books—1,000.
How to Contact/Writers: Nonfiction: Query; submit complete ms; submit outline/synopsis and sample chapters. Reports in 1 month on queries; 2 months on mss. Publishes a book "18 months after illustration is accepted." Will consider simultaneous submissions.
Illustration: Works with 4-6 illustrators/year. Will review ms/illustration packages. Will review artwork for future assignments.
How to Contact/Illustrators: Ms/illustration packages: Query; submit complete package. Query with samples, résumé, portfolio, tearsheets. Reports in 1 month. Return of originals negotiable.
Photography: Photographers should contact Philip Lee. Publishes photo essays and photo concept books. To contact, photographers should query with samples; query with resume of credits.
Terms: Pays authors royalty on retail price. Offers advances. Pays illustrators royalty on retail price. Photographers paid by the project. Sends galleys to author.
Tips: "Do your homework. Visit a bookstore or a library and find out what kind of children's books are being published. Should it be a picture book or story book? Is the story visual? Is the idea original? Are the characters well developed and believable? We specialize in multicultural stories. We would like to see more contemporary stories that are set in the U.S."

LERNER PUBLICATIONS CO., 241 First Ave. N., Minneapolis MN 55401. (612)332-3344. Fax: (612)332-7615. Book publisher. Editor: Jennifer Martin. Publishes 9 young reader titles/year; 62 middle reader titles/year; 5 young adult titles/year. 20% of books by first-time authors; 5% of books from agented writers. "Most books are nonfiction for children, grades 2 through 12."

Fiction: Middle readers: adventure, contemporary, folktales, health, hi-lo, history, multicultural, nature/environment, sports, suspense/mystery. Young adults: adventure, contemporary, folktales, health, history, multicultural, nature/environment, poetry, problem novels, sports, suspense/mystery. "Especially interested in books with ethnic characters." Recently published *Mystery in Miami Beach*, by Harriet K. Feder (grades 5 and up, mystery).

Nonfiction: Young readers, middle readers, and young adults: activity books, animal, biography, careers, health, history, nature/environment, sports, science/math, social studies, geography, social issues. Average word length: young readers—3,000; middle readers—7,000; young adults—12,000. Recently published *The Sacred Harvest*, by Gordon Regguimti with photos by Dale Kakkak (grades 3-6); *Clambake*, by Russell M. Peters with photos by John Madama (grades 3-6); *Flying Free*, by Philip S. Hart (grades 5 and up).

How to Contact/Writers: Fiction: Submit outline/synopsis and sample chapters. Nonfiction: Query; submit outline/synopsis and sample chapters. Reports on queries in 2-3 weeks; on mss in 2 months. Publishes a book 12-18 months after acceptance. Will consider simultaneous submissions.

Illustration: Works with 1-2 illustrators/year. Will review ms/illustration packages. Will review artwork for future assignments ("tend to work only with local talent"). Contact Art Director.

How to Contact/Illustrators: Query with samples and résumé to art director.

Photography: Photographers should contact Photo Research Department. Buys stock and assigns work. Model/property releases required. Publishes photo essays. To contact, photographers should query with samples.

Terms: Authors paid either royalty or outright purchase. Illustrators paid by the project. Sends galleys to authors. Book catalog available for 9×12 SAE and $1.90 postage; manuscript guidelines for 4×9 SAE and 1 first-class stamp.

Tips: Wants "straightforward, well-written nonfiction for children in grades 3 through 9 backed by solid current research or scholarship." No textbooks, poetry, workbooks, songbooks, puzzles, plays, religious material, fiction for adults, picture books or alphabet books. "Before you send your manuscript to us, you might first take a look at the kinds of books that our company publishes. We specialize in publishing high-quality educational books for children from second grade through high school. Avoid sex stereotypes (e.g., strong, aggressive, unemotional males/weak, submissive, emotional females) in your writing, as well as sexist language." (See also Carolrhoda Books, Inc.)

LIGUORI PUBLICATIONS, 1 Liguori Dr., Liguori MO 63057-9999. (314)464-2500. Fax: (314)464-8449. Book publisher. Estab. 1947. Editor-in-Chief: Rev. Paul Coury, C.S.S.R. Managing Editor: Audrey Vest. Publishes 1 middle reader title/year; 3 young adult titles/year. 10% of books by first-time authors.

Nonfiction: Young readers, middle readers, young adults: religion. Average word length: young readers—10,000; young adults—15,000.

How to Contact/Writers: Nonfiction: Query; submit outline/synopsis and sample chapters. Include Social Security number with submission. Reports on queries in 6 weeks; on mss in 6-8 weeks. Publishes a book 1 year after acceptance. Will consider electronic submissions via disk or modem.

Illustration: Editorial will review ms/illustration packages.
How to Contact/Illustrators: Ms/illustration packages: Query first.
Terms: Pays authors in royalties of 9% based on retail price. Book catalog available for 9 × 12 SAE and 3 first-class stamps; manuscript guidelines for #10 SAE and 1 first-class stamp.
Tips: Ms/illustrations "must be religious and suitable to a Roman Catholic audience."

LION BOOKS, PUBLISHER, Suite B, 210 Nelson, Scarsdale NY 10583. (914)725-2280. Imprint of Sayre Ross Co. Book publisher. Editorial contact: Harriet Ross. Publishes 5 middle reader titles/year; 10 young adult titles/year. 50-70% of books by first-time authors. Publishes books "with ethnic and minority accents for young adults, including a variety of craft titles dealing with African and Asian concepts."
Nonfiction: Activity, art/crafts, biography, history, hobbies, how-to, multicultural. Average word length: young adult—30,000-50,000.
How to Contact/Writers: Nonfiction: Query, submit complete ms. Reports on queries in 3 weeks; on ms in 2 months.
How to Contact/Illustrators: Reports in 2 weeks.
Terms: Pays in outright purchase—$500-5,000. Average advance: $750-2,000. Illustrators paid $500-1,500. Sends galleys to author. Book catalog is free on request.

LION PUBLISHING, (formerly Lion Publishing Corporation), 1705 Hubbard Ave., Batavia IL 60510. (708)879-0707. Book publisher. Estab. 1971. Publishes 8-10 children's books a year. 1% of books by first-time authors. "All books are written from a Christian perspective."
Fiction: Picture books: religion, folktales. Young adults: adventure, fantasy, problem novels, religion, science fiction, suspense/mystery. Average word length: picture books and young readers—1,000; middle readers—25,000; young adults—40,000. Recently published *Telling the Sea*, by Pauline Fisk (10-16, young adults, fantasy).
Nonfiction: All levels: nature/environment, reference, religion, social issues. Average word length: picture books and young readers—1,000; middle readers and young adults—"varies."
How to Contact/Writers: Fiction: Submit complete ms. Nonfiction: Submit outline/synopsis and 2-3 consecutive sample chapters. Reports on queries in 2-4 weeks; mss in 1-3 months. Publishes a book 18 months after acceptance.
Illustration: Works with 3-5 illustrators/year. Will review artwork for future assignments. Contact: Mary Horner, Publishing Assistant.
How to Contact/Illustrators: Illustrations only: query with samples.
Terms: Pays authors in variable royalties based on wholesale price. Sometimes buys ms outright. Pays illustrators by the project. Book catalog/manuscript guidelines for SAE and 2 first class stamps.
Tips: "Given Lion's ideology, it's imperative that the writer evidence an orthodox, Christian faith. The best chances are with those manuscripts that are written for *general* readers, not the Christian subculture. We see too many YA novels with a protagonist visiting relatives during the summer and discovering something significant about life."

LITTLE, BROWN AND COMPANY, 34 Beacon St., Boston MA 02108. (617)227-0730. Book publisher. Editor-in-Chief: Maria Modugno. Senior Editor: Stephanie O. Lurie. Art Director: Sue Sherman. Estab. 1837. Publishes 30% picture books/year; 10% young reader titles/year; 30% middle reader titles/year; 10% young adult titles/year. 10% of books by first-time authors; 50% of books from agented writers.
Fiction: Picture books: adventure, animal, contemporary, fantasy, folktales, history, humor, multicultural, nature/environment. Young readers: adventure, animal, contemporary, fantasy, history, humor, multicultural, nature/environment, science fiction, suspense/mystery. Middle readers: adventure, contemporary, fantasy, history, humor,

multicultural, nature/environment, science fiction, suspense/mystery. Young adults: contemporary, health, humor, multicultural, nature/environment, suspense/mystery. Multicultural needs include "any material by, for, and about minorities." No "rhyming texts, anthropomorphic animals that learn a lesson, alphabet and counting books, and stories based on an event rather than a character." Average word length: picture books—1,000; young readers—6,000; middle readers—15,000-25,000; young adults—20,000-40,000. Recently published *Letting Swift River Go*, by Jane Yolen (ages 4-8, picture book); *Through the Mickle Woods*, by Valiska Gregory (ages 4-8, picture book); *Howling for Home*, by Joan Carris (ages 7-9, first chapter book); *Dear Mom, Get Me Out of Here!*, by Ellen Conford (ages 8-12, middle reader).

Nonfiction: Picture books: animal, biography, concept, history, multicultural, nature/environment. Young readers: activity books, biography, multicultural. Middle readers: activity books, arts/crafts, biography, cooking, geography, history, multicultural. Young adults: multicultural, self-help, social issues. Average word length: picture books—2,000; young readers—4,000-6,000; middle readers—15,000-25,000; young adults—20,000-40,000. Recently published *Spreading Poison*, by John Langone (ages 10 and up, young adult); *Mary Cassatt*, by Robin Turner (ages 6-10, picture book).

How to Contact/Writers: Fiction: Submit complete ms. Nonfiction: Submit outline/synopsis and 3 sample chapters. Reports on queries and mss within 3 months. Publishes a book 18 months after acceptance. Will consider simultaneous submissions.

Illustration: Works with 40 illustrators/year. Will review ms/illustration packages. Will review artwork for future assignments.

How to Contact/Illustrators: Ms/illustration packages: complete ms with 1 piece of final art. Illustrations only: Query with samples/slides; provide résumé, promo sheet or tearsheets to be kept on file. Reports on art samples in 6-8 weeks. Original artwork returned at job's completion.

Photography: Photographers should contact Sue Sherman, art director. Works on assignment only. Model/property releases and captions required. Publishes photo essays and photo concept books. Uses 35mm transparencies. To contact, photographers should provide résumé, promo sheets or tearsheets to be kept on file.

Terms: Pays authors royalties of 3-10% based on retail price. Offers average advance payment of $2,000-10,000. Pays illustrators by the project (range: $1,500-5,000) or royalty of 3-10% based on retail price. Photographers paid by the project, by royalty based on retail price. Sends galleys to authors; dummies to illustrators. Book catalog, manuscript/artist's guidelines free on request.

Tips: "Publishers are cutting back their lists in response to a shrinking market and relying more on big names and known commodities. In order to break into the field these days, authors and illustrators will have to do their research into the competition and try to come up with something outstandingly different."

LODESTAR BOOKS, 375 Hudson St., New York NY 10014. (212)366-2627. Fax: (212)366-2011. Affiliate of Dutton Children's Books, a division of Penguin Books, USA, Inc. Estab. 1980. Editorial Director: Virginia Buckley. Senior Editor: Rosemary Brosnan. Publishes 10 picture books/year; 8-10 middle reader titles/year; 5 young adult titles/year (25 books a year). 5-10% of books by first-time authors; 50% through agents.

Fiction: Picture books: adventure, animal, contemporary, folktales, humor, multicultural, nature/environment. Young readers: adventure, animal, contemporary, fantasy, humor, multicultural, nature/environment. Middle reader: adventure, animal, contemporary, fantasy, folktales, humor, multicultural, nature/environment, science fiction, suspense/mystery. Young adult: adventure, contemporary, history, humor, multicultural, nature/environment, problem novels, science fiction. Multicultural needs include "well written books with good characterization. Prefer books by authors of same ethnic background as subject, but not absolutely necessary." No commercial picture books and no genre novels. Recently published *The Elephant's Wrestling Match*, by Judy Sierra with illustrations by Brian Pinkney (ages 5-8, picture book); *Leap Frog Friday*, by Ellen Leroe with illustrations by Dee deRosa (ages 7-10); *Crocodile Burning*, by Michael Williams (ages 12 up, a novel of young black South African's coming of age).

Nonfiction: Picture books: activity books, animal, concept, geography, history, multicultural, nature/environment, science, social issues. Young reader: animal, concept, geography, history, multicultural, nature/environment, science, social issues, sports. Middle reader: animal, biography, careers, geography, history, multicultural, music/dance, nature/environment, science, social issues, sports. Young adult: history, multicultural, music/dance, nature/environment, social issues, sports. Recently published *The Giant Book of Animal Worlds*, by Anita Ganeri with illustrations by John Butler (ages 7-10, giant board book on animal habitats); *Pilots*, by Peter Seymour with illustrations by Norm Ingersoll (ages 5-8, a pop-up and pull-tab book); *Terrorism: America's Growing Threat*, by Elaine Landau (ages 10-14, terrorists and terrorism past, present, and future).

How to Contact/Writers: Fiction: submit outline/synopsis and sample chapters or submit complete ms. Nonfiction: Query or submit outline/synopsis and sample chapters. Reports on queries in 1 month; on mss in 3 months. Publishes a book 1 year after acceptance. Will consider simultaneous submissions.

Illustration: Works with 12 illustrators/year. Will review ms/illustration packages. Will review work for future assignments.

How to Contact/Illustrators: Ms/illustration packages: Send "manuscript and copies of art (no original art, please)." Illustrations only: Query with samples; send portfolio or slides. Arrange a personal portfolio review. Reports back only if interested. Original art work returned at job's completion.

Photography: Purchases photos from freelancers.

Terms: Pays authors and illustrators in royalties of 5% each for picture books; 8% to author, 2% to illustrator for illustrated novel; and 10% for novel based on retail price. Sends galleys to author. Book catalog for SASE; manuscript guidelines for #10 SAE and 1 first class stamp.

Tips: Wants "well written books that show awareness of children's and young people's lives, feelings, and problems; arouse imagination and are sensitive to children's needs. Everyone is on the multicultural bandwagon. More books by black, Hispanic, Asian, and Native American writers. More novelty and interactional books; more tie-ins with audiocassettes."

*LOOK AND SEE PUBLICATIONS, P.O. Box 64216, Tucson AZ 85728-4216. (602)529-2857. Book publisher. "We self-publish the children's activity books we write." Publishes 2 young readers/year. Publishes "history and cultures of the Southwest national parks."

How to Contact/Writers: Nonfiction: Query. Reports on queries in 1 month.

Illustration: Works with 1-2 illustrators/year. Uses primarily b&w artwork only. "Most of the art we use is done in charcoal or pen & ink."

How to Contact/Illustrators: Ms/illustration packages: Query. Illustrations only: Query with samples. Reports back only if interested. Cannot return samples; samples filed. Originals not returned.

Terms: Pays illustrators by the project. Sends dummies to illustrators. Book catalog available for 4¼ × 9½ SAE and 1 first class stamp. Ms/artist's guidelines not available.

LOTHROP, LEE & SHEPARD BOOKS, 1350 Avenue of the Americas, New York NY 10019. (212)261-6500. Div. and imprint of William Morrow Co. Inc., Children's Fiction and Nonfiction. Editor-in-Chief: Susan Pearson. Publishes 60 total titles/year.

Fiction: All levels: various categories; no religion. Recently published *The Rainbabies*, by Laura Melmed, illustrated by Jim LaMarche (picture book); *His Royal Buckliness*, by Kevin Henkes (picture book).

Nonfiction: Recently published *Stegosaurs, The Solar Powered Dinosaurs*, by Helen Roney Sattler; *A Twilight Struggle: The Life of John Fitzgerald Kennedy*, by Barbara Harrison and Daniel Terris.
How to Contact/Writers: Fiction and nonfiction: Query; "no unsolicited mss."
Illustration: Editorial will review ms/illustration packages. Will review artwork for future assignments.
How to Contact/Illustrators: Ms/illustration packages: Write for guidelines first. Illustrations only: Query with samples; submit portfolio for review.
Terms: Method of payment: "varies." Manuscript/artist's guidelines free for SASE.
Tips: Currently seeking out picture books, early chapter novels, YA novels and nonfiction. "Multicultural books of all types" are popular right now.

LUCAS/EVANS BOOKS INC., 1123 Broadway, New York NY 10010. (212)929-2583. Executive Director: Barbara Lucas. Editor and Production Manager: Cassandra Conyers. Estab. 1984. Book packager specializing in children's books, preschool through high school age. Books prepared from inception to camera-ready mechanicals for all major publishers.
Fiction/Nonfiction: Particularly interested in series ideas, especially for middle grades and beginning readers. All subject categories except problem novels and textbooks considered. Recently published fiction titles: *You're My Nikki*, by Phyllis Rose Eisenberg (Dial); *Runa* and *The Book of Keepers*, by Ann Downer (Atheneum); and *Song for the Ancient Forest*, by J. Alison James (Atheneum). Recently published nonfiction titles: *Bees Dance and Whales Sing*, by Margery Facklam (Sierra Club); *Habitats of the World*, by Sheri Amsel (Raintree-Steck-Vaughn, series); *A Wetland Walk*, by Sheri Amsel (Millbrook).
How to Contact/Writers: Query. Reports on queries/mss in 2 months.
Illustration: Works with 15-20 illustrators/year. Will review ms/illustration packages. ("Query first.") Portfolios reviewed (bring, do not mail, original art). "Color photocopies of art welcome for our file." Art not necessary to accompany mss unless artist professionally trained.
How to Contact/Illustrators: Query with samples; provide résumé, promo sheet, slides, client list, tearsheets, arrange personal portfolio review.
Terms: Royalty-based contracts with advance based on retail price or outright purchase for authors and illustrators.
Tips: Prefer experienced authors and artists but will consider unpublished work. "There seems to be an enormous demand for early chapter books, although we will continue our efforts to sell to publishers in all age groups and formats. We are interested in series since publishers look to packagers for producing time-consuming projects."

LUCENT BOOKS, P.O. Box 289011, San Diego CA 92128-9009. (619)485-7424. Sister Company to Greenhaven Press. Book publisher. Editor: Bonnie Szumski. 50% of books by first-time authors; 10% of books from agented writers.
Nonfiction: Middle readers, young adults: education, health, topical history, nature/environment, sports, "any overviews of specific topics—i.e., political, social, cultural, economic, criminal, moral issues." No fiction. Average word length: 15,000-20,000. Published *The Persian Gulf War*, by Don Nardo (grades 6-12, history); *Photography*, by Brad Steffens (grades 5-8, history); *Rainforests*, by Lois Warburton (grades 5-8, overview).
How to Contact/Writers: Nonfiction: "Writers should query first, we do writing by assignment only. If you want to write for us, send SASE for guidelines." Reports on queries in 2 months. Publishes a book 6 months after acceptance.
Illustration: "We use photos, mostly." Uses primarily b&w artwork only. Will review ms/illustration packages. Will review artwork for future assignments. Preference: "7×9 format—4-color cover."

How to Contact/Illustrators: Ms/illustration packages: Query first. Illustrations only: Query with samples; provide résumé, business card, promotional literature or tearsheets to be kept on file.

Terms: "Fee negotiated upon review of manuscript." Sends galleys to authors. Manuscript guidelines free on request.

Tips: Books must be written at a 7-8 grade reading level. There's a growing market for quality nonfiction. Tentative titles: Free Speech, Tobacco, Alcohol, Discrimination, Immigration, Poverty, The Homeless in America, Space Weapons, Drug Abuse, Terrorism, MAD, Arms Race, Animal Experimentation, endangered species, AIDS, pollution, gun control, etc. The above list is presented to give writers an example of the kinds of titles we are seeking. If you are interested in writing about a specific topic, please query us by mail before you begin writing to be sure we have not assigned a particular topic to another author. The author should strive for objectivity. There obviously will be many issues on which a position should be taken—e.g. discrimination, tobacco, alcoholism, etc. However, moralizing, self-righteous condemnations, maligning, lamenting, mocking, etc. should be avoided. Moreover, where a pro/con position is taken, contrasting viewpoints should be presented. Certain moral issues such as abortion and euthanasia, if dealt with at all, should be presented with strict objectivity."

MARGARET K. McELDERRY BOOKS, 866 Third Ave., New York NY 10022. (212)702-7855. Imprint of Macmillan Publishing Co. Book publisher. Publisher: Margaret K. McElderry. Art Director: Nancy Williams. Publishes 10-12 picture books/year; 2-4 young reader titles/year; 8-10 middle reader titles/year; 5-7 young adult titles/year. 33% of books by first-time authors; 33% of books from agented writers.

Fiction: Picture books: folktales, multicultural. Young readers: multicultural. Middle readers: adventure, fantasy, humor, poetry. Young adult: contemporary, fantasy, humor. "Always interested in publishing picture books and beginning reader books which feature minority characters. We see too many rhymed picture book manuscripts which are not terribly original or special." Average word length: picture books—500; young readers—2,000; middle readers—10,000-20,000; young adults—45,000-50,000. Recently published *Look! Snow!*, by Kathryn O. Galbraith, illustrated by Nina Montezinos (ages 5-8); *The Beasts of Bethlehem*, by X.J. Kennedy, illustrated by Michael McCurdy (ages 6 up); *Bubble Trouble and Other Poems and Stories*, by Margaret Mahy (ages 8-12).

Nonfiction: Picture books: nature/environment. Young readers: biography, nature/environment. Middle readers: biography, history.

Average word length: picture books—500-1,000; young readers—1,500-3,000; middle readers—10,000-20,000; young adults—30,000-45,000. Recently published *Climbing Jacob's Ladder: Heroes of the Bible in African-America Spirituals*, selected by John Langstaff, illustrated by Ashley Bryan (all ages); *Natural History from A to Z*, by Tim Arnold (ages 10-14, basic concepts of biology); *Hiawatha: Messenger of Peace*, by Dennis Fradin (ages 7-11).

How to Contact/Writers: Fiction/nonfiction: Submit complete ms. Reports on queries in 2-3 weeks; on mss in 2-3 months. Publishes a book 12-18 months after acceptance. Will consider simultaneous (only if indicated as such) submissions.

Illustration: Works with 20-30 illustrators/year. Will review ms/illustration packages; design department will review artwork for future assignments (2 or 3 samples only).

How to Contact/Illustrators: Ms/illustration packages: Ms (complete) and 2 or 3 copies of finished art. Illustrations only: Query with samples; provide, promo sheet or tearsheets; arrange personal portfolio review. Reports on art samples in 6-8 weeks. Original artwork returned at job's completion.

Photography: Contact: Art Director. Looking for photos of children. Publishes photo essays and photo concept books. Works on assignment only. To contact, photographers should provide resume and promotional literature or tearsheets to be kept on file.

Terms: Pays authors averge royalty of 10% based on retail price. Pay for illustrators: by the project or royalty based on retail price. Photographers paid by the project. Sends galleys to authors; dummies to illustrators. Book catalog, manuscript/artist's guidelines free on request.

Tips: Sees "more sales of beginning chapter books; more sales of poetry books; constant interest in books for the youngest baby market." (See also Aladdin Books/Collier Books for Young Readers, Atheneum Publishers, Bradbury Press, Four Winds Press.)

MACMILLAN CHILDREN'S BOOKS, 866 Third Ave., New York NY 10022. Imprint of Macmillan Publishing Company. Contact: Submissions Editor. Publishes 45 picture books/year; 10 young readers books/year; 10 middle readers books/year; 5 young adult books/year. 5% or less of books by first-time authors; 33% from agented authors. "No primary theme—of a higher literary standard than mass market."

Fiction: All levels: adventure, anthology, animal, contemporary, fantasy, folktales, history, humor, multicultural, nature/environment, poetry, problem novels, science fiction, suspense/mystery. Does not want to see "topic" books, stories about bunnies or kittens, "New Age" themes. Recently published *Our Yard is Full of Birds*, by Anne Rockwell, with illustrations by Lizzy Rockwell (ages 2-7, picture book); *Meet Posy Bates*, by Helen Cresswell (grades 1-4, storybook); *Hats Off to John Stetson*, by Mary Blount Christian, with illustrations by Ib Ohlsson, (grades 2-6, historical fiction).

Nonfiction: Picture books, young readers, middle readers and young adults: animal, biography, history, music/dance, nature/environment, science. No fixed lengths! Recently published *The Macmillan Book of Baseball Stories*, by Terry Egan, Stan Friedmann and Mike Levine (grades 3 and up); *Frank Thompson: Her Civil War Story*, by Bryna Stevens (grades 5-9, biography); *Man and Mustang*, by George Ancona (grades 3-7, photo essay).

How to Contact/Writers: Fiction/nonfiction: Query. Submit complete ms ("only shorter works"). Submit outline/synopsis and 2 sample chapters. "For longer works, query with sample chapter and outline. All submissions must include SASE!" Reports on queries in 1-2 weeks; on mss in 2-6 weeks. Publishes a book 1-2 years after acceptance.

Illustration: Works with 45 illustrators/year. Will review ms/illustration packages. Will review artwork for future assignments. Contact Art Director.

How to Contact/Illustrators: Ms/illustration packages: Send complete ms with sample illustrations. Illustrations only: Query with samples and résumé; submit portfolio for review; drop off portfolio on specified days. "Should request guidelines for our portfolio review procedure—on a drop-off basis, or can mail it in." Reports back only if interested. Original artwork returned at job's completion. Publishes photo essays and photo concept books. Uses color and b&w prints.

Photography: Purchases photos from freelancers. "We do not work with stock agencies too much. Most of the photos we receive come with a manuscript, written by the photographer, or an author they're collaborating with."

Terms: Advance and royalties based on retail price negotiated at time of contract. Pays illustrators by the project or royalty based on retail price. Pays photographers by the project, per photo, royalty. Sends galleys to authors. Book catalog available for 9×12 SAE and $1.20 postage; ms guidelines available for SASE.

Tips: Wants "an original story that is not based on an overworked theme. With novels, good character development is essential."

Refer to the Business of Children's Writing & Illustrating for up-to-date marketing, tax and legal information.

MAGE PUBLISHERS INC., 1032-29th St. NW, Washington DC 20007. (202)342-1642. Book publisher. Editorial Contact: A. Sepehri. Publishes 2-3 picture books/year. 100% of books by first-time authors.

Fiction: Contemporary/myth, Persian heritage. Average word length: 5,000.

Nonfiction: Persian heritage. Average word length: 5,000.

How to Contact/Writers: Fiction/nonfiction: Query. Reports on queries/ms in 3 months. Will consider simultaneous submissions.

Illustration: Editorial will review ms/illustration packages submitted by authors/artists; ms/illustration packages. Will review artwork for possible future assignments.

How to Contact/Illustrators: Illustrations only: Send résumé and slides. Reports in 3 months. Original artwork returned at job's completion.

Terms: Pays authors in royalties. Sends galleys to authors. Book catalog free on request.

MAGINATION PRESS, 19 Union Square West, New York NY 10003. (212)924-3344. Brunner/Mazel, Inc. Book publisher. Editor-in-Chief: Susan Kent Cakars. Art Director: Millicent Fairhurst. Publishes 4-8 picture books and young reader titles/year. Publishes "books dealing with the psycho/therapeutic treatment or resolution of children's serious problems—written by mental health professionals."

Fiction: Picture books and young readers: concept, mental health, multicultural, problem novels, special needs. Recently published *Into the Great Forest: A Story for Children Away From Parents for the First Time*, by Irene Wineman Marcus and Paul Marcus, Ph.D. (ages 3-7); *What About Me? When Brothers & Sisters Get Sick*, by Allan Peterkin, M.D. (ages 4-8); *Little Tree: A Story for Children With Serious Medical Problems*, by Joyce C. Mills, Ph.D. (ages 4-8).

Nonfiction: Picture books and young readers: psychotherapy, concept, mental health, how-to, multicultural, special needs. Recently published *Putting on the Brakes: Young People's Guide to Understanting Attention Deficit Hyperactivity Disorder (ADHD)*, by Patricia O. Quinn, M.D. and Judith M. Stern, M.A. (ages 8-13).

How to Contact/Writers: Fiction/nonfiction: Submit complete manuscript. Reports on queries/mss: "up to 3 months (may be only days)." Publishes a book 1 year after acceptance.

Illustration: Works with 4-8 illustrators/year. Reviews illustration packages. Will review artwork for future assignments. Prefers b&w for text, full-color for cover.

How to Contact/Illustrators: Illustrations only: query with samples. Original artwork returned at job's completion.

Terms: Pays authors in royalties. Offers varied but low advance. Pay for illustrators: by the project, $2,000 max. Pays royalty, 2% max. Sends galleys to authors. Book catalog and manuscript guidelines on request with SASE.

MARCH MEDIA, INC., #256, 7003 Chadwick, Brentwood TN 37027. (615)370-3148. Independent book producer/agency. President: Etta G. Wilson. 25% of books by first-time authors.

Fiction: Picture books: animal, religion. Young readers: history, religion. Middle readers: folktales. Produced *Natalie Jean* series, by Kersten Hamilton (7-9, fiction); *Holt and the Teddy Bear*, by Jim McCafferty (7-10).

Nonfiction: Picture books: animal, religion. Young readers: animal, history. Middle readers: biography, history, religion.

How to Contact/Writers: Fiction: Submit outline/synopsis and sample chapters. Nonfiction: submit complete ms. Reports on queries in 1 month, on ms in 2 months. Will consider simultaneous submissions.

Illustration: Editorial will review ms/illustration packages. Will review artwork for future assignments.

How to Contact/Illustrators: Ms/illustration packages: "query first." Illustrations only: send tearsheets to be kept on file. Reports back only if interested. Original art work returned at job's completion.

Terms: Method of payment: "Either royalty or fee, depending on project and publisher's requirements."

Tips: Illustrators: "Be certain you can draw children. Study book design." Looking for manuscripts that present "a unique, imaginative exploration of a situation." Recent trend reflects "more nonfiction and better art."

MEADOWBROOK PRESS, 18318 Minnetonka Blvd., Deephaven MN 55391. (612)473-5400. Book publisher. Editorial Contact: Elizabeth Weiss. Publishes 7 young reader titles/year; 4 middle reader titles/year; 2 young adult titles/year. 25% of books by first-time authors; 8% of books from agented writers. Publishes nonfiction—"Childbirth and child care, humor, particularly relating to gift giving occasions, children's activity books, other how-to ideas, cookbooks and travel books."

Nonfiction: Young readers, middle readers, young adults: activity books, hobbies, education. No fiction picture books. Average word length: Young readers—8,200; Middle readers—8,200.

How to Contact/Writers: Nonfiction: Query, submit outline/synopsis and sample chapters or submit complete ms. Reports on queries/mss in 1 month. Publishes a book 9 months after acceptance. Will consider simultaneous submissions.

Illustration: Editorial will review ms/illustration packages. Jay Johnson, Managing Editor, will review artwork for future assignments.

How to Contact/Illustrators: Ms/illustration packages: Send "three sample chapters of ms with 1 piece of final art." Illustrations only: Send résumé and samples, promo sheet and client list. Reports back in 6 weeks. Original artwork returned at job's completion.

Terms: Pays authors in royalties of 5-7½% based on retail price. Offers average advance payment of $1,000-5,000. Pay for illustrators: $100-10,000; ¼-¾% of total royalties. Sends galleys for review to authors "sometimes." Book catalog, manuscript/artist's guidelines free on request.

Tips: Illustrators: "Develop a commercial style—compare your style to that of published authors, and submit your work when it is judged 'in the ball park.'" Looking for: "A children's book by objective observers, aimed at early elementary age kids which explains how to get into, e.g., science, astronomy, magic, collecting, hobbies."

MERIWETHER PUBLISHING LTD., 885 Elkton Dr., Colorado Springs CO 80907. Book publisher. Estab. 1969. Executive Editor: Arthur L. Zapel. Art Director: Tom Myers. "We do most of our artwork in-house; we do not usually publish for the children's elementary market." 75% of books by first-time authors; 5% of books from agented writers. Publishes primarily how-to activity books for teens.

Fiction: Humor, religion. "We are currently looking for a religious children's book at the primary level." No children's fiction at upper elementary levels.

Nonfiction: Middle readers: activity books, religion. Young adults: activity books, how-to church activities, religion, drama/theater arts. Average length: 200 pages. Recently published *Scenes That Happen,* by Mary Krell-Oishi; *Acting Natural,* by Peg Kehret; *Where Does God Live?,* by Ted Lazicki; *Get A Grip!* by L.G. and Annie Enscoe.

How to Contact/Writers: Nonfiction: Query or submit outline/synopsis and sample chapters. Reports on queries in 1 month; on mss in 6 weeks. Publishes a book 6-12 months after acceptance. Will consider simultaneous submissions.

Illustration: Works with 3 illustrators/year. Uses primarily black & white artwork only. Will review ms/illustration packages. Will review artwork for future assignments.

How to Contact/Illustrators: Ms/illustration packages: Query first. Illustrations only: query with samples; send resume, promo sheet or tearsheets. Reports on art samples in 4 weeks.

Terms: Pays authors in royalties of 10% based on retail or wholesale price. Pay for illustrators: by the project; royalties based on retail or wholesale price. Sends galleys to authors. Book catalog for SAE and $1 postage; manuscript guidelines for SAE and 1 first-class stamp.

Tips: "As indicated, we are currently looking for a unique concept for a children's book series relating to religion. It must be for the elementary level—applies to writers or illustrators, together or separately."

MERRILL PUBLISHING, 445 Hutchinson Ave., Columbus OH 43235. (614)841-3700. Fax: (614)841-3701. Imprint of Macmillan Publishing Co./College Division. Editor for Education: Linda Scharp. Publishes "educational books used by college students to teach them how to deal with children, children's special needs, and foundations of education. Publishes some children's literature books, and other disciplines in other divisions."

Illustration: Uses 30-40 illustrations/year for college level textbooks. Will review illustration packages. Contact Cover Designer Cathleen Norz at (614)841-3699.

How to Contact/Illustrators: Query with samples; submit portfolio for review; provide tearsheets. Reports in 1 week.

Photography: Photo Editor: Ann Vega. Uses photos of children, children with teachers at school, handicapped, children at play. Model/property release required with submissions. Uses color and b&w glossy prints and 35mm transparencies. Provide transparencies; submit portfolio for review.

Terms: Pays $300-1,000 by the project.

Tips: Wants "illustrations or photos depicting real life and some illustrations based on children's literature."

*JULIAN MESSNER, Children's Trade Division, 15 Columbus Circle, New York NY 10023. (212)373-8905. Imprint of Simon & Schuster. Book publisher. Editor: George Rubich. Publishes 4 young reader titles/year; 15 middle reader titles/year; 6 young adult titles/year. 25% of books by first-time authors; 50% of books from agented writers.

Nonfiction: Middle readers: animal, biography, history, hobbies, nature/environment, general science. Young adults: animal, biography, history, nature/environment, general science. Average word length: middle readers—30,000; young adults—40,000-45,000. Published *The Starry Sky*, Rose Wyler (5-7 years, science); *The Homeless*, by Elaine Landau (11-13 years, teenage nonfiction); *George Bush*, by George Sullivan (12-14 years, biography).

How to Contact/Writers: Nonfiction: Query. Reports on queries in 2 months; on mss in 3 months. Publishes a book 8 months after acceptance. Will consider simultaneous inquiries.

Illustration: Editorial will review ms/illustration inquiries submitted by authors with illustrations done by separate artists. Art Director, Carol Kuchta, will review an illustrator's work for possible use in author's texts.

How to Contact/Illustrators: Ms/illustration packages: Query first. Illustrations only: "Résumé and photocopies." Reports on art samples only if interested. Original artwork returned at job's completion.

Always include a self-addressed stamped envelope (SASE) or International Reply Coupon (IRC) with submissions.

Terms: Pays authors in royalties. Additional payment for ms/illustration packages. Sends galleys to authors.

■**METAMORPHOUS PRESS**, P.O. Box 10616, Portland OR 97210. (503) 228-4972. Book publisher. Acquisitions Editor: Lori Stephens. Estab. 1982. 10% of books from agented writers. Subsidy publishes 10%.
Nonfiction: Picture books: education. Young readers: education, music/dance. Middle readers: education, music/dance, self-help/esteem. Young adults: education, music/dance, self-help/esteem.
How to Contact/Writers: Fiction: Query. Nonfiction: Query; submit outline/synopsis and sample chapters. Reports on queries in 6-12 months. Publishes a book 1-2 years after acceptance. Will consider simultaneous and electronic submissions via disk or modem.
Illustration: Will review ms/illustration packages.
How to Contact/Illustrators: Ms/illustrations: Query. Illustrations only: "vitae with samples of range and style." Reports on art samples only if interested.
Terms: Pays authors royalty of 10% based on wholesale price. Illustrators paid by author. Sends galleys to authors; dummies to illustrators. Book catalog free on request.
Tips: Looks for "books that relate and illustrate the notion that we create our own realities, self-reliance and positive outlooks work best for us—creative metaphors and personal development guides given preference."

*****THE MILLBROOK PRESS**, 2 Old New Milford Rd., Brookfield CT 06804. (203)740-2220. Book publisher. Manuscript Coordinator: Tricia Bauer. Art Director: Judie Mills. Publishes 10 picture books/year; 40 young readers/year; 50 middle readers/year; 20 young adult titles/year. 10% of books by first-time authors; 10% of books from agented authors. Publishes curriculum-related nonfiction, primarily for the school library market.
Nonfiction: All levels: activity books, animal, arts/crafts, biography, careers, concept, geography, health, history, hobbies, multicultural, music/dance, nature/environment, reference, social issues, sports and science. No fiction or poetry. Average word length: picture books—minimal; young readers—5,000; middle readers—10,000; young adult/teens—20,000. Recently published *The Children's Animal Atlas*, by David Lambert (grades 2-6, reference book); *Experiments That Explore Recycling*, by Martin J. Gutnik (grades 5-8, science); *The Berlin Wall: How It Rose and Why It Fell*, by Doris Epler (grades 7-up, history).
How to Contact/Writers: Query. Submit outline/synopsis and 1 sample chapter. Reports on queries/mss in 1 month.
Illustration: Will review ms/illustration packages. Will review artwork for future assignments. Contact Judie Mills, art director.
How to Contact/Illustrators: Query. Submit 1 chapter of ms with 1 piece of final art. Illustrations only: Query with samples; provide résumé, business card, promotional literature or tearsheets to be kept on file. Reports back only if interested.
Terms: Pays author royalty 7% average based on wholesale price. Offers advances. Payment for illustrators varies. Sends galleys to authors. Book catalog for SAE; ms guidelines for SASE.

*****MISTY HILL PRESS**, 5024 Turner Rd., Sebastopol CA 95472. (707)823-7437. Book publisher. Editor-in-Chief: Sally Karste. Publishes 2 middle reader titles/year. 100% of books by first-time authors.
Fiction: Middle readers, young adults: history.
Nonfiction: Middle readers, young adults: history. Recently published *Trails to Poosey*, by Olive Cooke (young adults, historical fiction).

How to Contact/Writers: Fiction/nonfiction: Submit outline/synopsis and sample chapters. Reports on queries in 1 week; on mss in 4 weeks. Publishes a book 8 months after acceptance. Will consider simultaneous submissions.

Terms: Illustrators paid by the project. Sends galleys to authors.

Tips: "Historical fiction: substantial research, good adventure or action against the historical setting. Historical fiction only."

■**MOREHOUSE PUBLISHING CO.**, 871 Ethan Allen Hwy., Ridgefield CT 06877. (203)431-3927. Fax: (203)431-3964. Book publisher. Estab. 1884. Juvenile Books Editor: Jill Weaver. Publishes 10 picture books/year. 75% of books by first-time authors. Subsidy publishes 25%.

Fiction: All levels: religion.

Nonfiction: All levels: religion, moral message, family values. Picture books and young readers: religion.

How to Contact/Writers: Fiction/nonfiction: Submit outline/synopsis and sample chapters to Jill Weaver, P.O. Box 1321, Harrisburg PA 17105. Reports on queries in 4-6 weeks. Publishes a book 1 year after acceptance.

Illustration: Editorial will review ms/illustration packages.

How to Contact/Illustrators: Ms/illustration packages: 3 chapters of ms with 1 piece of final art. Illustrations only: Résumé, tearsheets. Reports on art samples in 4-6 weeks. Original artwork returned at job's completion. Send to Jill Weaver, P.O. Box 1321, Harrisburg PA 17105.

Terms: Pays authors "both royalties and outright." Offers average advance payment of $500. Sends galleys to authors. Book catalog free on request.

Tips: Writers: "Prefer authors who can do own illustrations. Be fresh, be fun, not pedantic, but let your work have a message." Illustrators: "Work hard to develop an original style." Looks for ms/illustrations "with a religious or moral value while remaining fun and entertaining."

■**JOSHUA MORRIS PUBLISHING**, 221 Danbury Rd., Wilton CT 06897. (203)761-9999. Fax: (203)761-5655. Subsidiary of Reader's Digest, Inc. Senior Editor: Sarah Black. Art Director: Patricia Jennings. "We publish mostly basic concept books and books for beginning readers. Most are in series of 4 titles and contain some kind of novelty element (i.e., lift the flap, die cut holes, book and soft toy, etc.) We publish 300-400 books per year." 5% of books by first-time authors; 5% of books from agented authors; 90% of books published on commission.

Fiction: Picture books and young readers: activity books, adventure, animal, concept, contemporary, fantasy, folktales, health-related, history, nature/environment, reference, religion, sports, suspense/mystery. Middle readers: animal, folktales, nature/environment, religion. Does not want to see poetry, short stories, science fiction. Average word length: picture books—300-400. Recently published *Whooo's There?*, by Lily Jones (ages 3-7, sound & light), *Ghostly Games*, by John Speirs, with additional text by Gill Speirs (ages 8-12, puzzle).

Nonfiction: Picture books, young readers and middle readers: activity books, animal, nature/environment, religion. Average word length: varies. Recently published *Alan Snow Complete Books (Dictionary, Atlas & Encyclopedia)*, by Alan Snow (ages 3-7, first reference); *Rain Forest Nature Search*, by Paul Sterry (ages 7-12, puzzle/activity).

How to Contact/Writers: Fiction: Query. Nonfiction: Query. Reports on queries in 1 month; reports on mss in 4 months. Publishes a book 12-18 months after acceptance. Will consider simultaneous submissions and previously published work.

Illustration: Will review ms/illustration packages. Will review artwork for future assignments. Contact Patricia Jennings, art director.

How to Contact/Illustrators: Ms/illustration packages: Query. Illustrations only: Query with samples (non-returnable). Provide résumé, promo sheet or tearsheets to be kept on file. Reports back only if interested. Original artwork returned (only if requested).

Photography: Photographers should contact Patricia Jennings, art director. Buys stock and assigns work. Uses photos of animals and children. Model/property releases required. Publishes photo concept books. Uses 4×6, glossy, color prints and 4×5 transparencies. To contact, photographers should provide résumé, promo sheet or tearsheets to be kept on file.

Terms: Pays authors royalty or outright purchase. Offers advances. Pays illustrators by the project or royalty. Photographers paid per photo.

Tips: Best bets with this market are "innovative concept and beginning readers, and books that have a novelty element."

MORROW JUNIOR BOOKS, 1350 Avenue of the Americas, New York NY 10019. Not interested in freelance work.

JOHN MUIR PUBLICATIONS, INC., P.O. Box 613, Santa Fe NM 87504-0613. (505)982-4078. Book publisher. Editorial Contact: Ken Luboff. Art Director: Ken Wilson. Publishes 25 middle reader nonfiction picture books/year.

Nonfiction: Middle readers: activity books, animal, arts/crafts, biography, concept, hobbies, multicultural, nature/environment, science, social issues. Average word length: middle readers—12,000-15,000. Recently published *Kidding Around Series* (16 titles), by different authors (middle readers); *Extremely Weird Series* (10 titles), by Sarah Lovett.

How to Contact/Writers: Query. Reports on queries/mss in 4-6 weeks. Publishes a book 8-12 months after acceptance. Will consider simultaneous submissions.

Illustration: Reviews illustration packages. Art Director, Ken Wilson, will review artwork for future assignments.

How to Contact/Illustrators: Ms/illustration packages: query, outline and 1 chapter for illustration; 4 original finished pieces and roughs of ideas. Illustrations only: submit résumé and samples of art that have been reproduced or samples of original art for style.

Photography: Purchases photos from freelancers. Buys stock images. Buys "travel, animal" photos.

Terms: Pays authors in royalties based on wholesale price. Offers advance. Some books are paid by flat fee for illustration. Pays illustrators by the project. Book catalog free on request.

Tips: "We want nonfiction books for 8- to 12-year-old readers that can sell in bookstores as well as gift stores, libraries and classrooms."

NAR PUBLICATIONS, P.O. Box 233, Barryville NY 12719. (914)557-8713. Book publisher. 50% of books by first-time authors; 5% of books from agented writers.

Fiction: "No young adult novels or books. Short picture books with limited text preferred."

How to Contact/Writers: Fiction/nonfiction: Query. Reports on queries in 3 weeks; mss in 1 month. Publishes book 9 months after acceptance. Will consider simultaneous and electronic submissions via disk.

Terms: Buys ms outright. Book catalog for 1 first class stamp and #10 SAE.

Tips: "We have only published two books for children. Preschool to age 8 has best chance of acceptance."

NATUREGRAPH PUBLISHER, INC., P.O. Box 1075, Happy Camp CA 96039. (916)493-5353. Contact: Barbara Brown. Publishes 2 adult titles/year, usable by young adults. ("We are not geared to young adult as such.") 100% of books by first-time authors.

Nonfiction: Animal, nature/environment, native American. Average word length: young adults—70,000.

How to Contact/Writers: Nonfiction: Query. Reports on queries/mss in 2 weeks. Publishes book 18 months after acceptance.
Terms: Pays authors in royalties of 10% based on wholesale price. Sends galleys to authors. Book catalog is free on request.

*NEW DISCOVERY BOOKS, 866 Third Ave., New York NY 10022. (212)702-9631. Imprint of Macmillan Children's Book Group. Book publisher. Associate Editor: Michael Ford. Publishes 40 middle readers/year. 20% of books by first-time authors; 10% of books from agented authors. Publishes "series and select single titles."
Nonfiction: Middle readers: biography, history, multicultural, science, social issues. Average word length: middle readers—10,000. Recently published *Cities At War: London*; *Great Battles and Sieges: Little Bighorn*; *The Warsaw Ghetto Uprising*.
How to Contact/Writers: Query. Submit outline/synopsis and 2 sample chapters. Reports on queries in 1 month; on mss in 2 months. Pubilshes book 1-1½ years after acceptance. Will consider simultaneous submissions.
Terms: Pays authors royalty of 5% maximum based on retail price. Offers advances (average amount: $2,000). Sends galleys to authors. Book catalog available for 9 × 12 SASE. Manuscript guidelines not available.

NORTH LIGHT BOOKS, 1507 Dana Ave., Cincinnati OH 45207. (513)531-2222. Book publisher. Contact: Children's Book Editor. Publishes 4-8 children's books/year. Majority of books by first-time authors. Publishes art and activity books for kids aged 6-11.
Nonfiction: Activity books: art and craft project and instruction books. "Not interested in fiction. Also not interested in low-priced coloring books." Recently published *Make Cards!*, by Kim Solga and *Make Costumes!* by Priscilla Hershberger (ages 6-11, art projects all part of art/activities for kids series).
How to Contact/Writers: Submit outline/synopsis and 1 sample chapter. Reports in 1 month. Publishes book 18 months to 2 years after acceptance.
Illustration: Will review ms/illustration packages. Will review artwork for future assignments. Contact: Children's Book Editor.
Terms: Pays author outright purchase. Offers advances. Pays illustrators by the project. Sends galley to authors. Book catalog free.
Tips: Author's best chance is with an art or activity book for preschoolers or for ages 6-11.

*NORTHLAND PUBLISHING, P.O. Box 1389, Flagstaff AZ 86002. (602)774-5251. Book publisher. Editor-in-Chief: Betti Albrecht. Art Director: David Jenney. Publishes 6 picture books/year; 2 young readers/year. 90% of books by first-time authors. Primary theme is Southwest regional, Native American folktales.
Fiction: Picture books and young readers: animal, folktales, multicultural, nature/environment. Middle readers: folktales ("Our Native American folktales are enjoyed by readers of all ages, child through adult"). Multicultural needs include "bilingual regional, translations, tales from other countries." No religion, science fiction, anthology. Average word length: picture books—800; young readers—1,500. Recently published *Antelope Woman: An Apache Folktale*, by Michael Lacapa (Native American folktale), ages 7 and up; *The Three Little Javelinas*, by Susan Lowell, illustrated by Jim Harris, ages 3-8, (Southwestern *Three Little Pigs*); *Turkey's Gift to the People*, by Ani Rucki, ages 5-9 (adaptation of Navajo story).
Nonfiction: Picture books and young readers: animal, multicultural, nature/environment. Average word length: picture books—1,500; young readers—1,500.
How to Contact/Writers: Fiction/nonfiction: Query; submit complete ms. Reports on queries in 1 month; on mss in 6 weeks. "Acknowledgment sent immediately upon receipt." If manuscript and art are complete at time of acceptance, publication takes 9 months; if not, usually 1 year. Will consider simultaneous submissions.

Illustration: Works with 6 illustrators/year. Will review ms/illustration packages. Will review artwork for future assignments. Uses color artwork only.

How to Contact/Illustrators: Ms/illustration packages: Submit ms with samples: slides or color photocopies. Illustrations only: Query with samples, promo sheet, slides, tearsheets. Reports in 1 month. Samples returned with SASE. Original artwork returned at job's completion.

Terms: Pays authors royalty of 8-12% based on net receipts. Offers advances. Pays illustrators by the project or royalty based on net receipts. "This depends so much on quality of work and quantity needed." Sends galleys to authors; dummies to illustrators. Ms guidelines available for SASE; artist's guidelines not available.

Tips: Receptive to "Native American folktales (must be retold by a Native American author)."

*NORTHWORD PRESS, INC., P.O. Box 1360, Minocqua WI 54548. (715)356-9800. Imprints: Willow Creek Press, Heartland Press. Editor-in-Chief: Greg Linder. Production Coordinator: Russ Kuepper. Publishes 3 picture books/year. 50% of books by first-time authors; 10% of books from agented authors. Publishes books pertaining to nature, wildlife and the environment.

Fiction: Picture books, young readers, middle readers: animal, nature/environment. Does not want to see "anything without a strong nature/animal focus; no moralizing animal/nature stories (didactic)."

Nonfiction: Picture books, young readers, middle readers: activity books, animal, nature/environment. Average word length: picture books—500-3,000; young readers—2,500-3,000. Recently published *Moose for Kids,* by Jeff Fair (ages 4-10, photo picture book); *Wild Animal Workbook,* by Hilton Snowdon (activity and coloring book, ages 4-10).

How to Contact/Writers: Fiction: Query. Nonfiction: Query; submit outline/synopsis and 1 sample chapter. Reports on queries in 2 months; reports on mss in 3 months. Publishes a book 9-12 months after acceptance. Will consider simultaneous submissions.

Illustration: Works with 1-3 illustrators/year. Will review ms/illustration packages. Will review artwork for future assignments. Contact Russ Kuepper, production coordinator.

How to Contact/Illustrators: Ms/illustration packages: Query. Submit 1 chapter of ms with 3 pieces of final art. Illustrations only: query with samples. Reports back only if interested. Original artwork returned at job's completion.

Photography: Photographers should contact Robert Baldwin, photo editor. Uses nature and wildlife photos, full-color. Buys stock and assigns work. Model releases required. Publishes photo concept books. Uses color prints and 35mm transparencies. To contact, query with samples.

Terms: Pays authors royalty based on wholesale price or outright purchase. Offers negotiable advances. Pays illustrators by the project. Pays photographer by the project, per photo or royalty. Sends galleys to authors. Book catalog available for 9×12 SAE and 2 first class stamps; ms guidelines available for SASE.

Tips: "The two key words are 'nature' and 'wildlife.' Beyond that, we're looking for fun, unusual, and unusually well-written manuscripts. We are expanding our children's line."

ODDO PUBLISHING, INC., P.O. Box 68, Fayetteville GA 30214. (404)461-7627. Book publisher. Estab. 1964. Contact: Editor. Publishes 3-6 picture books/year; 1-2 young reader titles/year; 1-2 middle reader titles/year. 10% of books by first-time authors.

 The asterisk before a listing indicates the listing is new in this edition.

Fiction: Picture books, young readers: adventure, animal, concept, contemporary, folk-tales, hi-lo, multicultural, nature/environment, special needs. Average word length: picture books—500; young readers—1,000; middle readers—2,000. Published *Wrongway Santa*, by Rae Oetting, illustrated by Art Shardin (grades 4-6, picture book).

Nonfiction: Picture books, young readers: activity books, animal, arts/crafts, concept, cooking, geography, health, hi-lo, hobbies, how-to, multicultural, nature/environment, science, special needs. Average word length: picture books—500; young readers—1,000; middle readers—2,000.

How to Contact/Writers: Fiction/nonfiction: Query; submit outline/synopsis and sample chapters. Reports on queries 1-2 months; on mss 2-3 months. Publishes a book 24 months after acceptance. Will consider simultaneous submissions.

Illustration: Works with 1-3 illustrators/year. Will review ms/illustration packages. Will review artwork for future assignments. Uses color artwork only.

How to Contact/Illustrators: Ms/illustration packages: Query first. Illustrations only: Query with samples. Reports on art samples only if interested.

Photography: "Rarely" purchases photos from freelancers. "At present, not looking."

Terms: Buys ms outright; "negotiable" price. Illustrators paid by the project. Sends galleys to authors "only if necessary." Book catalog available for 9 × 12 SAE and 9 first-class stamps.

Tips: "Wants books "with underlying educational value. Themes can be anything from fictional stories to nonfictional science, but must have a reason for being told. Educational value has been the most important trend in children's books. Parents more and more expect books to teach and not simply babysit."

OPEN HAND PUBLISHING INC., P.O. Box 22048, Seattle WA 98122. (206)447-0597. Book publisher. Contact: Pat Andrus. Publishes 1-3 children's books/year. 50% of books by first-time authors. Multi-cultural books: African-American theme or bilingual.

Fiction: Picture books: folktales, history and African American. Young readers and middle readers: history and African-American. Young adult/teens: African-American. Average word length: picture books—32-64 pages; young readers—64 pages; middle readers—64 pages; young adult/teens—120 pages.

Nonfiction: All levels: history and African-American. Average word length: picture books—32-64 pages; young readers—64 pages; middle readers—64 pages; young adult/teens: 64-120 pages.

How to Contact/Writers: Fiction/nonfiction: Query. Reports on queries in 3 weeks; reports on mss in 5 weeks. Publishes a book 12-18 months after acceptance. Will consider simultaneous submissions.

Illustration: Will review ms/illustration packages. Will review artwork for future assignments. Contact P. Anna Johnson, publisher.

How to Contact/Illustrators: Ms/illustration packages: Query. Illustrations only: Query with samples. Reports in 3 weeks. Original artwork returned "depending on the book."

Terms: Pays authors royalty of 5-15% based on wholesale price. Offers advances ("only under special circumstances"). Pays illustrators by the project; commission for the work. Sends galleys to authors. Book catalog available for SAE and 2 first class stamps; ms guidelines available for SASE and 1 first class stamp.

*ORCA BOOK PUBLISHERS, P.O. Box 3626 Stn. B, Victoria, British Columbia V8R 6S4 Canada. (604)380-1229. Book publisher. Children's Books Editor: Ann Featherstone. Publishes 6 picture books/year; 1 or 2 middle readers/year; 1 or 2 young adult titles/year. 25% of books by first time authors. "We only consider authors and illustrators who are Canadian or who live in Canada."

Fiction: Picture books: contemporary, folktales, humor, nature/environment, fairy tales. Middle readers: adventure, contemporary, history, multicultural, nature/environment, problem novels, special needs, suspense/mystery. Young adults: contemporary, history, multicultural, nature/environment, problem novels, special needs. "Please, no cute little woodland creatures looking for their mother, name, or home. Spare us also from *Alice in Wonderland* clones, where children meet talking animals that take them on 'exciting' adventures." Average word length: picture books—500-2,000; middle readers—25-35,000; young adult—35,000-60,000. Recently published *Thistle Broth*, by Richard Thompson, illustrated by Henry Fernandes; *Waiting for the Whales*, by Sheryl McFarlane, illustrated by Ron Lightburn.

Nonfiction: Picture books, young readers, middle readers: animal, nature/environment. We have enough whale stories to hold us for a while. Average word length: picture books—300-500; middle readers—2,000-3,000. Recently published *Siwiti-A Whale's Story*, by Alexandra Morton, photographs by Robin and Alexandra Morton (ages 6-12, animal).

How to Contact/Writers: Fiction: Submit complete ms if picture book; submit outline/synopsis and 3 sample chapters. Nonfiction: Query with SASE. "All queries or unsolicited submissions should be accompanied by a SASE." Reports on queries in 3-6 weeks; reports on mss in 1-3 months. Publishes book 12-18 months after acceptance.

Illustration: Works with 6 illustrators/year. Will review ms/illustration packages. Will review artwork for future assignments. Uses both b&w and color artwork.

How to Contact/Illustrators: Ms/illustration packages: Submit ms with 3-4 pieces of final art. "Reproductions only, no original art please." Illustrations only: Query with samples; provide resume, slides. Reports in 6-8 weeks. Samples returned with SASE; samples filed. Original artwork returned at job's completion if picture books.

Terms: Pays authors royalty of 5-10% if picture book based on retail price. Offers advances (average amount: $500). Pays illustrators royalty of 5% minimum based on retail price or advance on royalty of $500. Sends galleys to authors. Book catalog available for legal or 8½×11 manila SAE and 2 first class stamps. Ms guidelines available for SASE. Art guidelines not available.

Tips: "American authors and illustrators should remember that the US stamps on their reply envelopes cannot be posted in any country outside of the US."

ORCHARD BOOKS, 95 Madison Ave., New York NY 10016. (212)686-7070. Div. and imprint of Grolier, Inc. Book publisher. President and Publisher: Neal Porter. "We publish between 50 and 60 books yearly including fiction, poetry, picture books, and photo essays." 10-25% of books by first-time authors.

Nonfiction: "We publish nonfiction on a very selective basis."

How to Contact/Writers: Nonfiction: Submit outline/synopsis and sample chapters. Reports on mss in 2 months. Average length of time between acceptance of a book-length ms and publication of work "depends on the editorial work necessary. If none, about 8 months." Will only consider simultaneous submissions in rare instances.

Illustration: Editorial will review ms/illustration packages. "It is better to submit ms and illustration separately unless they are by the same person, or a pairing that is part of the project such as husband and wife."

How to Contact/Illustrators: Ms/illustration packages: 3 chapters of ms with 1 piece of final art, remainder roughs. Illustrations only: "tearsheets or photocopies or photostats of the work." Reports on art samples in 1 month. Original artwork returned at job's completion.

Terms: Pays authors in royalties "industry standard" based on retail price. Sends galleys to authors; dummies to illustrators. Book catalog free on request.

OUR CHILD PRESS, 800 Maple Glen Ln., Wayne PA 19087-4797. (215)964-0606. Book publisher. Contact: Carol Hallenbeck, President. 90% of books by first-time authors.

Fiction/Nonfiction: All levels: adoption, multicultural, special needs. Average word length: Open. Recently published *Don't Call Me Marda*, by Sheila Kelly Welch; *Is That*

Your Sister? by Catherine and Sherry Burin; *Oliver: A Story About Adoption*, by Lois Wickstrom.
How to Contact/Writers: Fiction/Nonfiction: Query or submit complete manuscript. Reports on queries/mss in 2 months. Publishes a book 6-12 months after acceptance.
Illustration: Works with 2 illustrators/year. Reviews ms/illustration packages. Will review artwork for future assignments.
How to Contact/Illustrators: Query first. Submit résumé, tearsheets and photocopies. Reports on art samples in 2 months. Original artwork returned at job's completion.
Terms: Pays authors in royalties of 5% based on wholesale price. Pays illustrators royalties. Book catalog for SAE (business envelope) and 52¢ postage.
Tips: Won't consider anything *not* related to adoption.

RICHARD C. OWEN PUBLISHERS, INC., 135 Katonah Ave., Katonah NY 10536. (914)232-3903. Book publisher. Editor: Janice Boland. Publishes 5 storybooks/year. 95% of books by first-time authors. Publishes "child focused, meaningful books about characters and situations with which five, six, and seven year old children can identify. We include multicultural stories that present minorities in a positive and natural way. Our stories show the diversity in America."
Fiction: Picture books that children will read themselves ("These are not lap books—they are books for 5-7 year olds to read by themselves; they have brief text and pictures on every page."): animal, contemporary (multicultural and minorities), Native American folktales, multicultural, nature/environment (American animals), poetry. Does not want to see holiday, religious themes, moral teaching stories. No talking animals with personified human characteristics, jingles and rhymes, holiday stories, alphabet books, lists without plots. No stereotyping. Average word length: picture books—up to 100 words.
Nonfiction: Picture books: animal, careers, multicultural and nature/environment. No "encyclopedic" type of information stories. Average word length: up to 100 words.
How to Contact/Writers: Fiction/nonfiction: Submit complete ms. *Must* request guidelines first. Reports on ms in 3 weeks. Publishes a book 2-3 years after acceptance. Will consider simultaneous submissions.
Illustration: Works with 2-3 illustrators/year.
How to Contact/Illustrators: Contact Janice Boland for illustrator guidelines first. Send color copies/reproductions or photos of art or provide tearsheets. Must request guidelines first. Reports in 1 month.
Photography: Photographers should contact Janice Boland. Wants photos that are child oriented; not interested in portraits. "Natural, bright, crisp and colorful—of children and of subjects and compositions attractive to children." Sometimes interested in stock photos for special projects. Uses color transparencies.
Terms: Pays authors royalties of 8% based on "monies we receive." Pays illustrators by the project (range: $800-1,000). Photographers paid by the project. Ms/artist guidelines available for SASE.
Tips: Seeking "a story that has charm, magic, impact and appeal; one that children living in today's society will want to read and reread; a book with a strong storyline, child-appealing language, action and interesting, vivid characters." Multicultural needs include "ethnic true-to-life tales, folktales, Indian legends and stories about specific culture environments. We want our books to reflect the rich cultural heritage of this country without stereotyping." Trend is toward "quality books that portray various cultures in rich and interesting ways; well-constructed and developed books that make these cultures accessible to all."

PACIFIC PRESS, P.O. Box 7000, Boise ID 83707. (208)465-2500. Fax: (208)465-2531. Book publisher. Acquisitions Editor: Marvin Moore. Publishes 2-4 picture books, 2-4 young readers, 2-4 middle readers, 4-6 young adult titles/year. 5% of books by first-

Close-up

Janice Boland
Editor
Richard C. Owen Publishers, Inc.
Katonah, New York

Once upon a time, Dick, Jane and Spot introduced children to the pleasure of reading. It was pretty dry, and while it taught the basic skills of reading it didn't go a long way toward producing life-long readers. But the times they are changing. Whole language curriculums, in which teachers use trade books instead of textbooks, are bumping basal readers aside in more and more classrooms throughout the United States, according to Janice Boland, editor of children's books for Richard C. Owen Publishers, Inc.

Whole language is opening a new market for writers of children's books in the U.S. This year Richard C. Owen Publishers will launch the American expansion of the Ready-to-Read series of brief trade-quality books for the classroom, she says.

Prior to that the company was the sole marketer and distributor for New Zealand's whole language Ready-to-Read series. The series features books designed to teach reading skills to 5- to 7-year-olds by providing them with books that have meaning to them and that they enjoy reading.

In an effort to create books that would better reach children here at home, the American expansion of the series imports the philosphy and format of the New Zealand books but uses American authors and themes.

"Our American expansion of Ready-to-Read is based on the philosophy of good literature in the classroom," Boland says. "We believe that children learn to read by reading, just like you learn to ride a bicycle by riding one."

The publisher's call for American authors, which began two years ago, has gotten a large response. More than 2,000 manuscripts have come through the editorial offices since the effort began. Of those manuscripts, the first two books in the series are in production, and the company plans to increase the number of titles published each year, she says.

Writing children's books for classroom application is not much different from writing for trade publishers, says Boland. Length of the manuscript is the primary difference. While many popular trade books run as long as 32 pages, the Ready-to-Read series calls for books just eight to 16 pages (or up to 100 words) long.

"We ask our authors to follow the prerequisites for writing a good trade book. Only do it with an economy of words," Boland says. "The character is most important, because children are most interested in, and identify with, the character in the story. Be clear, direct and focused. Keep your storyline simple but strong. Stories must be well-structured, which means they must have interesting beginnings, clear middles and satisfactory conclusions. And they should be written from the heart."

Boland, who began her career as an elementary school teacher and now teaches courses on writing and illustrating children's books, advises beginning authors to write in third person and past tense. "It's easier for the children," she says. Authors who receive writer's guidelines will find a request for a mix of both natural and book language. "Book language is the stylized or formal phrasing you find in books and natural language is the language children use and hear in everyday life. We like a balance of both in our books."

The company is seeking manuscripts that reflect the diversity and richness of culture in the United States to put an American spin on the Ready-to-Read series. Specifically, Boland says, they are looking for uniquely American fiction and nonfiction—stories about wildlife indigenous to North America, folk tales and retold Native American stories, and stories that portray minorities and alternative family structures in "positive, respectful, appealing and natural ways."

Successfully handling multicultural and contemporary themes requires that writers "get out there and see what's happening, have a connection with the children," Boland says. "It's wonderful to think about what childhood should be like, and it's wonderful to remember yours through rose-colored glasses, but those stories are not going to grab the children of today. Go to the children's room in the library and read what's being published. Make opportunities to be with children, visit a classroom, go to the playground, begin to look at the world through a child's eyes."

Boland has two caveats for prospective Richard C. Owen authors: don't stereotype and don't moralize. "All different types of people have wonderful things to contribute and that's what we want to show the children."

She encourages first-time authors to submit their material. Despite the volume of manuscripts coming in, each one is read, she says, and revisions can take a manuscript from the rejection pile to the book list. "If a story comes to us and I see a jewel hidden inside it, I ask the author if they want to pursue the project," Boland says. "I will work alongside the author helping to get the story to the point where it better fits our needs."

First-time authors most often have difficulty writing from a child's point of view, she says. To remedy that, she recommends that writers view the world from a child's perspective. "Climb a tree, lay under a coffee table. You'll be surprised how these exercises can peel away all those adult layers and put you in touch with the child within yourself," she says.

The company is also looking for American illustrators for the Ready-to-Read series. Illustrators should demonstrate an ability to draw 5- to 10-year-olds and to carry the character from page to page without inconsistencies, says Boland, who works with artists during production.

Writing and illustrating for children is a tough field, Boland acknowledges, reflecting on the years that preceded the publication of her first children's trade book. "It does take a lot of time, focus and dedication," she says. "But it's worth it. It's the greatest reward to see children's eyes light up when you are reading your book to them. It's a fulfilling and wonderful feeling."

—*Anne Bowling*

time authors. Seventh-day Adventist Christian publishing house which publishes books pertaining to religion, spiritual values (strong spiritual slant).

Fiction: All levels: religion. Does not want to see fantasy or totally non-factual stories. "We prefer true stories that are written in fiction style." Average word length: picture books—500-1,000; young readers—6,000-7,000; middle readers—25,000-33,000; young adult/teens—33,000-75,000. Published *Focus on the Edge*, by Heidi Borriuk (teens); *Mystery on Colton's Island*, by Mary Duplex (ages 8-12); *Rocky and Me*, by Paul Ricchiati (ages 4-6, picture/text for pre-school).

Nonfiction: All levels: activity books, animal, health, nature/environment and religion. "All manuscripts must have a religious/spiritual/health theme." Average word length: picture books—500-1,000; young readers—6,000-7,000; middle readers—25,000-33,000; young adult/teens—33,000-80,000. Recently published *Before I Was a Kid*, by Rita Stewart (age 4-6, picture/text for preschool).

How to Contact/Writers: Fiction: Submit complete ms; submit outline/synopsis and 2 sample chapters. Nonfiction: Query; submit complete ms; submit outline/synopsis and 2 sample chapters. Reports on queries in 2 weeks; reports on mss in 2 months. Publishes a book 6-12 months after acceptance. Will consider simultaneous submissions and electronic submissions via disk or modem.

Illustration: Will review ms/illustration packages. Will review artwork for future assignments. Contact: Tim Larson, book designer.

How to Contact/Illustrators: Ms/illustration packages: Submit complete package. Illustrations only: submit portfolio for review. Reports in 2 weeks. Original artwork returned at job's completion.

Terms: Pays authors royalty of 12-16% on wholesale price. Offers $300-500 advances. Pays illustrators by the project; 6% royalty on wholesale price. Sends galleys to authors. Book catalog available for 9×12 SASE. Ms guidelines available for SASE.

PANDO PUBLICATIONS, 5396 Laurie Lane, Memphis, TN 38120. (901)682-8775. Book publisher. Estab. 1988. Owner: Andrew Bernstein. Publishes 2-6 middle reader titles/year; 2-6 young adult titles/year. 20% of books by first-time authors.

Fiction: Animal, concept, folktales, history, nature/environment. No poetry, science fiction, religion.

Nonfiction: Middle readers, young adults: activity books, animal, arts/crafts, biography, concept, cooking, geography, history, hobbies, how-to, multicultural, nature/environment, reference, science, social issues, special needs, sports. Average length: middle readers—175 pages; young adults—200 pages.

How to Contact/Writers: Fiction/nonfiction: Prefers full ms. Reports on queries in 2 months; on mss in 3 months. Publishes a book 9 months after acceptance. Will consider simultaneous submissions. "Prefers" electronic submissions via disk or modem.

Illustration: Works with 2 illustrators/year. Editorial will review all illustration packages.

How to Contact/Illustrators: Ms/illustrations: Query first. Illustrations only: Query with samples. Reports on art samples in 1 month. Original artwork returned at job's completion.

Terms: Pays authors royalty of 7-10% based on retail price. Offers average advance payment of "⅓ royalty due on first run." Sends galleys to authors; dummies to illustrators. "Book descriptions available on request."

Tips: Writers: "Find an untapped market then write to fill the need." Illustrators: "Find an author with a good idea and writing ability. Develop the book with the author. Join a professional group to meet people—ABA, publisher's groups, as well as writer's groups and publishing auxiliary groups. Talk to printers." Looks for "how-to books, but will consider anything."

PARENTING PRESS, INC., P.O. Box 75267, Seattle WA 98125. (206)364-2900. Book publisher. Estab. 1979. Editorial Director: Alice Cummiskey. Publishes 2-3 picture books/year; 1-2 young reader titles/year; 1-2 middle reader titles/year. 40% of books by first-time authors.

Fiction: Picture books, young readers, middle readers: social skills books for children. "We rarely publish straight fiction." Recently published *First Day Blues*, by Peggy King Anderson with illustrations by Rebekah J. Strecker (ages 7-11); *On The Wings Of A Butterfly*, by Marilyn Maple, Ph.D. with illustrations by Sandy Haight (ages 6-11); *I'm Mad*, by Elizabeth Crary with illustrations by Jean Whitney (ages 3-9).

Nonfiction: Picture books: education, health, history, multicultural, social skills building. Young readers: education, health, history, nature/environment, social skills building books. Middle readers: health, social skills building. No books on "new baby, coping with a new sibling, cookbooks, manners." Average word length: picture books—500-800; young readers—1,000-2,000; middle readers—up to 10,000. Recently published *Kids To The Rescue*, by Maribeth and Darwin Boelts (ages 4-12).

How to Contact/Writers: Fiction: "We publish educational books for children in story format. *No straight fiction.*" Nonfiction: Query. Reports on queries in 4-6 weeks; mss in 1-2 months, "after requested." Publishes a book 10-11 months after acceptance. Will consider simultaneous submissions.

Illustrations: Works with 6 illustrators/year. Will review ms/illustration packages. "We do reserve the right to find our own illustrator, however." Will review artwork for future assignments.

How to Contact/Illustrators: Ms/illustration packages: Query. Illustrations only: Send "résumé, samples of art/drawings (no original art); photocopies or color photocopies okay." Original artwork returned at job's completion for illustrators under contract.

Terms: Pays authors in royalties of 4% based on net. Outright purchase of ms, "negotiated on a case-by-case basis. Not common for us." Offers average advance of $150. Pay for illustrators: by the project; 4% royalty based on net. Sends galleys to authors; dummies to illustrators. Book catalog/manuscript guidelines for #10 SAE and 1 first-class stamp.

Tips: Writers: "Query publishers who already market to the same audience. We often get manuscripts (good ones) totally unsuitable to our market." Illustrators: "We pay attention to artists who are willing to submit an illustration on speculation." Looking for "social skills building books for children, books that empower children, books that encourage decision making, books that are balanced ethnically and in gender."

PAULIST PRESS, 997 Macarthur Blvd., Mahwah NJ 07430. (201)825-7300. Fax: (201)825-8345. Book publisher. Estab. 1865. Editor: Kevin Lynch. Publishes 9-11 picture books/year; 6-7 young reader titles/year; 3-4 middle reader titles/year. 70% of books by first-time authors; 30% of books from agented writers.

Fiction: Picture books, young readers, middle readers: religious/moral. Average length: picture books—24 pages; young readers—24-32 pages; middle readers—64 pages. Published *A Bug From Aunt Tillie*, by Susan O'Keefe (ages 6-8, picture story book); *What Do You Do With the Rest of the Day, Mary Ann?*, by Eileen Lomasney (ages 5-7, picture book).

Nonfiction: Young readers, middle readers: religion. Published *Christopher Columbus: The Man Who Unlocked the Secrets of the World*, by Teri Martini (ages 9-12, biography).

How to Contact/Writers: Fiction/nonfiction: Submit complete ms. Reports on queries in 1 month; on mss in 2 months. Publishes a book 12-16 months after acceptance.

Illustration: Editorial will review all varieties of ms/illustration packages.

How to Contact/Illustrators: Ms/illustration packages: Complete ms with 1 piece of final art, remainder roughs. Illustrations only: Résumé, tearsheets. Reports on art samples in 6 weeks. Original artwork returned at job's completion, "if requested by illustrator."

Terms: Outright purchase: $65-100/illustration. Offers average advance payment of $450-$650. Factors used to determine final payment: Color art, b&w, number of illustrations, complexity of work. Pay for separate authors and illustrators: Author paid by royalty rate; illustrator paid by flat fee, sometimes by royalty. Sends galleys to authors; dummies to illustrators.

Tips: Not interested in reviewing novels. Looking for "concept books for young readers, ages 7-9."

Former Paulist Press Children's Book Editor Georgia Christo says the sophisticated drawing style and light strokes of Maywood, New Jersey, illustrator Mikki Machlin were ideal for the pages of Maria's Secret by June Toretta-Fuentes. Machlin created 15 pieces of art for the book, and she received $90 per inside illustration.

*PEARTREE, P.O. Box 14533, Clearwater FL 34629-4533. (813)531-4973. Book publisher. President: Barbara Birenbaum. Office Manager: H. Lapidus or Barbara Birenbaum. Publishes 1-5 young readers/year; 1-5 middle readers/year. 50% of books by first-time authors; subsidy publishes 50%. "Publishes shows on events (i.e. Liberty Centennial, Ground Hog Day, Thanksgiving) or general stories with 'lessons,' no Christian themes."

Fiction: Young readers: adventure, animal, contemporary, fantasy, hi-lo, humor, nature/environment, poetry, holidays. Middle readers: adventure, animal, fantasy, hi-lo, humor, multicultural, nature/environment, poetry, holidays. Does not want to see material on religion, science fiction, suspense, sports (per se), anthology.

How to Contact/Writers: Query. Reports on queries in 2 weeks; reports on mss in 3-6 months. Publishes book 9 months after acceptance. Will consider simultaneous submissions and previously published work.

Illustration: Works with 2 illustrators/year. Will review ms/illustration packages. Will review artwork for future assignments. Uses primarily b&w artwork with text.

How to Contact/Illustrators: Ms/illustration packages: Query; then submit ms with dummy. Illustrations only: Query with samples with SASE. Samples returned with SASE; samples filed ("if we anticipate an interest").

Terms: Pays author outright purchase. Other methods of payment include profits from sales of books. Pays illustrators by the project (range—$10 per illustration to $200 per book). Sends galleys to authors.

Tips: "We will consider publishing and marketing books as subsidy press when major houses reject titles. Be willing to get illustrations in books at minimum cost. Understand that small presses offer budding artists/writers chance to get in print and 'launch' careers on shoestring budgets."

PELICAN PUBLISHING CO. INC., 1101 Monroe St., Gretna LA 70053. (504)368-1175. Book publisher. Estab. 1926. Editor: Nina Kooij. Production Manager: Dana Bilbray. Publishes 6 picture books/year; 7 middle reader titles/year; 25% of books by first-time authors; 20% of books from agented writers.

Fiction: Picture books, young readers: folktales, health, history, nature/environment, religion. Middle readers: folktales, health-related, history, nature/environment, problem novels, religion, sports, suspense/mystery. Average word length: picture books—32 pages; middle readers—112 pages. Recently published *Cowboy Rodeo*, by James Rice (ages 5-8, describes origins and events of rodeos); *Little Freddie at the Kentucky Derby*, by Kathryn Cocqueyt, illustrated by Sylvia Corbett (ages 8-12, novel about a horse who wins Kentucky Derby).

Nonfiction: Young readers: biography, health, history, music/dance, nature/environment, religion. Middle readers: biography, cooking, health, history, music/dance, nature/environment, religion, sports. Published *Floridians All*, by George S. Fichter, illustrated by George Cardin (ages 8-12, collection of biographies on famous Florida figures).

How to Contact/Writers: Fiction/Nonfiction: Query. Reports on queries in 1 month; mss in 3 months. Publishes a book 12-18 months after acceptance.

Illustration: Works with 10-15 illustrators/year. Will review ms/illustration packages. Will review artwork for future assignments.

How to Contact/Illustrators: Ms/illustration packages: Query first. Illustrations only: query with samples (no originals). Reports on ms/art samples only if interested.

Terms: Pays authors in royalties; buys ms outright "rarely." Sends galleys to authors.

Tips: No anthropomorphic stories, pets stories (fiction or nonfiction), fantasy, poetry, science fiction, or romance. Writers: "Be as original as possible. Develop characters that lend themselves to series and always be thinking of new and interesting situations for those series. Give your story a strong hook—something that will appeal to a well-defined audience. There is a lot of competition out there for general themes." Looks for: "writers whose stories have specific 'hooks' and audiences, and who actively promote their work."

*PERFECTION LEARNING, 10520 New York Ave., Des Moines IA 50322. (515)278-0133. Book publisher. Senior Editor: Jody Cosson. Art Director: Dennis Clark. Publishes less than 10 picture books/year. Publishes nonfiction, hi-lo stories.
Fiction: All levels: adventure, animal, anthology, concept, contemporary, fantasy, folktales, health, hi-lo, history, humor, multicultural, nature/environment, problem novels, romance, science fiction, special needs, sports, suspense/mystery.
Nonfiction: All levels: activity books, animal, arts/crafts, biography, careers, concept, cooking, geography, health, hi-lo, history, hobbies, how-to, multicultural, music/dance, nature/environment, reference, science, self help, social issues, special needs, sports.
How to Contact/Writers: Fiction/nonfiction: submit outline/synopsis. Reports on queries in 3-4 months. Publishes a book 18 months after acceptance.
Illustration: Works with 15 illustrators/year. Will review artwork for future assignments.
How to Contact/Illustrators: Ms/illustration packages: Query. Illustrations only: Query with samples, promo sheet, portfolio, tearsheets; arrange personal portfolio review. Reports in 2 weeks. Samples returned with SASE.
Photography: Purchases photos from freelancers. Buys stock and assigns work. To contact, photographers should submit stock photo list.
Terms: Pays authors with outright purchase. Illustrators: pay negotiated project by project. Ms/artist's guidelines not available.

PERSPECTIVES PRESS, P.O. Box 90318, Indianapolis IN 46290. (317)872-3055. Book publisher. Estab. 1982. Publisher: Pat Johnston. Publishes 1-3 picture books/year; 1-3 young reader titles/year; 1-3 middle reader titles/year. 95% of books by first-time authors.
Fiction/Nonfiction: Picture books, young readers, middle readers: adoption, foster care, donor insemination or surrogacy. Recently published *Lucy's Feet*, by Stephanie Stein, illustrated by Kathryn A. Imlec.
How to Contact/Writers: Fiction/nonfiction: Query or submit outline/synopsis and sample chapters. Reports on queries in 2 weeks; on mss in 6 weeks. Publishes a book 6-10 months after acceptance. Will consider simultaneous submissions.
Illustration: Works with 1-2 illustrators/year. Will review artwork for future assignments.
How to Contact/Illustrators: Illustrators only: Submit promo sheet and client list. Reports on art samples only if interested.
Terms: Pays authors in royalties of 5-15% based on net sales or by outright purchase. Illustrators paid royalty or by the project. Sends galleys to authors; dummies to illustrators. Book catalog, manuscript guidelines available for #10 SAE and 2 first-class stamps.
Tips: "Do your homework! I'm amazed at the number of authors who don't bother to check that we have a very limited interest area and subsequently submit unsolicited material that is completely inappropriate for us. For children, we focus exclusively on issues of adoption and interim (foster) care, plus families built by donor insemination or surgery; for adults we also include infertility issues."

PHILOMEL BOOKS, 200 Madison Ave., New York NY 10016. (212)951-8700. Imprint of The Putnam & Grosset Group. Book publisher. Editor-in-Chief: Paula Wiseman. Editorial Director: Patricia Gauch. Editorial Contact: Laura Walsh. Art Director: Nanette Stevenson. Publishes 30 picture books/year; 5-10 young reader titles/year. 20% of books by first-time authors; 80% of books from agented writers.
Fiction: All levels: adventure, animal, fantasy, folktales, nature/environment, special needs, poetry, multicultural, history. Middle readers, young adults: problem novels. No concept picture books, mass-market "character" books, or series.
Nonfiction: All levels: arts/crafts, biography, history, multicultural, music/dance. "Creative nonfiction on any subject." Average length: "not to exceed 150 pages."

How to Contact/Writers: Fiction/nonfiction: Query; submit outline/synopsis and sample chapters; all other unsolicited mss responded to within 8-10 weeks. Reports on queries in 4-6 weeks. Publishes a book 2 years after acceptance.
Illustration: Works with 20-25 illustrators/year. Will review ms/illustration packages. Will review artwork for future assignments.
How to Contact/Illustrators: Ms/illustration packages: Query first. Illustrations only: query with samples. Send resume, promo sheet, portfolio, slides, client list, tearsheets or arrange personal portfolio review. Reports on art samples in 2 months. Original artwork returned at job's completion.
Terms: Pays authors in advance royalties. Average advance payment "varies." Illustrators paid by advance and in royalties. Sends galleys to authors; dummies to illustrators. Book catalog, manuscript/artist's guidelines free on request with SASE (9 × 12 envelope for catalog).
Tips: Wants "unique fiction or nonfiction with a strong voice and lasting quality. Discover your own voice and own story—and persevere." Looks for "something unusual, original, well-written. Fine art. The genre (fantasy, contemporary, or historical fiction) is not so important as the story itself, and the spirited life the story allows its main character. We are also interested in receiving adolescent novels, particularly novels that contain regional spirit, such as a story about a young boy or girl written from a southern, southwestern, or northwestern perspective."

PIPPIN PRESS, 229 E. 85th St., Gracie Station, Box 92, New York NY 10028. (212)288-4920. Fax: (212)563-5703. Children's book publisher. Estab. 1987. Publisher/President: Barbara Francis. Publishes 6-8 books/year. "Not interested in young adult books." *Query letter must precede all submissions.*
Fiction: Picture books, young readers, middle readers: adventure, animal, fantasy, folktales, humorous, multicultural, suspense/mystery. Multicultural needs include "original material rather than retellings or adaptations and written by a person of the particular ethnic group." Average word length: picture books—750-1,500; young readers—2,000-3,000; middle readers—3,000+. Recently published *A Weekend in the City*, by Lee Lorenz (ages 4-8). No YA books.
Nonfiction: Picture books, young readers, middle readers: animal, biography, history, multicultural, music/dance, nature/environment. Published *Benjamin Franklin and His Friends*, by Robert Quackenbush (ages 6-10); *Take Me to Your Liter*, by Charles Keller, illustrated by Gregory Filling (ages 7-11, science and math jokes). No YA books.
How to Contact/Writers: Fiction/nonfiction: Query with SASE. **No unsolicited mss.** Reports on queries in 2-3 weeks; on **solicited** mss in 6-8 weeks. Publishes a book 9-18 months after acceptance. Will consider simultaneous submissions.
Illustration: Works with 6-8 illustrators/year. Send query with SASE before sending any artwork.
How to Contact/Illustrators: Illustrations only: "Query. "I see illustrators by appointment." Reports on art samples only if interested. Original artwork returned at job's completion.
Terms: Pays authors in royalties. Pays illustrators royalties or by the project. Sends galleys to authors; dummies to illustrators. "The illustrator prepares the dummy on picture books; dummies for longer books prepared by the designer are submitted to the illustrator." Book catalog available for 6 × 9 SASE; manuscript/artist's guidelines for #10 SASE.
Tips: "We receive too many unsolicited mss even though our guidelines specify *query only*. We will be publishing more transitional books, i.e. picture storybooks for ages 7 to 10. and more imaginative nonfiction for ages 6-10. The market is glutted with mediocre and poor picture books. We are looking for chapter books, especially humorous ones, and will continue to publish writers and illustrators with track records."

PLAYERS PRESS, INC., P.O. Box 1132, Studio City CA 91614. (818)789-4980. Book publisher. Estab. 1965. Vice President/Editorial: R. W. Gordon. Publishes 2-10 young readers dramatic plays and musicals titles/year; 2-10 middle readers dramatic plays and musicals titles/year; 4-20 young adults dramatic plays and musicals titles/year. 35% of books by first-time authors; 1% of books from agented writers.
Fiction: "We use all categories (young readers, middle readers, young adults) but only for dramatic plays and/or musicals."
Nonfiction: "Any children's nonfiction pertaining to the entertainment industry, performing arts and how-to for the theatrical arts only."
How to Contact/Writers: Fiction/nonfiction: Submit plays or outline/synopsis and sample chapters of entertainment books. Reports on queries in 2-4 weeks; on mss in 3-4 months. Publishes a book 10 months after acceptance. No simultaneous submissions.
Illustration: Associate Editor will review an illustrator's work for future assignments.
How to Contact/Illustrators: Ms/illustration packages: Query first. Illustrations only: Send résumé, tearsheets, slides. Reports on art samples only if interested.
Terms: Pays authors in royalties of 2-20% based on retail price. Pay for illustrators: by the project; royalties range from 2-5%. Sends galleys to authors; dummies to illustrators. Book catalog available for $1.
Tips: Looks for "plays/musicals and books pertaining to the performing arts only."

*■POCAHONTAS PRESS, INC., 2805 Wellesley Ct., Blacksburg VA 24060-4126. (703)951-0467. Book Publisher. Editorial contact: Mary C. Holliman. Publishes 1-2 middle readers/year. Subsidy publishes 50%.
Nonfiction: All levels: biography, history, hobbies, nature/environment, sports. No preschool or fiction. Published *Quarter-Acre of Heartache*, by C.C. Smith (young adult, Indian battle to save reservation).
How to Contact/Writers: Query; submit outline/synopsis and sample chapters. Reports on queries in 3-4 weeks; mss in 1-2 months. Publishes a book "probably as much as a year" after acceptance.
Illustrations: Will review all varieties of manuscript illustration packages. Prefers "black ink, though will sometimes accept pencil drawings. No color."
Terms: Pays authors in royalties of 10% based on actual receipts. Pays illustrators either by the project $20/hour or in royalties of 5-10% based on actual receipts. Authors see galleys for review; illustrators see dummies for review. Book catalog free on request. Manuscript guidelines not available.
Tips: "Have respect for your child reader, and remember that the actual reader is often an adult. Don't talk down and make jokes or references that are beyond the child's experience. Please, avoid the caricature and the scary." Looks for "a story, well told, about a real person, not necessarily well known, who has done something interesting or unusual or achieved something from a poor start."

CLARKSON N. POTTER INC., Random House, 201 E. 50th St., New York NY 10022. (212) 572-6166. Senior Editor: Shirley Wohl.
Fiction: Picture books: adventure, animal, contemporary, fantasy, nature/environment, suspense/mystery. Young readers and middle readers: adventure, animal, contemporary, folktales, history, nature/environment, suspense/mystery. "We do nature and picture books for children through age 11."
Nonfiction: Picture books: animal, music/dance, nature/environment, sports. "We rarely do nonfiction for children."

The solid block before a listing indicates the market subsidy publishes manuscripts.

How to Contact/Writers: Fiction/nonfiction: *Agented work only*. Query with SASE only.
Illustrations: Will not accept unagented artwork.
Terms: Pays authors in royalties based on retail price.

THE PRESERVATION PRESS, 1785 Massachusetts Ave., NW, Washington DC 20036. (202)673-4057. Fax: (202)673-4172. Subsidiary of the National Trust for Historic Preservation. Book publisher. Director: Buckley Jeppson. Publishes 1 middle reader/year. 20% of books by first-time authors; 25% of books from agented authors; subsidy publishes 40%. Publishes books about architecture; "preservation of cultural sites and objects."
Nonfiction: Picture books, young readers, middle readers and young adults: activity books, history, architecture, American culture. Published *I Know That Building!*, by D'Alelio (middle reader, activities); *What It Feels Like to Be a Building*, by Wilson (young reader, architecture).
How to Contact/Writers: Nonfiction: Submit outline/synopsis and 1 sample chapter. Reports on queries in 3 weeks; reports on mss in 2 months. Publishes a book 12-18 months after acceptance. Will consider simultaneous submissions and previously published work.
Illustration: Will review ms/illustration packages.
How to Contact/Illustrators: Ms/illustration packages: Submit 1-2 chapters of ms with 3-4 pieces of final art. Reports in 3-4 weeks. Original artwork returned at job's completion.
Photography: Photographers should contact Janet Walker, managing editor. Uses architectural photos—interior and exterior. Model/property releases and photo captions required. Interested in stock photos. Publishes photo essays. Uses 5×7 or 8×10 glossy, b&w prints and 35mm, $2\frac{1}{4} \times 2\frac{1}{4}$, 4×5 and 8×10 transparencies. To contact, photographers should provide résumé, business card, promotional literature and tearsheets to be kept on file.
Terms: Pays authors royalty of 5-15% based on retail price. Offers advances of $800-1,600. Pays illustrators royalty of 3-10% based on retail price. Photographers paid royalty of 5-15% based on retail price. Sends galleys to authors; dummies to illustrators. Book catalog available for 9×12 SAE and 2 first class stamps.
Tips: Looks for "an energetic, hands-on approach for kids to gain an appreciation for the variety and depth of their American cultural heritage."

PRICE STERN SLOAN, 11150 Olympic Blvd., Los Angeles CA 90064. (310)477-6100. Book publisher. Assistant Editor: Cindy Chang. Publishes 0-1 picture books/year; 10-20 young reader titles/year; 5-10 middle reader titles/year; 0-1 young adult titles/year. 25% of books by first-time authors; 25% of books from agented writers. 50% from packagers.
Fiction: Picture books, young readers, middle readers, young adults: adventure, anthology, animal, contemporary, health-related, history, nature/environment, sports, suspense/mystery. "No fantasy/sci-fi, religious books, or poetry." Recently published *Adventures with Barbie #5-8*, by Suzanne Weyn (7-10, fiction series); *More Scary Stories*, by Q.L. Pierce (ages 7-10, scary short stories); *Magic Castle Clock* (ages 2-6; storybook with clock face and movable hands).
Nonfiction: Picture books, young readers, middle readers, young adults: activity books, animal, careers, health, hobbies, music/dance, nature/environment, sports. No religious books or textbooks. Recently published Nature Series Board Books by Suzanne Vasilak and Marshal Kieveach (8 mos.-2 yrs, board books); *Basic Scribbling*, by Will Howell (8 and up, drawing activity book); *Joker's Wild*, by Dian Smith (7-11, joke book).
How to Contact/Writers: Fiction/nonfiction: Query; submit outline/synopsis and 1-2 sample chapters. Reports on queries/mss in 2-3 months. Publishes a book 1 year after acceptance. Will consider simultaneous submissions and previously published work.

Illustration: Number of illustrations used for fiction/nonfiction: picture books—varies; young readers—2-7; middle readers—2-7. Editor will review ms/illustration packages. Will review artwork for future assignments.

How to Contact/Illustrators: Ms/illustration packages: Query; submit 1-2 chapters of ms with 1-2 pieces of final art (color copies—no original work). Illustrations only: Query with samples; provide resume, promo sheet, portfolio or tearsheets to be kept on file. Reports in 2-3 months.

Photography: Photographers should contact Art/Design Department. Buys stock and assigns work. Model/property release required. Publishes photo essays and photo concept books.

Terms: Pays authors royalty or outright purchase. Offers advances. Pays illustrators by project. Photographers paid by the project or per photo. Sends galleys to authors; dummies to illustrators. Book catalog available for 9 × 12 SAE and 5 first class stamps. Ms/artist's guidelines available.

Tips: "We don't have closed doors on any type of book. If it's good or special enough, we'll buy it. Parents are now willing to spend money on books to enhance the information a child would normally get in school."

PROMETHEUS BOOKS, 700 E. Amherst St., Buffalo NY 14215. Book publisher. Editor: Jeanne O'Day. Publishes 1 young reader title/year; 3 middle reader titles/year; 1 young adult title/year. 40% of books by first-time authors; 50% of books from agented writers. Publishes books on moral education, critical thinking, skepticism."

Fiction: All levels: sex education, moral education, critical thinking, science, skepticism. Average word length: picture books—2,000; young readers—10,000; middle readers—20,000; young adult/teens—60,000. Published *Girls Are Girls and Boys are Boys: So What's the Difference?*, by Sol Gordon (ages 8-12, sex education).

Nonfiction: All levels: sex education, moral education, critical thinking, science, skepticism. Average word length: picture books—2,000; young readers—10,000; middle readers—20,000; young adult/teens—60,000. Published *Wonder-workers! How They Perform the Impossible*, by Joe Nickell (ages 9-14, skepticism); *How Do You Know It's True?*, by Hy Ruchlis (ages 12-15, critical thinking); *Maybe Right, Maybe Wrong*, by Dan Barker (ages 7-12, moral education); *Science in a Nanosecond*, by Jim Haught (ages 10 and up, science).

How to Contact/Writers: Fiction/nonfiction: Submit complete ms with sample illustrations (b&w). Reports on queries in 1-2 months; mss in 2-3 months. Publishes a book 12-18 months after acceptance.

Illustration: Works with 2 illustrators/year. Editorial will review ms/illustration packages.

How to Contact/Illustrators: "Prefer to have full work (manuscript and illustrations); will consider any proposal." Include résumé, photocopies.

Terms: "Contract terms vary with projects." Pays authors royalties; author hires illustrator. Sends galleys to author. Book catalog is free on request.

Tips: Wants "secular moral education for young readers, including black & white illustrations."

*PUMPKIN PRESS PUBLISHING HOUSE, P.O. Box 139, Shasta CA 96087; (916)244-3456. Book publisher. President: Dick Bozzi. Or contact: Susan Olson Higgins. Publishes 2-3 picture books/year; 2-3 young readers/year; 1-2 middle readers/year.

Fiction: Picture books: adventure, animal, contemporary, fantasy, poetry. Young readers: adventure, fantasy, poetry. Middle readers: poetry. No science fiction.

Nonfiction: Picture books: activity books, animal, geography, history, music/dance, nature/environment, religion, science, social issues. Young readers: activity books, animal, arts/crafts, history, how-to, nature/environment, religion, science, social issues, sports.

How to Contact/Writers: Submit complete ms. Reports on queries in 5-8 weeks; on mss in 3 months.

Illustration: Works with 3 illustrators/year. Will review ms/illustration packages. Will review artwork for future assignments.

How to Contact/Illustrators: Ms/illustration packages: Submit ms with dummy. Original artwork returned at job's completion.

Photography: Purchases photos from freelancers. Contact Dick Bozzi. Work on assignment only.

Terms: Pays authors royalty or outright purchase. Pays illustrators and photographers by the project. Book catalog available for SASE. Ms/artist's guidelines not available.

Tips: "Fresh, fun, original manuscripts focused on pre-school to third-grade children."

*G.P. PUTNAM'S SONS, 200 Madison Ave., New York NY 10016. (212)951-8700. Imprint of Putnam and Grosset Group. Book publisher. Executive Editor: Refna Wilkin. Art Director: Nanette Stevenson. Publishes 40 picture books/year; 3 middle readers; 6 young adult titles. 5% of books by first-time authors; 50% of books from agented authors.

Fiction: Picture books: adventure, concept, contemporary, folktales, humor. Young readers: adventure, contemporary, folktales, history, humor, special needs, suspense/mystery. Middle readers: adventure, contemporary, history, humor, special needs, suspense/mustery. Young adults: contemporary, humor, problem novels, special needs. "Multicultural books should reflect different cultures accurately but unobtrusively." Regarding special needs, "stories about physically or mentally challenged children should portray them accurately and without condescension." No series, romances, sports fiction. Very little fantasy. Average word length: picture books – 200-1,500; middle readers – 10,000-30,000; young adults – 40,000-50,000. Recently published *Herbie Jones and Hamburger Head*, by Suzy Kline; *Mismatched Summer*, by C.S. Adler; *The Pennywhistle Tree*, by Doris Buchanan Smith.

Nonfiction: Picture books: concept multicultural. Young readers: biography, history, multicultural. Middle readers and young adults: biography, history, multicultural, social issues. No hard science, series. Average word length: picture books – 200-1,500; middle readers: 10,000-30,000; young adults: 30,000-50,000. Recently published *Bully for You, Teddy Roosevelt!*, by Jean Fritz; *What Do I Do Now?*, by Susan Kuklin; *A Grateful Nation: The Story of Arlington National Cemetery*, by Brent Ashabranner.

How to Contact/Writers: Fiction/nonfiction: Query; submit outline/synopsis and 3 sample chapters. Reports on queries in 1 month; on mss in 6-8 weeks. Publishes a book two years after acceptance. Will consider simultaneous submissions (if stipulated).

Illustration: Works with 40 illustrators/year. Will review ms/illustration packages. Will review artwork for future assignments.

How to Contact/Illustrators: Query. Reports in 6-8 weeks. Samples returned with SASE; samples filed. Original artwork returned at job's completion.

Terms: Pays authors royalty based on retail price. Pays illustrators by the project or royalty. Sends galleys to authors. Book catalog and ms guidelines available for SASE.

QUARRY PRESS, P.O. Box 1061, Kingston, Ontario K7L 4Y5 Canada. (613)548-8429. Book publisher. Publisher: Bob Hilderley. Publishes 4 picture books/year. 50% of books by first-time authors.

Fiction: Picture books: folktales. Published *Cathal the Giant Killer*, by Mary Alice Downie (grade 1-4, folklore); *My Underwear's Inside Out*, by Diane Dawber (grade 1-4, how to write poetry).

How to Contact/Writers: Fiction: Query; submit outline/synopsis and sample chapters. Reports on queries and mss in 3 months. Publishes a book 6 months-1 year after acceptance. Will consider electronic submissions via disk or modem.

Illustration: Will review ms/illustration packages. Will review artwork for future assignments. Contact: Melanie Dugan, managing editor.

How to Contact/Illustrators: Ms/illustration packages: Query; submit 10 pieces of art. Illustration only: Query with samples. Reports in 3 months. Original artwork returned at job's completion.

Terms: Pays authors royalty based on retail price. Pay for illustrators varies. Sends galleys to authors; dummies to illustrators. Book catalog available for 9×12 SAE and IRC or 2 first class Canadian stamps.

Tips: "Make it easy on us. We are inundated with material, so send a clear, easy-to-read letter/manuscript. Include name, address and phone number. Make sure proposals are clear and well organized."

RANDOM HOUSE BOOKS FOR YOUNG READERS, 8th Floor, 225 Park Ave. South, New York NY 10003. (212)254-1600. Random House, Inc. Book publisher. Vice President/Editor-in-Chief: Kate Klimo. Vice President/Executive Art Director: Cathy Goldsmith. 100% of books published through agents; 2% of books by first-time authors.

Fiction: Picture books: animal, easy-to-read, history, sports. Young readers: adventure, animal, easy-to-read, history, sports, suspense/mystery. Middle readers: adventure, history, science, sports, suspense/mystery.

Nonfiction: Picture books: animal. Young readers: animal, biography, hobbies. Middle readers: biography, history, hobbies, sports.

How to Contact/Writers: Fiction/nonfiction: **submit through agent only.** Publishes a book in 12-18 months. Will consider simultaneous submissions.

Illustration: Will review ms/illustration packages **(through agent only)**. Will review an illustrator's work for possible future assignments.

Terms: Pays authors in royalties; sometimes buys mss outright. Sends galleys to authors. Book catalog free on request.

■**READ'N RUN BOOKS**, P.O. Box 294, Rhododendron OR 97049. (503)622-4798. Subsidiary of Crumb Elbow Publishing. Book publisher. Publisher: Michael P. Jones. Publishes 3 picture books/year; 5 young reader titles/year; 2 middle reader titles/year; 5 young adult titles/year. 50% of books by first-time authors; 2% of books from agented writers. Subsidy publishes 10%.

Fiction: Will consider all categories for all age levels. Average word length: "Open."

Nonfiction: Will consider all categories for all age levels. Average word length: "Open."

How to Contact/Writers: For fiction and nonfiction: Query. Reports on queries/mss in 2 months "or sooner depending upon work load." Publishes a book about 8 months to a year after acceptance depending on workload and previously committed projects. Will consider simultaneous submissions.

Illustration: Reviews ms/illustration packages. Publisher, Michael P. Jones, will review illustrator's work for possible future assignments. "Black and white, 8×10 or 5×7 illustrations. No color work for finished artwork, but color work is great to demonstrate the artist's talents."

How to Contact/Illustrators: Query with sample chapter and several pieces of the artwork. "Artists should submit a good selection of their work, a résumé and a letter outlining their goals. Photocopies are fine." Reports on ms/art samples in 1-2 months. Original artwork returned at job's completion.

Photography: Photographers should contact Michael P. Jones. Looking for wildlife, history, nature. Model/property release required. Photo captions optional. Publishes photo essays and photo concept books. Uses 5×7 or 8×10 b&w prints; 4×5 or 35mm transparencies. To contact, photographers should query with samples.

Terms: Pays in published copies only. Sends galleys to authors; dummies to illustrators. Book catalog available for $2. Ms/artists' guidelines available for 1 first class stamp and #10 SAE.
Tips: "Don't give up. The field can seem cruel and harsh when trying to break into the market. Roll with the punches." Wants natural history and historical books. Sees trend toward "more computer generated artwork."

*REDBUD BOOKS, 1145 Sunrise Greetings Ct., P.O. Box 4699, Bloomington IN 47402. (812)336-9900. Imprint of Sunrise Publications. Book producer/packager. Editorial Coordinator: Laurie D. Hoover. Number of picture books published/year "varies." 50% of books by first-time authors.
Fiction: Picture books: adventure, animal, contemporary, fantasy, folktales, nature/environment, multicultural, poetry. Young readers: animal, contemporary, fantasy, folktales, nature/environment, multicultural, poetry. Recently co-produced *Basil of Bywater Hollow*, by Jill Baker (preschool-8 yrs., picture book).
Nonfiction: Picture books: animal, music/dance, nature/environment.
How to Contact/Writers: Fiction: Submit complete ms. Nonfiction: Query. Reports on queries in 3 weeks; reports on mss in 3-6 weeks. Will consider simultaneous submissions.
Illustration: Will review ms/illustration packages. Uses color artwork only.
How to Contact/Illustrators: "We already work with a number of outstanding illustrators, and are therefore mainly interested in receiving manuscripts. Truly determined illustrators are welcome to send illustrated packages, however." Ms/illustration packages: Submit complete package. Illustrations only: provide promotional literature or tearsheets to be kept on file. Reports back only if interested. Original artwork returned at job's completion.
Terms: Pays authors royalty based on retail price or outright purchase. Pay for illustrators varies, according to the style and level of detail of the artwork. Sends galleys to authors; dummies to illustrators. Ms guidelines available for SASE.
Tips: "We are a relatively new division of Sunrise Publications and are looking for talented authors. Our primary interest is picture book length fiction, especially stories with animal/environmental and holiday themes."

THE ROSEN PUBLISHING GROUP, 29 E. 21st St., New York NY 10010. (212)777-3017. Book publisher. Estab. 1950. Editorial Contact: Ruth Rosen. Publisher: Roger Rosen. Publishes 25 middle reader titles/year; 50 young adult titles/year. 35% of books by first-time authors; 3% of books from agented writers.
Nonfiction: Young adults: careers, hi-lo, multicultural, special needs, psychological self-help. No fiction. Average word length: middle readers—10,000; young adults—40,000. Recently published *Everything You Need to Know When a Parent is in Jail*, (high-lo, YA, The Need to Know Library); *The Value of Trust*, by Rita Mlios (YA The Encyclopedia of Ethical Behavior); *Careers as an Animal Rights Activist*, by Shelly Field (YA, The Career Series).
How to Contact/Writers: Nonfiction: Submit outline/synopsis and sample chapters. Reports on queries/mss in 1-2 months. Publishes a book 9 months after acceptance.
Photography: Purchases photos from freelancers. Contact Roger Rosen. Work on assignment only.
Terms: Pays authors in royalties or outright purchase. Sends galleys to authors. Book catalog free on request.
Tips: "Target your manuscript to a specific age group and reading level and write for established series published by the house you are approaching."

SAGEBRUSH BOOKS, (formerly Waterston Productions, Inc.), 25 NW Irving Ave., Bend OR 97701. (503)385-7025 or 800-779-7025. Book publisher. Editor: Emily Bonavia. Publishes 3 books/year. 50% of books by first-time authors. "We are seeking young adult and children's stories with a regional (Northwest) feel. We want to feature Northwest writers and illustrators, but will consider all mss received."

Fiction: Picture books and young readers: various subjects including adventure, anthology, animal, contemporary, fantasy, folktales, health-related, history, multicultural (Native American), nature/environment, poetry, science fiction, sports, suspense/mystery. Does not want to see "Stories that are written from an adult's perspective; stories that are cute or condescending." Average word length: picture books—200; young readers—1,500. Published *Letter City and the Alphabet Winds*, by Larry Kimmel (young reader); *Tea at Miss Jean's*, by Bispham Page (preschool—8 years, picture book); *Tale of Three Tractors, Jimmy the Beet Truck*, and *Big Cat the Proud*, by Molly Pearce (preschool, picture books).

Nonfiction: Picture books and young readers: activity books, animal, biography, history, nature/environment, sports. Average word length: picture books—200; young readers—1,500.

How to Contact/Writers: Fiction/nonfiction: Submit complete ms. Reports on queries/mss: 1-2 months. Publishes a book 7-9 months after acceptance. Will consider simultaneous submissions.

Illustration: Will review ms/illustration packages. Will review artwork for future assignments.

How to Contact/Illustrators: Ms/illustration packages: Submit complete package. Illustrations only: Send unsolicited art samples by mail. Reports in 4-6 weeks. Original artwork returned at job's completion.

Terms: Pays authors and illustrators royalty based on wholesale price or outright purchase. Offers advances. Sends galleys to authors. Book catalog available for 4×9½ SASE.

Tips: "Learn to view the world from a child's perspective by reading aloud to children." Wants a book that is written "from the heart—a story that presents an old idea in a new way. It must be obvious that the writer believes that a children's book requires the same skills and attention to detail as adult literature."

ST. ANTHONY MESSENGER PRESS, 1615 Republic St., Cincinnati OH 45210. (513)241-5615. Fax: (513)241-0399. Book publisher. Managing Editor: Lisa Biedenbach. 25% of books by first-time authors.

Nonfiction: Middle readers and young adults: religion. No fiction.

How to Contact/Writers: Nonfiction: Query, submit outline/synopsis and sample chapters. Reports on queries in 2-4 weeks; mss in 4-6 weeks. Publishes a book 12-18 months after acceptance.

Illustration: Editorial will review ms/illustration packages. "We design all covers and do most illustrations in-house." Uses primarily b&w artwork.

Terms: Pays authors in royalties of 10-12% based on net receipts. Offers average advance payment of $600. Sends galleys to authors. Book catalog, manuscript guidelines free on request.

Tips: "We're looking for programs to be used in Catholic schools and parishes—programs that have successful track records."

ST. PAUL BOOKS AND MEDIA, 50 St. Paul's Ave., Jamaica Plain MA 02130. (617)522-8911. Daughters of St. Paul. Book publisher. Estab. 1934. Children's Editor: Sister Anne Joan, fsp. Art Director: Sister Mary Joseph. Publishes 1-2 picture books/year; 1-2 young reader titles/year; 1-2 middle reader titles/year; 1-3 young adult titles/year. 20% of books by first-time authors.

Fiction: All levels: contemporary, religion. Average word length: picture books—150-300; young readers—1,500-5,000; middle readers—10,000; young adults—20,000-50,000.

Nonfiction: All levels: religion, devotionals, biography (saints). Average word length: picture books—200; young readers—1,500-5,000; middle readers—10,000; young adults—20,000-50,000.

How to Contact/Writers: Fiction/nonfiction: Submit outline/synopsis and sample chapters. Reports on queries in 3-8 weeks; on mss in 3 months. Publishes a book 2-3 years after acceptance. No simultaneous submissions.

Illustration: Works with 20 illustrators/year. Will review ms/illustration packages. Will review artwork for future assignments. Style/size of illustration "varies according to the title."

How to Contact/Illustrators: Ms/illustration packages: "Outline first with art samples." Illustrations only: Query with samples; send promo sheets or tearsheets. Reports on art samples in 3-8 weeks.

Photography: Photographers should contact Sister Annette Margaret. Buys stock images. Looking for children, animals—active interaction. Uses 4×5 or 8×10 b&w prints; 35mm or 4×5 transparencies.

Terms: Pays authors in royalties of 4-12% based on gross sales. Illustrations paid by the project. Photographers paid by the project, $15-200. Book catalog for 9×12 SAE and 4 first class stamps. Manuscript guidelines for legal-size SAE and 1 first class stamp.

Tips: "We are a Roman Catholic publishing house looking for devotional material for all ages (traditional and contemporary prayer-forms); obviously, material should be consonant with Catholic doctrine and spirituality!"

SCHOLASTIC INC., 730 Broadway, New York NY 10003. Not accepting unsolicited mss.

SCIENTIFIC AMERICAN BOOKS FOR YOUNG READERS, 41 Madison Ave., New York NY 10010. (212)576-9400. (212)689-2383. W.H. Freeman and Company. Book publisher. Publisher, Children's Books: Marc Gave. "Approximately 18-20 middle to YA titles are projected." 20% of books from agented authors. Publishes science, social science, math subjects.

Fiction: "We might consider fiction with a scientific slant if there is a real purpose in presenting the material in a fictionalized context."

Nonfiction: Middle readers and young adults/teens: biography, careers, health, nature/ environment, science, math, social science; all material should have a scientific slant. No books that are too similar to textbooks. Average word length: middle readers— 15,000+, young adult/teens—25,000+.

How to Contact/Writers: Fiction/nonfiction: Query. Reports on queries in 2-4 weeks; reports on mss in 1-2 months. Will consider simultaneous submissions.

Illustration: Will review ms/illustration packages. Will review artwork for future assignments. Contact Maria Epes, art director.

How to Contact/Illustrators: Ms/illustration packages: Query. Illustrations only: Query with samples; submit portfolio for review; provide tearsheets. Reports in 2-4 weeks.

Photography: Photographers should contact Marc Gave, publisher, children's books. Uses scientific subjects. Model/property release required. Interested in stock photos. May publish photo essays. Uses 35mm transparencies. To contact, photographers should query with samples; submit portfolio for review; provide tearsheets.

Terms: Pays authors royalty based on net wholesale price. Offers advances. Pays illustrators by the project or by royalty. Photographers paid by the project or per photo. Sends galleys to authors. Book catalog available in spring 1993. Ms and art guidelines available for SASE.

Tips: "Study the publishers' lists to find out who is publishing what. Don't send anything out to a publisher without finding out if the publisher is interested in receiving such material." Looking for well-researched, well-written, thoughtful but lively books on a focused aspect of science, social science (anthropology, psychology—not politics, history), with lots of kid interest, for ages 9 and up.

CHARLES SCRIBNER'S SONS, 866 Third Ave., New York NY 10022. (212)702-7885. Imprint of Macmillan Publishing Co. Book publisher. Senior Vice President/Editorial Director: Clare Costello. 35% of books from agented writers.
Fiction: Picture books, young readers: adventure, animal, contemporary, fantasy, folktales, nature/environment, science. Middle readers, young adults: adventure, animal, contemporary, fantasy, folktales, history, nature/environment, problem novels, science fiction, sports, suspense/mystery. Recently published *The Golden Deer*, by Hodges/San Souci (picture book); *Raw Head, Bloody Bones*, by Mary Lyons (ethnic tales).
Nonfiction: Picture books: animal, nature/environment. Young readers: animal, history, nature/environment. Middle readers, young adults/teens: animal, biography, history, nature/environment. Recently published *Sting*, by Adkins (science, how-to); *The Discoverers of America*, by Faber (young adult history).
How to Contact/Writers: Fiction: Submit outline/synopsis and sample chapters. Nonfiction: Query. Reports on queries in 4 weeks; mss in 10-14 weeks. Publishes a book 12-18 months after acceptance, "picture books longer." Will consider simultaneous (if specified when submitted) submissions.
Illustration: Editorial will review ms/illustration packages.
How to Contact/Illustrators: Ms/illustration packages: "Query first." Illustrations only: Send tearsheets. Reports back only if interested. Original artwork returned at job's completion.
Terms: Pays authors in royalties based on retail price. Sends galleys to authors; dummies to illustrators. Book catalog for 8×10 SAE; manuscript guidelines for legal-size SASE.

*SEACOAST PUBLICATIONS OF NEW ENGLAND, Suite 165, 2800A Lafayette Rd., Portsmouth NH 03801. Book publisher. Founder: Paul Jesep. Publishes 1-3 young readers/year. 100% of books by first-time authors. Mss *"must* have New England theme."
Fiction: Young readers: adventure, animal, contemporary, fantasy, folktales, history. Doesn't want fiction "not related to New England." Average word length: young readers—1,400. Recently published *Lady-Ghost of the Isles of Shoals*, illustrated by John Bowdren (ages 5-8).
Nonfiction: Young readers: biography, history. Average word length: 1,400. "If the right manuscript came along, it would need to be on New Hampshire history, for example, from the founding of the state to the present."
How to Contact/Writers: Fiction/nonfiction: Query. Reports on queries in 1 month; on mss in 1-3 months. Publishes a book 9 months after acceptance. Will consider simultaneous submissions.
Illustration: Works with 1-2 illustrators/year. Will review ms/illustration packages. Will review artwork for future assignments. Uses primarily b&w artwork.
How to Contact/Illustrators: Ms/illustration packages: Submit ms with 2 pieces of final art. Illustrations only: Query with samples; provide resume and client list. Reports in 6 weeks. Samples returned with SASE. Originals not returned.
Photography: Purchases photos from freelancers. Contact: Paul Jesep. Buys stock and assigns work. Wants photos of scenic New England. Model/property releases and captions required. Uses b&w prints. To contact, photographers should send cover letter and résumé.
Terms: Pays author outright purchase. Pays illustrators by the project (range: $100-300). Photographers paid per photo ($25 min.). Book catalog not available (hopefully available in late '93). Ms/artist's guidelines available for SASE.
Tips: Wants "a very unique New England theme—folklore about old New England—18th- or 19th-century Boston, marine life, pirates, ghosts, New Hampshire seacoast—the first book by Seacoast Publications was about the Isles of Shoals. Ironically no one

has ever written about the Shoals for children even though it is rich in New England history, ghost stories and pirates."

HAROLD SHAW PUBLISHERS, 388 Gundersen Dr., P.O. Box 567, Wheaton IL 60189. (708)665-6700. Book publisher. Estab. 1967. Dir. of Editorial Services: Ramona Cramer Tucker. Publishes 2 young adult titles/year. 10% of books by first-time authors; 5% of books from agented writers.
Fiction: Young adults: adventure, problem novels. Average length: young adults—112-250 pages. Recently published *The Sioux Society*, by Jeffrey Asher Nesbit (ages 13 and up, novel); *Light at Summer's End*, by Kimberly M. Ballard (ages 13 and up, novel).
How to Contact/Writers: Reports on queries in 2-4 weeks; on mss in 4-6 weeks. Publishes a book 1 year after acceptance. Will consider simultaneous submissions.
Terms: Pays authors in royalties of 5-10% based on retail price. Sends pages to authors. Book catalog available for SAE and $1.25; manuscript guidelines for SASE.
Tips: No longer accepts illustrator or photographer packages. Writers: "Read your stories to teens and to adults. You'll find that kids are the most honest." Wants "realistic books that focus on real needs of real characters." Looks for "a very unusual story which would make us change our minds about not picking up any more young adult books! It (the teen book market) is growing, but at the same time the quality of writing has been going down. There is a lot of 'fluff' on the market. Parents are now becoming more interested in books that meet needs and speak to the problems of today's world."

*SHOESTRING PRESS, Box 1223, Edmonton, Alberta T5J 2M4 Canada. Book publisher. Contact: Editor. Publishes 2 picture books/year; 1 young readers/year; 1 middle readers/year; 10 young adult titles/year. 40% of books by first-time authors; subsidy publishes 20%. No primary theme, publish various categories.
Fiction: Picture books, young readers, middle readers, young adults: adventure, folktales, Indian Legends. Average word length: picture books—3,000; young readers—7,500; middle readers—4,000; young adult—20,000.
Nonfiction: Picture books: geography, Indian Legends. Young readers, middle readers, young adults: Indian Legends.
How to Contact/Writers: Fiction: Query; submit outline/synopsis. Nonfiction: Query; submit outline/synopsis. Reports on queries in 4 months; reports on mss in 6 months. Publishes book 15 months after acceptance.
Illustration: Works with 2 illustrators/year. Will review ms/illustration packages. Will review artwork for future assignments. Uses primarily b&w artwork only. Prefers b&w.
How to Contact/Illustrators: Ms/illustration packages: query. Illustrations only: Query with samples; provide résumé, portfolio. Reports in 4 months. Samples returned with SASE; samples filed for 6 months. Originals not returned.
Terms: Pays authors royalty of 5-10% based on wholesale price. Pays illustrators royalty. Ms and art guidelines available for SASE.

*SIMON & SCHUSTER CHILDREN'S BOOKS, 15 Columbus Circle, New York NY 10023. (212)373-8500. Imprints: Little Simon, Simon & Schuster Books for Young Readers. Editor-in-Chief: Grace Clarke. Art Director: Lucille Chomowicz. Publishes 100 picture books/year; 8 young readers/year; 25 middle readers/year; 10 young adult titles/year.

"Picture books" are geared toward the preschool—8 year old group; *"Young readers"* to 5-8 year olds; *"Middle readers"* to 9-11 year olds; and *"Young adults"* to those 12 and up.

Fiction: Picture books: adventure, animal, concept, contemporary, fantasy, folktales, health, humor, multicultural, nature/environment, poetry, sports. Young readers: animal, contemporary, humor, mystery. Middle readers: adventure, animal, anthology, contemporary, fantasy, folktales, history, multicultural, nature/environment, science fiction, sports, mystery. Young adults: anthology, contemporary, fantasy, sports, suspense/mystery. Does not want to see horror, straight romance, mass market series ("Sweet Valley High" type). Average word length: picture books—wordless to 600 words; young readers—1,500; middle readers—2,000; young adult/teens—over 2,000. Recently published *Me And The End of the World*, by William Corbin (ages 8-12, middle-grade fiction); *Eamily Eyefinger*, by Duncan Ball and George Ulrich (ages 6-9, chapter book); *You Must Kiss a Whale*, by David Skinner (ages 11 and up, young adult).

Nonfiction: Picture books: animal, arts/crafts, biography, concept, geography, history, multicultural, nature/environment, science, social issues. Young readers: activity books, animal, biography, concept, geography, history, multicultural, music/dance, nature/environment, science, social issues. Middle Readers: activity books, animal, biography, concept, geography, history, multicultural, music/dance, nature/environment, science, social issues. Young adults: activity books, animal, biography, concept, geography, history, multicultural, music/dance, nature/environment, social issues. Does not want to see self-help books or poorly written manuscripts. Average word length: picture books—1,000; young readers—1,500; middle readers—2,000. Recently published *Antarctica*, by Laurence Pringle (ages 9 and up, geography); *Penguins*, by The Cousteau Society (preschool, picture book).

How to Contact/Writers: Fiction: Query; submit complete ms; submit through agent only. Nonfiction: Query; submit through agent only. Reports on queries in 3 weeks; reports on mss in 3 months. Publishes book 2 years after acceptance. Will consider simultaneous submissions and previously published work.

Illustration: Works with 35 illustrators/year. Will review ms/illustration packages only if illustrator is author. "Do not submit original art; copies only." Will review artwork for future assignments. Uses both b&w and color artwork. "No mural-size art, please."

How to Contact/Illustrators: Ms/illustration packages: Query; submit ms with dummy; submit ms with 2-3 pieces of final art. Illustrations only: Query with samples; provide portfolio, slides, tearsheets, arrange personal portfolio review, through agent. Reports only if interested. Samples returned with SASE; samples filed.

Photography: Purchases photos from freelancers. Works on assignment only. Model/property releases required. Uses 35 mm transparencies. To contact, photographers should send cover letter, résumé, published samples, slides, promo piece in color or b&w.

Terms: Pays authors royalty (varies). Pays illustrators royalty. Photographers paid royalty. Sends galleys to authors. Book catalog for 10 × 13 SAE; ms guidelines available. No artist's guidelines available.

Tips: "Present your manuscript as polished and professional as possible." Sees trend toward "multicultural, multi-ethnic and multi-generational" books.

*SOUNDPRINTS, 165 Water St., P.O. Box 679, Norwalk CT 06856. (203)838-6009. Book publisher. Editor: Dorothy Shillinglaw. Publishes 7 picture books/year. 15% of books by first-time authors; 30% of books from agented authors. Subjects published include North American wildlife and habitats.

Fiction: Picture books: animal. No fantasy or anthropomorphic animals. Average word length: picture books—800. Recently published *Seasons of a Red Fox*, by Susan Saunders with illustrations by Jo-Ellen Bosson (ages 5-9, picture book).

Nonfiction: Picture books: animal. No anthropomorphic animals or pets. Average word length: picture books—800; young readers—1,500. Recently published *After Columbus: The Horse's Return To America*, by Herman J. Viola with illustrations by Deborah Howland (ages 7-11, history picture book).

How to Contact/Writers: Fiction/nonfiction: Query. Reports on queries/mss in 1 month. Publishing time "Can vary from one to two years, depending on where it can be fitted into our publishing schedule." Will consider simultaneous submissions.

Illustration: Works with 4 illustrators/year. Will review ms/illustration packages "if subject matter is appropriate." Will review artwork for future assignments. Uses color artwork only. Books are approx. 8″×8″. Illustrations are usually full bleed two-page spreads.

How to Contact/Illustrators: Ms/illustration packages: Query. Illustrations only: Query with samples; provide resume, promo sheet. "If interest is generated, additional material will be requested." Reports in 1 month. Samples returned with SASE. Original artwork returned at job's completion.

Terms: Pays authors royalty or outright purchase. Offers advances. Pays illustrators by the project or royalty. Book catalog for 6½×11 SAE and 52¢ postage; ms guidelines for SASE. "It's best to request both guidelines and catalog. Both can be sent in self-addressed envelope at least 6½×11, with 52¢ postage."

Tips: Wants a book that "features North American wildlife and habitats with great accuracy while capturing the interest of the reader/listener."

THE SPEECH BIN, INC., 1766 Twentieth Ave., Vero Beach FL 32960. (407)770-0007. Fax: (407)770-0006. Book publisher. Contact: Jan J. Binney, Senior Editor. Publishes 10-12 books/year. 50% of books by first-time authors; less than 15% of books from agented writers. "Nearly all our books deal with treatment of children (as well as adults) who have communication disorders of speech or hearing or children who deal with family members who have such disorders (e.g., a grandparent with Alzheimer's or stroke)."

Fiction: Picture books: animal, easy-to-read, fantasy, health, special needs. Young readers, middle readers, young adult: health, special needs.

Nonfiction: Picture books, young readers, middle readers, young adults: activity books, health, textbooks, special needs. Recently published *Chatty Hats and Other Props*, by Denise Mantione; *Holiday Hoopla: Holiday Games for Language & Speech*, by Michele Rost; *Speech Sports*, by Janet M. Shaw.

How to Contact/Writers: Fiction/nonfiction: Query. Reports on queries in 4-6 weeks; 2-3 months on mss. Publishes a book 10-12 months after acceptance. "Will consider simultaneous submissions only if notified; too many authors fail to let us know if ms is simultaneously submitted to other publishers! We *strongly* prefer sole submissions."

Illustration: Works with 4-5 illustrators/year ("usually in-house"). Will review ms/illustration packages. Will review artwork for future assignments.

How to Contact/Illustrators: "Query first!" Submit tearsheets (no original art). Original artwork returned at job's completion.

Photography: Photographers should contact Jan J. Binney, senior editor. Buys stock and assigns work. Looking for all ages of people, occasional scenic shots. Model/property release required. Uses glossy b&w prints, 35mm or 2¼×2¼ transparencies. To contact, photographer should provide resume, business card, promotional literature or tearsheets to be kept on file.

Terms: Pays authors in royalties based on selling price. Pay for illustrators: by the project. Photographers paid by the project or per photo. Sends galleys to authors. Book catalog for 3 first class stamps and 9×12 SAE; manuscript guidelines for #10 SASE.

STANDARD PUBLISHING, 8121 Hamilton Ave., Cincinnati OH 45231. (513)931-4050. Book publisher. Director: Mark Plunkett. Creative Director: Coleen Davis. Publishes 25 picture books/year; 4 young reader titles/year; 8 middle reader titles/year; 4 young adult titles/year. 25% of books by first-time authors; 1% of books from agented writers. Publishes spiritual/religious books.

Fiction: Picture books: animal, contemporary, religion. Young readers: adventure, animal, contemporary, religion. Middle readers: adventure, contemporary, religion. Young adults: contemporary, religion. No poetry. Average word length: picture books—400; young readers—1,000; middle readers—25,000; young adults—40,000.

Nonfiction: Picture books, young readers: activity books, religion. Middle readers, young adults: religion. Average word length: picture books—400; young readers—1,000; middle readers—25,000; young adults—40,000.

How to Contact/Writers: Fiction/nonfiction: Query. Reports on queries in 3 weeks; on mss in 3 months. Publishes a book 18 months after acceptance. Will consider simultaneous and electronic submissions via disk or modem.

Illustration: Works with 20 illustrators/year. Will review ms/illustration packages. Will review artwork for future assignments (contact Coleen Davis, Creative Director).

How to Contact/Illustrators: Ms/illustration packages: Query. Illustrations only: Query with samples; arrange personal portfolio review. Reports on art samples in 3 weeks.

Photography: Photographers should contact Theresa Hayes. Looking for photos for bulletin covers. Model/property releases required. Uses 35mm and 2¼ × 2¼ transparencies. To contact, photographers should query with samples.

Terms: Pays authors in royalties of 5-12% based on wholesale price. Buys ms outright for $250-1,000. Offers average advance payment of $250. Photographers are paid $100-200 per photo. Sends galleys to authors. Book catalog available for 8½ × 11 SAE; manuscript guidelines for letter-size SASE.

Tips: "When writing children's books, make the vocabulary level correct for the age you plan to reach. Keep your material true to the Bible. Be accurate in quoting scriptures and references."

STAR BOOKS, INC., 408 Pearson St., Wilson NC 27893. (919)237-1591. Editorial Contact: Irene Burk Harrell. "We are still a new and growing company." All books are strongly Christian.

Fiction: All levels: adventure, animal, contemporary, fantasy, folktales, humor, poetry, problem novels, religion, romance, science fiction, special needs, sports, suspense/mystery. "All must be strongly Christian. Manuscripts must be somehow strongly related to the good news of Jesus Christ. Nothing dull or 'Sunday-schooly.' No Santa or Easter bunny." Recently published *Adventure of Captain Rhema*, by Barbara Grady Castle.

Nonfiction: All levels: biography, history, religion, social issues, special needs, sports. "All manuscripts must be strongly Christian."

How to Contact/Writers: Submit complete ms. Reports on queries/mss in 1-4 weeks. Publishes a book 6 months after acceptance ("longer if extensive editing needed"). *No* simultaneous submissions. "No books requiring colored illustrations." No curriculum materials.

Illustration: Works with 0-5 illustrators/year. Editorial will review ms/illustration packages. "We do not 'hire' illustrators. Prefer to see manuscript/illustration package. At present, we prefer informal black and white line art. As finances improve, we'll be interested in color."

How to Contact/Illustrators: Ms/illustration packages: send whole ms, 1-3 roughs of art. Submit art in ms packages only. Reports on art samples within a month. Original artwork returned at job's completion.

Terms: Pay: Authors get royalty of 10-15% based on retail price. "We issue contract for the whole (ms/illustration) package." Sends galleys to authors. Book catalog/guidelines available for #10 SAE and 2 first-class stamps.

Tips: "We want biblical values, conversation that sounds real, characters that come alive, exciting stories with 'behavior modification' strengths."

*STARBURST PUBLISHERS, P.O. Box 4123, Lancaster PA 17604. (717)293-0939. Editorial Director: Ellen Hake. Publishes 1-3 picture books/year. 50% of books by first-time authors; 10% of books from agented authors; subsidy publishes 10%. "Only looking for Bible-related books."
Nonfiction: Picture books and young readers: religion. Only interested in Bible related themes. Recently published *A Child's Guide to the Lord's Prayer*.
How to Contact/Writers: Nonfiction: Query; submit outline/synopsis. Reports on queries in 2-3 weeks; reports on mss in 6-8 weeks. Publishes a book less than 1 year after acceptance. Will consider simultaneous submissions.
Illustration: Works with 2 illustrators/year. Will review ms/illustration packages. Will review artwork for future assignments.
How to Contact/Illustrators: Ms/illustration packages: Query; submit ms with 3 pieces of final art. Illustrations only: Query with samples; provide résumé. Reports back only if interested. Cannot return samples. Original artwork returned at job's completion.
Terms: Pays authors royalty of 6-15% based on wholesale price. Pays illustrators by the project (range: $100 min.). Sends galleys to authors; dummies to illustrators. Book catalog available for 9×12 SAE and 3 first class stamps; ms guidelines available for SASE; artist's guidelines not available.

STEMMER HOUSE PUBLISHERS, INC., 2627 Caves Rd., Owings Mills MD 21117. (301)363-3690. Book publisher. Estab. 1975. President: Barbara Holdridge. Publishes 1-3 picture books/year. "Sporadic" numbers of young reader/middle reader/young adult titles/year. 60% of books by first-time authors.
Fiction: Picture books: animal, ecology, nature/environment. Young reader/middle reader: history. Recently published *Grandma's Band*, by Brad Bowles with illustrations by Anthony Clon (ages 4-6); *The Pied Piper*, by Sharon Chmeloy with illustrations by Pat and Robin DeWitt (ages 4-8).
Nonfiction: Picture book: animal, arts/crafts, biography, music/dance, nature/environment. Young reader: animal, arts/crafts, biography, music/dance, nature/environment. Recently published *The Hawaiian Coral Reef Coloring Book*, by Katherine Orr; *The First Teddy Bear*, by Helen Kay with illustrations by Susan Kranz.
How to Contact/Writers: Fiction/nonfiction: Query, submit outline/synopsis and sample chapters. Reports on queries in 6 weeks. Publishes a book 18 months after acceptance. Will consider simultaneous submissions.
Illustration: Will review ms/illustration packages. Will review artwork for future assignments.
How to Contact/Illustrators: Ms/illustration packages: "Query first, with several photocopied illustrations." Illustrations only: Send "tearsheets and/or slides (with SASE for return)." Reports in 2 weeks.
Terms: Pays authors in royalties of 4-6% based on wholesale price. Offers average advance payment of $300. Pay for illustrators: 4-5% royalty based on wholesale price. Sends galleys to authors. Book catalog for 9×12 SASE.
Tips: Writers: "Simplicity, literary quality and originality are the keys."

STEPPING STONE BOOKS, 225 Park Ave. S., New York NY 10003. (212)254-1600. Series of Random House, Inc. Book publisher. Contact: Stephanie Spinner.
Fiction: Young readers: "There are no restrictions on subject matter—we just require well-written, absorbing fiction." Length: 8,000-9,000 words. Audience: 7-9 year olds.
Illustration: Average number of illustrations used for fiction: young readers—10-15. Prefer b&w drawings.

STERLING PUBLISHING CO., INC., 387 Park Ave. South, New York NY 10016. (212)532-7160. Book publisher. Acquisitions Director: Sheila Anne Barry. Publishes 30 middle reader titles/year. 10% of books by first-time authors.

Illustrator Pat Porter of New York, New York, depicts the playfulness of these two boys as they battle each other in a pillow fight. The cover illustration was used by Stepping Stone Books for the book Slime Time *by Jim and Jane O'Connor.*

© 1990 Pat Porter

Nonfiction: Middle readers: activity books, animal, arts/crafts, geography, ghosts, hobbies, how-to, true mystery, nature/environment, reference, science, sports, humor, supernatural incidents. "Since our books are highly illustrated, word length is seldom the point. Most are 96-128 pages." Recently published *Sky Detective*, by Eileen Docekal, illustrated by David Eames (ages 8-12, astronomy facts and lore); *Dinosaur Dots*, by Monica Russo, illustrated by Monica Russo (ages 4-10, follow the dots book, with fascinating facts about each dinosaur); *Go Ahead—Make Me Laugh*, by Meridith Berk & Toni Vavrus, illustrated by Jeff Sinclair (ages 8-12, jokes, riddles, and other forms of humor).

How to Contact/Writers: Reports on queries in 1-8 weeks; on mss in 2-16 weeks. Publishes a book 6-18 months after acceptance. Will consider simultaneous submissions.

Illustration: Works with 6-10 illustrators/year. Will review ms/illustration packages. Will review artwork for future assignments.

How to Contact/Illustrators: Ms/illustration packages: "Query first." Illustrations only: "Send sample photocopies of line drawings; also examples of some color work." Original artwork returned at job's completion "if possible, but usually held for future needs."

Terms: Pays authors in royalties of up to 10% "standard terms, no sliding scale, varies according to edition." Pays illustrators by the project. Sends galleys to authors. Manuscript guidelines for SASE.

Tips: Looks for: "Humor, hobbies, science books for middle-school children." Also, "mysterious occurrences, activities and fun and games books."

*SUNBELT MEDIA, INC./EAKIN PRESS, P.O. Box 90159, Austin TX 78709. (512)288-1771. Fax: (512)288-1813. Book publisher. Estab. 1978. President: Ed Eakin. Publishes 2 picture books/year; 3 young readers/year; 10 middle readers/year; 2 young adult titles/

year. 50% of books by first-time authors; 5% of books from agented writers.
Fiction: Picture books: animal. Middle readers: history sports. Young adults: history, sports. Average word length: picture books—3,000; young readers—10,000; middle readers—15,000-20,000; young adults—20,000-30,000. "90 percent of our books relate to Texas and the Southwest."
Nonfiction: Picture books: animal. Middle readers and young adults: history, sports. Recently published *Build the Alamo*, (ages 4-10, picture book).
How to Contact/Writers: Fiction/nonfiction: Query. Reports on queries in 2 weeks; on mss in 6 weeks. Publishes a book 18 months after acceptance. Will consider simultaneous and electronic submissions via disk.
Illustration: Editorial will review all varieties of ms/illustration packages.
How to Contact/Illustrators: Ms/illustration packages: Query. Illustrations only: Tearsheets. Reports on art samples in 2 weeks.
Terms: Pays authors in royalties of 10-15% based on net to publisher. Pay for separate authors and illustrators: "Usually share royalty." Pay for illustrators: Royalty 10-15% based on wholesale price. Sends galleys to authors. Book catalog, manuscript/artist's guidelines for SASE.
Tips: Writers: "Be sure all elements of manuscript are included—include vitae of author or illustrator." **Submit books relating to Texas only.**

TAB BOOKS, Blue Ridge Summit PA 17294-0850. (717)794-2191. A division of McGraw-Hill, Inc. Book Publisher. Editor-in-Chief: Kim Tabor. Publishes 6 young reader titles/year; 6 young adult titles/year. 50% of books by first-time authors. 10% of books by agented authors.
Nonfiction: All levels: activity books, science. Young adults: arts/crafts, geography, hobbies, how-to, nature/environment, self help, special needs (mentally challenged).
How To Contact/Writers: Nonfiction: Query; submit outline/synopsis and sample chapters. Reports on queries in 2 months; mss in 3 months. Publishes a book 9-12 months after acceptance. Does not want to see fiction.
Illustration: Uses approximately 12 illustrators/year. Will review ms/illustration packages and artwork for future assignments.
How To Contact/Illustrators: Query first; submit resume, tearsheets, photocopies. Reports back only if interested. Originals returned to artist at job's completion.
Terms: "Terms vary from project to project." Book catalog and manuscript guidelines are free on request.
Tips: Looks for "science and craft topics which are fun and educational and include activities adult and children can work on together. Projects should be designed around inexpensive, household materials and should require under two hours for completion."

TAMBOURINE BOOKS, 1350 Avenue of the Americas, New York NY 10019. Imprint of William Morrow & Co. Inc. Book publisher. Editor-in-Chief: Paulette Kaufmann. Art Director: Golda Laurens. Publishes 50 picture books, 4 middle readers, 2 young adult titles/year.
Fiction/Nonfiction: No primary theme for fiction or nonfiction—publishes various categories.
How to Contact/Writers: Fiction/Nonfiction: Submit complete ms. Reports on mss in 1-3 months.
Illustration: Will review ms/illustration packages. Will review artwork for future assignments.
How to Contact/Illustrators: Ms/illustration packages: Submit complete package. Illustrations only: submit portfolio for review; provide résumé, business card, promotional literature or tearsheets to be kept on file. Original artwork returned at job's completion.

Terms: Pays authors royalty based on retail price. Offers advances. Pays illustrators royalty. Sends galleys to authors. Book catalog available for 9 × 12 SASE; ms guidelines available for SASE.

TEXAS CHRISTIAN UNIVERSITY PRESS, Box 30783, Fort Worth TX 76129. (817)921-7822. Book Publisher. Editorial contact: Judy Alter. Art Director: Tracy Row. Publishes 1 young adult title/year. 75% of books by first-time authors.
Fiction: Young adults/teens: Texas history. Average word length: 35,000-50,000. Recently published *Josefina and the Hanging Tree*, by Isabelle Ridout Marvin (grades 6-9); *Have Gun—Need Bullets*, by Ruby Tolliver (grades 6-9); *The Last Innocent Summer*, by Zinita Parsons Fowler (grades 6-9).
Nonfiction: Young adults/teens; Texas biography, Texas history. Average word length: 35,000-50,000.
How To Contact/Writers: Fiction/nonfiction: Query. Reports on queries in 2 weeks; mss in 2 months. Publishes a book 1-2 years after acceptance.
Illustration: Editor/Art Director Tracy Row will review artwork for future assignments.
How To Contact/Illustrators: Reports back to artists within 1 week. Originals returned to artist at job's completion.
Terms: Pays in royalty of 10% based on wholesale price. Illustrators are paid flat fee. Book catalog is free on request. Manuscript guidelines free on request.
Tips: "We look only at historical novels set in Texas."

*THISTLEDOWN PRESS LTD., 633 Main St., Saskatoon, Saskatchewan S7H 0J8 Canada. (306)244-1722. Book publisher. Contact: Patrick O'Rourke. Publishes numerous middle reader and young adult titles/year. "Thistledown originates books by Canadian authors only, although we have co-published titles by authors outside Canada. We do not publish children's picture books."
Fiction: Middle readers and young adults: anthology (short stories), mystery/adventure. Average word length: middle readers—35,000; young adult/teens—40,000. Recently published *The Blue Jean Collection*, by various authors (young adult, short story anthology); *Fish House Secrets*, by Kathy Stinson (young adult); *The Mystery of the Missing Will*, by Jeni Mayer (middle reader, mystery series).
How to Contact/Writers: Fiction: Submit outline/synopsis and sample chapters. Reports on queries/mss in 3 months. Publishes a book about one year after acceptance. No simultaneous submissions.
Terms: Pays authors in royalties based on retail price. Sends galleys to authors. Book catalog free on request. Manuscript guidelines for #10 envelope and IRC.

*TREASURE CHEST PUBLICATIONS, INC., 1802 W. Grant Rd., #101, Tucson AZ 85745. (602)623-9558. Book publisher and distributor. Production Manager: Nancie S. Mahan. Publishes 2 picture books/year; 1 young readers/year; 1 middle readers/year; 1 young adult title/year. All books must pertain to a particular region, Native Americans, Arizona/New Mexico topics, desert living.
Fiction: Picture books, young readers, middle readers and young adults: adventure, animal and multicultural. Does not want to see poetry, novels. Recently published *Malcolm Yucca Seed*, by Lynn Gessner (ages 8-12, Native American).
Nonfiction: Picture books, young readers: activity books, animal, arts/crafts, multicultural, nature/environment. Middle readers, young adults: activity books, animal, arts/crafts, cooking, hobbies, how-to, multicultural and nature.
How to Contact/Writers: Fiction: Query. Nonfiction: Query; submit outline/synopsis. Reports on queries in 3-4 weeks; reports on mss in 3-4 months. Publishes a book 6-12 months after acceptance "depending on amount of work needed."
Illustration: Works with 3 illustrators/year. Will review ms/illustrations packages. Will review artwork for future assignments. Uses both b&w and color artwork.

How to Contact/Illustrators: Ms/illustration packages: Query; submit ms with dummy. Illustrations only: Query with samples; provide résumé. Reports back only if interested. Samples returned with SASE. Copies kept on file.

Terms: Pays authors royalty of 10-15% based on wholesale price; "may split with illustrator." Offers advance (depends on work). Pays illustrators by the project; or royalty of 5-10%; "may split with author." Sends galleys to authors; dummies to illustrators. Book catalog available for SAE.

TROLL ASSOCIATES, 100 Corporate Dr., Mahwah NJ 07430. Book publisher. Editor: Marian Frances.

Fiction: Picture books: animal, contemporary, folktales, history, nature/environment, poetry, sports, suspense/mystery. Young readers: adventure, animal, contemporary, folktales, history, nature/environment, poetry, science fiction, sports, suspense/mystery. Middle readers: adventure, anthology, animal, contemporary, fantasy, folktales, health-related, history, nature/environment, poetry, problem novels, romance, science fiction, sports, suspense/mystery. Young adults: problem novels, romance and suspense/mystery.

Nonfiction: Picture books: activity books, animal, biography, careers, history, hobbies, nature/environment, sports. Young Readers: activity books, animal, biography, careers, health, history, hobbies, music/dance, nature/environment, sports. Middle readers: activity books, animal, biography, careers, health, history, hobbies, music/dance, nature/environment, religion, sports. Young adults: health, music/dance.

How to Contact/Writers: Fiction: Query or submit outline/synopsis and 3 sample chapters. Nonfiction: Query. Reports in 2-4 weeks.

Illustration: Will review ms/illustration packages. Will review artwork for future assignments. Contact Marian Frances, editor.

How to Contact/Illustrators: Illustrations only: query with samples; arrange a personal interview to show portfolio; provide resume, promotional literature or tearsheets to be kept on file. Reports in 2-4 weeks.

Photography: Model/property releases required. Interested in stock photos.

Terms: Pays authors royalty or by outright purchase. Pays illustrators by the project or royalty. Photographers paid by the project.

TROPHY BOOKS, 10 E. 53rd St., New York NY 10022. Subsidiary of HarperCollins Children's Books Group. Book publisher. Editorial Director: Erin Gathrid. Publishes 6-9 chapter books, 25-30 middle grade titles, 30 picture books, 12-15 young adult titles/year. "Trophy is primarily a paperback reprint imprint."

Fiction: No subject limitations. Published *Melusine*, by Lynne Reid Banks (YA, mystery); *My Brother Stealing Second*, by Jim Naughton (YA, suspense); and *R-T, Margaret, and the Rats of Nimh*, by Jane Conly (middle reader, fantasy adventure).

Nonfiction: All levels: animal, biography, music/dance, nature/environment. No careers, health, hobbies, religion, textbooks. Published *Now is Your Time*, by Walter Dean Myers (MG/YA, historical); *The King's Day*, by Aliki (picture book, historical/bio); *Fireflies in the Night*, Judy Hawes (Let's-Read-and-Find Out Science Picture book, early science).

How to Contact/Writers: Nonfiction: Submit complete ms (for picture and chapter books); submit outline/synopsis and 3 sample chapters (for middle grade and YA). Reports on queries in 2-3 weeks; reports on mss in 4-6 weeks. Will consider simultaneous submissions, electronic submissions via disk or modem, and previously published work.

Illustration: Will review artwork for future assignments.

How to Contact/Illustrators: Illustrations only: Query with samples (no originals). Reports in 3-4 weeks.

Photography: Photographers should contact David Saylor, art director. Photo captions required. To contact, photographers should query with samples.

Close-up

Seymour Simon
Writer
Great Neck, New York

If a subject is scientific in any way, be it planets, computers or animals, Seymour Simon has probably written about it. If he hasn't, he'll probably get around to it. Simon has written so many books that even he is not sure of the exact number. "I stopped counting after 100," he says. "But I know it's somewhere between 125 and 150."

Having been a science teacher for 23 years, Simon is familiar with how to relate to kids. In addition to being a teacher, he was a freelance writer who wrote magazine articles, including a four-page monthly science supplement for *Scholastic*. "Writing was something I had always done from early on. Writing books was simply an extension," he says.

Simon says he wrote his first book when he was a kid. "I wrote *Space Monsters* when I was in second grade. I even drew the pictures for the book and my teacher stapled the book together. Then she forced the class to listen to me as I read it to them," says Simon. Today, school children throughout the country read his books voluntarily.

His first published book, *Animals in Field and Laboratory* published in 1968 by McGraw-Hill, was about animal behavior. The book received rave reviews. "It was completely lost on me," says Simon. "I didn't realize how extraordinary it was until some other books came out and didn't receive that reception."

Getting that first book published was not too difficult, he says, because of his previous magazine credits. Also, he made sure to do everything right when contacting a potential publisher. "I followed all the directions that I had read from writing magazines," he says. "I wrote a letter of inquiry to McGraw-Hill, listing some of the things that I had written, and then I sent an outline and a couple of chapters—just the way one's supposed to. I got a call within a few weeks. They had liked what they had seen and offered me a contract."

Simon writes about a wide variety of subjects, never limiting himself to just one or two corners of science. Despite this, he claims he doesn't intentionally try to tailor his writing to kids' interests and advises writers not to write to fit a niche in the curriculum. "One of the things I really have found to be true is that I follow my own interests. I almost don't think about what kids are interested in. I have my own childlike enthusiasm about things. That's what I write about," he says.

"I wrote about computers at one time because I was really fascinated by computers. I had bought myself a computer before most people. Actually, I got it to play games with. But then I got so tired of playing games that I started to play with the computer as a computer. My interest in space dates back to the time I was a kid. Animal behavior was my major when I was in graduate school. So the fact that I still write books about space and animals is not strange because they are really two of my principal interests."

Simon also writes the Einstein Anderson series, fiction books where the main character solves mysteries with his scientific knowledge. "Fiction was something I had been writing when I initially started to write. It never occurred to me to write nonfiction. I was writing science fiction and mysteries. The Einstein Anderson books resulted from what I used to do when I was a teacher." At the end of the school year he would run out of things for the kids to do—so he would have to entertain them, he says. "I used to write these mystery stories, and in order to solve them the kids had to use some of the science that I had taught during the year. In addition, the books gave me the chance to use terrible puns that my students used to laugh at," says Simon.

Nonfiction children's books are much more appealing than they used to be, says Simon. He compares them to coffee-table books, saying they are now printed beautifully with stunning, oversized photographs. "When I began, science books really read like textbooks. I was really one of the few people writing in a conversational style." He goes on to say that these days, nonfiction writers are better, not only when it comes to writing in a conversational style, but also when it comes to depicting different types of children. "Early on, a lot of those books were sexist, addressed only to boys. If there were girls in the books, they were watching what the boys did. Also, you never saw minorities or physically disabled people," says Simon. Today the situation of portraying a variety of children has improved.

Simon works on several projects at once, not only with the writing but also doing his own photo research and paste-up. *Our Solar System*, a roundup of current information that for some reason or another didn't fit into his other books about planets, was published by Morrow in September 1992. Two books are slated for 1993, including *Weather* (Morrow), in which he took most of his own photographs, and *Wolves* (HarperCollins). *Earthwords*, a dictionary of ecology terms, is due out in spring 1994. He is also working on the first of a series of books on seasons for Hyperion.

Considering the countless number of books with his name on them, Simon knows what he's talking about when he advises writers to maintain an individual voice in what they write. "You're not going to come up with a topic nobody's ever thought of before. If nothing has ever been written about the topic, maybe it's because nobody is interested. The slant is what's important. An individual voice is important, especially a conversational style," he says.

Simon recalls a time when he was sitting on a panel with several other writers at a conference. "It occurred to me that we all had written books on a common subject, but the books were all still so different, it didn't matter."

—*Lisa Carpenter*

66 One of the things I really have found to be true is that I follow my own interests . . . . I have my own childlike enthusiasm about things. That's what I write about. **99**

—**Seymour Simon**

Terms: Sends galleys to authors. Ms guidelines available for SASE.

TROUBADOR BOOKS, 11150 Olympic Blvd. Los Angeles CA 90064. (310)477-6100. Imprint of Price Stern Sloan, Inc. Book publisher. Assistant Editor: Cindy Chang. Publishes informative, illustrated coloring books, activity books and punch-out-and-play sets (dioramas). 25% of books by first-time authors/illustrators; 25% of books by agented authors/illustrators; 50% of books from packagers. Troubador publishes no fiction titles.
Nonfiction: All levels: activity books, animals, careers, health, history, hobbies, music/dance, nature/environment, sports. Recently published *Great Plains Indians Action Set*, by Malcolm Whyte and Dan Smith (age 7-11, diorama); *Gross and Gruesome Games and Puzzles*, by Larry Evans (age 6-10, game/activity book); *World of Nature Invisibles*, by Larry Evans (age 8 and up, game/activity book).
How to Contact/Writers: Query. Reports in 2-3 months. Publishes a book 9 months to 1 year after acceptance. Will consider simultaneous submissions and previously published work.
Illustration: "There is no average number of illustrations used for our titles. Every project is unique." Will review ms/illustration packages. Will review artwork for future assignments. Contact Art Department.
How to Contact/Illustrators: Ms/illustration packages: Submit 1-2 chapters of ms with 1-2 photocopies. Illustrations only: Query with samples. Provide résumé, business card, promotional literature or tearsheets to be kept on file. Reports back only if interested.
Photography: Troubador does not normally use photography.
Terms: Pays authors royalty, outright purchase. Offers advances. Pays illustrators royalty or by projects. Sends galleys to authors; dummies to illustrators. General PSS guidelines available. Book catalog available for 9 × 12 SAE and five first class stamps.

TYNDALE HOUSE PUBLISHERS, INC., 351 Executive Dr., P.O. Box 80, Wheaton IL 60189. (708)668-8300. Book publisher. Children's editorial contact: Lucille Leonard. Children's illustration contact: Marlene Muddell. Publishes approximately 20 children's titles/year.
Fiction/Nonfiction: Currently overstocked in all categories. Send queries only. Is not accepting unsolicited mss for review.
Illustration: Full-color for book covers, black and white or color spot illustrations for some nonfiction.
How to Contact/Illustrators: Illustrations only: Send photocopies (color or b&w) of samples, résumé.
Terms: Pay for authors and illustrators: variable fee or royalty.
Tips: "All accepted mss will appeal to evangelical Christian children and parents."

THE VANITAS PRESS, Platslagarevägen 4 E 1, 22730 Lund, Sweden. Publisher: March Laumer. Publishes 2 young adult titles/year. "All our books, at the present time, are continuations of the American 'Oz' series of novels."
Fiction: Young adults: animal, humor. "Nothing can be considered except possible contributions to the Oz series." Young adults/teens: anthology, fantasy. Average word length: 60-100,000 words. Published *The Umbrellas of Oz* and *A Farewell to Oz*, by March Laumer; and *The Crown of Oz*, by Michael Michanczyk; (all for young to full adults, fantasies).
Nonfiction: Young adults: biography, how-to, multicultural, music/dance, nature/environment. Preparing a book entitled *The Salt Disagreements* and inviting "submissions dealing with the issue of salt/sodium in human diet — either accounts of personal experiences or scholarly investigations into the subject."
How to Contact/Writers: Query. Reports on mss in 2 weeks. Publishes book 6 months after acceptance. Will consider simultaneous submissions, electronic submissions via disk or modem, and previously published work.

Illustration: Will review ms/illustration packages. Will review artwork for future assignments. Uses primarily black & white artwork only. "Normal single book page size: vertical orientation."

How to Contact/Illustrators: Ms/illustration packages: Query. Illustration only: Query with samples. Reports immediately. Original artwork returned at job's completion.

Terms: Pays authors percentage of profits — if any or outright purchase up to $50. (For nonfiction, "a percentage on royalties earned from any publication of the work by houses *other than our own* — large-market publishers whether in the U.S.A. or abroad. Please write for details.") Pays illustrators percentage of profits. "A list of publication titles can be provided."

Tips: Wants "books that deal with changing cultures, living with one/two or more cultures (French/English, English/Spanish, or any combination of two or more languages and cultures). I would advise being willing to offer material without charge for the benefit derived from seeing one's early work in print. In much of small press publishing there simply isn't any profit to be shared; it's a 'for-the-love-of-it' operation. There's a very good chance of 'selling' us anything in the Oz-fantasy line." Trends: "I notice more concentration on pictures. Earlier, much-still-loved children's books were long, engrossable novels. Books now are wider-format, much thinner, and demand only of the reader an ability to look at pictures. Apparently reading ability is being played down."

VICTOR BOOKS, Scripture Press, 1825 College Ave., Wheaton IL 60187. (708)668-6000. Fax: (708)668-3806. Book publisher. Children's Editor: Liz Duckworth. Publishes 9 picture books/year; 10 middle readers/year. "No young readers at this point, but open to them." 50% of books by first-time authors; 10% of books from agented authors. All books are related to Christianity.

Fiction: Picture books: adventure, animal, contemporary, religion. Young readers: adventure, animal, contemporary, religion, science fiction, sports, suspense/mystery. Middle readers: adventure, contemporary, history, religion, sports, suspense/mystery. Does not want to see stories with "Christian" animals; no holiday legends. Published *Dr. Drabble's Phenomenal Antigravity Dust Machine*, by Sigmund Browner and Wayne Davidson (ages 4-7, picture book); *The Reluctant Runaway*, by Jeffrey Asher Nesbit (ages 8-12, middle reader); *Creature of the Mists*, by Sigmund Browner (ages 8-12, middle reader).

Nonfiction: Picture books: biography, religion. Young readers: biography, history, religion. Middle readers: biography, history, religion, sports. No ABC books or biographies of obscure/not well-known people.

How to Contact/Writers: Fiction/nonfiction: Submit complete ms for picture books. Submit outline/synopsis and 2 sample chapters for middle readers. Reports on queries in 1 month; reports on mss in 1½ months. Publishes a book 1½ years after acceptance. Will consider simultaneous submissions.

Illustration: Will review ms/illustration packages. Will review artwork for future assignments. Contact Paul Higdon, art director.

How to Contact/Illustrators: Ms/illustration packages: Submit complete package. Illustrations only: Submit portfolio for review. Provide résumé, promotional literature or tearsheets to be kept on file. Reports back only if interested. Does not return original artwork at job's completion.

Photography: Photographer should contact Paul Higdon, art director. Uses photos of children. Model/property releases required. Interested in stock photos. To contact, photographers should submit portfolio for review; provide résumé, promotional literature or tearsheets to be kept on file.

Terms: Pays authors royalty of 5-10% based on wholesale price, outright purchase $125-2,500. Offers advance "based on project." Pays illustrators by the project, royalty of 5% based on wholesale price. Photographers paid by the project, per photo. Sends galleys to authors. Book catalog available for 9 × 12 SAE and 2 first class stamps. Ms guidelines available for SASE.

Tips: "In general children's books I see trends toward increasingly high quality. In Christian children's books I see increasing commercial/cartoon characters—we're not interested in the latter."

*VICTORY PUBLISHING, 3504 Oak Dr., Menlo Park CA 94025. (415)323-1650. Book publisher. Publisher: Yolanda Garcia. 95% of books by first-time authors. "All books pertain to instruction of elementary age children—specifically bilingual—Spanish/English."

Fiction: Picture books and young readers: concept, fantasy, poetry. Middle readers: poetry. No religion, mystery, sports.

Nonfiction: Picture books, young readers and middle readers: activity books, arts/crafts, concept, cooking, how-to. No animals.

How to Contact/Writers: Fiction/nonfiction: Query. Submit outline/synopsis and 2 sample chapters. Reports on queries in 3 weeks; reports on mss in 1 month. Publishes a book 1 year after acceptance. Will consider simultaneous submissions and electronic submissions via disk or modem.

Illustration: Works with 2 illustrators/year. Will review ms/illustration packages. Contact Veronica Garcia, Illustrator.

How to Contact/Illustrators: Ms/illustration packages: Query. Illustration only: Query with samples; provide resume, promo sheet to be kept on file. Reports in 3 weeks or only if interested. Samples returned with SASE (if requested); samples filed. "Originals are purchased."

Photography: Purchases photos from freelancers. Work on assignment only.

Terms: Pays authors outright purchase (average amount: $100-500. Pays illustrators by the project or set amount per illustration depending on complexity. Photographers paid per photo (range: $5-20). Sends dummies to illustrators. Manuscript/artist guidelines not available.

Tips: Wants "teacher resources for elementary school—bilingual Spanish/English activity books."

VOLCANO PRESS, P.O. Box 270, Volcano CA 95689. (209)296-3345. Fax: (209)296-4515. Book publisher. President: Ruth Gottstein. Published 1 picture book in 1989; 3 in 1990.

Fiction: All levels: multicultural, nature/environment, special needs. Recently published *Berchick*, by Esther Silverstein Blanc, illustrated by Tennessee Dixon; *Mighty Mountain and the Three Strong Women*, by Irene Hedlund.

Nonfiction: All levels: health, history, multicultural, nature/environment, self help, social issues, special needs. Will consider feminist, social issues, Pacific-rim related (Asian) material for picture books, young readers and middle readers. Recently published *Save My Rainforest*, by Monica Zak, illustrated by Bengt-Arne Runnerstrom.

How to Contact/Writers: Nonfiction: Submit outline/synopsis and sample chapters. Reports on queries/mss in approximately 6 weeks. Publishes a book 1 year after acceptance. "Please always enclose SASE."

Illustration: Works with 2-3 illustrators/year. Will review ms/illustration packages. Will review artwork for future assignments.

How to Contact/Illustrators: Illustrations only: brief query with samples.

Terms: Pays authors royalty based on wholesale price. Pays illustrators by the project. Sends galleys to authors; dummies to illustrators. Book catalog for #10 SASE.

Tips: Considers "non-racist, non-sexist types of books that are empowering to women." Sees too much "fiction, trite fantasy, didactic and moralistic material, anthropomorphic male animal heroes."

Victory Publishing's Yolanda Garcia says she was searching for simple artwork to coincide with spelling words in the language book "Vocalitos" when she chose the work of 15-year-old Veronica Garcia, of Menlo Park, California. The illustrations are designed to help English-speaking readers remember Spanish words beginning with the letter "E."

© 1992 Victory Publishing

■**W.W. PUBLICATIONS**, P.O. Box 373, Highland MI 48357-0373. (813)585-0985. Subsidiary of American Tolkien Society. Independent book producer. Editorial Contact: Phil Helms. 75% of books by first-time authors. Subsidy publishes 75%.

Fiction/Nonfiction: All ages: fantasy, Tolkien-related.

How to Contact/Writers: Fiction: Query. Submit outline/synopsis of complete ms. Reports on queries in 4-6 weeks; 2-3 months on mss. Publishes a book 3-6 months after acceptance. Will consider simultaneous submissions.

Illustrations: Reviews all illustration packages. Prefers 8½ × 11 b&w and ink.

How to Contact/Illustrators: Query with samples. Reports on ms/art samples in 3 months. Original artwork returned at job's completion if requested.

Terms: Pays author free copies. Sends galleys to author if requested; dummies to illustrators. Book catalog for 1 first class stamp and #10 SAE.

Tips: "Tolkien oriented only."

WALKER AND CO., 720 Fifth Ave., New York NY 10019. (212)265-3632. Div. of Walker Publishing Co., Inc. Book publisher. Estab. 1959. Associate Editor: Mary Rich. Publishes 3-5 picture books/year; 10-15 middle readers/year; 15 young adult titles/year. 10-15% of books by first-time authors; 65% of books from agented writers.

Fiction: Picture books: fantasy, history. Young readers: animal, history, fantasy. Middle readers: fantasy, science fiction, history. Young adults: fantasy, history, science fiction. Published *Steam Train Ride*, by E.C. Mott (picture book); *Brother Night*, by V. Keller (young adult).

Nonfiction: Picture books, young readers, middle readers, young adults: animal, biography, education, history, hobbies, music/dance, nature/environment, religion, science, sports. Published *The Story of Things*, by S. Morrow (picture book history); *America Fights the Tide: 1942*, by John Devaney (young adult history).

How to Contact/Writers: Fiction/nonfiction: Submit outline/synopsis and sample chapters. Reports on queries/mss in 2-3 months. Will consider simultaneous submissions.

Illustration: Editorial will review ms/illustration packages.

How to Contact/Illustrators: Ms/illustration packages: 5 chapters of ms with 1 piece of final art, remainder roughs. Illustrations only: "Tearsheets." Reports on art samples only if interested. Original artwork returned at job's completion.

Terms: Pays authors in royalties of 5-10% based on wholesale price "depends on contract." Offers average advance payment of $2,000-4,000. Pays illustrators by the project, $500-5,000; royalties from 50%. Sends galleys to authors. Book catalog available for 9×12 SASE; manuscript guidelines for SASE.

Tips: Writers: "Keep writing, keep trying. Don't take rejections personally and try to consider them objectively. We receive 20 submissions a day. Can it be improved?" Illustrators: "Have a well-rounded portfolio with different styles." Looks for: "Science and nature series for young and middle readers."

WATERFRONT BOOKS, 86 Lake St., Burlington VT 05401. (802)658-7477. Book publisher. Publisher: Sherrill N. Musty. 100% of books by first-time authors.

Fiction: Picture books, young readers, middle readers, young adults; mental health, family/parenting, health, special issues involving barriers to learning in children.

Nonfiction: Picture books, young readers, middle readers, young adults: education, guidance, health, mental health, social issues. "We publish books for both children and adults on any subject that helps to lower barriers to learning in children: mental health, family/parenting, education and social issues. We are now considering books for children on bettering the environment."

How to Contact/Writers: Fiction/nonfiction: Query. Reports on queries in 2 weeks; on mss in 6 weeks. Publishes a book 6 months after acceptance.

Illustration: Editorial will review ms/illustration packages.

How to Contact/Illustrators: Ms/illustration packages: Query first. Illustrations only: Résumé, tearsheets. Reports on art samples only if interested.

Terms: Pays authors in royalties of 10-15% based on wholesale price. Pays illustrators by the job. Sends galleys to authors; dummies to illustrators. Book catalog available for #10 SAE and 1 first class stamp.

Tips: "Have your manuscript thoroughly reviewed and even copy edited, if necessary. If you are writing about a special subject, have a well-qualified professional in the field review it for accuracy and appropriateness. It always helps to get some testimonials before submitting it to a publisher. The publisher then knows she/he is dealing with something worthwhile."

WEIGL EDUCATIONAL PUBLISHERS, 2114 College Ave., Regina, Saskatchewan S4P 1C5 Canada. (306)569-0766. Book publisher. Publisher: Linda Weigl.

Fiction: Middle readers: folktales, multicultural.

Nonfiction: Young reader/middle reader/young adult: resources involving activity books, careers, education, health, history, nature/environment, social studies. Average word length: young reader/middle reader/young adult—64 pages. Recently published *Alberta Our Province*; *Citizenship in Action*; *Strategies for Career and Life Management—Student Journal*.

How to Contact/Writers: Nonfiction: Submit query and résumé. Reports on queries in 1 month; mss in 2-3 months. Publishes a book 2 years after acceptance. Will consider simultaneous submissions.

Illustration: Editorial will review ms/illustration packages. Will review artwork for future assignments.

How to Contact/Illustrators: Ms/illustration packages: "Query first." Illustrations only: Query with samples. Reports back only if interested or when appropriate project comes in.

Photography: Purchases photos from freelancers. Buys stock and assigns work. Wants political, juvenile, multicultural photos.

Terms: Authors paid royalty or outright purchase. Illustrators paid by the project. Sends galleys to author; sends dummies to illustrator. Book catalog free on request.

Tips: Looks for "a manuscript that answers a specific curriculum need, or can be applied to a curriculum topic with multiple applications (e.g., career education)."

*WHITEBIRD BOOKS, 200 Madison Ave., New York NY 10016. Putnam and Grosset Group. Book publisher. Senior Editor: Arthur Levine. Publishes 2 picture books/year. 50% of books by first-time authors.

Fiction: Picture books: folktales. Average word length: picture books—750. Recently published *The Singing Fir Tree: A Swiss Folktale*, by Marti Stone, illustrated by Barry Root (ages 4-8, picture book); *Chancay and the Secret of Fire: A Peruvian Folktale*, by Donald Charles (ages 4-8, picture book); *Quail Song: A Pueblo Indian Folktale*, by Valerie Carey, with illustrations by Ivan Barnett (ages 4-8, picture book).

How to Contact/Writers: Fiction: Query. Reports on queries in 2 weeks; reports on mss in 2-3 months. Publishes a book 1½-2 years after acceptance.

Illustration: Will review ms/illustration packages. Will review artwork for future assignments. Uses color artwork only.

How to Contact/Illustrators: Ms/illustration packages: Submit ms with dummy; submit ms with 2-3 pieces of final art. Illustrations only: Query with samples; provide resume, promo sheet, portfolio, tearsheets. Reports back only if interested. Samples returned with SASE; samples filed. Original artwork returned at job's completion.

Terms: Pays authors royalty based on retail price. Offers advances. Pays illustrators royalty based on retail price. Sends galleys to authors; dummies to illustrators. Book catalog available for SASE.

Tips: "In a word: *Research!* If you'd like to be published by Whitebird, read all the Whitebird titles you can get your hands on (a catalog will list these titles). But don't stop there—read dozens of folktales published recently by other companies to get a feeling for contemporary styles." Illustrators should submit "a gorgeously illustrated folktale from a culture that Whitebird has not yet explored. I am particularly interested in writers whose own ethnicity is reflected in their work."

ALBERT WHITMAN & COMPANY, 6340 Oakton St., Morton Grove IL 60053-2723. (708)581-0033. Book publisher. Editor-in-Chief: Kathleen Tucker. Publishes 30 picture books/year; 3 middle readers/year. 40% of books by first-time authors; 15% of books from agented authors. "We publish various categories, but we're mostly known for our concept books—books that deal with children's problems or concerns."

Fiction: Picture books: adventure, animal, contemporary, fantasy, folktales, health, nature/environment, poetry. Young readers and middle readers: adventure, animal, contemporary, fantasy, folktales, health, history, multicultural, nature/environment, poetry, problem novels, special needs, sports, suspense/mystery. Does not want to see "religion-oriented, ABCs, pop-up, romance, counting or any book that is supposed to be written in." Recently published *Savitri: A Tale of Ancient India*, retold by Aaron Shepard, illustrated by Vera Rosenberry (ages 6-11, picture book); *The Lion Who Had Asthma*, by Jonathan London, illustrated by Nadine Bernard Westcott (preschool-7, picture book).

Nonfiction: Picture books, young readers and middle readers: animal, careers, health, history, hobbies, multicultural, music/dance, nature/environment, special needs, sports. Does not want to see "religion, any books that have to be written in, biographies of living people." Recently published *Hamsters*, by Jerome Wexler (grades 2-8, young readers/middle readers); *Theodore Roosevelt Takes Charge*, by Nancy Whitelaw (ages 8 and up, middle readers).

How to Contact/Writers: Fiction/nonfiction: Submit complete ms. Reports on queries in 4-6 weeks; reports on mss in 2 months. Publishes a book 18 months after acceptance. Will consider simultaneous submissions "but let us know if it is one" and previously published work "if out of print."

Illustration: Will review ms/illustration packages. Will review artwork for future assignments. Contact Editorial. Uses more color art than b&w.

How to Contact/Illustrators: Ms/illustration packages: Submit all chapters of ms with any pieces of final art. Illustrations only: Query with samples. Send slides or tearsheets. Reports back only if interested. Original artwork returned at job's completion.

Photography: Photographers should contact editorial. Publishes books illustrated with photos but not stock photos—desires photos all taken for project. "Our books are for children and cover many topics; photos must be taken to match text. Books often show a child in a particular situation (e.g., a first communion, a sister whose brother is born prematurely.)" To contact, photographers should query with samples; send unsolicited photos by mail.

Terms: Pays authors royalty. Pays illustrators royalty. Offers advances. Sends galleys to authors; dummies to illustrators. Book catalog available for 9 × 12 SAE and 5 first class stamps. Ms guidelines available for SASE.

Tips: "In both picture books and nonfiction, we are seeking stories showing life in other cultures and the variety of multicultural life in the US. We also want fiction and nonfiction about mentally or physically challenged children—some recent topics have been AIDS, asthma, cerebral palsy."

WILLIAMSON PUBLISHING CO., Box 185, Charlotte VT 05445. (802)425-2102. Book publisher. Editorial Director: Susan Williamson. Publishes 8 young readers titles/year. 80% of books by first-time authors; 20% of books from agented authors. Publishes "very successful nonfiction series (Kids Can! Series) on subjects such as nature, creative play, arts & crafts, geography."

Nonfiction: Young readers: activity books, animal, arts/crafts, careers, geography, health, how-to, nature/environment, science, self-help. No textbooks. Published *The Kids Nature Book*, by Susan Milard (ages 4-10, activity/experiential); *Kids Create!*, by Laurie Carlson (ages 4-7, art & craft); and *Kids Learn America*, by Reed & Snow (ages 7-14, informational/activity).

How to Contact/Writers: Nonfiction: Query; submit outline/synopsis and 2 sample chapters. Reports in 2-3 months. Publishes book, "depending on graphics, about 9 months after acceptance." Will consider simultaneous submissions.

Illustration: Uses primarily black & white artwork only.

Terms: Pays authors royalty based on wholesale price. Offers advances. Sends galleys to authors. Book catalog available for 6 × 9 SAE and 4 first class stamps; ms guidelines available for SASE.

Tips: Interested in "creative, packed-with-interesting information, interactive learning books written to young readers ages 4-8. In nonfiction children's publishing, we are looking for authors with a depth of knowledge shared with children through a warm, embracing style—a respite in a rough world that tells not only how, but affirms that children can."

*WILLOWISP PRESS, 10100 SBF Dr., Pinellas Park FL 34666. Division of SBF Services, Inc. Book publisher. Writers contact: Acquisitions Editor. Illustrators contact: Art Director. Publishes 15-20 picture books/year; 6-8 young readers/year. 6-8 middle readers/year. 25% of books by first-time authors.

Fiction: Picture books: adventure, animal, contemporary, folktales, history, humor, rhymes, multicultural, nature/environment. Young readers: adventure, animal, contemporary, fantasy, folktales, history, humor, multicultural, nature/environment, sports, suspense/mystery. Middle readers: adventure, animal, anthology, contemporary, folktales, history, humor, multicultural, nature/environment, problem novels, romance, sports, suspense/mystery. Young adults: adventure, animal, anthology, contemporary, folktales, history, humor, multicultural, nature/environment, problem novels, romance, sports, suspense/mystery. No religious or violence. Average word length: picture books—350-1,000; beginning chapter books—3,000-4,000; middle readers—14,000-18,000; young adult—20,000-24,000. Recently published *Dead Wrong*, by Alida E. Young (grades 5 & up, novel); *The Haunted Underwear*, by Janet Adele Bloss (grades 3-5, novel); *Whatever I Do, The Monster Does Too!* by Tracey E. Dils (grades K-2, picture book).

Nonfiction: Picture books: activity books, animal, biography, geography, history, how-to, multicultural, nature/environment, reference, science. Young readers: activity books, animal, arts/crafts, biography, geography, history, how-to, multicultural, nature/environment, reference, science, sports. Middle readers: activity books, animal, biography, careers, geography, history, hobbies, how-to, multicultural, nature/environment, reference, science, social issues, sports. Young adults: animal, biography, careers, concept, geography, history, hobbies, how-to, multicultural, nature/environment, reference, science, social issues, sports. No religious. Recently published *A Look Around Endangered Animals*, by Ed Perez (ages K-3, environment); *People Who Shape Our World: Mother Teresa*, by Margaret Holland (grades 3 & up, biography); *Really Reading: When Dinosaurs Ruled the Earth*, by Martha Morss (grades 1-3, animal).

How to Contact/Writers: Fiction: Query. Submit outline/synopsis and 2 sample chapters. Nonfiction: Query. Submit outline/synopsis and 1 sample chapter. "Only *one* manuscript at a time! Do *not* send original work when querying." Reports on queries/mss in 6-8 weeks. Publishes a book 6 months to 1 year after acceptance. Will consider simultaneous submissions (if so noted). "SASE a must."

Illustration: Works with 10-12 illustrators/year. Will review ms/illustration packages "though almost all art is assigned independent of manuscript." Will review artwork for future assignments.

How to Contact/Illustrators: Ms/illustration packages: Query; submit ms with dummy. Illustrations only: Query with samples (samples that can be retained on file); provide resume. Reports in 2-3 months. Samples returned with SASE (and on request); samples filed. Original artwork not returned at job's completion.

Photography: Purchases photos from freelancers. Contact Acquisitions Editor. Buys stock and assigns work. Seeking photos related to environment, sports, animals. Photo captions required. Uses color slides. To contact, photographers should submit cover letter, resume, published samples, stock photo list.

Terms: Pays authors royalty or outright purchase. Offers advance. Pays illustrators by the project. Photographers paid by the project or per photo. "Our terms are highly variable, both in reference to royalties and outright purchase." Book catalog available for 9 × 12 SAE and 5 first class stamps. Ms guidelines available for SASE.

Tips: "Make sure the adult tone is not in evidence."

■**WINSTON-DEREK PUBLISHERS, INC.**, P.O. Box 90883, Nashville TN 37209. (615)321-0535. Book publisher. Estab. 1972. Editorial contact as follows: picture books: Matalyn Rose Peebles; young reader titles: Maggie Staton; middle reader/young adult titles: Kim Wohlenhaus. Publishes 35-40 picture books/year; 25-30 young reader titles/year; 10-15 middle reader titles/year; 10-15 young adult titles/year. 50% of books by first-time authors; 5% through agents. Subsidy publishes 20% of books/year.

Fiction: Picture books: contemporary, folktales, history, religion. Young readers: adventure, folktales, history, religion. Middle readers: adventure, contemporary, folktales, history, religion, suspense/mystery. Young adults: adventure, contemporary, folktales, history, problem novels, religion, suspense/mystery. Average word length: picture book—600-1200; young reader—3,000-5,000; middle reader—2,000; young adult—

10,000-40,000. Recently published *The Color of My Fur*, by Nanette Brophy.

Nonfiction: Picture books: biography, careers, religion, textbooks. Young readers, middle readers and young adults: biography, careers, history, religion, textbooks/basal readers, African American biographies. Average word length: picture book—600-800; young readers—2,500-4,000; middle reader—1,000-2,500; young adult—10,000-30,000.

How to Contact/Writers: Fiction: Query or submit outline/synopsis and sample chapters. Nonfiction: Submit complete ms. Reports on queries in 6 weeks; on mss in 8 weeks. Publishes a book 1 year after acceptance. Will consider simultaneous submissions.

Illustration: Editorial will review ms/illustration packages. Editor, J.W. Peebles, will review work for future assignments.

How to Contact/Illustrators: Ms/illustration packages: 3 chapters of ms with 1 piece of final art. Illustrations only: Send résumé and tearsheets. Reports in 3 weeks. Original artwork returned at job's completion.

Terms: Pays authors in royalties of 10-15% based on wholesale price. Also pays in copies. Separate authors and illustrators: 12½% royalty to writer and 2½% royalty to illustrator. Illustrators paid $30-150 or 2½-8½ royalty. Sends galleys to author; dummies to illustrator. Book catalog for SASE; ms/artist's guidelines free on request.

Tips: Illustrators: Use "action illustrations plus send good work and variety of subjects such as male/female; b&w." Looks for: "educational, morally sound subjects, multi-ethnic; historical facts."

WOMEN'S PRESS, 233-517 College Street, Toronto, Ontario M6G 4A2 Canada. (416)921-2425. Book publisher. Editorial Contact: Anne Decter and Angela Robertson. Publishes 1-2 picture books/year; 0-1 middle reader titles/year; 0-1 young adult titles/year. 60% of books by first-time authors. "We give preference to authors who are Canadian citizens or those living in Canada."

Fiction: Picture books: contemporary, social issues, health and family problems. Young readers, middle readers and young adults: contemporary, problem novels. Average word length: picture books—24 pages; young readers—70-80 pages; middle readers—60-70 pages; young adult/teens—80-150 pages. Published *Asha's Mums*, by Elwin & Paulse (4-8, picture-issue).

Nonfiction: Picture books: environment. Young adults: sex, health.

How to Contact/Writers: Fiction/Nonfiction: Query. Reports on queries in 1 month; reports on mss in 3-6 months. Publishes a book 1 year after acceptance.

Illustration: Editorial will review ms/illustration packages (Canadian only).

Terms: Pays authors in royalties of 10% min. based on retail price. Sends galleys to authors; dummies to illustrators. Book catalog and/or manuscript guidelines free.

WOODBINE HOUSE, 5615 Fishers Ln. Rockville MD 20852. (301)468-8800. Book publisher. Editor: Susan Stokes. Production Manager: Robin Dhawan. Publishes 0-2 picture books/year; 0-2 young adult titles/year. 100% of books by first-time authors. "All children's books are for or about children with disabilities."

Fiction: All levels: health-related and special needs (disability-related). "No fiction unless disability-related." Average word length: picture books—24 pages. Recently published *Charlie's Chuckle*, by Clara Berkus (ages 5-11); *My Brother, Matthew*, by Mary Thompson (ages 5-11); *Taking Charge: Teenagers Talk About Life and Disabilities*, by Kay Kriegsman et. al.

Nonfiction: All levels: special needs (disabilities). Does not want to see anything other than subjects about disabilities; "books written *primarily* to impart messages about people with disabilities to people without disabilities (Everyone's different and it's OK!' ")."

How to Contact/Writers: Fiction/nonfiction: Submit complete ms. Reports on queries in 3 weeks; reports on mss in 2-3 months. Publishes a book 18 months after acceptance. Will consider simultaneous submissions and previously published work.

Illustration: Works with 0-2 illustrators/year. Will review ms/illustration packages. Will review artwork for future assignments.
How to Contact/Illustrators: Ms/illustration packages: Submit entire ms with 2-3 pieces of art (color photocopies OK). Illustrations only: Query with samples; provide promo sheet, tearsheets. Reports back only if interested.
Terms: Pays authors royalty of 10-12% based on wholesale price. Offers advances of $0-3,000. Pays illustrators by the project. Sends galleys to authors. Book catalog available for 6×9 SAE and 3 first class stamps. Ms guidelines available for SASE.

*YMAA PUBLICATION CENTER, 38 Hyde Park Ave., Jamaica Plain MA 02130. (617)524-8892. Book publisher. Director Sales/Marketing: David Ripianzi. Publishes 2 middle readers/year. Publishes "morality stories, i.e., folktales (cultural themes)."
Fiction: Picture books, young and middle readers, young adults/teens: folktales, multicultural, sports. Multicultural needs for "books that identify the lifestyles and virtues of a particular culture." No science fiction, humor, poetry, religion, suspense, mystery.
Nonfiction: Picture books, young readers, middle readers and young adults: health, multicultural, sports.
How to Contact/Writers: Fiction/nonfiction: Query; submit outline/synopsis. Reports on queries/mss in 1 month. Publishes book 18 months after acceptance. Considers simultaneous submissions, electronic submissions via disk and previously published work.
Illustration: Works with one illustrator/year. Will review ms/illustration packages. Will review artwork for future assignments. Uses color artwork only.
How to Contact/Illustrators: Ms/illustration packages: Query; submit ms with dummy. Illustrations only: Query with samples, résumé. Reports in 1 month. Samples returned with SASE. Originals not returned.
Terms: Payment for authors negotiated. Payment for illustrators negotiated. Book catalog available.

JANE YOLEN BOOKS (See Harcourt Brace Jovanovich.)

Book Publishers/'92-'93 changes

The following markets are not included in this edition of *Children's Writer's & Illustrator's Market* for the reasons indicated within parentheses. If there is no reason given, it means the market did not respond to our requests for updated information for a 1993 listing.

Author's Connection Press, The (could not contact)
Beacon Press (not publishing children's books)
Bluestocking Press (not accepting queries)
Bold Productions (in-house staff only)
Cascade Pass Inc.
Child Graphics Press
Clyde Press
Crocodile Books, USA (not accepting unsolicited mss)
Delacorte Press and Doubleday Books for Young Readers
Dial Books for Young Readers (responded too late)
Enslow Publishers Inc.
Esoterica Press

Facts on File
Fiesta City Publishers
Haypenny Press
Ideals Publishing Corporation (not accepting unsolicited material)
Kendall Green Publications (not publishing children's books)
Kennebec River Press, Inc., The (not accepting unsolicited material)
Kingsway Publications (not publishing children's books)
Lester Publishing Limited (removed per request)
Midmarch Arts Press (not accepting unsolicited mss)
Mosaic Press (not accepting

unsolicited material)
Press of MacDonald & Reinecke, The
Review and Herald Publishing Association (removed per request)
Rosebrier Publishing Co.
Scholastic Hardcover
Shoe Tree Press
Sri Rama Publishing
Sunburst Books (only publishes reprints)
Tundra Books of Northern New York (not accepting unsolicited mss)
Voyageur Publishing Co., Inc. (suspended new publication activities)
Franklin Watts, Inc.

Magazines

For writers and illustrators who lack publication credits, magazines are an ideal place to break into the business. Collecting bylines and illustration credits is essential in building credibility in the children's field. Many magazine editors are partial to working with established writers or illustrators, but there is still room for the newcomer who has not made his mark on the publishing industry.

Much like the children's book publishing industry, children's magazines are succeeding in a time when many businesses are suffering economic turmoil. An article in the Feb. 2, 1992 issue of *Publisher's Weekly* reports that there are over 120 magazines for children ages two through 14, compared to just a few in the 1950s. The reasons for this vary. "Magazine articles can hold and expand a child's attention span, in itself an accomplishment in our electronically oriented society," the article states. "Magazines serve as an excellent bridge to books, and introducing kids to good magazines reinforces the idea that reading is not only necessary but enjoyable and exciting."

The popularity of kids' magazines

Possibly one of the reasons most juvenile magazines are surviving the crunch is children find them more appealing than in the past. Today there is a much more diverse selection that covers specific interests. Also, in order to accommodate children in a visually-oriented society, publishers have snazzed up their periodicals by increasing production qualities. Parents love magazines for their children because they view reading as a desirable alternative to watching television. Some children may not be patient enough to conquer whole books, but they may be willing to flip through the pages of a magazine until something attracts them.

Children today are more worldly and have a desire to know what's going on around them. Because magazines have the advantage of timeliness, they can expose children to current events in much less time than books and at less cost (the average one-year subscription is about the same as one hardcover picture book).

Another plus for the children's magazine industry is that teachers, in an effort to promote Whole Language theory, are utilizing fact-based educational periodicals as supplements in their classrooms. As a result, it's not unusual for children to want summer subscriptions, or even their own personal subscriptions after being initially exposed to certain magazines at school.

Do your homework

As children's writers and illustrators you must know what subjects appeal to kids. As a child, certain expressions and subject matter may have been interesting to you, but those same topics may not be interesting to the current generation of youths. As society changes so will the editorial content of many magazines. When submitting an article to a magazine, don't rely on your knowledge of that publication the way it looked 10-20 years ago. Do your research. If you are writing a story aimed at preteens, try to find a child in that age group who can read your story and give you feedback. In the August 1992 issue of *Children's Writer* Stan Zukowski, assistant editor at *Child Life* and *Children's Digest*, says "One of the reasons some writers get so many rejections is that they set their stories in today's world, but the actions and values are a generation late. It seems really obvious that they don't talk to children before they write the story."

In the June 1992 issue of *Children's Writer* Roxanne Camron, editor of *'Teen Magazine*, shares a similar problem with freelancers. Today's magazines for young women still cover the traditional topics, but they are more interested in tackling harder-hitting issues. "Girls always will be, and have been, first and foremost interested in boys. But some of the issues we deal with along those lines are different. For example, sexually transmitted diseases: You wouldn't have seen a focus on that as much in the past as you do now," says Camron. Writers and illustrators must note these trends when submitting work. Becoming familiar with the theme of a magazine will save valuable time for you, the freelancer submitting the work, and the editor who has to edit your material. Knowing the markets' needs also will save you money in postage. Without doing your homework your chances of selling material to an editor will dramatically decrease.

Needs of magazines

Some of the magazines listed here are informational, while others can be described as literary, religious-oriented or special interest. A few are adult magazines with special children's sections. There are many children's magazines that are not much more than promotions for toys, movies or television shows. You're not likely to find any of these in this book because they use licensed characters and are mostly produced in-house. Also, some of these types of magazines are more interested in generating revenue than enriching a young mind, and therefore concentrate more on product advertisement than literary or educational content.

The large circulation, ad-driven publications will generally offer a better pay rate than religious or nonprofit magazines. But smaller magazines may be more open to reviewing the work of newcomers. They can provide an excellent vehicle for you to compile clippings as you work your way toward the more lucrative markets. There is a drawback, though. It's not uncommon for juvenile magazines to purchase all rights to both stories and artwork. Though work for hire is generally frowned upon among freelancers, in the end selling all rights may prove to be advantageous. All of the magazines at the Children's Better Health Institute buy all rights, as does *Highlights*. However, these magazines are very reputable, and any clips acquired through them will be valuable.

A variety of manuscripts are needed by these markets. Classic subjects considered by many magazines include stories/features about the alphabet, outer space, computers and animals (even dinosaurs). As is with books, nonfiction features are very popular — especially photo features. Also, sports stories and descriptive articles on the way things work are marketable. Though trends tend to peak and fade quickly, current needs in the general interest magazine field are solid. They include historical fiction, retold folktales, mysteries, science fiction and fantasy. Multicultural material is very high in demand — editors can't seem to find enough of it. It appears efforts are strong to supply stories and artwork which include ethnic diversity. Don't expect demands for multicultural material to subside anytime soon.

Many kids' magazines sell subscriptions via direct mail or schools, so don't be surprised if you can't find a particular publication in the bookstore or at the newsstand. Be sure to send away for a sample copy of any magazine you're interested in working with. Most listings in this section have sample copies available and will be glad to send them upon request.

Once you have determined which magazines you are interested in contacting, take another look at the listing to review their preferred method of receiving submissions. Some may wish to see an entire manuscript; others may wish to see a query letter and outline, especially for nonfiction articles (with nonfiction articles, accompanying photographs are much welcomed). If you're an artist, review the listing for the types of samples you should send to the art director.

Finally, be sure you submit your best work. Though the magazine market is a good way for children's writers and illustrators to break in, it is not a junkyard for "less-than-your-best" material.

AIM MAGAZINE, America's Intercultural Magazine, P.O. Box 20554, Chicago IL 60620. (312)874-6184. Articles Editor: Ruth Apilado. Fiction Editor: Mark Boone. Art Director: Bill Jackson. Photo Editor: Betty Lewis. Quarterly magazine. Circ. 8,000. Readers are high school and college students, teachers, adults interested in helping, through the written word, to create a more equitable world. 15% of material aimed at juvenile audience.
Fiction: Young adults: history, multicultural, "stories with social significance." Wants stories that teach children that people are more alike than they are different. Does not want to see religious fiction. Buys 20 mss/year. Average word length: 1,000-4,000. Byline given.
Nonfiction: Young adults: interview/profile, multicultural, "stuff with social significance." Does not want to see religious nonfiction. Buys 20 mss/year. Average word length: 500-2,000. Byline given.
How to Contact/Writers: Fiction: Send complete ms. Nonfiction: Query with published clips. Reports on queries/mss in 1 month. Will consider simultaneous submissions.
Illustration: Buys 20 illustrations/issue. Preferred theme or style: Overcoming social injustices through nonviolent means. Will review ms/illustration packages. Reviews artwork for future assignments.
How to Contact/Illustrators: Ms/illustration packages: Query first. Illustrations only: Query with tearsheets. Reports on art samples in 2 months. Original artwork returned at job's completion "if desired." Credit line given.
Photography: Wants "photos of activists who are trying to contribute to social improvement."
Terms: Pays on publication. Buys first North American serial rights. Pays $15-25 for stories/articles. Pays in contributor copies if copies are requested. Pays $5-25/b&w cover illustration. Photographers paid by the project (range: $10-15). Sample copy $3.50.
Tips: "We need material of social significance, stuff that will help promote racial harmony and peace and (illustrate) the stupidity of racism."

*AMERICAN GIRL, Pleasant Company, P.O. Box 984, Middleton WI 53562-0984. (608)836-4848. Articles/Fiction Editor: Harriet Brown. Editor-in-Chief: Nancy Holyoke. Bimonthly magazine. Estab. 1992. Circ. 150,000+. "For girls ages 7-11. We run fiction and nonfiction, historical and contemporary."
Fiction: Middle readers (ages 7-11): contemporary, historical, multicultural, suspense/mystery, good fiction about anything. No preachy, moralistic tales or stories with animals

© 1992 George Harris

The shoddy butcher's shop in this illustration by George Harris, of Philadelphia, Pennsylvania, helps depict the type of businessman the elderly woman is confronting. The artwork was used in a story called "Aunt Chloe's Pride," published in the Summer 1992 issue of AIM Magazine.

as protagonists. Only a girl or girls as characters—no boys. Buys approx. 6 mss/year. Average word length: 1,000-3,000. Byline given.

Nonfiction: Any articles aimed at girls aged 7-11. Buys 3-10 mss/year. Average word length: 600. Byline sometimes given.

How to Contact/Writers: Fiction: Send complete ms. Nonfiction: Query with published clips. Reports on queries/mss in 4-6 weeks. Will consider simultaneous submissions.

Illustration: Works on assignment only.

Terms: Pays on acceptance. Buys first North American serial rights. Pays $500 minimum for stories; $300 minimum for articles. Sample copies for $4 (send to Margo Clark, General Manager). Writer's guidelines free for SASE.

Tips: "Keep (stories and articles) simple but interesting. Kids are discriminating readers, too. They won't read a boring or pretentious story."

*ASPCA ANIMAL WATCH, ASPCA, 424 E. 92nd St., New York NY 10128. (212)876-7700, ext. 4441. Visual Arts Editor: Dave McMichael. Quarterly magazine. Estab. 1951. Circ. 130,000. Focuses on animal issues. 15% of publication aimed at juvenile market.

Fiction: Young readers and middle readers: animal, animal protection, animal care. Average word length: 100-500. Byline given.
Nonfiction: Young readers and middle readers: animal, animal care, animal protection. Average word length: 100-500. Byline given.
Poetry: Wants to see animal care and animal protection.
How to Contact/Writers: Fiction/nonfiction: Query with published clips. Send complete ms. Reports on queries in 10 weeks; mss in 3 months. Publishes ms 1½ months after acceptance.
Illustration: Buys 5 illustrations/issue; 20 illustrations/year. Reviews ms/illustration packages; reviews artwork for future assignments; works on assignment only.
How to Contact/Illustrators: Illustrations only: Send tearsheets, quality photocopies to hold on file. Reports back only if interested. Samples kept on file. Originals returned upon job's completion. Credit line given.
Photography: Looking for animal care and animal protection. Model/property releases required. Uses 8 × 10, glossy color/b&w prints; 35mm, 2¼ × 2¼ and 4 × 5 transparencies. To contact, photographers should send stock list. Reports in 2 months.
Terms: Buys first North American serial rights and one-time rights for mss. Buys one-time rights for artwork/photographs. Pays $35-100 for stories and articles. Additional payment for ms/illustration packages. Pays illustrators $100-150/color cover; $50-100 color inside. Photographers paid per photo (range: $35-100). Sample copies for 9 × 12 SASE. Writer's guidelines not available. Illustrator's/photo guidelines for SASE.
Tips: Trends include "more educational, more interactive" material.

ATALANTIK, 7630 Deer Creek Dr., Worthington OH 43085. (614)885-0550. Articles/ Fiction Editor: Prabhat K. Dutta. Art Director: Tanushree Bhattacharya. Quarterly magazine. Estab. 1980. Circ. 400. "*Atalantik* is the first Bengali (Indian language) literary magazine published from the USA. It contains poems, essays, short stories, translations, interviews, opinions, sketches, book reviews, cultural information, scientific articles, letters to the editor, serialized novels and a children's section. The special slant may be India and/or education." 10% of material aimed at juvenile audience.
Fiction: Young reader: animal. Middle readers: history, humorous, problem solving, math puzzles, travel. Young adults: history, humorous, problem solving, romance, science fiction, sports, spy/mystery/adventure, math puzzles, travel. Does not want to see: "religious, political, controversial or material without any educational value." Sees too many animal stories. Buys 20-40 mss/year. Average word length: 300-1,000. Byline given, "sometimes."
Nonfiction: Middle readers: history, how-to, humorous, problem solving, travel. Young adults: history, how-to, humorous, interview/profile, problem solving, travel, puzzles. Does not want to see: "religious, political, controversial or material without any educational value." Wants to see more educational, math puzzles, word puzzles. Buys 20-40 mss/year. Average word length: 300-1,000. Byline given, "sometimes."
Poetry: Reviews 20-line humorous poems that rhyme; maximum of 5 submissions.
How to Contact/Writers: Fiction/nonfiction: Send complete ms. Reports on queries in 1 month; mss in 4 months. Will consider simultaneous submissions.
Illustration: Buys 4-20 illustrations/year. Prefers to review juvenile education, activities, sports, culture and recreation. Will review ms/illustration packages, including artwork for future assignments.
How to Contact/Illustrators: Ms/illustration packages: Send "complete manuscript with final art." Illustrations only: Query; send portfolio, client list. Reports only if interested. Credit line given.
Terms: Pays on publication. Buys all rights. Usually pays in copies for all circumstances. Sample copy $6. Writer's/illustrator's guidelines free with SAE and 1 first class stamp.
Tips: Writers: "Be imaginative, thorough, flexible and educational. Most importantly, be a child."

BOYS' LIFE, Boy Scouts of America, 1325 W. Walnut Hill Lane, Box 152079, Irving TX 75015-2079. (214)580-2000. Articles Editor: Doug Daniel. Fiction Editor: Kathleen DaGroomes. Art Director: Elizabeth Hardaway Morgan. Director of Design: Joseph P. Connolly. Monthly magazine. Estab. 1911. Circ. 1,300,000. *Boys' Life* is "a general interest magazine for boys 8 to 18 who are members of the Cub Scouts, Boy Scouts or Explorers. A general interest magazine for all boys."

Fiction: Middle readers: animal, contemporary, fantasy, history, humor, problem-solving, science fiction, sports, spy/mystery/adventure. Does not want to see "talking animals and adult reminiscence." Buys 12 mss/year. Average word length: 500-1,200. Byline given.

Nonfiction: Average word length: 500-1,200. Byline given.

How to Contact/Writers: Fiction/nonfiction: Send complete ms/query. Reports on queries/mss in 4-6 weeks.

Illustration: Buys 5-7 illustrations/issue; buys 23-50 illustrations/year. Will review ms/illustration packages; illustrator's work for possible future assignments. Works on assignment only.

How to Contact/Illustrators: Ms/illustration packages: "Query first." Illustrations only: Send tearsheets. Reports on art samples only if interested. Original artwork returned at job's completion. Buys first rights.

Tips: "I strongly urge you to study at least a year's issues to better understand type of material published. All submissions must be accompanied with SASE and adequate postage."

MARION ZIMMER BRADLEY'S FANTASY MAGAZINE, P.O. Box 249, Berkeley CA 94701. (415)601-9000. Managing Editor: Rachel Holmen. Fiction Editor: Marion Bradley. Quarterly magazine. Estab. 1988. Circ. 3,000 + . Publishes fantasy stories. "We are not a kiddie magazine but most of our work should not be unsuitable for bright children."

Fiction: Middle readers: fantasy. Young adults: contemporary, fantasy. Buys 50 + mss/year. Average word length: 500-5,000. Byline given. "No pen names—if a story isn't good enough to put real name on it, it's not good enough to print."

How To Contact/Writers: Send SASE for guidelines. "Care will be taken, but we cannot assume responsibility for unsolicited stories. If you want your manuscript returned, send a 9″ × 12″ SASE with sufficient postage. Rejected manuscripts without return postage will be thrown out. If you need to know we received your story, enclose a self-addressed stamped postal card. If your manuscript is rejected, it will be returned as soon as possible. If we do not return it within a month, we are holding it for possible use and will write to you as soon as we can." Reports on mss in 2-3 weeks. Average length of time between acceptance of mss and publication of work is 4 months. "No simultaneous submissions. I know no one can afford to have stuff tied up so I try to report by return mail if I can't use it."

Illustration: "Must be professional illustrators." Preferred theme/style: full page; double page spreads; ½, ⅓, ¼ page; illustration of the stories. No manuscript illustration packages. Credit line given.

How To Contact/Illustrators: "The best method is to send good quality black and white photocopies to Rachel Holmen for her files. Please send no more than five or six 8½ × 11 non-returnable samples. Most of the artwork we use is interior black and white pen-and-ink drawings, but other black and white media are acceptable." Include return address and phone number. Originals returned to artist at job's completion.

Terms: Pays on acceptance. Buys first magazine rights. Pays 3-10¢/word for stories. Pays illustrators $500-800 for color cover; $15-100 b&w inside. Sample copies for $3.50. Writer's guidelines free on request.

Tips: "Beware of dime-a-dozen subjects such as dragons, elves, unicorns, sea creatures, brute warriors, ghosts, and adventuring sorcerers/sorceresses. We get dozens of these kinds of stories every week, and we reject all but the *truly* unusual and well-written ones. We buy original fantasy with no particular objection to modern settings, but we do want action and adventure. The primary purpose of your story should be to entertain the reader; and although any good story has a central point behind the plot, the reader should be able to deduce it rather than having it thrust upon him. We prefer strong female characters, and will reject out of hand stories in which we find obvious or objectionable sexism. We do not favor strong language because, although we *are not* a magazine aimed at children or young adults, we do have many young readers. Nonfiction should be queried; it is done on commission only."

*BRILLIANT STAR, National Spiritual Assembly of the Baha'is of the United States, 915 Washington St., Evanston IL 60202. General Editor: Candace Moore Hill. Art Director: Pepper Peterson Oldziey. Bimonthly magazine. Estab. 1968. Circ. 2,300. A magazine for Bahá'í children that emphasizes the history, teachings and beliefs of the Bahá'í faith. We look for "sensitivity to multi-racial, multi-cultural audience and a commitment to assisting children in understanding the oneness of the human family." 90% of material aimed at juvenile audience.
Fiction: Young readers, middle readers: contemporary history, folktales, humorous, multicultural, nature/environment, problem solving, religious, sports, suspense/mystery. Does not want to see material related to traditional Christian holidays or to secular holidays such as Christmas, Easter or Halloween. Nothing that pontificates! Acquires 12-15 mss/year. Average word length: 250-1,000. Byline given.
Nonfiction: Young readers, middle readers: arts/crafts, biography, cooking, games/puzzles, geography, history, how-to, humorous, interview/profile, multicultural, nature/environment, problem-solving, religion, sports, travel. Multicultural needs include material about interracial groups working together. Does not want to see crafts or activities specific to holidays. Accepts 12-15 mss/year. Average word length: 250-750. Byline given.
Poetry: Reviews poetry. Word/line length open.
How to Contact/Writers: Fiction/nonfiction: Send complete ms. Reports in 2 months. Publishes ms 8-12 months after acceptance. Will consider simultaneous submissions and previously published work.
Illustration: "Illustrations for specific stories on assignment for Art Director." Will review ms/illustration packages; artwork for future assignments. Works on assignment only.
How to Contact/Illustrators: Illustrations only: Query; send resume, promo sheet, tearsheets. Reports on art samples in 2 months. Original artwork returned at job's completion. Credit line given.
Terms: *"Brilliant Star* cannot purchase art or stories at this time." Provides 2 copies of issue in which work appears. Sample copy with 9x12 SAE and 5 oz. worth of postage; writer's/illustrator's/photo guidelines free with SASE.
Tips: Writers: "Know the age range and interests of your reader. Read the magazine before you submit. Express a willingness to adapt a story to the editor's needs. A story from real life is always more interesting than what you think children should read. Avoid morals. Any writer who is willing to learn and study the Bahá'í faith in order to write a story from Bahá'í history will be most welcome and encouraged." Illustrators: "Don't be too cute. Get past the one thing you like to draw best and be ready to expand your range. Art director is open to reviewing general submissions. Need artists who can illustrate diversity of peoples without stereotyping, and in a sensitive way that affirms the beauty of different racial characteristics."

BUSINE$$ KIDS, (formerly Businesship), Suite 1080 E., 1300 I St., N.W., Washington D.C. 20005. Director of Corporate Communications: Michael J. Holmes. Quarterly newsletter. Estab. 1988. Circ. 75,000. "We cover stories about young entrepreneurs, how teens and preteens can become entrepreneurs, and useful information for effective business operation and management. Our goal is to help prepare America's youth for the complex and competitive world of business by sharing with them every possible business experience, the problems *and* the solutions. And while we're *serious* about business, we want them to know that business can be *fun*. 99% of material aimed at juvenile audience with one article aimed at parents in each issue."

Nonfiction: Middle readers: how-to, interview/profile, problem solving. Young adult/ teens: how-to, interview/profile, problem solving. "All must relate to business"; wants to see "more profiles and photos of kids ages 8-18 who have their own businesses." Buys 15 mss/year. "Our goal is 50% freelance." Average word length: 200-400. Byline: Listed as a contributing writer.

Poetry: Reviews free verse, light verse, traditional poetry; 25-50 lines.

Illustration: Reviews ms/illustration packages.

How to Contact/Writers: Nonfiction: Send complete ms. Reports on mss in 2 months.

Terms: Pays on publication. Buys all rights. Pays 15¢ word/unsolicited articles; $35-50 for puzzles/games; $15-20 for cartoons; $5-10 for b&w/8 × 10 photos. Writer's guidelines and sample copy available.

Tips: Looking for "any nonfiction pertaining to teens in the business world. How to choose, build, improve, market or advertise a business. When, and how, to hire (or fire) employees. Lots of profiles about successful young entrepreneurs. The latest in *any* field—entertainment, sports, medicine, etc.—where teens are making megabucks (or just movie money!). New products; book reviews on children and money; motivational articles; how-to invest/save money; news releases; tax information; stock market tips; bonds; banking; precious metals; cartoons; puzzles; poetry; games also sought."

*CALLIOPE, World History for Young People, Cobblestone Publishing, Inc., 7 School St., Peterborough NH 03458. (603)924-7209. Editor-in-Chief: Carolyn Yoder. Art Director: Ann C. Webster. Photo Editor: Francelle Carapetyan. Bimonthly magazine. "*Calliope* covers world history (East/West) and lively, original approaches to the subject are the primary concerns of the editors in choosing material."

Fiction: Middle readers and young adults: adventure, folktales, history, biographical fiction. Material must relate to forthcoming themes. Average word length: 800.

Nonfiction: Middle readers and young adults: arts/crafts, biography, cooking, games/ puzzles, history. Material must relate to forthcoming themes. Average word length: 300-800.

Poetry: Maximum line length: 100. Wants "clear, objective imagery. Serious and light verse considered."

How to Contact/Writers: "A query must consist of all of the following to be considered (please use nonerasable paper): a brief cover letter stating subject and word length of the proposed article; a detailed one-page outline explaining the information to be presented in the article; an extensive bibliography of materials the author intends to use in preparing the article; a self-addressed stamped envelope. Writers new to *Calliope* should send a writing sample with query. If you would like to know if your query has been received, please also include a stamped postcard that requests acknowledgment of receipt. In all correspondence, please include your complete address as well as a telephone number where you can be reached. A writer may send as many queries for one issue as he or she wishes, but each query must have a separate cover letter, outline, bibliography and SASE. Telephone queries are not accepted. Handwritten queries will not be considered. Queries may be submitted at any time, but queries sent well in advance of deadline *may not be answered for several months*. Go-aheads requesting material proposed in queries are usually sent five months prior to publication date. Unused queries will be returned approximately three to four months prior to publication date."

Illustration: Reviews artwork for future assignments.

How to Contact/Illustrators: Illustrations only: Send tearsheets, photocopies. Original work returned upon job's completion (upon written request).

Photography: Wants photos pertaining to any forthcoming themes. Uses b&w/color prints, 35 mm transparencies. To contact, photographers should send unsolicited photos by mail (on speculation).

Terms: Buys all rights for mss and artwork. Pays 10-17¢/word for stories/articles. Pays illustrators $10-125/b&w inside; $20-210/color inside. "Covers are assigned and paid on an individual basis." Photographers paid per photo (range $15-75). Sample copy for $3.95 and SASE with $1.05 postage. Writer's/illustrator's/photo guidelines for SASE.

CAREER WORLD, Curriculum Innovations Group, 60 Revere Dr., Northbrook IL 60062. (708)205-3000. Fax: (708)564-8197. Articles Editor: Carole Rubenstein. Art Director: Kristi Simkins. Monthly (school year) magazine. Estab. 1972. A guide to careers, for students grades 7-12.

Nonfiction: Young adults: education, how-to, interview/profile, career information. Byline given. Sample copies for 9 × 12 SAE and 3 first class stamps.

How to Contact/Writers: Nonfiction: query with published clips.

Illustration: Buys 5-10 illustrations/year. Reviews ms/illustration packages; reviews artwork for future assignments; works on assignment only.

How to Contact/Illustrators: Submit photocopies, resumes.

Terms: Pays on publication. Buys all rights. Sample copies free for 9 × 12 SAE and 3 first class stamps. Writer's guidelines free, but only on assignment.

CAREERS AND COLLEGES, (formerly Careers), E.M. Guild, 1001 Avenue of the Americas, New York NY 10018. (212)354-8877. Editor-in-Chief: June Rogoznica. Senior Editor: Don Rauf. Art Director: Roe LiBretto. Magazine published 4 times during school year (Sept., Nov., Jan., March). Circ. 600,000. This is a magazine for high school juniors and seniors, designed to prepare students for their futures.

Nonfiction: Young adults: how-to, humor, interview/profile, problem solving. Buys 30-40 mss/year. Average word length: 1,000-1,250. Byline given.

How to Contact/Writers: Nonfiction: Query. Reports on queries/mss in 6 weeks. Will consider electronic submissions via disk or modem.

Illustration: Buys 10 illustrations/issue; buys 40 illustrations/year. Will review ms/illustration packages. Works on assignment "mostly."

How to Contact/Illustrators: Ms/illustration packages: Query first. Illustrations only: Send tearsheets, cards. Reports on art samples only if interested. Original artwork returned at job's completion.

Terms: Pays 90 days after publication. Buys first North American serial rights. Pays $250-300 assigned/unsolicited articles. Additional payment for ms/illustration packages "must be negotiated." Pays $500-1,000/color illustration; $300-700 b&w/color (inside) illustration. Sample copy $2.50 with SAE and $1.25 postage; writer's guidelines free with SAE and 1 first-class stamp.

CAT FANCY, The Magazine for Responsible Cat Owners, Fancy Publications, P.O. Box 6050, Mission Viejo CA 92690. (714)855-3045. Articles Editor: Debbie Phillips-Donaldson. Art Director: Gayle McCormick. Monthly magazine. Estab. 1965. Circ. 317,000. "Our magazine is for cat owners who want to know more about how to care for their pets in a responsible manner. We want to see stories and articles showing children relating to or learning about cats in a positive, responsible way. We'd love to see more craft projects for children." 3% of material aimed at juvenile audience.

Fiction: Middle readers: animal (cat). Does not want to see stories in which cats talk. Buys 3-9 mss/year. Average word length: 750-1,000. Byline given.

Nonfiction: Middle readers: animal (cat), arts/crafts (cat-related). Buys 3-9 mss/year. Average word length: 450-1,000. Byline given.

Poetry: Reviews maximum of 64 short-line poems. "No more than 10 poems per submission please."

How To Contact/Writers: Fiction/nonfiction: Send complete ms—query is acceptable too. Reports on queries in 1-2 months; mss in 2-3 months. Average length of time between acceptance and publication of work: 4 months for juvenile material.

Illustration: Buys 3-6 illustrations/year. "Most of our illustrations are assigned or submitted with a story. We look for realistic images of cats done with pen and ink (no pencil)." Will review ms/illustration packages. Reviews artwork for future assignments.

How To Contact/Illustrators: Query first or send complete ms with final art. "Submit photocopies of work; samples of spot art possibilities." Reports in 2-3 months. Originals returned to artist at job's completion. Credit line given.

Photography: "Cats only, in excellent focus and properly lit. Send SASE for photo needs and submit according to them."

Terms: Pays on publication. Buys first North American serial rights. Buys one-time rights for artwork and photos. Pays $20-75/juvenile articles. Pays additional $45-100 for manuscript/illustration packages. $20-50/black and white (inside). Photographers paid per photo (range: $15-150). Sample copies for $4.50. Writer's/artist's guidelines free for #10 SAE and 1 first class stamp.

Tips: "Our 'Kids for Cats' department is most open. Perhaps the most important tip I can give is: Consider what 9 to 11 year olds want to know about cats and what they enjoy most about cats, and address that topic in a style appropriate for them. Writers, keep your writing concise, and don't be afraid to try again after a rejection. Illustrators, we use illustrations mainly as spot art; occasionally we make assignments to illustrators whose spot art we've used before."

CHICKADEE, for Young Children from OWL, Young Naturalist Foundation, 56 The Esplanade, Ste. 306, Toronto Ontario M5E 1A7 Canada. (416)868-6001. Editor: Lizann Flatt. Art Director: Tim Davin. Magazine published 10 times/year. Estab. 1979. Circ: 150,000. *Chickadee* is a "hands-on" publication designed to interest 3-9 year olds in the world and environment around them.

Fiction: Picture material, young readers: adventure, animal, fantasy, folktales, humorous, nature/environment, science fiction, sports. Does not want to see religious, anthropomorphic animal, romance material, material that talks down to kids. Buys 8 mss/year. Average word length: 200-800. Byline given.

Nonfiction: Picture material, young readers: animal, arts/crafts, cooking, games/puzzles, interview/profile, travel. Does not want to see religious material. Buys 2-5 mss/year. Average word length: 20-200. Byline given.

Poetry: Maximum length: 50 lines. Limit submissions to 5 poems.

How to Contact/Writers: Fiction/nonfiction: Send complete ms. SAE and $1 money order for answer to query and return of ms. Report on queries/mss in 2 months. Will consider simultaneous submissions.

Illustration: Buys 3-5 illustrations/issue; buys 40 illustrations/year. Preferred theme or style: realism/humor (but not cartoons). Reviews ms/illustration packages; reviews artwork for future assignments. Works on assignment only.

How to Contact/Illustrators: Ms/illustration packages: Story with sample of art. Illustrations only: Provide promo sheet or tearsheets to be kept on file. Reports on art samples only if interested. Credit line given.

Photography: Looking for animal (mammal, insect, reptile, fish, etc.) photos. Model/property releases required. Uses 35mm and 2¼ × 2¼ transparencies. Write to request photo package for $1 money order, attention Robin Wilner, Photo Researcher.

Terms: Pays on acceptance. Buys all rights for mss and artwork. Buys one-time rights for photos. Pays $25-250 for stories. Pays $500/color (cover) illustration; $100-650/color (inside). Photographers paid per photo (range: $100-350). Sample copy $4.50. Writer's guidelines free.

Tips: "Study the magazine carefully before submitting material. 'Read-to-me selection' most open to freelancers. Uses fiction stories. Kids should be main characters and should be treated with respect." (See listing for *Owl*.)

CHILD LIFE, Children's Better Health Institute, 1100 Waterway Blvd., Indianapolis IN 46202. (317)636-8881. Editor: Stan Zukowski. Art Director: Janet Moir. Magazine published 8 times/year. Estab. 1923. Circ. 80,000. "Adventure, humor, fantasy and health-related stories with an imaginative twist are among those stories we seek. We try to open our readers' minds to their own creative potential, and we want our stories and articles to reflect and encourage this."

Fiction: Middle readers: adventure, animal, contemporary, fantasy, folktales, health, history, humorous, multicultural, nature/environment, problem-solving, science fiction, sports, suspense/mystery. "Health and fitness is an ongoing need." Buys 30-35 mss/year. Average word length: 850. Byline given.

Nonfiction: Middle readers: animal, arts/crafts, biography, careers, cooking, games/puzzles, geography, health, history, hobbies, how-to, humorous, interview/profile, multicultural, nature/environment, problem solving, science, social issues, sports, travel. Average word length: 800. Byline given.

Poetry: Reviews poetry.

How to Contact/Writers: Fiction/nonfiction: Send complete ms. No queries please. Reports on mss in 8-10 weeks. Will not consider previously published material. Will consider simultaneous submissions. "But be professional—if you sell to another mag, let us know!"

Illustration: Buys 8-10 illustrations/issue; buys 65-80 illustrations/year. Preferred theme: "Need realistic styles especially." Reviews ms/illustration packages; reviews artwork for future assignments. Works on assignment only.

How to Contact/Illustrators: Illustrations only: Send query, resume and portfolio. Samples must be accompanied by SASE for response and/or return of samples." Reports on art samples only if interested. Credit line given.

Photography: Purchases photos with accompanying ms only.

Terms: Pays on publication. Writers paid 10-15 cents/word for stories/articles. Buys all rights. Illustrators paid $250/color cover; $30-70/b&w inside; $65-140 color inside. For artwork, buys all rights. Photographers paid per photo (range: $25-30). Buys one-time rights for photographs. Writer's/illustrator's guidelines free with SAE and 1 first class stamp.

Tips: "Writers must be as contemporary as possible in their treatment of modern children's characters. Many stories we receive sound as if they're from the 1950s. Illustrators simply *must* review copies of our magazines—current copies—or they'll not really understand what the individual titles need. Each of our mags is different." Trends include "multiculturalism, definitely. But 'African Americans' are not the only other cultural group in the US. We'd like to see how *all* cultures have influenced our American culture. Encyclopedic approaches are out. Relay pertinent information through the story—fiction or nonfiction. And for heaven's sake, use some dialogue! Let your characters do the talking—not the author."

CHILDREN'S DIGEST, Children's Better Health Institute, Box 567, Indianapolis IN 46206. (317)636-8881. Articles/Fiction Editor: Elizabeth Rinck. Art Director: Lisa Nelson. Magazine published 8 times/year. Estab. 1950. Circ. 125,000. For preteens; approximately 33% of content is health-related.

Fiction: Middle readers: animal, contemporary, fantasy, folktales, health, history, humorous, problem solving, science fiction, sports, suspense/mystery/adventure. Buys 25 mss/year. Average word length: 500-1,500. Byline given.

Nonfiction: Middle readers: animal, arts/crafts, biography, cooking, education, games/puzzles, health, history, how-to, humorous, interview/profile, nature/environment, problem solving, travel, sports. Buys 16-20 mss/year. Average word length: 500-1,200. Byline given.

Poetry: Maximum length: 20-25 lines.

How to Contact/Writers: Fiction/nonfiction: Send complete ms. Reports on mss in 10 weeks.

Illustration: Will review an illustrator's work for possible future assignments. Works on assignment only.

How to Contact/Illustrators: Ms/illustration packages: Query first. Illustrations only: Send résumé and/or slides or tearsheets to illustrate work; query with samples. Reports on art samples in 8-10 weeks.

Photography: Purchases photos with accompanying ms only. Model/property releases and photo captions required. Uses 35mm transparencies.

Terms: Pays on acceptance for illustrators, publication for writers. Buys all rights for mss and artwork; one-time rights for photos. Pays 10¢/word for accepted articles. Pays $225/color (cover) illustration; $24-100/b&w (inside); $60-125/color (inside). Photographers paid per photo (range: $10-75). Sample copy 75¢. Writer's/illustrator's guidelines for SAE and 1 first-class stamp. (See listings for *Children's Playmate, Humpty Dumpty's Magazine, Turtle Magazine* and *US Kids*.)

CHILDREN'S PLAYMATE, Children's Better Health Institute, Box 567, Indianapolis IN 46206. (317)636-8881. Articles/Fiction Editor: Elizabeth Rinck. Art Director: Steve Miller. Magazine published 8 times/year. Estab. 1929. Circ. 135,000. For children between 6 and 8 years; approximately 33% of content is health-related.

Fiction: Young readers: animal, contemporary, fantasy, folktales, history, humorous, science fiction, sports, suspense/mystery/adventure. Buys 25 mss/year. Average word length: 200-700. Byline given.

Nonfiction: Young readers: animal, arts/crafts, biography, cooking, games/puzzles, health, history, how-to, humorous, travel, sports. Buys 16-20 mss/year. Average word length: 200-700. Byline given.

Poetry: Maximum length: 20-25 lines.

How to Contact/Writers: Fiction/nonfiction: Send complete ms. Reports on mss in 8-10 weeks.

Illustration: Will review an illustrator's work for possible future assignments. Works on assignment only.

How to Contact/Illustrators: Ms/illustration packages: Query first. Illustrations only: Query with samples. Reports on art samples in 8-10 weeks.

Photography: Purchases photos with accompanying ms only. Model/property releases and photo captions required. Uses 35mm transparencies. Send completed ms with transparencies.

Terms: Pays on acceptance for illustrators, publication for writers. Buys all rights for mss and artwork; one-time rights for photos. Pays 10¢/word for assigned articles. Pays $225/color (cover) illustration; $25-100/b&w (inside); $60-125/color (inside). Photographers paid per photo (range: $10-75). Sample copy 75¢. Writer's/illustrator's guidelines for SAE and 1 first-class stamp. (See listings for *Children's Digest, Humpty Dumpty's Magazine, Turtle Magazine*.)

CLUBHOUSE, Your Story Hour, P.O. Box 15, Berrien Springs MI 49103. (616)471-3701. Articles/Fiction Editor, Art Director: Elaine Trumbo. Bimonthly magazine. Estab. 1949. Circ. 6,000.

Fiction: Middle readers, young adults: animal, contemporary, health, history, humorous, problem solving, religious, sports. Does not want to see science fiction/fantasy/

Halloween or Santa-oriented fiction. Buys 30 mss/year. Average word length: 800-1,300. Byline given.

Nonfiction: Middle readers, young adults: how-to. "We do not use articles except 200-500 word items about good health: anti—drug, tobacco, alcohol; pro—nutrition." Buys 6 mss/year. Average word length: 200-400. Byline given.

How to Contact/Writers: Fiction/nonfiction: Send complete ms. Reports on queries/mss in 6 weeks. Will consider simultaneous submissions.

Illustration: Buys 20-25 illustrations/issue; buys 120+ illustrations/year. Uses b&w artwork only. Will review artwork for future assignments. Works on assignment only.

How to Contact/Illustrators: Illustrations only: Send photocopies, tearsheets or prints of work to be kept on file. Reports on art samples in 6 weeks. Originals usually not returned at job's completion, but they can be returned if desired.

Terms: Pays "about 6 months after" acceptance for authors, within 2 months for artwork. Buys first and one-time rights for mss and artwork. Pays $25-35 for articles. "Writers and artists receive 2 copies free in addition to payment." Pays $30/b&w (cover) illustration; $7.50-25/b&w (inside). Sample copy for business SAE and 3 first-class stamps; writer's/illustrator's guidelines free for business SAE and 1 first class stamp.

Tips: Writers: "Take children seriously—they're smarter than you think! Respect their sense of dignity, don't talk down to them and don't write stories about 'bad kids.' Illustrators: "Keep it clean, vigorous, fresh—whatever your style. Send samples we can keep on file. Black and white line art is best."

COBBLESTONE, The History Magazine for Young People, Cobblestone Publishing, Inc., 7 School St., Peterborough NH 03458. (603)924-7209. Fax: (603)924-7380. Articles/Fiction Editor-in-Chief: Carolyn P. Yoder. Art Director: Ann C. Webster. Monthly magazine. Circ. 37,000. "*Cobblestone* is theme-related. Writers should request editorial guidelines which explain procedure and list upcoming themes. Queries must relate to an upcoming theme. Fiction is not used often, although a good fiction piece offers welcome diversity. It is recommended that writers become familiar with the magazine (sample copies available)."

Fiction: Middle readers, young adults: history. "Authentic historical and biographical fiction, adventure, retold legends, etc., relating to the theme." Buys 6-10 mss/year. Average word length: 800. Byline given.

Nonfiction: Middle readers, young adults: activities, games/puzzles (no word finds), history, interview/profile, travel. All articles must relate to the issue's theme. Buys 120 mss/year. Average word length: 300-1,000. Byline given.

Poetry: Up to 100 lines. "Clear, objective imagery. Serious and light verse considered." Pays on an individual basis. Must relate to theme.

How to Contact/Writers: Fiction/nonfiction: Query. "A query must consist of all of the following to be considered (please use nonerasable paper): a brief cover letter stating the subject and word length of the proposed article; a detailed one-page outline explaining the information to be presented in the article; an extensive bibliography of materials the author intends to use in preparing the article; a self-addressed stamped envelope. Writers new to *Cobblestone* should send a writing sample with query. If you would like to know if your query has been received, please also include a stamped postcard that requests acknowledgment of receipt. In all correspondence, please include your complete address as well as a telephone number where you can be reached. A writer may send as many queries for one issue as he or she wishes, but each query must have a separate cover letter, outline, bibliography, and SASE. Telephone queries are not accepted. Handwritten queries will not be considered. Queries may be submitted at any time, but queries sent well in advance of deadline *may not be answered for several months*. Go-aheads requesting material proposed in queries are usually sent five months prior to publication date. Unused queries will be returned approximately three to four months prior to publication date."

$\mathcal{P}$ox Stampede

Poems by:
Susan Anderson

The pox! The pox!
I've got the pox!
Behind my knees
Under my socks
Below my feet
Between my toes
Way down my throat
Inside my nose
I've got more pox
than hives have bees
or nests have birds
or forests trees.
This many pox
I do not need.
I'm going to start
a pox stampede.
I'll whistle, wave
my arms and shout:
"Giddup there pox.
We're movin' out!"

Susan D. Anderson, of Saratoga, California, teamed with illustrator Ron Hodgdon, of Talent, Oregon, to make their first sale, $15 each from Clubhouse Magazine. After "Pox Stampede" was published Anderson spoke with a publisher who wants to purchase a collection of her poems that are illustrated by Hodgdon.

Illustration: Buys 3 illustrations/issue; buys 36 illustrations/year. Preferred theme or style: Material that is simple, clear and accurate but not too juvenile. Sophisticated sources are a must. Will review ms/illustration packages; reviews artwork for future assignments; works on assignment only.
How to Contact/Illustrators: Illustrations only: Send photocopies, tearsheets, or other nonreturnable samples. "Illustrators should consult issues of *Cobblestone* to familiarize themselves with our needs." Reports on art samples in 1-2 months. Original artwork returned at job's completion (upon written request).
Photography: Contact Francelle Carapetyan, Picture Editor. Photos must relate to upcoming themes. To submit, send transparencies and/or color/b&w prints. Submit on speculation.
Terms: Pays on publication. Buys all rights to articles and artwork. Pays 10¢/word for assigned articles. Pays $10-125/b&w (inside) illustration; $20-210 for color (inside) illustration. Photographers paid $15-75. Sample copy $3.95 with 7½ × 10½ SAE and 5 first-

class stamps; writer's/illustrator's/photographer's guidelines free with SAE and 1 first-class stamp.

Tips: Writers: "Submit detailed queries which show attention to historical accuracy and which offer interesting and entertaining information. Be true to your own style. Study past issues to know what we look for. All feature articles, recipes, activities, fiction and supplemental nonfiction are freelance contributions." Illustrators: "Submit black and white samples, not too juvenile. Study past issues to know what we look for. The illustration we use is generally for stories, recipes and activities." (See listing for *Faces: The Magazine About People*; *Calliope: The World History Magazine for Young People*; *ODYSSEY: Science That's Out of This World.*)

COCHRAN'S CORNER, Cochran's Publishing Co., Box 2036, Waldorf MD 20604. (301)843-0485. Articles Editor: Ada Cochran. Fiction Editor/Art Director: Debby Thompkins. Quarterly magazine. Estab. 1986. Circ. 1,000. "Our magazine is open to most kinds of writing that is wholesome and suitable for young children to read. It is 52 pages, 8½×11, devoted to short stories, articles and poems. Our children's corner is reserved for children up to the age of 14. **Right now we are forced to limit our acceptance to subscribers only.**" 30% of material aimed at juvenile audience.

Fiction: Picture-oriented material: religious. Young readers: animal, fantasy, humorous, problem solving, religious. Middle readers: religious. Young adults: contemporary, history, religious, romance, science fiction. Does not want to see "anything that contains bad language or violence." Buys 150 mss/year. Average word length: 1,000 words maximum.

Nonfiction: Picture-oriented material: religious, travel. Young readers: animal, how-to, problem solving, religious, travel. Middle readers: religious, travel. Young adults: history, humorous, interview/profile, religious, travel. Does not want to see "editorials or politics." Buys 100 mss/year. Average word length: 150. Byline given.

Poetry: Reviews 20-line poetry on any subject.

How to Contact/Writers: Fiction/nonfiction: Send complete ms. Reports on mss in 3 months. Will consider simultaneous submissions.

Terms: "Payment is one contributor's copy for now, but we hope as we grow to begin paying." Sample copy $5 with 9×11 SASE. Writer's guidelines free for SASE.

Tips: Must subscribe to be published in this market ($12/years, $20/2 years).

CRICKET MAGAZINE, Carus Corporation, P.O. Box 300, Peru IL 61354. (815)224-6656. Articles/Fiction Editor-in-Chief: Marianne Carus. Art Director: Ron McCutchan. Monthly magazine. Estab. 1973. Circ. 100,000. Children's literary magazine for ages 7-14.

Fiction: Young readers, middle readers, and young adult: contemporary, fantasy, folk and fairy tales, history, humorous, science fiction, sports, suspense/mystery/adventure. Buys 180 mss/year. Maximum word length: 1,500. Byline given.

Nonfiction: Environment, history, how-to, biography/interview/profile, natural science, problem solving, science and technology, space, travel. Also arts/crafts, games/puzzles, experiments. Buys 180 mss/year. Average word length: 1,000. Byline given.

Poetry: Reviews 1-page maximum length poems. Prefers 5 or less submissions.

How to Contact/Writers: Send complete ms. Do not query first. Reports on mss in 3 months. Does not like but will consider simultaneous submissions. Please include SASE for return of mss.

Always include a self-addressed stamped envelope (SASE) or International Reply Coupon (IRC) with submissions.

Illustration: Buys 35 (14 separate commissions)/issue; 425 illustrations/year. Uses black and white or 2-color work only. Original artwork returned at job's completion. Preferred theme or style: "strong realism; strong people, especially kids; good action illustration; no cartoons. All media, but prefer other than pencil." Will review ms/illustration packages "but reserves option to re-illustrate."

How to Contact/Illustrators: Ms/illustration packages: complete manuscript with sample and query. Illustrations only: provide tearsheets or good quality photocopies to be kept on file. Please include SASE for return of samples. Reports on art samples in 2 months.

Photography: Purchases photos with accompanying ms only. Model/property releases required. Uses b&w, glossy prints.

Terms: Pays on publication. Buys first publication rights. Buys first publication rights plus promotional rights for artwork. Pays up to 25¢/word for unsolicited articles; up to $3/line for poetry. Pays $500/color cover; $75-150/b&w inside. Writer's/illustrator's guidelines free with SAE and 1 first class stamp.

Tips: Writers: "Read copies of back issues and current issues. Adhere to specified word limits. *Please* do not query." Illustrators: "Edit your samples. Send only your best work and be able to reproduce that quality in assignments. Put name and address on *all* samples. Know a publication before you submit—is your style appropriate?"

CRUSADER, Calvinist Cadet Corps, P.O. Box 7259, Grand Rapids MI 49510. (616)241-5616. Editor: G. Richard Broene. Art Director: Robert DeJonge. Magazine published 7 times/year. Circ. 13,000. "Our magazine is for members of the Calvinist Cadet Corps—boys aged 9-14. Our purpose is to show how God is at work in their lives and in the world around them."

Fiction: Middle readers, young adults: adventure, contemporary, humorous, nature/environment, problem solving, religious, sports, suspense/mystery. Does not want to see fantasy, science fiction. Buys 12 mss/year. Average word length: 800-1,500.

Nonfiction: Middle readers, young adults: animal, arts/crafts, biography, games/puzzles, hobbies, humorous, interview/profile, religious, science, sports. Buys 6 mss/year. Average word length: 400-900.

How to Contact/Writers: Fiction/nonfiction: Send complete ms. Reports on queries/mss in 3-5 weeks. Will consider simultaneous submissions.

Illustration: Buys 1 illustration/issue; buys 6 illustrations/year. Works on assignment only. Credit line given.

Terms: Pays on acceptance. Buys first North American serial rights; first rights; one-time rights; reprint rights. Pays 2-5¢/word for stories/articles. Sample copy free with 9×12 SAE and 3 first-class stamps.

Tips: Publication is most open to fiction: write for a list of themes (available yearly in January).

CURRENT HEALTH I, The Beginning Guide to Health Education, 60 Revere Dr., Northbrook IL 60062-1563. (708)205-3000. Monthly (during school year Sept.-May) magazine. "For classroom use by students, this magazine is curriculum specific and requires experienced educators who can write clearly and well at fifth grade reading level."

Nonfiction: Middle readers: nature/environment, problem solving, health. Buys 60-70 mss/year. Average word length: 1,000. "Credit given in staff box."

How to Contact/Writers: Nonfiction: Query with published clips and résumé. Publishes ms 6-7 months after acceptance.

Terms: Pays on publication. Buys all rights. Pays $100-150. ("More for longer features.") Writer's guidelines available only if writer is given an assignment.

Tips: Needs material about drug education, nutrition, fitness and exercise.

Close-up

Ron McCutchan
Art Director
Ladybug/Cricket Magazines
Peru, Illinois

This is the "golden moment" of children's literature, says Ron McCutchan, art director for both *Ladybug* and *Cricket* magazines. New publications are springing to life quickly, and art directors are experimenting with a variety of styles and media. This abundance of opportunity attracts thousands of artists vying for freelance assignments, so getting noticed takes more than luck and artistic skill. According to McCutchan—a man whose advice is as straightforward as his personality—you need to do your homework, approach art directors with a professional portfolio that showcases a variety of talents, be able to handle several subjects well, and provide memorable samples that can be kept on file.

McCutchan's office is crowded with file drawers stuffed with queries from illustrators, so he knows the market well. Yet given the plethora of mail he receives, he has little difficulty pinpointing artists suited for his magazines. He quickly rules out many would-be freelancers because their work is inappropriate for his publications. Before sending a query (consisting of a letter and samples), he advises all illustrators to be familiar with his and other magazines. "The worst thing you can do is send in material blind," he says. Instead, pick up a copy of the magazine on the newsstand or request a sample from the publisher. Then, page through it carefully, noting which kinds of work the art director prefers and the age group toward which the magazine is geared. Sending material to a publication that doesn't publish your type of art is a waste of everyone's time, and your money.

A designer and student of medieval history who made his way into magazine publishing via the sales department at Times Books, McCutchan seeks artists adept at "creating life on the page." He chooses freelance illustrators largely by the breadth of work they are capable of producing. He prefers to view portfolios that showcase a variety of media and styles, as long as each piece is well executed. Why? "Ideally, I'd like to send someone at least six assignments a year." McCutchan says. If he knows an illustrator is capable of more than just say, charcoal animal drawings, McCutchan can give the artist a variety of assignments. McCutchan accepts and assigns work in almost any medium, from watercolor (popular with editors), acrylic and scratchboard, to pencil (of which there is currently an abundance).

Still, some genres of children's art are absolutely essential, and should be included in every portfolio. Animals and people of all ethnic groups are universal elements in children's publications. Yet McCutchan also recommends that illustrators be skilled in developing scenes from a story. Whether in a direct-mail submission or in a portfolio, demonstrate that you can take a character from place to place in several scenes (include dummies or photocopies if necessary).

Perhaps due to his liberal arts training at the University of Illinois, but largely because of the broad subject range of his magazines, McCutchan also likes to see historical renderings. He advises illustrators to "get out of contemporary America." Include in your portfolio a scene from ancient Rome, for example. He wants to see evidence that an illustrator is "well-rounded," can think creatively and research a subject thoroughly.

McCutchan's final word of advice to illustrators is simple: although the recent boom in children's literature provides a market rich with opportunity, remember that budgets are forever shrinking. To make yourself and your work as attractive as possible, be sure that your query package is professional, but don't get too fancy, he warns. "If you go overboard, I might ask 'Can I afford you?' Let your work stand on its own." In your initial mailing, include only 8½ × 11-inch samples or slides of your artwork that can easily fit in a file drawer. And be sure to send a SASE if you want your work returned.

Be smart and leave an art director not only with a sense of your personality and ability, but with something memorable to keep. A clear, modest photocopy (clearly labeled with your name, address and telephone number) can tell as much about you as a slick, oversized promotional brochure, McCutchan stresses. The difference is, the latter item is less intimidating to an art director with a budget, easy to store and easy to find. In a market deluged with capable illustrators, these seemingly small details can make a huge difference.

—*Jennifer Hogan-Redmond*

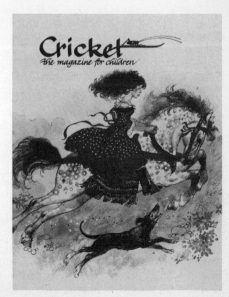

As art director for Cricket and Ladybug magazines, Ron McCutchan searches for artists who are adept at "creating life on the page." He prefers illustrators who can produce diverse subjects using a variety of media.

CURRENT HEALTH II, The Continuing Guide to Health Education, 60 Revere Dr., Northbrook IL 60062-1563. (708)205-3000. Monthly (during school year Sept.-May). "For classroom use by students, this magazine is curriculum specific and requires experienced educators who can write clearly and well at a ninth grade reading level."
Nonfiction: Young adults/teens: nature/environment, problem-solving, sports, health. Buys 70-90 mss/year. Average word length: 1,000-2,500. Byline given.
How to Contact/Writers: Nonfiction: Query with published clips and résumé. Reports on queries in 2 months. Publishes ms 6-7 months after acceptance.
Terms: Pays on publication. Buys all rights. Pays $100-150 for assigned articles, more for longer features. Writer's guidelines available only if writers are given an assignment.
Tips: Needs articles on drug education, nutrition, fitness and exercise.

DAY CARE AND EARLY EDUCATION, 351 Pleasant St., Suite 330, Northampton MA 01060. Articles/Fiction Editor: Randa Nachbar. Art Director: Bill Jobson. Quarterly magazine. Circ. 2,500. Magazine uses material "involving children from birth to age 7." 5% of material aimed at juvenile audience.
Fiction: Picture material, young readers: contemporary, fantasy, humorous, problem solving. Average word length: 1,000-3,000. Byline given.
Nonfiction: Picture material, young readers: animal, how-to, humorous, problem solving. Average word length: 1,000-3,000. Byline given.
How to Contact/Writers: Fiction/nonfiction: Send complete ms. Reports on queries in 1 month; mss in 2-3 months.
Illustration: Will review ms/illustration packages.
How to Contact/Illustrators: Ms/illustration packages: Send complete ms with final art. Reports on art samples only if interested. Original artwork returned at job's completion.
Terms: Pays in 2 copies. Free sample copy; free writer's guidelines.

DISCOVERIES, Children's Ministries, 6401 The Paseo, Kansas City MO 64131. (816)333-7000. Editor: Latta Jo Knapp. Executive Editor: Mark York. Weekly tabloid. *Discoveries* is a leisure reading piece for third and fourth graders. It is published weekly by the Department of Children's Ministries of the Church of the Nazarene. "The major purposes of *Discoveries* are to: provide a leisure reading piece which will build Christian behavior and values; provide reinforcement for Biblical concepts taught in the Sunday School curriculum. The focus of the reinforcement will be life-related, with some historical appreciation. *Discoveries*' target audience is children ages 8-10 in grades three and four. The readability goal is third to fourth grade."
Fiction: Young readers, middle readers: adventure, contemporary, problem-solving, religious. "Fiction — stories should vividly portray definite Christian emphasis or character-building values, without being preachy. The setting, plot and action should be realistic." Average word length: 500-700. Byline given.
How to Contact/Writers: Fiction: Send complete ms. Reports on mss in 6-8 weeks.
Illustration: "*Discoveries* publishes a wide variety of artistic styles, i.e. cartoon, realistic, montage, etc., but whatever the style, artwork must appeal to 8-10 year old children. It should not simply be child-related from an adult viewpoint. All artwork for *Discoveries* is assigned on a work for hire basis. Samples of art may be sent for review.
How to Contact/Illustrators: Illustrations only: send resume, portfolio, client list, tearsheets. Reports back only if interested. Credit line given.
Terms: Pays "approximately one year before the date of issue." Buys multi-use rights. Pays 5¢/word. Pays illustrators $75/color (cover). Contributor receives 4 complimentary copies of publication. Writer's/artist's guidelines free with #10 SAE.
Tips: "*Discoveries* is committed to reinforcement of the Biblical concepts taught in the Sunday School curriculum. Because of this, the themes needed are mainly as follows: faith in God, obedience to God, putting God first, choosing to please God, accepting

Jesus as Savior, finding God's will, choosing to do right, trusting God in hard times, prayer; trusting God to answer, Importance of Bible memorization, appreciation of Bible as God's Word to man, Christians working together, showing kindness to others, witnessing." (See listing for *Power and Light*.)

DISNEY ADVENTURES, The Walt Disney Company, 500 S. Buena Vista St., Burbank CA 91521. (818)973-4333. Associate Editor: Sarah Gallop. Monthly magazine. Estab. 1990. Circ. 350,000.
Fiction: Middle readers: adventure, contemporary, fantasy, humorous, science fiction, sports, suspense/mystery. Buys approx. 6-10 mss/year. Averge word length: 1,500-2,000. Byline given.
Nonfiction: Middle readers: animal, biography, games/puzzles, interview/profile, nature/environment and sports. Buys 100-150 mss/year. Average word length: 250-750. Byline given.
How to Contact/Writers: Fiction: Send complete manuscript. Nonfiction: Query with published clips. Reports in 1 month. Publishes ms 6-12 months after acceptance. Will consider simultaneous submissions and electronic submissions via disk or modem.
Illustration: Buys approx. 20 illustrations/issue; 250 illustrations/year. Reviews ms/illustration packages; reviews artwork for future assignments; works on assignment only.
How to Contact/Illustrators: Illustrations only: Provide resume, business card, promotional literature or tearsheets to be kept on file. Reports only if interested. Does not return original artwork.
Photography: Purchases photos separately. Model/property releases and captions required. Send "anything but originals—everything sent is kept on file." To contact, photographers should provide resume, business card, promotional literature or tearsheets to be kept on file. Reports only if interested.
Terms: Pays on acceptance. Buys all rights. Purchases all rights for artwork, various rights for photographs. Pays $250-750 for assigned articles. Pays illustrators $50 and up. Photographers paid $100 minimum per project, or $25 minimum per photo. Sample copies: "Buy on newsstand or order copies by calling 1-800-435-0715." Writer's guidelines for SASE.

DOLPHIN LOG, The Cousteau Society, 8440 Santa Monica Blvd., Los Angeles CA 90069. (213)656-4422. Editor: Beth Kneeland. Bimonthly magazine for children ages 7-15. Circ. 80,000. Entirely nonfiction subject matter encompasses all areas of science, natural history, marine biology, ecology, and the environment as they relate to our global water system. The philosophy of the magazine is to delight, instruct and instill an environmental ethic and understanding of the interconnectedness of living organisms, including people. Of special interest are articles on ocean- or water-related themes which develop reading and comprehension skills.
Nonfiction: Middle readers, young adult: animal, environmental, geography, nature/environment, science, ocean. Does not want to see talking animals. No dark or religious themes. "Writers continue to send us fiction. We do not publish fiction." Buys 10 mss/year. Average word length: 500-700. Byline given.
How to Contact/Writers: Do not send fiction. For nonfiction articles, query first. Reports on queries in 1 month; mss in 2 months.

Illustration: Buys 1 illustration/issue; buys 6 illustrations/year. Preferred theme or style: Biological illustration. Will review artwork for future assignments.

How to Contact/Illustrators: Illustrations only: Send promo sheet, slides. Reports on art samples in 8 weeks only if interested. Credit line given to illustrators.

Photography: Wants "sharp, colorful pictures of sea creatures. The more unusual the creature, the better."

Terms: Pays on publication. Buys first North American serial rights; reprint rights. Pays $25-150 for articles. Pays $25-200/color photos. Sample copy $2 with 9×12 SAE and 3 first class stamps. Writer's/illustrator's guidelines free with #10 SAE and 1 first class stamp.

Tips: Writers: "Write simply and clearly and don't anthropomorphize." Illustrators: "Be scientifically accurate and don't anthropomorphize. Some background in biology is helpful, as our needs range from simple line drawings to scientific illustrations which must be researched for biological and technical accuracy."

DYNAMATH, Scholastic Inc., 730 Broadway, New York NY 10003. (212)505-3000. Fiction Editor: Jackie Glasthal. Monthly magazine. Estab. 1981. Circ. 300,000. Purpose is "to make learning math fun, challenging and uncomplicated for young minds in a very complex world."

Fiction/nonfiction: All levels: anything related to math and science topics. Byline given sometimes.

How To Contact/Writers: Fiction/nonfiction: Query with published clips, send manuscript. Reports on queries in 6 weeks. Average length of time between acceptance and publication of work: 4 months. Will consider simultaneous submissions.

Illustration: Buys 4 illustrations/issue. Reviews ms/illustration packages.

How To Contact/Illustrators: Query first. Reports back in 2 months on submissions. Originals returned to artist at job's completion.

Terms: Pays on acceptance. Buys first North American serial rights.

*EQUILIBRIUM[10], Everyone's Entertainment, Eagle Publishing Productions, Box 162, Golden CO 80401. President: Gary Eagle. Quarterly magazine. Circ. 10,000. Material on or relating to balance is best. Material on antonyms (opposites) is even better but not required. 10% of material aimed at juvenile audience.

Fiction: Young readers, young adults: animal, contemporary, fantasy, history, humor, problem solving, religion, romance, science fiction, sports, spy/mystery/adventure. Buys 40 mss/year. Average word length: 500-2,000. Byline given sometimes.

Nonfiction: Middle readers, young adults: animal, history, how-to, humor, interview/profile, problem solving, religion, travel. Buys 60 mss/year. Average word length: 500-2,000. Byline given sometimes.

How to Contact/Writers: Fiction/nonfiction: Query first. SASE for answer to query. Reports on queries in 8 weeks; mss in 16 weeks. Will consider simultaneous, photocopied, computer printout and electronic submissions via disk (3.5 inch) or modem.

Illustration: Buys 10 illustrations/issue; buys 150 illustrations/year. Will review ms/illustration packages by authors/artists; ms/illustration packages submitted by authors with illustrations done by separate artists for a fee; illustrator's work for possible use with fiction/nonfiction articles. Works on assignment only.

How to Contact/Illustrators: Ms/illustration packages: Query first, (quick summary of ms) and final art included, captions too. Illustrations only: Send tearsheets, photographed, copied pieces. Reports on art samples in 3 months. Original artwork returned at job's completion.

Terms: Pays on publication. Buys second serial (reprint rights). Pays $50-100 for assigned/unsolicited articles (shorts). "Contributor copies are free with signed contract." Additional payment for ms/illustration packages within the $50-100 range; "photos help pay range." Pays $50-200/b&w (cover) illustration; $100-200/color (cover); $25/b&w

(inside); $50/color (inside). Sample copy free with 9×14 SAE and 5 first-class stamps. Writer's/illustrator's guidelines free with #10 SAE and 2 first-class stamps. "For serious inquiries, we offer a special package as an investment on your behalf. Besides author's guidelines, you'll receive: *Equilibrium* [10] Magazine; Generic Word Search; the Pyramid Edition (mini-newspaper); variety of pamphlets; business opportunities at our company; and any other future publications for $15. We will critique your work and query for $5."
Tips: Writers: "Be specific in your query as to why readers would enjoy your material. If on balance, state so. If on antonyms, state them. Shorter the better. Enter the Cheapstakes Sweepstakes Contest. Query with SASE."

EXPLORING, Boy Scouts of America, P.O. Box 152079, 1325 W. Walnut Hill Ln., Irving TX 75015-2079. (214)580-2365. Executive Editor: Scott Daniels. Art Director: Joe Connally. Photo Editor: Brian Payne. Magazine published "4 times a year—not quarterly." *Exploring* is a 12-page, 4-color magazine published for members of the Boy Scouts of America's Exploring program. These members are young men and women between the ages of 14-21. Interests include careers, computers, life skills (money management, parent/peer relationships, study habits), college, camping, hiking, canoeing.
Nonfiction: Young adults: interview/profile, problem solving, travel. Buys 12 mss/year. Average word length: 600-1,200. Byline given.
How to Contact/Writers: Nonfiction: Query with published clips. Reports on queries/mss in 1 week.
Illustration: Buys 3 illustrations/issue; buys 12 illustrations/year. Will review artwork for future assignments. Works on assignment only.
How to Contact/Illustrators: Reports on art samples in 2 weeks. Original artwork returned at job's completion.
Terms: Pays on acceptance. Buys first North American serial rights. Pays $300-500 for assigned/unsolicited articles. Pays $1,000/color (cover); $250-500/b&w (inside); $500-800/color (inside). Sample copy with 8½×11 SAE and 5 first-class stamps. Free writer's/illustrator's guidelines.
Tips: Looks for "short, crisp career profiles of 1,000 words with plenty of information to break out into graphics."

FACES, The Magazine About People, Cobblestone Publishing, Inc., 7 School St., Peterborough NH 03458. (603)924-7209. Fax: (603)924-7380. Editor-in-Chief: Carolyn P. Yoder. Art Director: Ann C. Webster. Photo Editor: Francelle Carapetyan. Magazine published 9 times/year (Sept.-May). Circ. 13,000. "Although *Faces* operates on a by-assignment basis, we welcome ideas/suggestions in outline form. All manuscripts are reviewed by the American Museum of Natural History in New York before being accepted. *Faces* is a theme-related magazine; writers should send for theme list before submitting ideas/queries."
Fiction: Middle readers, young adults: contemporary, folktales, history, multicultural, religious, anthropology. Does not want to see material that does not relate to a specific upcoming theme. Buys 9 mss/year. Maximum word length: 800. Byline given.
Nonfiction: Middle readers, young adults: arts/crafts, games/puzzles, history, interview/profile, religious, travel, anthropology. Does not want to see material not related to a specific upcoming theme. Buys 63 mss/year. Average word length: 300-800. Byline given.
How to Contact/Writers: Fiction/nonfiction: Query with published clips and 2-3 line biographical sketch. "Ideas should be submitted six to nine months prior to the publication date. Responses to ideas are usually sent approximately four months before the publication date."
Illustration: Buys 3 illustrations/issue; buys 27 illustrations/year. Preferred theme or style: Material that is meticulously researched (most articles are written by professional anthropologists); simple, direct style preferred, but not too juvenile. Reviews ms/illustration packages; reviews artwork for future assignments; works on assignment only.

How to Contact/Illustrators: Ms/illustration packages: Illustration is done by assignment. Roughs required. Illustrations only: Send samples of b&w work. "Illustrators should consult issues of *Faces* to familiarize themselves with our needs." Reports on art samples in 1-2 months. Original artwork returned at job's completion (upon written request).

Photography: Wants photos relating to forthcoming themes.

Terms: Pays on publication. Buys all rights for mss and artwork. Pays 10¢/word for assigned articles. Pays $10-125/b&w (inside) illustration. Covers are assigned and paid on an individual basis. Pays photographers $15-75/photo. Sample copy $3.95 with 7½×10½ SAE and 5 first-class stamps. Writer's/illustrator's/photo guidelines free with SAE and 1 first-class stamp.

Tips: "Writers are encouraged to study past issues of the magazine to become familiar with our style and content. Writers with anthropological and/or travel experience are particularly encouraged; *Faces* is about world cultures. All feature articles, recipes and activities are freelance contributions." Illustrators: "Submit black and white samples, not too juvenile. Study past issues to know what we look for. The illustration we use is generally for retold legends, recipes and activities." (See listing for *Cobblestone: The History Magazine for Young People*; *Calliope: The World History Magazine for Young People*; *ODYSSEY: Science That's Out of This World*.)

FAITH 'N STUFF, The Magazine For Kids, Guideposts Associates, Inc., 747 Third Ave., New York NY 10017. Editor: Mary Lou Carney. Articles Editor: Wally Metts. Fiction Editor: Lurlene McDaniel. Art Director: Mike Lyons. Photo Editor: Matt Russell. Bimonthly magazine. Estab. 1990. Circ. 120,000. "*Faith 'n Stuff: The Magazine for Kids* is published bimonthly by Guideposts Associates, Inc. for kids 7-12 years old (emphasis on upper end of that age bracket). It is a Bible-based, direct mail magazine that is *fun* to read. It is *not* a Sunday school take-home paper or a miniature *Guideposts*."

Fiction: Middle readers: adventure, animal, contemporary, fantasy, humorous, problem-solving, religious, science fiction, sports, suspense/mystery. Does not want to see preachy fiction. "We want real stories about real kids doing real things—conflicts our readers will respect; resolutions our readers will accept. Problematic. Tight. Filled with realistic dialogue and sharp imagery. No stories about 'good' children always making the right decision. If present at all, adults are minor characters and *do not* solve kids' problems for them." Buys approx. 10 mss/year. Average word length: 500-1,500. Byline given.

Nonfiction: Middle readers: animal, interview/profile. "Make nonfiction issue-oriented, controversial, thought-provoking. Something kids not only *need* to know, but *want* to know as well." Buys 10 mss/year. Average word length: 200-700. Bylines sometimes given.

How to Contact/Writers: Fiction: Send complete ms. Nonfiction: Query. Reports on queries in 6 weeks; on ms in 2 months.

How to Contact/Illustrators: Send promo sheet. Reports back only if interested. Credit line given.

Terms: Pays on acceptance. Buys all rights for mss. "Features range in payment from $150-350; fiction from $150-250. We pay higher rates for stories exceptionally well-written or well-researched. Regular contributors get bigger bucks, too." Additional payment for ms/illustration packages "but we prefer to acquire our own illustrations." Sample copies are $3.25. Writer's guidelines free for SASE.

Tips: "Make your manuscript good, relevant and playful. No preachy stories about Bible-toting children. *Faith 'n Stuff* is not a beginner's market. Study our magazine. (Sure, you've heard that before—but it's *necessary*!) Neatness *does* count. So do creativity and professionalism. SASE essential."

FFA NEW HORIZONS, The Official Magazine of the National FFA Organization, 5632 Mt. Vernon Memorial Hwy., Alexandria VA 22309. (703)360-3600. Fax: (703)360-5524. Articles Editor: Andrew Markwart. Bimonthly magazine. Estab. 1952. Circ. 400,000. "*FFA New Horizons* strives to strengthen the aims and purposes of FFA by bringing to our readers living examples of how these are being fulfilled daily by individual FFA members."
Nonfiction: Young adults: animal, biography, careers, education, health, hobbies, how-to, humorous, interview/profile, nature/environment, problem-solving, sports. "All stories must be directed toward teens and have an FFA connection. Does not want to see stories that have no FFA connection at all." Average word length: 600-1,000.
How to Contact/Writers: Nonfiction: Query with published clips. Send complete ms. Reports on queries/mss in 1 month. Publishes ms 2-4 months after acceptance. Will consider simultaneous submissions and electronic submissions via disk or modem.
Illustration: Buys 6 illustrations/year. Reviews ms/illustration packages; reviews artwork for future assignments; works on assignment only.
How to Contact/Illustrators: Ms/illustration packages: Query. Illustrations only: Query with samples. Reports in 1 month. Original work not returned upon job's completion.
Photography: Looking for "photos that show the FFA member and illustrate the story." Uses 5×7 color and b&w prints; 35mm transparencies. Reports in 1 month.
Terms: Pays on acceptance. Buys all rights for mss, artwork and photographs. Pay varies. Photographers paid per photo. Sample copies for 9×12 SAE and 5 first class stamps. Writer's/illustrator's/photo guidelines for SASE.

*FOR SENIORS ONLY, Campus Communications, Inc., 339 N. Main St., New City NY 10956. (914)638-0333. Articles/Fiction Editor: Judi Oliff. Art Director: Randi Wendelkin. Semiannual magazine. Estab. 1971. Circ. 350,000. Publishes career-oriented articles for high school students; college-related articles, and feature articles on travel, etc.
Fiction: Young Adults: health, humorous, sports, travel. Byline given.
Nonfiction: Young adults: careers, games/puzzles, health, how-to, humorous, interview/profile, social issues, sports, travel. Buys 4-6 mss/year. Average word length: 1,000-2,500. Byline given.
How to Contact/Writers: Fiction/nonfiction: Query; query with published clips; send complete ms. Publishes ms 2-4 months after acceptance. Will consider simultaneous submissions, electronic submissions via disk or modem and previously published work.
Illustration: Reviews ms/illustration packages; reviews artwork for future assignments.
How to Contact/Illustrators: Ms/illustration packages: Query; submit complete package with final art; submit ms with rough sketches. Illustrations only: Query; send slides. Reports back only if interested. Samples not returned; samples kept on file. Original work returned upon job's completion. Credit line given.
Photography: Model/property release required. Uses $5\frac{1}{2} \times 8\frac{1}{2}$ and $4\frac{7}{8} \times 7\frac{3}{8}$ color prints; 35mm and 8×10 transparencies. To contact, photographers should query with samples; send unsolicited photos by mail. Reports back only if interested.
Terms: Pays on publication. Buys exclusive magazine rights. Payment is byline credit. Writer's/illustrator's/photo guidelines for SASE.

THE FRIEND MAGAZINE, The Church of Jesus Christ of Latter-day Saints, 50 E. North Temple, Salt Lake City UT 84150. (801)240-2210. Managing Editor: Vivian Paulsen. Art Director: Richard Brown. Monthly magazine. Estab. 1971. Circ. 250,000. Magazine for 3-11 year olds.
Fiction: Picture material, young readers, middle readers: adventure, animal, contemporary, folktales, history, humorous, problem-solving, religious, ethnic, sports, suspense/mystery. Does not want to see controversial issues, political, horror, fantasy. Average word length: 400-1,000. Byline given.

Nonfiction: Picture material, young readers, middle readers: animal, arts/crafts, biography, cooking, games/puzzles, history, how-to, humorous, problem-solving, religious, sports. Does not want to see controversial issues, political, horror, fantasy. Average word length: 400-1,000. Byline given.
Poetry: Reviews poetry. Maximum line length: 20.
How to Contact/Writers: Fiction/nonfiction: Send complete ms. Reports on mss in 2 months.
How to Contact/Illustrators: Illustrators only: Query with samples; arrange personal interview to show portfolio; provide résumé and tearsheets for files.
Terms: Pays on acceptance. Buys all rights for mss. Pays 9-11¢/word for unsolicited articles. Contributors are encouraged to send for free sample copy with 9 × 11 envelope and 85¢ postage. Free writer's guidelines.
Tips: "The *Friend* is published by The Church of Jesus Christ of Latter-day Saints for boys and girls up to twelve years of age. All submissions are carefully read by the *Friend* staff, and those not accepted are returned within two months when a self-addressed stamped envelope is enclosed. Submit seasonal material at least eight months in advance. Query letters and simultaneous submissions are not encouraged. Authors may request rights to have their work reprinted after their manuscript is published."

*THE FUN ZONE, Highlights for Children, 803 Church St., Honesdale PA 18431. (717)253-1080. Editor: Jeff O'Hare. Monthly magazine. Estab. 1992. Circ. 350,000. The Fun Zone is a puzzle-oriented magazine for kids 6-13. "We feature sophisticated puzzles, engaging and exciting art, and a cast of interesting characters."
Nonfiction: "We are *puzzle* based. We will look at any type of article with a puzzle tie-in." Buys 15-20 mss/year; 3,000 puzzles/year. Word length: 375-500. No byline given.
How to Contact/Writers: Nonfiction: Send complete ms. Reports on queries/mss in 1 month. Will consider simultaneous submissions.
Illustration: Buys 45-55 illustrations/issue; 550 illustrations/year. Prefers humorous thru realistic/ink, watercolor, paint/any size (page size 8⅜ × 10⅞). Reviews ms/illustration packages; reviews artwork for future assignments.
How to Contact/Illustrators: Ms/illustration packages: Query. Illustrations only: Query; send promo sheet, client list, tearsheets. Reports back only if interested. Samples not returned; samples kept on file. Original work not returned upon job's completion. Credit line sometimes given.
Photography: Looking for puzzle photos. Model/property releases required. To contact, photographers should query with samples; send unsolicited photos by mail. Reports in 1 month.
Terms: Pays on acceptance. Buys all rights for artwork/photographs. Additional payment for ms/illustration packages. Sample copy free for 8½ × 11 SAE and 10 first class stamps. Writer's guidelines free for SASE.

THE GOLDFINCH, Iowa History for Young People, State Historical Society of Iowa, 402 Iowa Ave., Iowa City IA 52240. (319)354-3916. Fax: (319)335-3924. Editor: Deborah Gore Ohrn. Quarterly magazine. Estab. 1980. Circ. 2,500. "The award-winning *Goldfinch* consists of 10 to 12 nonfiction articles, short fiction, poetry and activities per issue. Each magazine focuses on an aspect or theme of history that occurred in or affected Iowa."
Fiction: Middle readers: adventure, animal, folktales, history. Fiction only on spec. Buys approx. 4 mss/year. Average word length: 500-1,500. Byline given.
Nonfiction: Middle readers: arts/crafts, biography, games/puzzles, history, how-to, interview/profile, travel. Uses 20-30 mss/year. Average word length: 500-1,500. Byline given.
Poetry: Reviews poetry. No minimum or maximum word length; no maximum number of submissions.

How to Contact/Writers: Fiction/nonfiction: Query with published clips. Reports on queries/mss in 2-4 weeks. Publishes ms 1 month-1 year after acceptance. Will consider electronic submissions via disk or modem.
Illustration: Buys 4 illustrations/issue; 20 illustrations/year. Uses b&w artwork only. Prefers cartoon, line drawing. Reviews ms/illustration packages; reviews artwork for future assignments; works on assignment only.
How to Contact/Illustrators: Ms/illustration packages: Query. Illustrations only: Query with samples. Reports in 2-4 weeks. Original work returned upon job's completion.
Photography: Types of photos used vary with subject. Model/property releases required with submissions. Uses b&w prints; 35mm transparencies. Query with samples. Reports in 2-4 weeks.
Terms: Pays on acceptance (artwork only). Buys all rights. Payment for manuscripts is in copies at this time. Pays illustrators $10-150. Photographers paid per photo (range: $10-100). Sample copies are $3. Writer's/illustrator's/photo guidelines free for SASE.
Tips: "The editor researches the topic and determines the articles. Writers, most of whom live in Iowa, work from primary and secondary research materials to write pieces. The presentation is aimed at children 8-14 and the writing of E.B. White is a model for the prose."

GUIDE MAGAZINE, Review and Herald Publishing Association, 55 West Oak Ridge Dr., Hagerstown MD 21740. (301)791-7000. Articles Editor: Jeannette Johnson. Art Director: Bill Kirstein. Weekly magazine. Estab. 1953. Circ. 40,000. "Ours is a weekly Christian journal written for 10- to 14-year-olds, presenting true stories relevant to the needs of today's young person, emphasizing positive aspects of Christian living."
Fiction: Middle readers, young adults: adventure, animal, contemporary, history, humorous, nature/environment, problem solving, religious, sports, suspense/mystery, character-building. "We like 'true-to-life,' that is, based on true happenings." No violence.
Nonfiction: Middle readers, young adults: animal, games/puzzles, history, how-to, humorous, nature/environment, problem solving, religious, social issues, sports, character-building. Does not want to see violence, hunting. Buys 300+ mss/year. Average word length: 500-600 minimum, 1,000-1,200 maximum. Byline given.
How to Contact/Writers: Nonfiction: Send complete ms. Reports in 1-2 weeks. Will consider simultaneous submissions. "We can only pay half of the regular amount for simultaneous submissions." Reports on queries/mss in 1 week.
Illustration: Buys 4-6 illustrations/issue; buys 350+ illustrations/year. Reviews artwork for future assignments. Works on assignment only.
How to Contact/Illustrators: Ms/illustration packages: "Art is by assignment only. Glad to look at portfolios." Illustrations only: Send tearsheets. Reports back only if interested. Original artwork returned at job's completion. Credit line given
Photography: Purchases photos by assignment only.
Terms: Pays on acceptance. Buys first North American serial rights; first rights; onetime rights; second serial (reprint rights); simultaneous rights. Pays 3-4¢/word for stories and articles. "Writer receives several complimentary copies of issue in which work appears." Pays $150-250/b&w (cover) illustration; $175-300/color (cover); $125-175/b&w (inside); 150-175/color (inside). Sample copy free with 5×9 SAE and 2 first-class stamps; writer's/illustrator's guidelines for SASE.

HICALL, Gospel Publishing House, 1445 Boonville Ave., Springfield MO 65802-1894. (417)862-2781, ext. 4349. Articles/Fiction Editor: Deanna Harris. Art Director: Richard Harmon. Quarterly newsletter (Sunday school take-home paper). Estab. 1920. Circ. 80,000. "Slant articles toward the 15- to 17-year-old teen. We are a Christian publication, so all articles should focus on the Christian's responses to life. Fiction should be realistic, not syrupy nor too graphic. Fiction should have a Christian slant also."

Fiction: Young adults: adventure, contemporary, fantasy, history, humorous, problem-solving, religious, romance, sports. Also wants fiction based on true stories. Buys 100 mss/year. Average word length 1,000-1,500. Byline given.

Nonfiction: Young adults: animal, biography, careers, education, games/puzzles, health, history, hobbies, how-to, humorous, nature/environment, problem solving, religious, sports. Buys 25 mss/year. Average word length: 1,000. Byline given.

Poetry: Reviews 20-line poetry. Limit submissions to 5 poems.

How to Contact/Writers: Fiction/nonfiction: Send complete ms. Do *not* send query letters. Reports on mss in 4-6 weeks. Will consider simultaneous submissions.

Illustration: Buys 10-30 illustrations/year. Uses color artwork only. "Freelance art used only when in-house art department has a work overload." Prefers to review "realistic, cartoon, youth-oriented styles." Will review artwork for future assignments. Works on assignment only. "Any art sent will be referred to the art department. Art department will assign freelance art."

How to Contact/Illustrators: Illustrations only: Query with samples; send "tearsheets, slides, photos. Résumé helpful." Reports in 4-6 weeks.

Photography: "Teen photos that look spontaneous. Ethnic and urban photos urgently needed." Uses color prints, 35mm, 2¼×2¼, 4×5 transparencies. To contact, send unsolicited photos by mail.

Terms: Pays on acceptance. For mss, buys first North American serial rights, first rights, one-time rights, second serial (reprint rights), simultaneous rights. For artwork, buys one-time rights for cartoons, all rights for assigned illustrations; one-time rights for photos. Pays 2-4¢/word for articles. Pays $35/b&w cover photo; $50/color cover photo; $25/b&w inside photo; $35/color inside photo. Sample copy free with 6×9 SASE. Writer's guidelines free with SASE.

HIGH ADVENTURE, Assemblies of God, 1445 Boonville Ave., Springfield MO 65802. (417)862-2781, Ext. 4181. Fax: (417)862-8558. Editor: Marshall Bruner. Quarterly magazine. Circ. 86,000. Estab. 1971. Magazine is designed to provide boys with worthwhile, enjoyable, leisure reading; to challenge them in narrative form to higher ideals and greater spiritual dedication; and to perpetuate the spirit of Royal Rangers through stories, ideas and illustrations. 75% of material aimed at juvenile audience.

Fiction: Buys 100 mss/year. Average word length: 1,000. Byline given.

Nonfiction: Articles: Christian living, devotional, Holy Spirit, salvation, self-help; biography; missionary stories; news items; testimonies, inspirational stories based on true-life experiences.

How to Contact/Writers: Fiction/nonfiction: Send complete ms. Reports on queries in 6-8 weeks. Will consider simultaneous submissions. Will review ms/illustration packages.

How to Contact/Illustrators: Ms/illustration packages: Send complete ms with final art. Illustrations only: "Most of our artwork is done in-house."

Terms: Pays on acceptance. Buys first and second rights. Pays 2-3¢/word for articles. Sample copy free with 9×12 SASE. Free writer's/illustrator's guidelines for SASE.

HIGHLIGHTS FOR CHILDREN, 803 Church St., Honesdale PA 18431. (717)253-1080. Manuscript Coordinator: Beth Troop. Art Director: Rosanne Guararra. Monthly (July-August issue combined) magazine. Estab. 1946. Circ. 2.8 million. Our motto is "Fun With a Purpose." We are looking for quality fiction and nonfiction that appeals to children, encourages them to read, and reinforces positive values. All art is done on assignment.

Fiction: Picture-oriented material: animal, contemporary, fantasy, history, humorous, problem solving. Young readers, middle readers: animal, contemporary, fantasy, history, humorous, problem solving, science fiction, sports, mystery/adventure. Does not want to see: war, crime, violence. Buys 150+ mss/year. Average word length: 400-800. Byline given.

Nonfiction: Picture-oriented material: animal, history, how-to, humorous, problem solving. Young readers, middle readers: animal, history, how-to, humorous, interview/profile, problem solving, foreign, science, nature, arts, sports. Does not want to see: trendy topics, fads, personalities who would not be good role models for children, guns, war, crime, violence. Buys 75+ mss/year. Maximum word length: 900. Byline given.

How to Contact/Writers: Send complete ms. Reports on queries in 4 weeks; mss in 4-6 weeks.

Illustration: Preferred theme or style: Realistic, some stylization, cartoon style acceptable. Works on assignment only.

How to Contact/Illustrators: Ms/illustration packages: Art is done on assignment only. Illustrations only: Photocopies, tearsheets, or slides. Résumé optional. Reports on art samples in 4 weeks.

Terms: Pays on acceptance. Buys all rights. Pays 14¢/word and up for unsolicited articles. "Illustration fees vary on size of job. Median range: $350-600. Pays more for covers." Writer's/illustrator's guidelines free on request.

Tips: Writers: "Analyze several issues of the magazines you want to write for. Send for writer's guidelines." Illustrators: "Fresh, imaginative work presented in a professional portfolio encouraged. Flexibility in working relationships a plus. Illustrators presenting their work need not confine themselves to just children's illustrations as long as work can translate to our needs. We also use animal illustrations, real and imaginary. We need party plans, crafts and puzzles—any activity that will stimulate children mentally and creatively. We are always looking for imaginative cover subjects."

HOBSON'S CHOICE, P.O. Box 98, Ripley OH 45167. (513)392-4549. Editor: Susannah C. West. Monthly magazine. Estab. 1974. Circ. 2,000. "*Hobson's Choice* is a science fiction magazine which also publishes science and technology-related nonfiction along with the stories. Although the magazine is not specifically aimed at children, we do number teenagers among our readers. Such readers are the type who might enjoy reading science fiction (both young adult and adult), attending science fiction conventions, using computers, and be interested in such things as astronomy, the space program, etc."

Fiction: Young adults: fantasy, folktales, science fiction. Buys 12-15 mss/year. Average word length 2,000-10,000.

Nonfiction: Young adults: biography, careers, education, how-to (science), interview/profile, math, science, informational science book review. Does not want to see crafts. Buys 8-10 mss/year. Average word length: 1,500-5,000. Byline given.

How to Contact/Writers: Fiction: Send complete ms. Nonfiction: query first. Reports on queries/mss in 2-3 months. ("After 16 weeks, author should feel free to withdraw ms from consideration.") Will consider submissions via disk (Macintosh MacWrite, WriteNow, IBM PC or compatible on 3½ disks).

"Picture books" are geared toward the preschool—8 year old group; "Young readers" to 5-8 year olds; "Middle readers" to 9-11 year olds; and "Young adults" to those 12 and up.

Illustration: Buys 2-5 illustrations/issue; buys 20-30 illustrations/year. Uses b&w artwork only. Prefers to review "science fiction, fantasy or technical illustration." Reviews ms/illustration packages; reviews artwork for future assignments.

How to Contact/Illustrators: Ms/illustration packages: "Would like to see clips to keep on file (b&w only, preferably photocopies)." Illustrations only: Query with tearsheets to be kept on file. "If we have an assignment for an artist, we will contact him/her with the ms we want illustrated. We like to see roughs before giving the go-ahead for final artwork." Reports in 2-3 months. Original artwork returned at job's completion, "sometimes, if requested. We prefer to retain originals, but a high-quality PMT or Velox is fine if artist wants to keep artwork." Credit line given.

Photography: Purchases photos with accompanying ms only. Uses b&w prints. Wants photos for nonfiction.

Terms: Pays 50% on acceptance (for art), 50% on publication. Pays 25% on acceptance (for writing), 75% on publication. Buys first North American serial rights; second serial (reprint rights). Buys first rights for artwork and photographs. Pays $20-100 for stories; $15-50 for articles. Payment for illustrations: Pays $25-50/b&w cover; $5-25/b&w inside. Sample copy $1.75; writer's/illustrator's guidelines free with business-size SAE and 1 first class stamp. "Specify fiction or nonfiction guidelines, or both." Tip sheet package for $1 and business-size envelope with 2 first class stamps (includes all guidelines and tips on writing science fiction and science nonfiction).

Tips: Writers: "Read lots of children's writing in general, especially specific genre if you're writing a genre story (SF, romance, mystery, etc.). We list upcoming needs in our guidelines; writers can study these to get an idea of what we're looking for." Illustrators: "Study illustrations in back issues of magazines you're interested in illustrating for, and be able to work in a genre style if that's the type of magazine you want to publish your work. Everything is open to freelancers, as almost all our artwork is done out-of-house. (We occasionally use public domain illustrations, copyright-free illustrations and photographs.)"

HOPSCOTCH, The Magazine for Girls, The Bluffton News Publishing and Printing Company, 103 N. Main St., Bluffton OH 45817. (419)358-4610. Editor: Marilyn Edwards. Bimonthly magazine. Estab. 1989. Circ. 8,000. For girls from 6 to 12 years, featuring traditional subjects—pets, games, hobbies, nature, science, sports etc.—with an emphasis on articles that show girls actively involved in unusual and/or worthwhile activities."

Fiction: Young readers and middle readers: adventure, animal, contemporary, fantasy, folktales, health, history, humorous, multicultural, nature/environment, problem solving, sports, suspense/mystery. Does not want to see stories dealing with dating, sex, fashion, hard rock music. Buys 24 mss/year. Average word length: 300-1,100. Byline given.

Nonfiction: Young readers and middle readers: animal, arts/crafts, biography, careers, cooking, games/puzzles, health, history, hobbies, how-to, humorous, interview/profile, math, multicultural, nature/environment, problem solving, science. Does not want to see pieces dealing with dating, sex, fashion, hard rock music. Buys 36 mss/year. Average word length: 400-1,100. Byline given.

Poetry: Reviews traditional, wholesome, humorous poems. Maximum word length: 400; maximum line length: 40. Will accept 6 submissions/author.

How to Contact/Writers: Fiction: Send complete ms. Nonfiction: Query, send complete ms. Reports on queries in 2 weeks; on mss in 1 month. Publishes ms 6 months after acceptance. Will consider simultaneous submissions.

Illustration: Buys 4-8 illustrations/issue; buys 24-48 illustrations/year. "Generally, the illustrations are assigned after we have purchased a piece (usually fiction). Occasionally, we will use a painting—in any given medium—for the cover, and these are usually seasonal." Uses b&w artwork only for inside; color for cover. Will review ms/illustration packages. Will review artwork for future assignments.

How to Contact/Illustrators: Query first or send complete ms with final art. Illustrations only: Send résumé, portfolio, client list and tearsheets. Reports on art samples in 2 weeks. Original artwork returned at job's completion. Credit line given.

Photography: Purchases photos separately (cover only) and with accompanying ms only. Looking for photos to accompany article. Model/property releases required. Uses 5×7, b&w prints; 35mm transparencies. Black and white photos should go with ms. Should have girl or girls age 6-12.

Terms: For manuscripts, pays a few months ahead of publication. For mss, artwork and photos, buys first North American serial rights; second serial (reprint rights). Pays $30-100 for stories/articles. "We always send a copy of the issue to the writer or illustrator." Text and art are treated separately. Pays $100-150/color cover; $10-20/b&w inside. Photographers paid per photo (range: $10-20; $150 for color cover photo). Sample copy for $3. Writer's/illustrator's guidelines free for #10 SASE.

Tips: "Please look at our guidelines and our magazine . . . and remember, we use far more nonfiction than fiction. Most welcome is the article that has a girl or girls directly involved in an interesting and/or worthwhile activity. If decent photos accompany the piece, it stands an even better chance of being accepted. We believe it is the responsibility of the contributor to come up with photos. Please remember, our readers are 6-12 years—most are 7-10—and your text should reflect that."

HUMPTY DUMPTY'S MAGAZINE, Children's Better Health Institute, 1100 Waterway Blvd., P.O. Box 567, Indianapolis IN 46206. (317)636-8881. Editor: Christine French Clark. Art Director: Lawrence Simmons. Magazine published 8 times/year—Jan/Feb; Mar; April/May; June; July/Aug; Sept; Oct/Nov; Dec. *HDM* is edited for kindergarten children, approximately ages 4-6. It includes fiction (easy-to-reads; read alouds; rhyming stories; rebus stories), nonfiction articles (some with photo illustrations), poems, crafts, recipes and puzzles. Much of the content encourages development of better health habits. We especially need material promoting fitness. "All but 2 pages aimed at the juvenile market. The remainder may be seasonal and/or more general."

Fiction: Picture-oriented material: animal, contemporary, fantasy, humorous, sports, health-related. Young readers: animal, contemporary, fantasy, humorous, science fiction, sports, suspense/mystery/adventure, health-related. Does not want to see bunny-rabbits-with-carrot-pies stories! Also, talking inanimate objects are very difficult to do well. Beginners (and maybe everyone) should avoid these. Buys 35-50 mss/year. Maximum word length: 700. Byline given.

Nonfiction: Picture-oriented material, young readers: animal, how-to, humorous, interview/profile, health-related. Does not want to see long, boring, encyclopedia rehashes. "We're open to almost any subject (although most of our nonfiction has a health angle), but it must be presented creatively. Don't just string together some facts." Looks for a fresh approach. Buys 6-10 mss/year. Prefers very short nonfiction pieces—500 words maximum. Byline given.

How to Contact/Writers: Send complete ms. Nonfiction: Send complete ms with bibliography if applicable. "No queries, please!" Reports on mss in 8-10 weeks.

Illustration: Buys 13-16 illustrations/issue; buys 90-120 illustrations/year. Preferred theme or style: Realistic or cartoon. Will review ms/illustration packages. Will review artwork for future assignments. Works on assignment only.

How to Contact/Illustrators: Ms/illustration packages: Send slides, printed pieces or photocopies. Illustrations only: Send slides, printed pieces or photocopies. Reports on art samples only if interested.

Terms: Writers: Pays on publication. Artists: Pays within 6-8 weeks. Buys all rights. "One-time book rights may be returned if author can provide name of interested book publisher and tentative date of publication." Pays about 10-20¢/word for stories/articles;

payment varies for poems and activities. Up to 10 complimentary issues are provided to author with check. Pays $250/color cover illustration; $30-70 per page b&w (inside); $55-110/2-color (inside); $65-140/color (inside). Sample copy for $1.25. Writer's/illustrator's guidelines free with SASE.

Tips: Writers: "Study current issues and guidelines. Observe, especially, word lengths and adhere to requirements. It's sometimes easier to break in with recipe or craft ideas, but submit what you do best. Don't send your first, second, or even third drafts. Polish your piece until it's as perfect as you can make it." Illustrators: "Please study the magazine before contacting us. Your art must have appeal to three- to seven-year-olds." (See listings for *Child Life, Children's Digest, Children's Playmate, Jack and Jill, Turtle Magazine*.)

*I.D., David C. Cook Publishing Co., 850 N. Grove Ave., Elgin IL 60120. (708)741-2400. Articles Editors: Douglas C. Schmidt, Lorraine Triggs. Art Director: Jeffrey P. Barnes. Photo Editor: Ruthie Corcoran. Weekly magazine. Estab. 1991. Circ. 100,000. "*I.D.* is a class-and-home paper for senior high Sunday school students."

Fiction: Young adults: adventure, contemporary, folktales, history, humorous, nature/environment, religious, science fiction, sports, suspense/mystery. "All must have religious, redeeming qualities." Buys approx. 12 mss/year. Average word length: 600-1,000.

Nonfiction: Young adults: animal, biography, careers, concept, games/puzzles, geography, health, history, hobbies, how-to, humorous, interview/profile, religion, science, social issues, sports. "Sometimes material sent to us is too 'preachy.' " Buys 12 mss/year. Average word length: 600-1,000. Byline sometimes given if written in the first person.

How to Contact/Writers: Send complete ms. Reports in 2 months. Publishes ms 15 months after acceptance. Will consider simultaneous submissions.

Illustrations: Buys 1 illustration/issue; 52 illustrations/year. Uses b&w and color artwork. Reviews ms/illustration packages; reviews artwork for future assignments; works on assignment only.

How to Contact/Illustrators: Ms/illustration package: Submit ms with rough sketches. Illustrations only: Query.

INSTRUCTOR MAGAZINE, Scholastic, Inc., 730 Broadway, New York NY 10003. (212)505-4927. Fax: (212)260-8595. Art Director: Drew Hires. Magazine published 9 times/year. Estab. 1891. Circ. 300,000. "*Instructor*'s primary audience is teachers grades K-8. Features and regular columns offer practical and professional information for educators."

Nonfiction: Young readers and middle readers: animal, arts/crafts, biography, careers, cooking, education, fashion, games/puzzles, health, history, hobbies, how-to, humorous, interview/profiles, nature/environment, problem-solving, religion, travel, sports. Buys fewer than 10 mss/year. Written for kids. Byline sometimes given.

Poetry: Reviews poetry.

How to Contact/Writers: Fiction/nonfiction: Send complete ms. Reports in 4-6 weeks. Publishes ms 3 months to 1 year after acceptance. Will consider electronic submissions via disk or modem.

Illustrations: Buys 19 illustrations/issue. Uses color artwork only. Prefers friendly/modern illustrations. Reviews artwork for future assignments; works on assignment only.

How to Contact/Illustrators: Ms/illustration packages: Query. Illustration only: Query with samples. Reports back only if interested. Original work returned upon job's completion (if requested).

Photography: Looking for photos on education. Model/property releases required; photo captions "helpful." To contact, query with samples. Reports back only if interested.

Terms: Pays on publication. Buys one-time rights for mss. Pays $20 and for assigned articles. "Published authors receive a complementary copy." Writer's guidelines for SASE.
Tips: "We're not a children's magazine."

INTERNATIONAL GYMNAST, Sundbysports, Inc., 225 Brooks, Box 2450, Oceanside CA 92054. (619)722-0030. Editor: Dwight Normile. Monthly publication. "We are a magazine about gymnasts for ages 9 and up."
Fiction: Young adults: problem solving and sports stories for gymnasts.
Nonfiction: Young adults: biography, health, interview/profile, sports. Gymnastics material only.
How to Contact/Writers: Query with published clips. Will consider simultaneous submissions (please advise).
Illustration: Will review ms/illustration packages. Uses b&w artwork only, but "very rarely." Usually prefers cartoons—8½×11 camera ready.
How to Contact/Illustrators: Ms/illustration packages: query first. Illustrations only: send slides or prints.
Photography: Looking for clear action/personality photos. Photo captions required. Uses 5×7 or 8×10, b&w, glossy prints; 35mm transparencies. To contact, send unsolicited photos by mail.
Terms: Pays on publication by arrangement. Buys one-time rights for mss, artwork and photos. Pays $15-25 for articles. Pays illustrators per b&w inside illustration (range: $10-15). Photographers paid per photo (range: $5-50).
Tips: "For us, gymnastics knowledge is necessary. Standard kidstuff with tenuous gym orientation doesn't cut it."

JACK AND JILL, Children's Better Health Institute, 1100 Waterway Blvd., Indianapolis IN 46206. (317)636-8881. Articles, Fiction Editor: Steve Charles. Art Director: Ed Cortese. Magazine published 8 times/year. Estab. 1938. Circ. 360,000. "Write entertaining and imaginative stories *for* kids, not just *about* them. Writers should understand what is funny to kids, what's important to them, what excites them. Don't write from an adult 'kids are so cute' perspective. We're also looking for health and healthy lifestyle stories and articles, but don't be preachy."
Fiction: Young readers: animal, contemporary, fantasy, history, humorous, problem solving. Middle readers: contemporary, humorous. Buys 30-35 mss/year. Average word length: 900. Byline given.
Nonfiction: Young readers: animal, history, how-to, humorous, interview/profile, problem solving, travel. Buys 8-10 mss/year. Average word length: 1,000. Byline given.
Poetry: Reviews poetry.
How to Contact/Writers: Fiction/nonfiction: Send complete ms. Reports on queries in 2 weeks; mss in 8-10 weeks. Will consider simultaneous submissions.
Terms: Pays on publication; minimum 10¢/word. Buys all rights.

JUNIOR TRAILS, Gospel Publishing House, 1445 Boonville Ave., Springfield MO 65802. (417)862-2781. Articles/Fiction Editor: Sinda S. Zinn. Art Director: Leonard Bailey. Quarterly magazine. Circ. 70,000. *Junior Trails* is an 8-page take-home paper for fifth and sixth graders. "Its articles consist of fiction stories of a contemporary or historical nature. The stories have a moral slant to show how modern-day people can work out problems in acceptable ways, or give examples in history from which we can learn."
Fiction: Middle readers: adventure, animal, contemporary, history, humorous, nature/environment, problem solving, religious, suspense/mystery. Does not want to see science fiction, mythology, ghosts and witchcraft. Wants to see more stories about "kids struggling with a problem in Christian living and solving it through biblical principles." Buys 100 mss/year. Average word length: 800-1,500. Byline given.

Nonfiction: Middle readers: animal, games/puzzles, history, how-to, problem solving, religious. Buys 30 mss/year. Average word length: 300-800. Byline given.

Poetry: Wants to see poetry with a religious emphasis.

How to Contact/Writers: Fiction/nonfiction: Send complete ms. Reports on queries in 2 weeks; mss in 4-6 weeks. Will consider simultaneous submissions.

Illustration: Uses color artwork only. Reviews artwork for future assignments.

How to Contact/Illustrators: Illustrations only: provide résumé, promo sheet or tearsheets to be kept on file; or arrange personal interview to show portfolio. Reports only if interested. Credit line sometimes given.

Photography: Uses 2¼ × 2¼ transparencies. To contact, photographers should query with samples; provide résumé, promo sheet or tearsheets to be kept on file. Wants photos of "children involved with activity or with other people."

Terms: Pays on acceptance. For mss, buys one-time rights. Buys all rights to artwork; one-time rights to photographs. Pays 2-3¢/word for articles/stories. Pays illustrators $150-200/color (cover). Photographers paid per photo (range: $30-100). Sample copy free with 9 × 12 SASE.

Tips: "Make the characters and situations real. The story should unfold through their interaction and dialogue, not narration. Don't fill up space with unnecessary details. We are always in need of good fiction stories." Looks for: "fiction that presents believable characters working out their problems according to Bible principles. Present Christianity in action without being preachy; articles with reader appeal, emphasizing some phase of Christian living, presented in a down-to-earth manner; biography or missionary material using fiction technique; historical, scientific or nature material with a spiritual lesson; fillers that are brief, purposeful, usually containing an anecdote, and always with a strong evangelical emphasis."

KEYNOTER, Key Club International, 3636 Woodview Trace, Indianapolis IN 46268. (317)875-8755. Articles Editor: Julie Carson Vitello. Art Director: James Patterson. Monthly magazine. Estab. 1915. Circ. 133,000. "As the official magazine of the world's largest high school service organization, we publish nonfiction articles that interest teenagers and will help our readers become better students, better citizens, better leaders."

Nonfiction: Young adults: how-to, humorous, problem solving. Does not want to see first-person accounts; short stories. Buys 15 mss/year. Average word length: 1,800-2,500. Byline given.

How to Contact/Writers: Nonfiction: Query. Reports on queries/mss in 1 month. Will consider simultaneous submissions.

Illustration: Buys 2-3 illustrations/issue; buys 15 illustrations/year. Will review ms/illustration packages. Works on assignment only.

How to Contact/Illustrators: Ms/illustration packages: "Because of our publishing schedule, we prefer to work with illustrators/photographers within Indianapolis market." Reports on art samples only if interested. Original artwork returned at job's completion if requested.

Terms: Pays on acceptance. Buys first North American serial rights. Pays $75-300 for assigned/unsolicited articles. Sample copy free with 8½ × 11 SAE and 65¢ postage. Writer's guidelines free with SAE and 1 first-class stamp.

Tips: "We are looking for light or humorous nonfiction, self-help articles." Also looking for articles about education reform, national concerns and trends, teen trends in music, fashion, clothes, ideologies, etc.

KID CITY, Children's Television Workshop, 1 Lincoln Plaza, New York NY 10023. (212)595-3456. Articles editor: Maureen Hunter-Bone; Fiction editor: Lisa Rao; Art director: Michele Weisman. Monthly magazine. Estab. 1971. Circ. 330,000 +.

Fiction: Middle readers: animal, contemporary, history, humorous, science fiction, sports, spy/mystery/adventure. Does not want to see "cutesie, overly moralistic, preachy material." Buys 3-4 mss/year. Average word length: 200-500. Byline given.

Nonfiction: Middle readers: animal, nature/environment, sports. Does not want to see puzzle and games submissions. Buys 12 mss/year. Average word length: 200-500. Byline given.

How to Contact/Writers: Fiction: Send complete ms. Nonfiction: Query or send complete ms. Reports on queries/mss in 4 weeks. Will consider simultaneous submissions (if notified).

Illustration: Buys 5+ illustrations/issue; 50-60 illustrations/year. Works on assignment only.

How to Contact/Illustrators: Artists send samples. Reports back only if interested. Originals returned to artist at job's completion.

Terms: Pays on acceptance. Buys all rights. Pays $75-300 for assigned/unsolicited articles. Pays $300-400 per page for inside color illustrations. Writer's guidelines free with SASE. Sample copy with 8×11 SASE and $1.50.

Tips: Writers: "Use concrete, colorful, direct language. We use short-short stories—2 pages, 100 lines at 45 characters per line." Illustrators: "Avoid the cute. Use hot colors. Don't make kids you illustrate look like kewpie dolls. Don't be afraid of detail. Use a sense of humor. Send lots of sample cards to art directors. Write or call to bring in portfolios." (See listing for *3-2-1 Contact*.)

*KIDS TODAY MINI-MAGAZINE, Today Publishing, Inc., 2724 College Park Rd., Allison Park PA 15101. Editor: Don DiMarco. Art/Photo Director: Kevin Metzger. Quarterly mini-magazine in newsletter format. Estab. 1988. Circ. 15,000. "The mini-magazine is intended for children, targeting but not limited to, grades 3, 4 and 5. The purpose of the publication is to stimulate within our young readership an interest and appreciation for the ability to communicate, learn and entertain through reading, writing and artistic skills. This is accomplished through an appealing mix of fiction nonfiction, poetry, puzzles, games, contests and activities."

Fiction: Young readers and middle readers: adventure, contemporary, history, humorous, science fiction, sports. "Material that is preachy in tone or focuses on violence, war, drugs or sex is not accepted. Material reflecting racial, religious or gender bias is inappropriate." Average word length: 300-600. Byline given.

Nonfiction: Young readers: arts/crafts, biography, games/puzzles, history, interview/profile, nature/environment, sports; middle readers: arts/crafts, games/puzzles, history, interview/provile, nature/environment, travel, sports. "We want material that will make a kid say, WOW! Of particular interests are articles about famous people, especially those who serve as ideal role models for children; articles about kids (unusual accomplishments—talents etc.); short pieces about inventions, sports, historical events and biographical sketches." Average word length: 200-500. Byline given.

Poetry: Featured in "Spotlight" section—for young authors only.

How to Contact/Writers: Fiction/nonfiction: Send complete ms. Reports on mss in 3 weeks. Publishes ms 6 months after acceptance. Reviews ms/illustration packages.

How to Contact/Illustrators: "Submit illustrations only with manuscript." Reports in 3 weeks. Does not return artwork.

Photography: Purchases photos with accompanying ms only. Model/property releases required. Uses b&w prints. Reports in 3 weeks.

Terms: Pays on publication. "For the most part we prefer to purchase all rights; however, on some items, we will consider purchasing first North American serial rights." Pays $10-25 for articles. "Some of our writers forego payment in lieu of multiple copies of publication." Sample copies for $1. Writer's guidelines for SASE.

Tips: "Our readership enjoys short articles and stories about a variety of subjects. Many publications offer complex layouts with commercial integration. Many disadvantaged children cannot afford the cost. *Kids Today* is different. It is distributed free and without advertising. It is simple and clean. The editorial philosophy of *Kids Today Mini-Magazine* is to recognize and celebrate imagination, creativity, distinctiveness and worth of all people, with particular emphasis on *all children*. All mss submitted are carefully reviewed. All material must be original and previously unpublished. Writer's should consider the nature of our mission prior to submitting material. The length of all material must be short. We are particularly interested in mss that are creatively devised to stimulate children to read, think and write. Subscriptions are mailed to any location in the U.S. for a contribution of $5 or more per 3 issues annually. *Kids Today* is produced and distributed by Today Publishing, Inc., a nonprofit, tax exempt organization."

LADYBUG, THE MAGAZINE FOR YOUNG CHILDREN, P.O. Box 300, 315 Fifth Street, Peru IL 61354. (815)224-6643. Editor-in-Chief: Marianne Carus. Associate Editor: Paula Morrow. Art Director: Ron McCutchan. Monthly magazine. Estab. 1990. Circ. 130,000. Literary magazine for children 2-6, with stories, poems, activities, songs and picture stories.
Fiction: Picture-oriented and young readers: adventure, animal, contemporary, fantasy, folktales, humorous, picture book texts. "Open to any easy fiction stories." Buys 50 mss/year. Average word length 300-750 words. Byline given.
Nonfiction: Picture-oriented and young readers: animal, arts/crafts, games/puzzles, activities, how-to, humorous, nature/environment. "Nonfiction in *Ladybug* will not be in article form, but rather in pictures with short captions." Buys 35 mss/year.
Poetry: Reviews 20-line maximum length poems; limit submissions to 5 poems. Uses lyrical, humorous, simple language.
How to Contact/Writers: Fiction/nonfiction: Send complete ms. Queries not accepted. Reports on mss in 3 months. Publishes ms up to 2 years after acceptance. Does not like, but will consider simultaneous submissions.
Illustration: Buys 12 illustrations/issue; 145 illustrations/year. Original artwork returned at job's completion. Uses color artwork only. Prefers "bright colors; all media, but use watercolor and acrylics most often; same size as magazine is preferred but not required." Reviews ms/illustration packages.
How to Contact/Illustrators: Ms/illustrations packages: "Manuscript with one or two rough sketches and some examples of finished artwork from other projects." Illustrations only: To contact, submit sample for review. "Tearsheets, good quality photocopies, C-prints; slides are somewhat less useful, but OK." Reports on art samples in 2 months.
Terms: Pays on publication. For mss, buys first publication rights; second serial (reprint rights). Buys first publication rights plus promotional rights for artwork. Pays up to 25¢/word. Pays $750 for color (cover) illustration, $200-300 for color (inside) illustration. Sample copy for $2. Writer's/illustrator's guidelines free for SAE and 1 first class stamp.
Tips: Writers: Has a need for "well-written read-aloud stories. Read copies of back issues and current issues. Set a manuscript aside for a few weeks, then reread before sending it off. Adhere to specified word limits." Illustrators: "Include examples, where possible, of children, animals, and—most important—action and narrative (i.e., several scenes from a story, showing continuity and an ability to maintain interest)."

LIGHTHOUSE, Lighthouse Publications, Box 1377, Auburn WA 98071-1377. Editor/Publisher: Tim Clinton. Bimonthly magazine. Estab. 1986. Circ. 300. Magazine contains timeless stories and poetry for family reading. 25% of material aimed at juvenile audience.
Fiction: Young readers, middle readers, young adults: animal, nature/environment, humor, problem-solving, sports, mystery/suspense. Young adults: romance. Does not want to see anything not "G-rated," any story with a message that is not subtly handled or stories without plots. Buys 18 mss/year. Average word length: 2,000. Byline given.

Poetry: Reviews poetry. Maximum line length: 50. Maximum number of submissions: 5.

How to Contact/Writers: Fiction: Send complete ms and SASE with sufficient postage for return of ms. Reports on mss in 2-3 months.

Terms: Pays on publication. Buys first North American serial rights; first rights. Pays $5-50. Sample copy for $3 (includes guidelines). Writer's guidelines free with regular SAE and 1 first class stamp.

Tips: "All sections are open to freelance writers—just follow the guidelines and stay in the categories listed above."

LISTEN, Celebrating Positive Choices, 1350 North Kings Rd., Nampa ID 83687. (208)465-2500. Monthly magazine. Circ. 70,000. *Listen* offers positive alternatives to drug use for its teenage readers.

Fiction: Young adults: contemporary, humorous, problem solving activities. Buys 12 mss/year. Average word length: 1,200-1,500. Byline given.

Nonfiction: Young adults: how-to, interview/profile, problem solving activities. Buys 50 mss/year. Average word length: 1,200-1,500. Byline given.

How to Contact/Writers: Fiction/nonfiction: Send complete ms. Reports on queries/mss in 2 months.

Terms: Pays on acceptance. Buys first North American serial rights. Pays 5-10¢ a word. Sample copy for $1 and SASE. Writer's guidelines free with SASE.

Tips: "*Listen* is a magazine for teenagers. It encourages development of good habits and high ideals of physical, social and mental health. It bases its editorial philosophy of primary drug prevention on total abstinence from alcohol and other drugs. Because it is used extensively in public high school classes, it does not accept articles and stories with overt religious emphasis. Four specific purposes guide the editors in selecting materials for *Listen*: 1) To portray a positive lifestyle and to foster skills and values that will help teenagers deal with contemporary problems, including smoking, drinking and using drugs. This is *Listen*'s primary purpose. 2) To offer positive alternatives to a lifestyle of drug use of any kind. 3) To present scientifically accurate information about the nature and effects of tobacco, alcohol and other drugs. 4) To report medical research, community programs and educational efforts which are solving problems connected with smoking, alcohol and other drugs. Articles should offer their readers activities that increase one's sense of self-worth through achievement and/or involvement in helping others. They are often categorized by three kinds of focus: 1) Hobbies. 2) Recreation. 3) Community Service."

*THE MAGAZINE FOR CHRISTIAN YOUTH!, United Methodist Publishing House, 201 Eighth Ave. S., Box 801, Nashville TN 37202. (615)749-6319. Articles Editor: Tony Peterson. Art Director: Phil Francis. Photo Editor: Phil Francis. Monthly magazine. Estab. 1985. Circ. 35,000. "*Youth!* is a leisure reading magazine whose purpose is to help teenagers develop Christian identity and live the Christian faith in their contemporary culture."

Fiction: Young adults: adventure, animal, contemporary, fantasy, health, history, humorous, multicultural, nature/environment, problem-solving, religious, romance, science fiction, sports, suspense/mystery. "We appreciate fiction that allows people of color to be main characters. We do not want occultic fiction. We appreciate realistic fiction that also takes Christian faith seriously." Buys 5-10 mss/year. Average word length: 500-2,000. Byline given.

Nonfiction: Young adults: animal, arts/crafts, biography, careers, concept, health, history, hobbies, how-to, humorous, interview/profile, multicultural, nature/environment, problem-solving, religion, science, social issues, sports, travel. Buys 10-30 mss/year. Average word length: 500-2,000. Byline given.

How to Contact/Writers: Fiction/nonfiction: Query; send complete ms. Reports on queries in 2 months; mss in 3 months. Will consider simultaneous and electronic submissions via disk or modem and previously published work.

Illustration: Reviews ms/illustration packages; reviews artwork for future assignments.

How to Contact/Illustrators: Ms/illustration packages: Query; submit ms with rough sketches. Illustrations only: Query; send promo sheet, portfolio, slides and tearsheets. Reports in 2 months. Samples returned with SASE. Samples filed. Original work returned upon job's completion. Credit line given.

Photography: Purchases photography from freelancers. Model/property release required. Uses b&w glossy prints; 35mm, 2¼ × 2¼ transparencies. To contact, photographers should query with samples; send unsolicited photos by mail; submit portfolio for review; provide business card, promotional literature and tearsheets. Reports in 2 months.

Terms: Buys first North American serial rights, first rights, one-time rights, reprint rights or all rights for mss. Purchases all rights for artwork; user rights for photographs. Pays $35-125. Additional payment for ms/illustation packages. Pays illustrators $50-150/ b&w cover; $25-50 b&w inside; $150-300/color cover; $50-150 color inside. Photographers paid per photo (range: $25-300). Writer's/illustrator's/photo guidelines for SASE.

Tips: "Refrain from talking down to teens, use 'your' instead of 'they' language. We rarely print fiction from adults."

MY FRIEND, A Magazine for Children, Daughters of St. Paul/St. Paul Books and Media, 50 St. Paul's Ave., Jamaica Plain, Boston MA 02130. (617)522-8911. Articles/ Fiction Editor: Sister Anne Joan, fsp. Art Director: Sister M. Joseph, fsp. Magazine published 10 times/year. Estab. 1979. Circ. 17,000. *"My Friend* is a magazine of inspiration and entertainment for a predominantly Catholic readership. We reach ages 6-12."

Fiction: Young readers, middle readers: adventure, contemporary, history, humorous, religious, suspense/mystery. Does not want to see poetry, animals as main characters in religious story, stories whose basic thrust would be incompatible with Catholic values. Buys 50 mss/year. Average word length: 450-750. Byline given.

Nonfiction: Young readers: arts/crafts, games/puzzles, health, hobbies, humor, religion. Middle readers: arts/crafts, games/puzzles, health, history, hobbies, how-to, humor, interview/profile, nature/environment, problem solving, religion, science, sports. Does not want to see material that is not compatible with Catholic values; no "new age" material. Buys 10 mss/year. Average word length: 450-750. Byline given.

How to Contact/Writers: Fiction/nonfiction: Send complete ms. Reports on queries in 1 month; mss in 1-2 months.

Illustration: Buys 8 illustrations/issue; buys 60-80 illustrations/year. Preferred theme or style: Realistic depictions of children, but open to variety! "We'd just like to hear from more illustrators who can do *humans*! (We see enough of funny cats, mice, etc.)" Looking for a "Bible stories" artist, too. Reviews ms/illustration packages; reviews artwork for future assignments.

How to Contact/Illustrators: Ms/illustration packages: Send complete ms with copy of final art. Illustrations only: Send résumé, promo sheet and tearsheets. Reports on art samples only if interested. Original artwork returned at job's completion. Credit line given.

Photography: Wants photos of "children at play or alone; school scenes."

Terms: Pays on acceptance for mss. Buys one-time rights for mss, artwork and photos. Pays $20-150 for stories/articles. Pays illustrators $50-100/b&w (inside); $50-175/color (inside). Sample copy free with 9 × 12 SAE and 4 first-class stamps. Writer's/illustrator's guidelines free with SAE and 1 first-class stamp.

Tips: Writers: "Right now, we're especially looking for science articles and stories that would appeal to boys. We are not interested in poetry unless it is humorous." Illustrators: "Please contact us! For the most part, we need illustrations for fiction stories."

NATURE FRIEND MAGAZINE, Pilgrim Publishers, 22777 State Road 119, Goshen IN 46526. (219)534-2245. Articles Editor: Stanley Brubaker. Monthly magazine. Estab. 1983. Circ. 11,000. "See our writer's guidelines *before* submitting articles."
Nonfiction: Picture books, young readers, middle readers, young adults: animal, nature. Does not want to see evolutionary material. Buys 50-80 mss/year. Average word length: 350-1,500. Byline given.
How to Contact/Writers: Nonfiction: Send complete ms. Reports on mss in 1-4 months. Will consider simultaneous submissions.
Illustration: Buys 10 illustrations/year. See samples of magazine for styles of art used. Will review ms/illustration packages.
Terms: Pays on publication. Buys one-time rights. Pays $15-75. Payment for ms/illustration packages: $15-40. Payment for illustrations: $15-80/b&w inside. Two sample copies for $3 with 7×10 SAE and 85¢ postage. Writer's/illustrator's guidelines for $1.
Tips: Looks for "main articles, puzzles and simple nature and science projects."

NEW ERA MAGAZINE, Official Publication for Youth of the Church of Jesus Christ of Latter-Day Saints, 50 E. North Temple Street, Salt Lake City UT 84150. (801)240-2951. Articles/Fiction Editor: Richard M. Romney. Art Director: B. Lee Shaw. Monthly magazine. Estab. 1971. Circ. 200,000. General interest religious publication for youth ages 12-18 who are members of The Church of Jesus Christ of Latter-Day Saints (Mormons).
Fiction: Young adults: contemporary, humorous, problem solving, religious, romance, science fiction. "All material must relate to Mormon point of view." Does not want to see formula pieces, articles not sensitive to an LDS audience. Buys 20 mss/year. Average word length: 250-2,500. Byline given.
Nonfiction: Young adults: biography, careers, education, fashion, games/puzzles, humorous, interview/profile, problem solving, religion, travel, sports; "general interest articles by, about and for young Mormons. Does not want to see formula pieces, articles not adapted to our specific voice and our audience." Buys 150-200 mss/year. Average word length: 250-2,000. Byline given.
Poetry: Reviews "30-line maximum" poems. Will accept 10 submissions/author.
How to Contact/Writers: Fiction/nonfiction: Query. Reports on queries/mss in 6-8 weeks. Publishes ms 1 year or more after acceptance. Will consider electronic submissions via disk.
Illustration: Buys 5 illustrations/issue; buys 50-60 illustrations/year. "We buy only from our pool of illustrators. We use all styles and mediums." Works on assignment only.
How to Contact/Illustrators: Illustrations only: Submit portfolio for review; provide resume, business card, promotional literature and tearsheets to be kept on file. Reports on art samples in 6-8 weeks. Original artwork returned at job's completion.
Terms: Pays on acceptance. For mss, buys first rights; other rights ("right to publish again in other church usage"). Buys all or one-time rights for artwork and photos. Pays $25-375 for articles. Pays illustrators and photographers "by specific arrangements." Sample copy for $1. Writer's guidelines free for SAE (business envelope and 1 first class stamp).
Tips: Open to "first-person and true-life experiences. Tell what happened in a conversational style."

NOAH'S ARK, A Newspaper for Jewish Children, 8323 Southwest Freeway, #250, Houston TX 77074. (713)771-7143. Articles/Fiction Editor: Debbie Israel Dubin. Monthly tabloid. Circ. 450,000. All submissions must have Jewish content and positive Jewish values. The newspaper is sent to more than 400 religious schools and submissions must be appropriate for educational use as well.
Fiction: Young readers, middle readers: contemporary, fantasy, folktales, health, history, humorous, nature/environment, religious, sports. Does not want to see Christian

Close-up

Carolyn Yoder
Editor-in-Chief
Cobblestone Publishing
Peterborough, New Hampshire

For writers interested in people, history and science, Cobblestone Publishing is fertile territory that harvests plenty of new opportunities each year. But only those who have done their work and taken the time to prepare their articles get published, according to Editor-in-Chief Carolyn Yoder, who oversees Cobblestone's four magazines.

"Our editorial focus is basically to offer an in-depth look at one subject, but also offers kids the multifaceted aspect of the subject," says Yoder. Because of this, it is important that each of the four magazines be factually accurate, especially since they are used heavily as educational supplements. *Cobblestone* focuses on American history, *Calliope* centers on world history, *Faces* on world cultures and *Odyssey* on science, space exploration and astronomy. All the magazines are targeted toward children ages 8-14, though it's not unheard of for some of the readers to be younger or older, says Yoder.

"We're a little different in that we really delve into one theme in all the magazines," says Yoder. "For the most part, the individual editors are in charge of the themes, but they do come in a variety of ways." Requests from readers is one way. Because of requests, *Cobblestone* did an issue on pirates. "Sometimes we take into account gaps in our own survey. Maybe we haven't done enough on contemporary twentieth century history or biography or something along that line." Also, she says themes are sometimes set around an anniversary year. "Last year all four magazines geared around the topic of Christopher Columbus, though we didn't really do anything exactly on him. In *Cobblestone* we did an issue on the legacy of Columbus; in *Faces* we did original people's first encounters; in *Calliope*, other explorations to the West; and in *Odyssey* we did a whole thing about exploration and new discoveries," says Yoder.

"I think the writing in our magazines is quite good, but I'd like to see more. Not only in our magazines, but in the future of children's literature. The need is for really good nonfiction writing for kids. Fiction tends to get emphasized. I don't think there's enough nonfiction and I don't think it's stressed enough in children's literature classes. Good quality research and writing style is due."

Yoder is a stickler for research and getting the facts straight. "*Faces* works with the Museum of Natural History, so we have a built-in consulting editor there. But all of the other magazines have consulting editors as well. They review the magazines for accuracy and tone. Also, we ask them to review our manuscripts." In addition, she says that two rounds of fact checking in-house as well as extensive research beforehand ensures accurate editorial content.

All of the magazines work on a query system where ideas for articles must be submitted with a very detailed outline and bibliography. The problem is, though, that too many writers submit queries displaying shoddy research and weak bibliographies. These people usually rely on about two or three sources that aren't reliable references, such as encyclopedias, according to Yoder. "There are misconceptions about writing a nonfiction article for a child. We look for complete, accurate information. A bad cover letter and outline won't give us a clear idea of how the article will shape up. You really have to convey to us that your article is going to be well thought out," she says.

She reminds writers that the guidelines and editorial calendars for the magazines are very exact. "If the article you're submitting doesn't adhere to those guidelines, we just don't have the time to make it worth our while."

Guidelines for illustrators and photographers are also available. Unlike a few years ago, there is now an art director and a picture editor on staff. Photo suggestions are also welcomed from writers with articles.

Yoder estimates she gets between 50 to 100 requests for guidelines per week, which indicates interest in these markets is out there. But before a writer can be interested in seeing his byline in print within one of the Cobblestone publications, he must be interested in writing about a topic that appeals to him. "Start with writing about something you like," says Yoder. "Don't try and stretch it."

— Lisa Carpenter

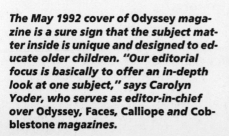

The May 1992 cover of Odyssey magazine is a sure sign that the subject matter inside is unique and designed to educate older children. "Our editorial focus is basically to offer an in-depth look at one subject," says Carolyn Yoder, who serves as editor-in-chief over Odyssey, Faces, Calliope and Cobblestone magazines.

and secular material. Buys 3 mss/year. Average word length: 650. Byline given.
Nonfiction: Young readers, middle readers: arts/crafts, biography, cooking (Jewish recipes), games/puzzles, history, how-to, interview/profile, nature/environment, religious, social issues. Does not want to see secular, Christian nonfiction. Buys 1 ms/year, "only because more not submitted." Average word length: 500. Byline given.
How to Contact/Writers: Fiction/nonfiction: Send complete ms. Report on mss 6-8 weeks.
Terms: Pays on acceptance. Buys first North American serial rights. Pays 5¢/word for stories/articles. Sample copy free with #10 SAE and 1 first-class stamp. Writer's guidelines free with SASE.
Tips: "Send appropriate material. We receive mostly inappropriate submissions; very few submissions have Jewish values as required."

*ODYSSEY, Science That's Out of This World, Cobblestone Publishing, Inc., 7 School St., Peterborough NH 03458. (603)924-7209. Editor: Eleanor B. Cochrane. Editor-in-Chief: Carolyn Yoder. Art Director: Ann C. Webster. Photo Editor: Francelle Carapetyan. Magazine published 10 times/year. Estab. 1979. Circ. 59,000. Magazine covers astronomy and space exploration for children ages 8-14. All material must relate to the theme of a specific upcoming issue in order to be considered.
Fiction: Middle readers and young adults: adventure, folktales, history, biographical fiction. Does not want to see anything not theme-related. Average word length: 750 maximum.
Nonfiction: Middle readers and young adults: arts/crafts, biography, cooking, games/puzzles (no word finds), science. Don't send anything not theme-related. Average word length: 200-750, depending on section article is used in.
How to Contact/Writers: "A query must consist of all of the following to be considered (please use nonerasable paper): a brief cover letter stating the subject and word length of the proposed article; a detailed one-page outline explaining the information to be presented in the article; an extensive bibliography of materials the author intends to use in preparing the article; a self-addressed stamped envelope. Writers new to *Odyssey* should send a writing sample with query. If you would like to know if your query has been received, please also include a stamped postcard that requests acknowledgment of receipt. In all correspondence, please include your complete address as well as a telephone number where you can be reached. A writer may send as many queries for one issue as he or she wishes, but each query must have a separate cover letter, outline, bibliography, and SASE. Telephone queries are not accepted. Handwritten queries will not be considered. Queries may be submitted at any time, but queries sent well in advance of deadline *may not be answered for several months*. Go-aheads requesting material proposed in queries are usually sent five months prior to publication date. Unused queries will be returned approximately three to four months prior to publication date."
Illustration: Reviews artwork for future assignments.
How to Contact/Illustrators: Illustrations only: send tearsheets, photocopies. Original artwork returned upon job's completion (upon written request).
Photography: Wants photos pertaining to any of our forthcoming themes. Uses b&w and color prints; 35mm transparencies. To contact, photographers should send unsolicited photos by mail (on speculation).
Terms: Buys all right for mss and artwork. Pays 10-17¢/word for stories/articles. "Covers are assigned and paid on an individual basis. Pays illustrators $10-125/b&w inside; $20-210/color (inside). Photographers paid per photo (range: $15-75). Sample copy for $3.95 and SASE with $1.05 postage. Writer's/illustrator's/photo guidelines for SASE.

ON THE LINE, Mennonite Publishing House, 616 Walnut Ave., Scottdale PA 15683. (412)887-8500. Editor: Mary Clemens Meyer. "Monthly in weekly parts" magazine. Estab. 1970. Circ. 10,000.

Fiction: Young adults: contemporary, history, humorous, problem-solving, religious, sports and suspense/mystery. "No fantasy or fiction with animal characters." Buys 60 mss/year. Average word length: 900-1,200. Byline given.

Nonfiction: Middle readers, young adults: animal, arts/crafts, biography, cooking, games/puzzles, health, history, hobbies, how-to, humorous, nature/environment, problem-solving. Does not want to see articles written from an adult perspective. Average word length: 200-600. Byline given.

Poetry: Wants to see light verse, humorous poetry. Maximum line length: 24 lines.

How to Contact/Writers: Fiction/nonfiction: Send complete ms. Reports on queries/mss in 1 month. Will consider simultaneous submissions.

Illustration: Buys 1-2 illustrations/issue; buys 52 illustrations/year. "Illustrations are done on assignment only, to accompany our stories and articles—our need for new artists is very limited."

How to Contact/Illustrators: Illustrations only: "Prefer samples they do not want returned; these stay in our files." Reports on art samples only if interested. Original art work returned at job's completion.

Photography: Looking for photography showing ages 12-14, both sexes, good mix of races, wholesome fun. Uses 8×10 glossy b&w prints. To contact, photographers should send unsolicited photos by mail.

Terms: Pays on acceptance. For mss buys one-time rights; second serial (reprint rights). Buys one-time rights for artwork and photos. Pays 2-5¢/word for assigned/unsolicited articles. Pays $25-50/color (inside) illustration. Photographers are paid per photo, $15-50 (cover). Sample copy free with 7×10 SAE. Free writer's guidelines.

Tips: "We will be focusing on the 12 and 13 age group of our 10-14 audience. (Focus was somewhat younger before.)"

OWL MAGAZINE, The Discovery Magazine for Children, Young Naturalist Foundation, Ste. 306, 56 The Esplanade, Toronto Ontario M5E 1A7 Canada. (416)868-6001. Editor: Debora Pearson. Managing Editor: Deena Waisberg. Art Director: Tim Davin. Magazine published 10 times/year. Circ. 160,000. "*OWL* helps children over eight discover and enjoy the world of science and nature. We look for articles that are fun to read, that inform from a child's perspective, and that motivate hands-on interaction. *OWL* explores the reader's many interests in the natural world in a scientific, but always entertaining, way."

Fiction: Middle readers, young adults: animal, contemporary, fantasy, humorous, science fiction, sports, suspense/mystery/adventure. Does not want to see romance, religion, anthropomorphizing. Average word length: 500-1,000. Byline given. "We publish only 3-4 pieces of fiction per year."

Nonfiction: Middle readers, young adults: animal, biology, high-tech, humor, interview/profile, travel. Does not want to see religious topics, anthropomorphizing. Buys 20 mss/year. Average word length: 200-1,500. Byline given.

How to Contact/Writers: Fiction/nonfiction: Query with published clips. Report on queries in 4-6 weeks; mss in 6-8 weeks.

Illustration: Buys 3-5 illustrations/issue; buys 40-50 illustrations/year. Uses color artwork only. Preferred theme or style: lively, involving, fun, with emotional impact and appeal. "We use a range of styles." Works on assignment only.

How to Contact/Illustrators: Illustrations only: Send tearsheets and slides. Reports on art samples only if interested. Original artwork returned at job's completion.

Photography: Looking for shots of animals and nature. "Label the photos." Uses 2¼×2¼ and 35mm transparencies. To contact, photographers should query with samples.

Terms: Pays on acceptance. For mss, artwork and photos buys first North American and world rights. Pays $200-500 (Canadian) for assigned/unsolicited articles. Pays up to

$650 (Canadian) for illustrations. Photographers are paid per photo. Sample copy $4.28. Free writers' guidelines.

Tips: Writers: "Talk to kids and find out what they're interested in; make sure your research is thorough and find good consultants who are doing up-to-the-minute research. Be sure to read the magazine carefully to become familiar with *OWL's* style." (See listing for *Chickadee*.)

*PETS TODAY, Moorshead Publications, 797 Don Mills Rd. 10th Floor, North York Ontario M3C 3S5 Canada. (416)696-5488. Editor: Janet Piotrowski. Quarterly magazine. Estab. 1991. Circ. 30,000. "*Pets Today* is for the average pet owner, interested in health, behaviors, training, human-animal bond of their pets (not just cats and dogs), and in all animal kingdom in general." 10% of publication aimed at juvenile market.
Fiction: All levels: animal. Buys approx. 4-6 mss/year. Average word length: 500-1,000. Byline given.
Nonfiction: All levels: animal. Buys 4-6 mss/year. Average word length: 500-1,000. Byline given.
How to Contact/Writers: Fiction/nonfiction: Query. Reports on queries/mss in 2-4 weeks. Publishes ms 6 months after acceptance. Will consider simultaneous submissions, electronic submissions via disk or modem and previously published work.
Illustration: Buys 1 illustration/issue; 10 illustrations/year. Uses b&w artwork only. Reviews ms/illustration packages; reviews artwork for future assignments; works on assignment only.
How to Contact/Illustrators: Ms/illustration packages: Query. Illustrations only: Query; send resume and client list. Reports in 2-4 weeks. Samples returned with SASE. Original work returned upon job's completion "depending on arrangement made." Credit line given.
Photography: Purchases photos with accompanying ms only or for cover only. For cover, wants photos that are vertical, color, with room for title, pets (alone, with other pets, with people)—otherwise, b&w photos with manuscripts." Model/property releases required; photo captions required. Uses b&w glossy prints; 35mm transparencies. To contact, photographers should query with samples; query with resume of credits; send unsolicited photos by mail. Reports in 2-4 weeks.
Terms: Pays on publication. Buys reprint rights and all rights for mss. Purchases one-time rights for artwork ("with some exceptions"); one-time rights for photographs. For stories/articles pays "flat rates at discretion of editor." Additional payment for ms/illustration packages. Pays illustrators $25/color cover; b&w inside. Photographers paid $25/photo. Sample copy for 9 × 12 SAE (Canadian stamps). Writer's/illustrator's/photo guidelines free for SAE (Canadian stamps or IRCs).

PIONEER, Brotherhood Commission, SBC, 1548 Poplar Ave., Memphis TN 38104. (901)272-2461. Articles Editor: Jeno C. Smith. Art Director: Jim Hornsby. Monthly magazine. Circ. 30,000. Magazine contains boy interests, sports, crafts, sports personalities, religious.
Nonfiction: Young adults: animal, arts/crafts, biography, careers, games/puzzles, geography, health, hobbies, how-to, nature/environment, sports. Buys 15 mss/year. Average word length: 400-600. Byline given.
How to Contact/Writers: Nonfiction: Send complete ms. Reports on queries in 4-6 weeks; mss in 2 months. Will consider simultaneous submissions.
Illustration: Buys 1-2 illustrations/issue; buys 12 illustrations/year. Will review ms/illustration packages. Reviews artwork for future assignments.
How to Contact/Illustrators: Ms/illustration packages: Send complete ms with final art. Illustrations only: Provide promo sheet to be kept on file. Reports back only if interested. Credit line given.

Photography: Purchases photography from freelancers.
Terms: Pays on acceptance. Buys one-time and reprint rights. Pays $25-35 for articles. Photographers paid per photo (range: $5-75). Sample copy free with #10 SAE and 3 first-class stamps. Writer's/illustrator's guidelines free with SAE and 1 first-class stamp.
Tips: Wants to see "teenagers in sports, nature, health, hobbies—no preachy articles."

POCKETS, Devotional Magazine for Children, The Upper Room, 1908 Grand, P.O. Box 189, Nashville TN 37202. (615)340-7333. Articles/Fiction Editor: Janet R. McNish. Art Director: Chris Schechner, Ste. 207, 3100 Carlisle Plaza, Dallas TX 75204. Magazine published 11 times/year. Estab. 1981. Circ. 72,000. "Stories should help children 6 to 12 experience a Christian lifestyle that is not always a neatly wrapped moral package, but is open to the continuing revelation of God's will."
Fiction: Young readers, middle readers: contemporary, fantasy, history, religious, "retold Bible stories." Does not want to see violence. Buys 26-30 mss/year. Average word length: 800-2,000. Byline given.
Nonfiction: Young readers, middle readers: history, interview/profile, religious, "communication activities." Does not want to see how-to articles. "Our nonfiction reads like a story." History is in form of role-model stories as is profile. Buys 10 mss/year. Average word length: 800-2,000. Byline given.
How to Contact/Writers: Fiction/nonfiction: Send complete ms. "Prefer not to deal with queries." Report on mss in 2-4 weeks. Will consider simultaneous submissions.
Illustration: Buys 30 illustrations/issue. Preferred theme or style: varied; both 4-color and 2-color. Will review artwork for future assignments. Works on assignment only.
How to Contact/Illustrators: Illustrations only: Send tearsheets and slides to Chris Schechner, Ste. 207, 3100 Carlisle Plaza, Dallas TX 75204. Reports on art samples only if interested. Original artwork returned at job's completion. Credit line given.
Photography: Purchases photography from freelancers.
Terms: Pays on acceptance. Buys first North American rights for mss; one-time rights for artwork and photos. Pays 12-15¢/word for stories/articles. Pays $500-600/color (cover) illustration; $50-400/color (inside); $50-250 (2-color). Pays $25 for color transparencies accompanying articles; $500 for cover photos. Sample copy free with 7×9 SAE and 4 first-class stamps. Writer's/illustrator's guidelines free with SAE and 1 first-class stamp.
Tips: "Ask for our themes first. They are set yearly in the fall. Also, we are looking for articles about real children involved in environment, peace, or similar activities."

*POWER AND LIGHT, Children's Ministries, 6401 The Paseo, Kansas City MO 64131. (816)333-7000. Editor: Beula Postlewait. Executive Editor: Mark York. Weekly tabloid. *Power and Light* is a leisure reading piece for fifth and sixth graders. It is published weekly by the Department of Children's Ministries of the Church of the Nazarene. "The major purposes of *Power and Light* are to: provide a leisure reading piece which will build Christian behavior and values; provide reinforcement for Biblical concepts taught in the Sunday School curriculum. The focus of the reinforcement will be life-related, with some historical appreciation. *Power and Light*'s target audience is children ages 11-12 in grades fifth and sixth. The readability goal is fifth to sixth grade."
Fiction: Middle readers: adventure, contemporary, problem-solving, religious. "Avoid fantasy, science fiction, abnormally mature or precocious children, personification of animals. Also, avoid extensive cultural or holiday references, especially those with a distinctly American frame of reference. Our paper has an international audience." Average word length: 500-700. Byline given.
How to Contact/Writers: Send complete ms. Reports on queries in 2-4 weeks; mss in 4-6 weeks. Publishes ms 2 years after acceptance.

Illustration: *Power and Light* publishes a wide variety of artistic styles, i.e., cartoon, realistic, montage, etc., but whatever the style, artwork must appeal to 11-12 year old children. Reviews artwork for future assignments.

How to Contact/Illustrators: Illustrations only: Query; send resume, portfolio. Reports back only if interested. Credit line given.

Terms: Pays on publication. "Payment is made approximately one year before the date of issue." Buys multiple use rights for mss and artwork. Pays 3.5-5¢/word for stories. Pays illustrators $50/b&w (cover); $75/color (cover); $50/b&w inside; $50-75/color (inside). Writer's/illustrator's guidelines for SASE.

Tips "Themes and outcomes should conform to the theology and practices of the Church of the Nazarene, Evangelical Friends, Free Methodist, Wesleyan, and other Bible-believing Evangelical churches."

*RACING FOR KIDS, Griggs Publishing Company Inc., P.O. Box 500, Concord NC 28026. (704)786-7132. Editor: Donna Cox. Monthly magazine. Estab. 1990. Circ. 10,000. Publication caters to kids interested in racing.

Nonfiction: Young readers: health, nature/environment, science, sports, auto racing. Middle readers and young adults: science, sports, auto racing. Buys 12-20 mss/year. Average word length: 400-1,200. Byline given.

How to Contact/Writers: Nonfiction: Query. Reports on queries in 1 month. Publishes ms 6-12 months after acceptance.

Terms: Pays on publication. Buys exclusive magazine rights for mss. Pays $50-150 for stories, $50-150 for articles. Additional payment for photos that accompany article.

Tips: "Know the subject matter, study publication."

R-A-D-A-R, Standard Publishing, 8121 Hamilton Ave., Cincinnati OH 45231. (513)931-4050. Editor: Margaret Williams. Weekly magazine. Circ. 150,000. *R-A-D-A-R* is a weekly take-home paper for boys and girls who are in grades 3-6. "Our goal is to reach these children with the truth of God's Word, and to help them make it the guide of their lives. Many of our features, including our stories, now correlate with the Sunday school lesson themes. Send for a quarterly theme list and sample copies of *R-A-D-A-R*. Keep in mind that others will be submitting stories for the same themes—this is not an assignment."

Fiction: Middle readers: animal, contemporary, history, humorous, problem solving, religious, sports, suspense/mystery/adventure. Does not want to see fantasy or science fiction. Buys 150 mss/year. Average word length: 400-1,000. Byline given.

Nonfiction: Middle readers: animal, history, how-to, humorous, interview/profile, problem solving, religious, travel. Buys 50 mss/year. Average word length: 400-1,000. Byline given.

Poetry: Reviews poetry. Maximum line length: 16.

How to Contact/Writers: Fiction/nonfiction: Send complete ms. Reports on queries/mss 6-8 weeks. Will consider simultaneous submissions, (but prefer not to). Reprint submissions must be retyped.

Illustration: Will review all illustration packages. Works on assignment only; there have been a few exceptions to this.

How to Contact/Illustrators: Illustrations only: Send résumé, tearsheets, or promo sheets; samples of art can be photocopied. Reports on art samples only if interested.

Photography: Purchases photos from freelancers. Model/property releases required. Send résumé, business card, promotional literature or tearsheets to be kept on file.

Terms: Pays on acceptance. Buys first rights, one-time rights, second serial, first North American; all rights to art. Pays 3-7¢/word for unsolicited articles, few are assigned. Contributor copies given "not as payment, but all contributors receive copies of their art/articles." Pays $70-125 for color illustrations; $125-150 for color cover; $40-60 for line art only. Photographers paid $125 maximum per photo. Sample copy and writer's guidelines free with 9⅜ × 4¼ SAE and 1 first-class stamp.

Tips: "Write about current topics, issues that elementary-age children are dealing with. Keep illustrations/photos current." (See listing for *Straight*.)

RANGER RICK, National Wildlife Federation, 8925 Leesburg Pike, Vienna VA 22184. (703)790-4000. Editor: Gerald Bishop. Design Director: Donna Miller. Monthly magazine. Circ. 890,000. "Our audience ranges from ages six to twelve, though we aim the reading level of most material at nine-year-olds or fourth graders."

Fiction: Middle readers: animal (wildlife), fantasy, humor, science fiction. Buys 4-6 mss/year. Average word length: 900. Byline given.

Nonfiction: Middle readers: animal (wildlife), conservation, outdoor adventure, humor. Buys 20-30 mss/year. Average word length: 900. Byline given.

How to Contact/Writers: Fiction: Query with published clips; send complete ms. Nonfiction: Query with published clips. Reports on queries/mss in 6 weeks.

Illustration: Buys 6-8 illustrations/issue; buys 75-100 illustrations/year. Preferred theme or style: nature, wildlife. Will review artwork for future assignments. Works on assignment only.

How to Contact/Illustrators: Illustrations only: Send résumé, tearsheets. Reports on art samples in 6 weeks. Original artwork returned at job's completion.

Terms: Pays on acceptance. Buys all rights (first North American serial rights negotiable). Pays up to $575 for full-length of best quality. For illustrations, buys one-time rights. Pays $250-1,000 for color (inside, per page) illustration. Sample copy $2. Writer's guidelines free with SASE.

Tips: "Fiction and nonfiction articles may be written on any aspect of wildlife, nature, outdoor adventure and discovery, domestic animals with a 'wild' connection (such as domestic pigs and wild boars), science, conservation, or related subjects. To find out what subjects have been covered recently, consult our annual indexes and the *Children's Magazine Guide*. These are available in many libraries. The National Wildlife Federation (NWF) discourages the keeping of wildlife as pets, so the keeping of such pets should not be featured in your copy. Avoid stereotyping of any group. For instance, girls can enjoy nature and the outdoors as much as boys can, and mothers can be just as knowledgeable as fathers. The only way you can write successfully for *Ranger Rick* is to know the kinds of subjects and approaches we like. And the only way you can do that is to read the magazine. Recent issues can be found in most libraries or are available from our office for $2 a copy."

*SASSY, 230 Park Ave., New York NY 10169. (212)551-9554. Fiction Editor: Christina Kelly. Art Director: Noel Claro. Monthly magazine. Estab. 1988. Circ. 650,000. Audience is teenage girls.

Fiction: Young Adults: quality fiction. Buys approx. 12 mss/year. Average word length: 1,000-2,000. Byline given.

How to Contact/Writers: Send complete ms. Reports in 3 months. Will consider simultaneous submissions.

SCHOLASTIC MATH MAGAZINE, Scholastic, Inc., 730 Broadway, New York NY 10003. (212)505-3135. Fax: (212)505-3377. Editor: Tracey Randinelli. Senior Designer: Leah Bossio. Art Director: Joan Michael. Magazine published 8 times/year, September-May. Estab. 1980. Circ. 265,000. "We are a math magazine for 7, 8, 9 grade classrooms. We present math in current, relevant, high-interest topics. Math skills we focus on include whole number, fraction, and decimal computation, percentages, ratios, proportions, geometry."

Nonfiction: Young adults: animal, arts/crafts, careers, cooking, fashion, games/puzzles, geography, health, history, hobbies, how-to, humorous, interview/profile, math, multicultural, nature/environment, problem solving, science, social issues, sports, travel. No fiction. Does not want to see "anything dealing with *very* controversial issues—e.g., teenage pregnancy, etc." Buys 20 mss/year. Byline given.

How to Contact/Writers: Query. Reports on queries in 2 months. Will consider simultaneous submissions.

Illustration: Buys 4 illustrations/issue; 56 illustrations/year. Prefers to review "humorous, young adult sophistication" types of art. Will review ms/illustration packages. Works on assignment only.

How to Contact/Illustrators: Ms/illustration packages: "Query first." Illustrations only: Query with samples; submit portfolio for review. Reports back only if interested. Original artwork returned at job's completion.

Terms: Pays on publication. Buys all rights for mss. Pays $25 for puzzles and riddles; maximum of $350 for stories/articles. Photographers are paid by the project.

Tips: "For our magazine, stories dealing with math concepts and applications in the real world are sought."

SCHOOL MAGAZINE, (BLAST OFF!, COUNTDOWN, ORBIT, TOUCHDOWN), New South Wales Dept. of School Education, Private Bag 3, Ryde NSW 2112 Australia. (02)808-9683. Editor: Jonathan Shaw. 4 monthly magazines. Circ. 200,000. *School Magazine* is a literary magazine that is issued to all N.S.W. primary public schools. Private schools and individuals subscribe for a small fee. We include stories, plays and poems. The 4 magazines issued each month are graded according to age level, 8-12 years.

Fiction: Young readers: animal, contemporary, fantasy, humorous. Middle readers: animal, contemporary, fantasy, humorous, problem solving, science fiction, suspense/mystery/adventure. Buys 30 mss/year. Average word length: 500-2,500. Byline given.

Poetry: Maximum length: 150 lines. Limit submissions to 10 poems.

How to Contact/Writers: Fiction: Send complete ms. SAE (IRC) for return of ms. Reports on queries in 2 weeks; on mss in 2 months. Publishes ms at least 6 months after acceptance.

Terms: Pays on acceptance. Buys first Australian serial rights. "Pays $137 per thousand words." Free sample copy.

SCHOOL MATES, USCF's Magazine For Beginning Chess Players, United States Chess Federation, 186 Rt. 9W, New Windsor NY 12553. (914)562-8350. FAX (914)561-CHES. Editor-in-Chief: Jennie Simon. Art Director: Jami Anson. Bimonthly magazine. Estab. 1987. Circ. 13,600. Magazine for beginning chess players. Offers instruction articles, features on famous players, scholastic chess coverage, games, puzzles, occasional fiction, listing of chess tournaments.

Fiction: Middle readers: problem-solving (chess related). Average word length: 1,000-5,000 words.

Nonfiction: Middle readers: games/puzzles, chess. "No *Mad Magazine* type humor. No sex, no drugs, no alcohol, no tobacco. No stereotypes. We want to see chess presented as a wholesome, non-nerdy activity that's fun for all. Good sportsmanship, fair play, and 'thinking ahead' in chess as in life are extremely desirable in articles. Also, celebrities who play chess."

Poetry: "We've just begun to consider publishing poetry." Wants to see poetry about chess!!

How to Contact/Writers: Send complete ms. Reports on queries/mss in 3 months

Illustration: Buys 2-3 illustrations/year. Prefers b&w, ink preferably, cartoons OK. Reviews ms/illustration packages; reviews artwork for future assignments.

How to Contact/Illustrators: Query first. Reports back only if interested. "Typically, a cover is credited while an illustration inside gets only the artist's signature in the work itself."

Photography: Purchases photos from freelancers. Wants "action shots of chess games, well-done portraits of popular chess players."
Terms: Pays on publication. Buys one-time rights for mss, artwork and photos. For stories/articles, pays $40 per 1,000 words. Pays illustrators $50-75/b&w cover; $25-45/b&w inside. Pays photographers per photo (range: $25-75). Sample copies are free for 9×12 SAE and 2 first class stamps. Writer's guidelines free on request.
Tips: Writers: "Lively prose that grabs and sustains kids' attention is desirable. Don't talk down to kids or over their heads. Don't be overly 'cute.' " Illustration/photography: "Whimsical shots are often desirable."

SCIENCE WEEKLY, Science Weekly Inc., Suite 202, 2141 Industrial Pkwy., Silver Spring MD 20904. (301)680-8004. Fax: (301)680-9240. Biweekly magazine. Estab. 1984. Circ. 250,000.
Nonfiction: All levels: education, problem-solving, science/math education. "Call for more information on freelancing needs."
Terms: Pays on publication. "Call for more information, writer's guidelines and training workshop."

SCIENCELAND, To Nurture Scientific Thinking, Scienceland Inc., #2108, 501 Fifth Ave., New York NY 10017-6102. (212)490-2180. Fax: (212)986-2077. Editor/Art Director: Al Matano. Magazine published 8 times/year. Estab. 1977. Circ. 16,000. This is "a content reading picture-book for K-3rd grade to encourage beginning readers; for teachers and parents."
Nonfiction: Picture-oriented material and young readers: animal, art/crafts, biography, careers, cooking, education, games/puzzles, health, history, how-to, nature/environment, problem solving. Does not want to see "unillustrated material."
Poetry: Reviews poetry. Maximum length: 12 lines.
How to Contact/Writers: Not interested in stories. *Must* be picture or full-color illustrated stories.
Illustration: Prefers to review "detailed, realistic, full color art. No abstracts." Uses "predominantly" color artwork. Will review ms/illustration packages; reviews artwork for future assignments.
How to Contact/Illustrators: Ms/illustration packages: "Query first." Illustrations only: Send unsolicited art by mail; provide resume, promotional literature or tearsheets to be kept on file. Reports back in 3-4 weeks. Original artwork returned at job's completion, "depending on material."
Photography: Wants to see "physical and natural science photos with children in scenes whenever possible." Model/property release and photo captions required. Uses 35mm transparencies. To contact, photographer should submit portfolio for review; provide resume, promotional literature or tearsheets to be kept on file.
Terms: Pays on publication. Buys first rights for mss, artwork and photos. Payment for ms/illustration packages: $50-500. Payment for illustrations: $25-300 color cover; $25-300 color inside. Photographers paid by the project. Sample copy free with 9×12 SASE.
Tips: "Must be top notch illustrator or photographer. No amateurs."

*SCOPE, Scholastic Inc., 730 Broadway, New York NY 10003. (212)505-3000. Editor: Laurem Tarshis. Art Director: Joy Makon. Biweekly magazine. Estab. 1964. Circ. 700,000. "*Scope* is directed at middle-school and high school students who often wish they weren't at school. Many are poor readers. *Scope* aims to motivate them to read and to think about their world."
Fiction: Middle readers, young adults: animal, contemporary, fantasy, humorous, problem solving, science fiction, sports and spy/mystery/adventure. Young adults: romance. Buys 20 mss/year. Average word length: 200-2,500. Byline given.

Nonfiction: Middle readers, young adults: animal, how-to, humorous, interview/profile and problem solving. Buys 35 mss/year. Average word length: 200-2,000. Byline "sometimes given."

How to Contact/Writers: Fiction: Send complete ms. Nonfiction: Query with published clips. Include Social Security number with submission. Reports on queries in 1 month; mss in 2 months.

Illustration: Buys 6-10 illustrations/issue; buys 100-150 illustrations/year. Preferred theme or style: "varies; prefer sophisticated, non-childish styles." Works on assignment only.

How to Contact/Illustrators: Ms/illustration packages: "Submit portfolio; leave samples/tearsheets." Illustrations only: "Submit portfolio; leave samples/tearsheets. Do not send any nonreturnable materials." Original artwork returned at job's completion.

Terms: Pays on acceptance. Pays $75-400 for assigned articles; $50-250 for unsolicited articles. Additional payment for ms/illustration packages. Sample copy for $1.75 with 9 × 12 SAE. Writer's guidelines free with SASE.

Tips: Illustrators: "Do not telephone art department. Submit portfolio of sample styles; leave samples/tearsheets to keep on file."

SEVENTEEN MAGAZINE, News America, 850 Third Ave., New York NY 10022. (212)759-8100. Managing Editor: Roberta Myers. Articles Editor: Sarah Patton. Fiction Editor: Joe Bargmann. Art Director: Annie Demchick. Monthly magazine. Estab. 1944. Circ. 1,750,000. "General interest magazine for teenage girls."

Fiction: Young adults: animal, contemporary, fantasy, history, humorous, problem-solving, religious, romance, science fiction, sports, spy/mystery/adventure, adult. "We consider all good literary short fiction." Buys 12-20 mss/year. Average word length: 900-3,000. Byline given.

Nonfiction: Young adults: animal, history, how-to, humorous, interview/profile, problem solving, religious, travel. Buys 150 mss/year. Word length: Lengths vary from 800-1,000 words for short features and monthly columns to 2,500 words for major articles. Byline given.

Poetry: Reviews poetry "only by teenagers younger than 21."

How to Contact/Writers: Fiction: Send complete ms. Nonfiction: Query with published clips or send complete ms. Reports on queries/mss in 3 weeks. Will consider simultaneous submissions.

Illustration: 1 illustration per short story. Will review ms/illustration packages. Illustrators paid by the project. Writer's guidelines for business-size envelope and 1 first-class stamp.

SHARING THE VICTORY, Fellowship of Christian Athletes, 8701 Leeds, Kansas City MO 64129. (816)921-0909. Fax: (816)921-8755. Articles Editor: John Dodderidge. Art Director: Frank Grey. Photo Editor: John Dodderidge. Monthly magazine. Estab. 1982. Circ. 55,000. "Purpose is to present to coaches and athletes, and all whom they influence, the challenge and adventure of receiving Jesus Christ as Savior and Lord."

Nonfiction: Young adults: interview/profile, sports. Buys 20-25 mss/year. Average word length: 400-900. Byline given.

Poetry: Reviews poetry. Maximum word length 50-75.

How to Contact/Writers: Nonfiction: Query with published clips. Reports in 3 weeks. Publishes ms 3 months after acceptance. Will consider simultaneous submissions, electronic submissions via disk or modem and previously published work.

Photography: Purchases photos separately. Looking for photos of sports action. Uses color, b&w prints and 35mm transparencies.

Terms: Pays on publication. Buys first rights and second serial (reprint rights). Pays $50-250 for assigned and unsolicited articles. Photographers paid per photo (range: $50-300). Sample copies for 9 × 12 SASE and $1. Writer's/photo guidelines for SASE.

Tips: "Be specific—write short. Take quality photos that are useable." Wants interviews and features. Interested in colorful sports photos.

SHOFAR, 43 Northcote Dr., Melville NY 11747. (516)643-4598. Managing Editor: Gerald H. Grayson. Magazine published monthly Oct. through May—double issues Dec./Jan. and April/May. Circ. 17,000. For Jewish children ages 9-13.
Fiction: Middle readers: cartoons, contemporary, humorous, poetry, puzzles, religious, sports. All material must be on a Jewish theme. Buys 10-20 mss/year. Average word length: 500-700. Byline given.
Nonfiction: Middle readers: history, humorous, interview/profile, religious. Buys 10-20 mss/year. Average word length: 500-1,000. Byline given.
How to Contact/Writers: Fiction/nonfiction: Send complete ms (preferred). Queries welcome. Submit holiday theme pieces at least 4 months in advance. Will consider simultaneous and electronic submissions via disk or modem (only Macintosh).
Illustration: Buys 3-4 illustrations/issue; buys 15-20 illustrations/year. Works on assignment only.
How to Contact/Illustrators: Ms/illustration packages: Query first. Illustrations only: Send tearsheets. Works on assignment only. Reports on art samples only if interested. Original artwork returned at job's completion.
Terms: Buys first North American serial rights or first serial rights. Pays on publication. Pays 7¢/word plus 5 contributor's copies. Photos purchased with mss at additional fees. Pays $25-100/b&w cover illustration; $50-150/color (cover). Sample copy free with 9 × 12 SAE and 3 first-class stamps. Free writer's/illustrator's guidelines.

THE SINGLE PARENT, Journal of Parents Without Partners, Inc., 8807 Colesville Rd., Silver Spring MD 20910-4346. (301)588-9354. Fax: (301)588-9216. Articles/Fiction Editor/Art Director: Rene McDonald. Bimonthly magazine. Estab. 1957. Circ. 100,000. Members of PWP are single parents who are divorced, widowed or never married. "All our material is related to this basic fact. We look at the positive side of our situation and are interested in all aspects of parenting, and the particular situation of single parenting." 10% of material aimed at juvenile audience.
Fiction: Young readers, middle readers, young adults: contemporary, humorous, problem solving, suspense/mystery/adventure (only stories with single parent angle). No "downers" or sports, romance, or anthropomorphic material. Buys 12 mss/year. Average word length: 800-1,500. Byline given.
Nonfiction: Young readers, middle readers, young adults: careers, cooking, education, health, history, humorous, interview/profile, problem-solving. "We do not ordinarily use nonfiction aimed at children, but could be persuaded by a particularly good piece." Does *not* want to see material unrelated to single-parent children and families. Average word length: 800-1,800. Byline given.
How to Contact/Writers: Fiction/nonfiction: Send complete ms. Reports on queries/mss in 6 weeks. Will consider simultaneous submissions. Scannable manuscripts are required.
Illustration: Buys 3 illustrations/issue. Preferred theme or style: Line art, sometimes with mechanicals. "Must fit trim size—8 × 10¾." No special preference for style. Will review ms/illustration packages. Works on speculation only.
How to Contact/Illustrators: Ms/illustration packages: Send complete ms with final art with prepaid return envelope. Illustrations only: Send nonreturnable samples in whatever form the artist prefers. Reports on art samples only if interested. Original artwork returned at job's completion.
Photography: Wants to see "child(ren) with one parent, children interacting, including angrily." Model/property release required. Uses 8 × 10 b&w prints, 35mm transparencies. To contact, photographer should query with samples; provide résumé, business card and tearsheets.

Terms: Pays on publication. Buys one-time rights to mss, artwork and photos. Pays $35-125 for unsolicited stories. Pays $125/color (cover) illustration; $50-75/b&w (inside); $50-75/color (inside). Sample copy $1.25 (first class postage). Writer's/illustrator's guidelines free with SASE.

Tips: Writers: "Study your target; do not submit material if you've never seen the magazine. In stories where the protagonist undergoes a behavior change, build up a credible reason for it. 'Comes to realize' is not a credible reason. Be aware of the age you are writing about and for. Include less fluff and more substance in attractive formats. We are overstocked at the moment with children's stories, but still buy one occasionally that we're unable to resist. Our greatest need is for articles for adults, in particular, articles on parenting from the single father's perspective." Illustrators: "Get examples of your work to as many editors as possible, but remember, there are hundreds of others doing the same thing. All samples are reviewed, and I put those that appeal to me in a separate file as potential illustrators for the magazine. To get into the 'may call on' file, provide me with nonreturnable samples that illustrate the broadest range of your work—I may not appreciate your cartoon style, but think your realistic style is super or vice versa."

SKIPPING STONES, A Multi-Cultural Children's Quarterly, P.O. Box 3939, Eugene OR 97403. (503)342-4956. Manging Editor: Arun N. Toké. Quarterly magazine. Estab. 1988. Circ. 3,000. "*Skipping Stones* is a multi-cultural nonprofit children's magazine designed to encourage cooperation, creativity and celebration of cultural and environmental richness. We encourage submissions by minorities and under-represented populations."

Nonfiction: All age groups: animal, nature/environment, problem-solving, religion and cultural celebrations, travel, and multicultural and environmental awareness. Does not want to see preaching or abusive language. Average word length: 300 words. Byline given.

How to Contact/Writers: Query. For nonfiction, send complete ms. Reports on queries in 2 months. Will consider simultaneous submissions. Please include your name on each page.

Illustration: Prefers b&w drawings especially by young adults. Will consider all illustration packages.

How to Contact/Illustrators: Submit complete ms with final art. Submit tearsheets. Reports back in 2 months (only if interested). Original artwork returned at job's completion.

Photography: B&w photos preferred, but color photos will be considered.

Terms: No payment; just a copy of the magazine containing work. Acquires one-time rights. Sample copy for $4 with SAE and 4 first class stamps. Writer's/illustrator's guidelines for 1 first class stamp and 4×9 SAE.

Tips: Wants material "meant for children," with multi-cultural or environmental awareness theme. "Think, live and write as if you were a child. Let the 'inner child' within you speak out—naturally, uninhibited." Wants "material that gives insight on cultural celebrations, lifestyle, custom and tradition, glimpse of daily life in other countries and cultures. Photos, songs, artwork are most welcome if they illustrate/highlight the points. Translations are welcome if your submission is in a language other than English. In 1993, our themes will include homeless and street children, world religions and cultures,

African-American experiences, Japan, a Spanish-English bilingual issue, Eastern Europe, death and loss, substance abuse, . ."

SPARK! Creative Fun for Kids, F&W Publications, 1507 Dana Ave., Cincinnati OH 45207. (513)531-2222. Fax: (513)531-2902. Editorial Director: Michael Ward. Art Director: Stephanie Redman. Published nine times per year. Estab. 1991. Circ. 80,000. "Publication devoted to nurturing creativity in 6- to 12-year-old children; publish art and writing projects that kids can do on their own or with minimal help from their parents."
Fiction: Young readers and middle readers: finish the adventure fantasies. Buys approx. 15-20 mss/year. Average word length: 300-800 words. Byline given.
Nonfiction: Young readers, middle readers: arts/crafts, games/puzzles and how-to. Buys 60-70 mss/year. Average word length: 250-500. Byline given.
Poetry: Maximum length: 100 words.
How to Contact/Writers: Fiction/nonfiction: Query with published clips. Reports in 1 month. Publishes ms 3 months after acceptance. Will consider simultaneous submissions and previously published work.
Illustration: Buys 5-7 illustrations/issue; 40 illustrations/year. Reviews ms/illustration packages; reviews artwork for future assignments; works on assignment only.
How to Contact/Illustrators: Illustrations only: provide résumé and tearsheets. Reports back only if interested. Original work returned upon job's completion. Credit line given.
Photography: Purchases photography from freelancers with accompanying ms only.
Terms: Pays on acceptance. Buys first North American serial rights. Purchases first North American rights for artwork and photos. Pays $50-250 for articles. Sample copies for $3 and SASE. Writer's guidelines free for SASE.
Tips: "Writers should understand the developmental levels of kids 6-12, and know how to structure articles and projects to meet their needs." Seeking "articles that describe, step-by-step, and illustrate creative projects for kids. Query with the entire articles and photos of the kid-produced projects."

STORY FRIENDS, Mennonite Publishing House, 616 Walnut Ave., Scottdale PA 15683. (412)887-5181. Fax: (412)887-3111. Editor: Marjorie Waybill. Art Director: Jim Butti. "Monthly in weekly issues magazine." Estab. 1905. Circ. 10,000. Story paper that reinforces Christian values for children ages 4-9.
Fiction: Young readers: contemporary, humorous, problem solving, religious, relationships. Buys 45 mss/year. Average word length: 300-800. Byline given.
Nonfiction: Picture-oriented and young readers: interview/profile, nature/environment. Buys 10 mss/year. Average word length: 300-800. Byline given.
Poetry: "I like variety—some long story poems and some four-lines."
How to Contact/Writers: Fiction/nonfiction: Send complete ms. Reports on mss in 2-3 weeks. Will consider simultaneous submissions.
Illustration: Works on assignment only.
Terms: Writer's guidelines free with SAE and 2 first class stamps.

STRAIGHT, Standard Publishing, 8121 Hamilton Ave., Cincinnati OH 45231. (513)931-4050. Articles/Fiction Editor: Carla J. Crane. "Quarterly in weekly parts" magazine. Circ. 60,000. *Straight* is a magazine designed for today's Christian teenagers.
Fiction: Young adults: adventure, contemporary, health, humorous, nature/environment, problem solving, religious, sports. Does not want to see science fiction, fantasy, historical. Buys 100-115 mss/year. Average word length: 1,100-1,500. Byline given.
Nonfiction: Young adults: careers, concept, health, how-to, humorous, interview/profile, nature/environment, problem solving, religious, science, social issues. Does not want to see devotionals. Buys 24-30 mss/year. Average word length: 500-1,000. Byline given.

Poetry: Reviews poetry from teenagers only.

How to Contact/Writers: Fiction/nonfiction: Query or send complete ms. Reports on queries in 1-2 weeks; mss in 4-6 weeks. Will consider simultaneous submissions.

Illustration: Buys 40-45 illustrations/year. Uses color artwork only. Preferred theme or style: Realistic, cartoon (full-color only). Will review ms/illustration packages "on occasion." Reviews artwork for future assignments. Works on assignment only.

How to Contact/Illustrators: Ms/illustration packages: Query first. Illustrations only: Submit portfolio or tearsheets. Reports back only if interested. Credit line given.

Photography: Purchases photos from freelancers. Looking for contemporary teenagers. Model/property release required. Uses 5×7 or 8×10 b&w prints and 35mm transparencies. To contact, photographer should send unsolicited photos by mail.

Terms: Pays on acceptance. For mss buys first North American rights; second serial (reprint rights). Buys full rights for artwork; one-time rights for photos. Pays 3-7¢ per word for stories/articles. Pays illustrators $150-250/color inside. Photographers paid per photo (range: $50-125). Sample copy free with business SASE. Writer's/illustrator's guidelines free with business SASE.

Tips: "The main characters should be contemporary teens who cope with modern-day problems using Christian principles. Stories should be uplifting, positive and character-building, but not preachy. Conflicts must be resolved realistically, with thought-provoking and honest endings. Accepted length is 1,100 to 1,500 words. Nonfiction is accepted. We use devotional pieces, articles on current issues from a Christian point of view, and humor. Nonfiction pieces should concern topics of interest to teens, including school, family life, recreation, friends, part-time jobs, dating and music." (See listing for *R-A-D-A-R*.)

*STREET TIMES, Outside In, 1236 SW Salmon, Portland OR 97205. Editor: Louis Folkman. Monthly newsletter. Estab. 1987. Circ. 800. Contains "resources, street life stories, poetry and art—designed as a pre-employment training tool for Portland street youth." 70% of publication aimed at juvenile market.

Nonfiction: Wants experiences of "other street youth or former street youth; difficulties of getting off the street."

Poetry: Reviews poetry.

How to Contact/Writers: Nonfiction: Send complete ms. Will consider simultaneous submissions and previously published work.

Illustration: Uses b&w artwork only.

How to Contact/Illustrators: Samples not returned; samples kept on file. Originals not returned upon job's completion.

Terms: Sample copies free for SASE.

SUPERSCIENCE BLUE, Scholastic, Inc., 730 Broadway, New York NY 10003. (212)505-3000. Editor: Kathy Burkett. Art Director: Susan Kass. Monthly (during school year) magazine. Estab. 1989. Circ. 375,000. "News and hands-on science for children in grades 4-6. Designed for use in a class setting; distributed by teacher. Articles make science fun and interesting for a broad audience of children. Issues are theme-based."

Nonfiction: Middle readers: animal, how-to (science experiments), nature/environment, problem solving, science topics. Does not want to see "general nature stories. Our focus is science with a *news* or *hands-on* slant. To date we have never purchased an unsolicited manuscript. Instead, we assign articles based on clips—and sometimes

 The asterisk before a listing indicates the listing is new in this edition.

queries." Write for editorial calendar. Average word length: 250-800. Byline sometimes given.

How to Contact/Writers: Nonfiction: Query with published clips. (Most freelance articles are assigned.) Reports on queries in 4-6 weeks. Publishes ms 4 months after acceptance.

Illustration: Buys 2-3 illustrations/issue; 10-12 illustrations/year. Works on assignment only.

How to Contact/Illustrators: Illustrations only: Send résumé and tearsheets. Reports on art samples only if interested. Original artwork returned at job's completion.

Terms: Pays on acceptance. Buys all rights. Pays $100-450. Illustrations only: $75+/ b&w (inside); $150-1,200/color (inside) (complicated spreads only). Writer's guidelines free on request.

Tips: Looks for "news articles and photo essays. Good journalism means always going to *primary* sources—interview scientists in the field, for example, and *quote* them for a more lively article."

TAKE 5, Back to the Bible, P.O. Box 82808, Lincoln NE 68501. (402)474-4567. Editor: Marcia Claesson. Quarterly devotional. Circ. approx. 25,000.

Nonfiction: Young adults: Commentaries on specific Bible passages. Write or call for further information. Writers must agree with Statement of Faith. Average word length: 200.

How to Contact/Writers: Send samples of devotionals. Reports in 2 weeks.

Terms: Buys first rights. Pays $15.

'TEEN MAGAZINE, Petersen Publishing Co., 8490 Sunset Blvd., Los Angeles CA 90069. (310)854-2950. Editor: Roxanne Camron. Managing/Fiction Editor: Karle Dickerson. Art Director: Laurel Finnerty. Monthly magazine. Estab. 1957. Circ. 1,100,000. "We are a pure junior high and senior high female audience. *'TEEN* teens are upbeat and want to be informed."

Fiction: Young adults: adventure, humor, problem-solving, romance and suspense/mystery. Does not want to see "that which does not apply to our market—i.e., science fiction, history, religion, adult-oriented." Buys 12 mss/year. Length for fiction: 10-15 pages typewritten, double-spaced.

Nonfiction: Young adults: how-to, humor, interview/profile, problem solving and young girl topics. Does not want to see adult oriented, adult point of view." Buys 25 mss/year. Length for articles: 10-20 pages typewritten, double-spaced. Byline given.

How to Contact/Writers: Fiction/nonfiction: Query. Reports on queries/mss in 10 weeks. Prefer submissions hard copy and disk.

Illustration: Buys 0-4 illustrations/issue. Preferred theme or style: "Various styles for variation. Use a lot of b&w illustration. Light, upbeat." Will review ms/illustration packages; artwork for future assignments.

How to Contact/Illustrators: Ms/illustration packages: "Query first." Illustrations only: "Want to see samples whether it be tearsheets, slides, finished pieces showing the style."

Terms: Pays on acceptance. Buys all rights. Pays $25-400 for assigned articles. Pays $25-250/b&w inside; $100-400/color inside. Writer's/illustrator's guidelines free with SASE.

Tips: Illustrators: "Present professional finished work. Get familiar with magazine and send samples that would be compatible with the style of publication." There is a need for artwork with "fiction/specialty articles. Send samples or promotional materials on a regular basis."

TEEN POWER, Scripture Press Publications, Inc., P.O. Box 632, Glen Ellyn IL 60138. (708)668-6000. Editor: Amy J. Cox. Quarterly magazine. Estab. 1965. "*Teen Power* is an eight-page Sunday School take-home paper aimed at 11-16 year olds in a conservative

Christian audience. Its primary objective is to help readers see how principles for Christian living can be applied to everyday life."

Fiction: Young adults: contemporary, humor, problem solving, religion, sports. Does not want to see "unrealistic stories with tacked-on morals. Fiction should be true-to-life and have a clear, spiritual take-away value." Buys 50 mss/year. Average word length: 400-1,200. Byline given.

Nonfiction: Young adults: how-to, humor, interview/profile, problem-solving, religion. Does not want to see "articles with no connection to Christian principles." Buys 30 mss/year. Average word length: 250-700. Byline given.

How To Contact/Writers: Fiction/nonfiction: Send complete ms. Reports on mss in 2 months. Average length of time between acceptance and publication of work: "at least one year." Will consider simultaneous submissions.

Terms: Pays on acceptance. Buys one-time rights. Pays $20-120 for articles. Sample copies and writer's guidelines for #10 SAE and 1 first class stamp.

3-2-1 CONTACT, Children's Television Workshop, One Lincoln Plaza, New York NY 10023. (212)595-3456. Articles Editor: Jonathan Rosenbloom. Fiction Editor: Curtis Slepian. Art Director: Al Nagy. Magazine published 10 times/year. Estab. 1979. Circ. 440,000. This is a science and technology magazine for 8-14 year olds. Features all areas of science and nature.

Fiction: "Our fiction piece is an on-going series called "The Time Team." So far it has been written in-house."

Nonfiction: Middle readers, young adults: animal, how-to, interview/profile. Does not want to see religion, travel or history. Buys 20 mss/year. Average word length: 750-1,000. Byline given.

How to Contact/Writers: Fiction/nonfiction: Query with published clips. Reports on queries in 3 weeks.

Illustration: Buys 15 illustrations/issue; buys 150 illustrations/year. Works on assignment only.

How to Contact/Illustrators: Illustrations only: Send tearsheets. Reports on art samples only if interested. Original artwork returned at job's completion.

Terms: Pays on acceptance. Pays $100-600 for assigned/unsolicited articles. Pays $500-1,000/color (cover) illustration; $150-300/b&w (inside); $175-350/color (inside). Sample copy for $1.75 and 8 × 14 SASE; writer's/illustrator's guidelines free with 8½ × 11 SASE.

Tips: Looks for "features. We do not want articles based on library research. We want on-the-spot interviews about what's happening in science now." (see listing for *Kid City*)

TOUCH, Calvinettes, P.O. Box 7259, Grand Rapids MI 49510. (616)241-5616. Editor: Joanne Ilbrink. Managing Editor: Carol Smith. Art Director: Chris Cook. Monthly (with combined issues May/June, July/Aug.) magazine. Circ. 15,200. "*Touch* is designed to help girls ages 9-14 see how God is at work in their lives and in the world around them."

Fiction: Middle readers, young adults: animal, contemporary, history, humor, problem solving, religion, romance. Does not want to see unrealistic stories and those with trite, easy endings. Buys 40 mss/year. Average word length: 400-1,000. Byline given.

Nonfiction: Middle readers, young adults: how-to, humor, interview/profile, problem solving, religion. Buys 5 mss/year. Average word length: 200-800. Byline given.

How to Contact/Writers: Fiction/nonfiction: Send complete ms. Reports on mss in 4 months. Will consider simultaneous submissions.

Illustration: Buys 1-2 illustrations/issue; buys 10-15 illustrations/year. Prefers illustrations to go with stories. Will review ms/illustration packages. Works on assignment only.

How to Contact/Illustrators: Ms/illustration packages: "We would prefer to consider finished art with a ms." Illustrations only: "A sample of work could be submitted in tearsheets or rough drafts." Reports on art samples only if interested.

Terms: Pays on publication. Buys first North American serial rights; first rights; second serial (reprint rights); simultaneous rights. Pays $20-50 for assigned articles; $5-30 for unsolicited articles. "We send complimentary copies in addition to pay." Pays $25-50/ b&w (cover) illustration; $15-25/b&w (inside) illustration. Writer's guidelines free with SASE.

Tips: Writers: "The stories should be current, deal with adolescent problems and joys, and help girls see God at work in their lives through humor as well as problem solving." Illustrators: Write for guidelines and our biannual update. It is difficult working with artists who are not local."

TQ, Teen Quest, Good News Broadcasting Assoc., Box 82808, Lincoln NE 68501. (402)474-4567. Fax: (402)474-4519. Editor: Christopher Lyon. Art Director: Victoria Valentine. Monthly (combined July/August issue) magazine. Estab. 1947. Circ. 55,000. "Ours is a magazine for Christian teenagers. Articles and fiction purchased from free-lancers must have a Christian basis, be relevant to contemporary teen culture, and be written in a style understandable and attractive to teenagers. Artwork must be likewise appropriate."

Fiction: Young adults: contemporary, fantasy, humor, problem solving, religion, romance, science fiction, sports, suspense/mystery/adventure. Buys 40 mss/year. Average word length: 1,500-3,000. Byline given.

Nonfiction: Young adults: how-to, humor, interview/profile, problem solving, religion, travel. Buys 30 mss/year. Average word length: 500-2,000. Byline given.

How to Contact/Writers: Fiction/nonfiction: Query. Reports on queries in 6 weeks; mss in 6-8 weeks. Will consider simultaneous submissions (indicate so).

Illustration: Buys 5 illustrations/issue; buys 50 illustrations/year. Preferred theme or style: "Realistic, somewhat contemporary, but not too far out of the mainstream." Works on assignment only.

How to Contact/Illustrators: Ms/illustration packages: Query only. Illustrations only: Send tearsheets. Reports on art samples only if interested. Original artwork returned at job's completion.

Terms: Pays on completion of assignment. Buys one-time rights. Pays 10-15¢/word for assigned articles; 7-12¢/word for unsolicited articles. Sample copy for 10 × 12 SAE and 5 first-class stamps; writer's/illustrator's guidelines for business-size envelope and 1 first-class stamp.

Tips: Fiction: be current; Christian message without being "preachy." "Most stories we buy will center on the lives and problems of 14 to 17 year-old characters. The problems involved should be common to teens (dating, family, alcohol and drugs, peer pressure, school, sex, talking about one's faith to nonbelievers, standing up for convictions, etc.) in which the resolution (or lack of it) is true to our readers' experiences. In other words, no happily-ever-after endings, last-page spiritual conversions or pat answers to complex problems. We're interested in the everyday (though still profound) experiences of teen life—stay away from sensationalism."

TURTLE MAGAZINE, For Preschool Kids, Children's Better Health Institute, P.O. Box 567, Indianapolis IN 46206. (317)636-8881. Editor: Christine Clark. Art Director: Bart Rivers. Monthly/bimonthly magazine, Jan./Feb., March, April/May, June, July/August, Sept., Oct./Nov., Dec. Circ. approx. 550,000. *Turtle* uses read-aloud stories, especially suitable for bedtime or naptime reading. Also used are poems, simple science experiments, and health-related articles. All but 2 pages aimed at juvenile audience.

Fiction: Picture-oriented material: adventure, animal, contemporary, folktales, health-related, seasonal stories with holiday themes, humorous, nature/environment, problem-solving, sports. "Need adaptations of folktales for Pokey Toes Theatre, a regular feature starring the Turtle character, Pokey Toes. Also needs action rhymes to foster creative movement." Does not want to see stories about monsters or scary things. Avoid stories in which the characters indulge in unhealthy activities like eating junk food. Buys 50 mss/year. Average word length: 200-600. Byline given.

Nonfiction: Picture-oriented material: animal, arts/crafts, games/puzzles, health, multicultural, nature/environment, science, sports. Buys 20 mss/year. Average word length: 200-600. Byline given.

How to Contact/Writers: Fiction/nonfiction: Send complete ms. "No queries, please." Reports on mss in 8-10 weeks.

Illustration: Buys 20-25 illustrations/issue; 160-200 illustrations/year. Prefers "realistic and humorous illustration." Reviews artwork for future assignments.

How to Contact/Illustrators: Illustrations only: Send promo sheet, slides, tearsheets. Reports back only if interested. Credit line given.

Photography: Purchases photos from freelancers with accompanying ms only.

Terms: Pays on publication. Buys all rights for mss/artwork; one-time rights for photographs. Pays 10-20¢/word for articles, depending upon length and quality. Pays $250/color (cover) illustration, $30-70/b&w (inside); $65-140/color (inside). Sample copy $1.25. Writer's/illustrator's guidelines free with SAE and 1 first-class stamp.

Tips: "We're beginning to edit *Turtle* more for the very young preschooler, so we're looking for stories and articles that are written more simply than those we've used in the past. Our need for health-related material, especially features that encourage fitness, is ongoing. Health subjects must be age-appropriate. When writing about them, think creatively and lighten up! Fight the tendency to become boringly pedantic. Nobody— not even young kids—likes being lectured. Always keep in mind that in order for a story or article to educate preschoolers, it first must be truly entertaining—warm and engaging, exciting, or genuinely funny. Understand that writing for *Turtle* is a difficult challenge." (See listings for *Children's Digest, Children's Playmate, Child Life, Humpty Dumpty's Magazine, Jack and Jill.*)

*2 HYPE AND HYPE HAIR, Word Up Publication, 63 Grand Ave., Suite 230, New York NY 10451. (201)487-6124. Art Director: Stuart Koban. Bimonthly magazine. Estab. 1990. Publishes articles about music (rap and R&B)—fashion, hair trends, health, grooming, games, contests—all dealing with music.

Nonfiction: Young adults: careers, fashion, games/puzzles, health, hobbies, how-to, interview/profile, problem-solving. Byline given.

How to Contact/Writers: Nonfiction: Query; query with published clips. Publishes ms 5 months after acceptance. Will consider electronic submissions via disk or modem.

Illustration: Buys 10 illustrations/issue. Illustrations should be done on 8½ × 11 paper. Reviews ms/illustration packages; reviews artwork for future assignments; works on assignment only.

How to Contact/Illustrators: Ms/illustration packages: Submit complete package with final art. Illustrations only: Send promo sheet, portfolio, tearsheets. Reports back only if interested. Samples not filed. Original work returned upon job's completion. Credit line given.

Photography: Model/property releases and photo captions required. Uses b&w and color prints. To contact, photographers should send unsolicited photos by mail. Reports back only if interested.

Terms: Pays on publication. Buys one-time rights to mss. Pays $75-100 for articles. Additional payment for ms/illustration packages. Pays illustrators $50-75. Photographers paid per photo (range $35-150). Writer's/illustrator's/photo guidelines free for SASE.

Tips: "Send fun ideas for people with short attention spans."

*U.S. KIDS, P.O. 567, Indianapolis IN 46202. (317)636-8881. Co-editors: Marta Partington and Steve Charles. Art Editor: Mary Pesca. Magazine published 8 times a year. Estab. 1987. Circ. 250,000.

Fiction: Young readers and middle readers: adventure, animal, contemporary, health, history, humor, multicultural, nature/environment, problem-solving, sports, suspense/mystery. "I see too many stories with no real story line. I'd like to see more mysteries." Buys approx. 8-16 mss/year. Average word length: 500-1,000. Byline given.

Nonfiction: Young readers and middle readers: animal, arts/crafts, cooking, games/puzzles, health, history, hobbies, how-to, humor, interview/profile, multicultural, nature/environment, science, social issues, sports, travel. Wants to see interviews with kids, ages 5-11, who have done something unusual or different. Buys 30-40 mss/year. Average word length: 500-1,000. Byline given.

Poetry: Maximum length: 32 lines.

How to Contact/Writers: Fiction: Send complete ms. Nonfiction: Query. Reports on queries and mss in 1 month. Publishes ms 6 months after acceptance. Will consider simultaneous submissions, electronic submissions via disk or modem and previously published work.

Illustration: Buys 8 illustrations/issue; 70 illustrations/year. Color artwork only. Reviews ms/illustration packages; reviews artwork for future assignments; works on assignment only.

How to Contact/Illustrators: Ms/illustration packages: Query. Illustrations only: Send résumé and tearsheets. Reports back only if interested. Samples returned with SASE; samples kept on file. Does not return originals. Credit line given.

Photography: Purchases photography from freelancers. Looking for photos that pertain to children ages 5-11. Model/property release required. Uses color and b&w prints; 35mm, $2\frac{1}{4} \times 2\frac{1}{4}$, 4×5 and 8×10 transparencies. To contact, photographers should provide résumé, business card, promotional literature or tearsheets to be kept on file. Reports back only if interested.

Terms: Pays on publication. Buys all rights for mss. Purchases all rights for artwork. Purchases one-time rights for photographs. Pays 10¢/word minimum. Additional payment for ms/illustration packages. Pays illustrators $140/page for color (inside). Photographers paid by the project or per photo (negotiable). Sample copies for $2.50. Writer's/illustrator/photo guidelines for SASE.

Tips: "Write clearly and concisely without preaching or being obvious. Send illustrations that apply to children's market. Draw children well."

VENTURE, Christian Service Brigade, P.O. Box 150, Wheaton IL 60189. (708)665-0630. Articles/Fiction Editor: Deborah Christensen. Art Director: Robert Fine. Bimonthly magazine. Estab. 1937. Circ. 23,000. The magazine is designed "to speak to the concerns of boys from a biblical perspective. To provide wholesome, entertaining reading for boys."

Fiction: Middle readers, young adults: adventure, contemporary, humor, nature/environment, problem-solving, religion, sports, suspense/mystery. Does not want to see fantasy, romance, science fiction or anything without Christian emphasis. "We see too much 'new kid in town' stories. We'd like to see more humor." Buys 12 mss/year. Average word length: 1,000-1,500. Byline given.

Nonfiction: Middle readers, young adults: animal, games/puzzles, geography, hobbies, how-to, humor, interview/profile, nature/environment, problem solving, religion, science, social issues, sports, travel. Buys 3 mss/year. Average word length: 1,000-1,500. Byline given.

How to Contact/Writers: Fiction/nonfiction: send complete ms. Reports on queries/mss in 1 week. Will consider simultaneous submissions.

Illustration: Buys 3 illustrations/issue; buys 18 illustrations/year. Will review ms/illustration packages; artwork for future assignments.

How to Contact/Illustrators: Ms/illustration packages: send complete ms. Illustrations only: Send promo sheet, portfolio, tearsheets or slides. Reports on art samples only if interested. Original artwork returned at job's completion. Credit line given.

Photography: Purchases photography from freelancers. Wants photos of boys 10-15 years old.

Terms: Pays on publication for mss, artwork and photos. Buys first North American serial rights; first rights; second serial (reprint rights). Pays $30-150 for stories/articles. Pays $75-125/b&w (cover) illustration—usually photos only; $35-250/b&w (inside) illustration (includes photos). Sample copy $1.85 with 9×12 SAE and 98¢ postage affixed. Writer's/illustrator's guidelines free with SAE and 1 first class stamp.

WITH, Faith & Life Press, Mennonite Publishing House, 722 Main, P.O. Box 347, Newton KS 67114. (316)283-5100. Editors: Eddy Hall, Carol Duerksen. Published 8 times a year. Circ. 5,800. Magazine published for teenagers, ages 15-18, in Mennonite congregations. "We deal with issues affecting teens and try to help them make choices reflecting an Anabaptist-Mennonite faith."

Fiction: Young adults: contemporary, fantasy, folktales, humor, nature/environment, problem solving, religion, sports. "Would like to see more humor and parables/allegories." Buys 10 mss/year. Average word length: 1,000-2,000. Byline given.

Nonfiction: Young adults: first-person teen personal experience (as-told-to), humor, nature/environment, problem-solving, religion, social issues. Buys 15-20 mss/year. Average word length: 500-1,500. Byline given.

Poetry: Wants to see religion, humor, nature. "We're cutting back on poetry." Maximum word length: 50.

How to Contact/Writers: Send complete ms. Query on first-person teen personal experience stories. Reports on queries in 1 month; mss in 3 months. Will consider simultaneous submissions.

Illustration: Buys 6-8 illustrations/issue; buys 50-60 illustrations/year. Uses b&w and 2-color artwork only. Preferred theme or style: Candids/interracial. Will review ms/illustration packages. Reviews artwork for future assignments.

How to Contact/Illustrators: Ms/illustration packages: Query first. Illustrations only: Query with portfolio or tearsheets. Reports on art samples only if interested. Original artwork returned at job's completion. Credit line given.

Photography: Looking for teens (ages 15-18), ethnic minorities, candids. Uses 8×10 b&w glossy prints. To contact, photographers should send unsolicited photos by mail.

Terms: Pays on acceptance. For mss buys one-time rights; second serial (reprint rights). Buys one-time rights for artwork and photos. Pays 4¢/word for unpublished manuscripts; 2¢/word for reprints. Will pay more for assigned as-told-to stories. Pays $25-50/b&w (cover) illustration; $20-35/b&w (inside) illustration. Photographers are paid per photo (range: $20-50 cover only). Sample copy for 9×12 SAE and $1.21 postage. Writer's/illustrator's guidelines free with SASE.

Tips: "We're hungry for stuff that makes teens laugh—fiction, nonfiction, and cartoons. It doesn't have to be religious, but must be wholesome."

WONDER TIME, Beacon Hill Press, 6401 The Paseo, Kansas City MO 64131. (816)333-7000. Editor: Lois Perrigo. Weekly magazine. Circ. 45,000. "*Wonder Time* is a full-color story paper for first and second graders. It is designed to connect Sunday School learning with the daily living experiences and growth of the primary child. Since *Wonder Time's* target audience is children ages six to eight, the readability goal is to encourage beginning readers to read for themselves. The major purposes of *Wonder Time* are to: Provide a life-related paper which will build Christian values and encourage ethical behavior and provide reinforcement for the biblical concepts taught in the Word Action Sunday School curriculum."

Fiction: Young readers: problem-solving, religion. Buys 52 mss/year. Average word length: 400-550. Byline given.

Poetry: Reviews religious poetry of 4-8 lines.
How to Contact/Writers: Fiction/nonfiction: Send complete ms. Reports on queries/mss in 6-8 weeks. Will consider simultaneous submissions.
Illustration: Buys 10-15 illustrations/year. Will review illustration packages. Works on assignment only.
How to Contact/Illustrators: Ms/illustration packages: Ms with sketch. Illustrations only: Samples of work. Reports on art samples only if interested.
Terms: Pays a minimum of $25 per story for rights which allow the publisher to print the story multiple times in the same publication without repayment. Sends complimentary contributor's copies of publication. Sample copy and writer's guidelines with 9½ × 12 SAE and 2 first class stamps.
Tips: "These basic themes reappear regularly: faith in God; putting God first; choosing to please God; understanding that Jesus is God's Son and our Savior; choosing to do right; asking forgiveness; trusting God in hard times; prayer: trusting God to answer; appreciation of the Bible as God's word to man; importance of Bible memorization; understanding both meanings of church: a place where we worship God, a fellowship of God's people working together; understanding each person's value to God and to others; showing love and kindness to others; enriching family life, including non-traditional family units; addressing current problems which children may face."

THE YOUNG CRUSADER, National WCTU, 1730 Chicago Ave., Evanston IL 60201. (708)864-1396. Managing Editor: Michael C. Vitucci. Published monthly except July and August. Estab. 1887. Circ. 3,500. The magazine is geared to the 6-12 year old child. It stresses high morals and good character. Nature and informational stories are also used. Above all, the stories should not be preachy or religious as the magazine is used in public schools.
Fiction: Middle readers: contemporary, problem-solving, positive character building. Does not want to see preachy, religious-type stories. Sees too many "trite old plots." Buys 4 mss/year. Average word length: 550-650. Byline given.
Nonfiction: Middle readers: animal, history, nature/environment, problem solving. Material should encourage "character building, good manners, good values." Buys 10 mss/year. Average word length: 550-650. Byline given.
How to Contact/Writers: Fiction/nonfiction: Send complete ms. Will consider simultaneous submissions. "I require submissions to be copies. If not used, the manuscript will be destroyed." Doesn't report back unless ms is published.
Terms: Pays on publication. "We buy any rights author wishes. We only publish once and the story reverts back to author." Pays ½¢/word for stories/articles; 10¢/line for poetry. Free sample copy.
Tips: "Don't write down to the child. Writers often underestimate their audience." Looks for: "nonfiction stories stressing good character and high morals."

YOUNG JUDAEAN, Hadassah Zionist Youth Commission, P.O. Box 173, Merion Station PA 19066. Editor: Steve Schasszin. Published 3 times a year (fall, winter, spring). Estab. 1910. Circ. 4,000. "Magazine is intended for members—age 9-12—of Young Judaea, which is the Zionist-oriented youth movement sponsored by the Hadassah Women's Organization."
Fiction: Middle readers: contemporary, fantasy, history, humor, science fiction, sports and spy/mystery/adventure. Does not want to see "any material that does *not* relate to Jewish themes. Also, no material whose Jewishness is theological rather than cultural." Buys 10-15 mss/year. Average word length: 500-1,500. Byline given.
Nonfiction: Middle readers, young adults: history, how-to, humor, interview/profile, problem solving and travel. Does not want to see "anything that preaches a particular theological outlook. Anything that is *not* related to Jewish life." Buys 30 mss/year. Average word length: 500-1,500. Byline given.

How to Contact/Writers: Fiction: Send complete ms. Nonfiction: Send complete ms or query.

Illustration: Buys 6 illustrations/issue. Preferred theme or style: "Lively and anecdotal." Will review ms/illustration packages; illustrator's work for possible future assignments.

How to Contact/Illustrators: Ms/illustration packages: Send complete ms with final art. Illustrations only: Send tearsheets. Original artwork returned at job's completion "if requested."

Terms: Pays on publication. Buys first North American serial rights. Pays $20-50 for assigned articles; $20-50 for unsolicited articles. Additional payment for ms/illustration packages is "manuscript plus $20 per illustration." Pays $20-40/b&w cover illustration, $20-30 b&w inside illustration. Sample copy $1 with SASE; free writer's/illustrator's guidelines.

YOUNG NATURALIST FOUNDATION (See listings for Chickadee, Owl.)

YOUNG SALVATIONIST, The Salvation Army, 615 Slaters Lane, P.O. Box 269, Alexandria VA 22313. (703)684-5500. Editor: Captain M. Lesa Salyer. Monthly magazine. Estab. 1984. Circ. 50,000. "We accept material with clear Christian content written for high school age teenagers. *Young Salvationist* is published by teenage members of The Salvation Army, a fundamental, activist denomination of the Christian Church."

Fiction: Young adults: multicultural, religion, sports (with Christian perspective). Buys 12-20 mss/year. Average word length: 750-1,200. Byline given.

Nonfiction: Young adults: religion—hobbies, how-to, interview/profile, multicultural, nature/environment, problem-solving, social issues. Buys 40-50 mss/year. Average word length: 750-1,200. Byline given.

Poetry: Reviews 16-20 line poetry dealing with a Christian theme. Send no more than 6 submissions.

How to Contact/Writers: Fiction/nonfiction: Query with published clips or send complete ms. Reports on queries in 2-3 weeks; mss in 1 month. Will consider simultaneous submissions.

Illustrations: Buys 2-3 illustrations/issue; 20-30 illustrations/year. Reviews ms/illustration packages; reviews artwork for future assignments.

How to Contact/Illustrators: Ms/illustration packages: "Query or send manuscript with art." Illustrations only: Query; send fesumé, promo sheet, portfolio, tearsheets. Reports on artwork in 2-3 weeks (with SASE). Original artwork returned at job's completion "if requested." Credit line given.

Photography: Purchases photography from freelancers. Looking for teens in action.

Terms: Pays on acceptance. For mss, buys first North American serial rights, first rights, one-time rights, second serial (reprint rights). Purchases one-time rights for artwork and photographs. For mss, pays 10¢/word. Pays $100-150 color (cover) illustration; $50-100 b&w (inside) illustration; $100-150 color (inside) illustration. Sample copy for 9 × 12 SAE and 3 first class stamps. Writer's/illustrator's guidelines free for #10 SASE.

Tips: "Ask for theme list/sample copy! Write 'up,' not down to teens. Aim at young *adults*, not children." Wants "less fiction, more 'journalistic' nonfiction."

YOUTH UPDATE, St. Anthony Messenger Press, 1615 Republic St., Cincinnati OH 45210. (513)241-5615. Articles Editor: Carol Ann Morrow. Art Director: Julie Lonneman. Monthly newsletter. Estab. 1982. Circ. 32,000. "Each issue focuses on one topic only. *Youth Update* addresses the faith and Christian life questions of young people and is designed to attract, instruct, guide and challenge its audience by applying the gospel to modern problems and situations. The students who read *Youth Update* vary in their religious education and reading ability. Write for average high school students. These students are 15-year-olds with a C+ average. Assume that they have paid attention to religious instruction and remember a little of what 'sister' said. Aim more toward 'table talk than teacher talk.' "

Nonfiction: Young adults: religion. Buys 12 mss/year. Average word length: 2,300-2,400. Byline given.

How to Contact/Writers: Nonfiction: Query. Reports on queries/mss in 6 weeks. Will consider computer printout and electronic submissions via disk.

Terms: Pays on acceptance. Buys first North American serial rights. Pays $325-400 for articles. Sample copy free with #10 SAE and 1 first class stamp.

Tips: "Read the newsletter yourself—3 issues at least. In the past, our publication has dealt with a variety of topics including: dating, Lent, teenage pregnancy, baptism, loneliness, rock and roll, confirmation and the Bible. When writing, use the *New American Bible* as translation. More interested in church-related topics."

$1,000-1,500/color (cover); $500-1,500/color (inside). Sample copy and writer's guidelines free on request.

Magazine Publishers/'92-'93 changes

The following markets are not included in this edition of *Children's Writer's & Illustrator's Market* for the reasons indicated. The phrase "did not respond" means the market was in the *1992 Children's Writer's & Illustrator's Market* but did not respond to our written and phone requests for updated information for a 1993 listing.

Challenges (removed per request)
Choices (did not respond)
Free Spirit (ceased publication)
Home Altar, The (did not respond)
National Geographic World (removed per request)
Nickelodeon (did not respond)
Racing for Kids (did not respond)
Sing Out! (receiving too many inappropriate submissions)
Sports Illustrated for Kids (did not respond)
Together Time (did not respond)
Voice (suspended publication)
YABA Framework (not accepting unsolicited material)
Zillions! (removed per request)

Audiovisual Markets

Videocassette recorders (VCRs) can now be found in millions of homes, as well as thousands of schools. With them comes a new means of entertaining and educating children. Because of this, video products are no longer sidelines in the children's market.

It used to be that video stores were the only place to buy videos, but now they are prominent items in books and toy stores as well. Also, people are purchasing reasonably-priced videos rather than renting them, and children's videos make up a major percentage of these purchases.

Though children's entertainment videos can be considered "babysitters," parents are equally interested in the educational advantages. For example, the mass market audience has responded strongly to interactive videos, or, read-alongs for children. One such series is the Bank Street Read-Along Story Videos, which combines live action with computer animation. In the Bank Street story videos, each story is told twice. The second version includes words printed on the screen so kids can read along.

New in this ever-expanding technological field are laser videodiscs, which are as much a threat to videotapes as compact discs were to records. They have clearer pictures than videotapes and digital sound. Laser videodiscs do not wear out, and therefore are good for repeated playing and are virtually childproof. They're used alone or in conjunction with a personal computer, making for an interactive teaching system.

The prognosis is good for the future of children's audiovisual products. Video production companies are just now starting to recognize the profit potential of the children's market. Many such production companies are included in this section and have a range of writing and animation needs that include educational and entertainment subjects. Educational films may not pay quite as much as those destined for entertainment distribution, but they are a good way to break in. Notice that video isn't the only format produced by production houses. Writers and illustrators may find themselves working on film projects, filmstrips or multi-media productions.

Be aware that audiovisual media rely more on the "visual" to tell the story. The script itself plays a secondary role and explains only what the visual message doesn't make clear to viewers. Thus, these markets may be more open to work-for-hire artists with specific skills, such as in animation, storyboarding and video graphics.

*ARTICHOKE PRODUCTIONS, 4114 Linden St., Oakland CA 94608. (510)655-1283. Producer/Director: Paul Kalbach. Estab. 1981. Production House (live action and computer graphics/animation). General audience. Produces films, videotapes.
Children's Writing: To submit, query with synopsis. Submissions returned with proper SASE. Reports back only if interested. Pay depends on project.
Illustration/Animation: Hires illustrators for character development. Types of animation produced: cel animation, stop motion, special effects, computer animation, video

graphics, live action. Art samples returned with proper SASE. Reports back only if interested.

BALL & CHAIN, 164 Fairfield Ave., Stamford CT 06902. (203)324-0018. Owner: Chuck Jepsen. Estab. 1978. Production company. Uses films, videotapes.
Children's Writing: Needs: animation scripts. To submit, query. Submissions are filed.
Illustration/Animation: Hires illustrators for animation. Types of animation produced: cel animation, special effects, motion control, live action. To submit, send demo tape. Art samples are filed.

BENNU PRODUCTIONS INC., 626 McLean Ave., Yonkers NY 10705. (914)964-1828. Fax: (914)964-2914. Producer: Wayne J. Keeley. Estab. 1985. Film and video production house. Audience: General public, businesses, schools, etc. Uses multimedia productions, films and videotapes. Children's productions: "Say No to Strangers," written by Wayne J. Keeley (video safety program for children); "Save Our Planet" written by Wayne J. Keeley/Chris Austermann (environmental eductional video for junior to senior high). 25% of writing is by freelancers; 25% of illustrating/animating by freelancers.
Children's Writing: Needs: Educational material on all relevant topics for all age levels. Subjects include: substance abuse, environment, history, health, science, art, etc. To submit, query. Submissions returned with proper SASE. Reports back only if interested. Pay varies.
Illustration/Animation: Hires illustrators for animation (computer and graphic), storyboarding, character development, live action, comprehensives, pencil testing. Types of animation produced: special effects, computer animation, video graphics, live action. To submit, send cover letter, résumé, demo tape (VHS) and business card. Art samples returned with proper SASE. Reports back only if interested. Pay varies.
Tips: "Educationally stimulating material should be submitted." Looks for "creativity, innovation, flexibility."

*BROADCAST QUALITY, INC., 5701 Sunset Dr. #316, South Miami FL 33143. (305)665-5416. President: Diana Udel. Estab. 1978. Video production and post production house. Produces videotapes. Recent children's productions: "It's Ours to Save—Biscayne National Park," written by Jack Moss, produced by Diana Udel/BQI, Betacam SP/1″ Master, (Environmental awareness for grades 4-7); "The Wildlife Show at Parrot Jungle," written by Amy Smith, produced by BQI, Betacam SP/1″ Master, (Hands on to Florida's Wildlife for K-8th grade). Uses 2-5 freelance writers/year; purchases various projects/year.
Tips: "Send a resume and demo reel. Seeks variety, knowledge of subject and audience."

CLEARVUE/eav, 6465 N. Avondale, Chicago IL 60631. (312)775-9433. Editor/Producer: Mary Watanabe. Estab. 1969. Type of company: production and distribution house. Audience: educational pre-school through high school. Uses filmstrips, slide sets, videotapes. 70% of illustrating/animating is by freelancers.
Children's Writing: "At this time we are only accepting for review *finished* video projects that we will consider for distribution." Query with resume. Reports back only if interested. Pays 5-10% royalty.
Illustration/Animation: Hires illustrators for: computer animation of company-owned filmstrips. Send cover letter, resume, demo tape (VHS). Reports in 2 weeks only if interested. Video samples returned. Guidelines/catalog free. Pay: "open."

 The asterisk before a listing indicates the listing is new in this edition.

Tips: "Programs must be designed for educational market—not home or retail. We are looking for good animators with equipment to scan in our filmstrips and animate the characters and action according to prepared directions that allow for artistic variations."

DIMENSION FILMS, 15007 Gault St., Van Nuys CA 91405. (818)997-8065. President: Gary Goldsmith. Estab. 1962. Production house. Audience: schools and libraries. Uses film strips, films, videotapes. 10% of writing is by freelancers; 100% of illustrating/animating is by freelancers.
Children's Writing: Needs: educational material and documentaries for kindergarten-12th-grade audience. Submission method: query. Submissions filed. Reports in a matter of weeks. "Call for guidelines." Pays in accordance with Writer's Guild standards.
Illustration/Animation: Hires illustrators for storyboarding, comprehensives. Types of animation produced: cel animation, video graphics, live action. Submission method: send cover letter and résumé. Reports in a matter of weeks. "Call for guidelines." Pays $30-60/frame.
Tips: Illustrators/animators: looking for "imagination, clarity and purpose." Portfolio should show "strong composition; action in stillness."

EDUCATIONAL VIDEO NETWORK, 1401 19th St., Huntsville TX 77340. (409)295-5767. Editor: Gary Edmondson. Estab. 1954. Production house. Audience: educational (school). Uses videotapes. 20% of writing by freelancers; 20% of illustrating/animating is by freelancers.
Children's Writing: Needs: "Educational material" for ages 9-11 and 12-18. Submission method: script with video or animation. Submissions returned with proper SASE. Reports in 1 month. Guidelines/catalog free. Pays writers in royalties or buys material outright.
Illustration/Animation: Hires illustrators for: acetate cels, animation. Types of animation produced: cel animation stills, video graphics, live action. Submission method: send cover letter and VHS demo tape. Art samples returned with proper SASE. Reports in 1 month. Guidelines/catalog free.
Tips: "Materials should fill a curriculum need in grades 6-12." Writers/scriptwriters: "Work must be of professional quality adaptable to video format." Illustrators/animators: Looks for "creativity. More live-action is being demanded. Go to school library and ask to review most popular AV titles."

*FILM CLASSIC EXCHANGE, 143 Hickory Hill Circle, Osterville MA 02655. (508)428-7198. President: J.H. Aikman. Estab. 1916. Distribution/production house. Audience: Pre-school through college. Produces films, videotapes. Recent children's productions: "The Good Deed," written by Wm. P. Pounder; illustrated by Karen Losaq. (Film on family values aimed at preschool.) "Willie McDuff's Big Day," written and illustrated by Joe Fleming. (Film on anti-drug aimed at ages 12+.) Uses 6 freelance writers and artists/year. Purchase 6 writing and 6 art projects/year.
Children's Writing: Needs: Preschool. Subjects include: anti-drug. Query with synopsis or submit completed script. Submissions are returned wtih proper SASE. Reports back only if interested. Buys material outright.
Illustration/Animation: Hires illustrators for cel/video animation, storyboarding, character development, live action, comprehensives, pencil testing. Types of animation produced: cel animation, clay animation, stop motion, special effects, computer animation, video graphics, motion control, live action. To submit, send cover letter, resume, demo tape (VHS), color print samples. Art samples returned with proper SASE. Reports back only if interested.
Tips: "Keep sending updated resumes/samples of work."

FINE ART PRODUCTIONS, 67 Maple St., Newburgh NY 12550. (914)561-5866. Director: Richie Suraci. Estab. 1989. "We cover every aspect of the film, video, publishing and entertainment industry." Audience: All viewers. Uses film strips, films, slide sets, video-tapes, multimedia productions, any format needed. Children's productions: "1991 Great Hudson River Revival," illustrated by various artists. (35mm film and print on environment, clearwater sailing ship.) "Wheel and Rock to Woodstock Bike Tour," written and illustrated by various artists. (Film, print, video on exercise, health, music and volunteerism.) Percent of freelance illustrators/animators used varies.
Children's Writing: To submit, query with synopsis, or submit synopsis/outline, completed script, résumé. Submissions are filed, or returned with proper SASE. Reports in 1 month if interested. Pay is negotiated.
Illustration/Animation: Hires illustrators for animation, storyboarding, character development, live action, comprehensives, pencil testing. Types of animation produced: cel animation, clay animation, stop motion, special effects, computer animation, video graphics, motion control, live action. To submit, send cover letter, résumé, demo tape (VHS or ¾"), b&w print samples, color print samples, tearsheets, business card. Art samples are filed, or returned with proper SASE. Reports in 1 month if interested. Guidelines/catalog for SAE. Pay is negotiated.

*GATEWAY PRODUCTIONS, INC., 3011 Magazine St., New Orleans LA 70115. (504)891-2600. President: William Manschot. Estab. 1970. Independent producer of educational audio-visual materials. Audience: students, grades 5-10. Produces film strips. Recent children's productions: "The Indians of Ohio," written and illustrated by W. Manschot. (Filmstrip on Ohio prehistory aimed at ages 9-13.) "All About Pennsylvania," written and illustrated by W. Manschot. (Six filmstrips on Pennsylvania social studies aimed at ages 9-13.)
Children's Writing: Needs: filmstrips, grades 5-8. Subjects include: general social studies: geography, history, economy, government (state studies). To submit, query. Submissions filed. Guidelines/catalog free on request.
Illustration/Animation: Hires illustrators for general graphic art. Art samples returned with proper SASE. Reports in 3 weeks.
Tips: "We are a *very* small company. I currently do *all* of the creative work. We would like, though, to increase our output, and we'd like to hear from people who could do essentially what I do, write *and* produce their own material upon our approval. We would then provide technical assistance, promotion, sales and distribution. Submit ideas for consideration. We would then discuss salability, suitability to our operation, costs and terms in general."

GREY FALCON HOUSE, Suite 443, 496-A Hudson St., New York NY 10014. (212)777-9042. Fax: (212)691-8661. President: Ann Grifalconi. Estab. 1972. Production house. Uses films strips, multimedia productions, films, videotapes. Recent children's productions: "The Underwear Champ" (film strips/video cassettes, the fictional story of how commercials are made for ages 9-14). "The Village of Round and Square Houses" (filmstrip and video cassettes about African village and myth). 50% of writing is by freelancers; 50% of illustrating/animating is by freelancers.
Children's Writing: Needs: new material on world subjects and folklores, myths; mostly fiction (7 and older). To submit, query with résumé. Submissions are filed, or returned with proper SASE. Reports back only if interested. Pay varies.
Illustration/Animation: Hires illustrators for animation. Types of animation produced: cel animation, clay animation, stop motion, special effects, computer animation, video graphics, motion control, live action. To submit, send résumé, b&w print samples, business card. Art samples are filed.

HOME, INC., 731 Harrison Ave., Boston MA 02118. (617)266-1386. Director: Alan Michel. Estab. 1974. Nonprofit video production and post production facility which produces some teen television programming for the local Boston market. Audience: teenagers, teachers, instructors, education administrators, parents, social workers and court intervention professionals. Uses videotapes. Children's productions: "Going to Court," written by Ken Cheeseman; graphics: Alan Michel (¾" videotape puppet drama explaining the court for ages 3 through teens). "Stand Back from Crack," written by Young Nation; graphics: Alan Michel (¾" videotape, anti-drug public service video for teen and pre-teen). 90% of writing is by freelancers; 15% of illustrating/animating is by freelancers.

Children's Writing: Needs: scripts, curriculum, educational support material for videos, proposal writing for elementary through high school. Subjects include social or cultural content/sometimes career or health care oriented. To submit, send synopsis/outline and résumé. Submissions are filed and cannot be returned. Reports back only if interested. Payment negotiated/commissioned.

Illustration/Animation: Hires illustrators for storyboarding and graphics. Types of animation produced: special effects, computer animation and video graphics. To submit send cover letter, résumé, VHS demo tape, b&w and color print samples. Samples are filed and not returned. Reports back only if interested. Payment negotiated. Pays $250-4,000/project for specialized animation.

Tips: "We look for cooperative associates who have a commitment to quality and to their profession. This includes their presentation and follow-through in their dealings with us prior to project engagement."

I.N.I. ENTERTAINMENT GROUP, INC., Suite 700, 11150 Olympic Blvd., Los Angeles CA 90064. (213)479-6755. Fax: (213)479-3475. President: Irv Holender. Director of Advertising: Linda Krasnoff. Estab. 1985. Producer/International Distributor. Audience: children of all ages. Uses films. Recent children's productions: "The Adventures of Oliver Twist," screenplay written by Fernando Ruiz (updated version of the Dickens tale for ages 4-12); "Alice Through the Looking Glass," screenplay written by James Brewer (updated and upbeat version of Carroll's for ages 4-12). 100% of writing is by freelancers; 100% of illustrating/animating is by freelancers.

Children's Writing: Needs: animation scripts/scripts. "Anything from fantasy to fable." To submit, query with synopsis. Submit synopsis/outline, completed script, résumé. Submissions returned with proper SASE. Reports back only if interested. Pay varies.

Illustration/Animation: Type of animation produced: computer animation. To submit, send cover letter, résumé, demo tape (VHS), color print samples, business card. Art samples are filed, returned with proper SASE or not returned. Reports back only if interested.

Tips: "We are gearing to work with fairytales or classic stories. We look for concise retelling of older narratives with slight modifications in the storyline, while at the same time introducing children to stories that they would not necessarily be familiar with. We don't hire illustrators for animation. We hire the studio. The illustrators that we hire are used to create the advertising art."

*JEF FILMS, 143 Hickory Hill Circle, Osterville MA 02655. (508)428-7198. President: Jeffrey H. Aikman. Estab. 1973. Production house. Audience: schools/libraries/video retailers. Produces slide sets, multimedia productions, films, videotapes. Recent children's productions: "The Reward," written and illustrated by Dennis Chatfield. (Film on animation aimed at pre-school.) "Kiddy Kartoon Korner," written by Carolyn Elckoff; illustrated by Bill Wicksdorf. (35mm film on animation aimed at ages 5-8.) Uses 20-24 freelance writers/year; purchases 20-24 writing projects/year. Uses 20-24 freelance artists/year; purchases 20-24 art projects/year.

Children's Writing: Needs: animation scripts for ages 5-8. Subjects include: tales with message. To submit, send synopsis/outline. Submissions returned with proper SASE. Reports in 2 months. Buys outright.

Illustration/Animation: Hires illustrators for cel/video/clay animation, storyboarding, character development, live action, comprehensives, pencil testing. Types of animation produced: cel animation, clay animation, stop motion, special effects, video graphics, motion control, live action. To submit, send cover letter, resume, demo tape (VHS), b&w print samples, color print samples, tearsheets, slides, promo sheet. Samples returned with proper SASE; samples filed. Reports in 2 months.

Tips: "Be persistent. We receive a great number of inquiries and can not always use everyone who submits work. Keep us updated on all new projects. Everything sent to us is kept on file. We look for unique styles unlike other works on market."

KENSINGTON FALLS ANIMATION, Suite 200, 2921 Duss Ave., Ambridge PA 15003. (412)266-0329. Fax: (412)266-4016. Producer: Michael Schwab. Estab. 1979. Animation studio. Audience: Entertainment, educational. Uses film strips, slide sets, films, videotapes. 100% of writing is by freelancers; 100% of illustrating/animating is by freelancers. Uses 5-20 freelance writers/year; purchases 5-20 writing projects/year. Uses 1-10 freelance artists/year.

Children's Writing: Needs: animation scripts, educational material. To submit, query with résumé. Submissions are filed. Reports back only if interested. Guidelines/catalog free on request. Writers paid in accordance with Writer's Guild standards.

Illustration/Animation: Hires illustrators for character animation, storyboarding, character development, pencil testing, background illustration, ink & paint production. Types of animation produced: cel animation, computer animation, video graphics. To submit, send cover letter, résumé, demo tape (VHS or ¾"). Art samples returned with proper SASE. Guidelines/catalog free on request. Pays: $10-50/hour for storyboarding/comp work; $20-50/hour for animation work.

Tips: "We offer apprenticeships."

*KIDVIDZ: SPECIAL INTEREST VIDEO FOR CHILDREN, 618 Centre St., Newton MA 02158. (617)965-3345. Partner: Jane Murphy. Estab. 1987. Home video publisher. Audience: pre-school and primary-age children, 4-12 years. Produces videotapes. Recent children's productions: "Let's Get a Move On!," written by Jane Murphy and Karen Tucker (home video, 1-inch master), a video guide to a family move, aimed at 4-year olds. "Squiggles, Dots & Lines," written by Jane Murphy and Karen Tucker (home video, 1-inch master). Uses 2 freelance writers/year. Uses 3 freelance artists/year. Submissions filed.

KJD TELEPRODUCTIONS, 30 Whyte Dr., Voorhees NJ 08043. (609)751-3500. Fax: (609)751-7729. President: Larry Scott. Creative Director: Kim Davis. Estab. 1989. Location production services (Betacam Sp) plus interformat edit and computer animation. Audience: industrial and broadcast. Uses slide sets, multimedia productions, videotapes. Children's productions: "Kidstuff," written by Barbara Daye; illustrated by Larry Scott (educational vignettes for ages 6-16). 10% of writing is by freelancers; 25% of animating/illustrating by freelancers.

Children's Writing: Needs: animation. To submit, query. Submissions are filed. Reports in 2 weeks. Pays royalty, outright purchase.

Illustration/Animation: Hires illustrators for animation. Types of animation produced: computer animation. To submit, send cover letter, résumé, demo tape (VHS or ¾"), b&w print samples, tearsheets, business card. Art samples are filed. Reports in 2 weeks. Pay varies.

MARSHMEDIA, P.O. Box 8082, Shawnee Mission KS 66208. (816)523-1059. Fax: (816)333-7421. Production Director: Joan K. Marsh. Estab. 1969. Production and marketing house. Audience: grades K-12. 100% of writing is by freelancers; 100% of illustrating/animating is by freelancers.
Children's Writing: Needs: educational materials, self-esteem stories for K-3: animal protagonist, significant geographical setting, strong non-sexist self-esteem message, 1,500 words. Submission method: query with synopsis and submit completed scripts, résumé. Submissions returned with proper SASE. Buys material outright.
Illustration/Animation: Submission method: send résumé and VHS demo tape. Art samples returned with proper SASE. Reports in 1 month.

NATIONAL GALLERY OF ART, Education Dept., Washington DC 20565. (202)737-4215. Fax: (202)-789-2681. Coordinator of Teacher Materials: Janna Eggebeen. Children's Coordinator: Kitty Walsh-Piper. Estab. 1941. Museum. Audience: teachers and students. Uses film strips, slide sets, videotapes, reproductions. Children's productions: "The Magic Picture Frame," written by Maura Clarkin (reproductions of paintings for NGA Museum Guide for ages 7-10). 75% of writing is by freelancers.
Children's Writing: Needs: educational material for all levels. Subjects include knowledge of art-making and art history. To submit, send résumé. Submissions are filed. Reports back only if interested. Guidelines/catalog not available. Buys material outright.

NEW & UNIQUE VIDEOS, 2336 Sumac Dr., San Diego CA 92105. (619)282-6126. Fax: (619)283-8264. Acquisitions Managers: Candy Love, Mark Schulze. Estab. 1985. Video production and distribution services. "Audience varies with each title." Uses films and videotapes. Children's productions: "Battle at Durango: The First-Ever World Mountain Bike Championships," written by Patricia Mooney; produced by Mark Schulze (VHS video mountain bike race documentary for 12 and over). "John Howard's Lessons in Cycling," written by John Howard; direction and camera by Mark Schulze (VHS video on cycling for 12 and over). 50% of writing is by freelancers; 85% of illustrating/animating is by freelancers.
Children's Writing: Needs: video scripts and/or completed videotape productions whose intended audiences may range from 1 and older. "Any subject matter focusing on a special interest that can be considered 'new and unique.'" To submit, query. Submissions are returned with proper SASE. Reports in 2-3 weeks. Payment negotiable.
Illustration/Animation: Hires illustrators for film or video animation. Types of animation produced: computer animation and video graphics. To submit, send cover letter. Art samples returned with proper SASE. Reports back in 2-3 weeks. Payment negotiable.
Tips: "As more and more video players appear in homes across the world, and as the interest in special interest videos climbs, the demand for more original productions is rising meteorically."

*TOM NICHOLSON ASSOC., INC., 8th Floor, 295 Lafayette St., New York NY 10012. (212)274-0470. Estab. 1987. Interactive multimedia developer. Audience: children. Produces multimedia.

Market conditions are constantly changing! If you're still using this book and it is 1994 or later, buy the newest edition of Children's Writer's & Illustrator's Market *at your favorite bookstore or order directly from Writer's Digest Books.*

Children's Writing: Needs: documentary film, animation scripts, educational/entertainment. Subjects include: science, humanities, nature, etc. To submit, send completed script, resume. Submissions filed. Reports back only if interested. Pay is negotiable.
Illustration/Animation: Hires illustrators for animation, storyboarding, character development, live action. Types of animation produced: cel animation, computer animation. To submit, send VHS demo tape, tearsheets, promo sheets. Art samples filed; not returned. Reports back only if interested.

NTC PUBLISHING GROUP, 4255 W. Touhy Ave., Lincolnwood IL 60646. (708)679-5500. Fax: (708)679-2494. Editorial Director: Richard Smith. Art Director: Karen Christoffersen. Estab. 1960. Type of company: publisher. Audience: all ages. Uses film strips, multimedia productions, videotapes, books and audiocassettes. Children's production: *Let's Learn English Picture Dictionary,* (versions in Spanish, French, German and Italian); illustrations by Marlene Goodman. For ages 7-11. 40% of writing is by freelancers; 50% of illustrating/animating is by freelancers.
Children's Writing: Needs: educational material for ages 5-14. Subjects include: "mostly foreign language, travel and English." Submission method: submit synopsis/outline, completed script, résumé and samples. Submission returned with proper SASE only. Reports in 2 months. Guidelines/catalog free. Pays writers in royalties or buys material outright—"depends on project."
Illustration/Animation: Hires illustrators for character development, comprehensives, pencil testing. Types of animation produced: stop motion, video graphics. Submission method: send cover letter, résumé, color print samples, tearsheets, business card. Art samples returned with proper SASE. Reports in 8 weeks. Guidelines/catalog free.
Tips: Looking for "experienced professionals only with proven track record in the *educational* field."

OLIVE JAR ANIMATION, 44 Write Place, Brookline MA 02146. (617)566-6699. Fax: (617)566-0689. Executive Producer: Matthew Charde. Estab. 1984. Type of company: animation studio. Audience: all ages. Uses films, videotapes. 75% of writing is by freelancers; 75% of illustrating/animating is by freelancers.
Illustration/Animation: Hires illustrators for animation (all types), storyboarding, pencil testing, design, ink paint, sculpture, illustration. Types of animation produced: cel and clay animation, stop motion, special effects. Submission method: send cover letter, résumé, demo tape, b&w print samples, color print samples, tearsheets, business card. Art samples are filed. Reports back only if interested. Pays flat rate according to job.
Tips: Looks for "someone who is really good at a particular style or direction as well as people who work in a variety of mediums. Attitude is as important as talent. The ability to work with others is very important."

THE PARTNERSHIP WORKS, (formerly Glyn/Net, Inc.), 10th Floor, 475 10th Ave., New York NY 10011. (212)629-6777. Executive Producer: Patrice Samara. Estab. 1968. Production house. Audience: Theme park entertainment, business video, TV and home video. Uses multimedia productions, videotapes. Children's productions: "Muppet Babies Video Story Books" with Jim Henson; illustrated by various artists (moral tales for 2 and up); "Ben Vereen's Kids Sing Along," written by Dennis Scott (series of participatory videos for ages 2 and up). 25% of writing is by freelancers; 100% of illustrating/animating is by freelancers.
Children's Writing: Needs: scripts, educational material, home videos for all ages. To submit, query with synopsis. "Do not call." Submissions are filed. Submissions cannot be returned. Reports in 1 month only if interested. Pays royalty (occasionally), buys material outright.

Illustration/Animation: Hires illustrators for animation, storyboarding, live action. Types of animation produced: stop motion, special effects, computer animation, video graphics, motion control, live action. Art samples are filed. Reports in 1 month if interested. Pay varies.

SEA STUDIOS, INC., 810 Cannery Row, Monterey CA 93940. (408)649-5152. Fax: (408)649-1380. Office Manager: Cindy Ignacio. Estab. 1985. Natural history video production company. Audience: general. Uses multimedia productions, videotapes. 50% of writing is by freelancers; 50% of illustrating/animating is by freelancers.
Children's Writing: Needs: educational material—target age dependent on project. To submit, send résumé (no phone calls please). Submissions returned with proper SASE. Reports back only if interested. Pay negotiable.
Illustration/Animation: To submit, send cover letter, résumé (no phone calls please). Art samples returned with proper SASE. Reports back only if interested.

SHADOW PLAY RECORDS & VIDEO, P.O. Box 180476, Austin TX 78718. (512)345-4664. Fax: (512)345-9734. President: Peter J. Markham. Estab. 1984. Children's music publisher. Audience: families with children ages 3-10. Uses videotapes. Children's productions: "Joe's First Video," written by Joe Scruggs; illustrated by various artists (VHS children's music videos for preschool-10 years). 5% of writing is by freelancers; 100% of illustrating/animating by freelancers.
Children's Writing: Needs: poems or lyrics for children's songs. To submit, send query. No unsolicited submissions accepted! Submissions returned with proper SASE. Reports in 6 weeks. Pays royalty or buys material outright.
Illustration/Animation: Hires illustrators for animation, storyboarding, live action, pencil testing. Types of animation produced: cel animation, clay animation, stop motion, special effects, computer animation, video graphics, live action. To submit, send cover letter, résumé, demo tape (VHS), color print samples, business card. Art samples returned with proper SASE. Reports in 6 weeks. Pay varies by project and ability of artist.

SISU HOME ENTERTAINMENT, Suite 402, 20 W. 38th St., New York NY 10018. (212)768-2197. Fax: (212)768-7413. President: Haim Scheinger. Estab. 1988. Video and audio manufacturers (production, distribution). Audience: Children (educational videos and entertainment videos). Uses videotapes and audio. Children's productions: "Lovely Butterfly—Chanuka," written by IETV (Israel Educational TV); illustrated by IETV (Jewish holiday-program for ages 2-5). 25% of writing is by freelancers.
Children's Writing: Needs are for publicity writing—all ages. To submit, arrange interview.
Illustration/Animation: Types of animation produced: clay animation, video graphics. To submit, send résumé. Art samples filed. Reports back only if interested.

STILES-BISHOP PRODUCTIONS INC., 3255 Bennett Dr., Los Angeles CA 90068. (213)883-0011. Fax: (213)466-5496. Contact: Katy Bishop. Estab. 1974. Production house. Audience: children. Uses videotapes and books. Children's productions: "The Cinnamon Bear" (audiotape and books of children's Christmas story for ages 2-10). 50% of writing is by freelancers; 100% of illustrating/animating is by freelancers.
Children's Writing: Needs: children's fiction for ages 2-11. Subjects include: all genres. To submit, send synopsis/outline, completed script, résumé, book. Submissions cannot be returned. Reports back only if interested. Pays negotiable royalty.
Illustration/Animation: Hires illustrators for animation and books. Types of animation produced: cel animation, computer animation, live action. To submit, send cover letter, résumé, VHS or ¾" demo tape, color print samples. Art samples are not returned. Reports back only if interested. Payment negotiable.

TREEHAUS COMMUNICATIONS, INC., 906 W. Loveland Ave., P.O. Box 249, Loveland OH 45140. (513)683-5716. President: Gerard A. Pottebaum. Estab. 1968. Type of company: production house. Audience: preschool through adults. Uses film strips, multimedia productions, videotapes. Children's production: *Seeds of Self-Esteem* series, written by Dr. Robert Brooks, Jane Ward and Gerard A. Pottebaum, includes two books for teachers, four in-service teacher training videos and 27 posters for children from primary grades through junior high school, distributed by American Guidance Service, Inc. 30% of writing is by freelancers; 30% of illustrating/animating is by freelancers.
Children's Writing: Needs: educational material/documentaries, for all ages. Subjects include: "social studies, religious education, documentaries on all subjects, but primarily about people who live ordinary lives in extraordinary ways." Submission method: query with synopsis. Submissions returned with proper SASE. Reports in 1 month. Guidelines/catalog for SAE. Pays writers in accordance with Writer's Guild standards.
Tips: Illustrators/animators: "Be informed about movements and needs in education, multi-cultural sensitivity." Looks for "social values, originality, competency in subject, global awareness."

*VIDEO AIDED INSTRUCTION, INC., 182 Village Rd., Roslyn Heights NY 11577. (516)621-6176. FAX: (516)484-8785. Contact: Peter Lanzer, President. Estab. 1983. Video publisher. Audience: grade 6 through adult. Uses videotapes. Recent children's productions: "Consumer Math," written by Dr. Harold Shane (math video for grade 6-adult). "Fractions," written by Peter Lanzer (math video for grade 6-adult). 50% of writing is by freelancers.
Children's Writing: Needs: educational material for all age levels on all school subjects. Query. Submissions are filed. Reports in 1 month. Guidelines/catalog free on request. Pays royalty; buys material outright.
Illustration/Animation: Types of animation produced: video graphic, live action. Guidelines/catalog free on request.

Audiovisual Companies/'92-'93 changes

The following markets are not included in this edition of *Children's Writer's & Illustrator's Market* for the reasons indicated. The phrase "did not respond" means the market was in the *1992 Children's Writer's & Illustrator's Market* but did not respond to our written and phone requests for updated information for a 1993 listing.

Aerial Image Video Services (did not respond)
Bes Creative (did not respond)

John Gati Film Effects, Inc. (unable to contact)
A.J. Shalleck Productions, Inc. (removed per request)

Bill Wadsworth Productions (unable to contact)

Audiotapes

In recent years, efforts have been made to promote children's audiovisual products, both spoken-word and musical. Those efforts have paid off, for today children's cassettes and book/cassette packages make up a significant presence in most bookstore and library inventories.

There are many indicators that the popularity of audiotapes is more than a passing fad. The art of storytelling is becoming more popular, so much that large storytelling festivals are held each year throughout the country—the largest being each October in Jonesborough, Tennessee. Most large publishers house audio departments and produce cassettes from their own backlists. Spoken word cassette/book packages are loved by children who enjoy having stories read to them (with today's two-career families, parents don't have as much time to read to their kids). Book/cassette packages also expedite the development of reading skills among children by allowing them to read the book simultaneously with the recorded narration. Though story tapes aren't produced with the intention of being a replacement for reading, they do make an excellent supplement.

One trend in story tapes is for celebrities such as Robin Williams, Judy Collins, Meryl Streep and Jack Nicholson to do the narrations. Also, established authors are recording their own creations. Jeff Brown, executive producer of *We Like Kids!* in Juneau, Alaska, says his children's radio show provides a forum for parents and children wishing to hear music and stories before they buy them. The show incorporates both storytelling and music into its programming as a way of educating and entertaining kids. Brown discusses his station, KTOO, and its use of freelancers in a close-up article on page 230.

Producers of children's music tapes are striving to record contemporary material tackling modern day issues (such as drug prevention), and with the same production qualities as recorded material for adults. Even grown-ups like to listen to some of the music currently being produced for children. This is no accident. Adults are more likely to purchase children's music they find tolerable—in other words, music they can bear to listen to over and over again (that's usually the way kids like to play it).

Flashier packaging is evident in audiocassettes in order to make them more appealing. Also, with the saturation of compact disc players in households nationwide, it is foreseen the majority of children's audio packages will soon be available on compact disc.

Represented in this section are book publishers, sheet music publishers and recording companies looking for good story material and unique children's music to record. There are some that are interested in reviewing both. Study each listing to determine what subject matter is preferred and what age levels material should be geared to. Pay rates will, for the most part, be based on royalties for writers and songwriters or, for recording musicians, on recording contracts.

*ALISO CREEK PRODUCTIONS, INC., P.O. Box 8174, Van Nuys CA 91409. (818)787-3203. President: William Williams. Record company, book publisher. Estab. 1987.
Music: Releases 2 LPs-cassettes; and 2 CDs/year. Member of ASCAP. Records 20 children's songs/year. Works with composers, lyricists, team collaborators. For songs recorded pays musicians/artists on record contract and songwriters on royalty contract. Call first and obtain permission to submit material. Submit 3-5 songs with lyric sheets on demo cassette. SASE/IRC for return of submission. Reports in 3 weeks. Recently recorded songs: *Brontosaurus Stomp,* by Bob Menn and William Williams, recorded on Aliso Creek Records label (dixieland music for ages 3-8); *What Makes a Car Go, Dad?,* by Bob Menn and William Williams, recorded on Aliso Creek Records label (Gilbert & Sullivan type of music for ages 3-8).
Tips: "We're looking for music in a variety of styles that doesn't talk down to children or isn't preachy, but does convey positive values or educate."
Stories: Publishes 2 book/cassette packages/year; 2 cassettes/CDs/year. 100% of stories are fiction. Will consider all types of fiction, but story and songs must be related. "We publish musical plays on cassette aimed at ages 3-8." Will consider all types of nonfiction aimed at ages 3-8. Authors are paid negotiable royalty based on retail price; outright purchase of ms. Submit both cassette tape and ms. Reports on queries in 3 weeks. Catalog is free for #10 SAE and 1 first class stamp. Recently published *Take a Trip with Me,* by Bob Menn and William Williams, narrated by Kevin Birkbeck and Katy Morkri (ages 3-8); *Move!,* by Bob Men and William Williams, narrated by Katy Morkri (ages 3-8), a family adjusts to moving to a different city.
Tips: "We publish song and story cassettes with an illustrated lyric book so we need writers and illustrators to create a unified product."

AMERICAN MELODY, P.O. Box 270, Guilford CT 06437. (203)457-0881. President: Phil Rosenthal. Music publisher, record company (American Melody), recording studio, book publisher. Estab. 1985.
Music: Releases 4 LPs/year. Member of BMI. Publishes 20 children's songs/year; records 30 children's songs/year. Works with composers, lyricists, team collaborators. For music published pays standard royalty of 50%; for songs recorded pays musicians/artists on record contract, musicians on salary for inhouse studio work, and songwriters on royalty contract. Call fist and obtain permission to submit material. Submit demo cassette. SASE/IRC for return of submission. Reports in 1 month. Recorded songs: *The Bremen Town Song,* by Max Showalter and Peter Walker, recorded by Max Showalter on American Melody label (folk music for ages 2-10); *Calico Pie,* by Phil Rosenthal, recorded by Phil Rosenthal on American Melody label (bluegrass music for ages 1-8).
Music Tips: "Submit as nice a demo as possible, with lyrics understandable."
Stories: "Plan to publish 2 book/cassette packages/year." 100% of stories are fiction. Will consider all kinds of genres for ages 2-10. For nonfiction, considers biography and history. Authors are paid royalties based on wholesale price. Submit both cassette tape and manuscript. Reports on queries/mss in 1 month. Catalog is free on request. Recorded story tapes: *The Gold Dog,* by Lev Ustinov, narrated by Max Showalter (fairy tales for ages 4-12); *Tales from the First World,* written and narrated by Sylvia and Jeff McQuillan (adaptations of folktales for ages 2-12).

*ART AUDIO PUBLISHING COMPANY/TIGHT HI-FI SOUL MUSIC, 9706 Cameron Ave., Detroit MI 48211. (313)893-3406. President: Albert M. Leigh. Music publisher. Estab. 1962.
Music: Works with composers and lyricists. For music published pays standard royalty of 50%. Submit demo tape by mail; unsolicited submissions OK. Submit demo cassette with 1-3 songs, lyric and/or lead sheet. SASE/IRC for return of submission. Reports in 2 weeks.

Music Tips: "We are looking for songs with a strong hook, strong words. We are looking for hits, such as *Little Teddy Bear, Duckey Lucky* or *Chicken Little*. Can be songs or musical stories for movie sound tracks. Videocassette top sales and rentals and also for major record companys, uptempo dance. All lyrics are up-front: Words are clearly understandable."

BRENTWOOD MUSIC, INC., 316 Southgate Court, Brentwood TN 37027. (615)373-3950. Fax: (615)373-0386. Creative Director: Ed Kee. Music publisher, book publisher, record company, children's video. Estab. 1980.
Music: Releases 40 cassettes/year; 24-30 CDs/year. Member of ASCAP, BMI and SESAC. Publishes 60-120 children's songs/year. Works with composers. For music published pays standard royalty of 50% of net receipts. Submit demo cassette tape by mail; unsolicited submissions OK; 2 songs and lyric sheet or lead sheet. "No music can be returned unless you include a self-addressed, stamped envelope. Do not send stamps or postage only. If you want it back, send an *envelope* big enough to hold all material and the *proper* postage. No exceptions." Reports in 3-6 months.
Stories: Will consider fictional animal, fantasy or adventure aimed at preschool through 3rd or 4th grades. Author's pay is negotiable. Query. Reports in 1 week.

*CENTER FOR THE QUEEN OF PEACE, 3350 Highway 6, Suite 412, Houston TX 77478. Music publisher, book publisher and record company. Record labels include Cosmotone Records. Estab. 1984.
Music: Releases 1 single, 1 12-inch single and 1 LP/year. Member of ASCAP. Works with team collaborators. For music published pays negotiable royalty; for songs recorded pays musicians on salary for inhouse studio work, songwriters on royalty contract. Write for permission to submit material. "Will respond only if interested."

*CHILDREN'S MEDIA PRODUCTIONS, P.O. Box 40400, Pasadena CA 91114. (818)797-5462. President: C. Ray Carlson. Video publisher. Estab. 1983. Works with composers and/or lyricists. For songs recorded pays musicians/artists on record contract. Write for permission to submit material.
Music Tips: "We use original music and songs only for videos.We serve markets worldwide and must often record songs in foreign languages. So avoid anything provincially *American*. Parents choose videos that will '*teach* for a lifetime' (our motto) rather than entertain for a few hours. They *avoid* that which is usually seen on Saturday a.m. TV."

THE CHRISTIAN SCIENCE PUBLISHING SOCIETY, One Norway Street, Boston MA 02115. (617)450-2033. Fax: (617)450-2017. General Publications Product Manager: Rhoda M. Ford. Book publisher "but we do issue some recordings." Estab. 1898.
Music: Releases 2 audio cassettes/year; 1 CD/year. Hires staff writers for children's music. Works with team collaborators. Submit query letter with proposal, references, résumé. Does not return unsolicited submissions. Reports in 2 months.
Stories: Publishes 1-2 book/cassette packages/year; 1 audio tape/year. 100% of stories are nonfiction. Will consider nonfiction for beginning readers, juveniles, teens based on the Bible (King James Version). Authors are paid royalty or outright purchase of manuscript, "negotiated with contract." Submit query letter with proposal, references and résumé. Include Social Security number. Reports on queries in 2 months. Trade Kit available.

 The asterisk before a listing indicates the listing is new in this edition.

Tips: "Since we are part of The First Church of Christ, Scientist, all our publications are in harmony with the teachings of Christian Science."

THE CUTTING CORPORATION, 4940 Hampden Lane, Bethesda MD 20814. (301)654-2887. Vice President Mary Cutting. Children's audio book producer. Estab. 1971.
Stories: Publishes 10 audio tapes/year. 100% of stories are fiction. Will consider adventure, fantasy, fairy tales. Story tapes aimed at ages 3-8. For nonfiction, considers history. Story tapes aimed at ages 3-8. Authors are paid by outright purchase of manuscript. Submit casssette tape of story. Reports on queries in 1 week; on mss in 1 month. Recorded story tapes: *Frolics Dance*, by Soundprints Corporation, narrated by Tom Chapin (ages 5-8, animal); *Beaver at Long Pond*, by Soundprints Corporation, narrated by Red Grammer (ages 5-8, nature).

DISCOVERY MUSIC, 5554 Calhoun Ave., Van Nuys CA 91401. (818)782-7818. Fax: (818)782-7817. C.E.O. David Wohlstadter. Record company (Discovery Music). Estab. 1985.
Music: Releases 2-3 LPs and 2-3 CDs/year. Records approximately 45 songs/year. For songs recorded pays musicians/artists on record contract, musicians on salary for in-house studio work, songwriters on royalty contract (percentage royalty). Submit demo tape by mail; unsolicited submissions OK. Submit demo cassette with cover letter. Cannot return material. Reporting on submissions "varies." Recently recorded songs: *Put Yourself Together, Humpty* and *Jack & Jill's Better Scheme*, both by Dennis Hysom, recorded by Discovery Music on Discovery Music label (children's music for ages 3-8).

DOVE AUDIO, 301 N. Cañon Dr., Beverly Hills CA 90210. (213)273-7722. Fax: (213)273-0365. Customer Service Supervisor: Maryann Camarillo. Audio book publisher. Estab. 1985.
Stories: Publishes approx. 100/year (audio tapes only). 50% of stories are fiction; 50% nonfiction. Submit through agent only. Reports in 2 weeks. Catalog is free on request. Recorded story tapes include *Ryan White: My Own Story*, by Ryan White, narrated by Lukas Haas (ages 8 and up, biography).

DUTTON CHILDREN'S BOOKS, 375 Hudson St., New York NY 10014. (212)366-2600. Fax: (212)366-2011. Senior Vice President and Publisher: Christopher Franceschelli. Book publisher.
Stories: Publishes 3 book/cassette packages/year. 100% of stories are fiction. Will consider animal and fantasy. Story tapes aimed at ages 2-10. Authors are paid 5-12% royalties based on retail price; outright purchase of $2,000-20,000; royalty inclusive. Average advance $3,000. Submit outline/synopsis and sample chapters through agent. Reports on queries in 3 weeks; on mss in 6 months. Catalog is available for 8 × 11 SAE and 8 first class stamps. Ms guidelines available for #10 SAE and 1 first class stamp. Children's story tapes include *Noah's Ark*, narrated by James Earl Jones.
Story Tips: "Do not call publisher. Get agent. Celebrity readers sell."

*MARTIN EZRA & ASSOCIATES, 45 Fairview Ave., Lansdowne PA 19050. (215)622-1600. President: Martin Ezra. Producer. Estab. 1968.
Music: Submit demo tape by mail; unsolicited submissions OK. Submit demo cassette (VHS videocassette if available). Lyric or lead sheets not necessary.
Stories: Will consider all types of fiction and nonfiction. Submit cassette tape of story.

FINE ART PRODUCTIONS, 67 Maple St., Newburgh NY 12550. (914)561-5866. Contact: Richie Suraci. Music publisher, record company, book publisher. Estab. 1989.
Music: Member of ASCAP and BMI. Publishes and records 1-2 children's songs/year. Hires staff writers for children's music. Works with composers, lyricists, team collabora-

tors. For music published pays standard royalty of 50% or other amount; for songs recorded pays musicians/artists on record contract, musicians on salary for inhouse studio work, songwriters on varying royalty contract. Submit ½" demo tape by mail; unsolicited submissions OK. Submit demo cassette. Not neccessary to include lyric or lead sheets. SASE/IRC for return of submission. Reports in 3-4 months.
Stories: Publishes 1 book/cassette package and 1 audio tape/year. 50% of stories are fiction; 50% nonfiction. Will consider all genres for all age groups. Authors are paid varying royalty on wholesale or retail price. Submit both cassette tape and manuscript. Reports in 3-4 months. Catalog is not available. Ms guidelines free with SASE.

FRONTLINE MUSIC GROUP/FMG BOOKS, Box 28450, Santa Ana CA 92799. (714)660-3888. Fax: (714)660-3899. Executive Vice President: Brian Tong. Music publisher, record company, book publisher. Record labels include Alma, Vineyard, Asaph, Frontline Kids. Estab. 1985.
Music: Releases 80-100 singles/year; 40-50 LPs/year; 40-50 CDs/year. Member of ASCAP and BMI. Publishes and records 50-60 children's songs/year. Hires staff writers for children's music. Works with composers, lyricists, team collaborators. For music published pays standard royalty of 50%; for songs recorded pays musicians/artists on record contract, musicians on salary for inhouse studio work, and songwriters on royalty contract. Submit cassette demo tape and lyric sheet by mail—unsolicited submissions OK. Requirements: only Christian material, no fantasy stuff. SASE for return of submissions. Reports in 3-4 weeks.
Tips: Songwriters: "Submit fresh material that is relevant to today's issues." Trends in children's music: "Age groupings are becoming more specialized. There is a distinct difference in likes and dislikes between 6-10 and 10-13 year olds and 14-16 year olds."
Stories: Publishes 2-4 book/cassette packages/year. 100% of stories are fiction. Will consider fictional animal, fantasy, history, sports and suspense/mystery/adventure stories aimed at all juvenile audiences "if Christian." Will consider nonfictional Bible stories aimed at all juvenile audiences. Authors are paid in royalties based on retail price. Submit complete ms. SASE for return of ms. Reports on queries in 4-6 weeks; mss in 6-8 weeks. Book catalog, ms guidelines not available.
Tips: Writers: "Be unusual." Trends in children's reading material: "More sophistication."

GORDON MUSIC CO. INC./PARIS RECORDS, P.O. Box 2250, Canoga Park CA 91306. (818)883-8224. Owner: Jeff Gordon. Music publisher, record company. Estab. 1950.
Music: Releases 3-4 CDs/year. Member of ASCAP and BMI. Publishes 6-8 children's songs/year; records 10-15 children's songs/year. Works with composers, lyricists, team collaborators. For music published pays standard royalty of 50%; for songs recorded, arrangement made between artist and company. Call first and obtain permission to submit. Submit 3-4 videocassette tapes, lyric and lead sheets. Does not return unsolicited submissions. Recorded children's songs: *Izzy, the Pest of the West*, recorded by Champ on Paris label.

HOME, INC., 731 Harrison Ave., Boston MA 02118. (617)266-1386. Director: Alan Michel. Nonprofit video production company. Estab. 1973.
Music: Paymaster through to AFTRA/SAG. Works with composers, lyricists, team collaborators. For music published pay negotiated on a project-by-project basis. Submit demo tape by mail; unsolicited submissions OK. Submit demo cassette with 3-6 songs.

Refer to the Business of Children's Writing & Illustrating
for up-to-date marketing, tax and legal information.

"I am usually looking for versatility and range in demos submitted." Cannot return material. Reports back only if interested in the work. Recorded songs: *Going to Court*, music only by Don Dinicola, recorded by Don Dinicola used on video tape as sound track (country for preschool-preteen); *Stand Back From Crack*, by Young Nation, recorded by Frank King, used on video tape (rap for teen).

Music Tips: "We are not a publisher or record company. We work with independent publishers who are attempting to meet some social need through communications. We specialize in developing teen and preteen related programming."

Stories: Publishes 5 videos/year. 100% of stories are fiction. Will consider drama, music videos, public service announcements, training for preteens and teens. For nonfiction, considers animal, education and others as may be needed. Payment negotiated. Submit outline/synopsis and sample chapters with résumé. If interested, reports in 2-3 weeks (if solicited only).

MAMA-T ARTISTS/THE FOLKTELLERS, P.O. Box 2898, Asheville NC 28802. (704)258-1113. Contact: Amy D. Mozingo. Inhouse publisher of storytelling tapes. Estab. 1981.

Stories: Publishes audio tapes only. 75% of stories are fiction; 25% nonfiction. Will consider all genres for varying age groups. Authors are paid 2-8% royalties based on retail price; outright purchase of $1,000 (so far have only done once). Average advance $100. Submit complete ms—"we do all performing ourselves." Reports on queries/mss in 2-3 months. Catalog is free on request. Recently recorded story tapes: *Story for the Road*, narrated by The Folktellers (traditional and contemporary stories for children of all ages).

MELODY HOUSE, INC., 819 NW 92nd St., Oklahoma City OK 73114. (405)840-3383. Fax: (405)840-3384. President: Stephen Fite. Record company (Melody House). Estab. 1972.

Music: Releases 6 LPs/year. Records 72 children's songs/year. Works with composers, lyricists, team collaborators. For songs recorded pays musicians on salary for inhouse studio work or standard mechanical royalty per song. Submit demo tape by mail; unsolicited submissions OK. Submit demo cassette (5 songs or more) with lyric and lead sheets. SASE/IRC for return of submission. Reports in 2 months. Recorded songs: *Blues for My Blue Sky*, by Stephen Fite, recorded by Al Rasso on Melody House label (rhythm and blues for ages 4-8); *What A Beautiful World*, by Al Rasso, recorded by Stephen Fite on Melody House label (ballad for ages 4-8).

Music Tips: "The music and the lyrics should reach out and grab the child's attention. Children are much more sophisticated in their listening than their parents were at the same age. Children's music is definitely taking on the characteristics of the pop market with the sounds and even the hype in some cases. Even some of the messages are now touching on issues such as divorce/separation, the environment and social consciousness, both in the U.S. and the world."

NEW DAY PRESS, 2355 E. 89th St., Cleveland OH 44106. (216)795-7070. Chair, Editorial Committee: Charlotte Durant. Book publisher. Estab. 1972.

Stories: Publishes "1 or less" book/cassette packages/year. 50% of stories are fiction; 50% are nonfiction. Will consider historical African-American fiction and nonfiction only aimed at ages 10 and up. Buys mss outright for $100-250. Query. Book catalog free on request. Recorded story tape: *Fireside Tales*, written by Mary Shepard-Moore and narrated by Carolyn Gordon (African-American History for 6-12 year olds).

*OAK STREET MUSIC, 108-93 Lombard Ave., Winnipeg, Manitoba R3B 3B1 Canada. (204)957-0085. Record company. Estab. 1987.

Music: Releases 8 LPs-cassettes/year; 3 CDs/year. Member of SOCAN and PROCAN. Records 30 children's songs/year. Works with team collaborators. For songs recorded

pays musicians/artists on record contract; songwriters on royalty contract. Submit demo tape by mail; unsolicited submissions OK. Include demo cassette (VHS videocassette if available); minimum 2-5 songs; not necessary to include lyric or lead sheets. SASE/IRC for return of submission. Recently recorded songs: *You Can Count On Me*, by Sammy Cahn, recorded by Fred Punner on Oak Street Music label (children's music for ages 2-10); *Oo Babba Loo*, by Markus, recorded by Fred Punner on Oak Street Music label (children's music for ages 2-10).
Stories: Publishes 2 book/cassette packages/year. 50% of stories are fiction; 50% nonfiction. Interested in all types of fiction for "older" children (ages 5-8). Interested in all types of nonfiction. Submit both cassette tape and ms.
Tips: "Listen to our products for an idea of what we need or choose a specific artist like Fred Punner to write for."

*PASSING PARADE MUSIC, P.O. Box 872, West Covina CA 91790. Owner/Operator: Kelly D. Lammers. Music publisher. Estab. 1972.
Music: Member of ASCAP. Publishes 3-6 children's songs/year. Works with composers, lyricists, team collaborators. For music published pays standard royalty of 50%. Submit demo tape by mail; unsolicited submissions OK. Submit demo cassette with maximum of 3 songs and lyric sheet. SASE/IRC for return of submission. Reports in 4-6 weeks. Recently published songs: *Let Me Be a Kid for Just Awhile*, by K. Lammers and D. Lammers, recorded by The Neighborhood Kids (anti-drug children's song for ages 6-15); *The Happy Song*, by Jim Pash, recorded by Jim Pash and The Neighborhood Kids on the Koinkidink label (instrumental music for kids of all ages).
Tips: "We would like all children's material to have a positive and uplifting theme or message."

PETER PAN INDUSTRIES, 88 St. Francis St., Newark NJ 07105. (201)344-4214. Fax: (201)344-0465. Vice President of Sales: Shelly Rudin. Music publisher, record company. Record labels include Parade Music, Compose Music, Peter Pan. Estab. 1927.
Music: Releases 20 singles/year; 10 12-inch singles; 45 LPs/year; 45 CDs/year. Member of ASCAP and BMI. Publishes 50 children's songs/year; records 80-90 songs/year. Works with composers, lyricists, team collaborators. For music published pays standard royalty of 50%; for songs recorded pays musicians/artists on record contract, songwriters on royalty contract. Making contact: Submit a 15 IPS reel-to-reel demo tape or VHS videocassette by mail—unsolicited submissions OK. SASE (or SAE and IRCs) for return of submissions. Reports in 4-6 weeks.
Stories: Publishes 12 book/cassette packages/year. 90% of stories are fiction; 10% nonfiction. Will consider all genres of fiction and nonfiction aimed at 6-month to 9-year olds. Authors are paid in royalties based on wholesale price. Making contact: Query. Reports on queries in 4-6 weeks. Book catalog, manuscript guidelines free on request.
Tips: "Tough business but rewarding. Lullabies are very popular."

PLANETARY PLAYTHINGS, P.O. Box 66, Boulder Creek CA 95006. (408)338-2161. Fax: (408)338-9861. Vice President of Sales and Marketing: Kathy White. Music publisher, book publisher, record company. Estab. 1989.
Music: Releases 3 LPs and 3 CDs/year. Member of ASCAP. Publishes and records 2 children's songs/year. Works with composers. For music published pays standard royalty of 50%; for songs recorded pays musicians on salary for inhouse studio work. Call first and obtain permission to submit material. Submit demo cassette. Cannot return material. Reports in 1 month. Published and recorded songs: *Heart Way*, written and recorded by Deborah Razman on Planetary Productions label (relaxation for ages 3-7); *Heart Zones*, written and recorded by Doc Lew Childre on Planetary Productions label (stress reduction, learning enhancement ages 5-21).
Stories: Publishes 8 book/cassette packages/year. 70% of stories are fiction; 30% nonfiction. Will consider adventure stories aimed at 5 to teen audience. For nonfiction, consid-

ers education aimed at teen audience. Submit query. Reports on queries in 1 month; on mss in 2 months. Catalog is free on request.

Tips: "We are a consortium of 40 artists, writers, musicians, educators and business professionals who have common ownership of the business. All of our books and tapes are created inhouse. We do not usually publish works by outside people but we are open to sharing ideas and having contact with others in the industry. If you have any questions, please call 1-800-372-3100."

*QUIET TYMES, INC., Suite 521, 2121 S. Oneida St., Denver CO 80224. (303)757-5545. Fax: (303)757-3679. Vice President: Cathy Gavend. Record company. Estab. 1987.

Music: "We've released 2 audiocassette tapes since our company began. We are now working on our third." Works with composers, teams collaborators. For music published pays royalties; pays musicians/artists on record contract. Write for permission to submit material. Submit demo tape. SASE/IRC for return of submission. Reports in 6 weeks. Recently recorded *Sleepy Angels*, by Jim Oliver (mothers-to-be to age 10; but enjoyed by all); *The Baby Soother*, by Roger Wannell (sounds for infants to 1½ years).

RHYTHMS PRODUCTIONS/TOM THUMB MUSIC, P.O. Box 34485, Los Angeles CA 90034. President: R.S. White. Record company, cassette and book packagers. Record label, Tom Thumb—Rhythms Productions. Estab. 1955.

Music: Member of ASCAP. Works with composers and lyricists. For songs recorded pays musicians/artists on record contract, songwriters on royalty contract. Submit a cassette demo tape or VHS videotape by mail—unsolicited submissions OK. Requirements: "We accept musical stories. Must be produced in demo form, and must have educational content or be educationally oriented." Reports in 2 months. Recently recorded: *Adventures of Professor Whatzit & Carmine Cat*, by Dan Brown and Bruce Crook (6 book and cassette packages); and *First Reader's Kit* (multimedia learning program); all on Tom Thumb label.

*CHARLES SEGAL MUSIC, 16 Grace Rd., Newton MA 02159. (617)969-6196. Contact: Charles Segal. Music publisher and record company. Record labels include Spin Record. Estab. 1980.

Music: Publishes 36 children's songs/year. Works with composers and/or lyricists, team collaborators. For music published pays standard royalty of 50%; for songs recorded pays musicians/artists on record contract. Submit demo tape by mail.; unsolicited submissions OK. Submit demo cassette if available with 1-3 songs and lyric or lead sheets. Reports in 6-7 weeks. Recently recorded songs: *Animal Concert*, by Colleen Hay, recorded by Concert Kids on CBS label (sing along for ages 4-13); *Everyday Things*, recorded by Charles Segal on MFP label (kids pop music for ages 6-15).

Music Tips: "Must be of educational value, entertaining easy listening. The lyrics should not be focused on sex, killing, etc.

Stories: Publishes 6 book/cassette packages/year. 50% of stories are fiction; 50% nonfiction. Will consider all genres aimed at ages 6-15. For nonfiction, considers all aimed at ages 6-15. Authors are paid royalty. Submit complete ms or submit both cassette tape and ms. Reports on queries in 6 weeks; on mss in 2 months.

Story Tips: "I always look for the experienced writer who knows where he's going and not beating around the bush; in other words, has a definite message—a simple, good storyline."

Market conditions are constantly changing! If you're still using this book and it is 1994 or later, buy the newest edition of Children's Writer's & Illustrator's Market *at your favorite bookstore or order directly from Writer's Digest Books.*

Close-up

Jeff Brown
Executive Producer
We Like Kids!
Juneau, Alaska

Jeff Brown preaches the gospel of children's radio. "I believe that it has a higher purpose than just entertaining kids," he says. He has been involved with children's radio, and Juneau, Alaska's public radio station KTOO ever since coming to Juneau from Los Angeles in 1975. KTOO has always been involved in doing children's programming, and Brown was brought into continual contact with those creating it. As he became more involved in children's radio he actively sought out nationally broadcast programming for his station. But looking through the satellite offerings from National Public Radio (NPR), he found there were no regular weekly offerings for children. So, Brown, Judy Hall and Jan Conitz decided to create their own. *We Like Kids!* was offered to NPR and has been on the network weekly for four years.

We Like Kids! not only seeks to entertain and educate, but to provide a forum for parents and children wishing to hear music or stories before buying them. "It's hard for the kids and the parents, who are looking for a way to make an intelligent choice about the music and stories their children listen to," says Brown. Through the show and a monthly newsletter listing all the songs and stories used, Brown hopes to expose the show's audience to a fast-growing body of music and stories.

The show itself is a weekly half-hour program featuring Brown's alter ego, Professor Sphagnum Moss, his companion Alpine Annie (co-producer Hall) and children from the Juneau area. The group gathers in the "Electronic Mystery Lab" and shares songs, stories and thoughts on selected topics with their listeners. A single topic is chosen as the theme of each show, and appropriate music and stories are chosen by Brown and Hall from their recording library.

Although each show does have a specific theme, Brown and Hall are constantly seeking quality music and stories for their recording library. "Our goal is to encourage people who are making songs and stories now to continue to do so," says Brown. They feature many new artists on the show to create a wide variety as well as opportunity for the musical artists and storytellers featured. "There's a bunch of great people out there, and very few people who aren't worthy of air-play," Brown says.

The show features children's music in all styles. However, the stories are somewhat different. *We Like Kids!* features storytelling rather than producing stories submitted by authors. Brown has often received stories in print from authors. "A lot of the submissions that we've received have been from writers who think that we produce the stories ourselves," he says. "When we get something from a writer, we'll read a cover letter that says, 'We've read that you're looking for stories. Here's a bunch.' We have probably gotten five to ten of those letters.

"The people we feature on the show are tellers of stories who present stories in a dramatic and sometimes musical way. Those are the kind of submissions we're looking for—people who tell stories and invite people to travel along with them."

Brown seeks music and storytelling tapes that are for sale either directly from the artist or commercially through a record company or distributor. "We send a letter (to authors sending stories in printed form) saying if you have commercially available cassettes out, please send those rather than the written word," Brown says. "Hopefully, the authors are also storytellers in the audio market who have cassettes out." Consequently, high quality recording is important for both music and stories submitted to Brown.

Music, stories, funny characters and topically oriented material add up to a great show in a struggling format. Radio for children is scarce and not well-supported by funding agencies like the Corporation for Public Broadcasting. However, Brown remains optimistic. "People who do things with kids are some of the most supportive people I've ever seen," he says. "It's a whole different world from pop music, and everybody in it knows that it's a big battle."

—*Michael Oxley*

We Like Kids! *co-producers Jeff Brown and Judy Hall not only aim their weekly radio show at kids, but they also include children in the studio work. Here, kids from Juneau, Alaska help with production of stories and music on the air.*

A.J. SHALLECK PRODUCTIONS, INC., Guinea Rd., Brewster NY 10509. President: Alan J. Shalleck. Audiovisual production house, children's home video/film. Estab. 1981.
Music: Hires staff writers for children's music. Works with composers, lyricists; teams collaborators.
Stories: Publishes 5-15 book/cassette packages and audio tapes/year. 80% of stories are fiction. Will consider various genres for appropriate age group; pre-K-3rd grade. Authors are paid by outright purchase. Average advance $500-1,000. Query. Recorded story tapes: *Classic Titles* (Goldilocks, Henny Penny, etc.), by various authors, narrated by Fred Newman (classic and original stories for pre-K-3rd grade); *Curious George Various*, by Margret Rey and A. Shalleck (children's fiction for pre-K-3rd grade).
Story Tips: "We are noticing more stories involving present social problems."

SONG WIZARD RECORDS, P.O. Box 931029, Los Angeles CA 90093. (213)461-8848. Fax: (213)461-0936. Owner: Dave Kinnoin. Music publisher, record company. Record label Song Wizard Records. Estab. 1987.
Music: Releases 1 cassette/year. Member of ASCAP. Records 12 songs/year. Publishes 20 songs/year. Works with composers, lyricists and team collaborators. For music published pays negotiable royalty; for songs recorded pays songwriters on royalty contract (negotiable). Write for permission to submit material. Submit demo cassette with 3 songs and lyric sheet. "Put name, address, phone number and copyright notice on all pieces of submission." SASE/IRC for return of submission. Reports in 6 months or sooner. Recently recorded songs: "Dunce Cap Kelly," written and recorded by Dave Kinnoin on Song Wizard Records label (pop rock for ages 7-12).
Music Tips: "Be startlingly fresh with pure rhymes and poetic devices that live happily with singability. If someone sends me a song that is so amazing I can't refuse it, I'll use it or pass it to someone else who may."

SOUND PUBLICATIONS, INC., Suite 108, 10 E. 22nd St., Lombard IL 60148. (708)916-7071. President: Cheryl Basilico. Music publisher, record company. Record labels include Sound Publications. Estab. 1991.
Music: Releases 10 LPs/year. Publishes and records 50 children's songs/year. For music published pays standard royalty of 50%; songs recorded on joint venture. Call or write for permission to submit material. Submit demo cassette with 3-5 songs, lyric sheet. "Music is to be educational." SASE/IRC for return of submission. Reports in 3 months.

SOUNDPRINTS, a Division of Trudy Management Corporation, 165 Water St., P.O. Box 679, Norwalk CT 06856. (203)838-6009. Editor: Dorothy Shillinglaw. Book publisher. Estab. 1988.
Stories: Publishes 6-7 book/cassette packages/year. Almost 100% of stories are fiction. Will consider realistic animal stories for preschool-3rd grade. For nonfiction, considers animal for preschool-3rd grade. Query with SASE. Reports in 2 weeks on queries; 1 month on mss. Catalog free on request. Ms guidelines free with SASE. Published and recorded story tapes: *Jackrabbit and the Prairie Fire*, by Susan Saunders, narrated by Peter Thomas (black-tailed jackrabbit on the Great Plains for preschool-3rd grade); *Seasons of a Red Fox*, by Susan Saunders, narrated by Peter Thomas (the first year in the life of a red fox for preschool-3rd grade).
Tips: "Be realistic. Much of what I get is not worth reading."

TRENNA PRODUCTIONS, P.O. Box 2484, Malibu CA 90265. (310)457-2583. Fax: (213)457-6998. President: Trenna Daniells. Children's audio story cassette publisher. Estab. 1981.
Music: Releases 4 LPs/year. Works with composers. For music published pays per project. Submit demo tape by mail; unsolicited submissions OK. Submit demo cassette.

SASE/IRC for return of submission. Recorded music: *Be True To Yourself*, by composer Jimmy Hammer, recorded by Trenna Daniells on Trenna Productions (for ages 4-9); *No More Nightmares*, by composer Jimmy Hammer, recorded by Trenna Daniells on Trenna Productions (ages 4-9).

WATCHESGRO MUSIC PUBLISHING CO., BMI. Watch Us Climb, ASCAP. 900 19th Ave. South, Suite 106, Nashville TN 37212. (615)329-3991. President: Eddie Lee Carr. Music publisher, record company. Record labels include Interstate 40 Records, Tracker Records. Estab. 1970.
Music: Releases 10 singles/year; 5 12-inch singles/year; 1 LP/year; 1 CD/year. Publishes 15 children's songs/year; records 4 children's songs/year. Works with composers, lyricists. For music published pays standard royalty of 50%; for songs recorded pays musicians/artists on record contract, musicians on salary for inhouse studio work. Write or call first and obtain permission to submit a cassette tape. Does not return unsolicited material. Reports in 1 week.

WE LIKE KIDS!, produced by KTOO-FM, 224 4th St., Juneau AK 99801. (907)586-1670. Fax: (907)586-3612. Producers: Jeff Brown or Judy Hall. Producer of nationwide children's radio show.
Music: Releases 50+ programs/year. Member of Children's Music Network; National Association for the Preservation and Perpetuation of Storytelling. Submit demo tape by mail; unsolicited submissions OK. Submit demo cassette vinyl, CD.
Music Tips: "The best advice we could give to anyone submitting songs for possible airplay is to make certain that they give their best performance and record it in the best way possible. A mix of well-honed songwriting skills, an awareness of a variety of international musical styles, and the advent of home studios have all added up to a delightful abundance of quality songs and stories for children."
Stories: "Our show is based on themes most of the time. Send us your recorded stories."

WORLD LIBRARY PUBLICATIONS INC., 3815 N. Willow Dr., Schiller Park IL 60176. (708)678-0621. General Editor: Nicholas T. Freund. Music publisher. Estab. 1945.
Music: Publishes 10-12 children's songs/year. Works with composers. For music published pays 10% of sales. Making contact: Submit demo cassette tape and lead sheet by mail; unsolicited submissions OK. "Should be liturgical. We are primarily a Roman Catholic publisher." Reports in 3 months. Published children's songs: "Let the Children Come to Me," written and recorded by James V. Marchconda on WLP cassette 7845 label (religious/catechetical); "Gather You Children," written by Peter Finn and James Chepponis (religious/catechetical); and "Mass of the Children of God," written by James V. Marchionda on WLP Cassette 7664 label (liturgical).

*ZACK PRESS, STILES-BISHOP PRODUCTIONS INC., 3255 Bennett Dr., Los Angeles CA 90068. (213)883-0011. Editor: Kathryn Bishop. Book publisher. Estab. 1991.
Stories: Publishes 1 book/cassette package/year; 1 cassette/CD/year. 100% of stories are fiction. Will consider fantasy and adventure fiction stories for ages 6-9. Will consider animal stories, biographies, history and sports nonfiction stories for ages 6-9. Authors are paid 5-10% royalties based on wholesale price. Query, submit through agent only. Reports on queries in 2 weeks; on mss in 1 month. Recently recorded *The Cinnamon Bear*, by Heisch (ages 3 and up, fantasy).

Scriptwriter's Markets

There are rumors that children are less discriminating than adults, and therefore not as picky about the plays they view. The reality is children are about the cruelest critics there are. Most adults will sit patiently and watch a dull play just to be polite, but for the most part, kids don't care about being polite and are less inhibited at visibly expressing their dissatisfaction. One way to assure against a bored audience is to use plenty of rhythm, repetition and effective dramatic action. Avoid using subplots and unnecessary dialogue, which will add to the length of the play. Most plays for children average less than an hour.

"Fourth wall" plays, or plays where actors perform as if they are not aware of the audience, are still the standard in this field. But because of the competition of movies and television, interactive plays which involve the audience are gaining more acceptance.

The U.S. population is comprised of a multitude of ethnic subcultures. Be aware of this when writing plays for children. You might have a better chance at selling a script if it reflects racial diversity.

Since many theater groups produce plays with limited budgets, scripts containing elaborate staging and costumes might not meet their needs. Also, many children's plays are touring productions that consist of three to six actors. There might be more characters in your play than available actors, so think about how the roles can be doubled up. Also, touring theaters want simple sets that can be easily transported. To become more familiar with the types of plays the listed markets are looking for, contact them about their specific needs. Some will have catalogs available.

Plays using adult roles *and* plays with children's roles are being solicited by the markets in this section. Note the listings contain percentages of how many plays produced are for adult roles, and how many are for children's roles.

Payment for playwrights usually comes in the form of royalties, outright payments or a combination of both. The pay scale isn't going to be quite as high as screenplay rates, but playwrights *do* benefit by getting to watch their work performed live by a variety of groups employing a multitude of interpretations.

*A.D. PLAYERS, 2710 W. Alabama, Houston TX 77098. (713)526-2721. Literary Manager: Martha Doolittle.Estab. 1967. Produces 3-4 children's plays/year in new Children's Theatre Series; 1 musical/year. Produces children's plays for professional productions. 99-100% of plays/musicals written for adult roles; 1-0% for juvenile roles. "Need minimal, portable sets for proscenium arena stage with no fly space and small wing space." Recently produced *Joshua And The Ta Ra Ta Raa Ta Raaa*, by Jeannette Clift George — musical telling of Joshua and his march around the walls of Jericho for ages 5-100; *A Little Something*, by Sharla R. Boyce — two sisters learning the true meaning of Christmas for ages 5-100. Does not want to see large cast or set requirements, New Age themes. Will consider simultaneous submissions and previously performed work. Submission method: query with synopsis, character breakdown and set description; no tapes until requested. Reports in 6 months-1 year. Purchases some residual rights. Pay negotiated. Submissions returned with SASE.
Tips: "Children's musicals tend to be large in casting requirements. For those theaters with smaller production capabilities, this can be a liability for a script. Try to keep it

small and simple, especially if writing for theaters where adults are performing for children. We are interested in material that reflects family values, emphasizes the importance of responsibility in making choices, encourages faith in God and projects the joy and fun of telling a story."

ART EXTENSIONS THEATER, 11144 Weddington, N. Hollywood CA 91601. (818)760-8675. Fax: (818)508-8613. Artistic Director: Maureen Kennedy Samuels. Estab. 1991. Produces 2 children's plays/year; 1 children's musical/year. Small budget. Equity waiver. 90% of plays/musicals written for adult roles; 10% for juvenile roles. Produced plays: *Cirquedula — Working without Annette*, (by Debbie Devine) about fear of change for ages 7-12. Will consider simultaneous submissions and previously performed work. Submission method: query with synopsis, character breakdown and set description; submit complete ms and score. Reports in 2 weeks. Pays writers in royalties of 5-10%; pays $10-25/performance. SASE for return of submission.

ARTREACH TOURING THEATRE, 3074 Madison Rd., Cincinnati OH 45209. (513)871-2300. Fax: (513)871-2501. Artistic Director: Kathryn Schultz Miller. Estab. 1976. "ArtReach has cast requirement of 3: 2 men and 1 woman. Sets must look big but fit in large van." Professional theater. Produced plays: *Young Cherokee*, by Kathryn Schultz Miller — history and culture of early Cherokee tribe as seen through the eyes of a young brave, for primary students and family audiences; *The Trail of Tears*, by Kathryn Schultz Miller — a companion play to *Young Cherokee* depicting story of Cherokee removal and unjust destruction of their culture, for intermediate through adult audiences. Does not want to see musicals, holiday plays, TV type scripts (about drugs, child abuse etc.) or fractured fairy tales. Will consider simultaneous submissions and previously performed work. Submission method: query with synopsis, character breakdown and set description. Reports in 10 days to 6 weeks. Author retains rights. Pays writers in royalties. SASE for return of submission.
Tips: "Type script in professional form found in *Writer's Market*. Do not submit plays that are less than 45 pages long. Look to history, culture or literature as resources."

BAKER'S PLAYS, 100 Chauncy St., Boston MA 02111. (617)482-1280. Fax: (617)482-7613. Associate Editor: Raymond Pape. Estab. 1845. Publishes 5-8 children's plays/year; 2-4 children's musicals/year. 80% of plays/musicals written for adult roles; 20% for juvenile roles. Subject matter: "Touring shows for 5-8 year olds, full lengths for family audience and full lengths for teens." Submission method: Submit complete ms, score and tape of songs. Reports in 3-8 months. Rights obtained on mss: worldwide rights. Pays writers in royalties (amount varies) or $10-100/performance.
Tips: "Know the audience you're writing for before you submit your play anywhere. 90% of the plays we reject are not written for our market."

*BOARSHEAD: MICHIGAN PUBLIC THEATER, 425 S. Grand Ave., Lansing MI 48933. (517)484-7800. Artistic Director: John Peakes. Estab. 1966. Produces 4 children's plays/year. Produces children's plays for professional production. Majority of plays written for adult roles. Recently produced plays: *1,000 Cranes*, by Amy Schultz — radiation death years after Hiroshima for ages 6-15; *Charlotte's Web*, by E.B. White — pigs 'n stuff for ages 6-12. Does not want to see musicals. Will consider previously performed work. Submission method: query with synopsis, character breakdown and set description. Include 10 pgs. of representative dialogue. Reports in 2 weeks for query; 4 months for

 The asterisk before a listing indicates the listing is new in this edition.

submissions. Pays writers $15-25/performance. Submissions returned with SASE. If no SASE, send SASPC for reply.

CHILDREN'S STORY SCRIPTS, Baymax Productions, Suite 130, 2219 W. Olive Ave., Burbank CA 91506. (818)563-6105. Fax: (818)563-2968. Editor: Deedra Bebout. Estab. 1990. Produces 3-10 children's scripts/year. "Except for small movements and occasionally standing up, children remain seated in Readers Theatre fashion." Publishes scripts sold to schools, camps, churches, scouts, hotels, cruise lines, etc.; wherever there's a program to teach or entertain children. "All roles read by children except K-2 scripts, where kids have easy lines, leader helps read the narration." Subject matter: Scripts on all subjects. Targeted age range—K-8th grade, 5-13 years old. Recently published: *How To Hide An Elephant*, by Marcia Clemmitt—nature's camouflaging of animals for grades 1-3. *The Story of Io*, by Deanna Peters—Greek myth for grades 5-8. No "sweet, syrupy, predictable stories or full-length theatrical scripts for regular proscenium productions." Accepts simultaneous submissions. Submission method: submit complete ms. Reports in 2 weeks. Rights obtained on mss: All rights; authors retain copyrights. Pays writers in royalties; 10-15% on sliding scale, based on retail price. SASE for reply and return of submission.
Tips: "Children's Story Scripts are essentially *prose* stories broken into parts. Descriptive narration is mixed with character dialogue. The scripts are meant to be read aloud. All the children enter at the beginning and remain in place throughout the performance. We do not hit the kids over the head with the moral or purpose of a script. We provide discussion questions which can be used after the performance to address the purpose of the story. Writer's guidelines packet available for business-sized SASE with two first-class stamps. Guidelines explain what Children's Story Scripts are, give four-page examples from two different scripts, give list of suggested topics for scripts."

*THE CHILDREN'S THEATRE COMPANY, 2400 Third Ave. S., Minneapolis MN 55404. (612)874-0500. Artistic Director: Jon Cranney. Estab. 1965. Produces 9 children's plays/ year; 1-3 children's musicals/year. Produces children's plays for professional, not-for-profit productions. 60% of plays/musicals written for adult roles; 40% for juvenile roles in all productions. Recently produced plays: *Ramona Quimby*, by Len Jenkin—family life of the Quimbys for all ages; *On the Wings of the Hummingbird: Tales of Trinidad*, by Beverly Smith-Dawson—life in Trinidad during carnival for all ages. Does not want to see plays written for child performers only. Will consider simultaneous submissions and previously performed work. Submission method: submit complete manuscript and score (if a musical). Reports in 2-6 months. Rights negotiable. Pays writers in royalties (2%). Submissions returned with SASE.
Tips: "The Children's Theatre Company rarely (if ever) produces unsolicited manuscripts; we continue a long tradition of producing new works commissioned to meet the needs of our audience and catering to the artistic goals of a specific season. Though the odds of us producing submitted plays are very slim, we always enjoy the opportunity to become acquainted with the work of a variety of artists, particularly those who focus on young audiences."

CIRCA '21 DINNER THEATRE, P.O. Box 3784, Rock Island IL 61204-3784. (309)786-2667. Director of Children's Theatre: Debbie Alley. Estab. 1977. Produces 2-3 children's plays/year; 3 children's musicals/year. "Prefer a cast no larger than 10." Produces children's plays for professional productions. 95% of plays/musicals written for adult roles; 5% written for juvenile roles. Submission method: query with synopsis, character breakdown, tape and set description. Reports in 3 months. Payment negotiable.

I.E. CLARK, INC., P.O. Box 246, Schulenburg TX 78956. Fax: (409)743-4765. Estab. 1956. Publishes 3 children's plays/year; 1 or 2 children's musicals/year. Medium to large casts preferred. Publishes plays for all ages. Published plays: *Wind of a Thousand Tales*, by John Glore (a young girl who doesn't believe in fairy tales) for ages 5-12; *Rock'n'Roll Santa*, by R. Eugene Jackson (Santa's reindeer form a rock band) for ages 4-16. Does not want to see plays that have not been produced. Will consider simultaneous submissions and previously performed work. Submission method: submit complete ms and audio or video tape. Reports in 6-8 months. Purchases all rights. Pays writers in negotiable royalties. SASE for return of submission.
Tips: "We publish only high quality literary works."

COMMUNITY CHILDREN'S THEATRE OF KANSAS CITY INC., 8021 E. 129th Terrace, Grandview MO 64030. (816)761-5775. Contact: Blanche Sellens. Estab. 1951. Produces 5 children's plays/year. Prefer casts of between 6-8. Produces children's plays for amateur productions for ages K-6. Produced play: *Red Versus the Wolf*, by Judy Wolferman — musical for K-6 audience. Submission method: query first then submit complete ms. Reports in a matter of months. "Winning script is performed by one of the units for two years."
Tips: "Write for guidelines and details for The Margaret Bartle Annual Playrwriting Award."

CONTEMPORARY DRAMA SERVICE, Division of Meriwether Publishing Ltd., 885 Elkton Dr., Colorado Springs CO 80907. (719)594-4422. Fax: (719)594-9916. Editor: Arthur Zapel. Estab. 1979. Publishes 45 children's plays/year; 5 children's musicals/year. 15% of plays/musicals written for adult roles; 85% for juvenile roles. Recently published plays: *The Way It Is*, by Lucile McIntyre, an ensemble play about the realities of being high school students; *You're Someone Special*, a collection of playlets about self-esteem for high school performers; *The Littlest Donkey* by Rhonda Wray, an Easter play for children performers. "We do not publish plays for elementary level except for church plays for Christmas and Easter. All of our secular plays are for teens or college level." Does not want to see "full-length, 3-act plays or plays with dirty language." Will consider simultaneous submissions or previously performed work. Submission method: query with synopsis, character breakdown and set description; "query first if a musical." Rights obtained on mss: all first rights. Payment varies according to type: royalty or purchase. SASE for return of submission.

THE COTERIE, 2450 Grand, Kansas City MO 64108. (816)474-6785. Fax: (816)545-6500. Artistic Director: Jeff Church. Estab. 1979. Produces 7 children's plays/year; 1 children's musical/year. "Prefer casts of between 5-7, no larger than 15." Produces children's plays for professional productions. 80% of plays/musicals written for adult roles; 20% for juvenile roles. "We do *not* produce puppet shows, although we may use puppets in our plays. We produce original plays, musicals and literary adaptations for ages 5 through adult." Produced plays: *Amelia Lives*, by Laura Annawyn Shamas — one-woman show on Amelia Earhart for 6th grade through adult audience; *Dinosaurus*, by Ed Mast and Lenore Bensinger — Mobil Oil workers discover cavern of dinosaurs, for ages 5 through adult audience. "We do *not* want to see 'camp' adaptations of fairytales." Submission method: query with synopsis, character breakdown and set description. Reports immediately if interested in seeing more material. Rights obtained on mss: "negotiable." Pays writers in royalties per play of approximately $500-1,500; SASE for return of submission.
Tips: "We're interested in adaptations of classic literature with small casts, simple staging requirements, strong thematic, character and plot development, and also 'risky' issues (i.e. teen pregnancy, substance abuse, race relations, etc.). There is a need for non-condescending material for younger age groups (5-8) and for middle school (ages 9-13)."

CREEDE REPERTORY THEATRE, P.O. Box 269, Creede CO 81130. (719)658-2541. Fax: (719)658-2343. Artistic Director: Richard Baxter. Estab. 1966. Produces 1-2 children's plays/year. Limited to 4-6 cast members and must be able to tour. Produces children's plays for summer, school or professional productions. 100% of plays/musicals written for adult roles. Publishes plays for ages K-12. Produced plays: *Prairie Dog Tales*, by Ric Averill and the Seem-to-Be Players—country western folktales for ages K-6; *Tortilla Soup*, by Joe Hayes—fables of New Mexico for ages K-12. Will consider simultaneous submissions and previously performed work. Query first, submit complete ms and score, or query with synopsis, character breakdown and set description. Reports in 12 months. Pays writers in 5% royalties; pays $25-30 per performance.

DRAMATIC PUBLISHING, INC., 311 Washington St., Woodstock IL 60098. (815)338-7170. Fax: (815)338-8981. Estab. 1885. Publishes 105 plays/year, 110 musicals/year children and young adults. Recently published plays/musicals: *Secret Garden*, by Pamela Sterling—newly published adaptation with optional underscoring for elementary to adult; *Johnny Tremain* by Lola H. and Coleman A. Jennings—portrays turbulent times of Revolutionary Boston, adapted from Esther Forbes' book for middle elementary to adults. Will consider simultaneous submissions and previously performed work. Submission method: Query with synopsis, character breakdown and set description; send script, (with a cassette if a musical) and include an SASE if wish to have submission returned. Reports in 3-4 months. Pays writers in royalties.
Tips: "Scripts should be from ½ to 1½ hours long, and not didactic or condescending. Original plays dealing with hopes, joys and fears of today's children are preferred to adaptations of old classics."

ELDRIDGE PUBLISHING CO. INC., P.O. Box 216, Franklin OH 45005. (513)746-6531. Editor: Nancy Vorhis. Estab. 1906. Publishes approximately 25 children's plays/year (5 for elementary; 20 for junior and senior high); 2-3 high school musicals/year. Prefers simple staging; flexible cast size. We "publish for middle, junior and high school, all genres." Recently published plays: *Dirty Dealings in Dixie*, by Craig Sodaro—parody on Gone With The Wind, a hilarious melodrama for high school age; *Fly Away Home*, by Peg Sheldrick—effects of divorce on a teen's family at Christmas, for junior and senior high school audience. Submission method: submit complete ms, score and tape of songs (if a musical). Reports in 2 months. Rights obtained on mss: all dramatic rights. Pays writers 10% of copy sales or 35% of royalties; buys material outright for $150-300.
Tips: "We're always on the lookout for large-cast comedies which provide a lot of fun for our customers. But other more serious topics which concern teens, as well as intriguing mysteries, and children's theater programs are of interest to us as well. We know there are many new talented playwrights out there and we look forward to reading their fresh scripts."

ENCORE PERFORMANCE PUBLISHING, P.O. Box 692, Orem UT 84059. (801)225-0605. Estab. 1978. Publishes 6-10 children's plays/year; 6-10 children's musicals/year. Prefers equal male/female ratio if possible. Adaptations for K-12 and older. Recently published plays: *Puss In Boots*, by Greg Palmer—classic English Panto style retelling of tale for 8-adult (family); *Commedia Princess And The Pea*, by Lane Riosley and Rebecca Bycus—Commedia D'ell Arte retelling of Andersen classic for ages 6-14. Will only consider previously performed work. Looking for issue plays and unusual fairy tale

---

Always include a self-addressed stamped envelope (SASE) or International Reply Coupon (IRC) with submissions.

adaptations. Submission method: query first. Purchases all publication and production rights. Author retains copyright. Pays writers in royalties (50%). SASE for return of submission.

Tips: "Give us issue and substance, be controversial without offence. Use a laser printer! Don't send old manuscripts. Make yours look the most professional."

FLORIDA STUDIO THEATRE, 1241 N. Palm Ave., Sarasota FL 34236. (813)366-9017. Artistic Director: Richard Hopkins. Estab. 1980. Produces 3 children's plays/year; 1-3 children's musicals/year. Produces children's plays for professional productions. 50% of plays/musicals written for adult roles; 50% for juvenile roles. "Prefer small cast plays that use imagination more than heavy scenery." Will consider simultaneous submissions and previously performed work. Submission method: query with synopsis, character breakdown and set description. Reports in 3 months. Rights negotiable. Pay negotiable. Submissions returned with SASE.

Tips: "Children are a tremendously sophisticated audience. The material should respect this."

THE FREELANCE PRESS, P.O. Box 548, Dover MA 02030. (508)785-1260. Estab. 1979. Produces 3 musicals and/or plays/year. Casts are comprised of young people, ages 8-15, and number 25-30. "We publish original musicals on contemporary topics for children and adaptations of children's classics (e.g., Velveteen Rabbit, Rip Van Winkle)." Published plays: *Velveteen Rabbit*, based on story of same name for ages 8-11; *Monopoly*, 3 young people walk through board game, the winner gets to choose where he/she wants to live (ages 11-15). No plays for adult performers. Will consider simultaneous submissions and previously performed work. Submit complete ms and score with SASE. Reports in 3 months. Pays writers 10% royalties. SASE for return of submission.

SAMUEL FRENCH, INC., 45 W. 25th St., New York NY 10010. (212)206-8990. Fax: (212)206-1429. Editor: Lawrence Harbison. Estab. 1830. Publishes 2 or 3 children's plays/year; "variable number of musicals." Subject matter: "All genres, all ages. No puppet plays. No adaptations of any of those old 'fairy tales.' No 'Once upon a time, long ago and far away.' No kings, princesses, fairies, trolls, etc." Submission method: submit complete ms and demo tape (if a musical). Reports in 2-8 months. Rights obtained on mss: "Publication rights, amateur and professional production rights, option to publish next 3 plays." Pay for writers: "book royalty 10%; professional production royalty 90%; amateur production royalty 80%." SASE for return of submissions.

Tips: "Children's theater is a very tiny market, as most groups perform plays they have created themselves or have commissioned."

*EMMY GIFFORD CHILDREN'S THEATER, 3504 Center St., Omaha NE 68105. Artistic Director: James Larson. Estab. 1949. Produces 9 children's plays/year; 1 children's musical/year. Produces children's plays for professional productions. 100% of plays/musicals written for adult roles. Need plays with small casts, no fly space necessary. Recently produced plays: *Pippi Longstocking*; *Bye Bye Birdie*. Does not want to see adult plays. Will consider simultaneous submissions, electronic submissions via disk or modem, or previously performed work. Submission method: query first. Reports in 6 months. Pays writers in royalties (6%). Submissions returned with SASE.

THE GREAT AMERICAN CHILDREN'S THEATRE COMPANY, P.O. Box 92123, Milwaukee WI 53202. (414)276-4230. Fax: (414)276-2214. Artistic Director: Teri Solomon Mitze. Estab. 1975. Produces 2 children's plays/year. Produces children's plays for professional productions; 100% written for adult roles. Produced plays: *The Secret Garden*, by Brett Reynolds—children's classic for ages K-8; *Charlie & the Chocolate Factory*, by Richard R. George—children's classic for ages K-8. Will consider previously performed work. Submission method: query with synopsis, character breakdown and set description. Reports in weeks. Rights and payment negotiable.

HAYES SCHOOL PUBLISHING CO. INC., 321 Pennwood Ave., Wilkinsburg PA 15221. (412)371-2373. Fax: (412)371-6408. Estab. 1940. Wants to see supplementary teaching aids for grades K-12. Will consider simultaneous and electronic submissions. Query first with synopsis, character breakdown and set description, or with complete ms and score. Reports in 3-4 weeks. Purchases all rights. Pays writers by outright purchase. SASE for return of submissions.

HONOLULU THEATRE FOR YOUTH, 2846 Ualena St., Honolulu HI 96819. (808)839-9885. Fax: (808)839-7018. Artistic Director: Pamela Sterling. Estab. 1955. "Cast size should be limited to 10; 6 is ideal." Produces 6 children's plays/year. Subject matter: Looks for plays "celebrating cultures of the Pacific Rim, especially. Also, plays that deal with issues of concern to today's young audiences (varying in age from 6-18)." Recently produced plays: *The Council*, by William S. Yellow Robe Jr.—man's relationship with the environment for 10 years through adult; *The Giant's Baby*, Allan Ahlberg—"modern" fairytale for ages 5 years through adult. Will consider simultaneous submissions and previously performed work. Submission method: query first with cast requirements and synopsis. SASE required for each script requested. Pays writers in royalties (4%) and by commission fee ($2,000-5,000).
Tips: "Obviously, smaller casts, less technical machinery, more imaginative use of resources. I have to balance a season with some 'title' recognition, i.e. adaptations of well-known books of fairy-tales, but I am more interested in good, *original* theatrical literature for young audiences."

*INDIANA REPERTORY THEATRE, 140 W. Washington, Indianapolis IN 46204. (317)635-5277. Artistic Director: Libby Appel. Estab. 1971. Produces 3 children's plays/year. Produces children's plays for professional productions. 100% of plays written for adult roles. "Limit 8 cast, 75 min. running time." Recently produced plays: *Huck Finn's Story*, by Aurand Harris for grades 3-8; *Secret History of the Future*, by James Still—Columbus quintcentenary historical encounter play for grades 6-8. Does not want to see preschool and K-4 material. Will consider previously performed work. Submission method: query with synopsis, character breakdown and set description to Janet Allen, Assoc. Artistic Director. Reports in 6 months. Pays writers negotiable royalty (6%) or commission fee. Submissions returned with SASE.

*THE MUNY STUDENT THEATRE, 560 Trinity, St. Louis MO 63130. (314)862-1255. Artistic Director: Larry Pressgrove. Estab. 1914. Produces 5 children's plays/year; 1 or 2 children's musicals/year. "We produce a touring and mainstage season September-May and offer extensive theater classes throughout the entire year." 100% of plays/musicals written for adult roles; 40% for juvenile roles. Prefers cast of four or five equity actors, children's parts unlimited. "Tour sets limited in size; mainstage sets limited only by budget." Recently produced plays: *Flat Stanley*, by Jeff Brown/adapted by Larry Pressgrove, (based on children's book for ages K-3); *BOCON!*, written by Lisa Loomer, (a young boy's travels from El Salvador to Los Angeles for ages 4-6). Will consider simultaneous submissions and previously performed work. Submission method: query with synopsis, character breakdown and set description. Rights negotiable.
Tips: "We emphasize diverse ethnic and cultural backgrounds. Tour shows should fit into the school curriculum. The Muny Student Theatre's mission is to introduce theater to young people, to encourage creative learning and to develop future theater audiences. The company is now one of the most comprehensive theater education programs in Missouri. Each year the company reaches over 100,000 students through its resident touring company, professional story tellers, mainstage productions and theater classes."

THE NEW CONSERVATORY CHILDREN'S THEATRE COMPANY & SCHOOL, 25 Van Ness Ave., San Francisco CA 94102. (415)861-6988. Executive Director: Ed Decker. Estab. 1981. Produces 6-10 children's plays/year; 1-2 children's musicals/year. Limited budget. Produces children's plays as part of "a professional theater arts training program for youths ages 4-19 during the school year and two summer sessions. The New Conservatory also produces educational plays for its touring company." 100% written for juvenile roles. "We do not want to see any preachy or didactic material." Submission method: query with synopsis, character breakdown and set description, or submit complete ms and score. Reports in 3 months. Rights obtained on mss: "negotiable." Pays writers in royalties. SASE for return of submission.
Tips: Trends: "Addressing socially relevant issues for young people and their families."

NEW PLAYS INCORPORATED, P.O. Box 5074, Charlottesville VA 22905. (804)979-2777. Artistic Director: Patricia Whitton. Estab. 1964. Publishes 4 plays/year; 1 or 2 children's musicals/year. Publishes "generally material for kindergarten through junior high." Recently published *Play With Shakespeare*, by Linda Buyson — scenes and adaptations for junior high and high school performers for junior high and high school teachers and students; *Cinderella: The World's Favorite Fairy Tale*, by Lowell Swortzell — dramatizations of Cinderella in China, Russia, and American Indian folklore for elementary school. Does not want to see "adaptations of titles I already have. No unproduced plays; junior high improvisations." Will consider simultaneous submissions and previously performed work. Submissions method: submit complete ms and score. Reports in 2 months. Purchases exclusive rights to sell acting scripts. Pays writers in royalties (50% of production royalties; 10% of script sales). SASE for return of submission.

NEW YORK STATE THEATRE INSTITUTE, P.A.C. 266, 1400 Washington Ave., Albany NY 12222. (518)442-5399. Fax: (518)442-5318. Producing Director: Patricia B. Snyder. Estab. 1976. Produces 1-2 children's plays and 1-2 children's musicals/year. Produces family plays for professional theater. 90% of plays/musicals are written for adult roles; 10% for juvenile roles. Does not want to see plays for children only. Submission method: submit complete ms and tape of songs (if a musical). Reports in 2-3 months. Rights obtained on mss: "varies." Pay for writers: "fees vary in nature and in degree." SASE for return of submission.
Tips: Writers should be mindful of "audience *sophistication!*"

THE OPEN EYE: NEW STAGINGS, 270 W. 89th St., New York NY 10024. (212)769-4142. Artistic Director: Amie Brockway. Estab. 1972 (theater). Produces plays for a family audience. Most productions are with music, but are not musicals. "Casts are usually limited to six performers because of economic reasons. Technical requirements are kept to a minimum for touring purposes." Professional productions using members of Actor's Equity Association. 100% of plays/musicals written for adult roles. Recently produced plays: *A Woman Called Truth*, by Sandra Fenichel Asher — a play celebrating the life of Sojourner Truth for ages 8 through adult; *Death and Life of Sherlock Holmes*, by Suzan L. Zeder — several Arthur Conan Doyle stories woven together for ages 8 through adult. "No videos or cassettes. We accept only one script per playwright per year." Will consider previously performed work. Submit complete ms and score. Reports in 3-6 months. Rights agreement negotiated with author. Pays writers by one time fee or royalty negotiated with publisher. SASE for return of submission.
Tips: "We are seeing a trend toward plays that are appropriate for a family audience and that address today's multicultural concerns."

PIONEER DRAMA SERVICE, P.O. Box 22555, Denver CO 80222. (303)759-4297. Fax: (303)759-0475. Editor: Steven Fendrich. Estab. 1960. Publishes 7 children's plays/year; 2 children's musicals/year. Subject matter: Publishes plays for ages 9-high school. Published plays/musicals: *Nutcracker*, by Patrick R. Dorn and Bill Francoeur—unique Christmas musical for ages 10 and up; *The Empty Chair*, by Tim Kelly—one-act anti-drug drama for teens and up; *A Little Bit of Magic*, by Gail and Grant Golden—small cast musical ideal for touring for audiences 5 and up; casts 10 and up. Does not want to see "script, scores, tapes, pics and reviews." Submission method: query with synopsis, character breakdown and set description. Reports in 2 months. Rights obtained on mss: all rights. Pays writers in royalties (10% on sales, 50% royalties on productions); or buys material outright for $200-1,000.

PLAYERS PRESS, INC., P.O. Box 1132, Studio City CA 91614-0132. (818)789-4980. Vice President: R. W. Gordon. Estab. 1965. Publishes 5-25 children's plays/year; 2-15 children's musicals/year. Subject matter: "We publish for all age groups." Published musical: *Rapunzel N' the Witch*, by William-Alan Landes—musical for grades 4-12. Submission method: query with synopsis, character breakdown and set description; include #10 SASE with query. Reports in 6-9 months. Rights obtained on mss: stage, screen, TV rights. Payment varies; outright purchases are available upon written request.
Tips: "Entertainment quality is on the upswing and needs to be directed at the world, no longer just the USA."

THE PLAYHOUSE JR., 222 Craft Ave., Pittsburgh PA 15213. (412)621-4445. Director: Wayne Brinda. Estab. 1949. Produces 5 children's plays/year including 1 children's musical/year. Produces children's plays for semi-professional with a college theater department: 99% of plays/musicals written for adult roles; 1% written for juvenile roles. Recently produced plays: *The Secret Garden*, by Pam Sterling—adaptation of classic story for 3rd grade through middle school; *The Velveteen Rabbit*—adaptation of story for K-3rd grade. Does not want to see "strong social problem plays." Will consider simultaneous submissions or previously produced work. Submission method: query with synopsis, character breakdown and set description; first drafts. Reports in 3 weeks. Rights obtained on mss: "performance rights—negotiable." Pays writers commission/royalty. SASE for return of submission.

PLAYS, THE DRAMA MAGAZINE FOR YOUNG PEOPLE, 120 Boylston St., Boston MA 02116. (617)423-3157. Managing Editor: Elizabeth Preston. Estab. 1941. Publishes 70-75 children's plays/year. "Props and staging should not be overly elaborate or costly. Our plays are performed by children in school." 100% of plays written for juvenile roles. Subject matter: Audience is lower grades through junior/senior high. Published plays: *Moonlight Is When*, by Kay Arthur, about a shy young researcher who finds romance in an unexpected place—the Museum of Natural History; *Express to Valley Forge*, by Earl J. Dias, about a courageous patriot who saves the day for George Washington's army; and *Kidnapped*, a dramatization of the Herman Melville classic, adapted by Adele Thane. Send "nothing downbeat—no plays about drugs, sex or other 'heavy' topics." Submission methods: query first on adaptations of folk tales and classics; otherwise submit complete ms. Reports in 2-3 weeks. Rights obtained on mss: all rights. Pay rates vary, on acceptance. Guidelines available; send SASE. Sample copy $3.
Tips: "Above all, plays must be entertaining for young people with plenty of action and a satisfying conclusion."

PLAYS FOR YOUNG AUDIENCES, P.O. Box 22555, Denver CO 80222. (303)759-4297. Fax: (303)759-0475. Editor: Steven Fendrich. Estab. 1989. Publishes 3 children's plays/ year; 1 children's musical/year. Subject matter: Publishes plays for preschool-8th grade audience. Produced plays: *A Little Bit of Magic*, by Gail and Grant Golden—audiences pre-school and up, casting 10 and up—small cast musical, ideal for touring; *The Dancing Snowman*, by R. Eugene Jackson and Carl Alette, audiences pre-school and up, cast-10 and up—musical; *Nutcracker*, by Patrick R. Dorn and Bill Francoeur, ages 10 and up—unique Christmas musical. Does not want to see script, score, tape, pictures and reviews. Submission method: query first; query with synopsis, character breakdown and set description. Reports in 2 months. Rights obtained on mss: all rights. Pays writers in royalties of 10% in sales, 50% on productions; or buys material outright for $200-1,000.

*ST. LOUIS BLACK REPERTORY COMPANY, Suite 10 F, 634 N. Grand Blvd., St. Louis MO 63103. (314)534-3807. Artistic Director: Ron Himes. Estab. 1976. Produces 4 children's plays/year. "The St. Louis Black Rep is a professional production company which includes a mainstage and touring component. The touring component produces 3-4 plays per year for young audiences." 100% of plays written for adult roles. "The touring shows are designed to be flexible and totally self-contained." Recently produced/published *Anansi The Spider*, by Al Bostick (a West African folk-character's quest to own all the world's stories, for ages K-6); *TaKunda*, by Charles Smith (a play for junior high students to adults dealing with the South African struggle). Will consider previously performed work. Submit complete ms; query with synopsis, character breakdown and set description; submit complete ms and score (if musical). Rights are mutually agreed upon via contract. Pays writers per performance ($20-35). Submissions returned with SASE.
Tips: "Our touring company consists of 4-5 actors, therefore we need plays written for at least four or a maximum of five characters. If a play calls for more than five roles, the actors must be able to double and interchange them."

STAGE ONE: THE LOUISVILLE CHILDREN'S THEATRE, 425 W. Market, Louisville KY 40202. (502)589-5946. Fax: (502)589-5779. Producing Director: Moses Goldberg. Estab. 1946. Produces 10 children's plays/year 1-3 children's musicals/year. Stage One is an Equity company producing children's plays for professional productions. 100% of plays/musicals written for adult roles. "Sometimes do use students in selected productions." Produced plays: *Bridge to Terabithia*, by Katherine PataSon, Stephanie Tulan, music by Steven Leibman—deals with friendship and the acceptance of tragedy, for 9 year old through adult audience; *Babar*, by Thomas Olson (adaptation)—story about the adventures of an elephant for 4-12 year old audience. Submission method: submit complete ms, score and tape of songs (if a musical); include the author's résumé if desired. Reports in 3-4 months. Pays writers in royalties or per performance.
Tips: Looking for "stageworthy and respectful dramatizations of the classic tales of childhood, both ancient and modern; plays relevant to the lives of young people and their families; and plays directly related to the school curriculum."

TADA!, 120 W. 28th St., New York NY 10001. (212)627-1732. Artistic Director: Janine Trevens. Estab. 1984. Produces 3-4 children's plays/year; 3-4 children's musicals/year. "All actors are children, ages 6-17." Produces children's plays for professional, year-round theater. 100% of plays/musicals written for juvenile roles. Produced plays: *The Gift of Winter*, book by Michael Slade, music by David Evans, lyrics by Faye Greenberg—how the very first snowfall came to happen for 2 through adults; *Rabbit Sense*, book by Davidson Lloyd, music by John Kroner, lyrics by Gary Gardner—several Brer Rabbit stories told with new relevance by weaving them through a modern day story in an urban setting for 2 through adults. Submission method: query with synopsis, character breakdown and set description; submit complete ms, score and tape of songs (if a musical). Reports in 3 months. Rights obtained on mss: "Depends on the piece." Pays writers in royalties. SASE for return of submissions.
Tips: "Too many authors are writing productions, not plays. Our company is multiracial and city-oriented. We are not interested in fairy tales."

THEATRE FOR YOUNG AMERICA, 7204 W. 80th St., Overland Park KS 66204. (913)648-4600. Artistic Director: Gene Mackey. Estab. 1974. Produces 10 children's plays/year; 3-5 children's musicals/year. We use a "small cast (4-7), open thrust stage." Theatre for Young America is a professional equity company. 80% of plays/musicals written for adult roles; 20% for juvenile roles. Produced plays: *The Wizard of Oz*, by Jim Eiler and Jeanne Bargy—for ages 6 and up; *A Partridge in a Pear Tree*, by Lowell Swortzell—deals with the 12 days of Christmas, for ages 6 and up; *Three Billy Goats Gruff*, by Gene Mackey and Molly Jessup—Norwegian folk tales, for ages 6 and up. Submission method: query with synopsis, character breakdown and set description. Reports in 2 months. Rights obtained on mss: "production, tour rights in local area." Pays writers in royalties or $10-50/per performance.
Tips: Looking for "cross-cultural material that respects the intelligence, sensitivity and taste of the child audience."

THEATREWORKS/USA, 890 Broadway, New York NY 10003. (212)677-5959. Artistic Director: Jay Harnick. Estab. 1960. Produces 4 musicals/year. Cast of 5 actors. Play should be 1 hour long, tourable. Professional children's theatre comprised of adult equity actors. 100% of musicals are written for adult roles. Produced musicals: *Harriet the Spy*, by James Still/Kim Olan/Alison Hubbard (adaptation of Louise Fitzhugh book)—grades 4-8; *Harold and the Purple Crayon*, by Jane Shepard/Jon Ehrlich/Robin Pagerbin (adaptations of picture book by Crockett Johnson)—ages K-3. No fractured, typical "kiddy theatre" fairy tales. Will consider previously performed work. Query first with synopsis, character breakdown and set description. Reports in 6 months. Pays writers 6% royalties. SASE for return of submission.

*WEST COAST ENSEMBLE, 6240 Hollywood Blvd., Hollywood CA 90028. (213)871-8673. Artistic Director: Les Hanson. Estab. 1982. Produces 2 children's plays/year; 1 children's musical/year. "We operate under an Equity Theatre for Young Audiences contract or under the Los Angeles 99-seat Theatre Plan. 90% of plays/musicals written for adult roles; 10% for juvenile roles. Prefers simple sets; casts of no more the eight. There are no limits on style or subject matter. Will consider simultaneous submissions (no more than two) and previously performed work. Submission method: submit complete ms, submit complete ms and score (if a musical). Purchases exclusive rights to perform play/musical in Southern California. Pays writers per performance ($25-50). Submissions returned with SASE.

THE YOUNG COMPANY, P.O. Box 225, Milford NH 03055. (603)673-4005. Literary Manager: Blair Hundertmark. Estab. 1984. Produces 10-12 children's plays/year; 1-2 children's musicals/year. "Scripts should not be longer than an hour, small cast preferred; very small production budgets, so use imagination." The Young Company is a professional training program associated with American Stage Festival, a professional theater. Produced plays/musicals: *Dancing on the Ceiling*, by Austin Tichenor—adaptation of Kafka's *Metamorphosis*, for ages 7 and up; *High Pressure Zone*, music by Andrew Howard, book and lyrics by Austin Tichenor—musical about addictive behavior, for middle school and older audience; *The First Olympics*, by Eve Muson and Austin Tichenor—deals with mythology/Olympic origins, for 6 year old through adult audience. Does not want to see condescending material. Submission method: Query with synopsis, character breakdown and sample score. Rights obtained on mss: first production credit on all future materials. Pays small fee and housing for rehearsals.
Tips: Looks for "concise and legible presentation, songs that further dramatic action. Develop material with strong marketing possibilities. See your work in front of an audience and be prepared to change it if your audience doesn't 'get it.' Don't condescend to your audience. Tell them a *story*."

Special Markets

Over 90% of children's-only bookstores carry ancillary products such as posters, coloring books, greeting cards, puzzles and games in their inventories. Booksellers have discovered sidelines are valuable in a couple of different ways: First, they act as bait to lure customers who might not visit the bookstore if it only carried books. Prominently displayed sidelines increase the visual attractiveness and enhance the image of a bookstore. As a result, the more inviting atmosphere is more likely to draw people in. Second, booksellers like selling sidelines because they offer a higher margin of profit than books, therefore making them a good source of supplemental revenue. Bookstore owners are especially interested in sidelines which are book-related or education-oriented.

One area for freelancers to make a heavy profit for their work is in the game industry. In the July 1992 issue of *Children's Book Insider*, Randice-Lisa Altschul says some companies pay royalties that can reach six figures for games. Altschul, who owns around 1,500 copyrights to game ideas, says even the smaller games can net a creator between $50,000 and $100,000 in royalties. The problem is "there's a 99.9 percent rejection rate in the game industry, even if it's the greatest idea in the world," she says. In order to sell your ideas you must create a game that is unique.

What follows is a list of special markets that produce various sidelines for children and are interested in using the services of freelancers. Sidelines consist of a potpourri of products, so needs among these markets may greatly vary. Read through the listing carefully to determine subject needs and methods of submission. This year there are 30 new markets in this section, giving you greater opportunity to find a place to sell your work. If more specific guidelines are available from the company, write to request them.

*ALEF JUDAICA, 3384 Motor Ave., Los Angeles CA 90034. (310)202-0024. Owner: Guy Orner. Greeting card and paper products company. Publishes Judaica card line, Judaica gift wrap and party goods. Publishes greeting cards (Hanukkah card line) and novelties (Hanukkah party goods).
Illustration: Needs freelance illustration for children's greeting cards and party goods. Makes about 80 illustration assignments/year. To contact, send published samples and portfolio. Reports in 1 month. Keeps materials on file. For children's greeting cards, pays flat fee of $250. For other artwork, pay "depends on how complicated the project is." Pays on acceptance. Buys all rights. Credit line sometimes given.
Tips: 25% of products are made for kids or have kids' themes. Seasonal material should be submitted 1 year in advance.

*AMCAL, 2500 Bisso Ln., #500, Concord CA 94520. (415)689-9930. Fax: (415)689-0108. Editor/Art Director: Jennifer DeCristoforo. Estab. 1975. 80% of material written and 100% illustrated by freelancers. Buys 10 freelance projects/year; receives 150 submissions/year. Greeting cards, calendars, desk diaries, boxed Christmas cards. "AMCAL publishes high quality full color, narrative and decorative art for a wide market from traditional to contemporary. We are currently seeking delightful illustrations and verses for greeting cards. Juvenile illustration should have some adult appeal. We don't publish cartoon, humorous or gag art, or bold graphics. We sell to small, exclusive gift retailers." Greeting cards: "unrhymed, with a simple, direct sentiment."

Making Contact & Terms: "Submissions are always accepted for future lines." Reports in 1 month. Pays on acceptance. Pay negotiable/usually advance on royalty. Guideline sheets for #10 SASE and 1 first class stamp.

*AMERICAN ARTS & GRAPHICS, INC., 10915 47th Ave. W., Mukilteo WA 98275. (206)353-8200. Licensing Director: Shelley Pedersen. Estab. 1948. Paper products company. Publishes and distributes posters.
Illustration: Needs freelance illustration for children's posters. Makes 3-4 illustration assignments/month; 30/year. "Prefers airbrush, to fit a 22"×34" format—fantasy, cute or funny animals. Other popular children and teen subjects." Uses color artwork only. To contact, send cover letter, color photocopies and slides. Reports in 1 week. Returns material with SASE. Materials sometimes filed. Pay is negotiable—usually $500-1,000. Pays on acceptance. Buys exclusive product rights. Credit line given. Artist's guidelines available for SASE.
Photography: Purchases photography from freelancers. Buys stock and assigns work. Buys 30 stock images/year; makes 12 assignments/year. Wants "exotic sports cars, cute and/or funny animals, wildlife (especially tigers, panthers), sports." Uses 2¼×2¼ and 4×5 transparencies. To contact, send cover letter, slides and portfolio. Reports in 1 week. Materials returned with SASE. Materials sometimes filed. Pays $500-1,000 advance against 10% royalties. Pays on acceptance. Buys exclusive product rights. Credit line given. Photographer's guidelines available for SASE.

*AMPERSAND PRESS, 691 26th St., Oakland CA 94612. (415)663-9163. Creative Director: Gillian Lowell. Estab. 1973. Publisher of games, puzzles, books, etc.—"science and environmental stuff. Specializing in educational games for children." Publishes coloring books, puzzles, games and posters.
Illustration: Needs freelance illustration for games, puzzles, books, (nature related). Makes 2-6 illustration assignments/year. To contact, send cover letter and promo piece. To query with specific ideas, write to request disclosure form first. Reports back only if interested. Returns materials with SASE. Materials filed. "We pay differently for each component of the project." Pays on acceptance or publication. Buys one-time rights, reprint rights or all rights. Credit line sometimes given.
Photography: Purchases photography from freelancers. Buys stock images. Buys 2-10 stock images/year. To contact, send cover letter with promo piece. Reports back only if interested. Materials returned with SASE. Materials filed. Pays on usage. Buys one-time rights. Credit line sometimes given. Photographer's guidelines not available.
Tips: 90% of products are made for kids or have kids' themes. Seasonal material should be submitted 10-12 months in advance.

ARISTOPLAY, LTD., P.O. Box 7529, Ann Arbor MI 48107. (313)995-4353. Fax: (313)995-4611. Product Development Director: Lorraine Hopping Egan. President: Jan Barney Newman. Art Director: Jack Thompson. Estab. 1980. Produces educational board games and card decks, activity kits—all educational subjects.
Writing: Needs freelance writing for games and question cards. Makes 2-4 writing assignments/year. To contact, send cover letter, resume and writing samples. Reports in 2 months. For writing assignments, pays by the hour (range: $10-20) or by the project (range: $200-1,000). Pays on acceptance. Buys all rights. Credit line given.
Illustration: Needs freelance illustration for games and card decks. Makes 2-6 illustration assignments/year. "Often hire designers, as well as illustrators." To contact, send

The asterisk before a listing indicates the listing is new in this edition.

cover letter, resume, published samples or color photocopies. Reports back only if interested. For artwork, pays by the project, $500-5,000. Pays on acceptance (½-sketch, ½-final). Buys all rights. Credit line given.

Tips: "Creating board games requires a lot of back and forth in terms of design, illustration, editorial and child testing; the more flexible you are, the better. Also, factual accuracy is important." Target age group 4-14. "We are an educational game company. Writers and illustrators working for us must be willing to research the subject and period of focus."

A/V CONCEPTS CORP., 30 Montauk Blvd., Oakdale NY 11769. (516)567-7227. Fax: (516)567-8745. Editor: Laura Solimene. Art Director: Philip Solimene. Estab. 1969. "We are an educational publisher. We publish books for the K-12 market—primarily, language arts and math and reading."

Writing: Needs freelance writing for classic workbooks: adaptations from fine literature. Makes 5-10 assignments/year. To contact, send cover letter and writing samples. Reports in 2 weeks. For other writing assignments, pays by the project ($1,000). Pays on publication. Buys all rights. No credit line given.

Illustration: Needs freelance illustration for classic literature adaptations. Makes 5-10 illustration assignments/year. Needs "super hero-like characters in four-color and b&w—some cartoons needed." To contact, send cover letter and photocopies. Reports back in 2 weeks. For other artwork, pays by the project ($250). Buys all rights. No credit line given.

THE AVALON HILL GAME CO., 4517 Harford Rd., Baltimore MD 21214. (301)254-9200. Fax: (301)254-0991. President: Jack Dott. Editor: A. Eric Dott. Art Director: Jean Baer. Estab. 1958. 50% of material written and illustrated by freelancers. Buys 50 freelance projects/year; receives 500 submissions annually. Produces comic books (*Tales From the Floating Vagabond*), a magazine for girls ages 7-14 and an extensive line of games.

Writing: Makes 6 writing assignments/month; 36/year. To contact send cover letter, résumé, client list, writing samples. Reports back only if interested. Pays on publication. Buys all rights. Credit line sometimes given.

Illustration: Makes 2-3 illustration assignments/month; 30/year. Prefers styles pertaining to general interest topics for girls. To contact send cover letter, résumé, published samples, portfolio. Reports in 1 month. Pays on acceptance. Buys all rights. Credit line sometimes given.

*AVANTI PRESS, INC., 2500 Penobscot Bldg., Detroit MI 48226. (313)961-0022. Submit images to this address: Avanti, Suite 602, 84 Wooster, New York NY 10012 (212)941-9000. Picture Editor: Susan Evans. Estab. 1979. Greeting card company. Publishes photographic greeting cards—nonseasonal and seasonal.

Photography: Purchases photography from freelancers. Buys stock and assigns work. Buys approx. 50-75 stock images/year. Makes approx. 20-30 assignments/year. Wants "narrative, storytelling images, graphically strong and colorful!" Uses b&w/color prints; 35mm, 2¼ × 2¼ and 4 × 5, transparencies. To contact, "Call for submission guidelines—no originals!!" Reports in 2 weeks. Returns materials with SASE. "We pay either a flat fee or a royalty which is discussed at time of purchase." Pays on acceptance. Buys exclusive product rights (world-wide card rights). Credit line given. Photographer's guidelines for SASE.

Tips: At least 50% of products have kids' themes. Submit seasonal material 9 months-1 year in advance. "All images submitted should express some kind of sentiment which either fits an occasion or can be versed and sent to the recipient to convey some feeling."

bePUZZLED/LOMBARD MARKETING, INC., 45 Wintonbury Avenue, Bloomfield CT 06002. (203)286-4226. Fax: (203)286-4229. Editor/Art Director: Luci Seccareccia. New Product Development: Susan Hardersen and Laurel Pepin. Estab. 1987. Publishes jigsaw puzzle mysteries, games-mystery, mystery word puzzles, mystery entertainment.
Writing: Needs freelance writing for short mystery stories. Makes 10-15 writing assign- · ments/year. To contact, send cover letter, resume, client list and writing samples. Reports back only if interested. Pays by the project (range: $200-1,000). Pays on publication. Buys all rights.
Illustration: Needs freelance illustration for jigsaw puzzles. Makes 25-30 illustration assignments/year. Preferences announced when needed. To contact, send cover letter, resume, client list and non-returnable samples. Reports back only if interested. Pays by the project ($50). Pays after completion. Buys all rights.

*RUSS BERRIE & COMPANY, INC., 111 Bauer Dr., Oakland NJ 07436. (201)337-9000. Director, Greeting Cards: Angelica Urra. Estab. 1963. Greeting card and paper products company. Manufactures "all kinds of paper products and impulse gifts—photo frames, mugs, buttons, trolls, baby gift products, cards, plush, ceramics, etc."
Writing: Needs freelance writing for children's greeting cards and other children's products (T-shirts, buttons, bookmarks, stickers). Makes 10-50 writing assignments/month. Tired of children's greeting card writing which talks down to kids. To contact, send writing samples. Reports in 2-3 months. Materials returned with SASE. Files materials "if we think there may be interest later." For greeting cards, pays flat fee of $50-100 per piece of copy. For other writing, pays by the project. Pays on acceptance. Buys all rights or exclusive product rights. Writer's guidelines for SASE.
Illustration: Needs freelance illustration for children's greeting cards and other children's products. Makes 10-50 illustration assignments/month. Artwork should be "contemporary, eye catching, colorful—professional." To contact, send client list, published samples, photocopies, slides and/or promo piece. To query with specific ideas, send tight roughs. Reports in 2 months. Returns material with SASE. Files material "if future interest is anticipated." For greeting cards, pays flat fee of $250-500. Pays on acceptance. Buys all rights or exclusive product rights. Credit line sometimes given. Artist's guidelines for SASE.
Photography: Purchases photography from freelancers. Buys stock and assigns work. Buys 100 stock images/year. Makes 100 assignments/year. Photos should be "humorous with animals or children; unusual, eye catching, interesting, contemporary—not too arty." Uses b&w prints; 35mm, 2¼×2¼, 4×5 and 8×10 transparencies. To contact, send slides, client list, published samples, promo piece, portfolio, prints. Reports in 2 months. Materials returned with SASE. Files photos "if there will be future interest." Pays per photo or by the project. Pays on acceptance. Buys all rights or exclusive product rights. Credit line sometimes given. Photographer's guidelines for SASE.
Tips: One third products are made for kids or have kids' themes. Seasonal material should be submitted 18 months in advance. Using more "freelance illustrators and freelance writers who can submit a concept rather than single piece of writing. We are upbeat, with a large, diverse baby/children's line. Send all material to greeting card director—if it is for another product it will be passed along to the appropriate department."

BRILLIANT ENTERPRISES, 117 W. Valerio St., Santa Barbara CA 93101. Art Director: Ashleigh Brilliant. Estab. 1967. Greeting cards: wide range of humorous concepts. Greeting cards: unrhymed.
Making Contact & Terms: Reports in 3 weeks. Purchases all rights. Pays on acceptance. Pay for greeting cards $40 minimum. Writer's/illustrator's guideline sheet for $2 and SAE.

*BURGOYNE INC., 2030 E. Byberry Rd., Philadelphia PA 19116. (215)677-8000. Art Director: Michael Burd. Creative Director: Jeanna Lane. Estab. 1907. Greeting card company. Publisher of Christmas cards.

Illustration: Interested in illustrations for children's greeting cards. To contact, send cover letter. To query with specific ideas, send slides, published samples or original art. Reports in 2 months. Materials filed. Pays on acceptance. Buys greeting card US rights. Credit line sometimes given. Artist's guidelines for SASE.

Tips: "We are looking for new traditional Christmas artwork with a detailed children's book look."

COLLECTOR'S GALLERY, P.O. Box 410, Long Lake MN 55356. (612)476-0241. Fax: (612)476-6799. President, Creative Director: Polly McCrea. Estab. 1980. 15% of material illustrated by freelancers. Buys 4 freelance projects/year; receives 35 submissions/year. Produces make-your-own greeting card kits and activity pads with games which can be played over and over (example: jumbo tic tac toe). "I'm not looking for freelance artwork at this time, but am interested in children's game materials."

Making Contact & Terms: Submit seasonal special games and puzzles 6-9 months in advance. SASE. Reports in 3-4 weeks. Buy all rights on accepted material. Pays on acceptance. Pays $30-75 for puzzles. Illustrator's guidelines for SASE.

Tips: "Small activity games played with paper and pen, that can go on small notepads sell best." Target age group: 6-12.

CONTEMPORARY DESIGNS, 213 Main St., Gilbert IA 50105. (515)232-5188. Fax: (515)232-3380. Editor and Art Director: Sallie Abelson. Estab. 1977. 25% of material is written by freelancers; 20% illustrated by freelancers. Buys 50 freelance projects/year; receives 150 submissions/year. Publishes greeting cards, coloring books and puzzles and/or games. "Greeting cards should be funny — for children who go to camp."

Making Contact & Terms: Submit seasonal material 1 year in advance. SASE. Reports in 1 month. Buys all rights on accepted material. Pays on acceptance. Pays $40 for greeting cards; negotiable amount for coloring books and puzzles. Writer's/illustrator's guidelines for SASE.

Tips: "Greeting cards for campers and Jewish markets only. Puzzles, games and coloring books should be Judaic."

CREATE-A-CRAFT, P.O. Box 330008, Fort Worth TX 76163-0008. (817)292-1855. Contact: Editor. Estab. 1967. Produces greeting cards, giftwrap, games, calendars, posters, stationery and paper tableware products for all ages. Works with 3 freelance artists/year. Buys 3-5 designs/illustrations/year. Prefers artists with experience in cartooning. Works on assignment only. Buys freelance designs/illustrations mainly for greetings cards and t-shirts. Also uses freelance artists for calligraphy, P-O-P displays, paste-up and mechanicals. Considers pen & ink, watercolor, acrylics and colored pencil. Prefers humorous and "cartoons that will appeal to families. Must be cute, appealing, etc. No religious, sexual implications or off-beat humor." Produces material for all holidays and seasons; submit 6 months before holiday.

Making Contact & Terms: For guidelines and sample cards, send $2.50 and #10 SASE. Contact only through artist's agent. Samples are filed. Samples not filed are not returned. Reports only if interested. Write to schedule an appointment to show a portfolio, which should include original/final art, final reproduction/product, slides, tearsheets, color and b&w. Original artwork is not returned to the artist after job's completion. "Payment depends upon the assignment, amount of work involved, production costs, etc. involved in the project." Buys all rights.

Tips: "Demonstrate an ability to follow directions exactly. Too many submit artwork that has no relationship to what we produce."

*DESIGN DESIGN INC., P.O. Box 2266, Grand Rapids MI 49501. (616)774-2448. President: Don Kallil. Estab. 1986. Greeting card company.
Writing: Needs freelance writing for children's greeting cards. For greeting cards, prefers both rhymed and unrhymed verse ideas. To contact, send cover letter and writing samples. Reports in 3 weeks. Materials returned with SASE. Materials not filed. Pays flat fee or royalty. Pays on publication. Buys all rights or exclusive product rights; negotiable. No credit line given. Writer's guidelines for SASE.
Illustration: Needs freelance illustration for children's greeting cards. Makes 30 illustration assignments/month. Uses color artwork only. To contact, send published samples, color photocopies and slides. Reports in 3 weeks. Returns materials with SASE. Materials not filed. Pays flat fee or royalty. Pays on publication. Buys all rights or exclusive product rights; negotiable. No credit line given. Artist's guidelines available for SASE.
Photography: Purchases photography from freelancers. Buys stock and assigns work. Uses 4×5 transparencies. To contact, send cover letter with slides, stock photo list, published samples and promo piece. Reports in 3 weeks. Materials returned with SASE. Materials not filed. Pays per photo or royalties. Pays on usage. Buys all rights or exclusive product rights; negotiable. No credit line given. Photographer's guidelines for SASE.

ECLIPSE COMICS, P.O. Box 1099, Forestville CA 95436. (707)887-1521. Fax: (707)887-7128. Editor-in-Chief: Catherine Yronwode. Art Director: Rich Powers. Submissions: Valarie Jones. "Publishes comic books, graphic albums, trading cards, books and posters for young adult and adult market. Most are fictional, but we also have factual, educational lines." Estab. 1978.
Writing: Makes approx. 100 writing assignments/year. To contact, send cover letter, writing samples and short proposal or query. Reports in 2 months. Payment varies—"impossible to answer as books, comic books, trading cards all have different rates. We always pay an advance and royalty." Pays on acceptance. Rights negotiable. Credit line given.
Illustration: Makes approx. 100 illustration assignments/year. To contact, send cover letter, published samples, photocopies, portfolio and promo piece. "See our artist's guidelines first—send SASE #10 envelope." Reports in 2 months. "Pay varies by project—all jobs pay an advance plus royalty." Pays on acceptance. Rights negotiable. Credit line given.
Tips: "Send for writers'/artists' guidelines before submitting work. Painters interested in remaining on file for trading cards, send slides, promo pieces—color only."

*ENGLISH CARDS, LTD., 40 Cutter Mill Rd., Great Neck NY 11021. (510)487-7370. Contact: Douglas Evans. Estab. 1965. Greeting card company. "Greeting cards—birthday, get well, anniversary, friendship, thank you notes, invitations, announcements, boxed stationery. Full line of Christmas cards. All cards are sold in a box to retail outlets."
Illustration: Needs freelance illustration for children's greeting cards. Wants "safari animals, juvenile; bright colors (watercolor)—purple, pink vivid colors. Teddys, balloon designs." Uses color artwork only. To contact, send cover letter and published samples. To query with specific ideas, send pencil sketches with color written out. Reports in 2-4 weeks. Materials filed. For greeting cards, pays flat fee of $150. For other artwork, pays by the project. Pays on acceptance. Buys all rights.
Photography: Purchases photography from freelancers. Buys stock images. Wants "clean, vivid, emotional, happy scenes of family, friends, *warmth*!" Uses prints and 4×5 transparencies. To contact, send stock photo list. Reports in 2-4 weeks. Keeps materials on file. Pays on acceptance. Buys all rights.

EPHEMERA BUTTONS, P.O. Box 490, Phoenix OR 97535. Estab. 1980. 90% of material written and 10% illustrated by freelancers. Buys over 200 freelance projects/year; receives over 2,000 submissions/year. Novelty pin back buttons with slogans and art. Need simple and bold line art that would work on a button.
Making Contact & Terms: SASE for return of submission. Reports in 3 weeks. Material copyrighted. Pays on publication. Pays $25 per slogan or design. Guideline sheets for #10 SAE and 1 first class stamp.
Tips: Looks for "very silly and outrageously funny slogans. We also are looking for provocative, irreverent and outrageously funny *adult* humor, and politically correct/ incorrect slogans."

*EVERYTHING PERSONALIZED, INC., P.O. Box 650610, Vero Beach FL 32965. Vice President: Jim St. Clair. Estab. 1981. Personalized wood toy manufacturer. Specializes in personalized puzzles, games, accessories. Manufactures novelties (coat hangers and stools), puzzles and games.
Illustration: Makes 1-3 illustration assignments/year. Prefers screen pattern designs for puzzles and games. Uses both b&w and color artwork. To contact, send cover letter, published samples, photocopies, promo piece. To query with specific ideas, cover letter or phone. Reports only if interested. Returns materials if accompanied with SASE. Pays a flat fee or royalties. For other artwork, pays by the project (range: negotiable). Pays on acceptance. Rights negotiable. Credit line given. Artist's guidelines not available.

FANTAGRAPHICS BOOKS, INC., 7563 Lake City Way NE, Seattle WA 98115. (206)524-1967. Fax: (206)524-2104. Submissions Editor: Robert Boyd. Art Director: Dale Yarger. 100% of material written and illustrated by freelancers. Estab. 1975. Buys 10-15 freelance projects/year; receives 300+ submissions/year. Comic books: "We print comics of quality mostly aimed at adults, but a few for younger readers. We like projects that come wholly from the creator (writer and artist); any subject or style they use is fine. The only thing an illustrator should be aware of is that we rarely print comics in color; we prefer black-and-white art. All submissions must be accompanied with a SASE."
Making Contact & Terms: Submit seasonal comic books 9 months in advance. Reports in 6 weeks. Purchases one-time rights. Pays on publication. Pays 4% minimum for comic books. Guideline sheets for #10 SASE.

FAX-PAX USA, INC., 37 Jerome Ave., Bloomfield CT 06002. (203)242-3333. Fax: (203)242-7102. Editor: Stacey L. Savin. Estab. 1990. Buys 1 freelance project/year. Publishes educational picture cards. Needs include U.S. history. Uses rhymed verse.
Making Contact & Terms: Buys all rights. Pays on publication. Cannot return material.
Tips: "Well written, interesting US history sells best."

FOR KIDS' SAKE PUBLISHERS, P.O. Box 70182, Eugene OR 97401-0111. Editor: Patrick G. Harrison. Estab. 1989. Produces coloring books (illustrated children's poems suitable for coloring; environmental and inspiring themes) and posters (simple, but appealing to the child's heart in all of us). "Need writers of children's poems suitable for coloring with environmental and inspiring themes. Need illustrators interested in doing coloring book style drawings." Uses rhymed verse.
Making Contact & Terms: Submit seasonal special coloring books 1 year in advance. SASE. Reports in 2 months. Buys all rights (but negotiable). Pays on publication (with small advance). Pays $25 minimum for coloring books + % royalty. Pays "per illustrated poem. If poet and illustrator are 2 people: split pay and royalty." Writer's/illustrator's guidelines for $2 or 9×12 SASE (75¢ postage).
Tips: Wants illustrated poems suitable for coloring. Target age group 8-12. "We look for coloring books that combine poetry and art."

*FOTOFOLIO/ARTPOST, 536 Broadway, New York NY 10012. (212)226-0923. Editorial Director: Ron Schick. Estab. 1976. Greeting card company. Also publishes fine art and photographic postcards, notecards, posters, calendars. New children's line.
Illustration: Needs freelance illustration for children's greeting cards, calendars and coloring books. To contact, send cover letter, published samples, photocopies, slides, promo piece. Reports back only if interested. Returns materials with SASE. Materials not filed. Rights negotiable. Credit line given. Artist's guidelines not available.
Photography: Purchases photography from freelancers. Buys stock images. To contact, send cover letter, slides, stock photo list, published samples and promo piece. Reports back only if interested. Returns material with SASE. Pays on usage. Rights negotiable. Credit line given. Photographer's guidelines not available.

*GALISON BOOKS, 36 W. 44th St., Suite 910, New York NY 10036. (212)354-8840. Editorial Director: Sharon Kalman. Estab. 1978. Paper products company. Publishes museum-quality gift products, including notecards and jigsaw puzzles. Publishes children's greeting cards, puzzles, blank journals, address books.
Illustration: Needs freelance illustration for children's greeting cards, jigsaw puzzles. Makes 30 illustration assignments/year. Wants scenes "preferably from already published children's books." Uses color artwork only. To contact, send cover letter, published samples and color promo piece. To query with specific ideas, write to request disclosure form first. Reports back only if interested. Returns materials with SASE. Materials filed. For greeting cards, pays flat fee of $250-1,000 or royalty of 2% for 3-5 years. For other artwork, pays by the project (range: $250-1,000) or royalty of 2%. Pays on publication. Buys one-time rights; negotiable. Credit line given. Artist's guidelines not available.
Photography: Purchases photography from freelancers. Buys stock images. Buys 40 stock images/year. Uses 35mm, 2¼×2¼ and 4×5 transparencies. To contact, send cover letter, stock photo list, published samples and color promo piece. Reports back only if interested. Returns materials with SASE. Materials filed. Pays $250/photo. Pays on publication. Buys one-time rights; negotiable. Credit line given. Photographer's guidelines available for SASE.
Tips: 10% of products are made for kids or have kids' themes. Seasonal material should be submitted 6 months in advance.

*THE GIFT WRAP COMPANY, 28 Spring Ave., Revere MA 02151. (617)284-6000. Produce Development and Marketing Coordinator: Pamela Gilman. Estab. 1904. Paper products company. "We manufacture gift wrap and ribbons. Also sell greeting cards (Christmas only)/gift bags."
Illustration: Needs freelance illustration for gift wrap and gift bag designs. Number of illustration assignments "depends on our needs" — 20 maximum/year. Looking for baby prints, juvenile birthday, wedding and shower. Uses color artwork only. To contact, send cover letter, resume, color photocopies and non-returnable art. Reports back only if interested. Returns materials with SASE. Materials filed. Pays by the project (range: $150-300). Pays on acceptance. Buys all rights. No credit line given.

Market conditions are constantly changing! If you're still using this book and it is 1994 or later, buy the newest edition of Children's Writer's & Illustrator's Market *at your favorite bookstore or order directly from Writer's Digest Books.*

Yours Free

with your introductory subscription to

Writer's® DIGEST

You'll gather a wealth of information and inspiration from children's writers, critics and editors when you get your hands on *The Basics of Writing for Children and Young Adults.*

It's your **FREE** gift when you subscribe to the world's leading magazine for writers!

A peek inside this exclusive new guide: What children's book editors want from you in the '90s...Paula Danziger's successful approach to honesty and young-adult writing...the skillful blend of research and imagination in writing kids' nonfiction... how to break into the children's drama market...mastering teen talk...and so much more.

Your Monthly Guide to Getting Published

Subscribe to the magazine thousands of successful authors have come to rely on for instruction and inspiration in all areas of writing. From generating plot ideas to overcoming writer's block. From setting the right tone for your audience to crafting powerful dialogue.

Not only can **Writer's Digest** make you a better writer, it can also make you a better *paid* writer! Learn the tricks of top-dollar freelancers, like how to slant your writing for multiple sales. How to negotiate contracts with editors and publishers. How to profit from magazine trends.

And, like clockwork, each monthly issue will keep you privy to the latest information on which markets are hungry for your work, how much they're paying, and how to contact the right people.

Let the world's leading how-to magazine for writers be your monthly guide to getting published! Subscribe today by using the post-paid card below.

Tips: 20-30% of products are made for kids or have kids' themes. Seasonal material should be submitted 4 months in advance. "We look for general designs that will fill our mass market and upscale lines."

GREAT AMERICAN PUZZLE FACTORY, INC., 16 South Main St., S. Norwalk CT 06854. (203)838-4240. Fax: (203)838-2065. Art Director: Pat Duncan. Estab. 1976. 100% illustrated by freelancers. Buys 30 freelance projects/year; receives 300 submissions/year. Produces puzzles.
Making Contact & Terms: Not interested in seasonal. SASE. Reports in 2 weeks. Rights vary. Pays on publication. Pay varies.
Tips: Wants "whimsical, fantasy" material. Target age group: 4-12.

*GREAT SEVEN, INC., 3838 Del Amo Blvd., #202, Torrance CA 90503. (310)371-4555. Vice President: Ronald Chen. Estab. 1984. Paper products company. Publishes educational and fun stickers for children and teenager market.
Illustration: Needs freelance illustration for children's fun stickers. Makes 120 illustration assignments/year. Wants "kid themes." To contact, send published samples and b&w photocopies. To query with specific ideas, write to request disclosure form first. Reports back only if interested. Returns material with SASE. Materials filed. Pays on acceptance. Buys all rights. No credit line given. Artist's guidelines not available.
Tips: 100% of products are made for kids or have kids' themes. Seasonal material should be submitted 10 months in advance.

*HANDPRINT SIGNATURE, P.O. Box 22682, Portland OR 97222. (503)295-1925. President: Paula Carlson. Greeting card company. "Manufacturer of greeting cards especially designed for kids to send. Each card to be 'signed' with a child's hand print or footprint."
Illustration: Needs freelance illustration for children's greeting cards. Makes 12 illustration assignments/year. "All art must tie in with general theme of Handprint Signature – cards for kids to send. Pure colors." To contact, send cover letter, resume, color photocopies and acknowledgement that he/she has seen and understands Handprint Signature card line. Reports in 1 month. Returns materials with SASE. Materials not filed. For greeting cards, pays flat fee of $50-125. For other artwork, pays by the project (range: $50-1,000). Pays on publication. Buys exclusive product rights. No credit line given. Artist's guidelines not available.
Tips: 100% of products are made for kids or have kids' themes. Seasonal material should be submitted 1 year in advance. "I expect to publish 9 designs by a different artist each year. Even though this artist's work must tie in with other artists already published, the design and presentation must stand out as his or her own unique interpretation."

HIGHLIGHTS FOR CHILDREN, The Fun Zone, Activity Books, 803 Church St., Honesdale PA 18431. (717)253-1080. Fax: (717)253-0179. Editor: Kent L. Brown Jr. Art Director: Rosanne Guararra. Puzzle Editor: Jeff O'Hare. Estab. 1946. 90% of materials freelance written and illustrated. Receives 7,000-8,000 submissions annually. Needs "independent activities targeting children 5-12 years in age. We favor visually stimulating puzzles free of violent themes."
Making Contact & Terms: Special puzzle submissions accepted year-round. SASE for return of submission. Reports in 1-2 months. Purchases all rights. Pays on acceptance. Writer's guidelines for SASE.
Tips: Looking for "codes, matching, crosswords, dot-to-dots, math and logic puzzles, hidden pictures, mazes, quizzes, riddles." Illustrators: "In illustration almost any range of art is accepted these days. Children are more sophisticated now in terms of graphics and design – the illustrator should be aware of this."

INTERCONTINENTAL GREETINGS LTD., 176 Madison Ave., New York NY 10016. (212)683-5830. Contact: Robin Lipner. Estab. 1964. 100% of material freelance written and illustrated. Bought over 200 freelance projects last year. Received "thousands" of submissions last year. Produces greeting cards and scholastic products (notebooks, pencil cases). Needs "humorous writing for greeting cards only. Greeting card (style) artwork in series of three or more. We use very little writing except for humor."
Making Contact & Terms: Accepts seasonal/holiday material year-round. SASE for return of submissions. Reports in 1 month. Purchases world rights under contract (for 2 years). Pays on publication. Pays $30-100 for greeting cards (per usage) and $80-200 for puzzles (per usage). "We hope to use each piece 2-20 times." Writer's/illustrator's guidelines available for SASE.
Tips: Target age group for juvenile cards: ages 1-10. Illustrators: "Use clean colors, not muddy or dark."

*JILLSON & ROBERTS GIFTWRAP, INC., 5 Watson Ave., Irvine CA 92718. (714)859-8781. Art Director: Max Bromwell. Estab. 1973. Paper products company. Makes giftwrap/giftbags.
Illustration: Needs freelance illustration for children's giftwrap. Makes 6-12 illustration assignments/year. Wants children/baby/juvenilel/themes. To contact, send cover letter. To query with specific ideas, write to request disclosure form first. Reports in 1 week. Returns material with SASE. Materials filed. For wrap and bag designs, pays flat fee of $250. Pays on publication. Rights negotiable. No credit line given. Artist's guidelines for SASE.
Tips: 20% of products are made for kids or have kids' themes. Seasonal material should be submitted up to 1 month in advance. "We produce two lines of giftwrap per year: 1 everyday line and 1 Christmas line. The closing date for everyday is June 30th and Christmas is September 15."

*LUCY & COMPANY, 7711 Lk. Ballinger Way NE, Edmonds WA 98925. (206)775-8826. Art Director: Noelle Rigg. Estab. 1977. Paper products company. Publishes greeting cards, calendars, books, gift items, tote bags, announcements, invitations. Publishes childrens'greeting cards (Lucy & Me line), magnets, coloring books, posters, calendars, children's stories, scrapbooks.
Writing: Needs freelance writing for children's greeting cards and books. Makes 2 writing assignments/month; 24/year. For greeting cards, prefers unrhymed verse ideas. Looks for greeting card writing which is sweet and slightly humorous. Tired of greeting card writing which is mushy. Other needs for freelance writing include children's stories. To contact, send client list and writing samples. To query with specific ideas, write to request disclosure form first. Reports back only if interested. Materials returned with SASE. Materials filed. Pays on publication. Buys reprint rights; negotiable. Credit line sometimes given. Writer's guidelines not available.
Illustration: Needs freelance illustration for children's greeting cards, wrap, bags, invitations, books. Makes 6 illustration assignments/month. Needs "ecological, detailed, animals, characters." Uses color artwork only. To contact, send client list, published samples, photocopies and promo piece. To query with specific ideas, write to request disclosure form first. Reports back only if interested. Returns materials with SASE. Materials filed. Pays flat fee or by the project. Pays on publication. Rights negotiable. Credit line given. Artist's guidelines for SASE.
Tips: 80% of products are made for kids or have kids' themes. Seasonal material should be submitted 6 months in advance.

*MAGIC MOMENTS GREETING CARDS, 10 Connor Rd., Deer Park NY 11729. (516)595-2300 ext. 1206. Contact: Art Director. Estab. 1938. Greeting card company. Publish and wholesale greeting cards.

Illustration: Needs freelance illustration for children's greeting cards. Uses color artwork only. To contact, send color photocopies and slides. Reports in 1 week. Returns materials with SASE. Materials not filed. For greeting cards, pays flat fee of $75-135. Pays on acceptance. Buys exclusive product rights. No credit line given. Artist's guidelines not available.

MAYFAIR GAMES, 5641 Howard St., Niles IL 60714. (708)647-9650. Fax: (708)647-0939. Editorial Director: Ray Winninger. Art Director: Maria Paz Cabardo. Estab. 1981. 100% of material is written and illustrated by freelancers. Buys 25 freelance projects/year; receives 100 submissions/year. Produces games under DC Heroes license and role playing and strategy games for teens and adults.
Making Contact & Terms: SASE. Reports in 2 months. Pays on acceptance and publication. Writer's guideline sheet for SASE.
Tips: Target age group: 14-40 years.

*P.S. GREETINGS/FANTUS PAPER PRODUCTS, 4459 W. Division St., Chicago IL 60651. (312)384-0909. Art Director: Kevin Lahvic. Greeting card company. Publishes boxed and individual counter cards. Publishes greeting cards (Kards for Kids—counter; Kids Kards—boxed; Christmas).
Writing: Needs freelance writing for children's greeting cards. Makes 1-10 writing assignments/year. Looks for writing which is "appropriate for kids to give to relatives." To contact, send writing samples. Reports in 6 months. Material returned only if accompanied with SASE. Materials filed. For greeting cards, pays flat fee. Pays on acceptance. Buys all rights. Credit line sometimes given. Writer's guidelines for SASE.
Illustration: Needs freelance illustration for children's greeting cards. Makes 50-100 illustration assignments/year. "Open to all mediums, all themes—use your creativity!" To contact, send published samples (up to 20 samples of any nature) and photocopies. Reports in 6 months. Returns materials with SASE. Materials filed. For greeting cards, pays flat fee. Pays on acceptance. Buys all rights. Credit line sometimes given. Artist's guidelines for SASE.
Photography: Purchases photography from freelancers. Buys stock images. Buys 10-20 stock images/year. Wants florals, animals, seasonal (Christmas, Easter, Valentines, etc.). Uses transparencies (any size). To contact, send slides. Reports in 6 months. Materials returned with SASE. Materials filed. Pays on acceptance. Buys all rights. Credit line sometimes given. Photographer's guidelines for SASE.
Tips: "Only 7% of products are made for kids or have kids' themes, so it needs to be great stuff!" Seasonal material should be submitted 6 months in advance. "We are open to all creative ideas—generally not fads, however. All mediums are considered equally. We have a great need for 'cute' Christmas subjects."

*PALM PRESS, INC., 1442A Walnut St., Berkeley CA 94709. (510)480-0502. Assistant Photo Editor: Courtney Murphree. Estab. 1980. Greeting card company. Publishes high quality blank and greeting cards from photos.
Photography: Purchases photography from freelancers. Buys stock images. Buys 15 stock images/year. Wants unusual images for birthday cards, new baby, friendship, get well, Valentines, Mother's Day, Christmas. Uses 35mm, 2¼ × 2¼ and 4 × 5 transparencies. Reports in 2 weeks. Materials returned with SASE. Pays per photo (range $150-1,000), or royalties of 6½%. Pays on usage. Buys exclusive product rights. Credit line given. Photographer's guidelines for SASE.
Tips: 15% of products are made for kids or have kids' themes. Seasonal material should be submitted 1½ years in advance.

*PAPER IMPRESSIONS, P.O. Box 157, Poway CA 92074. (619)679-7282. Creative Director: Robert Chisholm. Estab. 1990. Greeting card and paper products company. Publishes greeting cards, notes, gift enclosures, framed prints and invitations.
Illustration: Wants "soft, romantic scenes including florals, bears, lace, armoirs etc.—usually in watercolor." Uses color artwork only. To contact, send published samples, photocopies and slides. To query with specific ideas, write to request disclosure form first. Reports back only if interested. Returns materials with SASE. Materials filed. For greeting cards, pays flat fee of $200-300, or advance of $200-300 against 5% royalty for life of card. Pays 30 days of receipt. Rights purchased negotiable. No credit line given. Artist's guidelines not available.
Tips: Seasonal material should be submitted 9 months in advance.

PEACEABLE KINGDOM PRESS, 1051 Folger Ave., Berkeley CA 94710. (510)644-9801. Fax: (510)644-9805. Art Director: Olivia Hurd. Estab. 1983. Produces posters and greeting cards. Uses images from classic children's books.
Illustration: Needs freelance illustration for children's greeting cards and posters. Makes 5 illustration assignments/month; 60/year. To contact, send cover letter and color photocopies. Submit seasonal posters and greeting cards 6 months in advance. Reports in 3 weeks. Buys rights to distribution worldwide. Pays on publication with advance. Pays 5-10% of wholesale for greeting cards.
Tips: "We only choose from illustrations that are from published children's book illustrators, or commissioned art by established children's book illustrators."

*PEACOCK PAPERS, INC., 273 Summer St., Boston MA 02210. New Product Manager: Mia Miranda. Estab. 1982. Manufactures children's T-shirts and sweatshirts, wrappings (papers, bags).
Writing: Needs freelance writing for apparel (T's & sweats). Makes 8-10 writing assignments/year. To contact, send cover letter. To query with specific ideas, submit on 8½×11 paper, double spaced. Reports in 3 weeks. Materials returned with SASE. Materials filed. Pays $35 for 1st use. Pays on acceptance. Buys exclusive product rights. No credit line given. Writer's guidelines for SASE.
Tips: "Send only *original*, one-liners (quick reads) that relate to *all* children."

*PIECES OF THE HEART, P.O. Box 56163, Sherman Oaks CA 91413. (818)995-3273. President: Jill Gaines. Estab. 1988. Greeting card company. Publishes greeting cards and puzzles.
Illustration: Needs freelance illustration for children's greeting cards. Makes 1 illustration assignment/year. Uses color artwork only. To contact, send cover letter. To query with specific ideas, write to request disclosure form first. Reports back only if interested. Returns materials with SASE. Materials filed. For greeting cards, pays flat fee of $200-750. Pays on acceptance. No credit line given. Artist's guidelines not available.
Tips: 50% of products are made for kids or have kids' themes. Seasonal material should be submitted 8 months in advance.

*RED FARM STUDIO, 1135 Roosevelt Ave., P.O. Box 347, Pawtucket RI 02862. (401)728-9300. Creative Director: Lisa Harter Saunders. Estab. 1965. Social expression paper products. "Publish greeting cards—watercolors of nautical, traditional everyday, and Christmas subjects; realistic styles."
Illustration: Needs freelance illustration for children's subject greeting cards, color books and paintables. Makes 20 illustration assignments/month; 250/year. Prefers "watercolor, realistic styles yet cute and fluffy." For first contact, request art guidelines with SASE. Reports in 2-4 weeks. Returns materials with SASE. Appropriate materials are kept on file. For full color painting pays flat fee of $200-275. For black and white artwork, pays flat fee of $150-175 per page for b&w color books and paintables. Pays

on acceptance. Buys all rights. No credit line given but artist may sign artwork. Artist's guidelines for SASE.

Tips: 20% of products are made for kids or have kids' themes. Majority of freelance assignments made during January-May/yearly.

RIVERCREST INDUSTRIES, P.O. 771662, Houston TX 77215. (713)789-5394. Fax: (713)789-9666. Editor: Harry Capers. Estab. 1981. 100% of material airbrushed by freelancers. Buys 2 freelance projects/year. Produces games and books. Interested in someone to handle airbrush on completed illustrations.

Making Contact & Terms: SASE. Pays on acceptance.

Tips: Produces holiday games and juvenile books. Target age groups 2-7 for books; 6-adult for games.

*RUBBER STAMPEDE, 2542 Tenth St., Berkeley CA 94710. (510)843-8910. Fax: (510)843-5906. Art Director: Kent Lytle. Estab. 1978. 50% of material written by freelancers; 50% illustrated by freelancers. Buys 25 freelance projects/year; receives 50 submissions/year. Produces puzzles. Themes: nature, Victorian, teddy bears, cute animals, fantasy.

Making Contact & Terms: Submit seasonal special games, puzzles or comic books 4 months in advance. Reports in a month. Buys all rights. Pays on acceptance.

Tips: Target age group 3 to 103.

*SHULSINGER SALES, INC., 50 Washington St., Brooklyn NY 11201. (718)852-0042. Art Director: Patty Segovia. Estab. 1950. Greeting card and paper products company. "We are a Judaica company, distributing products such as greeting cards, books, paperware, puzzles, games, novelty items—all with a Jewish theme." Publishes greeting cards, novelties, coloring books and puzzles.

Writing: Looks for greeting card writing which can be sent by children to adults and sent by adults to children (of all ages). To contact, send cover letter. To query with specific ideas, write to request disclosure form first. Reports in 2 weeks. Materials returned with SASE. Materials filed. For greeting cards, pays flat fee (this includes artwork). Pays on acceptance. Buys exclusive product rights. Writer's guidelines not available.

Illustration: Needs freelance illustration for children's greeting cards, books, novelties, games. Makes 10-20 illustration assignments/year. "The only requirement is a Jewish theme." To contact, send cover letter and photocopies, color if possible. To query with specific ideas, write to request disclosure form first. Reports in 2 weeks. Returns materials with SASE. Materials filed. For children's greeting cards, pays flat fee (this includes writing). For other artwork, pays by the project. Pays on acceptance. Buys exclusive product rights. Credit line sometimes given. Artist's guidelines not available.

Tips: 40% of products are made for kids or have kids' themes. Seasonal material should be submitted 6 months in advance.

STANDARD PUBLISHING, 8121 Hamilton Ave., Cincinnati OH 45231. (513)931-4050. Fax: (513)931-0904. Acquisitions Editor: Mark Plunkett. Art Director: Richard Briggs. Estab. 1866. Publishes children's books and teacher helps for the religious market. Publishes coloring books, puzzles, games and activity books.

Writing: Needs freelance writing for children's books. Makes 5-12 writing assignments/year. Reports in 2 months. Pays on acceptance. Buys all rights. Credit line given.

Illustration: Needs freelance illustration for puzzle, activity books, teacher helps. Makes 5-7 illustration assignments/year. Freelance artwork needed for activity books, etc. (b&w line art). To contact, send cover letter and photocopies. Reports back only if interested. Pays on acceptance. Buys all rights. Credit line given.

Tips Looks for "Bible-oriented" material for a preschool-6th grade audience.

*THE STRAIGHT EDGE, INC., 296 Court St., Brooklyn NY 11231. (718)643-2794. President: Amy Epstein. Estab. 1983. Manufactures placemats, puzzles, rugs on educational theme for children, ages 6 months and up.
Illustration: Needs freelance illustration for placemats and puzzles. Makes approx. 6-10 illustration assignments/year. Wants "line art; no rendering; realistic drawings with a sense of humor." Uses color artwork only. To contact, send cover letter and b&w photocopies. Reports back only if interested. Does not return materials. Materials filed. For artwork, pays by the project (range: $350-400 per mechanical per design). Pays on completion of mechanical. Buys exclusive product rights. No credit line given.

*SUNRISE PUBLICATIONS, INC., P.O. Box 4699, Bloomington IN 47402. (812)336-9900. Fax: (812)336-8712. Editors: Lori Teesch/Sheila Gerber. Art Review Coordinator: Laurie Hoover. Estab. 1974. Buys 600 + freelance projects/year. Receives 1,000 + /year. Greeting card lines: general greetings, holidays, note cards. Greeting cards: unrhymed verse.
Making Contact & Terms: Submit seasonal greeting cards 6-8 months in advance. Reports in 10 weeks. Material copyrighted. Pays on acceptance. Pay for greeting cards $35-125 (versing); $350 per design. Guideline sheets for #10 SAE and 1 first class stamp.
Tips: "Bright, festive, not-too-wordy versing; occasion specific illustration."

*TLC GREETINGS, 615 McCall Rd., Manhattan KS 66502. (913)776-4041. Creative Director: Michele Johnson. Estab. 1986. Greeting card company. Publishes greeting cards and gift items. "We do a few children's cards—working at doing more."
Writing: Needs freelance writing for children's greeting cards. Makes 4 writing assignments/year. Prefers unrhymed verse ideas. Looks for greeting card writing with new, innovative approaches. Other need for freelance writing includes iron-on transfers, mugs, notepads. To contact, send cover letter and writing samples. To query with specific ideas, write to request disclosure form first. Reports in 1 month. Materials returned with SASE. For greeting cards, pays flat fee. For other writing, pays by the project (range $50-150). Pays on acceptance. Purchases all rights. Credit line sometimes given. Writer's guidelines for SASE.
Illustration: Needs freelance illustration for children's greeting cards. "We are now just looking to publish children's cards." Uses color artwork only. To contact, send cover letter, published samples, photocopies and promo pieces. To query with specific ideas, write to request disclosure form first. Reports in 1 month. Returns materials with SASE. Materials filed. For greeting cards, pays flat fee of $100-200. For artwork, pays by the project (range $100-200). Pays on publication. Buys all rights. Credit line given. Artist's guidelines for SASE.
Tips: 5% of products are made for kids or have kids' themes (but looking to expand). Seasonal material should be submitted 6 months in advance.

*UNITED PLASTIC PRODUCTS, 102 N. Duncan Rd., Champaign IL 61821. (217)359-5400. President: Ron Smith. Estab. 1960. Plastic products manufacturer. Prints plastic table covers, table skirting, aprons, bibs (adult and child), gloves and boots. Manufactures: children's bibs (printed with animals).
Illustration: Makes 1 illustration assignment/year. Uses black & white artwork only. To contact, send cover letter. To query with specific ideas, write to request disclosure

Refer to the Business of Children's Writing & Illustrating for up-to-date marketing, tax and legal information.

form first. Material not filed. Pays on acceptance. Buys one-time rights. Credit line sometimes given—depends on project.

Tips: About 3% of the products are made for kids or have kids' themes. Seasonal material should be submitted 6 months in advance.

WARNER PRESS, P.O. Box 2499, Anderson IN 46018. Editor: Cindy Maddox. Product Editor: Robin Fogle. Senior Product Designer: John Silvey. Art Director: Dianne Deckert. Estab. 1880. Publishes children's greeting cards, coloring and activity books, puzzles, games and posters, all religious-oriented. "Need fun, up-to-date stories for coloring books, with religious emphasis. Also considering activity books for Sunday school classroom use."

Writing: Needs freelance writing for children's greeting cards, coloring and activity books. To contact, request guidelines first. Reports in 6 weeks. For greeting cards, pays flat fee (range: $20-35). Pays on acceptance. Buys all rights. Credit line sometimes given.

Illustration: Needs freelance illustration for children's greeting cards, and coloring, activity books. Wants religious, cute illustrations. To contact, send published samples, photocopies and slides. Reports back only if interested. For greeting cards, pays flat fee (range: $250-300). Pays on acceptance. Buys all rights. Credit line given.

Tips: Write for guidelines before submitting. Unsolicited material that does not follow guidelines will not be reviewed.

Special Markets/'92-'93 changes

The following markets are not included in this edition of *Children's Writer's & Illustrator's Market* for the reasons indicated. The phrase "did not respond" means the market was in the *1992 Children's Writer's & Illustrator's Market* but did not respond to our written and phone requests for updated information for a 1993 listing.

Colormore, Inc. (did not respond)

Kingdom Puzzles (did not respond)

Lamont Publishing (unable to contact)

David Mekelburg & Friends (did not respond)

Northwest Corner, Inc. (did not respond)

Price Stern Sloan (removed per request)

Young Writer's/ Illustrator's Markets

As writers and illustrators trying to tackle the markets in this section, many of you won't exactly fit the mold of a typical freelancer. You probably have not received the litany of rejection letters that most writers collect over time. You won't have years of experience to draw upon when seeking topics to write about. For that matter most of you have not received a high school diploma. The 46 listings in this section (10 of which are new this year) are special because they seek work from talented youths.

Some of the magazines in this section are exclusively for children; others are adult magazines that have set aside special sections to feature the work of younger writers and illustrators. Since most juvenile magazines are distributed through schools, churches and home subscriptions, some of the smaller, literary magazines here may not be easily found in the bookstore or library. In such a case, you may need to contact the magazine to see if a sample copy is available, and what the cost might be. It is important for writers and artists to be familiar with the editorial needs of magazines they are interested in submitting to.

Be advised that it is important to send a self-addressed stamped envelope (SASE) with proper postage affixed with each submission. This way, if the market is not interested in your work, they will send it back to you. If you do not send the SASE with your submission, you probably won't get your work back. If your work is rejected the first time you send it out, be assured you are not the first one this has happened to. Many of our best known writers and artists were turned down more times than they can count at the beginning of their careers, yet went on to be successful at their craft. The key to becoming published lies in persistence as well as talent. Keep sending out stories and artwork as you continue to improve your craft. Someday, an editor may decide your work is just what he needs.

As the adult writers and artists have been advised in other parts of this book, refer to the Business of Children's Writing & Illustrating at the beginning of this book if you're not sure what steps to take when submitting your work.

THE ACORN, 1530 7th St., Rock Island IL 61201. (309)788-3980. Newsletter. Estab. 1989. Audience consists of "kindergarten-12th grade, teachers and other adult writers." Purpose in publishing works for children: to expose children's manuscripts to others and provide a format for those who might not have one. Children must be K-12 (put grade on manuscripts). Guidelines available on request.

Magazines: 50% of magazine written by children. Uses 6 fiction pieces (500 words), 6 nonfiction pieces (500 words), 20 pieces of poetry (32 lines). Pays 1 copy of the issue the work is in. Sample copy $2. Subscription $10 for 6 issues. Submit mss to Betty Mowery, editor. Send complete ms. Will accept typewritten, legibly handwritten and/or computer printout. SASE. Reports in 1 week.

Artwork/Photography: Publishes artwork by children. Looks for "all types; size 4×5. Use black ink in artwork." Pays in 1 copy of issue the work is in. Submit artwork either with manuscript or separately to Betty Mowery. SASE. Responds in 1 week.

Tips: "My biggest problem is not having names on the manuscript. If the manuscript gets separated from the cover letter, there is no way to know whom to respond to. Also, adults who submit will often go over word limit—we are a small publication and cannot handle more than wordage previously stated. I will use fiction or nonfiction by adults, but it must relate to something that will help children with their writing—submitting or publishing, as well as just entertain. Manuscripts without SASE will not be returned."

*AMERICAN GIRL, P.O. Box 984, Middleton WI 53562-0984. (608)836-4848. Bimonthly magazine. Audience consists of girls ages 7-12 who are joyful about being girls. Must be 7-12 years old, no proof needed of original work. Writer's guidelines not available.
Magazines: 5% of magazine written by young people. "Only two pages of each issue are set aside for children and articles are answers to a question or request that has appeared in a previous issue of *American Girl*." Pays in copies. Submit to Harriet Braun, editor. Will accept legibly handwritten ms. SASE. Reports in 2 months.

BOODLE, P.O. 1049, Portland IN 47371. (219)726-8141. Magazine published quarterly. "Each quarterly issue offers children a special invitation to read stories and poems written by others. Children can learn from the ideas in these stories and the techniques of sharing ideas in picures and written form. Audience is ages 6-12. We hope that publishing children's writing will enhance the self-esteem of the authors and motivate other children to try expressing themselves in this form." Submission requirements: "We ask that authors include grade when written, current grade, name of school, and a statement from parent or teacher that the work is original."
Magazines: 95% of magazine written by children. Uses 12 short stories (100-500 words), 1 mostly animal nonfiction piece (100-500 words), 25 poems (50-500 words), 2 puzzles and mazes (50-500 words). Pays 2 copies of issue. Submit mss to Mavis Catalfio, editor. Submit complete ms. Will accept typewritten and legibly handwritten mss. Include SASE.
Artwork/Photography: Wants "mazes, cartoons, drawings of animals or seasons or sports which will likely match a story or poem we publish." Pays 2 copies of issue. "Drawings should be done in black ink or marker." Submit artwork to Mavis Catalfio. Reports in 2 months.
Tips: "Submit seasonal materials at least 6 months in advance. We love humor and offbeat stories. We seldom publish sad or depressing stories about death or serious illness."

BOYS' LIFE, 1325 Walnut Hill Ln., P.O. Box 152079, Irving TX 75015-2079. (214)580-2366. Magazine published monthly. Audience consists of children 7-17. *Boys' LIfe* is published by the Boy Scouts of America to make available to children 7-17 the highest caliber of fiction and nonfiction, to stimulate an interest in good reading and to promote the principles of scouting. Requirements to be met before work is published: must be 18 or under. Guidelines available on request.
Magazines: Small percentage of magazine written by young people. Uses hobby and collecting tips for "Hobby Hows" and "Collecting" columns. Pays $5/tip. Uses jokes for "Think & Grin" column. Pays choice of $2 or copy of *Scout Handbook* or *Scout Field-book*/joke. Several times/year uses personal stories (500 words maximum) for "Readers' Page." Pays $25. Submit mss to column. Submit complete ms. Will accept typewritten and legibly handwritten mss and computer disk submissions.

The asterisk before a listing indicates the listing is new in this edition.

CHALK TALK MAGAZINE, Chalk Talk Publishing, 1550 Mills Rd., RR2, Sidney, BC V8L351 Canada. (604) 656-1858. Monthly magazine. Estab. 1988. *"Chalk Talk* gives children the opportunity to become published authors and inspires an enthusiasm for the written word. It is written by children for children."
Magazine: Submissions welcome from all children ages 5 to 14. The magazine contains "fun and imaginative stories and poems, true life experiences, book reviews, ecology news and concerns, and contains something different every month. Send in as many contributions as you like at one time and as often as you wish." IRCs for return of ms. Contributors are not paid for their submissions.
Artwork/Photography: "Artwork reproduces best from plain paper drawn in dark crayon, felt pen or pencil."

CHICKADEE MAGAZINE, Suite 306, 56 The Esplanade, Toronto, Ontario M5E 1A7 Canada. (416)868-6001. Magazine published 10 times/year. *"Chickadee* is for children aged 3-9. It's purpose is to entertain and educate children about science and nature in the world around them. We publish children's drawings to promote creativity and to give readers of all ages the chance to express themselves. Drawings must follow the topics that are given each month." Children are asked to provide their age and return address.
Artwork/Photography: Publishes artwork by children. Mail submissions with name, age and return address for thank you note. Submit to Mitch Butter, Chirp editor. Reports in months.

CHILDREN'S ALBUM, Kids Creative Fun Magazine, EGW Publishing, P.O. Box 6086, Concord CA 94524. (510)671-9852. *"Children's Album* is a bimonthly publication for kids, ages 7-12, to encourage their creativity, fun and excitement, through writing, reading, art, crafts, games and puzzles with an attempt to capture that age group's sense of humor, personalities, and sensibilities. Writer's guidelines available on request.
Magazines: 80% of magazine written by children. Uses 10 short stories (250-500 words), 10 poems (length varies). Pays in 1 year subscription. Submit mss to Margo Lemas, editor. Submit complete ms. Will accept typewritten, legibly handwritten mss. SASE. Reports in 2-4 weeks.
Artwork/Photography: Publishes artwork and photos by children; submit artwork on 8½ × 11 paper. Pays in 1 year subscription. SASE. Reports in 2-4 weeks.

CHILDREN'S DIGEST, P.O. Box 567, Indianapolis IN 46206. (317)636-8881. Magazine. Published 8 times/year. Audience consists of preteens. Purpose in publishing works by children: to encourage children to express themselves through writing. Requirements to be met before work is published: require proof of originality before publishing stories. Writer's guidelines available on request.
Magazines: 10% of magazine written by children. Uses 1 fiction story (about 200 words), 6-7 poems, 15-20 riddles, 7-10 letters/issue. "There is no payment for manuscripts submitted by readers." Submit mss to *Children's Digest* (Elizabeth A. Rinck, editor). Submit complete ms. Will accept typewritten, legibly handwritten, computer printout mss. "Readers whose material is accepted will be notified by letter. Sorry, no materials can be returned."

CHILDREN'S PLAYMATE, P.O. Box 567, Indianapolis IN 46206. (317)636-8881. Magazine. Estab. 1928. Audience consists of children between 6 and 8 years of age. Purpose in publishing works by children: to encourage children to write. Writer's guidelines available on request.
Magazines: 10% of magazine written by children. Uses 6-7 poems, 8-10 jokes, 8-10 riddles/issue. "There is no payment for manuscripts submitted by children." Submit mss to *Children's Playmate* (Elizabeth A. Rinck, editor). Submit complete ms. Will accept

typewritten, legibly handwritten, computer printout mss. "If a child's work is published, he/she will be notified by a letter. No material may be returned."
Artwork/Photography: Publishes artwork by children. "Prefers dark-colored line drawings on white paper. No payment for children's artwork published." Submit artwork to *Children's Playmate*.

CLUBHOUSE, P.O. Box 15, Berrien Springs MI 49103. (616)471-9009. Director of Publications: Elaine Trumbo. Magazine. Estab. 1949. Publishes 1 section by kids in each issue, bimonthly. "Audience consists of kids 9-14; philosophy is God loves kids, kids are neat people." Purpose in publishing works by children: encouragement; demonstration of talent. Requirements to be met before work is published: age 9-14; parent's note verifying originality.
Magazines: 1/16th of magazine written by children. Uses adventure, historical, everyday life experience (fiction/nonfiction-1,200 words); health-related short articles; poetry (4-24 lines of "mostly mood pieces and humor"). Payment for ms: prizes for children, money for adult authors. Query. Will accept typewritten, legibly handwritten, computer printout mss. "Will not be returned without SASE." Reports in 6 weeks.
Artwork/Photography: Publishes artwork by children. Looks for all types of artwork-white paper, black pen. Pays in prizes for kids. Send black pen on white paper to Elaine Trumbo, editor. SASE—"won't be returned without SASE."
Tips: "All items submitted by kids are held in a file and used when possible. We normally suggest they do not ask for return of the item."

CREATIVE KIDS, P.O. Box 6448, Mobile AL 36660. (205)478-4700. Editor/Publisher: Fay L. Gold. Magazine published 8 times/year (Oct.-May). Estab. 1979. "All of our material is by children, for children." Purpose in publishing works by children: to "create a product that is good enough for publication and to offer an opportunity for children to see their work in print." Requirements to be met before work is published: ages 5-18—must have statement by teacher or parent verifying originality. Writer's guidelines available on request. SASE required.
Magazines: Uses "about 6" fiction stories (200-750 words); "about 6" nonfiction stories (200-750 words); poetry, plays, ideas to share 200-750 words/issue. Pays in free magazine. Submit mss to Fay L. Gold, editor. Will accept typewritten, legibly handwritten mss. Reports in 1 month. SASE required.
Artwork/Photography: Publishes artwork by children. Looks for "any kind of drawing, cartoon, or painting." Pays in "free magazine." Send original or a photo of the work to Fay L. Gold, editor. No photocopies. Reports in 1 month. SASE required.
Tips: "*Creative Kids* is a magazine by kids, for kids. The work represents children's ideas, questions, fears, concerns and pleasures. The material never contains racist, sexist or violent expression. The purpose is to encourage youngsters to create a product that is good enough for publication. A person may submit one or more pieces of work. Each piece must be labeled with the student's name, birth date, grade, school, home address, and school address. Include a photograph, if possible. Recent school pictures are best. Material submitted to *Creative Kids* must not be under consideration by any other publication. Items should be carefully prepared, proofread and double checked. All activities requiring solutions must be accompanied by the correct answers. We're looking for current topics of interest: nutrition, ecology, cleaner environment, etc."

*CREATIVE WITH WORDS, *We Are Writers, Too!*, Creative With Words Publications, P.O. Box 223226, Carmel CA 93922. Editor: Brigitta Geltrich. Semiannual anthology. Estab. 1975. "We publish the creative writing of children." Audience consists of children, schools, libraries, adults, reading programs. Purpose in publishing works by children: to offer them an opportunity to get started in publishing. "Work must be of quality, original, unedited, and not published before; age must be given (up to 19 years old)."

SASE must be enclosed with all correspondence and mss. Writer's guidelines available on request.

Books: Considers all categories except those dealing with death and murder. Uses fairy tales, folklore items (1,000 words); poetry (not to exceed 20 lines, 46 characters across). Published *We Are Writers, Too!* (anthology, children of all ages); *A Scary Halloween!* (children and adults of all ages); *A CWW Easter!* and *Seasons and Holidays!* (anthology, children and adults of all ages). Pay: 20% off each copy of publication in which fiction or poetry by children appears. Submit mss to Brigitta Geltrich, editor. Query; teacher or parent must submit; teacher and/or parents must verify originality of writing. Will accept typewritten and/or legibly handwritten mss. SASE. Reports in 2 months after deadline.

Artwork/Photography: Publishes artwork and computer artwork by children (language art work). Pay: 20% off every copy of publication in which work by children appears. Submit artwork to Brigitta Geltrich, editor.

ESSENTIAL NEWS FOR KIDS, P.O. Box 26908, Tempe AZ 85285-6908. (602)345-READ. Newspaper published monthly. Audience consists of children, grades K-8, their families and educational community. Philosophy is to "stimulate a positive attitude toward learning and experiencing. Support kids' creativity. Emphasize genuine, self-esteem building content. Our purpose is to be a leader in unlocking the potential of today's children and developing their self-esteem." Students must be grades K-8, and may submit original work from any major market as an *Essential News For Kids* correspondent. Writer's guidelines available on request.

Magazines: Nonfiction news and features (uses 10 pieces per zone, 75-100 words); also uses for each issue: short poems (10-15/zone), letters to the editor (6-10/zone, 50 words), and reviews (4-6/zone, 75-100 words). Pays free copy. Children submit mss to Janet Cooper, Cub Reporter/Program Director. Submit complete manuscript. Will accept typewritten, legibly handwritten and/or floppy disk (Mac). Reports in 2 months. Sample issue $1.

Artwork/Photography: Publishes artwork and photos by children. Pays free copy. Submit artwork to Janet Cooper.

*FAMILYFUN, P.O. Box 929, North Hampton MA 01060. (413)585-0444. Magazine. Purpose in publishing works by young people: entertainment. Must be 5-15 years old, will call to verify proof of original work. Writer's guidelines not available.

Magazines: 5% of mgazine written by young people. Uses 1 fiction story (about 100-200 words, 30 nonfiction stories (length varies)/issue. Submit mss to Greg Lauzon, senior editor. Submit complete ms. Will accept legibly handwritten mss. SASE. Reports in 2 months.

Artwork: Publishes artwork and photography by children. Pays with certificate of recognition and one issue. Reports in 2 months.

FREE SPIRIT PUBLISHING INC., Suite 616, 400 First Ave. North, Minneapolis MN 55401. (612)338-2068. Publishes 3-8 books/year since starting in 1983. "We specialize in SELF-HELP FOR KIDS™. Our main interests include the development of self-esteem, self-awareness, creative thinking and problem solving abilities, assertiveness, and making a difference in the world. Children have a lot to share with each other. They also can reach and teach each other in ways adults cannot. Children only need an adult's signature assuring authenticity for the cartoon and writing contests we sponsor." Writer's guidelines available on request (specify student guidelines).

Books: Publishes psychology, self-help, how-to, education. Pays advance and royalties. Submit mss to Judy Galbraith, publisher. Send query. Will accept typewritten mss. Reports in 3-4 months.

Magazines: 20% of magazine written by children. Uses 2-5 nonfiction articles and survey responses. Word length: 100-800. Contest winners receive money and books." Submit complete ms to Elizabeth Salzmann, editorial assistant. Will accept typewritten, legibly handwritten mss Reports in 2 months.

Artwork/Photography: "We run a cartoon contest annually. Write for details." Contest winners receive a cash prize, and their entries are published. Winners also get a T-shirt and a book. Request rules and entry form in September or October (contest deadline is 1 November).

*THE FUN ZONE, Highlights for Children, 803 Church St,. Honesdale PA 18431. (717)253-1080. Monthly magazine. Audience consists of children ages 5-12. Publication is designed to provide learning through puzzles and fun. Purpose in publishing works by young people: so children may share with other children. Parental letter required stating originality of work. Writer's guidelines available upon request.

Magazines: 5-10% of magazine written by young people. Uses puzzles and letters. Query. Will accept legibly handwritten mss. SASE. Reports in 1 month.

FUTURIFIC, INC., the Foundation for Optimism, Futurific, 150 Haven Ave., T-3, New York NY 10032. Publisher: B. Szent-Miklosy. (212)297-0502. Magazine published monthly. Audience consists of people interested in an accurate report of what is ahead. "We do not discriminate by age. We look for the visionary in all people. They must say what will be. No advice or 'may-be.' " Sample copy for $5 postage and handling. Writer's guidelines available on request.

Magazines: Submit mss to B. Szent-Miklosy, publisher. Will accept typewritten, legibly handwritten, computer printout, 5½ inch Word Perfect diskette mss.

Artwork/Photography: Publishes artwork by children. Looks for "what the future will look like." Pay is negotiable. Send b&w drawings or photos. Submit artwork to B. Szent-Miklosy, publisher.

THE GOLDFINCH, 402 Iowa Ave., Iowa City IA 52240. (319)335-3916. Magazine published quarterly. Audience is fifth and sixth graders. "Magazine supports creative work by children: research, art, writing." Submitted work must go with the historical theme of each issue.

Magazines: 10-20% written by children. Uses at least 1 nonfiction essay, poem, story/issue (500 words). Pays complimentary copies. Submit mss to Deborah Gore Ohrn, editor. Submit complete ms. Will accept typewritten, legibly handwritten, computer disk (Apple) mss. Reports in 1 month.

Artwork/Photography: Publishes artwork/photographs by children. Art and photos must be black and white. Pays complimentary copies. Query first to Deborah Gore Ohrn.

HIGH SCHOOL WRITER, P.O. Box 718, Grand Rapids MN 55744. (218)326-8025. Magazine published monthly during the school year. "The *High School Writer* is a magazine written by students *for* students. All submissions must exceed usual and customary standards of decency." Purpose in publishing works by children: "To provide a real audience for student writers — and text for study." Submissions by junior high and middle school students accepted for our junior edition. Senior high students' works are accepted for our senior high edition. Students attending schools that subscribe to our publication are eligible to submit their work." Writer's guidelines available on request.

Magazines: Uses fiction, nonfiction (1,000 words maximum) and poetry. Submit mss to Roxanne Kain, editor. Submit complete ms, teacher must submit. Will accept typewritten, computer generated (good quality) mss.

Tips: "Submissions should not be sent without first obtaining a copy of our guidelines. Also, submissions will not be considered unless student's school subscribes."

HIGHLIGHTS FOR CHILDREN, 803 Church St., Honesdale PA 18431. (717)253-1080. Magazine published monthly (July-August issue combined). "We strive to provide wholesome, stimulating, entertaining material that will encourage children to read. Our audience is children 2-12." Purpose in publishing works by children: to encourage children's creative expression. Requirements to be met before work is published: age limit is 15.

Magazines: 15-20% of magazine written by children. Features which occur occasionally: "What Are Your Favorite Books?" (8-10 per year), Recipes (8-10 per year), "Science Letters" (15-20 per year). Special features which invite children's submissions on a specific topic: "Tell the Story" (15-20 per year), "You're the Reporter" (8-10 per year), "Your Ideas, Please" (8-10 per year), "Endings to Unfinished Stories" (8-10 per year). Submit complete mss to the Editor. Will accept typewritten, legibly handwritten, computer printout mss. Responds in 3-6 weeks.

Artwork/Photography: Publishes artwork by children. No cartoon or comic book characters. No commercial products. Submit black-and-white artwork for "Our Own Pages." Color for others. Features include "Creatures Nobody Has Ever Seen" (5-8 per year) and "Illustration Job" (18-20 per year). Responds in 3-6 weeks.

*KIDS BOOKS BY KIDS, Beyond Words Publishing, Inc., Route 3, Box 492B, Hillsboro OR 97123. (503)647-5109. Book publisher. Publishes 1-2 books by children per year. Looks for "books that encourage creativity and an appreciation of nature in children." Wants to "encourage children to write, create, dream and believe that it is possible to be published. The books must be unique, be of national interest and the child must be personable and promotable."

Books: Publishes stories and joke books. Publisher not accepting unsolicited ms at this time.

*KIDS TODAY MINI-MAGAZINE, 2724 College Park Rd., Allison Park PA 15101. A mini-magazine in newsletter format. Quarterly. Targets kids in grades 3-5. "To recognize and celebrate imagination, creativity, distinctiveness and worth of all people, with particular emphasis on *all* children. To stimulate within our young readership an interest and appreciation for the ability to communicate, learn and entertain through reading, writing and artistic skills." The Spotlight feature is reserved for publication of creative writing submitted by children ages 6-11. Writer's guidelines available on request.

Magazines: 25% of magazine written by young people. Uses 2 short stories (150-250 words), 12 poems (up to 100 words)/issue. Pays certificate of publication and contributor copies. Submit mss to Don DiMarco, editor. Submit complete ms. Will accept typewritten and legibly har.dwritten mss. SASE if author wants work returned. Reports in 3 weeks.

Artwork/Photography: Publishes artwork only when submitted with written work. Two children may submit as a team. Photos should be b&w 8½×11. "We respond to all young writers, offering positive reinforcement, even if work is not accepted."

KIDSART, P.O. Box 274, Mt. Shasta CA 96067. (916)926-5076. Newsletter published quarterly. Publishes "hands-on art projects, open-ended art lessons, art history, lots of child-made art to illustrate." Purpose in publishing works by children: to "provide achievable models for kids—give young artists a forum for their work. We always phone before publishing works to be sure it's OK with their folks, name's spelled correctly, etc."

Artwork/Photography: Publishes artwork/photographs by children. Any submissions by children welcomed. Pays free copies of published work. Submit artwork/photos to Kim Solga, editor. SASE desired, but not required. Reports in 3-4 weeks.

THE MCGUFFEY WRITER, 5128 Westgate Dr., Oxford OH 45056. (513)523-5565. Magazine published 3 times per year. "We publish poems and stories by children that compel the editors to read them to the end because of extraordinary originality of content or facility with language given the age of the child author." Purpose in publishing works by children: to reward by recognition those who strive to create in words and/or drawings and to motivate other children to try to meet a standard set in a sense by their peers. Requirements: be in grades K-12, no geographic restriction, originality must be attested to by adult parent or teacher. Writer's guidelines available on request.

Magazines: Uses 3-4 fiction short stories (800-2,000 words), 5-8 poems (varying length). Pays 2 free copies. Submit mss to Submissions Editor. Teacher submission preferred. "Send copy—we do not return submissions." Will accept typewritten form and legible handwriting. Responds in 3 months.

Artwork/Photography: Publishes black & white illustrations to fit 7½ × 8 page—any theme. Pays 2 contributor copies. Submit art and photographs to Linda Sheppard, art editor. Responds in 3 months.

MERLYN'S PEN: The National Magazine of Student Writing, P.O. Box 1058, East Greenwich RI 02818. (401)885-5175. Magazine. Published every 2 months during the school year, September to May. "We publish 150 manuscripts annually by students in grades 7-12. The entire magazine is dedicated to young adults' writing. Our audience is classrooms, libraries and students from grades 7-12." Requirements to be met before work is published: writers must be in grades 7-12 and must follow submission guidelines for preparing their manuscripts. When a student is accepted, he/she, a parent and a teacher must sign a statement of originality.

Magazines: Uses 15 short stories, plays (fiction); 8 nonfiction essays; 10 pieces of poetry; letters to the editor; editorials; reviews of previously published works; reviews of books, music, movies. No word limit on any material. Pays for ms in three copies of the issue and a paperback copy of *The Elements of Style* (a writer's handbook). Also, a discount is offered for additional copies of the issue. Submit complete ms. Will only accept typewritten mss. "All rejected manuscripts have an editor's constructive critical comment in the margin." Reports in 10 weeks.

Artwork/Photography: Publishes artwork by young adults, grades 7-12. Looks for black and white line drawings, cartoons, color art for cover. Pays in 3 copies of the issue to the artist, and a discount is offered for additional copies. Send unmatted original artwork. Reports in 10 weeks.

Tips: "All manuscripts and artwork must be submitted with a cover sheet listing: name, age and grade, home address, home phone number, school name, school phone number, school address, teacher's name and principal's name. SASE must be large enough and carry enough postage for return."

MY FRIEND, 50 St. Paul's Ave., Jamaica Plain, Boston MA 02130. (617)522-8911. Magazine published 10 times/year. Audience consists of children ages 6-12, primarily Roman Catholics. Purpose in publishing works by children: to stimulate reader participation and to encourage young Catholic writers. Requirements to be met before work is published: accepts work from children ages 6-16. Requirements regarding originality included in guidelines. Writer's guidelines available for SASE.

Tips: "Our 'Junior Reporter' feature gives young writers the chance to do active research on a variety of topics. Children may ask for an 'assignment' or suggest topics they'd be willing to research and write on. This would be mainly where our interest in children's writing would lie."

THE MYTHIC CIRCLE, Mythopoeic Society, P.O. Box 6707, Altadena CA 91001. Editor: Tina Cooper and Christine Lowentrout. Art Director: Lynn Maudlin. Magazine published quarterly. Circ. 150. Fantasy writer's workshop in print featuring reader comments in each issue. 5% of publication aimed at juvenile market.

Nonfiction: How-to, interview/profile. "We are just starting with nonfiction—dedicated to how to write and publish." Buys maximum of 4 mss/year. Average word length: 250-2,000. Byline given.

How to Contact/Writers: Fiction: send complete ms. Nonfiction: query. SASE (IRC) for answer to query and return of ms. Reports on queries/mss in 2 months. Will consider photocopied, computer printout (dark dot matrix) and electronic submissions via disk (query for details).

Artwork/Photography: Buys 10 illustrations/issue; buys 30 illustrations/year. Preferred theme or style: fantasy, soft science fiction. Reports on art samples in 3-6 weeks. Original artwork returned at job's completion (only if postage paid).

Terms: Pays on publication. Buys one-time rights. Pays in contributor copies. Sample copy $6.50. Writer's guidelines free with SAE and 1 first-class stamp.

Tips: "We are a good outlet for a story that hasn't sold but 'should' have—good feedback and tips on improvement."

THE PIKESTAFF FORUM, P.O. Box 127, Normal IL 61761. (309)452-4831. Magazine published annually; "we hope to eventually get out two issues per year. The basic audience of *The Pikestaff Forum* is adult; in each issue we have a Young Writers feature publishing writing and artwork by young people aged 7 through 17. Purpose in publishing works by children: Our purpose is twofold: (1) to put excellent writing by young people before the general public, and (2) to encourage young people in developing their self-confidence and powers of literary expression. Requirements to be met before work is published: Work must be by young people aged 7 through 17; it must be original, previously unpublished, and submitted by the authors themselves (we do *not* wish parents or teachers to submit the work); the person's age at the time the piece was written must be stated and SASE must be included." Writer's guidelines available on request.

Magazines: 10% of magazine written by children. Uses 1-3 fiction stories, 7-10 poems/issue. Poetry always welcome. Author or artist receives three free copies of the issue in which the work appears, and has the option of purchasing additional copies at a 50% discount. Submit mss to Robert D. Sutherland, editor/publisher. Submit complete ms. Will accept typewritten, legibly handwritten, computer printout mss. SASE. Reports in 3 months.

Artwork/Photography: Publishes artwork by children. No restrictions on subject matter; "should be free-standing and interesting (thought-provoking). *Black and white only* (dark image); we cannot handle color work with our format." Artist receives three free copies of the issue in which the work appears, and has the option of purchasing additional copies at a 50% discount off cover price. In black and white, clearly marked with artist's name, address and age at the time the work was created. Submit artwork to Robert D. Sutherland, editor/publisher. Reports in 3 months. "We do not wish teachers to submit for their students, and we do not wish to see batches of works which are simply the product of school assignments."

SHOFAR MAGAZINE, 43 Northcote Dr., Melville NY 11747. (516)643-4598. Magazine.

Magazines: 10-20% of magazine written by young people. Uses fiction/nonfiction (500-750 words), Kids Page items (50-150 words). Pays 7-10¢/word. Submit mss to Gerald Grayson, managing editor. Submit complete ms. Will accept typewritten, legibly handwritten mss and computer disk (Mac only). SASE. Reports in 4-6 weeks.

Artwork/Photography: Publishes artwork and photography by children. Pays "by the piece, depending on size and quantity." Submit original with SASE. Reports in 4-6 weeks.

SKIPPING STONES, Multicultural Children's Quarterly, P.O. Box 3939, Eugene OR 97403. (503)342-4956. Articles Editor: Arun N. Toke. Fiction Editor: Amy Klauke. Quarterly magazine. Estab. 1988. Circulation 3,000-4,000. "*Skipping Stones* is a multicultural, nonprofit, children's magazine to encourage cooperation, creativity and celebration of cultural and environmental richness. It offers itself as a creative forum for communication among children from different lands and backgrounds."
Magazine: Fiction accepted only by young writers (under 19 years of age). Word length for fiction: 2 pages. Byline given.
Poetry: Publishes poetry by young, unpublished writers.
How to Contact/Writers: Send complete manuscript. Reports on queries in 1 month; on ms in 2 months. Accepts simultaneous submissions.
Artwork/Photography: Will review all varieties of manuscript/illustration packages. Black and white photos preferred. Reports back to artists in 3 months.
Terms: "We are not able to pay cash. We are glad to give a few copies of the magazine in which your contribution is published." Sample copy for $4 and 8½×11 SAE with 4 first class stamps.
Tips: "Let the 'inner child' within you speak out—naturally, uninhibited." Wants "material that gives insight on cultural celebrations, lifestyle, custom and tradition, glimpse of daily life in other countries and cultures. Photos, songs, artwork are most welcome if they illustrate/highlight the points. Upcoming special features: Eastern Europe, African-American experience, drugs and substance abuse, religions and cultures from around the world, death and loss, Spanish-English bilingual issue, Japan, street children and rainforests."

SKYLARK, 2200 169th St., Hammond IN 46323. (219)989-2262. Editor: Pamela Hunter. Children's Editor: Catherine Bukovich. Annual magazine. Circ. 500-750. 15% of material aimed at juvenile audience. Presently accepting material *by* children. "*Skylark* wishes to provide a vehicle for creative writing of all kinds, by all ages, particularly ages five through eighteen, especially in our area, which has not ordinarily provided such an outlet. Children need a place to have their work published alongside that of adults." Parent or teacher verification required for authors 18 and under. Writer's guidelines available upon request.
Magazines: 15% of magazine written by young people. Uses animal, friends, families, life experiences, mystery. Does not want to see material about Satan worship, graphic sex. Uses 4 fiction stories (1,200 words max.), 1 nonfiction story (1,200 words max.), 25 poems, (20 lines max.). Pay in contributor's copies. Submit ms to Children's Editor. Submit complete ms. Will accept typewritten ms only. SASE. Reports in 6 months. Byline given.
Artwork/Photography: Publishes artwork/photos by children. Looks for "photos of animals, landscapes and sports, and artwork to go along with text." Pay in contributor's copies. All artwork and photos must be b&w, 8½×11, unlined paper. Submit artwork/photos to Children's Editor. SASE. Reports in 6 months.

THE SOW'S EAR POETRY JOURNAL, 245 McDowell St., Bristol TN 37620. (615)764-1625. Magazine published quarterly. "Our audience includes serious poets throughout the USA. We publish school-aged poets in each issue to encourage young writers and to show our older audience that able young poets are writing. We request young poets to furnish age, grade, school and list of any previous publication." Writer's guidelines available on request.
Magazines: 3% of magazine written by children. Uses 1-5 poems (1 page). Pays 1 copy. Submit complete ms. Will accept typewritten, legibly handwritten mss. SASE. Reports in 3 months.
Artwork/Photography: Publishes artwork and photographs by children. "Prefer line drawings. Any subject or size that may be easily reduced or enlarged. Must be black &

white." Pays 1 copy. Submit artwork to Mary Calhoun, Graphics Editor. SASE. Reports in 4 months.

*SPARK!, 1507 Dana Ave., Cincinnati OH 45207. (513)531-2222. Magazine. Published 9 times/year. Editorial philosophy: to provide fun, creative art and writing activities to stimulate children's imagination. Audience consists of 6 to 12 year olds. Purpose in publishing works by young people: to show kid-produced samples with how-to features (used as examples and as encouragement that "you can do it, too") and to share kids' original work with other kids across the country—an art and writing forum. Age requirements must be met; artist must sign "Artwork Verification" form. Writer's guidelines not available.
Artwork/Photography: Publishes artwork and photography by children. "We request children's stories/artwork to be featured in our column, 'Show & Tell.'" Submit to Show & Tell, 1507 Dana Ave., Cincinnati, OH 45207, Beth Struck, Managing Editor. Responds if artwork is to be published in Show & Tell; however, all kids who submit work receive a thank-you postcard.

SPRING TIDES, 824 Stillwood Dr., Savannah GA 31419. (912)925-8800. Annual magazine. Audience consists of children 5-12 years old. Purpose in publishing works by children: to encourage writing. Requirements to be met before work is published: must be 5—12 years old. Writers guidelines available on request.
Magazines: Uses 12-24 pieces of material per issue. Submit complete ms. Will accept typewritten mss. SASE.
Artwork/Photography: Publishes artwork by children. "We have so far used only local children's artwork because of the complications of keeping and returning pieces."

STONE SOUP, The Magazine by Children, Children's Art Foundation, P.O. Box 83, Santa Cruz CA 95063. (408)426-5557. Articles/Fiction Editor, Art Director: Ms. Gerry Mandel. Magazine published 5 times/year. Circ. 15,000. "We publish fiction, poetry and artwork by children through age 13. Our preference is for work based on personal experiences and close observation of the world." Purpose in publishing works by children: to encourage children to read and to express themselves through writing and art. Writer's guidelines available upon request.
Magazines: 100% of magazine written by children. Uses animal, contemporary, fantasy, history, problem solving, science fiction, sports, spy/mystery/adventure fiction stories. Uses 5-10 fiction stories (100-2,500 words), 5-10 nonfiction stories (100-2,500 words), 2-4 poems. Does not want to see classroom assignments and formula writing. Buys 65 mss/year. Byline given. Pays on acceptance. Buys all rights. Pays $10 each for stories and poems, $15 for book reviews. Contributors also receive 2 copies. Sample copy $2. Free writer's guidelines. "We don't publish straight nonfiction, but we do publish stories based on real events and experiences." Send complete ms. Will accept typewritten, legibly handwritten mss. SASE. Reports in 1 month.
Artwork/Photography: Publishes any type, size or color artwork/photos by children. Pays $8 for b&w illustrations. Contributors receive 2 copies. Sample copy $2. Free illustrator's guidelines. Send originals if possible. SASE. Reports in 1 month. Original artwork returned at job's completion. All artwork must be by children through age 13.

STRAIGHT MAGAZINE, Standard Publishing, 8121 Hamilton Ave., Cincinnati OH 45231. (513)931-4050. Magazine published weekly. Estab. 1951. Magazine includes fiction pieces and articles for Christian teens 13-19 years old to inform, encourage and uplift them. Purpose in publishing works by children: to provide them with an opportunity to express themselves. Requirements to be met before work is published: must submit their birth date and Social Security number (if they have one). Writer's guidelines available on request, "included in regular guidelines."

Magazines: 15% of magazine written by children. Uses fiction (500-1,000 words); personal experience pieces (500-700 words); poetry (approx. 1 poem per issue). Pays flat fee for poetry; per word for stories/articles. Submit mss to Carla J. Crane, editor. Submit complete ms. Will accept typewritten and computer printout mss. Reports in 4-6 weeks.

Artwork/Photography: Publishes artwork by children. Looks for "anything that will fit our format." Pays flat rate. Submit artwork to Carla Crane, editor. Reports in 4-6 weeks.

SUNSHINE MAGAZINE, Henrichs Publications, Inc., P.O. Box 40, Sunshine Park, Litchfield IL 62056. (217)324-3425. Magazine published monthly. Goal is to "to promote goodwill, a positive attitude and a cheerful, wholesome approach to everyday living. Audience is all the family." Purpose in publishing works by children: "to encourage writing, reading and communication among children."

Magazines: "Two pages/issue written by children. Submit complete ms." Uses fiction, nonfiction and poetry (up to 200 words). Pays in copies. Submit mss to Peggy Kuethe, associate editor. Submit complete ms. Will accept typewritten, legibly handwritten, computer printout mss. SASE. Reports in 3 months.

TEXAS HISTORIAN, Texas State Historical Association, 2/306 Sid Richardson Hall, Univ. Station, Austin TX 78731. (512)471-1525. Articles Editor: David De Boe. Magazine published 4 times a year in February, May, September and November. Estab. 1940. Circ. 2,000. "The *Texas Historian* is the official publication of the Junior Historians of Texas. Articles accepted for publication must be written by members of the Junior Historians of Texas." 75% of material directed to children.

Nonfiction: Young adult: history. Average word length: 2,500.

THUMBPRINTS, 928 Gibbs St., Caro MI 48723. (517)673-6653. Newsletter published monthly. "Our newsletter is designed to be of interest to writers and allow writers a place to obtain a byline." Purpose in publishing works by children: to encourage them to seek publication of their work. Statement of originality required. Writer's guidelines available on request, "same guidelines as for adults."

Newsletter: Percentage of newsletter written by children "varies from month to month." Pays in copies. Submit ms to Janet Ihle, editor. Submit complete ms or have teacher submit. Will accept typewritten and computer printout mss. Reports in 6-8 weeks.

Artwork/Photography: Publishes artwork by children. Looks for art that expresses our monthly theme. Pays in copies. Send pencil or ink line drawings no larger than 3 × 4. Submit artwork to Janet Ihle, editor. SASE. Reports in 3 months.

Tips: "We look forward to well written articles and poems by children. It's encouraging to all writers when children write and are published."

TURTLE, Ben Franklin Literary & Medical Society, Children's Better Health Institute, 1100 Waterway Blvd., P.O. Box 567, Indianapolis IN 46206. (317)636-8881. Magazine. "*Turtle* is a health-related magazine geared toward children from ages 2-5. Purpose in publishing works by children: we enjoy giving children the opportunity to exercise their creativity." Requirements to be met before work is published: for ages 2-5, publishes artwork or pictures that they have drawn or colored all by themselves. Writer's guidelines available on request.

Artwork/Photography: Publishes artwork by children. There is no payment for children's artwork. All artwork must have the child's name, age and complete address on it. Submit artwork to *Turtle* Magazine Editorial Director: Christine Clark. "No artwork can be returned."

*VIRGINIA WRITING, Longwood College, 201 High St., Farmville VA 23909. (804)395-2160. Magazine published twice yearly. *"Virginia Writing* publishes prose, poetry, fiction, nonfiction, art, photography, music, and drama from Virginia high school students and teachers. The purpose of the journal is to publish 'promise.' The children must be attending a Virginia high school, preferably in no less than 9th grade (though some work has been accepted from 8th graders). Originality is strongly encouraged. The guidelines are also in the front of our magazine." No profanity or racism accepted.
Magazines: 85% of magazine written by children. Uses approx. 17 nonfiction short stories, 56 poems and prose/issue. Submit mss to Billy C. Clark, Founder and Editor. All works: submit complete ms. Will accept typewritten mss. Reports as soon as possible.
Artwork/Photography: Publishes artwork by children. All types of artwork, including that done on computer. Color slides of artwork are acceptable. All original work is returned upon publication in a non-bendable, well protected package. Submit artwork to Billy C. Clark. Reports as soon as possible.
Tips: "All works should be submitted with a cover letter describing student's age, grade and high school currently attending."

*VOICES OF YOUTH, P.O. Box JJ, Sonoma CA 95476. (707)938-8314. Publishes 4 magazines/year by high school youths. Purpose in publishing works by young people is to provide a forum for expression and acknowledge ideas and great work. Must be in grades 9-12, does not insist upon proof of original work. Writer's guidelines available on request.
Magazines: Uses 35-50 fiction pieces (length varies), 35-50 nonfiction pieces (length varies), 35-50 poetry and prose pieces (length varies)/issue. Pays with complementary copy when article appears. Submit mss to Michael John, editor. Submit complete ms. Will accept typewritten mss. SASE.
Artwork/Photography: Publishes artwork and photography by children. Send a copy of artwork and SASE.

WHOLE NOTES, P.O. Box 1374, Las Cruces NM 88004. (505)382-7446. Magazine published twice yearly. "We look for original, fresh perceptions in writing. General audience. We try to recognize excellence in creative writing by children as a way to encourage and promote imaginative thinking." Writer's guidelines available on request.
Magazines: Every fourth issue is 100% by children. Uses 1-3 fiction short, short stories—any kind (length open), 30 poems/issue (length open). Pays 2 complimentary copies. Submit mss to Nancy Peters Hastings, editor. Submit complete ms. Will accept typewritten, legibly handwritten mss. SASE. Reports in 3 weeks.
Artwork/Photography: Publishes artwork and photographs by children. Looks for black and white line drawings which can easily be reproduced; b&w photos. Pays complimentary copy of issue. Send clear photocopy. Submit artwork to Nancy Peters Hastings, editor. SASE. Reports in 3 weeks.
Tips: Sample issue is $3.

WOMBAT: A JOURNAL OF YOUNG PEOPLE'S WRITING AND ART, 365 Ashton Dr., Athens GA 30606. (706)549-4875. Published 4 times a year. "Illiteracy in a free society is an unnecessary danger which can and must be remedied. *Wombat,* by being available to young people and their parents and teachers, is one small incentive for young people to put forth the effort to learn to read and write (and draw) better, to communicate better, to comprehend better and—hopefully—consequently, to someday possess greater discernment, judgment and wisdom as a result. "Purpose in publishing works by children: to serve as an incentive, to encourage them to work hard at their reading, writing and—yes—drawing/art skills, to reward their efforts." Requirements to be met before work is published: ages 6-16; all geographic regions; statement that work is original.

Magazines: 95% of magazine written by children. Have one 2-4 page "Guest Adult Article" in most issues/when available (submitted). Uses poetry; any kind of fiction (3,000 words maximum, shorter preferred) but avoid extreme violence, religion or sex (approaching pornography); any kind of nonfiction of interest to 6-16 year olds (3,000-4,000 words); cartoons, puzzles and solutions, jokes and games and solutions. Pays in copies and frameable certificates. Submit mss to Publisher: Jacquelin Howe. Submit complete ms. Teacher can submit; parents, librarians, students can submit. Will accept typewritten, legibly handwritten, computer printout mss. Responds in 1-2 weeks with SASE; up to 1 year with seasonal or holiday works (past season or holiday). Written work is not returned. SASE permits *Wombat* to notify sender of receipt of work.

Artwork/Photography: Publishes artwork by children. Looks for: works on paper, not canvas. Photocopies OK if clear and/or reworked for clarity and strong line definition by the artist. Pays in copies and frameable certificates. Submit artwork to Publisher: Jacquelin Howe. "Artwork, only, will be returned if requested and accompanied by appropriate sized envelope, stamped with sufficient postage."

Tips: *"Wombat* is, unfortunately, on 'hold' probably throughout this entire school year; therefore, we are asking people to please query as to when/if we will resume publication, before subscribing or submitting works to *Wombat* right now."

*THE WRITERS' SLATE, (The Writing Conference, Inc.), P.O. Box 664, Ottawa KS 66067. (913)242-1059. Magazine. Publishes 3 issues/year. *The Writers' Slate* accepts original poetry and prose from students enrolled in kindergarten through twelfth grade. The audience is students, teachers and librarians. Purpose in publishing works by young people: to give students the opportunity to publish and to give students the opportunity to read quality literature written by other students. Writer's guidelines available on request.

Magazines: 90% of magazine written by young people. Uses 10-15 fiction; 1-2 nonfiction; 10-15 other. Submit mss to Carlee N. Vieux, Editor, P.O. Box 734, Garden City, KS 67846. Submit complete ms. Will accept typewritten mss. Reports in 1 month.

Artwork/Photography: Publishes artwork by young people. Bold, black, student artwork may accompany a piece of writing. Submit to Carlee N. Vieux, Editor. Reports in 1 month.

YOUNG VOICES MAGAZINE, P.O. Box 2321, Olympia WA 98507. (206)357-4683. Magazine published bimonthly. *"Young Voices* is by elementary and middle school/junior high students for people interested in their work." Purpose in publishing work by young people: to provide a forum for their creative work. Send age, grade and school with submission. "Home schooled writers *definitely* welcome, too." Writer's guidelines available on request.

Magazines: Uses 20 fiction stories, 5 reviews, 20 poems per issue. Pays $3-5 on acceptance. Submit mss to Steve Charak, Publisher. Submit complete ms. Will accept typewritten, legibly handwritten mss. SASE. Reports in 3 months.

Artwork/Photography: Publishes artwork and photography by children. "Prefer work that will show up in black and white." Pays $3-5 on acceptance. Submit artwork to Steve Charak. SASE. Reports in 3 months.

Refer to the Business of Children's Writing & Illustrating for up-to-date marketing, tax and legal information.

Contests & Awards

Publication is not the only way to get your work recognized. Contests really can be viable vehicles to gain recognition in the industry. Placing in a contest or winning an award truly validates the time spent on a craft, including writing and illustrating. Even for those who don't place, many competitions offer the chance to obtain valuable feedback from judges and other established writers or artists.

Not all of these contests are geared strictly for professionals. Many are designed for "amateurs" who haven't yet been published. Still others are open only to students. Contests for students in this section are marked with a double dagger (‡).

Be sure to study the guidelines and requirements for each contest. Regard entry deadlines as gospel and note whether manuscripts and artwork should be unpublished or previously published. Also, be aware that awards vary with each contest. Where one contest may award a significant monetary amount, another may award a certificate or medal instead of money.

You will notice that some contests require nominations. For published authors, competitions provide an excellent means for promoting your work. If your book is eligible for a contest or award, have the appropriate people at your publishing company nominate or enter your work for consideration. Then make sure enough copies of your work are sent to the contest judges and any other necessary people affiliated with the competition.

Read through the listings that interest you, then send away for more information to acquire specifics about the types of written or illustrated material reviewed, word length and any qualifications you should know about, such as who retains the rights to prize-winning material.

JANE ADDAMS CHILDREN'S BOOK AWARD, Jane Addams Peace Association, % Jean Gore, 980 Lincoln Place, Boulder CO 80302. (212)682-8830. Contest/Award Director: Jean Gore. Annual contest/award. Estab. 1953. "The Jane Addams Children's Book Award is presented annually for a book that most effectively promotes the cause of peace, social justice, world community, and the equality of the sexes and all races." Previously published submissions only; year previous to year the award is presented. Deadline for entries: April 1. SASE for contest/award rules and entry forms. No entry fee. Awards a certificate to the author and seals for book jackets to the publisher (at cost). Judging by a committee of children's librarians. Works displayed at an award ceremony.

AIM Magazine Short Story Contest, P.O. Box 20554, Chicago IL 60620. (312)874-6184. Contest Directors: Ruth Apilado, Mark Boone. Annual contest. Estab. 1983. Purpose of the contest: "We solicit stories with social significance. Youngsters can be made aware of social problems through the written word and hopefully they will try solving them." Unpublished submissions only. Deadline for entries: August 15. SASE for contest rules and entry forms. SASE for return of work. No entry fee. Awards $100. Judging by editors. Contest open to everyone. Winning entry published in fall issue of *AIM*. Subscription rate $10/year. Single copy $2.50

*AIP SCIENCE WRITING AWARD, American Institute of Physics, 335 E. 45th St., New York NY 10017. (212)661-9404. Contact: Joan Wrather. Annual contest/award. Purpose of the contest/award: Awarded to articles, books, or booklets about physics and/or astronomy intended for children up to age 15. Previously published only. Submissions made by the author or by the author's agent. Deadline for entries: October. SASE for contest/award rules and entry forms. No entry fee. Awards $3,000 plus certificate. Judging by panel named by AIP.

‡AMHA MORGAN ART CONTEST, American Morgan Horse Assoc., Box 960, Shelburne VT 05482. (802)985-4944. Communications Director: Tracey Holloway. Annual contest/award. The art contest consists of three categories: Morgan art (pencil sketches, oils, water colors, paintbrush), Morgan cartoons, Morgan speciality pieces (sculptures, carvings). Unpublished submissions only. Deadline for entries: December 1. Contest/award rules and entry forms sent upon request. Entries not returned. Entry fee is $2. Awards $50 first prize in 3 divisions and AMHA ribbons to top 5 places in 6 categories. "All work submitted becomes property of The American Morgan Horse Association. Selected works may be used for promotional purposes by the AMHA." Requirements for entrants: "We consider all work submitted." Works displayed at the annual convention. This year the Morgan Horse Association, Inc. will be sponsoring two judgings. The first will be divided into three age groups: 13 years and under, 14-21 years and adult. The second judging will be divided into three categories and open to all ages. The top 5 places will receive official Art Contest Ribbons. Each art piece must be matted, have its own application form and its own entry fee.

*THE AMY WRITING AWARDS, The Amy Foundation, 3798 Capital City Blvd., Lansing MI 48906. Director: James Russell. Annual contest/award. Estab. 1984. "The purpose is to recognize creative, skillful writing that presents in a sensitive thought-provoking manner the biblical position on issues affecting the world today." Previously published submissions only; must be published between January 1 and December 31 each calendar year. Submissions made by the author. Deadline for entries: January 31st the year following publication. SASE for contest/award rules. "Entry forms not required." No entry fee. Awards $10,000 first prize and $24,000 additional cash awards. Judging by the Amy Awards Committee and a panel of distinguished judges. Right to use for promotion of Amy Writing Awards acquired. "Entry must contain one passage of scripture and be published in a secular non-religious publication." Works will be published in annual booklet.

*MARGUERITE DE ANGELI PRIZE, Doubleday Books for Young Readers, 666 Fifth Ave., New York NY 10103. Annual. Estab. 1992. Unpublished submissions only. Submissions made by author. Deadline for entries: June 30, 1993. SASE for contest/award rules and entry forms. Awards one Doubleday hardcover and Dell paperback book contract, including an advance and royalties, will be awarded annually to encourage the writing of fiction that examines the diversity of the American experience in the same spirit as the works of Marguerite de Angeli. The award consists of a $1,500 cash prize and a $3,500 advance against royalties. Judging will be done by editors of Doubleday Books for Young Readers. The contest is open to U.S. and Canadian writers who have not previously published a novel for middle-grade readers. Foreign-language mss are

The double dagger before a listing indicates the contest is for students.

not eligible. Translations are not eligible. Results will be announced no later than October 30, 1993.

*‡ARTS RECOGNITION AND TALENT SEARCH (ARTS), National Foundation for Advancement in the Arts, 3915 Biscayne Blvd., Miami FL 33137. (305)573-0490. Contact: Sherry Thompson. Open to students/high school seniors or 17 and 18 yr. olds. Annual contest/award. Estab. 1981. "Created to bring exceptional young artists to a higher plateau of excellence, Arts Recognition and Talent Search (ARTS) is an innovative national program of the National Foundation for Advancement in the Arts (NFAA). Established in 1981, ARTS touches the lives of gifted young people across the country, providing financial support, scholarships and goal-oriented artistic, educational and career opportunities. Each year, from a pool of 5,000-7,500 applicants, an average of 250 ARTS awardees are chosen for NFAA support by panels of distinguished artists and educators. Each ARTS applicant, generally a high school senior, 17-18 years of age, has special talent in music, dance, theater, visual arts or creative writing." Submissions made by the student. Deadline for entries: June 1 and October 1 (late). SASE for contest/award rules and entry forms. Entry fee is $25/35 (late) Fee waivers available based on need. Awards $100/$500/$1,500 and $3,000 – unrestricted cash grants. Judging by a panel of authors and educators recognized in the field. Rights to submitted/winning material: NFAA/ARTS retains the right to duplicate work in an anthology or in Foundation literature unless otherwise specified by the artist. Requirements for entrants: Artists must be high school seniors or, if not enrolled in high school, must be 17 or 18 yrs. old. Works will be published in an anthology distributed during ARTS Week, the final adjudication phase which takes place in Miami.

‡BAKER'S PLAYS HIGH SCHOOL PLAYWRITING CONTEST, Baker's Plays, 100 Chauncy St., Boston MA 02111. (617)482-1280. Contest Director: Raymond Pape. Annual contest. Estab. 1990. "To acknowledge playwrights at the high school level and to insure the future of American Theatre by encouraging and supporting those who are its cornerstone: young playwrights." Unpublished submissions only. Deadline for entries: January 31. SASE for contest rules and entry forms. No entry fee. Awards $500 to the first place playwright and Baker's Plays will publish the play under the Best Plays from the High School Series. $250 to the second place playwright with an honorable mention and $100 to the third place playwright with an honorable mention in the series. Judged anonymously. Open to any high school student. The first place playwright will have his/her play published in an acting edition the September following the contest. The work will be described in the Baker's Plays Catalogue, which is distributed to 50,000 prospective producing organizations. "Plays must be accompanied by the signature of a sponsoring high school drama or English teacher, and it is recommended that the play receive a production or a public reading prior to the submission. Please include a SASE."

MARGARET BARTLE ANNUAL PLAYWRITING AWARD, Community Children's Theatre of Kansas City, 8021 E. 129th Terrace, Grandview MO 64030. (816)761-5775. Chairperson: Mrs. E. Morley Sellens. Annual contest/award. Estab. 1947. "Community Children's Theatre of Kansas City, Inc. was organized in 1947 to provide live theater for elementary aged children. We are now recognized as being one of the country's largest organizations providing this type of service." Unpublished submissions only. Deadline for entries: end of January. SASE for contest/award rules and entry forms. SASE for return of entries. No entry fee. Awards $500. Judging by a committee of five. "CCT reverves the right for one of the units to produce the prize winning play for two years. The plays are performed before students in elementary schools. Although our 5 to 12 year old audiences are sophisticated, gratuitous violence, mature love stories, or slang are not appropriate – cursing is Not Acceptable. In addition to original ideas, subjects that usually provide good plays are: legends, folklore, historical incidents, biographies, and adaptations of children's classics."

*BAY AREA BOOK REVIEWER'S ASSOCIATION (BABRA), %Chandler & Sharp, 11A Commercial Blvd., Novato CA 94949. (415)883-2353. Fax: (415)883-4280. Contact: Jonathan Sharp. Annual award for outstanding book in children's literature, open to Bay Area authors, northern California from Fresno north. Annaual contest/award. Estab. 1981. "BABRA presents annual awards to Bay Area (northern California) authors annually in fiction, nonfiction, poetry, and children's literature. Purpose is to encourage Bay Area writers and stimulate interest in books and reading." Previously published submissions only. Submissions nominated by publishers; author or agent could also nominate published work. Deadline for entries: December. Send 3 copies of the book to Jonathan Sharp. No entry fee. Awards $100 honorarium and award certificate. Judging by voting members of the Bay Area Book Reviewer's Association. Books that reach the "finals" (usually 3-5 per category) displayed at annual award ceremonies (March or April).

THE IRMA S. AND JAMES H. SIMONTON BLACK BOOK AWARD, Bank Street College of Education, 610 West 112th Street, New York NY 10025. (212)222-6700. Contact: Linda Greengrass. Annual award. Estab. 1972. Purpose of the award: "The award is given each spring for a book for young children, published in the previous year, for excellence of both text and illustrations." Entries must have been published during the previous calendar year. Deadline for entries: January after book is published. "Publishers submit books to us by sending them here to me at the Bank Street library. Authors may ask their publishers to submit their books. Out of these, three to five books are chosen by a committee of older children and adults. These books are then presented to children in selected second, third and fourth grade classes here and at a few other cooperating schools on the East Coast. These children are the final judges who pick the actual award. The award is a scroll (one each for the author and illustrator, if they're different) with the recipient's name and a gold seal designed by Maurice Sendak."

BOOK PUBLISHERS OF TEXAS, Children's/Young People's Award, The Texas Institute of Letters, P.O. Box 9032, Wichita Falls TX 76308-9032. (817)689-4123. Contact: James Hoggard. Send to above address for list of judges to whom entries should be submitted. Annual award. Purpose of the award: "to recognize notable achievement by a Texas writer of books for children or young people or by a writer whose work deals with a Texas subject. The award goes to the author of the winning book, a work published during the calendar year before the award is given. Judges' list available each October. Deadline is first postally operative day of January." Previously published submissions only. SASE for award rules and entry forms. No entry fee. Awards $250. Judging by a panel of three judges selected by the TIL Council. Requirements for entrants: The writer must have lived in Texas for two consecutive years at some time, or the work must have a Texas theme.

THE BOSTON GLOBE-HORN BOOK AWARDS, The Boston Globe & The Horn Book, Inc., The Horn Book, 14 Beacon St., Boston MA 02108. (617)227-1555. Contest/Award Directors: Stephanie Loer and Anita Silvey. Writing Contact: Stephanie Loer, children's book editor for *The Boston Globe*, 298 North St., Medfield MA 02052. Annual contest/award. Estab. 1967. "Awards are for picture books, nonfiction and fiction. Up to three honor books may be chosen for each category." Books must be published between July 1, 1992 through June 30, 1993. Deadline for entries: May 1. "Publishers usually nominate books." Award winners receive $500 and silver engraved bowl, honor book winners receive a silver plate." Judging by three judges involved in children's book field who are chosen by Anita Silvey, editor-in-chief for *The Horn Book* and Stephanie Loer, children's book editor for *The Boston Globe*. "*The Horn Book* publishes speeches given at awards ceremonies. The book must be available/distributed in the U.S. The awards are given at the fall conference of the New England Round Table of Children's Librarians."

BUCKEYE CHILDREN'S BOOK AWARD, State Library of Ohio, 65 S. Front St., Columbus OH 43266-0334. (614)644-7061. Nancy Short, Chairperson. Correspondence should be sent to Floyd C. Dickman at the above address. Award every two years. Estab. 1981. Purpose of the award: "The Buckeye Children's Book Award Program was designed to encourage children to read literature critically, to promote teacher and librarian involvement in children's literature programs, and to commend authors of such literature, as well as to promote the use of libraries. Awards are presented in the following three categories: Grades K-2, Grades 3-5 and Grades 6-8." Previously published submissions only. Deadline for entries: February 1. "The nominees are submitted by this date during the even year and the votes are submitted by this date during the odd year. This award is nominated and voted upon by children in Ohio. It is based upon criteria established in our bylaws. The winning authors are awarded a special plaque honoring them at a banquet given by one of the sponsoring organizations. The BCBA Board oversees the tallying of the votes and announces the winners. The book must have been written by an author, a citizen of the United States and originally copyrighted in the U.S. within the last three years preceding the nomination year. The award-winning books are displayed at the Columbus Metropolitan Library in Columbus, OH."

‡**BYLINE MAGAZINE STUDENT PAGE**, P.O. Box 130596, Edmond OK 73013. (405)348-5591. Contest/Award Director: Marcia Preston, publisher. Estab. 1981. "We offer student writing contests on a monthly basis, September through June, with cash prizes and publication of top entries." Previously unpublished submissions only. Deadline for entries varies. Entry fee varies. Awards cash and publication. Judging by qualified editors and writers. "We publish top entries in student contests. Winners' list published in magazine dated 3 months past deadline." Send SASE for details.

CALDECOTT AWARD, Association for Library Service to Children, division of the American Library Association, 50 E. Huron, Chicago IL 60611. (312)280-2163. Executive Director ALSC: Susan Roman. Annual contest/award. Estab. 1938. Purpose of the contest/award: to honor the artist of the most distinguished picture book for children published in the U.S. (Illustrator must be U.S. citizen.) Must be published year preceding award. Deadline for entries: December. SASE for contest/award rules and entry forms. Entries not returned. No entry fee. "Medal given at ALA Annual Conference during the Newbery/Caldecott Banquet."

*****CALIFORNIA BOOK AWARDS**, The Commonwealth Club of California, 595 Market St., San Francisco CA 94105. (415)597-6700. Directors: James L. Coplan or Annie Hayflick. Annual contest/award. Estab. 1931. Purpose of the contest/award: to promote "the encouragement and production of literature in California." Previously published submissions only. Submissions made by the author or the author's agent. Must be published between January and December of the previous year. Deadline for entries: January 31. SASE for contest/award rules. No entry fee. Award is presentation of a medal. Judging by club jury members, comprised of men and women prominent in academia and other areas related to writing. Requirements for entrants: Illustration is judged in conjunction with prose. Announcement of winners published in Club newsletter.

 The asterisk before a listing indicates the listing is new in this edition.

*CALIFORNIA WRITERS' CONFERENCE AWARDS, California Writers' Club, 2214 Derby St., Berkeley CA 94705. (510)841-1217. "Ask for contest rules before submitting entries." Contest/award offered every two years. Next conference, July 23-25, 1993. Purpose of the contest/award: "the encouragement of writers." Categories: adult fiction, adult nonfiction, juvenile fiction or nonfiction, poetry and scripts. Unpublished submissions only. SASE for contest/award rules and entry forms. SASE for return of entries. Fee possible, but not yet determined. Awards: "First prize in each category is free tuition to the Conference; second and third prizes cash." Judging by "published writer-members of California Writers' Club." Requirements for entrants: "Open to any writer who is not a member of California Writers' Club. Winners in previous contests of California Writers' Club not eligible."

*‡CALIFORNIA YOUNG PLAYWRIGHTS CONTEST, Playwrights Project, P.O. Box 2068, San Diego CA 92112. (619)232-6188. Director: Deborah Salzer. Open to Californians under age 19. Annual contest/award. Estab. 1985. "Our organization, and the contest, are designed to nurture promising young writers. We hope to develop playwrights and audiences for live theater. We also teach playwriting." Submissions required to be unpublished and not produced professionally. Submissions made by the author. Deadline for entries: usually May 1. "Call for exact date." SASE for contest/award rules and entry form. No entry fee. Award is professional productions of 3-5 short plays each year, with a royalty award of $100 per play. Judging by professionals in the theater community, a committee of 5-7; changes somewhat each year. Works performed "in a professional theater in San Diego, most likely the Cassius Carter Centre Stage of the Old Globe Theatre. Writers submitting scripts of 10 or more pages may receive a detailed script evaluation letter if requested."

‡CANADIAN AUTHOR CREATIVE WRITING CONTEST, CA&B/Canadian Authors Association, Suite 500, 275 Slater St., Ottawa, Ontario K1P 5H9 Canada. (613)233-2846. Fax: (613)235-8237. Contest/Award Director: Diane Kerner. Annual contest/award. Estab. 1983. Categories: fiction, nonfiction, poetry. Unpublished submissions only (except in school paper). Deadlines posted on entry forms. Entry form carried in fall and winter issues of *Canadian Author*. Form must come from magazine. "Teacher nominates and may only nominate ONE student." Entries not returned. No entry fee. Awards $100 for each fiction, poetry and nonfiction — teachers get matching award. Judging by *Canadian Author* staff-selected judges. Contest open to high school, private school, college and university students. Works published in summer issue of magazine.

CHILDREN'S BOOK AWARD, Sponsored by Federation of Children's Book Groups. 30 Senneleys Park Rd., Northfield Birmingham B31 1AL England. (021)427-4860. Coordinator: Jenny Blanch. Purpose of the contest/award: "The C.B.A. is an annual prize for the best children's book of the year judged by the children themselves." Categories: (I) picture books, (II) short novels, (III) longer novels. Estab. 1980. Previously unpublished submissions only. Deadline for entries: December 31. SASE for contest rules and entry forms. Entries not returned. Awards "a magnificent silver and oak trophy worth over $6,000 and a portfolio of children's work." Silver dishes to each category winner. Judging by children. Requirements for entrants: Work must be fiction and published during the current year (poetry is ineligible). Work will be published in our current "Pick of the Year" publication.

CHILDREN'S READING ROUND TABLE AWARD, Children's Reading Roundtable of Chicago, 3930 North Pine Grove, #1507, Chicago IL 60613. (312)477-2271. Annual award. Estab. 1953. "Annual award to individual who has made outstanding contributions to children's books. Individual is nominated by membership, and selected by a committee from the membership, and finalized by a special committee of members, as well as nonmembers of CRRT." Awards a recognition certificate and stipend of $250. Award recipients have been authors, editors, educators and illustrators. "Note that our award recognizes *contributions* to children's literature. This includes people who are neither writers nor illustrators."

THE CHRISTOPHER AWARD, The Christophers, 12 E. 48th St., New York NY 10017. (212)759-4050. Christopher Awards Coordinator: Peggy Flanagan. Annual contest/award. Estab. 1969 (for young people; books for adults honored since 1949). "The award is given to works, published in the calendar year for which the award is given, that 'have achieved artistic excellence, affirming the highest values of the human spirit.' They must also enjoy a reasonable degree of popular acceptance." Previously published submissions only; must be published between January 1 and December 31. Deadline for entries: "books should be submitted all year." Entries not returned. No entry fee. Awards a bronze medallion. Books are judged by both reading specialists and young people. Requirements for entrants: "only published works are eligible and must be submitted during the calendar year in which they are first published."

*CITY OF FOSTER CITY WRITERS' CONTEST, Foster City Arts and Culture Committee, 650 Shell Blvd., Foster City CA 94404-2501. Chairman: John Hauer. Annual contest/award. Estab. 1974. Contest open to all writers—no age or geographic limit. Categories include Best Story for Children—2,000 word limit. Unpublished submissions only. Submissions made by the author. Deadline for entries: November 1. SASE for contest/award rules and entry form. Entry fee $10/entry. Award is $300 each category. Judging by Peninsula Press Club—California. No illustrated manuscripts.

THE COMMONWEALTH CLUB'S BOOK AWARDS CONTEST, The Commonwealth Club of California, 595 Market St., San Francisco CA 94105. (415)597-6700. Executive Director: James D. Rosenthal. Annual contest. Estab. 1932. Purpose of the contest is the encouragement and production of literature in California. Juvenile category included. Previously published submission; must be published from January 1 to December 31. Deadline for entries: January 31. SASE for contest rules and entry forms. No entry fee. Awards gold and silver medals. Judging by the Book Awards Jury. The contest is only open to California writers/illustrators. "The award winners will be honored at the Annual Book Awards Luncheon."

‡CRICKET LEAGUE, *Cricket*, the Magazine for Children, 315 5th Street, Peru IL 61354. (815)224-6643. Address entries to: Cricket League. Monthly. Estab. 1973. "The purpose of Cricket League contests is to encourage creativity and give children an opportunity to express themselves in writing, drawing, painting, or photography. There are two contests each month. Possible categories include story, poetry, art, or photography. Each contest relates to a *specific theme* described on each *Cricket* issue's Cricket League page. Entries which do not relate to the current month's theme cannot be considered." Unpublished submissions only. Deadline for entries: the 25th of each month. Cricket League rules, contest themes and submission deadline information can be found in the current issue of *Cricket*. "We prefer that children who enter the contests subscribe to the magazine, or that they read *Cricket* in their school or library." No entry fee. Awards certificate suitable for framing and children's books or art/writing supplies. Judging by *Cricket* Editors. Obtains right to print prize-winning entries in magazine. Requirements for entrants: Any child age 14 or younger can enter. Restrictions of mediums for illustrators: Usually artwork must be black and white only. Refer to contest rules in current *Cricket* issue. Winning entries are published on the Cricket League pages in the *Cricket* magazine 3 months subsequent to the issue in which the contest was announced.

DELACORTE PRESS PRIZE FOR A FIRST YOUNG ADULT NOVEL, Delacorte Press, Books for Young Readers Department, 666 Fifth Ave., Dept BFYR, New York NY 10103. (212)765-6500. Annual award. Estab. 1982. Purpose of the contest/award: To encourage the writing of contemporary young adult fiction. Previously unpublished submissions only. Manuscripts sent to Delacorte Press may not be submitted to other publishers while under consideration for the prize. "Entries must be submitted between Labor Day and New Year's Day of the following year. The real deadline is a December 31 postmark. Early entries are appreciated." SASE for contest/award rules. No entry fee. Awards a $1,500 cash prize and a $6,000 advance against royalties on a hardcover and paperback book contract. Judged by the editors of the Books for Young Readers Dept. of Delacorte Press. Rights acquired "only if the entry wins or is awarded an Honorable Mention." Requirements for entrants: The writer must be American or Canadian and must *not* have previously published a YA novel. He may have published anything else.

Tips: "Books (manuscripts) should have a contemporary setting and be suitable for ages 12-18, and be between 100 and 224 pages long. *Summaries are urgently requested.*"

*VIOLET DOWNEY BOOK AWARD, National Chapter of Canada IODE, Suite 254, 40 Orchard View Blvd., Toronto, Ontario M5R 1B9 Canada. (416)487-4416. Contest/Award Director: Suzanne Williams. Annual contest/award. Estab. 1985. Purpose of the contest/award: to name the best children's book, by a Canadian, published in Canada for ages 5-13, over 500 words. Previously published submissions only. Submissions made by author, author's agent, any one may submit. Must have been published during calendar year 1992. Deadline for entries: Jan. 31, 1993. SASE for contest/award rules and entry forms. No entry fee. Awards $3,000. Judging by a panel of six, four IODE members and 2 professionals.

DREXEL CITATION, Drexel University, College of Information Studies, Philadelphia PA 19104. (215)895-2474. Director: Shelley G. McNamara. Annual award. Purpose of the award: "The Drexel citation is an award that was established in 1963 and has been given at irregular intervals since that time to honor Philadelphia authors, illustrators, publishers or others who have made outstanding contributions to literature for children in Philadelphia. The award is co-sponsored by The Free Library of Philadelphia. The recipient is selected by a committee representing both the College of Information Studies and The Free Library of Philadelphia. There is only one recipient at any given time and that recipient is recognized at an annual conference on children's literature presented each year in the spring on the Drexel campus. The recipient receives an individually designed and hand-lettered citation at a special award luncheon during the conference."

SHUBERT FENDRICH MEMORIAL PLAYWRIGHTING CONTEST, Pioneer Drama Service, Inc., P.O. Box 22555, Denver CO 80222. (303)759-4297. Director: Steven Fendrich. Annual contest/award. Estab. 1990. Purpose of the contest/award: "To encourage the development of quality theatrical material for educational and community theater." Previously unpublished submissions only. Deadline for entries: March 1st. SASE for contest/award rules and entry forms. No entry fee. Awards $1,000 royalty advance and publication. Judging by Editors. All rights acquired when work is published. Restrictions for entrants: Any writers currently published by Pioneer Drama Service are not eligible.

*DOROTHY CANFIELD FISHER CHILDREN'S BOOK AWARD, Vermont Department of Libraries, Vermont State PTA and Vermont Congress of Parents and Teachers, % Southwest Regional Library, Pierpoint Ave., Rutland VT 05701. Chairman (currently): Barbara Ellingson. Annual contest/award. Estab. 1957. Purpose of the contest/award: to encourage Vermont children to become enthusiastic and discriminating readers by providing them with books of good quality by living American authors published in the current year. Previously published entries are not eligible. Deadline for entries: "January of the following year." SASE for contest/award rules and entry forms. No entry fee. Awards a scroll presented to the winning author at an award ceremony. Judging is by the children grades 4-8. They vote for their favorite book. Requirements for entrants: "The book must be copyrighted in the current year. It must be written by an American author living in the U.S."

‡FLORIDA STATE WRITING COMPETITION, Florida Freelance Writers Assoc., P.O. Box 9844, Fort Lauderdale FL 33310. (305)485-0795. Juvenile Chairman: Jean Pollack. Annual contest/award. Estab. 1984. Picture Books/under 6 years: 400 words maximum. Short Fiction: all age groups judged together/ages 7-10 — 400-900 words; ages 12 and up — 2,000 words maximum. Rebus: Picture words circled, no artwork — 400 words maximum. Florida Maritime Heritage Program Award for nonfiction, any age group, about Florida's maritime heritage. Book Chapter, fiction or nonfiction: ages 7-10 — 1,000 words maximum; ages 12 and up — 3,000 words maximum. Previously unpublished submissions only. Entry fee is $5 (members), $7 (non-members). Awards $100 first prize, certificates for second through fifth prizes. Judging by teachers, editors and published authors. Judging criteria: Interest and readability within age group, writing style and mechanics, originality, salability. Deadline: March 15. For copy of official entry form, send #10 SASE.

‡4-H ESSAY CONTEST, American Beekeeping Federation, Inc., P.O. Box 1038, Jesup GA 31545. (912)427-8447. Contest Director: Troy H. Fore. Annual contest. For an essay discussing "New Honey Promotion Ideas." Unpublished submissions only. Deadline for entries: before April 30. No entry fee. 1st place: $250; 2nd place: $100; 3rd place: $50. Judging by American Beekeeping Federation's Essay Committee. "All National entries become the property of the American Beekeeping Federation, Inc., and may be published or used as it sees fit. No essay will be returned. Essayists *should not* forward essays directly to the American Beekeeping Federation office. Each state 4-H office is responsible for selecting the state's winner and should set its deadline so state judging can be completed at the state level in time for the winning state essay to be mailed to the ABF office before April 30, 1993."

DON FREEMAN MEMORIAL GRANT-IN-AID, Society of Children's Book Writers, P.O. Box 66296, Mar Vista Stn., Los Angeles CA 90066. Estab. 1974. Purpose of award: to "enable picture book artists to further their understanding, training and work in the picture gook genre."Applications and prepared materials will be accepted between January 15-February 15. Grant awarded and announced on June 15. SASE for contest/award rules and entry forms. SASE for return of entries. No entry fee. Annually awards one grant of $1,000 and one runner-up grant of $500. "The Grant-In-Aid is available to both full and associate members of the SCBW who, as artists, seriously intend to make picture books their chief contribution to the field of children's literature."

*GOLD MEDALLION BOOK AWARDS, Evangelical Christian Publishers Association, Suite 101, 3225 S. Hardy Dr., Tempe AZ 85282. (602)966-3998. Fax: (602)966-1944. Director: Doug Ross. Annual contest/award. Estab. 1978. Categories include Preschool Children's Books, Elementary Children's Books, Youth Books. "All entries must be evangelical in nature and cannot be contrary to ECPA's Statement of Faith (stated in official rules)." Deadlines for entries: December 1. SASE for contest/award rules and entry form. "The work must be submitted by the publisher." Entry fee is $250 for non-members. Awards a Gold Medallion plaque.

GOLDEN KITE AWARDS, Society of Children's Writers and Illustrators, P.O. Box 66296, Mar Vista Station, Los Angeles CA 90066. (818)347-2849. Coordinator: Sue Alexander. Annual contest/award. Estab. 1973. "The works chosen will be those that the judges feel exhibit excellence in writing, and in the case of the picture-illustrated books—in illustration, and genuinely appeal to the interests and concerns of children. For the fiction and nonfiction awards, original works and single-author collections of stories or poems of which at least half are new and never before published in book form are eligible—anthologies and translations are not. For the picture-illustration awards, the art or photographs must be original works (the texts—which may be fiction or nonfiction—may be original, public domain or previously published). Deadline for entries: December 15. SASE for contest/award rules. Self-addressed mailing label for return of entries. No entry fee. Awards statuettes and plaques. The panel of judges will consist of two children's book authors, a children's book artist or photographer (who may or may not be an author), a children's book editor and a librarian." Requirements for entrants: "Must be a member of SCBW." Works will be displayed "at national conference in August." Books to be entered, as well as further inquiries, should be submitted to: The Society of Children's Book Writers, ℅ Sue Alexander, 6846 McLaren, Canoga Park, CA 91307.

HIGHLIGHTS FOR CHILDREN FICTION CONTEST, 803 Church St., Honesdale PA 18431. (717)253-1080. "Mss should be addressed to Fiction Contest. Editor: Kent L. Brown Jr." Annual contest/award. Estab. 1980. Purpose of the contest/award: to stimulate interest in writing for children and reward and recognize excellence. Unpublished submissions only. Deadline for entries: February 28; entries accepted after January 1 only. SASE for contest/award rules and entry forms. SASE for return of entries. No entry fee. Awards 3 prizes of $1,000 each in cash, (or, at the winner's election, attendance at the Highlights Foundation Writers Workshop at Chautauqua). Judging by *Highlights* editors. Winning pieces are purchased for the cash prize of $1,000 and published in *Highlights*. Requirements for entrants: contest open to any writer. Winners announced in June.
Tips: "This year's contest is for sports stories for children. Length up to 900 words. Stories for beginning readers should not exceed 500 words. Stories should be consistent with *Highlights* editorial requirements. No violence, war, crime or derogatory humor."

‡HOOT AWARDS, WRITING CONTEST, PHOTO CONTEST, POETRY CONTEST, COVER CONTEST, *Owl Magazine,* 56 The Esplanade, Toronto, ON M4V 1G2 Canada. (416)868-6001. Annual contest/award. Purpose of the annual contests/awards: "to encourage children to contribute and participate in the magazine. The Hoot Club Awards recognizes excellence in an individual or group effort to help the environment." Unpublished submissions only. Deadlines change yearly. Prizes/awards "change every year. Often we give books as prizes." Winning entries published in the magazine. Judging by art and editorial staff. Entries become the property of the Young Naturalist Foundation (*Owl Magazine*). "The contests and awards are open to children up to 14 years of age."

AMELIA FRANCES HOWARD-GIBBON MEDAL, Canadian Library Association, Ste. 602, 200 Elgin St., Ottawa ON K2P 1L5 Canada. (613)232-9625. Chairperson, Canadian Association of Children's Librarians. Annual contest/award. Estab. 1971. Purpose of the contest/award: "the main purpose of the award is to honor excellence in the illustration of children's book(s) in Canada. To merit consideration the book must have been published in Canada and its illustrator must be a Canadian citizen or a permanent resident of Canada." Previously published submissions only; must be published between January 1 and December 31. Deadline for entries: February 1. SASE for contest/award rules and entry forms. Entries not returned. No entry fee. Awards a medal. Judging by selection committee of members of Canadian Association of Children's Librarians.

Requirements for entrants: illustrator must be Canadian or Canadian resident. Winning books on display at CLA Headquarters.

*INDIAN PAINTBRUSH BOOK AWARD, Wyoming Library Assoc., P.O. Box 1387, Cheyenne WY 82003. (307)632-7622. Contest/Award Director: Laura Grott. Annual contest/award. Estab. 1986. Purpose of contest/award: to encourage the children of Wyoming to read good books. Previously published submissions only. Deadline for entries: April 1. Books can only be submitted for the nominations list by the children of Wyoming. No entry fee. Awards a plaque. Judging by the children of Wyoming (grades 4-6) voting from a nominations list of 20. Requirements for entrants: only Wyoming children may nominate; books must be published in last 5 years, be fiction, have good reviews; final list chosen by a committee of librarians.

INTERNATIONAL READING ASSOCIATION CHILDREN'S BOOK AWARD, Sponsored by the Institute for Reading Research-International Reading Association, 800 Barksdale Rd., P.O. Box 8139, Newark DE 19714-8139. (302)731-1600. Fax: (302)731-1057. Public Information Associate: Wendy L. Russ. Annual contest/award. "The IRA Children's Book Awards will be given for a first or second book, either fiction or nonfiction, in 2 categories (younger readers: ages 4-10; older readers: ages 10-16+) to 2 authors who show unusual promise in the children's book field." To submit a book for consideration, send 10 copies to: Mary Dupuis, Penn State University, 243 Chambers Building. University Park, PA 16802. Must be published during the calendar year. Deadline for entries: December 1 of each year. SASE for contest/award rules and entry forms. Awards a $1,000 stipend and medal. Award is presented each year at annual convention.

IOWA CHILDREN'S CHOICE AWARD, Iowa Educational Media Association, 9 Coventry Lane #3, Muscatine IA 52761. (319)262-8219. Director: Beth Elshoff. Annual contest/award. Estab. 1979. Purpose of the contest/award: to encourage children to read more and better books; to provide an avenue for positive dialogue between teacher, parent and children about books and authors; to give recognition to those who write books for children. "Writers and illustrators *do not 'enter'* their works themselves. A committee of teachers, librarians and students choose the books that are on the list each year. The list is narrowed down to 20-25 books based on set criteria." The award is unique in that it gives children an opportunity to choose the book to receive the award and to suggest books for the yearly reading list. Deadline for entries: February 15. "Students in grades 3-6 throughout Iowa nominate." Awards a brass-plated school bell. Judging by "students in grades 3-6 throughout Iowa."

*IOWA TEEN AWARD, Iowa Educational Media Association, P.O. Box 524, Holland IA 50642. (319)824-6788. Co-Chairmen: Don Osterhaus. Annual contest/award. Estab. 1983. Previously published submissions only. Purpose of contest/award: to allow students to read high quality literature and to have opportunity to select their favorite from this list. Must have been published "in last 3-4 years." Deadline for entries: August 1. No entry fee. "Media specialists, teachers and students nominate possible entries." Awards a brass apple. Judging by students in 6-9th grades. Requirements: To be of recent publication, so copies can be ordered for media center collections and to be nominated by media specialists on a scale of 1-5. Works displayed "at participating schools in Iowa."

IUPUI YOUTH THEATRE PLAYWRITING COMPETITION AND SYMPOSIUM, Indiana University-Purdue University at Indianapolis, 525 North Blackford Street, Indianapolis IN 46202. (317)274-2095. Director: Dorothy Webb. Entries should be submitted to W. Mark McCreary, Literary Manager. Contest/award every two years. Estab. 1983. Purpose of the contest/award: "To encourage writers to create artistic scripts for young

GET YOUR WORK INTO THE RIGHT BUYERS' HANDS!

You work hard... and your hard work deserves to be seen by the right buyers. With constant changes in the industry, it's difficult to know who those buyers are. That's why you'll want to keep up-to-date with the most current edition of this indispensable market guide.

Totally Updated Each Year

Keep ahead of the changes by ordering *1994 Children's Writer's & Illustrator's Market* today. You'll save yourself the frustration of getting manuscripts and artwork returned in the mail, stamped MOVED: ADDRESS UNKNOWN. And of NOT submitting your work to new listings because you don't know they exist. All you have to do to order the upcoming 1994 edition is complete the attached post card and return it with your payment or charge card information. Order now, and there's one thing that won't change from your *1993 Children's Writer's & Illustrator's Market* -- the price! That's right, we'll send you the 1994 edition for just $18.95. *1994 Children's Writer's & Illustrator's Market* will be published and ready for shipment in February 1994.

Don't let another opportunity slip by...get a jump on the industry with the help of *1994 Children's Writer's & Illustrator's Market*. Order today! You deserve it!

(See other side for more helpful children's writing books)

More Books to Help You Get Published!

The Children's Writer's Word Book
This handy reference book offers everything you need to ensure your writing speaks to your young audience, including word lists, a thesaurus of listed words and reading levels for a variety of synonyms. You'll also find samples of writing for each reading level, and guidelines for sentence length, word usage and theme at each level. 352 pages/$19.95/hardcover

Writing for Children & Teenagers
Filled with practical know-how and step-by-step instruction, including how to hold a young reader's attention, where to find ideas, and vocabulary lists based on age level. This third edition provides all the tips you need to flourish in today's children's literature market. 265 pages/$12.95/paperback

The Children's Picture Book: How to Write It, How to Sell It
If you'd like to try your hand at writing children's picture books, this guide is for you. It answers virtually every question about the writing and selling process: how to choose a subject, plot a story, work with artists and editors, and market your book. Includes advice from professional picture book writers and editors, plus a list of agents who handle picture books.. 189 pages/$19.95/paperback

How to Write & Illustrate Children's Books
A truly comprehensive guide that demonstrates how to bring freshness and vitality to children's text and pictures. Numerous illustrators, writers, and editors contributed their expert advice. 143 pages/$22.50/hardcover

Use the coupon on the other side to order these books today!

audiences. It provides a forum through which each playwright receives constructive criticism of his/her work and where selected writers participate in script development with the help of professional dramaturgs, directors and actors." Unpublished submissions only. Submissions made by author. Deadline for entries: September 1, 1994. SASE for contest/award rules and entry forms. No entry fee. "Awards will be presented to the top ten finalists. Four cash awards of $1,000 each will be received by the top four playwrights of whose scripts will be given developmental work culminating in polished readings showcased at the Symposium held on the IUPUI campus. Major publishers of scripts for young audiences, directors, producers, critics and teachers attend this Symposium and provide useful reactions to the plays. If a winner is unable to be involved in preparation of the reading and to attend the showcase of his/her work, the prize will not be awarded. Remaining finalists will receive certificates." Judging by professional directors, dramaturgs, publishers, university professors. Write for guidelines and entry form.

THE EZRA JACK KEATS NEW WRITER AWARD, Writing Contact: Hannah Nuba, Director, %The New York Public Library Early Childhood Resource and Information Center, 66 Leroy St., New York NY 10014. (212)929-0815. Biennial contest/award. Estab. 1986. Purpose of the contest/award: "Award to writers of books done in the tradition of Ezra Jack Keats that appeal to very young children, capture universal qualities of childhood in a multicultural world and portray strong family relationships." Previously published submissions only: Must be published the year of contest or the year before. Deadline for entries: December. SASE for contest/award rules and entry form. Entries not returned. No entry fee. Awards silver Ezra Jack Keats Medal and $500. "Books that reflect the tradition of Ezra Jack Keats: represent the multicultural nature of the world and extend the child's awareness and understanding of other cultural/ethnic groups; capture the universal qualities of childhood; portray strong family relationships; appeal to children ages 9 and under. The author should have published no more than six books. Picture books are judged on the outstanding features of the the text. Candidates need not be both author and illustrator."

KERLAN AWARD, Kerlan Collection, 109 Walter Library, 117 Pleasant St. SE, University of Minnesota, Minneapolis MN 55455. (612)624-4576. Curator: Karen Nelson Hoyle. Annual award. Estab. 1975. "Given in recognition of singular attainments in the creation of children's literature and in appreciation for generous donation of unique resources to the Kerlan Collection." Previously published submissions only. Deadline for entries: November 1. Anyone can send nominations for the award, directed to the Kerlan Collection. No materials are submitted other than the person's name. No entry fee. Award is a laminated plaque. Judging by the Kerlan Award Committee—three representatives from the University of Minnesota faculty (from the College of Education, the College of Human Ecology, and the College of Liberal Arts); one representative from the Kerlan Collection (ex officio); one representative from the Kerlan Friends; one representative from the Minnesota Library Association. Requirements for entrants: open to all who are nominated. Anyone can submit names. "For serious consideration, entrant must be a published author and/or illustrator of children's books (including young adult fiction) and have donated original materials to the Kerlan Collection."

*CORETTA SCOTT KING AWARD, Coretta Scott King Task Force, Social Responsibility Round Table, American Library Association, 50 E. Huron St., Chicago IL 60611. "The Coretta Scott King Award is an annual award for a book that conveys the spirit of brotherhood espoused by M.L. King, Jr.—and also speaks to the Black experience—for young people. There is an award jury that judges the books—reviewing over the year—and making a decision in January. A copy of an entry must be sent to each juror. Acquire jury list from SRRT office in Chicago."

*JANUSZ KORCZAK AWARDS, Joseph H. and Belle R. Braun Center for Holocaust Studies, Anti-Defamation League, 823 United Nations Plaza, New York NY 10017. (212)490-2525. Fax: (212)867-0779. Contest/Award Director: Dr. Dennis B. Klein. Contest/award usually offered every two years. Estab. 1980. Purpose of contest/award: "The award honors books about children which best exemplify Janusz Korczak's principles of selflessness and human dignity." Previously published submissions only; for 1993, books must have been published in 1992. SASE for contest/award rules and entry forms. No entry fee. Awards $1,000 cash and plaque (first prize); plaque (Honorable Mention). Judging by an interdisciplinary committee of leading scholars, editors, literary critics and educators. Requirements for entrants: Books must meet entry requirements and must be published in English for 1993 or in Polish. No entries are returned. They become the property of the Braun Center. Press release will announce winners.

*LANDERS THEATRE CHILDREN'S PLAYWRITING AWARD, Landers Theatre, 311 E. Walnut, Springfield MO 65806. (417)869-3869. Contact: Mick Denniston. Contest/award offered every two years. Estab. 1992. Purpose of the contest/award: to produce full-fledged mainstage production of new musicals for young audiences. Unpublished submissions only. Submissions made by the author. Deadline for entries: November 1, 1993. SASE for contest/award rules and entry forms. No entry fee. Awards $5,000 plus full production. Judging by theater artistic staff and panel. Performed in a Spring, 1994 production.

‡ELIAS LIEBERMAN STUDENT POETRY AWARD, Poetry Society of America, 15 Gramercy Park, New York NY 10003. (212)254-9628. Contest/Award Director: Elise Paschen. Annual contest/award. Purpose of the contest/award: Award is for the best unpublished poem by a high or preparatory school student (grades 9-12) from the U.S. and its territories. Unpublished submissions only. Deadline for entries: December 31. SASE for contest/award rules and entry forms. Entries not returned. No entry fee. Award: $100. Judging by a professional poet. Requirements for entrants: Contest open to all high school and preparatory students from the U.S. and its territories. School attended, as well as name and address, should be noted. Line limit: none. "The award-winning poem will be included in a sheaf of poems that will be part of the program at the award ceremony, and sent to all PSA members."

MAGAZINE MERIT AWARDS, Society of Children's Book Writers, Suite 159, 323 E. Matilija St., #112, Ojai CA 93023. (805)646-4337. Award Coordinator: Dorothy Leon. Annual award. Estab. 1988. "For outstanding original magazine work for young people published during that year and having been written or illustrated by members of SCBW." Previously published submissions only. Entries must be submitted between January 31 and December 15 of the year of publication. SASE for award rules and entry forms. No entry fee. Must be a SCBW member. Awards plaques and honor certificates for each of the three categories. Judging by a magazine editor and two "full" SCBW members. "Every magazine work for young people by an SCBW member—writer, artist or photographer—is eligible during the year of original publication. In the case of co-authored work, both authors must be SCBW members. Members must submit their own work. Required are: 4 copies each of the published work and proof of publication (may be contents page) showing the name of the magazine and the date of issue." Brochures may be obtained by writing to the address above. The SCBW is a professional organization of writers and illustrators and others interested in children's literature. Membership is open to the general public at large.

‡1993 MANNINGHAM POETRY TRUST STUDENT CONTESTS, National Federation of State Poetry Societies, Inc., Box 607, Green Cove Springs FL 32043. (904)284-0505. Chairman: Robert E. Dewitt. Estab. 1980. Purpose of the contest/award: "two separate contests: grades 6-8; grades 9-12. Poems can have been printed and can have won previous awards. Deadline for entries: April 15, 1993. "Submit one poem neatly typed on standard typewriter paper. Submit one original and one copy. On copy only, type: (1) name (2) complete home mailing address (3) school (4) grade. Student's teacher must certify originality. Awards $50 first; $30 second; $20 third; and five honorable mentions of $5 each. Winners will be announced at the 1993 NFSPS convention, and checks will be mailed shortly beforehand. Send SASE if you wish to receive a winner's list.

VICKY METCALF BODY OF WORK AWARD, Canadian Authors Association, Suite 500, 275 Slater St., Ottawa, ON K1P 5H9 Canada. (613)233-2846. Fax: (613)235-8237. Attn: Awards Chair. Annual contest/award. Estab. 1963. Purpose: to honor a body of work inspirational to Canadian youth. Deadline for entries: December 31. SASE for contest/ award rules and entry forms. Entries not returned. No entry fee. Awards $10,000 and certificate. Judging by panel of CAA-appointed judges including past winners. "The prizes are given solely to stimulate writing for children by Canadian writers," said Mrs. Metcalf when she established the award. "We must encourage the writing of material for Canadian children without setting any restricting formulas."

VICKY METCALF SHORT STORY AWARD, Canadian Authors Association, Suite 500, 275 Slater St., Ottawa, ON K1P 5H9 Canada. (613)233-2846. Fax: (613)235-8237. Attn: Awards Chair. Annual contest/award. Estab. 1979. Purpose: to honor writing by a Canadian inspirational to Canadian youth. Previously published submissions only; must be published between January 1 and December 31. Deadline for entries: December 31. SASE for contest/award rules and entry forms. Entries not returned. No entry fee. Awards $3,000 to Canadian author and $1,000 to editor of winning story if published in a Canadian periodical or anthology. Judging by CAA-selected panel including past winners.

THE MILNER AWARD, Atlanta-Fulton Public Library/Friends of the Atlanta Fulton Public Library, One Margaret Mitchell Square, Atlanta GA 30303. (404)730-1710. Exec. Director: Rennie Jones Davant. Annual contest/award. Estab. 1983. Purpose of the contest/award: "The Milner Award is an annual award to a living American author of children's books. Selection is made by the children of Atlanta voting for their favorite author during Children's Book Week." Previous winners not eligible. "The winning author is awarded a specially commissioned work of the internationally famous glass sculptor, Hans Frabel, and a $1,000 honorarium." Requirements for entrants: "Winner must be an American author, able to appear personally in Atlanta to receive the award at a formal program." No submission process.

‡MISSISSIPPI VALLEY POETRY CONTEST, North American Literary Escadrille, P.O. Box 3188, Rock Island IL 61204. Director: Sue Katz. Annual contest. Estab. 1971. Purpose: "To provide children, students, adults, Sr. Citizens, ethnic groups and teachers the opportunity to express themselves in verse and poetry on a regional and national scale." Categories for adults, and high school, junior high and elementary students. Unpublished submissions only. Deadline for entries: September 15. SASE for contest rules and entry forms. Entry fee of $3 student, $5 adult will cover up to 5 poems submitted. Awards cash from $50-175. Requirements for entrants: Open to any student or adult poet, writer or teacher.

NATIONAL JEWISH BOOK AWARD FOR CHILDREN'S LITERATURE, JCCA Jewish Book Council, 15 E. 26th St., New York NY 10010. (212)532-4949. Awards Coordinator: Dr. Marcia W. Posner. Annual contest/award. Estab. 1950. Previously published submissions only; must be published in 1991 for 1992 award. Deadline for entries: November

19. SASE for contest/award rules and entry forms. Entries not returned. No entry fee. Awards $750. Judging by 3 authorities in the field. Requirements for entrants: contest for best Jewish children's books, published only for ages 8-14. Books will be displayed at the awards ceremony in NYC in June.

NATIONAL JEWISH BOOK AWARD—PICTURE BOOKS, (Marcia & Louis Posner Award), Jewish Book Council, 15 E 26th St., New York NY 10010. (212)532-4949. Awards Coordinator: Dr. Marcia W. Posner. Annual contest/award. Estab. 1980. Previously published submissions only; must be published the year prior to the awards ceremony—1991 for 1992 award. Deadline for entries: November 19. SASE for contest/award rules and entry forms. Entries not returned. No entry fee. Awards $750. Judging by 3 authorities in the field. Requirements for entrants: subject must be of Jewish content, published. Works displayed at the awards ceremony.

‡NATIONAL PEACE ESSAY CONTEST, for high school students, United States Institute of Peace, P.O. Box 27720, Central Station, Washington DC 20038-7720. (202)429-3846. Contest Director: Hrach Gregorian. Annual contest. Estab. 1987. "The writing competition gives students the opportunity to do valuable research and writing on a topic of importance to the future of peace with freedom and justice." "Submissions, instead of being published, can be a classroom assignment"; previously published entries must have appeared between September 1 and February 1, 1992. Deadline for entries: February 1 (postmark deadline). "The opening and closing dates vary only slightly. Interested students, teachers and others may write or call to receive free contest kits. Please do not include SASE." No entry fee. State Level Awards are college scholarships in the following amounts: 1st place $500; 2nd place $250; 3rd place $100. National winners are selected from among the 1st place state winners. National winners receive 1st place $10,000, 2nd $5,000 and 3rd $3,500 in college scholarships. Judging is conducted by education professionals from across the country and by the Board of Directors of the United States Institute of Peace. "All submissions become property of the U.S. Institute of Peace to use at its discretion. The U.S. Institute of Peace may use, at its discretion and without royalty or any limitation, any winning essay. Students grades 9-12 in the U.S., its territories and overseas schools may submit essays for review by completing the application process. Please—no illustrations. National winning essays for each competition will be published by the U.S. Institute of Peace for public consumption."

‡THE 1993 NATIONAL WRITTEN & ILLUSTRATED BY . . . AWARDS CONTEST FOR STUDENTS, Landmark Editions, Inc., P.O. Box 4469, Kansas City MO 64127. (816)241-4919. Contest/Award Director: Teresa Melton. Annual awards contest with 3 published winners. Estab. 1986. Purpose of the contest/award: to encourage and celebrate the creative efforts of students. There are three age categories (6-9 years of age; 10-13; and 14-19). Unpublished submissions only. Deadline for entries: May 1, 1993. Contest rules available for self-addressed, business-sized envelope, stamped with 58¢ postage."Need to send a self-addressed, sufficiently stamped book mailer with book entry" for its return. Entry fee of $1. Prize: "Book is published." Judging by national panel of educators, editors, illustrators and authors. "Each student winner receives a publishing contract allowing Landmark to publish the book. Copyright is in student's name and student receives royalties on sale of book. Books must be in proper contest format and submitted with entry form signed by a teacher or librarian. Students may develop their illustrations

 The double dagger before a listing indicates the contest is for students.

in any medium of their choice, as long as the illustrations remain two-dimensional and flat to the surface of the paper." Works will be published in 1994 in Kansas City, Missouri for distribution nationally and internationally.

THE NENE AWARD, Hawaii Association of School Librarians and Hawaii Library Association, Children and Youth Section, Haleiwa Elementary School, 66-505 Haleiwa Rd., Haleiwa HI 96712. (808)637-4995. Award Director: Janet Yap. Estab. 1964. "The Nene Award was designed to help the children of Hawaii become acquainted with the best contemporary writers of fiction, become aware of the qualities that make a good book and choose the best rather than the mediocre." Previously published submissions only. Books must have been copyrighted not more than six years prior to presentation of award. Work is nominated. Awards Koa plaque. Judging by the children of Hawaii. Books must be fiction, written by a living author, copyrighted not more than six years ago and suitable for children in grades 4, 5 and 6.

NEWBERY MEDAL AWARD, Association for Library Service to Children—division of the American Library Association, 50 E Huron, Chicago IL 60611. (312)280-2163. Executive Director, ALSC: Susan Roman. Annual contest/award. Estab. 1922. Purpose of the contest/award: for the most distinguished contribution to American children's literature published in the U.S. Previously published submissions only; must be published prior to year award is given. Deadline for entries: December. SASE for contest/award rules and entry forms. Entries not returned. No entry fee. Medal awarded at banquet during annual conference. Judging by Newbery Committee.

*THE NOMA AWARD FOR PUBLISHING IN AFRICA, Kodansha Ltd., % Hans Zell Associates, 11 Richmond Rd., P.O. Box 56, Oxford OX1 3EL England. (0865)511428. Telex: 94012872ZELLG. Fax: (0865)793298 or (0865)311534. Secretary of the Managing Committee: Hans M. Zell. Annual contest/award. Estab. 1979. Purpose of contest/ award: To encourage publications of works by African writers and scholars in Africa, instead of abroad, as is still too often the case at present. Categories of books eligible for the Award are scholarly or academic, books for children, literature and creative writing, including fiction, drama and poetry. Previously published submissions only. 1994 Award given for book published in 1993. Deadline for entries: end Feb. 1994. Submissions must be made through publishers. Conditions of entry and submission forms are available from the secretariat. Entries not returned. No entry fee. Award is $5,000. Judging by the Managing Committee (jury): African scholars and book experts and representatives of the international book community. Chairman: Professor Abiola Irele. Requirements for entrants: author must be African, and book published in Africa. "Winning titles are displayed at appropriate international book events."

THE SCOTT O'DELL AWARD FOR HISTORICAL FICTION, 1418 E. 57th St., Chicago IL 60637. Award Director: Mrs. Zena Sutherland. Annual contest/award. Estab. 1981. Purpose of the contest/award: "To promote the writing of historical fiction of good quality." Previously published submissions only; must be published between January 1 and December 31 of each year. Deadline for entries: December 31. "Publishers send books, although occasionally a writer sends a note or a book." SASE for contest/award rules and entry forms. No entry fee. Award $5,000. Requirements for entrants: "Must be published by a U.S. publisher in the preceding year; must be by an American citizen; must be set in the North or South American continent; must be historical fiction."

*‡OHIO GENEALOGICAL SOCIETY ESSAY/ART CONTEST, Ohio Genealogical Society, P.O. Box 2625, Mansfield OH 44906. (419)522-9077. Annual contest. Estab. 1985. Purpose of the contest: "The purpose is to foster an interest in the child's ancestry and heritage. The essay division requires knowledge of proper research techniques, documentation, proper grammar and footnoting. The art division includes paintings, songs, poetry, needlework, photography, etc. and is designed to encourage creativity involving a family's heritage." Unpublished submissions only. Deadline for entries: March 1. SASE for contest rules and entry forms. No entry fee. Monetary awards. OGS reserves the right to print winning essays and photographs of winning art entries. Contestants retain all rights to copyright or any material submitted. Requirements for entrants: "Children submitting entries must be a member of OGS, or child/grandchild/great grandchild of an OGS member if living out of state. All children living in Ohio are eligible to enter, regardless of OGS membership." There are 2 divisions—junior division includes students in third grade through the age of 13; senior division are students over 13 through seniors in high school.

OHIOANA BOOK AWARDS, Ohioana Library Association, 1105 State Departments Bldg., 65 S. Front St., Columbus OH 43215. (614)466-3831. Director: Linda R. Hengst. Annual contest/award. "The Ohioana Book Awards are given to books of outstanding literary quality. Up to 6 Book Awards are given each year. Awards may be given in the categories of: fiction, nonfiction, children's literature, poetry and books about Ohio or an Ohioan. Books must be received by the Ohioana Library during the calendar year prior to the year the Award is given and must have a copyright date within the last two calendar years." Deadline for entries: December 31. SASE for contest/award rules and entry forms. No entry fee. Winners receive citation and glass sculpture. "Any book that has been written or edited by a person born in Ohio or who has lived in Ohio for at least five years" is eligible.

HELEN KEATING OTT AWARD FOR OUTSTANDING CONTRIBUTION TO CHILDREN'S LITERATURE, Church and Synagogue Library Association, P.O. Box 19357, Portland OR 97280. (503)244-6919. Chair of Committee: Lillian Koppin. Annual contest/award. Estab. 1980. "This award is given to a person or organization that has made a significant contribution to promoting high moral and ethical values through children's literature." Deadline for entries: February 1. "Recipient is honored in July during the conference." Awards certificate of recognition and a conference package consisting of registration, meals and housing and a complementary 1 year membership. "A nomination for an award may be made by anyone. It should include the name, address and telephone number of the nominee plus the church or synagogue relationship where appropriate. Nominations of an organization should include the name of a contact person. A detailed description of the reasons for the nomination should be given, accompanied by documentary evidence of accomplishment. The person(s) making the nomination should give his/her name, address and telephone number and a brief explanation of his/her knowledge of the nominee's accomplishments. Elements of creativity and innovation will be given high priority by the judges.

*PEN CENTER USA WEST AWARD FOR CHILDREN'S LITERATURE, PEN Center USA West, Suite 41, 672 S. Lafayette Park Place, Los Angeles CA 90057. (213)365-8500. Contact: Chair of the Awards Committee. Open to published authors. Annual contest/award. Estab. 1982. Purpose of the contest/award: "To recognize the work of published writers who live west of the Mississippi. The 1993 awards are for *books published in 1992.*" Categories include Children's Literature. Previously published submissions only. Submissions made by the author, author's agent or publishers. Deadline for entries: December 31. SASE for contest/award rules. Cash award, at least $500, and plaque. Judging by awards committee.

PLEASE TOUCH MUSEUM BOOK AWARD, Please Touch Museum, 210 N. 21st St., Philadelphia PA 19103. (215)963-0667. Child Development Specialist: Marzy Sykes, Ph.D. Annual award. Estab. 1985. Purpose of the award: "To recognize and encourage the publication of books for young children that are of the highest quality and will aid them in enjoying the process of learning through books. Awarded to a picture book that is particularly imaginative and effective in exploring a concept or concepts with children 36 months or younger." Previously published submissions only. "To be eligible for consideration a book must: (1) Explore and clarify an idea for young children. This could include the concept of numbers, colors, shapes, sizes, senses, feelings, etc. There is no limitation as to format. (2) Be distinguished in both text and illustration. (3) Be published within the last year by an American publisher. (4) Be written by an American author." Deadline for entries: April 30. SASE for award rules and entry forms. No entry fee. Judging by selected jury of children's literature experts, librarians, literacy officials and child development specialists. Education store purchases books for selling at Book Award Celebration Day and throughout the year.

*EDGAR ALLAN POE AWARD, Mystery Writers of America, Inc., 17 E. 47th St., 6th Floor, New York NY 10017. (212)888-8171. Executive Director: Priscilla Ridgway. Annual contest/award. Estab. 1945. Purpose of the contest/award: to honor authors of distinguished works in the mystery field. Previously published submissions only. Submissions made by the author, author's agent; "normally by the publisher." Must be published the year of the contest. Deadline for entries: December 1 "except for works only available in the month of December." SASE for contest/award rules and entry forms. No entry fee. Awards ceramic bust of "Edgar" for winner; scrolls for all nominees. Judging by professional members of Mystery Writers of America (writers). Requirements for entrants: Authors "must have been published/produced. Nominee press release sent after first Wednesday in February. Winner press release sent day of Edgar Banquet, held in late April."

‡PUBLISH-A-BOOK CONTEST, Raintree Steck-Vaughn Publishers. Send written entries: PAB Contest, P.O. Box 27010, Austin TX 78755. Annual contest/award. Estab. 1984. Purpose of the contest/award: to stimulate 4th, 5th and 6th graders to write outstanding stories for children. Unpublished submissions only. Deadline for entries: January 31. SASE for contest/award rules and entry forms. "Entries must be sponsored by a teacher or librarian." Entries not returned. No entry fee. Grand prizes: Raintree will publish four winning entries. Each winner will receive a $500 advance against an author royalty contract and ten free copies of the published book. The sponsor named on each of these entries will receive 20 free books from the Raintree catalog. Honorable mentions: each of the twenty honorable mention writers will receive $25. The sponsor named on each of these entries will receive ten free books from the Raintree Steck-Vaughn catalog. Judging by an editorial team. Contract issued for Grand Prize winners. Payment and royalties paid. Requirements for entrants: contest is open only to 4th, 5th and 6th graders enrolled in a school program in the United States or other countries. Books will be displayed and sold in the United States and foreign markets. Displays at educational association meetings, book fairs. "We also have a separate contest for children in grades 2 and 3, established in 1989. All of the above is the same with the exception of the grades, and number of winners will be one." For information: Contact Elaine-Johnston, (512)795-3217, Fax (512)795-3229.

*THE AYN RAND INSTITUTE'S ANTHEM ESSAY CONTEST, P.O. Box 6099, Dept. DB, Inglewood CA 90312. (310)306-9232. Contest/Award Director: Dr. Michael S. Berliner. Contest Coordinator: Donna Montrezza. Open to students. Annual. Estab. 1992. Purpose of award: "To encourage analytical thinking and writing excellence, and to introduce young people to the philosophic meaning of Ayn Rand's novelette *Anthem*." Deadline: March 30. SASE for contest/award rules and entry forms. No entry fee. Total prizes: $5,000. One first prize of $1,000. Ten second prizes of $200. Twenty third prizes of $100. Judging: All papers are first read by a national testing service in Oakland, CA;

semi-finalist and finalist papers are read by a panel of writers, professors and high school teachers. Rights to submitted or winning entries: Entry becomes property of the Ayn Rand Institute and will not be returned. Open to all 9th and 10th graders in high school. The Institute publishes the winning essay in its fall newsletter.

‡THE AYN RAND INSTITUTE'S *FOUNTAINHEAD* ESSAY CONTEST, The Ayn Rand Institute, P.O. Box 6004, Dept. DB, Inglewood CA 90312. (310)306-9232. Contest Director: Dr. Michael S. Berliner. Annual contest. Estab. 1986. "To introduce high school juniors and seniors to the fiction and nonfiction writings, as well as the ideas, of Ayn Rand, novelist and philosopher. To encourage well-organized, analytic writing; to place issues important to young people, such as independence and integrity, before them." Unpublished submissions only. Deadline for entries: April 15. Contest rules and entry forms available to high school juniors and seniors for SASE. No entry fee. Awards one first prize $5,000 cash; 5 second prizes $1,000 each; 10 third prizes $500 each. Judging by 1) Educational Testing Service, 2) a panel of writers, professors and professional people, 3) winner is selected from top entries by a university professor. Submitted or winning entries become property of the Ayn Rand Institute. Entrant must be in last two years of secondary school. The Institute publishes the winning essay in its newsletter.

‡ANNA DAVIDSON ROSENBERG AWARD FOR POEMS ON THE JEWISH EXPERIENCE, Judah L. Magnes Museum, 2911 Russell St., Berkeley CA 94705. (510)849-2710. Poetry Award Coordinator: P. Friedman. Annual award. Estab. 1986-87. Purpose of the contest/award: to encourage poetry in English on the Jewish experience. Previously unpublished submissions only. Deadline for entries: August 31. SASE for contest/award rules and entry forms by July 31. SASE for list of winners. Awards $100-1st Prize, $50-2nd Prize, $25-3rd Prize; honorable mention certificates; $25 Youth Commendation (poets under 19). Judging by committee of 3. There will be a reading of winners in December at Museum. Prospective anthology of winning entries. Write for entry form and guidelines *first*; entries must follow guidelines and be accompanied by entry form. *Please do not phone.*

CARL SANDBURG LITERARY ARTS AWARDS, Friends of the Chicago Public Library, Harold Washington Library Center, 400 S. State St., Chicago IL 60605. (312)747-4907. Annual contest/award. Categories: fiction, nonfiction, poetry, children's literature. Published submissions only; must be published between June 1 and May 31 (the following year). Deadline for entries: September 1. SASE for contest/award rules. Entries not returned. No entry fee. Awards medal and $1,000 prize. Judging by authors, reviewers, book buyers, librarians. Requirements for entrants: native born Chicagoan or presently residing in the six county metropolitan area. Two copies must be submitted by September 1. All entries become the property of the Friends.

‡THE SCHOLASTIC ART AWARDS, 730 Broadway, New York NY 10003. (212)505-3402. Program Manager: Diane McNutt. Director: Susan Ebersole. Annual award. Estab. 1922. Purpose: encouragement and recognition of student achievement in the visual arts."There are 15 categories: painting, drawing, computer graphics, video, film and animation, 2-D design, 3-D design, mixed media, printmaking, fiber arts and textile design, sculpture, ceramics, jewelry and metalsmithing, photography. Seniors only may submit art and photography portfolios. Awards consist of cash awards, scholarships and prizes. Unpublished submissions only. Some areas have sponsors who conduct a regional preliminary judging and exhibition." SASE for award rules and entry forms. Entry fees and deadlines vary depending on region in which a student lives. Judging by art educators, artists, photographers and art administrators. All publication rights are given to Scholastic Inc. (for one year). Requirements for entrants: students in grades 7-12. National winners work on exhibition during the summer. "Write to The Scholastic Art

Awards, 730 Broadway, New York NY 10003 for information."

‡SCHOLASTIC WRITING AWARDS, Scholastic, Inc., 730 Broadway, New York NY 10003. (212)505-3402. Program Manager: Diane McNutt. Director: Susan Ebersole. Annual award. Estab. 1923. Purpose of award: "Encouragement and recognition of young writers." Open to students in grades 6-12. Group I (Grades 6, 7, 8, 9). Group II— grades 10,11,12. There are 7 categories: short story, short short story, essay/nonfiction/persuasive writing, dramatic script, poetry, humor and science fiction. Seniors only may submit portfolios representing their best group of writing. Awards consist of cash awards, scholarships and prizes. Selected works will be published in Scholastic magazines. Unpublished submissions only. Entires must be postmarked by Janauary 15, 1993 except those from central Pennsylvania. Deadlines are indicated on entry forms. All publication rights are given to Scholastic Inc. for two years. Send SASE for guidelines and entry forms to: The Scholastic Writing Awards, Cooper Station, P.O. Box 665, New York, NY 10276-0665. The Scholastic Writing Awards hold all publishing rights for winning entries for two years.

SCIENCE WRITING AWARD IN PHYSICS AND ASTRONOMY, The American Institute of Physics, 335 E. 45th St., New York NY 10017. (212)661-9404. Contact: Manager, Public Information Division. For information contact the Public Information Division. Annual contest/award. Estab. 1987. Purpose of the contest/award: to stimulate and recognize writing that improves children's understanding and appreciation of physics and astronomy. Previously published submissions only; must be published between October 1 and September 30 (the following year). Deadline for entries: October 10. "Entries may be submitted by the publisher as well as the author." Entries not returned. No entry fee. Awards $3,000 and an engraved chair. Judging by a committee selected by the Governing Board of the AIP. Requirements for entrants: "entries must be articles or books, written in English or English translations, dealing primarily with physics, astronomy or related subjects directed at children, from preschool ages up to fifteen years old. Entries must have been available to and intended for young people. Your signature on submission will constitute your acceptance of the contest rules. Postmarked no later than January 31."

‡SEVENTEEN FICTION CONTEST, 9th Fl., 850 Third Ave., New York NY 10022. Fiction Editor: Joe Bardmann. Annual contest/award. Estab. 1945. Unpublished submissions only. Deadline for entries: April. SASE for contest/award rules and entry forms. Entries not returned. No entry fee. Awards cash prize. Judging by "external readers, in-house panel of editors." If first prize, acquires first North American rights for piece to be published. Requirements for entrants: "Our annual fiction contest is open to anyone between the ages of 13 and 21 on April 30. Submit only original fiction that has never been published in any form other than in school publications. Stories should be between 1,500 and 3,000 words in length (six to twelve pages). All manuscripts must be typed double-spaced on a single side of paper. Submit as many original stories as you like, but each story must include your full name, address, birth date and signature in the top right-hand corner of the first page. Your signature on submission will constitute your acceptance of the contest rules."

CHARLIE MAY SIMON BOOK AWARD, Arkansas Elementary School Council, Arkansas Dept. of Education, #4 Capitol Mall, Room 301B, Little Rock AR 72201. (501)682-4371. Award Director: James A. Hester. Annual contest/award. Estab. 1970. Purpose of contest/award: to promote reading—to encourage reading of quality literature and book discussion. Previously published submissions only; must be published between January 1 and December 31 of calendar year; all books must have recommendations from 3 published sources. "Books are selected based on being published in previous calendar year from time of committee work; *Horn Book* is used as selection guide." No entry fee. Awards a medallion. Contest open to entry by any writer, provided book is printed in year being considered.

*SOCIETY OF MIDLAND AUTHORS AWARDS, Society of Midland Authors, % Jim Bowman, 152 N. Scoville, Oak Park IL 60302-2642. (708)383-7568. Contact: Andrew Patner. Annual contest/award. Estab. 1915. Purpose of contest/award: "To stimulate creative literary effort, one of the goals of the Society. There are seven categories, including children's fiction and children's nonfiction." Previously published submissions only. Submissions made by the author or author's agent. Must be published during calendar year. Deadline for entries: January 15. SASE for contest/award rules and entry forms. No entry fee. Award is plaque given at annual dinner, cash. Judging by panel of three per category, writers for the most part. "Award is for book published in the awards year or play professionally produced in that year for the first time." Author to be currently residing in the Midlands, i.e., Illinois, Indiana, Iowa, Kansas, Michigan, Minnesota, Missouri, Nebraska, North Dakota, South Dakota, Ohio, or Wisconsin.

GEORGE G. STONE CENTER FOR CHILDREN'S BOOKS RECOGNITION OF MERIT AWARD, George G. Stone Center for Children's Books, The Claremont Graduate School, 131 E. 10th St., Claremont CA 91711-6188. (714)621-8000 ext. 3670. Contest/ Award Director: Doty Hale. Annual contest/award. Estab. 1965. Purpose of the contest/ award: given to an author or illustrator of a children's book or for a body of work for the "power to please and expand the awareness of children and teachers as they have shared the book in their classrooms." Previously published submissions only. SASE for contest/award rules and entry forms. Entries not returned. No entry fee. Awards a scroll by artist Richard Beasley. Judging by a committee of teachers, professors of children's literature and librarians. Requirements for entrants: "nominations are made by students, teachers, professors and librarians. Award made at annual Claremont Reading Conference in spring (March)."

*JOAN G. SUGARMAN CHILDREN'S BOOK AWARD, Washington Independent Writers Legal and Educational Fund, Inc., 733 15th St. NW, #220, Washington DC 20005. (202)347-4973. Director: Isolde Chapin. Open to residents of D.C., Maryland, Virginia. Contest/award offered every two years. Estab. 1987. Purpose of contest/award: to recognize excellence in children's literature, ages 1-15. Previously published submissions only. Submissions made by the author or author's agent; publishers. Must be published 1992-93 (for 1994 award). Deadline for entries: January 31, 1994. SASE for contest/award rules and entry forms. No entry fee. Awards $500-1,000. Judging by selected experts in children's books. Requirements for entrants: publication of material; residence in D.C., Maryland or Virginia. Works displayed at reception for award winners.

*SYDNEY TAYLOR BOOK AWARD, Association of Jewish Libraries, %National Foundation of Jewish Culture, 330 7th Ave., New York NY 10001. Chairman: Michlean J. Amir. Annual contest/award. Estab. 1973. Purpose of the contest/award: to "recognize books of quality in the field of Judaic books for children in two categories: picture books for young children, and older children's books." Previously published submissions only. Submissions made by publisher. Must be published January-December of the year being judged. Deadline for entries: February 15. SASE for contest/award rules and entry forms. No entry fee. Awards plaque and $300-500. Judging by a committee of six librarians. Requirements for entrants: "Subject matter must be of Judaic content."

SYDNEY TAYLOR MANUSCRIPT COMPETITION, Association of Jewish Libraries, 15 Goldsmith St., Providence RI 02906. (401)274-1117. Director: Lillian Schwartz. Annual contest. Estab. 1985. Purpose of the contest: "This competition is for unpublished writers of fiction. Material should be for readers aged 8-11 years, with universal appeal that will serve to deepen the understanding of Judaism for all children, revealing positive aspects of Jewish life." Unpublished submissions only. Deadline for entries: January 15. SASE for contest rules and entry forms. No entry fee. Awards $1,000. Judging by qualified judges from within the Association of Jewish Libraries. Requirements for entrants: Must be an unpublished fiction writer. "AJL assumes no responsibility for publication, but hopes this cash incentive will serve to encourage new writers of children's stories with Jewish themes for all children."

‡TIME EDUCATION PROGRAM STUDENT WRITING AND ART COMPETITION, *TIME* Magazine, Time Education Program, Box 1000, Mt. Kisco NY 10549-0010. (800)882-0852. Annual contest. "The aims of this competition are reflective of *TIME* Magazine's basic mission—to communicate ideas and information with intelligence, style and meaning." Previously unpublished submissions only. Deadlines for entries: February 1 of each year. SASE for contest rules and entry forms. No entry fee. Awards for writing: Grand Prize: $5,000 scholarship; First Prize: $2,500 scholarship; 2 Awards for Excellence: $1,000 scholarship each. Awards for Cover Art: Grand Prize: $5,000; First Prize: $2,500; 2 Awards for Excellence: $1,000 each. Awards for Cartoon Art: Grand Prize: $5,000; First Prize: $2,500; 2 Awards for Excellence; $1,000 each. Judging by *TIME* editorial staffers and educators. Rights to submitted material acquired or purchased. Open to any high school or college student in the U.S. or Canada. "Submissions must be no larger than 11 × 17; original 2 dimensional pieces." Works published in May 1993 issue of *TimeLines*.

‡VEGETARIAN ESSAY CONTEST, The Vegetarian Resource Group, P.O. Box 1463, Baltimore MD 21203. (410)366-VEGE. Address to Vegetarian Essay Contest. Annual contest. Estab. 1985. Unpublished submissions only. Deadline for entries: May 1 of each year. SASE for contest rules and entry forms. No entry fee. Awards $50 savings bond. Judging by awards committee. Acquires right for The Vegetarian Resource' Group to reprint essays. Requirements for entrants: ages 19 and under. Winning works may be published in Vegetarian Journal, instructional materials for students. "Submit 2-3 page essay on any aspect of vegetarianism, which is the abstinence of meat, fish and fowl. Entrants can base paper on interviewing, research or personal opinion. Need not be vegetarian to enter."

*‡VERY SPECIAL ARTS YOUNG PLAYWRIGHTS PROGRAM, Very Special Arts Education Office, John F. Kennedy Center for the Performing Arts, Washington D.C. 20566. (202)628-2800. Janet Rice Elman, Program Manager. Annual contest/award. Estab. 1984. "All scripts must address or incorporate some aspect of disability." Unpublished submissions only. Deadline changes each year according to production date. Write to Young Playwrights Coordinator for contest/award rules and entry forms. No entries returned. No entry fee. Judging by Artists Selection Committee. "Very Special Arts retains the rights for videotaping and broadcasting on television and/or radio." Requirements for entrants: Scripts must be written by students between the ages of 12 and 18. "Script will be selected for production at the John F. Kennedy Center for the Performing Arts, Washington D.C."

Market conditions are constantly changing! If you're still using this book and it is 1994 or later, buy the newest edition of Children's Writer's & Illustrator's Market at your favorite bookstore or order directly from Writer's Digest Books.

THE STELLA WADE CHILDREN'S STORY AWARD, *Amelia* Magazine, 329 E St., Bakersfield CA 93304. (805)323-4064. Editor: Frederick A. Raborg, Jr. Annual contest/award. Estab. 1988. Purpose of the contest/award: "with decrease in the number of religious and secular magazines for young people, the juvenile story and poetry must be preserved and enhanced." Unpublished submissions only. Deadline for entries: August 15. SASE for contest/award rules. Entry fee is $5 per adult entry; there is no fee for entries submitted by young people under the age of 17, but such entry must be signed by parent, guardian or teacher to verify originality. Awards $125 plus publication. Judging by editorial staff. Previous winners include Maxine Kumin and Sharon E. Martin. "We use First North American serial rights only for the winning manuscript." Contest is open to all interested. If illustrator wishes to enter only an illustration without a story, the entry fee remains the same. Illustrations will also be considered for cover publication. Restrictions of mediums for illustrators: no restrictions, though submitted photos should be no smaller than 5 × 7. Illustrations (drawn) may be in any medium. "Winning entry will be published in the most appropriate issue of either *Amelia*, *Cicada* or *SPSM&H* — subject matter would determine such. Submit clean, accurate copy."

WASHINGTON POST/CHILDREN'S BOOK GUILD AWARD FOR NONFICTION, % Patricia Markun, 4405 "W" St. NW, Washington DC 20007. (202)965-0403. Annual contest/award. Estab. 1977. Purpose of contest: "to encourage nonfiction writing for children of literary quality. Awarded for the body of work of a leading American nonfiction author." No entry fee. Awards $1000 and an engraved crystal cube (paperweight). Judging by a jury of Children's Book Guild librarians and authors and a *Washington Post Book World* editor. "One doesn't enter. One is selected."

‡WE ARE WRITERS, TOO!, Creative With Words Publications, P.O. Box 223226, Carmel CA 93922. Contest/Award Director: Brigitta Geltrich. Annual contest/award. Estab. 1975. Unpublished submissions only. Deadline for entries: June 15 and December 31. SASE for contest/award rules and entry forms. SASE for return of entries "if not winning poem." No entry fee. Awards publication is an anthology. Judging by selected guest editors and educators. Contest open to children only (up to and including 19 years old). Writer should request contest rules. SASE with all correspondence. "Age of child must be stated and manuscript must be verified of its authenticity."

WESTERN HERITAGE AWARDS, National Cowboy Hall of Fame, 1700 NE 63rd St., Oklahoma City OK 73111. (405)478-2250. Director of Public Relations: Dana Sullivant. Annual contest/award. Estab. 1961. Purpose of the contest/award: The WHA is presented annually to encourage the accurate and artistic telling of great stories of the West. Categories include fiction, nonfiction, children's books, poetry. Must have been published in previous contest year. Previously published submissions only; must be published the calendar year before the awards are presented. Deadline for entries: December 31. SASE for contest/award rules and entry forms. Entries not returned. No entry fee. Awards a Wrangler award. Judging by a panel of judges selected each year with distinction in various fields of western art and heritage. Requirements for entrants: the material must pertain to the development or preservation of the West, either from a historical or contemporary viewpoint. Historical accuracy is vital. There is an autograph party preceding the awards. Film clips are shown during the awards presentation.

LAURA INGALLS WILDER AWARD, Association for Library Service to Children — a division of the American Library Association, 50 E. Huron, Chicago IL 60611. (312)280-2163. Executive Director, ALSC: Susan Roman. Contest/award offered every 3 years. Purpose of the contest/award: to recognize an author or illustrator whose books, published in the U.S., have over a period of years made a substantial and lasting contribution to children's literature. Awards a medal. Judging by committee which chooses several authors—winner is chosen by vote of ALSC membership.

*‡PAUL A. WITTY OUTSTANDING LITERATURE AWARD, International Reading Association, Special Interest Group, Reading for Gifted and Creative Learning, School of Education, P.O. Box 32925, Fort Worth TX 76129. (817)921-7660. Contest/Award Director: Dr. Cathy Collins Block. Annual contest/award. Estab. 1979. Categories of entries: poetry/prose at elementary, junior high and senior high levels. Unpublished submissions only. Deadline for entries: February 1. SASE for contest/award rules and entry forms. SASE for return of entries. No entry fee. Awards $25 and plaque, also certificates of merit. Judging by 2 committees for screening and awarding. Works will be published in Reading Association publications. "The elementary students' entries must be legible and may not exceed 1,000 words. Secondary students' prose entries should be typed and may exceed 1,000 words if necessary. At both elementary and secondary levels, if poetry is entered, a set of 5 poems must be submitted. All entries and requests for applications must include a self-addressed, stamped envelope."

PAUL A. WITTY SHORT STORY AWARD, International Reading Association, 800 Barksdale Rd., P.O. Box 8139, Newark DE 19714-8139. (302)731-1600. Chair of Committee: Barbara D. Stoodt, 5011 Manning Dr., Greensboro NC 27410. Annual contest. Estab. 1986. Purpose of award: "The entry must be an original short story appearing in a young children's periodical that regularly publishes short stories for children. (These would be periodicals generally aimed at readers to about age twelve.) The awarded short story should serve as a reading and literary standard by which readers can measure other writing and should encourage young readers to read by providing them with enjoyable and profitable reading." Previously published submissions only. Deadline for entries: "The entry must have been published for the first time in the eligibility year; the short story must be submitted during the calendar year of publication; thus a story will be considered but one time; the story may be entered into the award competition by its publisher. A story may be entered into the competition by members of the subcommittee or other members of IRA. Anyone wishing to nominate a short story should send it to the designated Paul A. Witty Short Award Subcommittee Chair by November 15. The chair will then request that the publisher send ten copies of the story in manuscript form by the stated deadline. Both fiction and nonfiction writing are eligible; each will be rated according to characteristics that are appropriate for the genre." Interested authors should send inquiry to Barbara D. Stoodt. Award is $1,000 and recognition at the annual IRA Convention. Deadline for completed entries to the subcommittee chair is December 15.

ALICE LOUISE WOOD OHIOANA AWARD FOR CHILDREN'S LITERATURE, Ohioana Library Association, 1105 State Departments Bldg., 65 S. Front St., Columbus OH 43215. (614)466-3831. Director: Linda R. Hengst. Annual award. Estab. 1991. Purpose of the award: "Award of $1,000 to an Ohio author whose body of work has made, and continues to make, a significant contribution to literature for children or young adults." SASE for award rules and entry forms. Requirements for entrants: "Born in Ohio, or lived in Ohio for a minimum of five years; established a distinguished publishing record of books for children and young people; body of work has made, and continues to make, a significant contribution to the literature for young people; through whose work as a writer, teacher, administrator, or through community service, interest in children's literature has been encouraged and children have become involved with reading."

WORK-IN-PROGRESS GRANTS, Society of Children's Book Writers & Illustrators, P.O. Box 66296, Mar Vista Station, Los Angeles CA 90066. Annual contest. "The SCBW Work-In-Progress Grants have been established to assist children's book writers in the completion of a specific project." Five categories: 1. General Work-In-Progress Grant. 2. Grant for a Contemporary Novel for Young People. 3. Nonfiction Research Grant. 4. Grant for a work whose author has never had a book published. 5. Grant for a picture book writer. Requests for applications may be made beginning October 1. Completed applications accepted February 1-May 1 of each year. SASE for applications for grants. In any year, an applicant may apply for any of the grants except the one awarded for a work whose author has never had a book published. (The recipient of this grant will be chosen from entries in all categories.) Five grants of $1,000 will be awarded annually. Runner-up grants of $500 (one in each category) will also be awarded. "The grants are available to both full and associate members of the SCBW. They are not available for projects on which there are already contracts." Previous recipients not eligible to apply.

YOUNG PEOPLE'S LITERATURE AWARDS, Friends of American Writers, 1634 N. Wood St., Chicago IL 60622. (312)235-2686. Chairperson: Ms. Marianne Duignan. Annual award. Estab. 1960. Purpose: "To encourage neophyte writers of quality prose for young readers." Previously published submissions only. Deadline for entries: December 15. "At maximum, the entry must be the third published prose work by the writer. To receive an award in 1993, publication must have been in 1992." SASE for awards rules and entry forms. No entry fee. Awards cash of at least $400 to the writer; certificate of merit to the publisher.

YOUNG READER'S CHOICE AWARD, Pacific Northwest Library Association, 133 Suzzallo Library, FM-30, University of Washington, Graduate School of Library and Information Science, Seattle WA 98195. (206)543-1897. Secretary: Carol Doll. Award Director: Named annually. Annual contest/award for published authors. Estab. 1940. Purpose of the contest/award: "To promote reading as an enjoyable activity and to provide children an opportunity to endorse a book they consider an excellent story." Previously published submissions only; must be published 3 years before award year. Deadline for entries: February 1. SASE for contest/award rules and entry forms. No entry fee. Awards a silver medal, struck in Idaho silver. "Children vote for their favorite (books) from a list of titles nominated by librarians, teachers, students and other interested persons."

*THE ANNA ZORNIO MEMORIAL CHILDREN'S THEATER PLAYWRITING AWARD, University of New Hampshire Theater Resource for Youth Program, Department of Theater and Dance, Paul Creative Arts Center, University of New Hampshire, Durham NH 03824. Contact: Carol Lucha-Burns. Annual contest/award. Estab. 1979. Purpose of the contest/award: "to honor the late Anna Zornio, an alumna of The University of New Hampshire, for dedication to and inspiration of children's theater playwriting." Unpublished submissions only. Submissions made by the author. Deadline for entries: April 15 (subject to change). SASE for contest/award rules and entry forms. No entry fee. Awards $250 plus guaranteed production. Judging by faculty committee. Acquires rights to campus production. Requirements for entrants: Open to all playwrights in the U.S. and Canada. Write for details.

Resources

Clubs/Organizations

Children's writers and illustrators can benefit from contacts made through organizations such as the ones listed in this section. Professional organizations provide a writer or artist with a multitude of educational, business and legal services. Much of these services come in the form of newsletters, workshops or seminars that provide tips about how to be a better writer or artist, types of business records to keep, health and life insurance coverage you should carry or organizational competitions to be aware of.

You will notice that some of these organizations welcome anyone with an interest, while others are open to professionals only. Still, others have varying levels of membership such as the Society of Children's Book Writers & Illustrators. SCBWI offers associate memberships to those with no publishing credits. Those who have had work for children published are full members. Feel free to write for more information regarding any group that sounds interesting. Be sure to inquire about membership qualifications as well as services offered to members.

An added benefit to being a member of an organization includes being able to network with others with similar interests, creating a support system to help you through tight creative and financial periods. Important contacts can be made through your peers, and as it is in any business, knowing the right people can definitely help your career. Membership in a writer's or artist's group also presents to a publisher an image of being serious about your craft. Of course, this provides no guarantee that your work will be published, but it offers an added dimension of credibility and professionalism.

*AMERICAN ALLIANCE FOR THEATRE & EDUCATION, Theatre Dept., Arizona State University, Tempe AZ 85287-3411. (602)965-6064. Administrative Director: Katherine Krzys. Purpose of organization: to promote standards of excellence in theater and drama/theater education by providing the artist and educator with a network of resources and support, a base for advocacy, and access to programs and projects that focus on the importance of drama in the human experience. Membership cost: $68 annually for individual in U.S. and Canada, $75 annually for foreign, $95 annually for organization, $38 annually for students, $48 annually for retired people. Annual conference in Boston, August 4-8, 1993. Newsletter published quarterly, must be member to subscribe. Contests held for unpublished play reading project and annual awards for best play for K-8 and one for secondary audience. Award plaque and stickers for published playbooks. Published list of unpublished plays deemed worthy of performance in newsletter and press release.

ARIZONA AUTHORS ASSOCIATION, 3509 E. Shea Blvd., #117, Phoenix AZ 85028-3339. (602)996-9706. President: Gerry Benninger. Purpose of organization: Membership organization offering professional, educational and social opportunities to writers and authors. Membership cost: $40/yr. professional and associate; $50/yr. affiliate; $25/yr. student. Different levels of membership include: Professional: published writers; Associate: writers working toward publication; Affiliate: professionals in publishing industry; student: full-time students. Workshops/conferences: monthly educational workshops; contact office for current calendar. Newsletter provides information useful to writers (markets, book reviews, calendar of meetings and events) and news about members. Non-member subscription $25/yr. Sponsors Annual Literary Contest. Awards include total of $1,000 in prizes in several categories. Contest open to non-members.

ASSITEJ/USA, New Stagings for Youth, 270 West 89th St., New York NY 10024. (212)769-4141. Editor, TYA TODAY: Amie Brockway. Purpose of organization: service organization for theaters focused on productions for young audiences. Also serves as US Center for International Association of Theatre for Children and Young People. Membership Cost: $100 for organizations with budgets below $99,999; $200 for organizations with budgets of $100,000-$399,999; $300 for organizatons with budgets over $400,000; $50 annually/individual; $25 students and retirees; $65 for foreign organizations or individuals; $30 for library rate. Different levels of membership include: organizations, individuals, students, retirees, corresponding, library rates. Sponsors workshops or conferences. Publishes newsletter that focuses on information on field in US and abroad.

THE AUTHORS GUILD, 29th Floor, 330 W. 42nd St., New York NY 10036-6902. (212)563-5904. Executive Director: Helen Stephenson. Purpose of organization: membership organization of 6,700 members that offers services and information materials intended to help authors with the business and legal aspects of their work, including contract problems, copyright matters, freedom of expression and taxation. Qualifications for membership: book author published by an established American publisher within 7 years or any author who has had three works, fiction or nonfiction, published by a magazine or magazines of general circulation in the last 18 months. Associate membership also available. Annual dues: $90. Different levels of membership include: associate membership with all rights except voting available to an author who has work in progress but who has not yet met the qualifications for active membership. This normally involves a firm contract offer from a publisher. Workshops/conferences: "The Guild and Authors League of America conduct several symposia each year at which experts provide information, offer advice, and answer questions on subjects of interest and concern to authors. Typical subjects have been the rights of privacy and publicity, libel, wills and estates, taxation, copyright, editors and editing, the art of interviewing, standards of criticism and book reviewing. Transcripts of these symposia are published and circulated to members." Symposia open to members only. "The *Author's Guild Bulletin*, a quarterly journal, contains articles on matters of interest to writers, reports of Guild activities, contract surveys, advice on problem clauses in contracts, transcripts of Guild and League symposia, and information on a variety of professional topics. Subscription included in the cost of the annual dues."

THE AUTHORS RESOURCE CENTER, Box 64785, Tucson AZ 85740-1785. (602)325-4733. Executive Director: Martha R. Gore. Purpose of organization: to help writers understand the business and professional realities of the publishing world—also have literary agency (opened March 1, 1987) that markets members' books to publishers. Qualifications for membership: serious interest in writing or cartooning. Membership cost: $60 per year for aspiring and published members. "Professional development workshops are open to members at a discount and to the general public. TARC instructors are actively publishing and often have academic credentials. The *Tarc Report* is published bimonthly and includes information about markets, resources, legal matters, writers workshops, reference sources, announcement of members' new books, reviews and other news important to members. Subscription included in membership fee. *TARC* was established in 1984. Interested only in books for people of color."

*CALIFORNIA WRITERS' CLUB, 2214 Derby St., Berkeley CA 94705. (510)841-1217. Secretary: Dorothy V. Benson. Purpose of organization: "We are a nonprofit professional organization open to writers to provide writing and market information and to promote fellowship among writers." Qualifications for membership: "publication for active members; expected publication in five years for associate members." Membership cost: entry fee, $20; annual dues $25. (Entry fee is paid once.) Workshops/conferences: "Biennial summer conference, July 23-25, 1993, at Asilomar, Pacific Grove, CA; other conferences are held by local branches as they see fit." Conferences open to nonmembers. "Newsletter, which goes out to all CWC members, to newspapers and libraries, publishes the monthly meetings upcoming in the eight branches, plus the achievements of members, and market and contest opportunities." Sponsors contest. CWC's "major contest is for nonmembers, every two years, and first prize in each of 5 categories is free tuition to the biennial conference; second and third prizes are cash."

CANADIAN AUTHORS ASSOCIATION, 275 Slater St. #500, Ottawa, Ontario K1P 5H9 Canada. (613)233-2846. Fax: (613)235-8237. Contact: National Director. Membership is divided into two categories for individuals: Member (voting): Persons engaged in writing in any genre who have produced a sufficient body of work; Associate (nonvoting): Persons interested in writing who have not yet produced sufficient material to qualify for full membership, or those who, though not writers, have a sincere interest in Canadian literature. Persons interested in learning to write may join the Association for one year at a reduced rate. Membership cost: $100 members, $100-associates, $60-introductory rate. Workshops/conferences: 72nd Annual Conference, June 17-20, 1993 in Vancouver, B.C. "The conference draws writers, editors and publishers together in a congenial atmosphere providing seminars, workshops, panel discussions, readings by award-winning authors, and many social events." Open to nonmembers. Publishes a newsletter for members only. Also publishes a quarterly journal and a bienniel writer's guide available to nonmembers. "The Association created a major literary award program in 1975 to honor writing that achieves literary excellence without sacrificing popular appeal. The awards are in four categories—fiction, (for a full-length novel); nonfiction (excluding works of an instructional nature); poetry (for a volume of the works of one poet); and drama (for a single play published or staged). The awards consist of a handsome silver medal and $5,000 in cash; they are funded by Harlequin Enterprises, the Toronto-based international publisher." Contest open to nonmembers. Also contests for writing by students and for young readers (see Vicky Metcalf and Canadian Author awards); sponsors Air Canada Awards.

*CANADIAN SOCIETY OF CHILDREN'S AUTHORS, ILLUSTRATORS AND PERFORMERS, (CANSCAIP), P.O. Box 280, Station L, Toronto ON M4S 2HS Canada. (416)654-0903. Secretary: Bernice Bacchus. Purpose of organization: development of Canadian children's culture and support for authors, illustrators and performers working in this field. Qualifications for membership: *Members*—professionals who have been published (not self-published) or have paid public performances/records/tapes to their credit. *Friends*—share interest in field of children's culture. Membership cost: no initial dues but members' fees due each January. Currently, members' dues—$50 annually; friends'—$20; (friends) institutions'—$25. Sponsors workshops/conferences. Publishes

The asterisk before a listing indicates the listing is new in this edition.

newsletter: profiles of members; news round-up of members' activities countrywide; market news; news re awards, grants, etc; columns related to professional concerns.

THE CHILDREN'S BOOK COUNCIL, INC., 568 Broadway, New York NY 10012. (212)966-1990. Purpose of organization: "A nonprofit trade association of children's and young adult publishers, CBC promotes the enjoyment of books for children and young adults, and works with national and international organizations to that end. The CBC has sponsored National Children's Book Week since 1945." Qualifications for membership: Trade publishers of children's and young adult books are eligible for membership. Membership cost: "Individuals wishing to receive mailings from the CBC (our semi-annual newsletter, CBC FEATURES, and our materials brochures) may be placed on our mailing list for a one-time-only fee of $45. Publishers wishing to join should contact the CBC for dues information." Sponsors workshops and conferences. Publishes a newsletter with articles about children's books and publishing. Listings of free or inexpensive materials from publishers.

CHILDREN'S READING ROUND TABLE OF CHICAGO, #1507, 3930 N. Pine Grove, Chicago IL 60613. (312)477-2271. Information Chairperson: Marilyn Singer. Purpose of organization: "to support activities which foster and enlarge children and young adults' interest in reading and to promote good fellowship among persons actively interested in the field of children's books." Qualifications for membership: "Membership is open to anyone interested in children's books. There are no professional qualifications; however, the majority of our members are authors, freelance writers, illustrators, librarians, educators, editors, publishers and booksellers." Membership cost: $15 for year (July 1 through June 30), applicable to members within our Chicago meeting area; Associate Membership $10, limited to persons outside the Metropolican Chicago Area or who are retired. "All members have same privileges, which include attendance at meetings; newsletter, *CRTT Bulletin*; yearbook published biennially; and access to information about CRRT special activities." Workshops/conferences: Children's Reading Round Table Summer Seminar for Writers & Illustrators, given in odd-numbered years. The 2-day seminar, at a Chicago college campus, usually in August, features guest speakers and a variety of profession-level workshops, manuscript critiquing and portfolio appraisal. Enrollment is open to members and nonmembers; one fee applicable to all. Meals included, housing extra. Also, Children's Reading Round Table Children's Literature Conference, given in even-numbered years. One-day program, at a Chicago college campus, usually in early September. Program includes guest authors and educators, variety of workshops, exhibits, bookstore, lunch. Enrollment open to members and nonmembers; one fee applicable to all. *CRRT Bulletin, Children's Reading Round Table of Chicago* is published seven times a year, in advance of dinner meetings, and contains articles; book reviews; special sections of news about authors and artists, librarians and educators, publishers and booksellers. An Opportunity Column provides information about professional meetings, workshops, conferences, generally in the Midwest area. The *Bulletin* is available to members on payment of dues. Sample copies may be requested. Awards: "We do give an honorary award, the Children's Reading Round Table Annual Award, *not* for a single book or accomplishment but for long-term commitment to children's literature. Award includes check, lifetime membership, plaque. Nominations can be made *only* by CRRT members; nominees are not limited to membership."

CHRISTIAN WRITERS GUILD, 260 Fern Lane, Hume Lake CA 93628. (209)335-2333. Director: Norman B. Rohrer. Purpose of organization: a 48-unit home study, 3-year correspondence course. Qualifications for membership: the ability to think clearly and a commitment to editorial communication. Membership cost: $495 total: $35 down, $15/month. Different levels of membership. "One can join for $45 annually to receive help on his or her editorial projects." Sponsors workshops and conferences. "Conference held at Hume Lake each year for certain in July, then elsewhere as we have invitations." Publishes a small sheet called the "Quill o' the Wisp."

*EDUCATION WRITERS ASSOCIATION, 1001 Connecticut Ave. NW, Washington DC 20036. (202)429-9680. Assistant Director: Bert Menninga. Purpose of organization: professional association of education reporters. Qualifications for membership: primarily engaged in education writing. Membership cost: $50—annually. Levels of membership include: Active (working press); associate—$50. Foundation; institutional—$250. Sponsors workshops/conferences. Publishes *Education Reporter*—national newsletter pertinent to education reporters; and *High Strides*—urban middle grades. Nonmembers may subscribe. Subscription $50; $45 (H.S.). Sponsors National A contest. Awards include $250 1st prizes in 17 categories; plaques, certificates; $1,000 grand prize. Contest open to nonmembers.

FLORIDA FREELANCE WRITERS ASSOCIATION, P.O. Box 9844, Fort Lauderdale FL 33310. (305)485-0795. Executive Director: Dana K. Cassell. Purpose of organization: to act as a link between Florida writers and buyers of the written word; to help writers run more effective communications businesses. Qualifications for membership: "None—we provide a variety of services and information, some for beginners and some for established pros." Membership cost: $90/year. Sponsors annual conference held third weekend in May. Publishes a newsletter focusing on market news, business news, how-to tips for the serious writer. Non-member subscription: $39—does not include Florida section—includes national edition only. Sponsors contest: annual deadline March 15. Guidelines available fall of year. Categories: juvenile, adult nonfiction, adult fiction, poetry. Awards include cash for top prizes, certificate for others. Contest open to nonmembers.

GRAPHIC ARTISTS GUILD, 11 West 20th St., New York NY 10011. (212)463-7730. Executive Director: Paul Basista. Purpose of organization: "To unite within its membership all professionals working in the graphic arts industry; to improve the economic and social conditions of professional artists and designers; to improve industry standards." Qualification for full membership: 51% of income derived from artwork. Associate members include those in allied fields, students and retirees. Initiation fee: $25. Full memberships $100-175/year. Associate membership $55-95/year. Sponsors "Eye to Eye," a national conference exploring the relationships between artists/artists and artists/clients. Publishes *Graphic Artists Guild Handbook, Pricing and Ethical Guidelines*. "Advocates the advancement and protection of artists' rights and interests."

THE INTERNATIONAL WOMEN'S WRITING GUILD, P.O. Box 810, Gracie Station, New York NY 10028. (212)737-7536. Executive Director & Founder: Hannelore Hahn. IWWG is "a network for the personal and professional empowerment of women through writing." Qualifications: open to any woman connected to the written word regardless of professional portfolio. Membership cost: $35 annually; $45 annually for foreign members. "IWWG sponsors 13 annual conferences a year in all areas of the U.S. The major conference is held in August of each year at Skidmore College in Saratoga Springs NY. It is a week-long conference attracting more than 300 women internationally." Also publishes a 28-page magazine, *Network*, 6 times/year; offers health insurance at group rates.

*THE JEWISH PUBLICATION SOCIETY, 1930 Chestnut St., Philadelphia PA 19103-4599. (215)564-5925. Editor-in-Chief: Dr. Ellen Frankel. Children's Editor: Bruce Black. Purpose of organization: "to publish quality Jewish books and to promote Jewish culture and education. We are a non-denominational, nonprofit religious publisher. Our children's list specializes in fiction and nonfiction with substantial Jewish content for preschool through young adult readers." Qualifications for membership: "One must purchase a membership of at least $25 which entitles the member to purchase a certain unit number of our books. Our membership is nondiscriminatory on the basis of religion, ethnic affiliation, race or any other criteria." Levels of membership include: JPS member, $25; Associate, $50; Friend, $100; Fellow, $125; Senior member, $200; Sustaining member, $500. "The *JPS Bookmark* reports on JPS Publications; activities of members, authors and trustees; JPS projects and goals; JPS history; children's books and activities." All members receive *The Bookmark* with their membership.

LEAGUE OF CANADIAN POETS, 24 Ryerson Ave., Toronto, Ontario M5T 2P3 Canada. (416)363-5047. Fax: (416)860-0826. Executive Director: Edita Petrauskaite. President: Blaine Marchand. Inquiries to Administrative Assistant: Clive Thompson. The L.C.P. is a national organization of published Canadian poets. Our constitutional objectives are to advance poetry in Canada and to promote the professional interests of the members. Qualifications for membership: full — publication of at least one book of poetry by a professional publisher; associate membership — an active interest in poetry, demonstrated by several magazine/periodical publication credits. Membership fees: full — $175/year, associate — $60. Holds an Annual General Meeting every spring; some events open to nonmembers. "We also organize reading programs in schools and public venues. We publish a newsletter which includes information on poetry/poetics in Canada and beyond. Also publish the books *Poetry Markets for Canadians*; *Who's Who in the League of Canadian Poets*; *When is a Poem* (teaching guide) and its accompanying anthology of Canadian Poetry *Vintage*; plus a series of cassettes. We sponsor a National Poetry Contest, open to Canadians living here and abroad." Rules: Unpublished poems of any style/subject, under 75-lines, typed, with name/address on separate sheet. $6 entry fee (includes GST) per poem. $1,000-1st prize, $750-2nd, $500-3rd; plus best 50 published in an anthology. Inquire with SASE. Contest open to Canadian nonmembers. Organizes two annual awards: The Gerald Lampert Memorial Award for the best first book of poetry published in Canada in the preceding year and The Pat Lowther Memorial Award for the best book of poetry by a Canadian woman published in the preceding year. Deadline for both the poetry contest and award is January 31 each year. Send SASE for more details.

NATIONAL STORY LEAGUE, 3516 Russell #6, St. Louis MO 63104. (314)773-5555. Board Member, Story Art Contributor: E.G. Stirnaman. Purpose of organization: to promote the art of storytelling. Qualifications for membership: the wish to become a good storyteller and to work at it. Annual dues: $15. Publishes a magazine of story art. Non-member subscription: $5. Sponsors storywriting contest (original). Awards include cash and publication. Contest open to nonmembers.

NATIONAL WRITERS CLUB, Ste. 620, 1450 S. Havana, Aurora CO 80012. (303)751-7844. Executive Director: Sandy Whelchel. Purpose of organization: association for freelance writers. Qualifications for membership: associate membership — must be serious about writing; professional membership — published and paid (cite credentials). Membership cost: $50-associate; $60-professional; $15 setup fee for first year only. Workshops/conferences: TV/Screenwriting Workshops, NWC Annual Conferences, Literary Clearinghouse, Editing and Critiquing services, Local Chapters. National Writer's School. Open to nonmembers. Publishes industry news of interest to freelance writers; how-to articles; market information; member news and networking opportunities. Nonmember subscription $18. Sponsors poetry contest; short story/article contest; novel contest; nonfiction book proposal contest. Awards cash awards for top three winners; books and/or certificates for other winners; honorable mention certificate places 11-20. Contests open to nonmembers.

NATIONAL WRITERS UNION, Suite 203, 873 Broadway, New York NY 10003. (212)254-0279. National Director: Anne Wyville. Purpose of organization: Advocacy for freelance writers. Qualifications for membership: "Membership in the NWU is open to all qualified writers, and no one shall be barred or in any manner prejudiced within the Union on account of race, age, sex, sexual preference, disability, national origin, religion or ideology. You are eligible for membership if you have published a book, play, three articles, five poems, one short story or an equivalent amount of newsletter, publicity, technical, commercial, government or insitutional copy. You are also eligible for membership if you have written an equal amount of unpublished material and you are actively writing and attempting to publish your work." Membership Dues: Annual writing income under $5,000, $55/year; annual writing income $5,000-25,000, $95/year; annual writing income over $25,000, $135/year. National union newsletter quarterly, issues related to freelance writing and to union organization. Nonmember subscription: $15.

THE NEBRASKA WRITERS GUILD, P.O. Box 30341, Lincoln NE 68503-0341. (402)477-3804. President: Diane L. Kirkle. Purpose of organization: to provide support and information to professional and aspiring writers. "To be an active member, you must meet at least one of these criteria: have published and placed on sale through regular channels one or more books; have received payment for 5,000 words of prose published in magazines or newspapers of 2,500 circulation or more; have written for television, radio or other media seen or heard by an authenticated audience of 2,500 or more; present evidence of a continuous body of poetry to be judged on the basis of number and quality of publications, regardless of payment or circulation. If you don't qualify as an active member but are interested in the publishing industry, you may join the NWG as an Associate Member." Membership cost: Active and Associate member, $15/year; youth member (has same benefits as Assoc. member but for people under 18), $7/year. Different levels of membership include: Active member—professional writers; Associate member—aspiring writers, editors, publishers, librarians, etc.; Youth member—18 or younger. Workshops/conferences: two conferences/year—April to October. Publishes newsletter. Provides market and how-to information and news about the Guild and its members.

PEN AMERICAN CENTER, 568 Broadway, New York NY 10012. (212)334-1660. Purpose of organization: "To foster understanding among men and women of letters in all countries. International PEN is the only worldwide organization of writers and the chief voice of the literary community. Members of PEN work for freedom of expression wherever it has been endangered." Qualifications for membership: "The standard qualification for a writer to join PEN is that he or she must have published, in the United States, two or more books of a literary character, or one book generally acclaimed to be of exceptional distinction. Editors who have demonstrated commitment to excellence in their profession (generally construed as five years' service in book editing), translators who have published at least two book-length literary translations, and playwrights whose works have been professionally produced, are eligible for membership. An application form is available upon request from PEN Headquarters in New York. Candidates for membership should be nominated by two current members of PEN. Inquiries about membership should be directed to the PEN Membership Committee. Friends of PEN is also open to writers who may not yet meet the general PEN membership requirements. PEN sponsors more than fifty public events at PEN Headquarters in New York, and at the branch offices in Boston, Chicago, Houston, San Francisco and Portland, Oregon. They include tributes by contemporary writers to classic American writers, dialogues with visiting foreign writers, symposia that bring public attention to problems of censorship and that address current issues of writing in the United States, and readings that introduce beginning writers to the public. PEN's wide variety of literary programming reflects current literary interests and provides informal occasions for writers to meet each other and to welcome those with an interest in literature. Events are all open to the public and are usually free of charge. The Children's Book Authors' Committee sponsors regular public events focusing on the art of writing for children and young adults and on the diversity of literature for juvenile readers. The *PEN*/Norma Klein Award was established in 1991 to honor an emerging children's book author. National union newsletter covers PEN activities, features interviews with international literary figures, transcripts of PEN literary symposia, reports on issues vital to the literary community. All PEN publications are available by mail order directly from PEN American Center. Individuals must enclose check or money order with their order. Subscription: $8 for 4 issues; sample issue $2. Pamphlets and brochures all free upon request. Sponsors several competitions per year. Monetary awards range from $700-12,750.

*THE PLAYWRIGHTS' CENTER, 2301 Franklin Ave. E., Minneapolis MN 55406. (612)332-7481. Outreach Director: Sally MacDonald. Purpose of organization: Service organization for playwrights, offering development, classes, grants. Qualifications for membership: General members pay $35 fee; Associate and Core members apply for membership through a peer selection panel. Membership cost: $35 annually. Levels of membership include: General: space in calendar, discounts on classes, automatic notification of fellowships and grant opportunities; Associate: a one-year term with access to developmental lab (and all the above); Core: a 7-year term (see above). Sponsors workshops/conferences. Publishes newsletter: playwrights' center activities and programs; members' achievements. Sponsors contests: PlayLabs developmental workshops; McKnight, Jerome fellowships; Jones commissions; McKnight Advancement grants; exchanges and other opportunities by application. Awards include developmental services, cash awards. Contest open to non-members. Contact: Lisa Stevens, Public Relations/Membership Director.

PUPPETEERS OF AMERICA, INC., #5 Cricklewood Path, Pasadena CA 91107. (818)797-5748. Membership Officer: Gayle Schluter. Purpose of organization: to promote the art of puppetry. Qualifications for membership: interest in the art form. Membership cost: single adult, $35; junior member, $20; retiree, $25; group or family, $55; couple, $45. Sponsors workshops/conferences. Publishes newsletter. *The Puppetry Journal* provides news about puppeteers, puppet theatres, exhibitions, touring companies, technical tips, new products, new books, films, television, and events sponsored by the Chartered Guilds in each of the eight P of A regions. Subscription: $30.

SAN DIEGO WRITERS/EDITORS GUILD, 3235 Homer Street, San Diego CA 92106. (619)223-5235. Treasurer: Peggy Lipscomb. "The Guild was formed January, 1979 to meet the local writers' needs for assignments and editors who seek writers. The use of the Guild as a power to publicize poor editorial practices has evolved. We hope to meet writers' needs as we become aware of them and as members are willing to provide services." Activities include: monthly social meetings with a speaker, monthly newsletter, membership directory, workshops and conferences, other social activities. Qualifications for membership: published book; three published, paid pieces (nonfiction, fiction, prose, poetry), paid editor, produced screenplay or play, paid and published translations, public relations, publicity or advertising. "All professional members must submit clear evidence of work and a brief résumé. After acceptance, member need not requalify unless membership lapses." Membership cost: $25 annual fees, $40 member and spouse, $12.50 full-time student and out-of-state or county member. Different levels of membership include: associate and professional. Publishes a newsletter giving notice of meetings, conferences, contests.

SCIENCE FICTION AND FANTASY WRITERS OF AMERICA, INC., 5 Winding Brook Dr. #1B, Guilderland NY 12084. (518)869-5361. Executive Secretary: Peter Dennis Pautz. Purpose of organization: to encourage public interest in science fiction literature and provide organization format for writers/editors/artists within the genre. Qualifications for membership: at least one professional sale or other professional involvement within the field. Membership cost: annual active dues—$50; affiliate—$35; one-time installation fee of $10; dues year begins July 1. Different levels of membership include: affiliate requires one professional sale or professional involvement; active requires three professional short stories or one novel published. Workshops/conferences: annual awards banquet, usually in April or May. Open to nonmembers. Publishes newsletter. Nonmember subscription: $15 in U.S. Sponsors SFWA Nebula® Awards for best published SF in the categories of novel, novella, novelette, and short story. Awards trophy.

SOCIETY OF CHILDREN'S BOOK WRITERS AND ILLUSTRATORS, Box 66296, Mar Vista Station, Los Angeles CA 90066. (818)347-2849. Chairperson, Board of Directors: Sue Alexander. Purpose of organization: to assist writers and illustrators working or interested in the field. Qualifications for membership: an interest in children's literature and illustration. Membership cost: $40/year. Different levels of membership include: full membership—published authors/illustrators; associate membership—unpublished writers/illustrators. Workshops/conferences: 30-40 events around the country each year. Open to nonmembers. Publishes a newsletter focusing on writing and illustrating children's books. Sponsors grants for writers and illustrators who are members.

SOCIETY OF ILLUSTRATORS, 128 E. 63rd St., New York NY 10021. (212)838-2560. Director: Terrence Brown. Purpose of organization: To promote interest in the art of illustration for working professional illustrators and those in associated fields. "Cost of membership: Initiation fee—$200. Annual dues for Non-Resident members (those living more than 125 air miles from SI's headquarters) are $226. Dues for Resident Artist Members are $384 per year, Resident Associate Members $447." Different levels of membership include: *Artist Members* "shall include those who make illustration their profession" and through which they earn at least 60% of their income. *Associate Members* are "Those who earn their living in the arts or who have made a substantial contribution to the art of illustration." This includes art directors, art buyers, creative supervisors, instructors, publishers and like categories. "All candidates for membership are admitted by the proposal of one active member and sponsorship of four additional members. The candidate must complete and sign the application form which requires a brief biography, a listing of schools attended, other training and a résumé of his or her professional career." Candidates for *Artist* membership, in addition to the above requirements, must submit examples of their work. Sponsors The Annual of American Illustration. Awards include gold and silver medals. Open to nonmembers. Deadline: October 1. Sponsors "The Original Art." Deadline: mid-July. Call for details.

SOCIETY OF MIDLAND AUTHORS, % Bowman, 152 N. Scoville, Oak Park IL 60302. (708)383-7568. President: Jim Bowman. Purpose of organization: create closer association among writers of the Middle West; stimulate creative literary effort; maintain collection of members works; encourage interest in reading and literature by cooperating with other educational and cultural agencies. Qualifications for membership: to be author or co-author of a book demonstrating literary style and published by a recognized publisher or author of published or professionally produced play and be identified through birth or residence with IL, IN, IA, KS, MI, MN, MO, NE, ND, OH, SD or WI. Membership cost: $25/year dues. Different levels of membership include: regular—published book authors; associate, nonvoting—not published as above but having some connection with literature, such as librarians, teachers, publishers, and editors. Workshops/conferences: program meetings, Newberry Library, Chicago, held 5 times a year, featuring authors, publishers, editors or the like individually or on panels. Usually 2nd Tuesday of October, November, January, February and March. Also holds annual awards dinner at Drake Hotel, Chicago, in May. Publishes a newsletter focusing on news of members and of general items of interest to writers. Non-member subscription: $5. Sponsors contests. "Annual awards in 7 categories, given at annual dinner in May. Monetary awards for books published or plays performed professionally in previous calendar year. Send SASE to contact person for details." Contest open to non-members.

SOCIETY OF SOUTHWESTERN AUTHORS, P.O. Box 30355, Tucson AZ 85751-0355. President: Don Young. Purpose of organization: fellowship among members of the writing profession, recognition of members' achievements, to stimulate further achievement, and to assist persons seeking to become professional writers. Qualifications for membership: proof of publication of a book, articles, TV screenplay, etc. Membership cost: $25 initiation plus $10/year dues. Workshops/conferences: The Society of Southwestern Authors annual Writers' Conference, traditionally held the last Saturday of January at the University of Arizona. Publishes a newsletter, *The Write Word*, about members' activities and news of interest to them. Each spring a contest for beginning writers is sponsored. Applications are available in February. Send SASE to the P.O. Box.

TEXTBOOK AUTHORS ASSOCIATION, Box 535, Orange Springs FL 32182. (904)546-1000. Executive Director: Mike Keedy. Purpose of organization: to address the professional concerns of text authors. Qualifications for membership: all authors and prospective authors are welcome. Membership cost: $50. Workshops/conferences: being formulated. Newsletter focuses on all areas of interest to text authors.

WESTERN WRITERS OF AMERICA, INC., 2800 N. Campbell, El Paso TX 79902-2522. (915)532-3222. Secretary/Treasurer: Francis L. Fugate. Purpose: an organization of professional writers helping to preserve the spirit and reality of the West. Qualifications of membership: must be a published writer. Membership cost: $60/year. Different levels of membership include: Associate—must be published, 5 magazine articles or 1 book; active—must be published, 30 magazine articles or 3 books. Workshops/conferences: Annual convention is held the last full week of June. Publishes a newsletter that keeps the members in touch with each other. WWA sponsors the Owen Wister Award for lifetime achievement in Western literature. Annual Spur Awards go to authors of the best Western writing in a variety of categories including juvenile fiction and nonfiction. This competition is open to non-members. "We also publish *The Roundup Quarterly*; non-members can subscribe for $30 per year."

*THE WRITERS ALLIANCE, P.O. Box 2014, Setauket NY 11733. Executive Director: Kiel Stuart. Purpose of organization: "A support/information group for all types of writers." Membership cost: $15/year, payable to Kiel Stuart. A group membership costs $25. Different levels of membership include: corporate/group—$25, individual—$15. Publishes newsletter for all writers who use (or want to learn about) computers. Non-member subscription $15—payable to Kiel Stuart.

WRITERS CONNECTION, Suite 180, 1601 Saratoga-Sunnyvale Rd., Cupertino CA 95014. (408)973-0227. Editor: Jan Stiles; Vice President/Program Director: Meera Lester. Purpose of organization: to provide services and resources for writers. "We publish

---

Always include a self-addressed stamped envelope (SASE) or International Reply Coupon (IRC) with submissions.

three regional market guides for writers." Qualifications for membership: interest in writing or publishing. Membership cost: $40/year. Workshops/conferences: Selling to Hollywood, August; Get That Novel Started; Writing the Children's Picture Book. Publishes a newsletter focusing on writing and publishing (all fields except poetry), how-to, markets, contests, tips, etc. Non-member subscription: $18/year.

Clubs and Organizations/'92-'93 changes

The following markets are not included in this edition of *Children's Writer's & Illustrator's Market* for the reasons indicated. The phrase "did not respond" means the market was in the *1992 Children's Writer's & Illustrator's Market* but did not respond to our written and phone requests for updated information for a 1993 listing.

Action for Children's Television (did not respond)

Lewis Carroll Society of North America (did not respond)

International Black Writers (unable to contact)

Workshops

Whether you're a professional with a desire to fine-tune your craft, or a novice yearning to build fundamental skills, there are workshops offered for children's writers and illustrators of all levels. Conferences are great places to pick up solid information on a variety of topics, including successful techniques in writing and illustrating and trends in children's publishing. Some workshops even touch on business issues of concern to freelancers, such as changes in tax and copyright laws.

Be aware that not every workshop included here directly relates to juvenile writing or illustrating, but information acquired can be utilized in creating material for children. Illustrators may be interested in general painting and drawing workshops. Though they are not listed in this book, a plethora of them are held each year. Artists can find a detailed directory of art workshops offered nationwide each year in the March issue of *The Artist's Magazine*.

Listings in this section will provide you with information describing what courses are offered, where and when, and the costs. Some of the national writing and art organizations also offer regional workshops throughout the year. Write for information.

THE ART & BUSINESS OF HUMOROUS ILLUSTRATION, Cartoon Art Museum, 665 3rd St., San Francisco CA 94107. (415)546-3922. Director: Valerie Cox. Writer and illustrator workshops geared toward professional levels. "Class focus is on cartooning, but we do cover some marketing topics about children's books." Workshops held fall and spring. Length of each session: 10 weeks. Maximum class size: 30. Cost of workshop: $145, includes art and writing instruction. Write for more information.

*AUTUMN AUTHORS' AFFAIR X, 1507 Burnham Ave., Calumet City IL 60409. (708)862-9797. President: Nancy McCann. Writer workshop geared toward beginner, intermediate, advanced levels. Emphasizes writing for children and young adults. Annual workshop. Workshops held generally the fourth weekend in October. Cost of workshop: $65 for one day, $100 for weekend. Write for more information.

*BE THE WRITER YOU WANT TO BE—MANUSCRIPT CLINIC, 23350 Sereno Ct., Villa 30, Cupertino CA 95014. (415)691-0300. Contact: Louise Purwin Zobel. Writer and illustrator workshops geared toward beginner, intermediate, advanced levels. "Participants may turn in manuscripts at any stage of development to receive help with structure and style, as well as marketing advice. Manuscripts receive some written criticism and an oral critique from the instructor, as well as class discussion." Annual workshop. Usually held in the spring. Length of each session: 1-2 days. Registration limited to 20-25 people. Cost of workshop: $40-65/day, depending on the campus; includes an extensive handout.

*BENNINGTON WRITING WORKSHOPS, Bennington College, Bennington VT 05201. (802)442-5401, ext. 241. Assistant Director of Special Programs: Priscilla Hodgkins. Writer and illustrator workshops geared toward beginner, intermediate, advanced, and professional levels. Classes offered include fiction, nonfiction and poetry. Annual workshop. Workshops divided into two two-week sessions. Participants can attend one or both. Registration limited to 100-150. Last year's cost of workshop: two weeks tuition

$785, room and board $440; four weeks tuition $1,250, room and board $775. Must provide writing sample, resume of related experience, application form and $25 application fee. Write for more information.

BIOLA UNIVERSITY WRITERS INSTITUTE, 13800 Biola Ave., LaMirada CA 90639. (800)75WORDS. Director: Gretchen Passantino. Writer and illustrator workshops geared toward beginner, intermediate and advanced levels. Emphasizes nonfiction books and articles; fiction (short and long); poetry; children's books. Classes/courses offered include: basic magazine article writing, advanced fiction techniques and sell what you write. Workshops held July 25-28, 1993; 6 week classes, video correspondence course and ms critique service are held all year. Length of each session: 1-2 hours. Cost of workshop: $300; includes tuition and meals. "We take anyone with a desire to write."

*BLUE RIDGE WRITERS CONFERENCE, 1942 Avon Rd., Roanoke VA 24015. (703)345-6671. Chairperson: Liz Jones. Writer workshops geared toward beginner, intermediate levels. Illustrator workshops geared toward beginner level. Annual workshop. Workshops held first Saturday in October. Length of each session: one day. Registration limited to 200. Cost of workshop: 2 workshops, lunch, reception $40; includes keynote address. No requirements prior to registration unless submitting work for critique. Write for more information. "We are a small conference dedicated to inspiring writers and assisting publication. Children's literature is *not* covered every year."

*THE BROCKPORT WRITERS FORUM SUMMER WORKSHOPS, Lathrop Hall, State University of New York College at Brockport, Brockport NY 14420. (716)395-5713. Director: Dr. Stan Rubin. Writer workshops geared toward intermediate level. Classes offered include Children's Writing and Writing for Young Adults. Workshops held in July. Length of each session: 6 days. Registration limited to 10-15/genre (60-80 total in all genres offered). Cost of workshop: approx. $400; includes all seminars, readings, guest writers, editors, etc.; access to videotape library; breakfast, some lunches and dinners. Individual conference. Requirements: Submission of ms in progress or representative finished work. Write for more information. "Our workshop has run for 12 years drawing participants from New York State and around the U.S. We are a small, pleasant village on the banks of the Erie Canal, 10 miles from Lake Ontario. Our airport is Rochester International." The children's/YA workshop is *not* offered annually.

CAPE LITERARY WORKSHOPS, Cape Cod Writers Conference, Route 132, West Barnstable MA 02668. (508)775-4811. Executive Director: Marion Vuilleumier. Writer and illustrator workshops geared toward intermediate, advanced levels. Summer workshops offered in children's book writing and children's book illustration. Workshops held in July and early August. Conference held third week in August. Intensive workshops meet Monday-Friday from 9-1. Class sizes limited. Cost of workshop: $395; includes registration and tuition. Materials, room and board extra. "It is not necessary to have works-in-progress but those who do will find these workshops especially helpful. Participants are encouraged to send current work in advance." Send for brochure for more information on workshops and accommodations.

CHILDREN'S BOOK PUBLISHING: A COMPREHENSIVE BOOK ILLUSTRATION WORKSHOP, Rice University, P.O. Box 1892, Houston TX 77251-1892. (713)527-4803. Contact: Workshop Coordinator. Illustrator workshops geared toward intermediate,

 The asterisk before a listing indicates the listing is new in this edition.

advanced, professional levels. "This workshop is intended for persons with a background in art who wish to begin or advance their careers in children's book illustration. Award-winning illustrator Diane Stanley will take participants through the entire process of illustrating a book for children, using both lectures and hands-on work to guide them." Workshop held in July and August. Length of each session: 9:00 a.m.-12:00 p.m.; 1:00-4:00 p.m. Workshops held on Rice University campus. Cost of workshop: $375. Fee does not include supplies; a supply list will be provided. Write for more information.

CHILDREN'S BOOK PUBLISHING: AN INTENSIVE WRITING & EDITING WORKSHOP, Rice University, P.O. Box 1892, Houston TX 77251-1892. (713)527-4803. Contact: Workshop Coordinator. Writer workshops geared toward beginner, intermediate, advanced, professional levels. "Lectures and laboratories designed to help writers take their writing projects from the idea stage to the publishing market." Classes/courses offered include: Picture books from the writer's point of view; Writing nonfiction books; Plotting—from idea to end. Workshops held July, August. Length of each session: Morning lectures: 9:00 a.m.-11:45 a.m.; Afternoon laboratories: 1:00-4:15 p.m. Workshops held on Rice University campus. "Submission of a ms is optional, but must be submitted according to guidelines." Write for more information.

NINTH ANNUAL CHILDREN'S LITERATURE CONFERENCE, Hofstra University, U.C.C.E., 205 Davison Hall, Hempstead NY 11550. (516)463-5016. Writers/Illustrators Contact: Lewis Shena, director, Liberal Arts Studies. Writer and illustrator workshops geared toward beginner, intermediate, advanced, professional levels. Emphasizes: fiction, nonfiction, poetry, submission procedures, picture books. Workshops held April 3, 1993, 9:30 a.m.-4:30 p.m. Length of each session: 1 hour. Maximum class size: 35. Cost of workshop: approximately $50; includes 2 workshops, reception, lunch, panel discussion with guest speakers, e.g. "What An Editor Looks For." Write for more information. Co-sponsored by Society of Children's Book Writers.

*CLARION SCIENCE FICTION & FANTASY WRITING WORKSHOP, Lyman Briggs School, E-28 Holmes Hall, MSU, East Lansing MI 48825-1107. (517)353-6486. Administrative Assistant: Mary Sheridan. Writer and illustrator workshop geared toward intermediate levels. Emphasizes science fiction and fantasy. "An intensive workshop designed to stimulate and develop the talent and techniques of potential writers of speculative fiction. Previous experience in writing fiction is assumed. Approximately 20 participants will work very closely together over a six-week period, guided by a series of professional writers of national reputation." 1993 Workshop—June 20-July 31. Length of session: six weeks. Class size: 17-20. Cost of tuition (7 credits of upper-level course work): $500-600 for Michigan resident, $1,300-1,400 for non-Michigan resident (depending on residence and educational status). Lodging (single room) and meal costs are being negotiated. Requirements prior to registration: submission of two manuscripts (up to 2,500 words each) for review, and a completed application form with a $25 application fee. Write for more information.

*CREATIVE COLLABORATIVE, P.O. Box 2201, La Jolla CA 92038. (619)459-8897. Director: Penny Wilkes. Writer workshops geared toward intermediate, advanced levels. "Writing topics are geared to stimulating the creative spark and following it through to story development. Sharing of ideas and collaborating to enhance everyone's efforts become the keys to this workshop." Workshops held periodically from October-May. Length of each session: half- to full-day sessions. Registration limited to 20 students. Cost of workshop: $75; includes morning creativity session, afternoon writing and reading. Requirements prior to registration: story submittal (1,500 words) or excerpts not to exceed 5 pages. Write for more information.

DRURY COLLEGE/SCBWI WRITING FOR CHILDREN WORKSHOP, Drury College, Springfield MO 65802. (417)865-8731. Assistant Director, Continuing Education: Lynn Doke. Writer and illustrator workshop geared toward beginner, intermediate, advanced, professional levels. Emphasizes all aspects of writing for children and teenagers. Classes/courses offered include: "Between Author and Editor: One Editor's View," "Marketing Yourself," "An Editor Works with Illustrators," "No Place for Cowards: Writing Tough Scenes," "Picture Books, or How to Write for Little Bitty Short People," "Digging Up the Bones: Researching the Nonfiction Book," "Children's Interests: What's In It for Me? and Who's In It for You?" and "Skywalking: Poetry that Kids Love." One-day workshop held in November. Length of each session: 1 hour. Manuscript and portfolio consultations (by appointment only). Maximum class size: 25-30. $45 registration fee; individual consultations $25. Send SASE for more information.

*DUKE UNIVERSITY WRITERS' WORKSHOP, P.O. Box 90703, Durham NC 27708-0703. Director: Marilyn Hartman. "There are various small groups based on level and genre." Writer workshops geared toward beginner, intermediate, advanced, professional levels. Classes offered include short short fiction, creative nonfiction, poetry, novel, etc. Annual workshop. Workshops held June 20-25, 1993. Length of each session: five days. Registration limited to 10 in each small group. Cost of workshop: $345; includes registration, instruction materials, a few social meals. "Workshop sections are small; participants work a lot. We're low on large-group stuff, high on productivity."

EDUCATION WRITERS ASSOCIATION NATIONAL SEMINAR, 1001 Connecticut Ave. NW, Washington DC 20036. (202)429-9680. Administrative Assistant: Kristina Blakey. Writer workshops geared toward beginner, intermediate, advanced and professional levels. Emphasizes topics in education, education writing, investigative reporting in education, narrative writing. Workshops held April 14-18, 1993 in Boston (annual meeting); regional conferences. Length of each session: 4 days/1 day. Cost of workshop: $195 for annual meeting; includes some meals. Write for more information.

FLORIDA STATE WRITERS CONFERENCE, P.O. Box 9844, Ft. Lauderdale FL 33310. (305)485-0795. Executive Director: Dana K. Cassell. Writer workshops geared toward beginner, intermediate, advanced and professional levels. Emphasizes juvenile, novels, books, articles, business management and legal writing. Workshops held third weekend in May. Length of each session: 1 hour. Maximum class size: varies according to topic. Accommodations are typical hotel facilities. Cost of workshop: varies (single-day through complete packages). Write for more information.

FLORIDA SUNCOAST WRITERS' CONFERENCE, Dept. of English, Univ. of South Florida, Tampa FL 33620. (813)974-2421. Director: Ed Hirshberg. Writer and illustrator workshops geared toward intermediate, advanced, professional levels. Workshops held first weekend in February. 30-100 class sizes. Cost of workshop: $95; $75 students; includes all sessions, receptions, panels. Conference is held on St. Petersburg campus of U.S.F.

GREEN LAKE CHRISTIAN WRITERS CONFERENCE, American Baptist Assembly, Green Lake WI 54941-9300. (800)558-8898. Vice President of Program: Dr. Arlo R. Reichter. Writer workshops geared toward beginner, intermediate and advanced levels. Emphasizes poetry, nonfiction, writing for children, fiction. Classes/courses offered include: same as above plus one-session or two-session presentations on marketing, devotional writing and retelling Bible stories. Workshops held July 10-17, 1993. Length of conference: Saturday dinner through the following Saturday breakfast. Maximum class size: 20. Writing and/or art facilities available: housing, conference rooms, etc. "No special equipment for writing." Cost of workshop: $80; includes all instruction plus room and meals as selected. Write for more information. "The conference focuses on helping writers to refine their writing skills in a caring atmosphere utilizing competent, caring faculty. This annual conference has been held every year since 1948."

*HEART OF AMERICA WRITERS' CONFERENCE, JCCC, 12345 College Blvd., Overland Park KS 66210. (913)469-3838. Director: Judith Choice. Writer workshops geared toward beginner, intermediate, advanced, professional levels. Annual workshop. Workshops held in late March 1993. Length of each session: 1-3 hrs. Registration limited to 250. Cost of workshop: $100; includes lunch, reception. Write for more information.

HIGHLIGHTS FOUNDATION WRITERS WORKSHOP AT CHAUTAUQUA, Dept. CWL, 711 Court St., Honesdale PA 18431. (717)253-1192. Conference Director: Jan Keen. Writer workshops geared toward beginner, intermediate and advanced levels. Classes/courses offered include: "Children's Interests," "Writing Dialogue," "Beginnings and Endings," "Rights, Contracts, Copyrights," "Science Writing." Workshops held July 17-24, 1993, Chautauqua Institution, Chautauqua, NY. Maximum class size: 100. Write for more information.

*HOFSTRA UNIVERSITY SUMMER WRITERS' CONFERENCE, Hofstra University, UCCE, 205 Davison Hall, Hempstead NY 11550-1090. (516)463-5016. Director of Liberal Arts Studies: Lewis Shena. Writer workshops geared toward beginner, intermediate, advanced, professional levels. Classes offered include fiction, nonfiction, poetry, science fiction, children's literature, stage and screenwriting. Children's writing faculty has included Pam Conrad, Johanna Hurwitz, Tor Seidler and Jane Zalben, with Maurice Sendak appearing as guest speaker. Annual workshop. Workshops held July 12-23, 1993. Length of each session: Each workshop meets for 2½ hours daily for a total of 25 hours. Students can register for a maximum of 3 workshops, schedule an individual conference with the writer/instructor and submit a short ms. (less than 10 pages) for critique. Enrollees may register as certificate students or credit students. Cost of workshop: certificate students enrollment fee is approx. $575 plus $26 registration fee; two-credit student enrollment fee is approx. $775 undergraduate and $815 graduate; four-credit student enrollment fee is approx. $1,440 undergraduate and $1,500 graduate. On-campus accommodations for the sessions are available for approx. $300/person. Certificate students may attend any of the five workshops, a private conference and special programs and social events. Credit students may attend only the workshops they have registered for (a maximum of two for two credits each) and the special programs and social events.

*ILLUSTRATION & WRITING OF CHILDREN'S BOOKS WORKSHOP, Office of Special Programs, Hartwick College, Oneonta NY 13820. (607)431-4415. Program Coordinator: Gladys Freeland. Workshops geared toward all levels of illustrators. Writers welcome, too, but must have some drawing ability. Workshops generally held mid-July. Two-week intensive program. Maximum class size: 12-14. Cost of workshop: $1,250. Due to limited enrollment, applications are screened. Applicant must complete a Supplemental Application and Profile Questionnaire. Write for brochure.

*INTERNATIONAL WOMEN'S WRITING GUILD, IWWG, P.O. Box 810, Gracie Station, New York NY 10028. (212)737-7536. Executive Director: Hannelore Hahn. Writer and illustrator workshops geared toward beginner, intermediate, advanced, professional levels. Annual workshops. Workshops held in August. Length of each session: 1½ hours for an entire week. Registration limited to 400. Cost of workshop: $300. Write for more information. "This workshop always takes place at Skidmore College in Saratoga Springs, NY."

THE IUPUI NATIONAL YOUTH THEATRE PLAYWRITING SYMPOSIUM, 525 N. Blackford St., Indianapolis IN 46202. (317)274-2095. Literary Manager: W. Mark McCreary. "The purpose of the Symposium is to provide a forum in which we can examine and discuss those principles which characterize good dramatic literature for young people and to explore ways to help playwrights and the promotion of quality drama. Publishers, playwrights, directors, producers, librarians and educators join together to examine issues central to playwriting. The symposium will showcase four new plays selected from 125 scripts submitted in the 1992 Playwriting Competition." Length of each ·session: Feb. 26-27, 1993.

*I'VE ALWAYS WANTED TO WRITE BUT—BEGINNERS' CLASS, 23350 Sereno Ct., Villa 30, Cupertino CA 95014. (415)691-0300. Contact: Louise Purwin Zobel. Writer and illustrator workshops geared toward beginner, intermediate levels. "This seminar/ workshop starts at the beginning, although the intermediate writer will benefit, too. There is discussion of children's magazine and book literature today, how to write it and how to market it. Also, there is discussion of other types of writing and the basics of writing for publication." Annual workshops. "Usually several times a year; fall, winter and spring." Sessions last 1-2 days. Cost of workshop: $45-65/day, depending on the campus; includes extensive handout. Write for more information.

*MAPLE WOODS COMMUNITY COLLEGE WRITERS' CONFERENCE, 2601 NE Barry Rd., Kansas City MO 64156. (816)734-4878. Coordinator, Continuing Education: Pattie Smith. Writer workshops geared toward beginner, intermediate levels. Various writing topics and genres covered. Will be held in fall. Length of each session: 1 hour. Maximum class size: 100. Cost of workshop: $40; includes lunch.

MIDLAND WRITERS CONFERENCE, Grace A. Dow Memorial Library, 1710 W. St. Andrews, Midland MI 48640. (517)835-7151. Conference Co-chairs: Margaret Allen or Eileen M. Finzel. Writer and illustrator workshops geared toward beginner, intermediate, advanced and professional levels. "We always have one session each on children's, poetry and basics." Classes/courses offered include: romance writing, how to write poetry, writing for the wonder age (youth), your literary agent/what to expect, choosing a powerful setting and writing popular fiction. Workshops held June 12, 1993. Length of each session: concurrently, four one-hour and two-hour sessions. Maximum class size: 40. "We are a public library." Cost of workshop: $45; $35 seniors and students. Choice of workshops and the keynote speech given by a prominent author (last year Mary Higgins Clark). Write for more information.

*MISSISSIPPI VALLEY WRITERS CONFERENCE, Augustana College, Rock Island IL 61265. (309)762-8985. Conference Director: David R. Collins. Writer workshops geared toward beginner, intermediate, advanced, professional levels. Classes offered include Juvenile Writing—one of nine workshops offered. Annual workshop. Workshops held June 6-11, 1993; usually it is the second week in June each year. Length of each session: Monday through Friday, one hour each day. Registration limited to 20 participants/ workshop. Writing facilities available: college library. Cost of workshop: $25 registration; $35 to participate in one workshop, $60 in two, $30 for each additional; $20 to audit a workshop. Write for more information.

MOUNT HERMON CHRISTIAN WRITERS CONFERENCE, Mount Hermon Christian Conference Center, P.O. Box 413, Mount Hermon CA 95041. (408)335-4466. Director of Public Affairs: David R. Talbott. Writer workshops geared toward beginner, intermediate, advanced and professional levels. Emphasizes religious writing for children via books, articles; Sunday school curriculum; marketing. Classes/courses offered include: Suitable Style for Children; Everything You Need to Know to Write and Market Your

Children's Book; Take-Home Papers for children. Workshops held annually over Palm Sunday weekend: April 2-6, 1993. Length of each session: 5-day residential conferences held annually. Maximum class size: 45, but most are 10-15. Conference center with hotel-style accommodations. Cost of workshop: $450-$560 variable; includes tuition, resource notebook, refreshment breaks, full room and board for 13 meals and 4 nights. Write for more information.

*THE NATIONAL WRITERS CLUB 1993 CONFERENCE, Suite 620, 1450 S. Havana, Aurora CO 80012. (303)751-7844. Executive Director: Sandy Whelchel. Writer workshops geared toward beginner, intermediate, advanced, professional levels. Classes offered include marketing, agenting, "What's Hot in the Market." Annual workshop. Workshops held in June 1993. Length of each session: 50-minute sessions for 2½ days. Write for more information.

*CHRISTOPHER NEWPORT UNIVERSITY WRITERS' CONFERENCE, 50 Shoe Lane, Newport News VA 23606-2998. (804)594-7158. Coordinator: Doris Gwaltney. Writer workshops geared toward beginner, intermediate, professional levels. Emphasizes all genres. Length of each session: 2¼ hours. Maximum class size: 35. Cost of workshop: $65. Includes "Celebration of the Arts" on April 2, 1993, from 7-9 pm.

*101 WAYS TO MARKET YOUR BOOK, P.O. Box 152281, Arlington TX 76015. (817)468-9924. Seminar Director: Mary Bold. Writer workshops geared toward beginner, intermediate levels. Classes offered include heavy emphasis on how books are marketed to the public and how author and publisher can work together in promoting new titles. Annual workshop. Workshops held usually, spring and fall. Length of each session: ½ day. Cost of workshop: $40-50; includes lunch and materials. No prior requirements. Write for more information. "I am a charter member of the national organization for conference directors, Writers' Conferences & Retreats (WCR). Many of my seminars (for both writers and publishers) are sponsored by area universities and learning centers, as well as by the National Association of Independent Publishers."

OZARK CREATIVE WRITERS, INC. CONFERENCE, 6817 Gingerbread Ln., Little Rock AR 72204. (501)565-8889. President: Peggy Vining. Writer's workshops geared to all levels. "All forms of the creative process dealing with the literary arts. This year we have expanded to songwriting." Always the second weekend in October at Inn of the Ozarks in Eureka Springs AR (a resort town). Morning sessions are given to main attraction author . . . six one-hour satellite speakers during each of the two afternoons. Two banquets. "Approximately 125 to 150 attend the conference yearly . . . many others enter the creative writing competition." Cost of workshop: $25-30. "This does not include meals or lodging. We do block off fifty rooms prior to September 1 for OCW guests." Write for contest rules for entering competition. "Reserve early."

*PROFESSIONALISM IN WRITING SCHOOL, Parkview Baptist Church, 5805 S. Sheridan, Tulsa OK 74145. Registrar: Donna Johnson. Writer workshops geared toward all levels. Illustrator workshops geared toward beginners, intermediate and advanced. Emphasizes manuscript preparation, writing for series (books), teen fiction, picture books, copyright, cartooning and free verse. Workshops held third weekend in March. Length of each session: 1 hr. Maximum class size: 50. Cost of workshop: $125; includes meals, awards banquet, hand-out materials, magazine guidelines. Writers should contact Myrna Marshall, 1320 N. 157 E. Ave., Tulsa OK 74116-2432.

ROBERT QUACKENBUSH'S CHILDREN'S BOOK WRITING AND ILLUSTRATING WORKSHOP, 460 East 79th St., New York NY 10021. (212)744-3822. Contact: Robert Quackenbush. Writer and illustrator workshops geared toward beginner, intermediate,

FREE Sample Issue

CHILDREN'S WRITER

The Monthly Newsletter for the **BOOMING CHILDREN'S MARKET!**

W hether you're writing for yourself or creating a best-seller, CHILDREN'S WRITER covers the spectrum monthly. It gives you up-to-the-minute information you can't beg, borrow or buy anywhere else.

More than that, CHILDREN'S WRITER deals with the current questions and problems you're most likely to encounter—and it covers all the major markets that buy freelance writing.

"CHILDREN'S WRITER is full of information and articles that touch every writer, published or unpublished," says Patricia Clauson, Batavia, NY. "I think of it as a support group. When your newsletter arrives, everything comes to a halt! It's my favorite companion at the lunch table. I really *do* devour it… It's a wonderful newsletter."

"It helped me get an article accepted…."

"CHILDREN'S WRITER is a great source of reference for me and even helped me get an article accepted for publication," reports Karen Muller, E. Northport, NY. "*Hob-Nob's* request for non-fiction pieces in the February 1992 CHILDREN'S WRITER was a definite break for me. Thanks for helping my dream come true!"

"The articles about squeezing time out for writing and developing skills were most helpful," writes Carolyn Beck, Rialto, CA, "as I am a busy mother of three young children.…As someone getting started at the business of writing, *The Marketplace* section cuts through all the overwhelming array of data to sift through to find an editor who will use my work."

FREE Sample Issue

To get your free issue, just complete the reverse side and mail. *There is no obligation!*

BUSINESS REPLY MAIL

FIRST CLASS   PERMIT NO. 10   WEST REDDING, CT

POSTAGE WILL BE PAID BY ADDRESSEE

CHILDREN'S WRITER®

Subscription Department
95 Long Ridge Road
West Redding, CT 06896-9975

advanced, professional levels. Emphasizes picture books from start to finish. Classes/ courses offered include: fall and winter courses, extend 10 weeks each — 1½ hour/week; July workshop is a full five day (9 a.m.-4 p.m.) extensive course. Workshops held fall, winter and summer. Maximum class size: 8. Writing and/or art facilities available: work on the premises; art supply store nearby. Cost of workshop: $650 for instruction. Write for more information.

*READER'S DIGEST WRITER'S WORKSHOP, Northern Arizona University, P.O. Box 4092, Flagstaff AZ 86011-4092. (602)523-3232. Associate to the President: Ray Newton. Writer workshops geared toward beginner, intermediate, advanced, professional levels. Classes offered include major emphasis on nonfiction magazine articles for major popular publications. Annual workshops in various locations in US. Workshops held May 21-22 on the University of Nevada-Reno campus. Length of each session: intensive two-day sessions, each approx. 1 hr. Registration limited to 250. Writing facilities available: usually computers and other writing facilities. Cost of workshop: $50 first half day; $100 second full day; $140 if person attends both days; includes all registration fees, materials and two major meals, plus refreshment breaks. "Participants will have opportunity for one-on-one sessions with major editors, writers representing national magazines, including the *Reader's Digest.*" Write for more information.

SAN DIEGO STATE UNIVERSITY WRITERS' CONFERENCE, The College of Extended Studies, San Diego CA 92182. (619)594-5152. Extension Director: Jan Wahl. Writer workshops geared toward beginner, intermediate and advanced levels. Emphasizes nonfiction, fiction, screenwriting, advanced novel writing. Classes/courses offered include: Learning to Think Like an Editor; Writing for Television and Motion Pictures; Writing Children's Nonfiction and Picture Books. Workshops held third weekend in January each year. Length of each session: 50 minutes. Maximum class size: 100. Cost of workshop: 1991 fees were $177; included Saturday reception, 2 lunches and all sessions. Write for more information.

SCBWI NEW ENGLAND CONFERENCE, location varies from year to year. Regional Advisor: Don Gallo. (203)523-5795. Writer/illustrator workshops geared toward all levels. Emphasizes writing and illustrating for the children's market. One-day workshop usually held in the Spring includes keynote speakers and many workshops. Length of each session: 8-5 p.m. Conference limit: 250. "Specific cost yet to be determined; usually includes all-day conference, lunch. Conference is open to both published and unpublished writers and illustrators of children's books (and magazines) and anyone else interested in those aspects of children's books." Write for more information on date and location of 1993 conference.

SEMINARS FOR WRITERS, % Writers Connection, Ste. 180, 1601 Saratoga-Sunnyvale Rd., Cupertino CA 95014. (408)973-0227. Fax: (408)973-1219. Program Director: Meera Lester. Writer's workshops geared toward beginner, intermediate levels. Length of each session: six-hour session usually offered on a Saturday. Maximum class size: 30-35. Occasional seminars on writing for children (approximately 1-2 per year). Bookstore of writing, reference and how-to books. Monthly newsletter by subscription. Write for more information.

SOCIETY OF CHILDREN'S BOOK WRITERS & ILLUSTRATORS — FLORIDA REGION, 2000 Springdale Blvd., Apt. F-103, Palm Springs FL 33461. (407)433-1727. Florida Regional Advisor: Jean Shirley. Writer and illustrator workshops geared toward beginner, intermediate, advanced and professional levels. Subjects to be announced. Workshop held in the meeting rooms of the Palm Springs Public Library, 217 Cypress Lane, Palm Springs FL. Maximum class size: 100. Cost of workshop: $30 for members, $35 for nonmembers. Write for more information. "We plan to give one conference a year to be held on the second Saturday in September."

*SOCIETY OF CHILDREN'S BOOK WRITERS & ILLUSTRATORS – HAWAII, 2908 Robert Pl., Honolulu HI 96816. (808)737-6963. Regional Advisor: Ruth Brantley. Writer and illustrator conferences geared toward beginner, intermediate, advanced, professional levels. Write for more information.

*SOCIETY OF CHILDREN'S BOOK WRITERS & ILLUSTRATORS – INDIANA RETREAT, 4810 Illinois Rd., Fort Wayne IN 46804. (219)436-2160. Conference Director: Betsy Storey. Writer and illustrator workshops geared toward beginner, intermediate, advanced, professional levels. Classes offered include "Nuts and Bolts for Beginners"; "First Sales"; "Professionalism, Writing the Picture Book"; and "Nonfiction for Children." All are geared to children's writers and illustrators. Workshops held annually; June 25-27, 1993. Length of each session: 45 minutes to 1½ hours. Cost of workshop: approx. $225; includes accommodations, meals and workshops. Write for more information. "Ms and portfolio critiques by published writers and illustrators will be offered at additional charge."

*SOCIETY OF CHILDREN'S BOOK WRITERS & ILLUSTRATORS – MID-ATLANTIC WRITERS' ANNUAL CONFERENCE, P.O. Box 1707, Midlothian VA 23112. (804)744-6503. Writers contact Regional Advisor: Mrs. T.R. Hollingsworth. Illustrators contact: Carol Bock. Writer workshops geared toward all levels. Illustrator workshops geared toward beginner, intermediate levels. Annual workshop. Workshops held in fall of each year. Length of each session: one day. Registration limited to 100. Writing and/or art facilities available: writing contest, display of illustrations. Cost of workshop: $55-60; includes breakfast coffee, luncheon, afternoon soft drinks. Write for more information.

*SOCIETY OF CHILDREN'S BOOK WRITERS & ILLUSTRATORS – ROCKY MOUNTAIN CHAPTER SUMMER RETREAT, Franciscan Center, Colorado Springs CO 80919. Program Chairman: Linda White, 1712 Morning Dr., Loveland, CO 80537. Writer workshop geared toward beginner, intermediate, advanced, professional levels. Annual workshop. Workshops held July 23-25, 1993. Length of session: Friday-Sunday. Registration limited to 60. Cost of workshop: approx. $160. Participants may submit writing to be critiqued by speakers (additional fee charged). Write for more information. Speakers will be Dian Curtis Regan and Lee Wardlow.

*SOCIETY OF CHILDREN'S BOOK WRITERS & ILLUSTRATORS – WISCONSIN THIRD ANNUAL FALL RETREAT, 26 Lancaster Ct., Madison WI 53719-1433. (608)271-0433. Regional Advisor: Sheri Cooper Sinykin. Writer workshops geared toward beginner, intermediate, advanced, professional levels. Classes offered include: Pre-publication Secrets; Post-Publication Problems; workshops on craft; author-editor dialogues on the revision process; working relationships; marketing. "The entire retreat is geared *only* to children's book writing." Annual workshop. Workshops held November 5-7, 1993. Length of each session: 1-2 hours; retreat lasts from Friday evening to Sunday afternoon. Registration limited to approx. 60 people. Cost of workshop: usually $160-180 for

SCBWI members, higher for non-members; includes room, board, book, and program. "We strive to offer an informal weekend with an award-winning children's writer and an editor from a trade house in New York."

SOUTHERN CALIFORNIA SOCIETY OF CHILDREN'S BOOK WRITERS & ILLUSTRATORS DAY, 11943 Montana Ave. #105, Los Angeles CA 90049. (213)820-5601, 457-3501. Regional Advisor: Judith Enderle. Illustrator workshops geared toward beginner, intermediate, advanced, professional levels. Emphasizes illustration and illustration markets. Conference includes: presentations by art director, children's book editor, and panel of artists/author-illustrators. Workshops held annually in the fall. Length of session: full day. Maximum class size: 100. "Editors and art directors will view portfolios. We want to know if each conferee is bringing a portfolio or not." SCBWI Membership: $40/yr. "This is a chance for illustrators to meet editors/art directors and each other. Writers Day held in the spring. National conference for authors *and* illustrators held every August."

*SOUTHERN CALIFORNIA WRITERS CONFERENCE * SAN DIEGO, 3745 Mt. Augustus Ave., San Diego CA 92111. (619)277-7302. Director: Betty Abell Jurus. Writer workshops geared toward beginner, intermediate, advanced levels. Workshops offered include fiction, nonfiction, film and (marketing) business. Also speakers and agents' and editors' panels. Conference is annual on 4-day Martin Luther King weekend. Length of each session: Days, 2-hours; evenings, 2-4-hours. Cost of conference: Approx. $425, includes conference and hotel accommodations; approx. $200, conference without hotel. Write or phone for more information.

SPLIT ROCK ARTS PROGRAM, University of Minnesota, 306 Wesbrook Hall, 77 Pleasant St. SE, Minneapolis MN 55455. (612)624-6800. Registrar: Vivien Oja. Writer and illustrator workshops geared toward intermediate, advanced, professional levels. Workshops offered in writing and illustrating books for children and young people. 1993 workshops begin July 11. Length of each session: One week intensive, Sunday night to Saturday noon. two college credits available. Maximum class size: 16. Workshops held on the University of Minnesota-Duluth campus. Cost of workshop: $290-345; includes tuition and fees. Amounts vary depending on course fee, determined by supply needs, etc. "Moderately priced on-campus housing available." Complete catalogs available March 15. Call or write anytime to be put on mailing list. Some courses fill very early.

*STATE OF MAINE WRITERS' CONFERENCE, 16 Colby Ave., Ocean Park ME 04063. (207)934-5034 (summer). (413)596-6734 (winter). Chairman: Richard F. Burns. Writer workshops geared toward beginner, intermediate, advanced levels. Emphasizes poetry, prose, mysteries, editors, publishers, etc. Annual workshop. Workshops held last week of August; August 17-20, 1993. Cost of workshop: $70; include all sessions and banquet, snacks, poetry booklet. Write for more information.

MARK TWAIN WRITERS CONFERENCE, 921 Center St., Hannibal MO 63401. (314)221-2462. Director: James C. Hefley. Writer workshops geared toward beginner, intermediate and advanced levels. Emphasizes fiction, nonfiction, photography. Workshops covering poetry, humor, Mark Twain, newspapers, freelancing, the autobiography and working with an agent. Workshops held in June. Length of each session: 50-90 minutes. Maximum class size: 12-20. Writing facilities available: computers. Cost of workshop: $325; includes all program fees, room, meals and group photo. Write for more information.

UNIVERSITY OF KENTUCKY WOMEN WRITERS CONFERENCE, 106 Frazee Hall, University of Kentucky, Lexington KY 40506-0031. (606)257-3295. Conference Director: Betty Gabehart. Writer workshops geared toward beginner, intermediate, advanced, professional levels. Classes/courses offered include: annual ms workshops for poets, playwrights, children's writers, short fiction writers. Workshops held in October. Length of session: 3 hours. Cost of workshop: $10-25/day; includes registration. Submit ms by deadline, 3 months before conference. 20 pages maximum; 4 poems maximum/6 pages; essays/10 pages maximum. "Write to obtain brochure, available mid-August, 1992, outlining daily events, visiting writers bio info, registration costs/procedures."

VASSAR INSTITUTE OF PUBLISHING AND WRITING: CHILDREN'S BOOKS IN THE MARKETPLACE, Box 300, Vassar College, Poughkeepsie NY 12601. (914)437-5900. Program Coordinator: Maryann Bruno. Director: Barbara Lucas. Writer and illustrator workshops geared toward beginner, intermediate, advanced, professional levels. Emphasizes "the editorial, production, marketing and reviewing processes, on writing fiction and nonfiction for all ages, creating the picture book, understanding the markets and selling your work." Classes/courses offered include: "Writing Fiction," "The Editorial Process," "How to Write a Children's Book and Get It Published." Workshop in June. Length of each session: 3½-hour morning critique sessions, afternoon and evening lectures. Maximum class size: 50 (with three instructors). Cost of workshop: approximately $700, includes room, board and tuition for all critique sessions, lectures, and social activities. "Proposals are pre-prepared and discussed at morning critique sessions. Art portfolio review given on pre-prepared works." Write for more information. "This conference gives a comprehensive look at the publishing industry as well as offering critiques of creative writing and portfolio review."

*VENTURA/SANTA BARBARA (CA) SPRING MINI-CONFERENCE AND FALL WORK-SHOP, 1658 Calle La Cumbre, Camarillo CA 93010. (805)482-1075. Regional Advisor: Jean Stangl. Writer workshops geared toward beginner, intermediate, advanced, professional levels. "We invite editors, authors and author/illustrators. We have had speakers on the picture book, middle grade, YA, magazine, religious markets and photographer for photo essay books. Both fiction and nonfiction are covered." Semiannual workshops. Workshop held in February and October. Length of each session: 9:30 am-4 pm on Saturdays. Cost of workshop: $40; includes all sessions and lunch. Write for more information.

*WELLS WRITERS' WORKSHOP, 69 Broadway, Concord NH 03301. (603)225-9162. Coordinator: Victor Andre Levine. Writer workshops geared toward beginner, intermediate levels. "Sessions focus on careful plot preparation, as well as on effective writing (characterization, dialogue and description), with lots of time for writing." Workshops offered twice a year. Workshops held May 16-21, 1993; September 12-17, 1993. Length of each session: 5 days. Registration limited to 6. Writing facilities available: space, electrical outlets, resident MS-Dos computer. Cost of workshop: $550; includes tuition, housing and basic food items. Write for more information. "I invite interested writers to call or write. I'd be happy to meet with them if they're reasonably close by. Workshop stresses the importance of getting the structure right when writing stories for children."

WESLEYAN WRITERS CONFERENCE, Wesleyan University, Middletown CT 06459. (203)347-9411, ext. 2448. Director: Anne Greene. Writer workshops geared toward beginner, intermediate, advanced and professional levels. "This conference is useful for writers interested in how to structure a story, poem, or nonfiction piece. Although we don't always offer classes in writing for children, the advice about structuring a piece is useful for writers of any sort, no matter who their audience is." Classes in the novel, short story, fiction techniques, poetry, journalism and literary nonfiction. Guest speakers and panels offer discussion of fiction, poetry, reviewing, editing and publishing. Individual manuscript consultations available. Workshops held annually the last week in June. Length of each session: 6 days. "Usually, there are 100 participants at the

Conference." Classrooms, meals, lodging and word processing facilities available on campus. Cost of workshop: tuition—$415, room—$85, meals (required of all participants)—$165. "Anyone may register; people who want financial aid must submit their work and be selected by scholarship judges." Write for more information.

WESTERN RESERVE WRITERS AND FREELANCE CONFERENCE, Lakeland Community College, 7700 Clocktower Dr., Mentor OH 44060. (216)953-7080. Coordinator: Lea Leever Oldham. Writer workshops geared toward beginner, intermediate, advanced, professional levels. Emphasizes fiction, photography, greeting card writing, science fiction and fantasy writing, poetry. Classes/courses offered include: Writing For Children in Whole Language & Curriculum. Workshops held in mid-September. Length of each session: 7 hrs. Cost of workshop: $39; includes sessions and lunch. Critiques available at $10 per 10 pages. Other workshops held in late March or early April. Write for more information at 34200 Ridge Road #110, Willoughby OH 44094. (216)943-3047.

WILLAMETTE WRITERS ANNUAL WRITERS CONFERENCE, 9045 SW Barbur Blvd, Suite 5A, Portland OR 97219. (503)452-1542. Writer workshops geared toward beginner, intermediate, advanced, professional levels. Emphasizes all areas of writing. Opportunities to meet one-on-one with leading literary agents and editors. Workshops held in August.

*WRITER'S SEMINAR, College Development Center, Anoka Ramsey Community College, 11200 Mississippi Blvd., Coon Rapids MN 55433. (612)422-3303. Instructor: Peter Davidson. Writer workshops geared toward beginner level. Annual workshop. Workshops held in October. Length of session: 6½ hrs.; 8:30 a.m.-3:30 p.m. Registration limited to 35. Cost of workshop: $59; includes workshop booklet and handouts. Write for more information.

*WRITING BOOKS FOR CHILDREN, Nathan Mayhew Seminars of Martha's Vineyard, P.O. Box 1125, Vineyard Haven MA 02568. (508)693-6603. Director: Cynthia Riggs. Writer and illustrator workshops geared toward intermediate and advanced levels. Annual workshop. Workshops held in mid-August, Friday-Sunday from 9 am-4 pm. Registration limited to 25. Overnight accommodations available on campus. Cost of workshop: $175. Write for more information.

WRITING FOR YOUNG PEOPLE, 1908 S. Goliad, Amarillo TX 79106. (806)353-4925. Writer and illustrator workshops geared toward beginner, intermediate levels. Emphasizes "varying aspects of writing for the children's market, especially technique and marketing." Workshops held in October. Length of each session: one-day conference or workshop (8:30-4:00). Cost of workshop: approx. $45. Location—Region XVI Education Service Center, Amarillo, TX. "Our event is a one-day conference with 3-4 speakers experienced in some facet of the children's market (authors, editors, librarians, booksellers, illustrators)." Sponsored by Society of Children's Book Writers & Illustrators, West Texas Chapter.

WRITING MULTICULTURAL BOOKS FOR CHILDREN AND YOUNG ADULTS, The Authors Resource Center & The Artists Resource Center, P.O. Box 64785, Tucson AZ 85728. Director: Martha Gore. Writer workshops geared toward beginner, intermediate, advanced, professional levels. Emphasizes children's books for all multicultural children. "Dates to be announced." Length of each session: 3 hrs., plus meeting time with published authors. Maximum class size: 20. Bookstore setting. Cost of workshop: $50, plus materials. No requirements prior to registration. Send SASE for details. "This is an opportunity for writers to learn about the fastest growing segment of the children's market. Participants will be invited to submit their work for possible representation by the TARC Literary Agency."

Workshops/'92-'93 changes

The following markets are not included in this edition of *Children's Writer's & Illustrator's Market* for the reasons indicated. The phrase "did not respond" means the market was in the *1992 Children's Writer's & Illustrator's Market* but did not respond to our written and phone requests for updated information for a 1993 listing.

Annual Arizona Christian Writers Conference (did not respond)
Antioch Writers' Workshop (did not respond)
Cartoonist at Work, The (did not respond)
Maritime Writers' Workshop

(did not respond)
Mystery Writers of America (did not respond)
Port Townsend Writer's Conference (did not respond)
Rutgers University One-On-One Plus (did not respond)

Seattle Pacific Christian Writers Conference (did not respond)
Write to Sell Writer's Conference (did not respond)
Writers Studio Spring Writers Conference (did not respond)

Glossary

AAR. Association of Author's Representatives (merger of Society of Author's Representatives and Independent Literary Agents Association, Inc.).

Advance. A sum of money a publisher pays a writer prior to the publication of a book. It is usually paid in installments, such as one-half on signing the contract; one half on delivery of a complete and satisfactory manuscript. The advance is paid against the royalty money that will be earned by the book.

AIMP. Association of Independent Music Publishers.

All rights. The rights contracted to a publisher permitting a manuscript's use anywhere and in any form, including movie and book-club sales, without additional payment to the writer.

Anthropomorphization. To attribute human form and personality to things not human (such as animals).

ASAP. Abbreviation for as soon as possible.

ASCAP. American Society of Composers, Authors and Publishers. A performing rights organization.

B&W. Abbreviation for black and white artwork or photographs.

Backlist. A publisher's list of books not published during the current season but still in print.

Biennially. Once every two years.

Bimonthly. Once every two months.

Biweekly. Once every two weeks.

Bleed. Area of a plate or print that extends beyond the actual trimmed sheet to be printed.

BMI. Broadcast Music, Inc. A performing rights organization.

Book packager. Draws all elements of a book together, from the initial concept to writing and marketing strategies, then sells the book package to a book publisher and/or movie producer. Also known as book producer or book developer.

Business-size envelope. Also known as a #10 envelope, it is the standard size used in sending business correspondence.

Camera-ready. Art that is completely prepared for copy camera platemaking.

Caption. A description of the subject matter of an illustration or photograph; photo captions include names of people where appropriate. Also called cutline.

Clean-copy. A manuscript free of errors and needing no editing; it is ready for typesetting.

Contract. A written agreement stating the rights to be purchased by an editor or art director and the amount of payment the writer or illustrator will receive for that sale.

Contributor's copies. Copies of the issues of magazines sent to the author or illustrator in which his/her work appears.

Copy. Refers to the actual written material of a manuscript.

Copyediting. Editing a manuscript for grammar usage, spelling, punctuation, and general style.

Copyright. A means to legally protect an author's/illustrator's work. This can be shown by writing ©, your name, and year of work's creation.

Cover letter. A brief letter, accompanying a complete manuscript, especially useful if responding to an editor's request for a manuscript. A cover letter may also accompany a book proposal. A cover letter is not a query letter.

Cutline. See caption.

Disk. A round, flat magnetic plate on which computer data is stored.

Division. An unincorporated branch of a company.

Dot-matrix. Printed type in which individual characters are composed of a matrix or pattern of tiny dots.

Dummy. Hand-made mock-up of a book.

Final draft. The last version of a "polished" manuscript ready for submission to the editor.

First North American serial rights. The right to publish material in a periodical before it appears in book form, for the first time, in the United States or Canada.

Flat fee. A one-time payment.

GAG. Graphic Artists Guild.

Galleys. The first typeset version of a manuscript that has not yet been divided into pages.

Gatefold. A page larger than the trim size of a book which is folded so as not to extend beyond the edges.

Genre. A formulaic type of fiction, such as adventure, mystery, romance, science fiction or western.

Glossy. A black and white photograph with a shiny surface as opposed to one with a non-shiny matte finish.

Gouache. Opaque watercolor with an appreciable film thickness and an actual paint layer.

Halftone. Reproduction of a continuous tone illustration with the image formed by dots produced by a camera lens screen.

Hard copy. The printed copy of a computer's output.

Hi-Lo. Abbreviation for high interest, low reading level, as it pertains mostly to beginning adult readers.

Illustrations. May be artwork, photographs, old engravings. Usually paid for separately from the manuscript.

Imprint. Name applied to a publisher's specific line or lines of books.

IRC. International Reply Coupon; purchased at the post office to enclose with text or artwork sent to a foreign buyer to cover his postage cost when replying or returning work.

Keyline. Identification, through signs and symbols, of the positions of illustrations and copy for the printer.

Kill fee. Portion of the agreed-upon price the author or artist receives for a job that was assigned, worked on, but then canceled.

Layout. Arrangement of illustrations, photographs, text and headlines for printed material.

Letter-quality submission. Computer printout that looks like a typewritten manuscript.

Line drawing. Illustration done with pencil or ink using no wash or other shading.

LORT. League of Resident Theaters.

Mechanicals. Paste-up or preparation of work for printing.

Middle reader. The general classification of books written for readers 9-11 years of age.

Modem. A small electrical box that plugs into the serial card of a computer, used to transmit data from one computer to another, usually via telephone lines.

Ms, mss. Abbreviation for manuscript(s).

One-time rights. Permission to publish a story in periodical or book form one time only.

Outline. A summary of a book's contents in 5-15 double spaced pages; often in the form of chapter headings with a descriptive sentence or two under each one to show the scope of the book.

Package sale. The editor buys manuscript and illustrations/photos as a "package" and pays for them with one check.

Payment on acceptance. The writer or artist is paid for his work at the time the editor or art director decides to buy it.

Payment on publication. The writer or artist is paid for his work when it is published.

Photocopied submissions. Submitting photocopies of an original manuscript instead of sending the original. Do not assume that an editor who accepts photocopies will also accept multiple or simultaneous submissions.

Photostat. Black-and-white copies produced by an inexpensive photographic process using paper negatives; only line values are held with accuracy. Also called stat.

Picture book. A type of book aimed at the preschool to 8-year-old that tells the story primarily or entirely with artwork.

PMT. Photostat produced without a negative, somewhat like the Polaroid process.

Print. An impression pulled from an original plate, stone, block, screen or negative; also a positive made from a photographic negative.

Proofreading. Reading a manuscript to correct typographical errors.

Query. A letter to an editor designed to capture his/her interest in an article or book you purpose to write.

Reading fee. An arbitrary amount of money charged by some agents and publishers to read a submitted manuscript.

Reporting time. The time it takes for an editor to report to the author on his/her query or manuscript.

Reprint rights. Permission to print an already published work whose rights have been sold to another magazine or book publisher.

Response time. The average length of time it takes an editor or art director to accept or reject a manuscript or artwork and inform you of the decision.

Rights. What you offer to an editor or art director in exchange for printing your manuscripts or artwork.

Rough draft. A manuscript which has been written but not checked for errors in grammar, punctuation, spelling or content. It usually needs revision and rewriting.

Roughs. Preliminary sketches or drawings.

Royalty. An agreed percentage paid by the publisher to the writer or illustrator for each copy of his work sold.

SASE. Abbreviation for self-addressed, stamped envelope.

SCBWI. Society of Children's Book Writers & Illustrators.

Second serial rights. Permission for the reprinting of a work in another periodical after its first publication in book or magazine form.

Semiannual. Once every six months.

Semimonthly. Twice a month.

Semiweekly. Twice a week.

Serial rights. The rights given by an author to a publisher to print a piece in one or more periodicals.

Simultaneous submissions. Sending the same article, story, poem or illustration to several publishers at the same time. Some publishers refuse to consider such submissions. No simultaneous submissions should be made without stating the fact in your letter.

Slant. The approach to a story or piece of artwork that will appeal to readers of a particular publication.

Slush pile. What editors call the collection of submitted manuscripts which have not been specifically asked for.

Software. Programs and related documentation for use with a particular computer system.

Solicited manuscript. Material which an editor has asked for or agreed to consider before being sent by the writer.

SPAR. Society of Photographers and Artists Representatives, Inc.

Speculation (Spec). Writing or drawing a piece with no assurance from the editor or art director that it will be purchased or any reimbursements for material or labor paid.

Subsidiary rights. All rights other than book publishing rights included in a book contract, such as paperback, book club and movie rights.

Subsidy publisher. A book publisher who charges the author for the cost of typesetting, printing and promoting a book. Also vanity publisher.

Synopsis. A brief summary of a story or novel. If part of a book proposal, it should be a page to a page and a half, single-spaced.

Tabloid. Publication printed on an ordinary newspaper page turned sideways.

Tearsheet. Page from a magazine or newspaper containing your printed art, story, article, poem or ad.

Thumbnail. A rough layout in miniature.

Transparencies. Positive color slides; not color prints.

Unsolicited manuscript. A story, article, poem, book or artwork sent without the editor's or art director's knowledge or consent.

Vanity publisher. See subsidy publisher.

Word length. The maximum number of words a manuscript should contain as determined by the editor or guidelines sheet.

Word processor. A computer that produces typewritten copy via automated typing, text-editing, and storage and transmission capabilities.

Young adult. The general classification of books written for readers ages 12-18.

Young reader. The general classification of books written for readers 5-8 years old.

Recommended Books & Publications

Children's Writer's & Illustrator's Market recommends the following reading material to stay informed of market trends as well as to find additional names and addresses of buyers of juvenile material. Many of the publications recommended here incorporate business-oriented material with information about how to write or illustrate more creatively and skillfully. Most are available in a library or bookstore or from the publisher.

Books of interest

THE ART OF WRITING FOR CHILDREN: SKILLS & TECHNIQUES OF THE CRAFT. Epstein, Connie C. Archon Books, 1991.

THE ARTIST'S FRIENDLY LEGAL GUIDE. Conner, Floyd; Karlen, Peter; Perwin, Jean; Spatt, David M. North Light Books, 1991.

THE CHILDREN'S PICTURE BOOK: HOW TO WRITE IT, HOW TO SELL IT. Roberts, Ellen E.M. Writer's Digest Books, 1984.

GETTING STARTED AS A FREELANCE ILLUSTRATOR OR DESIGNER. Fleischman, Michael. North Light Books.

GUIDE TO WRITING FOR CHILDREN. Yolen, Jane. The Writer, 1989.

HOW TO SELL YOUR PHOTOGRAPHS & ILLUSTRATIONS. Gordon, Elliott & Barbara. North Light Books.

HOW TO WRITE, ILLUSTRATE, AND DESIGN CHILDREN'S BOOKS. Gates, Frieda. Lloyd-Simone Publishing Company, 1986.

HOW TO WRITE A CHILDREN'S BOOK & GET IT PUBLISHED. Seuling, Barbara. Charles Scribner's Sons, 1991.

HOW TO WRITE AND ILLUSTRATE CHILDREN'S BOOKS. Bicknell, Treld Pelkey; Trotman, Felicity, eds. North Light Books, 1988.

ILLUSTRATING CHILDREN'S BOOKS. Hands, Nancy S. Prentice Hall Press, 1986.

SUCCESS KITS FOR ARTISTS AND ILLUSTRATORS. Crawford, Tad. North Light Books.

THE WRITER'S ESSENTIAL DESK REFERENCE. Neff, Glenda, ed. Writer's Digest Books, 1991.

A WRITER'S GUIDE TO A CHILDREN'S BOOK CONTRACT. Flower, Mary. Fern Hill Books, 1988.

WRITING BOOKS FOR CHILDREN. Yolen, Jane. The Writer, Inc., 1983.

WRITING BOOKS FOR YOUNG PEOPLE. Giblin, James Cross. The Writer, Inc., 1990.

WRITING FOR CHILDREN & TEENAGERS. Wyndham, Lee & Madison, Arnold. Writer's Digest Books, 1988.

WRITING WITH PICTURES: HOW TO WRITE AND ILLUSTRATE CHILDREN'S BOOKS. Shulevitz, Uri. Watson-Guptill Publications, 1985.

Publications of interest

BYLINE. Preston, Marcia, ed. P.O. Box 130596, Edmond OK 73013.

BOOK LINKS. American Library Association. 50 E. Huron St., Chicago IL 60611.

CHILDREN'S BOOK INSIDER. Backes, Laura, ed. 254 E. Mombasha Road, Monroe NY 10950.

CHILDREN'S WRITER. Susan Tierney, ed. The Institute of Children's Literature. 95 Long Ridge Rd., West Redding CT 06896-1124.

THE FIVE OWLS. 2004 Sheridan Ave., S., Minneapolis MN 55405.

THE HORN BOOK MAGAZINE. Silvey, Anita, ed. The Horn Book, Inc., 14 Beacon St., Boston MA 02108.

THE LION AND THE UNICORN: A CRITICAL JOURNAL OF CHILDREN'S LITERATURE. The Johns Hopkins University Press—Journals Publishing Division, Suite 275, 701 W. 40th St., Baltimore MD 21211-2190.

ONCE UPON A TIME . . . . Baird, Audrey, ed. 553 Winston Court, St. Paul MN 55118.

SOCIETY OF CHILDREN'S BOOK WRITERS & ILLUSTRATORS BULLETIN. Mooser, Stephen; Oliver, Lin, eds. Society of Children's Book Writers & Illustrators, Box 66296, Mar Vista Station, Los Angeles CA 90066.

Age-Level Index

Book Publishers

The age-level index is set up to help you more quickly locate book and magazine markets geared to the age group(s) for which you write or illustrate. Read each listing carefully and follow the publisher's specific information about the type(s) of manuscript(s) each prefers and the style(s) of artwork each wishes to review.

Picture books (preschool-8-year-olds)

Advocacy Press
Aegina Press/University Editions
Africa World Press
African American Images
Aladdin Books/Collier Books for Young Readers
Alyson Publications, Inc.
American Bible Society
Arcade Publishing
Atheneum Publishers
Barrons Educational Series
Behrman House Inc.
Black Moss Press
Boyds Mills Press
Bradbury Press
Bright Ring Publishing
Candlewick Press
Capstone Press Inc.
Carolina Wren Press/Lollipop Power Books
Carolrhoda Books, Inc.
Chariot Books
Charlesbridge
Childrens Press
China Books
Chronicle Books
Clarion Books
Cloverdale Press
Cobblehill Books
Concordia Publishing House
Coteau Books Ltd.
Council for Indian Education
Crown Publishers (Crown Books for Children)
Crystal River Press
CSS Publishing
Davis Publications, Inc.
Dawn Publications
Denison Co. Inc., T.S.
Discovery Enterprises, Ltd.
Distinctive Publishing Corp.
Dorling Kindersley, Inc.
Dutton Children's Books
Eerdmans Publishing Company, Wm. B.
Farrar, Straus & Giroux
Four Winds Press
Free Spirit Publishing
Friendship Press, Inc.
Gage Educational Publishing Company
Geringer Books, Laura
Gibbs Smith, Publisher
Godine, Publisher, David R.
Golden Books
Gospel Light Publications
Greenwillow Books
Grosset & Dunlap, Inc.
Harbinger House, Inc.
Harcourt Brace Jovanovich
HarperCollins Children's Books
Harvest House Publishers
Hendrick-Long Publishing Company
Holiday House Inc.
Holt & Co., Inc., Henry
Homestead Publishing
Houghton Mifflin Co.
Humanics Publishing Group
Huntington House Publishers
Hyperion Books for Children
Jalmar Press
Jewish Lights Publishing
Jewish Publication Society
Jordan Enterprises Publishing Co., Inc.
Joy Street Books
Just Us Books, Inc.
Kar-Ben Copies, Inc.

Knopf Books for Young Readers
Kruza Kaleidoscopix, Inc.
Lee & Low Books, Inc.
Lion Publishing
Little, Brown and Company
Lodestar Books
Lothrop, Lee & Shepard Books
McElderry Books, Margaret K.
Macmillan Children's Books
Mage Publishers Inc.
Magination Press
March Media, Inc.
Metamorphous Press
Millbrook Press, The
Morehouse Publishing Co.
Morris Publishing, Joshua
Muir Publications, Inc, John
NAR Publications
North Light Books
Northland Publishing
NorthWord Press, Inc.
Oddo Publishing, Inc.
Open Hand Publishing Inc.
ORCA Book Publishers
Orchard Books
Our Child Press
Owen Publishers, Inc., Richard C.
Pacific Press
Parenting Press, Inc.
Paulist Press
Pelican Publishing Co. Inc.
Perfection Learning
Perspectives Press
Philomel Books
Pippin Press
Pocahontas Press, Inc.
Potter Inc., Clarkson N.
Preservation Press, The
Price Stern Sloan
Prometheus Books
Pumpkin Press Publishing House
Putnam's Sons, G.P.
Quarry Press
Random House Books for Young
   Readers
Read'n Run Books
Redbud Books
Sagebrush Books
St. Paul Books and Media
Scribner's Sons, Charles
Shoestring Press
Simon & Schuster Children's Books
Speech Bin, Inc., The
Standard Publishing

Star Books, Inc.
Starburst Publishers
Stemmer House Publishers, Inc.
Sunbelt Media, Inc./Eakin Press
TAB Books
Tambourine Books
Treasure Chest Publications, Inc.
Troll Associates
Trophy Books
Troubador Books
Tyndale House Publishers, Inc.
Victor Books
Victory Publishing
Volcano Press
Walker and Co.
Whitebird Books
Whitman & Company, Albert
Williamson Publishing Co.
Willowisp Press
Winston-Derek Publishers, Inc.
Women's Press
Woodbine House
YMAA Publication Center

Young readers (5-8-year-olds)

Addison-Wesley Publishing Co.
Advocacy Press
Aegina Press/University Editions
Africa World Press
African American Images
Aladdin Books/Collier Books for
   Young Readers
Alyson Publications, Inc.
American Bible Society
Appalachian Mountain Club Books
Arcade Publishing
Atheneum Publishers
Barrons Educational Series
Behrman House Inc.
Bethel Publishing
Boyds Mills Press
Bradbury Press
Bright Ring Publishing
Candlewick Press
Capstone Press Inc.
Carolina Wren Press/Lollipop Power
   Books
Carolrhoda Books, Inc.
Chariot Books
Chicago Review Press
Childrens Press
China Books
Chronicle Books

Sagebrush Books
St. Paul Books and Media
Scribner's Sons, Charles
Seacoast Publications of New England
Shoestring Press
Simon & Schuster Children's Books
Soundprints
Speech Bin, Inc., The
Standard Publishing
Star Books, Inc.
Starburst Publishers
Stemmer House Publishers, Inc.
Stepping Stone Books
TAB Books
Treasure Chest Publications, Inc.
Troll Associates
Trophy Books
Troubador Books
Tyndale House Publishers, Inc.
Victor Books
Victory Publishing
Volcano Press
W.W. Publications
Walker and Co.
Weigl Educational Publishers
Whitman & Company, Albert
Williamson Publishing Co.
Willowisp Press
Winston-Derek Publishers, Inc.
Women's Press
Woodbine House
YMAA Publication Center

Middle readers (9-11-year-olds)

Addison-Wesley Publishing Co.
Advocacy Press
Aegina Press/University Editions
Africa World Press
African American Images
Aladdin Books/Collier Books for Young Readers
Alyson Publications, Inc.
American Bible Society
Appalachian Mountain Club Books
Arcade Publishing
Archway Paperbacks/Minstrel Books
Atheneum Publishers
Avon Books
Bancroft-Sage Publishing, Inc.
Barrons Educational Series
Behrman House Inc.
Bethel Publishing

Blue Heron Publishing, Inc.
Boyds Mills Press
Bradbury Press
Breakwater Books
Bright Ring Publishing
Candlewick Press
Capstone Press Inc.
Carolrhoda Books, Inc.
Chariot Books
Chicago Review Press
Childrens Press
China Books
Chronicle Books
Clarion Books
Cloverdale Press
Cobblehill Books
Concordia Publishing House
Council for Indian Education
Crestwood House
Crossway Books
Crown Publishers (Crown Books for Children)
Crystal River Press
CSS Publishing
Davenport, Publishers, May
Davis Publications, Inc.
Dawn Publications
Denison Co. Inc., T.S.
Dillon Press, Inc.
Discovery Enterprises, Ltd.
Distinctive Publishing Corp.
Dutton Children's Books
Eerdmans Publishing Company, Wm. B.
Farrar, Straus & Giroux
Four Winds Press
Free Spirit Publishing
Friendship Press, Inc.
Geringer Books, Laura
Godine, Publisher, David R.
Golden Books
Gospel Light Publications
Greenhaven Press
Greenwillow Books
Harcourt Brace Jovanovich
HarperCollins Children's Books
Harvest House Publishers
Hendrick-Long Publishing Company
Herald Press
Holiday House Inc.
Holt & Co., Inc., Henry
Homestead Publishing
Houghton Mifflin Co.
Huntington House Publishers

Hyperion Books for Children
Incentive Publications, Inc.
Jewish Lights Publishing
Jewish Publication Society
Jones University Press/Light Line
    Books, Bob
Jordan Enterprises Publishing Co.,
    Inc.
Joy Street Books
Just Us Books, Inc.
Kar-Ben Copies, Inc.
Knopf Books for Young Readers
Kruza Kaleidoscopix, Inc.
Lee & Low Books, Inc.
Lerner Publications Co.
Liguori Publications
Lion Publishing
Little, Brown and Company
Lodestar Books
Lothrop, Lee & Shepard Books
Lucas/Evans Books Inc.
Lucent Books
McElderry Books, Margaret K.
Macmillan Children's Books
March Media, Inc.
Meadowbrook Press
Meriwether Publishing Ltd.
Messner, Julian
Metamorphous Press
Millbrook Press, The
Misty Hill Press
Morehouse Publishing Co.
Morris Publishing, Joshua
Muir Publications, Inc, John
New Discovery Books
North Light Books
Northland Publishing
NorthWord Press, Inc.
Oddo Publishing, Inc.
Open Hand Publishing Inc.
ORCA Book Publishers
Orchard Books
Our Child Press
Pacific Press
Pando Publications
Parenting Press, Inc.
Paulist Press
Peartree
Pelican Publishing Co. Inc.
Perfection Learning
Perspectives Press
Philomel Books
Pippin Press
Players Press, Inc.

Pocahontas Press, Inc.
Potter Inc., Clarkson N.
Preservation Press, The
Price Stern Sloan
Prometheus Books
Pumpkin Press Publishing House
Putnam's Sons, G.P.
Random House Books for Young
    Readers
Read'n Run Books
St. Anthony Messenger Press
St. Paul Books and Media
Scientific American Books For Young
    Readers
Scribner's Sons, Charles
Shoestring Press
Simon & Schuster Children's Books
Speech Bin, Inc., The
Standard Publishing
Star Books, Inc.
Stemmer House Publishers, Inc.
Sterling Publishing Co., Inc.
Sunbelt Media, Inc./Eakin Press
TAB Books
Tambourine Books
Thistledown Press Ltd.
Treasure Chest Publications, Inc.
Troll Associates
Trophy Books
Troubador Books
Tyndale House Publishers, Inc.
Victor Books
Victory Publishing
Volcano Press
W.W. Publications
Walker and Co.
Weigl Educational Publishers
Whitman & Company, Albert
Williamson Publishing Co.
Willowisp Press
Winston-Derek Publishers, Inc.
Women's Press
Woodbine House
YMAA Publication Center

Young adults (12 and up)

Addison-Wesley Publishing Co.
Aegina Press/University Editions
Africa World Press
African American Images
Aladdin Books/Collier Books for
    Young Readers
Alyson Publications, Inc.

American Bible Society
Appalachian Mountain Club Books
Arcade Publishing
Archway Paperbacks/Minstrel Books
Atheneum Publishers
Avon Books
Bandanna Books
Barrons Educational Series
Behrman House Inc.
Bethel Publishing
Blue Heron Publishing, Inc.
Boyds Mills Press
Bradbury Press
Breakwater Books
Candlewick Press
Chariot Books
Chicago Review Press
Childrens Press
Chronicle Books
Clarion Books
Cloverdale Press
Cobblehill Books
Concordia Publishing House
Council for Indian Education
Crossway Books
Crystal River Press
CSS Publishing
Davenport, Publishers, May
Davis Publications, Inc.
Dawn Publications
Discovery Enterprises, Ltd.
Distinctive Publishing Corp.
Dutton Children's Books
Farrar, Straus & Giroux
Free Spirit Publishing
Friendship Press, Inc.
Geringer Books, Laura
Golden Books
Gospel Light Publications
Greenhaven Press
Greenwillow Books
Grosset & Dunlap, Inc.
Harcourt Brace Jovanovich
HarperCollins Children's Books
Harvest House Publishers
Hendrick-Long Publishing Company
Herald Press
Holiday House Inc.
Holt & Co., Inc., Henry
Homestead Publishing
Houghton Mifflin Co.
Hunter House Publishers
Huntington House Publishers
Hyperion Books for Children

Incentive Publications, Inc.
Jewish Lights Publishing
Jewish Publication Society
Jones University Press/Light Line
    Books, Bob
Jordan Enterprises Publishing Co.,
    Inc.
Joy Street Books
Knopf Books for Young Readers
Lerner Publications Co.
Liguori Publications
Lion Books, Publisher
Lion Publishing
Little, Brown and Company
Lodestar Books
Lothrop, Lee & Shepard Books
Lucas/Evans Books Inc.
Lucent Books
McElderry Books, Margaret K.
Macmillan Children's Books
Meadowbrook Press
Meriwether Publishing Ltd.
Messner, Julian
Metamorphous Press
Millbrook Press, The
Misty Hill Press
Morehouse Publishing Co.
Naturegraph Publisher, Inc.
North Light Books
NorthWord Press, Inc.
Open Hand Publishing Inc.
ORCA Book Publishers
Orchard Books
Our Child Press
Pacific Press
Pando Publications
Paulist Press
Pelican Publishing Co. Inc.
Perfection Learning
Perspectives Press
Philomel Books
Players Press, Inc.
Pocahontas Press, Inc.
Preservation Press, The
Price Stern Sloan
Prometheus Books
Putnam's Sons, G.P.
Read'n Run Books
Rosen Publishing Group, The
St. Anthony Messenger Press
St. Paul Books and Media
Scientific American Books For Young
    Readers
Scribner's Sons, Charles

Magazine Publishers

Picture books (preschool-8-year-olds)

Young readers (5-8-year-olds)

Middle readers (9-11-year-olds)

Cat Fancy
Child Life
Children's Digest
Clubhouse
Cobblestone
Cochran's Corner
Cricket Magazine
Crusader
Current Health I
Discoveries
Disney Adventures
Dolphin Log
DynaMath
Equilibrium10
Faces
Faith 'n Stuff
Friend Magazine, The
Fun Zone, The
Goldfinch, The
Guide Magazine
High Adventure
Highlights for Children
Hopscotch
Instructor Magazine
Jack and Jill
Junior Trails
Kid City
Kids Today Mini-Magazine
Lighthouse
My Friend
Nature Friend Magazine
Noah's Ark
Odyssey
On The Line
Owl Magazine
Pets Today
Pockets
Power and Light
Racing for Kids
R-A-D-A-R
Ranger Rick
School Magazine, Blast Off!, Count-
   down, Orbit, Touchdown
School Mates
Science Weekly
Scope
Shofar
Single Parent, The
Skipping Stones
Spark!
Superscience Blue
Take 5
3-2-1 Contact
Touch

U.S. Kids
Venture
Young Crusader, The
Young Judaean

Young adults (12 and up)

Aim Magazine
Atalantik
Boys' Life
Bradley's Fantasy Magazine, Marion
   Zimmer
Busines$ Kids
Calliope
Career World
Careers And Colleges
Clubhouse
Cobblestone
Cochran's Corner
Cricket Magazine
Crusader
Current Health II
Dolphin Log
DynaMath
Equilibrium10
Exploring
Faces
FFA New Horizons
For Seniors Only
Guide Magazine
Hicall
High Adventure
Hobson's Choice
I.D.
International Gymnast
Keynoter
Lighthouse
Listen
Magazine for Christian Youth!, The
My Friend
Nature Friend Magazine
New Era Magazine
Odyssey
On The Line
Owl Magazine
Pets Today
Pioneer
Racing for Kids
Sassy
Scholastic Math Magazine
School Mates
Science Weekly
Scope
Seventeen Magazine

"Picture books" are geared toward the preschool — 8 year old group; *"Young readers"* to 5-8 year olds; *"Middle readers"* to 9-11 year olds; and *"Young adults"* to those 12 and up.

Index

Other Books of Interest
for Children's Writers and Illustrators

Annual Market Books

Artist's Market, edited by Lauri Miller $22.95

Guide to Literary Agents and Art/Photo Reps, edited by Roseann Shaughnessy $18.95

Humor & Cartoon Markets, edited by Bob Staake & Roseann Shaughnessy $18.95

Novel & Short Story Writer's Market, edited by Robin Gee (paper) $19.95

Photographer's Market, edited by Michael Willins $22.95

Poet's Market, edited by Michael J. Bugeja & Christine Martin $19.95

Songwriter's Market, edited by Michael Oxley $19.95

Writer's Market, edited by Mark Kissling $26.95

Writing for Children

The Children's Picture Book: How to Write It, How to Sell It, by Ellen E. M. Roberts (paper) $19.95

The Children's Writer's Word Book, by Alijandra Mogilner $19.95

Families Writing, by Peter R. Stillman (paper) $12.95

How to Write & Illustrate Children's Books, by Treld Pelkey Bicknell & Felicity Trotman $22.50

Writing for Children & Teenagers, 3rd Edition, by Lee Wyndham/Revised by Arnold Madison (paper) $12.95

Writing Young Adult Novels, by Hadley Irwin & Jeannette Eyerly $14.95

Illustration

Painting Watercolor Portraits that Glow, by Jan Kunz $27.95

Putting People in Your Paintings, by J. Everett Draper (paper) $19.95

Reference Books

Beginning Writer's Answer Book, edited by Kirk Polking (paper)$13.95

Business & Legal Forms for Authors & Self Publishers, by Tad Crawford (paper) $15.95

The Complete Guide to Self-Publishing, by Tom & Marilyn Ross (paper) $16.95

Creative Techniques for Photographing Children, by Vik Orenstein (paper) $24.95

Getting Started as a Freelance Illustrator or Designer, by Michael Fleischman (paper) $16.95

How to Sell Your Photographs & Illustrations, by Elliott & Barbara Gordon (paper) $16.95

How to Write a Book Proposal, by Michael Larsen (paper) $11.95

How to Write with a Collaborator, by Hal Bennett with Michael Larsen $11.95

Knowing Where to Look: The Ultimate Guide to Research, by Lois Horowitz (paper) $18.95

12 Keys to Writing Books that Sell, by Kathleen Krull (paper) $12.95

The 29 Most Common Writing Mistakes & How to Avoid Them, by Judy Delton (paper) $9.95

Word Processing Secrets for Writers, by Michael A. Banks & Ansen Dibell (paper) $14.95

The Writer's Book of Checklists, by Scott Edelstein (self-cover) $16.95

The Writer's Digest Guide to Manuscript Formats, by Dian Dincin Buchman & Seli Groves $18.95

The Writer's Guide to Everyday Life in the 1800s, by Marc McCutcheon $18.95

Graphics/Business of Art

Airbrushing the Human Form, by Andy Charlesworth (cloth) $19.95

Artist's Friendly Legal Guide, by Conner, Karlen, Perwin & Spatt (paper) $18.95

Basic Graphic Design & Paste-Up, by Jack Warren (paper) $14.95

Business & Legal Forms for Fine Artists, by Tad Crawford (paper) $12.95

Business & Legal Forms for Illustrators, by Tad Crawford (paper) $15.95

Color Harmony: A Guide to Creative Color Combinations, by Hideaki Chijiiwa (paper) $15.95

Complete Airbrush & Photoretouching Manual, by Peter Owen & John Sutcliffe (cloth) $24.95

The Complete Book of Caricature, by Bob Staake (cloth) $18.95

The Complete Guide to Greeting Card Design & Illustration, by Eva Szela (cloth) $29.95

Creative Ad Design & Illustration, by Dick Ward (cloth) $32.95

The Creative Artist, by Nita Leland (paper) $21.95

Design Rendering Techniques, by Dick Powell (cloth) $29.95

Dynamic Airbrush, by David Miller & James Effler (cloth) $29.95

Getting It Printed, by Beach, Shepro & Russon (paper) $29.50

The Graphic Artist's Guide to Marketing & Self Promotion, by Sally Prince Davis (paper) $15.95

Handbook of Pricing & Ethical Guidelines — 7th Edition, by Graphic Artists Guild (paper) $22.95
How to Draw & Sell Cartoons, by Ross Thomson & Bill Hewison (cloth) $18.95
How to Draw & Sell Comic Strips, by Alan McKenzie (cloth) $19.95
How to Succeed as an Artist in Your Hometown, by Stewart Biehl (paper) $24.95
How to Understand & Use Design & Layout, by Alan Swann (paper) $21.95
The Professional Designer's Guide to Marketing Your Work, by Mary Yeung (cloth) $29.95
Type: Design, Color, Character & Use, by Michael Beaumont (paper) $19.95
Typewise, by Kit Hinrichs with Delphine Hirasuna (cloth) $39.95

Watercolor
Painting Nature's Details in Watercolor, by Cathy Johnson (paper) $22.95
Tony Couch Watercolor Techniques, by Tony Couch (paper) $14.95
Tony Couch's Keys to Successful Painting, by Tony Couch $27.95
Watercolor Painter's Solution Book, by Angela Gair (paper) $19.95
Watercolor Tricks & Techniques, by Cathy Johnson (paper) $21.95
Watercolor Workbook, by Bud Biggs & Lois Marshall (paper) $22.95
Watercolor: You Can Do It!, by Tony Couch (cloth) $29.95
Watercolorist's Complete Guide to Color, by Tom Hill $27.95

Mixed Media
Colored Pencil Drawing Techniques, by Iain Hutton-Jamieson (cloth) $24.95
Exploring Color, by Nita Leland (paper) $24.95
Getting Started in Drawing, by Wendon Blake (cloth) $24.95
Keys to Drawing, by Bert Dodson (paper) $21.95
The North Light Illustrated Book of Painting Techniques, by Elizabeth Tate (cloth) $29.95
Oil Painting: Develop Your Natural Ability, by Charles Sovek (cloth) $29.95
Painting Animals Step-by-Step, by Barbara Luebke-Hill $27.95
Painting Outdoor Scenes in Watercolor, by Richard K. Kaiser $27.95
Painting Seascapes in Sharp Focus, by Lin Seslar (paper) $22.95
Painting Your Vision in Watercolor, by Robert A. Wade $27.95
Pastel Painter's Pocket Palette, by Rosalind Cuthbert $16.95
Pastel Painting Techniques, by Guy Roddon (paper) $19.95
The Pencil, by Paul Calle (paper) $19.95
Realistic Figure Drawing, by Joseph Sheppard (paper) $19.95
Sketching Your Favorite Subjects in Pen & Ink, by Claudia Nice $22.95
Decorative Painting for Children's Rooms, by Rosie Fisher (cloth) $29.95

A complete catalog of Writer's Digest Books, North Light Books and Betterway Books is available **FREE** by writing to the address shown below. To order books directly from the publisher, include $3.00 postage and handling for 1 book, $1.00 for each additional book. Allow 30 days for delivery.

Writer's Digest Books/North Light Books
1507 Dana Avenue, Cincinnati, Ohio 45207
Credit card orders call TOLL-FREE
1-800-289-0963

Write to this same address for information on *Writer's Digest* magazine, Writer's Digest Book Club, Writer's Digest School, Writer's Digest Criticism Service, North Light Book Club, Graphic Artist's Book Club, *The Artist's Magazine, HOW* Magazine and *Story* Magazine.

Prices subject to change without notice.